D1037419

Handbook of Research on ePortfolios

Ali Jafari
Indiana University-Purdue University Indianapolis, USA

Catherine Kaufman
ePortConsortium, USA

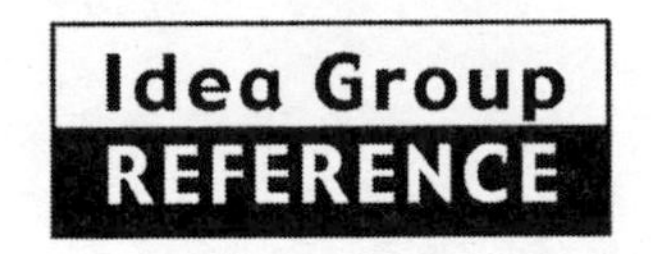

IDEA GROUP REFERENCE
Hershey · London · Melbourne · Singapore

Acquisitions Editor:	Michelle Potter
Development Editor:	Kristin Roth
Senior Managing Editor:	Amanda Appicello
Managing Editor:	Jennifer Neidig
Copy Editor:	Maria Boyer
Typesetter:	Sharon Berger
Cover Design:	Lisa Tosheff
Printed at:	Yuchak Printing Inc.

Published in the United States of America by
Idea Group Reference (an imprint of Idea Group Inc.)
701 E. Chocolate Avenue, Suite 200
Hershey PA 17033
Tel: 717-533-8845
Fax: 717-533-8661
E-mail: cust@idea-group.com
Web site: http://www.idea-group-ref.com

and in the United Kingdom by
Idea Group Reference (an imprint of Idea Group Inc.)
3 Henrietta Street
Covent Garden
London WC2E 8LU
Tel: 44 20 7240 0856
Fax: 44 20 7379 3313
Web site: http://www.eurospan.co.uk

Library of Congress Cataloging-in-Publication Data

Handbook of research on ePortfolios / Ali Jafari and Catherine Kaufman, editors.
p. cm.
Summary: "This handbook investigates a variety of ePortfolio uses through case studies, the technology that supports the case studies, and it also explains the conceptual thinking behind current uses as well as potential uses"--Provided by publisher.
ISBN 1-59140-890-3 (hardcover) -- ISBN 1-59140-891-1 (ebook)
1. Electronic portfolios in education. 2. Internet in education. I. Jafari, Ali. II. Kaufman, Catherine, 1953- .
LB1029.P67H36 2006
791.43'3--dc22

2006009293

British Cataloguing in Publication Data
A Cataloguing in Publication record for this book is available from the British Library.

List of Contributors

Table of Contents

Section II
ePortfolio Case Studies

Detailed Table of Contents

Section I
ePortfolio Thinking and Technology

This section includes a series of chapters focusing on the conceptual aspects of electronic portfolio systems and elaborates on how the innovative use of the ePortfolio can advance teaching and learning. Authors present their views of the current and potential uses for such systems in an effort to define the "big picture" for practical applications of ePortfolios. Chapters are written by conceptual thinkers, including academic leaders such as provosts within the higher education institutions, administrators within departments of education responsible for K-12 education, and experts in countries where ePortfolio usage is promoted by government. The section finally explores the technological aspects of the ePortfolio framework surrounding how the ePortfolio system as a new application software can be designed, built, and developed to operate either within an existing learning management system or as an independent enterprise systems, and authors discuss topics such as technical standards and functional interoperability among such systems.

This chapter presents an overview of 11 different ways in which electronic portfolios can support the teaching and learning process. Too often, discussion about the general instructional nature of electronic portfolios is reduced to two distinct roles: portfolios as a means of assessing specific student performance, and portfolios as a showcase for outstanding student accomplishments. This chapter summarizes how electronic portfolios can contribute to the design and implementation of effective instruction in many ways by assuming a variety of roles that go beyond a traditional approach to portfolio use in the classroom. These roles include artifact creation as meaningful context, goal-setting, practice with a purpose, examples and non-examples, assessment, reflection, communication, instructor planning and management tool, learner organization tool, interdisciplinary teaching and learning, and historical records/stories as role models. Examples of portfolio requirements and assessment strategies from a higher education teacher preparation program are used to illustrate these different roles.

portfolios in order to increase academic learning. Specifically, the authors recommend that electronic portfolios provide the means for students to set learning goals, monitor and regulate their progress toward these goals, as well as develop their self-assessment skills. Additionally, they suggest that these goals be focused on learning objectives rather than performance objectives.

This chapter examines the challenges and benefits of using reflection in ePortfolios, and reviews strategies for teaching and encouraging deep reflection. It includes a brief history of the use of reflection in portfolios, summaries of the main types of reflection, and general approaches for the development of student reflection. Barriers to successful reflection, such as inexperienced students and faculty, student fear and distrust of reflection, formulaic responses, and time constraints will be examined, and solutions will be proposed. The effects of the ePortfolio on reflection and the possibilities offered by technological advances and new software also will be reviewed. The chapter argues that faculty must carefully construct reflection learning objectives if they expect meaningful summative or formative assessment to take place. The author hopes that the discussion of prompts, scaffolding, cycling, and other mining techniques will help instructors transform reflection theory into practice.

This chapter includes three main themes, answering basic questions of "Why," "Where," and "How" that are asked when discussing the development of career portfolios during a student's academic program. The reasons why portfolios in general should be created are discussed primarily in the Rationale section. Following this is a description of ongoing programs at two universities where portfolios are an integral part of the curriculum for students in two diverse departments: Media Communications in a School of Professional Studies, and Management Information Systems in a School of Business. Finally, there is an outline of the portfolio development process with concrete suggestions on the steps to follow, the design process, and modes of distribution.

An ePortfolio is frequently seen as a space for electronically compiling and storing student work. After completing assignments, students generally submit their ePortfolio to an instructor, prospective employer, or other assessor. This chapter questions if the typical use of ePortfolios could be modified to create opportunities to encourage students (elementary school through graduate school) to engage in critical thinking, provide feedback to their peers, and/or other opportunities to contribute to the learning process.

In the 21st century, we talk of knowledge as the new currency, and knowledge building as the work to be done in learning organizations. While knowledge building is activity directed outward towards the creation of

This chapter examines the concept and the uses of electronic portfolios as pedagogical tools for adult learners, particularly in UK Higher Education, where it is part of the personal development plan (PDP) agenda on lifelong learning and widening participation. Its development relies on an environment that favors the learners' active involvement in the learning process as well as learning outcomes through reflection and collaborative participation. A better understanding of the pedagogical implications of such portfolios and their learning processes is needed and will be discussed in this chapter.

The goal of this chapter is to help the reader learn to use research and evaluative data to select which activities improve an ePortfolio initiative; accelerate the pace at which people within an institution begin to use ePortfolios for those activities; and limit the cost, stress, and risk associated with carrying out those activities, including the ePortfolio infrastructure that supports them.

The possible uses of student ePortfolios are varied, complex, and novel, making it difficult for scholars and professionals alike to capture an overall picture of this new technology. This chapter will address this concern by presenting a very straightforward overview of student ePortfolio functions, according to what have been identified as their five most basic functions: (1) storage, (2) information management, (3) connections, (4) communication, and (5) development. Each of these functions will be clarified with examples of practical applications, grounded in the real needs of undergraduate students at the University of California at Berkeley. Taken together, the functionality of student ePortfolios, if used to its full potential, could transform higher education by placing students at the center of their learning, better prepared to draw connections across subject matters and across the many realms of student life.

This chapter describes eLearning tools that focus the learner's attention on meaning, rather than rote learning of text and rehearsing problem-solving procedures. These tools are the Interactive Concept Discovery Learning Tool and the Meaning Equivalence Reusable Learning Object (MERLO). Results of several evaluative implementations of these novel instructional methodologies, which encourage learners to interact directly with the conceptual content of to-beLearned material, demonstrate their potential to enhance learning outcomes and to provide authentic, credible, evidence-based demonstration of mastery of learning and formative assessments of learning processes and outcomes for inclusion in "learning ePortfolios."

This chapter provides case studies of embedding the ePortfolio in the curricula of two medical schools in the UK, one of which is outcomes based, while the other uses a series of patient scenarios to inform the teaching of clinical skills within a curriculum that emphasizes the scientific basis of medicine. These case studies describe the implementation, evaluation, and process of embedding the portfolio within the respective curricula. They also illustrate the flexibility of a component-based ePortfolio to serve different pedagogic requirements. Research and evaluation issues are discussed, including an action-research approach with "fine-tuning" of technical features and pedagogy during the evaluation phase.

The purpose of this chapter is to describe the use of an electronic learning journal in the portfolio process and the construction of a digital portfolio. The authors discuss the problems that have arisen during the learning and tutoring process of various traditional (paper) learning journals. The problems of traditional learning journals and their tutoring have been the following: (1) low extent of tutoring and evaluation during the process; (2) when the learning journal is the object of external assessment, it is not used as a tool for profound reflection (private vs. public dimensions of the learning journal); and (3) there has been a lack of a user-friendly tools with which to construct a Web-based learning portfolio. In this chapter the authors discuss the basic elements of ONNI–The Learning Journal, as well as how this electronic tool can help in solving the problems mentioned above. ONNI is presently being experimented on at the University of Kuopio, but it will also be developed to become a tool for every Finnish college student and to better support learning from peers as well as lifelong learning.

The study reported here explored the use of an ePortfolio in teacher education, focusing on its possibilities for development of competencies in technology. The goal was to assess this competency development over a three-month period and to examine pre-service teachers' perception of the ePortfolio as a learning tool. Results show that pre-service teachers' competencies with technology increase while working on the ePortfolio and that they respond favorably to the ePortfolio as a learning tool. Pre-service teachers feel that the ePortfolio fosters reflection and the development of organizational skills and self-esteem while giving them better chances of finding employment. Solutions and recommendations about improving the use of an ePortfolio as a learning tool in a teacher education program are proposed.

their students, and highlights why ePortfolios are becoming more popular for supporting learners and learning. The authors aim to provide a context for ePortfolios in the UK, discuss the drivers for change, identify some of the issues faced by institutions, and highlight some of the differences in ePortfolio adoption between the UK and other countries.

MAPS, the Managed Assessment Portfolio System (see http://www.maps-ict.com), is a Web-based ePortfolio system that was developed to help both teachers and learners, initially with a focus of helping to raise standards in the teaching and learning of information and communications technology in the UK. MAPS has since developed into a system covering all stages and subjects of school education, and is now being used in further education contexts. This chapter plots the progress of MAPS from an initial sketch idea to its present form: supporting over 57,000 student portfolios. The authors then draw out a number of lessons learned from such extensive use. The chapter finishes with a look at forthcoming ePortfolio issues and consideration of the requirements of lifelong learning ePortfolios.

This chapter outlines the implementation of electronic portfolio technology as part of a university initiative to improve learning. The implementation of electronic portfolios, via Epsilen Software, is discussed in terms of key features deemed necessary by Bowling Green State University's assessment committee. One of the key features of the software is the matrix. This matrix is discussed in terms of its use for documenting student learning on the university's learning outcomes. Reactions from current users are also provided. The chapter concludes by providing the current status of electronic portfolio usage at the university and a discussion of future plans for the software.

This exploratory study examines if student perceptions and ePortfolio products match faculty beliefs that ePortfolios are influential learning experiences. Multiple methods of data collection (survey about values and uses of ePortfolios, and content analysis of the quality of ePortfolios) are used to triangulate the results. Student ePortfolios are reviewed for level of difficulty, uniqueness, design, and depth of reflection. Multiple raters help ensure reliability. Bivariate analysis as descriptive statistics is used to determine if any relationship exists between ePortfolio rubric score and academic credits earned in computer technology courses. This research aims to inform the development process of ePortfolios across university campuses, and suggests that the investment of time and resources in this authentic assessment process is yielding some valuable results.

This chapter introduces the Queensland University of Technology (QUT) ePortfolio project as an example of a successful collaboration and integration strategy within a higher education context. Following extensive piloting and testing, the portfolio was released to all students and staff late in 2004, and by May 2005 in excess of 10,000 portfolios had been commenced. This chapter will present insights into this project which reveal some key collaboration and integration strategy decisions that were taken by both the university and the portfolio design team. In order to support these insights, preliminary student, academic, and employer feedback is provided based on research carried out from 2003 to 2005. The authors hope that this chapter will provide insights that will enable other institutions to enjoy similar success.

This chapter examines the creative production context as a vehicle to reveal the issues, problems, and complexities that may be encountered when working with ePortfolios. We utilize metaphors from the creative arts as tools to provide new perspectives and insights that may not otherwise occur in other disciplines to provide a unique critique of the performativity of ePortfolios. Through reference to case studies drawn from drama, dance, music, new media, and the visual arts, the authors' research has problematized ePortfolios from the teacher, student, institutional, and pedagogical perspectives. They identify the issues and propose approaches to resolving them, and illustrate how these ideas derive from creative arts knowledge and outline how they are transferable to other disciplines using ePortfolios based on rich media forms of presentation. In conclusion, they examine the performing arts as temporal art forms attuned to the unfolding of a narrative and examine the notion that the audience experiences the reading of a portfolio as a performance.

When an institution-wide electronic student portfolio "goes public" beyond the campus, the processes of its conceptualization, development, implementation, and evaluation appear seamlessly successful. Similar to a published manuscript, all is in place, and the tortuous paths of creation are invisible. Yet we can learn from both the steps and missteps of any innovation. This chapter describes the evolution of the Indiana University (IU) student electronic portfolio from its initial conception as a first-year "electronic report card" of student learning of core skills to a fully integrated enterprise system that enhances, documents, certifies, and evaluates learning.

This case study illustrates a community-based constructive learning approach to ePortfolio development, and the subsequent phenomena and outcomes that came from the initial implementation. The authors discuss why and how an ePortfolio system was chosen, as well as faculty engagement, student engagement, and recommendations to others based on the University of Texas at San Antonio experience.

This project focused on student development in the freshman year as displayed in students' ePortfolios. The experimental design allowed analysis of student attitudes about ePortfolios with results that may be useful to faculty and students at other institutions. Researchers found that careful alignment of an ePortfolio with the learning goals of a course can help students to adapt easily to the new technology and recognize it as a useful academic tool.

This chapter reports on a pilot study which examined how student teachers of a one-year Post Graduate Certificate in Education course in Northern Ireland developed reflective ePortfolios and then used them to embed ICT in their first (Induction) year as qualified teachers. Two central themes emerged. First, the process of constructing the ePortfolio developed confidence among the beginning teachers which supported them when faced with the challenges of starting teaching. Second, the ePortfolio was used to ease the transition from Initial Teacher Education to Induction, but where there is a lack of critical reflection, barriers to professional development can emerge. These issues are discussed within the context of technology policy, teacher training, and emerging technology in Northern Ireland.

The chapter describes the Tecnológico de Monterrey implementation of an original ePortfolio model at the Mexico City campus. This model is grounded on student reflection in three broad areas of students' lives designed by Jesus Meza, PhD. The implementation was launched in August 2002, with 60 students studying two different majors. By January 2005, the number of student portfolios had grown to 5,000, covering 18 different majors. According to the mission of the Tecnológico de Monterrey for the year 2015, the authors consider that the ePortfolio model will evolve into a comprehensive communication tool reflecting the personal, academic, and professional achievements of the community at the Tecnológico de Monterrey.

For every creator of a portfolio, there needs to be a reader. In this chapter, we look at several samples of how the issue of audience has affected a digital portfolio system. Our samples come from high school and elementary schools, and from the original research on digital portfolios in the 1990s to schools using them

Foreword

This is the first book to be published with an entire focus on the ePortfolio. It will not be the last, because it comes at a very propitious moment when important forces are converging—forces that are causing us to re-examine where learning takes place and how it could be assessed, how work and knowledge should be managed, who we really are as we present ourselves to the world, how we use technology for teaching and learning. This thing we call the ePortfolio is a flashpoint at the convergence of imperatives and opportunities in the management of learning for human and social capital development. And it is a great source of inspiration as we re-evaluate our hopes and expectations for eLearning and for lifetime learning policies.

Why should it be that, when we combine two familiar words—electronic and portfolio—paradigms shift? In the field of education and training, we are relatively familiar with portfolio assessment of learning, with reflective teaching and learning, with self-assessment and self-directed learning, project learning, digital storytelling, technology-assisted evaluation, competence-based assessment, marking rubrics, prior learning assessment, blended learning, learning outcomes, evaluation practices, lifelong and lifewide learning. In the field of information and communication technologies, we are relatively aware of privacy concerns, access issues, new media and media convergence, eGovernment, eLearning, eCommerce, social networking, blogging, and podcasting. In the field of career and human resources management, we are relatively committed to skills gap analysis and targeted training, return on investment in learning systems, recognition of foreign credentials, the value of personal skills inventories as career transition and bridging mechanisms, skills outsourcing, and niche marketing. In public policy areas, we remain concerned about youth who are non-completers of formal education, adult illiteracy rates, the over-credentialing of the workplace, skills shortages, immigration practices, allocation of increasingly scare resources. The power of the ePortfolio, in my view, is that it combines the best of all we know from all these concerns and commitments put towards the new promotion and management of learning for the benefit of individuals and society at large.

Well, that is the theory at least. For several years now, ePortophiles like me and Ali Jafari and Serge Ravet have been hypothesizing the many and varied benefits of ePortfolios for individuals, institutions, business enterprises, and entire nations. This book is important because it moves us beyond speculation with research and practical experience. It is establishing critical benchmarks in the application of ePortfolios, largely in the context of formal education, but moving as well into the workforce and workplace.

Here is where I feel compelled to state clearly that an ePortfolio must have the capacity to include and place value on all forms of learning: formal, informal, non-formal, accidental, and incidental. In the workplace, then, an ePortfolio can accommodate work experience and non-formal training. And in the broader sense, all ePortfolios should incorporate learning from family and community responsibilities, reading and travel, troubles, and triumphs. That is what Dr. Jafari's next book will likely be about.

Recognizing the potential of the ePortfolio, there are two organizations promoting two important missions. The Learning Innovations Forum d'Innovations d'Apprentissage (LIfIA) in the Americas, together with the European Institute for E-Learning (EIfEL) in the European Union, actively advocate for:

- an ePortfolio for every citizen by 2010, and
- one ePortfolio for life.

Thanks to this book, more and more people will understand what we are talking about. We early adopters are still faced with very basic questions: *What IS an ePortfolio? What are you talking about?* This field is so exciting to us because our understanding of ePortfolios changes and improves at a very rapid rate—perhaps because of the international nature of the communication and commitment to ePortfolios, the resulting leapfrogging of concepts and applications between the Americas, Europe, and Australia.

It does feel like a family, and that is a good thing. In my view, we have a limited window to get this ePortfolio thing right. We did not get eLearning right. In encouraging and supporting "a thousand flowers to bloom," we have ended up with species of products and services that cannot and do not exist in the same ecosystem. And the end users—the learners and the purchasers—are the ones who pay for that inconsistency in approach and quality. The ePortfolio is so important that we cannot afford to have early adopters face the same problems and challenges that we have faced with eLearning. For that reason, it is critically important that we welcome everyone into the ePortfolio community. By continuous sharing of ideas and issues, we have been able to inculcate the importance of interoperability and transportability in ePortfolio systems—"one ePortfolio for life." We have opened lines of communication and collaboration by emphasizing that there is a giant new "industry" developing, with room and a role for anyone who is interested. We are working on promoting the value of quality standards within a competitive business environment, on developing systems that involve the agency that receives and processes individual ePortfolios, on meeting the needs of target audiences like Aboriginal peoples, seniors, healthcare workers, skilled immigrants, early school leavers ... working until "every citizen has an ePortfolio."

Here I feel compelled to be clear that the word "ePortfolio" has almost become a code word for a variety of very important concepts: the digital archive from which a purpose-driven ePortfolio can be created, the digital identity that links us to our own learning and to others, the management of time past, present, and future; social networking and social capital development; human capital development and management. It may go without saying, but we need to respect and promote the notion that an ePortfolio can be one of many different things depending on audience perspective and purpose. There can be no ePigeonhole for ePortfolios!

In my view, the ePortfolio is the tool to bring about the radical transformation of learning systems that futurists have been advocating for. We have been adamantly writing and speaking about the necessity to rethink how learning is delivered, to whom and by whom, how important non-formal and informal learning are. The ePortfolio may be the tool that we have been waiting for.

After considerable research and reflection, I have concluded that the ePortfolio represents the single greatest innovation in the use of learning technologies and transformation tools for the following reasons:

1. **The ePortfolio is eLearning at its Finest:** the best, least complicated, most appropriate use of ICT for learning and learning management on an individual and a societal basis.
2. **It is an Elegant Use of Inelegant Technologies:** using complex technological developments in simple, practical ways. Unlike most eLearning, the ePortfolio tool is typically user friendly and appealing with great and immediate utility.
3. **An ePortfolio System Can Do What Computers Do Best:** sorting and matching. It increases effectiveness and efficiency in learning assessment, staff recruitment and advancement, project implementation. It is a critical knowledge management tool in the digital age.
4. **It is a Learning Leveler:** it can be made accessible to each and every person regardless of skill levels and personal assets, and there is seldom a substantial cost involved. An ePortfolio can be as ubiquitous and equalizing as the Internet itself.
5. **It Focuses on "The Positive":** archiving and showcasing what a person knows and can do. The outcome of an ePortfolio is "look what I've achieved!" Rather than being deficit based, it is asset based.

6. **It Can Become a Complete Description of a Person's "Human Capital":** acquired skills and knowledge, including and going far beyond those represented by formal credentials. An ePortfolio incorporates learning from formal, informal, non-formal, accidental, and incidental learning environments.
7. **It is a More Accurate Description of a Person's "Human Capital":** being competency based, it does not assume or imply competence or use proxies for learning.
8. **For Teaching Purposes, It Builds on Best Practices in Designing, Delivering, and Assessing Skills and Knowledge:** authentic assessment is a cornerstone of the ePortfolio.
9. **For Learning Purposes, It is Appropriate for All Lvels and Types of Learners:** it builds on best practices in how people learn and shows positive change in the acquisition of new skills and knowledge. Reflective learning is another cornerstone of the ePortfolio process.
10. **It is Equally Adoptable in Both Formal and Informal Learning Situations:** teachers and instructors can use it for alternative assessment of learning aimed at accreditation. Lifelong learners can use it to understand and record ongoing acquisition of insight and competencies.
11. **It is Endlessly Scalable:** from the individual to an entire business or nation. This is in part because of interoperable technologies, and in part because of common learning and learning management needs at all levels.
12. **It Can be Both Deeply Private and Universally Accessed:** while the content of an ePortfolio is the sole property of the person or body creating it, the ePortfolio can be shared by them in many controlled ways or podcast to the world.
13. **It is a Comfortable Means of Communication Between Learners and Teachers/Mentors/Advisors and Friends:** it is exploratory and constructivist, rather than definitive and judgmental.
14. **It Can be a Critical Transformation Tool for Learning Systems:** to outcomes-based, learning-centered learning. It puts accountability for learning into the hands of the learner.
15. **It Enhances Creativity and Problem Solving:** with the ePortfolio, there are many ways to explore and present learning.
16. **It Can be, at One Time, Both a Teaching and Learning Tool:** with the ePortfolio creator both learning through reflection and teaching through sharing the acquired insight and competencies.
17. **The ePortfolio, as a Teaching/Learning Tool, Creates a Unique Balance Between Structured and Unstructured Learning:** the tool guides but does not limit learners.
18. **It Has Endless Utility to Individuals and Those They Engage with:** people of all ages can use it as a personal knowledge management tool, recording achievements, targeting new learning requirements, even making application for advance standing in formal learning environments. Employers can use it to understand and manage an entire workforce of any size, for identifying human resource needs and best utilizing human capital. Communities of place, interest, or practice can inventory entire competency banks and human capital resources for development and marketing purposes.

As you read this book, see if you do not agree with me. This book is important because it will launch new conversations and debates, generate new teams and research themes, support policy and practice initiatives.

Moving beyond hype and conjecture, I will offer my final advice. You ask, if we want to explore and promote the ePortfolio, *Where do we start?* With professional educators. Until and unless teachers, instructors, professors, and administrators have their own ePortfolios, they will not have the credibility or commitment to expect learners to develop and use ePortfolios. They—you—are the audience for this book, and I hope you are either inspired or compelled to create your own digital archive, your ePortfolio presentation of yourself, your own digital identity.

Dr. Kathryn Chang Barker
President, FuturEd Consulting Education Futurists, Inc., Canada
Chair, Learning Innovations Forum d'Innovations d'Apprentissage, Canada
ePortofile

* * *

As this book demonstrates through scientific studies and informed testimonies, the ePortfolio is currently effecting a quiet revolution in the world of learning. It is clear that the exciting initiatives being implemented in the higher education sector will be of relevance to other educational sectors, the world of work, and the community at large. The ability to connect different learning episodes (diachronic) and contexts at any given time (synchronic) is one of the main challenges ahead of us if we wish to reap all the benefits promised by the ePortfolio and revealed in the different chapters of this book. Interoperability, technical and organizational, will be critical to ensure that the ePortfolio plays the role of lifelong learning companion.

It has been estimated that by 2010 almost half of new jobs created will require tertiary-level education and almost 40% upper-secondary education. This will demand re-thinking education and training: how and where people learn, the roles of learners and those who support them, and the tools that will promote optimal learning. We feel that this re-think will mean an end to the "compartmentalization" of learning. The knowledge society will recognize the organic link between the learning citizen, the learning organization, and the learning territory: an open system of learning that embraces formal and informal, professional and cultural learning in the same dynamic.

Those involved in learning and training are looking for tools to transform the learning experience, to enable learners to become autonomous and enjoy a truly personalized development path. It is our view that the ePortfolio is one of the most significant tools for achieving this goal at all levels. It will support the realization of "portfolio careers" and act as an instrument for social inclusion, allowing all to "tell their story" and celebrate their achievements.

This is why, back in 2003, I suggested fixing as an objective for 2010 "*ePortfolio for all*." This was not just a question of numbers (x millions of people with an ePortfolio), but of creating the conditions for a continuum in the learning space where someone starting an ePortfolio at school, college, university, or work would not have to throw away the investment of several years when moving from one episode of life to another one. Even if in 2010 every citizen does not have an ePortfolio (which is very likely!), we should like to live in a world where every one of us is *entitled* to have an ePortfolio and is able to use it during our lifelong and lifewide learning journey. The ePortfolio will be our faithful digital companion, reflecting our digital identity and supporting our learning, and enabling transactions with others in a variety of social networks.

The *ePortfolio for all* campaign is a catalyst for change. It is about quality, not quantity. For example, while ePortfolios are already being used by job seekers, very few employers are *ePortfolio-aware*. Human resource professionals, familiar with the use of résumés to select candidates, have yet to progress to the analysis and evaluation of ePortfolios in their recruitment procedures. Even fewer have introduced ePortfolios as a tool to support learning, career planning, and development in-house. Greater progress is being made by professional bodies with mandatory continuing professional development, as a growing number are using ePortfolios to support CPD, and in some cases, like the Royal College of Nursing in the UK, using them for professional re-accreditation. ePortfolios are tools for the reflective practitioners *extracting learning from the workplace*, sharing their reflections with their peers to contribute to the development of learning communities.

Diachronic continuity, from kindergarten to school, college, university, and the world of work, and synchronic continuity of the learning landscape (Tosh & Werdmuller, 2004) through the different learning environments, from the personal learning space to the different learning communities, learning organizations, cities, and regions, will only be possible through a voluntary and concerted effort. Learning is about " ... establishing new premises (i.e., paradigms, schemata, mental models, or perspectives) to override the existing ones" (Nonaka & Takeucki, 1995). This applies to individuals, communities, organizations, as well as regions.

Informed policies are required, and we need a roadmap for the actions to engage across sectors, organizations, and countries. We need to demonstrate how the ePortfolio is a component key to today's top policy agendas—for lifelong learning, for the development of literacy and citizenship, for transparency of qualifications and workers' mobility in an increasingly global world, as well as continuing professional development.

If we look at Europe, we can see how regional, national, and European policies are critical factors in creating the conditions for extensive ePortfolio development that goes beyond the boundaries of classrooms, organizations or sectors. The most ambitious instance is Wales, now a politically independent province of the UK, which is offering an ePortfolio to all three million Welsh citizens. This initiative is an element of the vision of Wales as a *learning country,* providing every citizen with the infrastructure to record and exploit their learning achievements. Launched in November 2004, Careers Wales Online now has more than 80,000 regular users. The Welsh initiative sits alongside a series of other initiatives in the UK; for example, the ePortfolio is one of the top priorities of England's integrated eStrategy. I am very pleased to note that we are now moving away from explicit and separate *eLearning strategies* to *eStrategies for learning*. This is certainly more in line with EIfEL's vision of eLearning being the eTransformation of all the processes linked to all forms of learning, and not a separate entity.

Wales and England are not alone. Last September, the Computing Austrian Society had a meeting with representatives from different ministries to develop an eLearning strategy (which is in fact an eStrategy for learning) and decided to place the ePortfolio at the heart of this new eStrategy. Other countries, such as The Netherlands, are more advanced in their implementation of ePortfolios across sectors. The Dutch play a leading role in the initiatives in the field of human resources, in particular through the European chapter of HR-XML, the human resources standardization body which has published several specifications relevant to ePortfolios in the field of work, such as HR-Résumé, a specification that would allow an ePortfolio to be published on online recruitment services, when supporting this industry format.

While European countries are moving forward, some faster than others, Europe as a whole is also moving forward. Since 2000, national education policies, although still independent, are coordinated through the European Union by way of a series of resolutions bearing the name of the cities where they have been adopted: Bologna (common higher education area), Maastricht (Common Qualification Framework). The issues at stake are transparency, quality, recognition of informal and non-formal learning, and mobility of learners and workers as Europe responds to twenty-first century challenges.

One of the key instruments in meeting this challenge is Europass[1], an umbrella name given to a coordinated portfolio of documents, in a standardized format, for presenting and exchanging information about learners' history. The objective is to improve communication between job applicants and employers, regardless of borders, and help citizens make their qualifications and competencies clearly and easily understood throughout Europe. Europass should facilitate occupational mobility—between countries and sectors—and promote and add value to mobility in education and training. The European Commission estimates that three million citizens will use Europass by 2010.

The relation between an ePortfolio and Europass is twofold:

- **Europass Documents Can be Built from the Contents of an ePortfolio:** for example, the European CV could be built from the collection of information collected in an ePortfolio, or a certificate could be awarded from the assessment of an ePortfolio, generating a certificate supplement.

- **Europass Documents can Feed ePortfolio Repositories:** for example, a Diploma Supplement issued by a university, which is in fact a transcript of study in higher education, could be "posted" (or a reference to the transcript held by the university) on the ePortfolio of the students and could then be used by the prospective worker to feed in the CV sent to potential employers (the CV being the front page of the job-application ePortfolio).

By the end of 2005, every university will be obliged to deliver a Diploma Supplement to every student who requests one. Paper based initially, it is clear that as the initial source of information is based in information systems, paper transcripts will soon be replaced by the transfer of records from one establishment to another—for example, for registering at another university or to extract the information relevant to a résumé placed on the Internet to find a job.

In order to achieve this goal, it is critical to insure the interoperability of the records published by the different universities. The European Commission is co-funding TELCERT, a research project dedicated to measuring the conformance of the information produced or consumed by learning systems against specifications, building (almost) automatically test suites from initial specifications and standards. Those who attended the first ePortfolio 'plugfest' during the 3rd International E-Portfolio Conference at Cambridge (UK) were able to witness that six of the ePortfolio systems present were interoperable using relevant standards, such as UK-LeaP or (parts of) IMS-ePortfolio. We hope that we will soon be able to demonstrate that ePortfolio systems are conformant to HR-XML specifications and Europass specifications.

I believe that interoperability is critical for supporting much of the most interesting practice happening at the crossroads of different contexts in a lifelong and lifewide continuum. Interoperability is not only designed to make things easier for administrators of organizational and corporate information systems. Indeed, interoperability is also intended for us as ePortfolio owners who, being in charge of managing and administering our personal information systems, want a central location from which we can decide who can see what personal information about us. This information might be distributed, and in the near future reside on my personal computer (or server) in a peer-to-peer environment, but what I need is a central location from where all the information is aggregated and accessed under my control.

Here are seven things that I hope my ePortfolio—or let's call it my personal, lifelong, and lifewide learning landscape—will be able to do, and for which interoperability is a critical issue:

1. I want to be able to **aggregate,** in a central location, all key information about myself, such as the trail left in various information systems of organizations I have been dealing with, from kindergarten to nursing home (and eventually I want to reduce the size of this trail to its minimum!). *This requires standardized data format as well as protocols (e.g., SAML) ensuring that I control who has access to what piece of information.*
2. I want to be able to fully **exploit** the contents of my ePortfolio, using a multiplicity of services, for example, *cross-reference* the contents of my ePortfolio with standards of competence hosted by an industry sector governing body in order to present a file for accreditation of prior work experience; search or apply for a job. *This also requires a standardized data format as well as protocols across applications, such as those defined by the Open Knowledge Initiative (OKI).*
3. I want to be able to **profile** the readers of my multifaceted ePortfolio to present them with relevant information: faculty with curricular and (some) extracurricular activities; and employers with relevant information on competencies, experiences, and personal values without having to expose my gender or ethnic origin. This latter point is critical in some countries or sectors where prejudices are still prevalent. *This will probably require some kind of hand-shaking protocol (tell me who you are and I'll tell you more about me!) between personal information systems and the creation of "circles of trust" that will accredit visitors with the appropriate rights.*
4. I want to be able to **share** different parts of my ePortfolio across different communities having their own "aggregator" of individual ePortfolios, providing a seamless environment of individual and

community ePortfolios—for example, professional communities, communities of practice, and organizational ePortfolios used for quality assurance or accreditation. *Some communities are already using RSS aggregators, but one of the most promising technologies is probably the semantic Web, starting with (enriched) specifications such as FOAF (Friend of a Friend).*

5. I want an ePortfolio **intelligent** enough to automatically update some of its contents and presentations; for example, when I create an item about a new work experience, having my résumé automatically updated (but still have the ability to edit it manually, if I wish) or like wikis, (semi-) automatically cross-reference documents, so that when I have an item on a particular work experience, and if I write a reflection where the name of the employer is mentioned, create a link between the name and the item. *There is nothing really special here, so can't the suppliers just do it?*
6. I want an ePortfolio **flexible** enough to let me choose if I want to fill in information using forms (because I am lazy, I lack imagination, or on a more positive note, since I prefer starting with disconnected pieces of content and provide the context later) or through a blog or a free-form editor that lets me structure (like the outline mode of a word processor) and enrich its contents with tags (e.g., mark parts of a text "evidence" or "reflection"), giving me the ability to start with the "context" from which I then aggregate linked pieces of contents. *Here again, there is nothing really special, so why not do it?*
7. I want an ePortfolio **resilient** enough so that when a primary source of information disappears or when technical standards evolve, I am still able to access it, for example, access a record from a start-up that went bust. *This requires mechanisms such as caching (the type of service offered by Google) and replication.*

I believe that part of the realization of my seven wishes will derive from an architecture that will be a combination of peer-to-peer networks (with the contents of my ePortfolio cached in a databank) and client-server technologies to interact with various institutions and organizations.

But making my wishes come true would not be possible without the hard work of ePortfolio practitioners and publishers, who, as the authors of this book demonstrate, are exploring with a curious and open mind this still almost virgin territory. I believe that the contents of this book, bearing witness to the transformational impact of ePortfolios and generating stimulating reflections on the nature of twenty-first century learning, will make a major contribution to the cartography of this new territory and help us to get the necessary political commitment to achieve our 2010 goal: (interoperable) *ePortfolio for all!*

Serge Ravet
Chief Executive, European Institute for e-Learning (EIfEL), France

ENDNOTE

[1] The Europass suite of documents consists of a CV, a language portfolio; a record of trans-national mobility experiences; the Europass Diploma Supplement (EDS, part of a worldwide initiative with the support of UNESCO) issued—along with a higher education diploma—by the university or institution outlining the student's educational pathway in terms relevant to potential employers, and the Europass Certificate Supplement, a version of the EDS for vocational education

REFERENCES

Nonaka, I., & Takeucki H. (1995). *The knowledge-creating company.* Oxford, UK: Oxford University Press.

Tosh, D., & Werdmuller B. (2004, September). Creation of a learning landscape: Weblogging and social networking in the context of e-folios. In *E-Portfolio 2004 Proceedings.* France: EIfEL.

Preface

The concept for this book started in the early days of the ePortConsortium, when the consortium members were working on the development of the Electronic Portfolio White Paper (2003). Based on the positive, supportive reaction to that white paper, Catherine Kaufman, the longtime coordinator of ePortConsortium, and I decided to investigate the massive research being done worldwide on the subject of electronic portfolios, or ePortfolios. We invited all national and international members of the ePortConsortium, EPAC, and other ePortfolio groups and individual professionals to submit proposals for authoring chapters on one of three categories: ePortfolio thinking, ePortfolio technology, and ePortfolio case studies. As the proposal submission deadline approached, we received a tremendous response from experts around the world to our call for chapters. After we notified the publisher that we would likely not be able to accept some excellent and authoritative chapters due to our page limitation, the publisher suggested changing the book format to that of a handbook so that we could be more comprehensive in our publication. As a result, this book has developed to become the very first handbook on the subject of research on ePortfolios.

Other matters influenced the decision to develop this book. First, it was the obligation we felt as the director and the coordinator of the ePortConsortium to provide a service: to improve the global knowledge and understanding of the use of ePortfolios, and in doing so, to offer a better understanding of the concepts, technology, and standards surrounding the new ePortfolio paradigm and its future. We thought the development of a complete collection of current knowledge and examples of ePortfolio uses could benefit the entire ePortfolio community, from the conceptual thinkers to technologists to the end users. Second, in order to be able to better define the ePortfolio and to itemize its expected requirements and functionalities, we needed to survey international experts about the growing knowledge and existing examples of ePortfolios. I believed a review of the information and data ultimately presented as chapters within this book would assist us in defining the ePortfolio and painting its bigger picture as perceived by the various stakeholders.

ePORTFOLIO OPPORTUNITES AND CHALLENGES IN 2005

Although 2005 is almost a decade since the concept and technology of ePortfolio was introduced, the ePortfolio still faces two major challenges that should be addressed, and resolving those challenges would result in opportunities to conduct research and investigations and thus develop better conceptual and technical environments which make the ePortfolio a more accepted and integrated application into our learning, teaching, and professional practices. Before discussing the challenges, however, I should mention that this is only my personal perspective as to these issues, not necessarily the analysis of any of those authors who contributed chapters in this book.

I believe 2005 was yet another year where the advancement of the idea of ePortfolio among potential end users ended with limited success. Although some reports suggest that a large percentage of some communities are seriously using ePortfolio services or programs, according to my observation, as well as the much more systematic and documented research by Jo Paoletti of the University of Maryland (Paoletti, 2006), the picture is not as rosy as many would like the world to believe. Student "use" of ePortfolio in some of these reports simply means that students have created ePortfolio accounts, as requested or required by an instructor or administrator, yet those students are not necessarily updating those accounts after creation, much less maintaining, developing, improving, or sharing them. In some other cases, the data suggests that the majority of students who participated in a trial offering or beta testing simply abandoned the application. The important data to investigate and report is how many of the end users continued to use and maintain their portfolios after the trial period ended—for instance, after the mandate for using the ePortfolio to fulfill the requirement of a course ended. This suggests one of the two primary challenges that the ePortfolio is still facing in 2005: the current ePortfolio solutions and systems are not "sticky" to the end users—that is, the ePortfolio does not draw the end user back time and again, and thus has not become integrated into the lives of end users. I believe this is a very important element and one of the major expectations that many academic officers have.

The lack of stickiness being experienced with the ePortfolio has not been a challenge in some of the other new technologies introduced in academia; for example, the course management system (CMS). Once a faculty member used a course management system to complement a course, he most likely wanted to continue using it over and over, and in fact, many times faculty suggested ways to make it a better system and asked for more support. Students demonstrated this same high level of interest in CMS quickly after initial exposure to the system. It did not take more than two years before CMS was accepted as a sticky, useful tool, as compared to the ePortfolio which is experiencing a much longer time before acceptance, much less full implementation.

The stickiness problem of the current ePortfolio packages should not be seen as a long-term problem, though, nor should we allow it to cause us to question the usefulness and importance of ePortfolios in learning and beyond. In fact, this is an opportunity for us to continue our progress toward inventing a total solution package that "works" with sticky effect (Jafari, 2004). The "working" requirement has been our second challenge. An ePortfolio solution must offer all expected functional and technical requirements in a transparent and user-friendly environment. It must be able to integrate with other technology systems (such as CMS, SIS, and Campus Portals) in order to offer an interoperable "working" environment. For example, in order for an ePortfolio system to certify the authenticity of a learning artifact such as a student term paper, the ePortfolio system must be able to interoperate with a CMS system through which a student is presenting his term paper to the course instructor. We must recognize that the technology of the ePortfolio and the incorporated software code are only components of the whole package. We should further consider the incentives and support we must offer students and faculty to encourage use, as well as evaluate the internal academic policies and community role requirements that need to be satisfied to endorse official implementation. In addition, we have to substantiate the software costs and maintenance expenses so that administrators are persuaded of the efficacy of the ePortfolio. Finally, most notably, we must address the human aspects of the system to stimulate personal interest so that all have an understanding of how lifelong use and sharing of ePortfolios can both create and promote wide-ranging future opportunities.

THE KILLER APPLICATION

In 1995, Pierre Omdyar, the creator of eBay, came up with the idea of using the Internet as a totally new concept or a new paradigm of electronic trade, selling and buying "stuff" online. Here I see a similarity between eBay and the ePortfolio. Around the same time that Omdyar conceptualized eBay, some provosts and academic leaders thought of using technology or the Internet to present portfolio "stuff" online, called ePortfolio. What Omdyar invented, however, was a total package, an environment, the eBay system, not just the concept of eCommerce or lines of computer codes. Although many people have acknowledged his main invention as a software environment or the computer codes that run the eBay engine, in reality the invention was a total system package. He created a new market, the eCommerce paradigm, one that was not already in place. He invented a new method that can be used to establish trust among sellers and buyers using the feedback notion, something that was not needed or used in a traditional trade. Once an eBay user conducts a bad transaction, the entire community becomes aware of negative feedback in the matter of one click, and therefore that user has less chance of conducting any more business within that community. Omdyar built incentives into his model for eBay users to follow the rules that he developed, and the eBay community automatically rejects those who do not follow the rules. Omdyar's system is carefully designed around the human aspects, with a full understanding of people's expectations for usability, for trust, for communication, and finally, and I would argue most importantly, for stickiness. You will hardly find a person that uses eBay once or twice and does not stick to it to continue the use. This level of stickiness is almost here for CMS. But is it here for ePortfolios?

Although there are many good ePortfolio systems and packages available today, I believe the field of ePortfolio is still waiting for another Pierre Omdyar to invent a "sticky" ePortfolio package solution that "works." I see more and more commercial systems coming to the commercial or open source market, either as a stand-alone ePortfolio management system or as an add-on component to existing CMS software; however, I do not believe any of the current packages and solutions today are as sticky as the CMS was in the late nineties. In fact, I am one of those who have been trying to invent an ePortfolio solution for the last five years. Since late 2000, I have been using all of my CyberLab resources and all of my passion and R&D capacity to invent an ePortfolio solution called Epsilen Environment (www.epsilen.com, 2005). However, I am not yet sure if I have come up with that total solution package needed today. Currently, we are working on the third version of the Epsilen Environment, the third system, with some integrated eBay and even Amazon conceptual functionality, with the hope that it will turn on the light and offer that "sticky" solution that we badly need to make our ePortfolio dreams come to reality, to make the ePortfolio "work."

WHAT CAN YOU DO?

Practice what you preach. If you are reading this book, you most likely know about the ePortfolio and should appreciate its usefulness and applications in learning, teaching, and other aspects of your life. If you believe the ePortfolio has potential, use it and create your own ePortfolio site now. This is the best way to better understand the ePortfolio potential and to advance its concepts and usefulness to others. I continue seeing ePortfolio enthusiasts, developers, and researchers at various conferences making conference presentations on ePortfolios, or even selling ePortfolio software at tradeshows—but who have not even created an ePortfolio site for themselves! An observer might ask, "If you believe the ePortfolio is useful, why don't you use it yourself?"

I have been using my personal ePortfolio site for several years and find it to be very effective as a primary tool for my collaboration, teaching, research, and professional networking. This has given me two advantages: first, it is a very useful tool that makes my day-to-day job easier and more enjoyable; second, I continue to discover new applications and uses for the ePortfolio as I use it more often and more seriously. Many of the features presented in the Epsilen Environment ePortfolio I discovered as the result of my own ePortfolio use. I like it and use it so much that I have placed the Web address of my ePortfolio in my e-mail signature block. When people ask me for a look at this paper, that conference presentation, this project, that course, I simply give them the Web address of my ePortfolio. In some cases, I give them an access code to gain access to materials that I do not want the public or other groups to see.

HOW TO USE THIS BOOK

This book consists of two primary sections. Section I includes a number of chapters focusing on the conceptual aspects of ePortfolio, written by conceptual thinkers, academic administrators, and researchers, as well as a limited number of chapters which address the technical aspects of ePortfolios. Creative thinkers such as those who authored chapters in this section should be considered as the inventors of the ePortfolio. Their vision, combined with their subject matter expertise and their administrative responsibilities, have given birth to this new technology environment called ePortfolio. Few authors tackled the issue of program technology, but we expect that in the future, as more technology systems, solutions, and standards are developed, commercialized, and implemented, more experts will produce manuscripts that concentrate on those topics.

Section II consists of a series of ePortfolio case studies reporting on various ePortfolio initiatives and projects being explored, tested, and implemented in a range of educational institutions across the world. We have divided Section II into three subsections, with the initial chapters focusing on ePortfolio initiatives, exploring projects such as campus initiatives or committee work to understand and study the feasibility of ePortfolio implementation, followed by the second subsection of case studies reporting on a test or trial of an ePortfolio system for limited members or groups within an institution, and finally the third subsection examining case studies of full implementation of an ePortfolio project.

Each case study offers lessons learned, those caused by good or bad decisions, along with the perceptions of end users. A close examination of these case studies will certainly assist those inventing, researching, or participating in new ePortfolio projects by offering guidelines and suggestions for building a more successful ePortfolio project.

Our hope is that the readers of this book will come to realize the opportunities and challenges presented by the ePortfolio, and that by reviewing the discussions and case studies of international experts, they will advance their own awareness, development, or implementation of what we believe will soon be acknowledged by all as the next most valuable lifelong tool for individuals and institutions worldwide.

Ali Jafari, PhD
Director of CyberLab and Professor of Engineering and Technology
Purdue School of Engineering and Technology at IUPUI
Indiana University-Purdue University Indianapolis (IUPUI), USA
ePortfolio: http://jafari.iupui.epsilen.com

REFERENCES

Electronic Portfolio White Paper. (2003). Retrieved from http://www.eportconsortium.org/Uploads/whitepaperV1_0.pdf

Epsilen Environment. (2005). Retrieved from http://www.epsilen.org

Jafari, A. (2004). The sticky ePortfolio system: Tackling challenges and identifying attributes. *EDUCAUSE Review, 39*(3), 38-48.

Paoletti, J. (2006). ePortfolio thinking: The challenge of the public research university. In *Handbook of research on ePortfolio* (pp. 565-573). Hershey, PA: Idea Group Reference.

ADDITIONAL SOURCES

CyberLab. (2005). Retrieved from http://cyberlab.iupui.edu

ePortConsortium. (2005). Retrieved from http://www.eportconsortium.org

Acknowledgments

The editors are deeply grateful for the collaboration, cooperation, and contributions of the chapter authors who made this handbook a reality. They would further like to thank all the members of the ePortConsortium, both the academic and corporate members, whose donations and support help maintain the important work of the ePortConsortium and provided the incentive for the editors to produce this book.

Ali Jafari, IUPUI, USA
Catherine W. Kaufman, ePortConsortium, USA

Section I

ePortfolio Thinking and Technology

This section includes a series of chapters focusing on the conceptual aspects of electronic portfolio systems and elaborates on how the innovative use of the ePortfolio can advance teaching and learning. Authors present their views of the current and potential uses for such systems in an effort to define the "big picture" for practical applications of ePortfolios. Chapters are written by conceptual thinkers, including academic leaders such as provosts within the higher education institutions, administrators within departments of education responsible for K-12 education, and experts in countries where ePortfolio usage is promoted by government. The section finally explores the technological aspects of the ePortfolio framework surrounding how the ePortfolio system as a new application software can be designed, built, and developed to operate either within an existing learning management system or as an independent enterprise systems, and authors discuss topics such as technical standards and functional interoperability among such systems.

Chapter I
Instructional Roles of Electronic Portfolios

Greg Sherman
Radford University, USA

ABSTRACT

This chapter presents an overview of 11 different ways in which electronic portfolios (ePortfolios) can support the teaching and learning process. Too often, discussion about the general instructional nature of ePortfolios only focuses on two distinct roles: portfolios as a means of assessing specific student performance, and portfolios as a showcase for outstanding student accomplishments. This chapter summarizes how ePortfolios can contribute to the design and implementation of effective instruction in many different ways by assuming a variety of roles that go beyond a traditional approach to portfolio use in the classroom. These roles include artifact creation as meaningful context, goal-setting, practice with a purpose, examples and non-examples, assessment, reflection, communication, instructor planning and management tool, learner organization tool, interdisciplinary teaching and learning, and historical records/stories as role models. Examples of portfolio requirements and assessment strategies from a higher education teacher preparation program are used to illustrate these different roles.

INTRODUCTION

Electronic portfolios (ePortfolios) can play a variety of roles within any given educational environment. Teachers might use ePortfolios as a means of assessing student achievement by designing portfolio artifact requirements that reflect the successful learning and application of specific skills. Similarly, ePortfolios can be used to showcase outstanding student achievement in general if the required portfolio artifacts are designed to communicate the "best work" of students rather than the learning of specific outcomes. And because ePortfolio artifacts can be accessible via computer networks, the portfolio development experience can be used to ensure learner accountability as teachers, other students, parents, and even total strangers examine specific portfolio content.

Assessment, showcasing best practice, and learner accountability constitute some of the more common ways in which ePortfolios can be used within an educational environment. But these different roles represent just a small sample of the many different ways in which ePortfolios can support student learning. After designing and implementing ePortfolio requirements for different teacher education programs throughout the past 10 years, I have discovered that the true value of ePortfolios lies in the variety of ways portfolio artifact requirements can support the instructional process by defining effective instructional strategies.

The purpose of this chapter is to present a broad picture regarding how ePortfolios might be used to help facilitate learning within typical K-12 or higher education environments. In most cases, the roles presented in this chapter represent the application of instructional strategies designed to facilitate the learning of specific outcomes. The instructional strategies described within each role are consistent with those presented in many instructional design models, including the essential elements of effective instruction (Hunter, 1982), the systematic design of instruction (Dick & Carey, 1996), the conditions for learning (Gagné & Driscoll, 1988), and the constructivist-oriented models of Jonassen, Peck, and Wilson (1999).

Each of the following sections presents a single role along with a description of how portfolios playing such roles can be used to support effective instruction. Additionally, examples from the application of ePortfolio requirements within a preservice-teacher education program are provided to clarify specifically how ePortfolios might be used within typical instructional settings.

ROLES

Role 1: Artifact Creation as Instructional Context

Regardless of what role an ePortfolio might play within a typical learning experience, there is one thing that all ePortfolios have in common: the learners must *create* portfolio elements or artifacts to be presented within the portfolio itself. Artifacts might be developed specifically for an electronic format (like a Web page with annotated hyperlinks), or the artifacts might initially represent specific things that were not developed for inclusion in an electronic environment, such as a science project involving living organisms. In a case such as this, learners might communicate the essence of the science project within an electronic environment by capturing a series of digital images, generating digital graphs and charts, developing electronic documents that detail the design and data collection procedures, and so forth. But whether or not a learner decides to configure a piece of non-digital work to be displayed within an ePortfolio or develop something specifically for electronic delivery, the actual act of creating something for inclusion in an ePortfolio becomes a context for learning and applying a variety of skills.

A good illustration of how the act of creation can help define meaningful learning environments can be found in a closer examination of the requirements for a teacher preparation portfolio. Figure 1 presents an example of some ePortfolio requirements that could be used within a typical teacher preparation program. These sample ePortfolio requirements were designed to document and communicate the learning of skills reflected in a number of national standards for professional educators, such as the Interstate New Teacher Assessment and Support Consortium's (INTASC's) core teacher education standards (see http://www.ccsso.org) and the International Society for Technology in Education's (ISTE's) national educational technology standards for teachers (see http://cnets.iste.org/teachers). Today, many pre-service teachers must develop such portfolios in order to communicate accomplishments throughout their teacher preparation programs. One common artifact in this type of portfolio is a lesson plan or unit study (an example of this is presented in "Portfolio Component 7: Problem-Based Learning Instructional Material" within Figure 1). This type of artifact might include a description of the lesson plan itself, copies of instructional materials developed, and possibly a report detailing how effective the lesson was after being implemented within a field experience assignment. Initially, a portfolio artifact like this might consist of a word-processed lesson plan, materials developed from a variety of media, and a separate report that presents achievement data in tabular form. Creating an ePortfolio artifact that presents this information might involve scanning documents to create digital pictures, converting word-processed pages to Web pages, and taking digital pictures of non-digital material. And all this information would need to be organized and stored within some type of digital media environment, such as a Web site or CD-ROM. This act of "creation" would necessitate the learning and/or application of a variety of skills related to the use of the technologies needed to make it all happen.

If you examine the list of basic skills that all teachers should be able to perform as recommended by ISTE, you would find that the act of successfully creating such electronic artifacts from existing teacher education material would provide evidence that the teacher candidate had mastered all the skills inherent in the "Technology Operations and Concepts" category. And more importantly, these skills would have been learned and/or applied within an environment that was meaningful for the learners—that is, to successfully communicate their lesson or unit plans to their supervisors and possibly peers.

Role 2: Goal-Setting/ Instructional Scaffolding

If providing a concrete creation-oriented context for the learning of specific skills is one of the most important roles that ePortfolios can serve within the teaching and learning process, then using ePortfolio requirements as a means of setting personal learning goals would probably rank a close second in terms of instructional importance. Clearly articulating the goals of a new learning experience constitutes one of the most important instructional strategies that should be included within any instruction. And providing learners with a detailed picture of all the artifacts that are expected to be included in an ePortfolio represents a very comprehensive way to communicate instructional goals. For example, professional education students who are expected to develop an ePortfolio based on the artifacts presented in Figure 1 are not only provided with a clear picture of what their portfolios should include, but the descriptions of each artifact also provide some direction with respect to individual assignments that will eventually lead to the creation of specific artifacts.

In order to develop an artifact that meets minimum design criteria, learners often require a more detailed development rubric or guideline. An example of this is presented in Figure 2. This chart presents criteria for the creation of material that will be projected (i.e., Microsoft PowerPoint presentations). These guidelines would be used to evaluate an artifact corresponding to the "Portfolio Component 4: Professional Presentations" in Figure 1. Understanding the specific requirements of an assignment in clear detail not only helps support learners by clarifying instructional goals, but the design requirements themselves can act as instructional support mechanisms for learners, providing them with opportunities to compare their progress to the project requirements. This type of support, often referred to as "metacognitive scaffolding" (Hannafin, Land, & Oliver, 1999), in combination with clear instructional goals, constitutes very effective instructional strategies for learners of all ages.

Role 3: Practice with a Purpose

Another important instructional role that an ePortfolio might play within any given learning experience relates closely to the first role (providing a context for learning and applying specific skills). If teachers require portfolios to be electronic in order to provide a context for learning and applying technology-related skills, then the act of successfully creating digital artifacts will no doubt require practice using various types of technology to successfully accomplish all required tasks. Lots of practice. Instead of assigning word-processing, scanning, and Web development lessons simply for the sake of learning how to scan or use a word processor, the journey toward successful portfolio development can be rich with practice using technology for a very definite purpose.

Role 4: Examples and Non-Examples

One of the most important instructional strategies for learning both knowledge and procedural skills is the availability of examples as well as non-examples that illustrate information, concepts, and rules (Gagné & Driscoll, 1988; Merrill & Tennyson, 1994). And one of the greatest strengths of ePortfolios is the ability to access portfolio content relatively easily. Most teachers and students appreciate the ability to have samples of unacceptable, acceptable, and outstanding work associated with specific assignments. ePortfolios provide teachers with the opportunity to easily collect and organize copies of specific artifact samples that have been evaluated and categorized. Because the artifacts are electronic, they can be readily edited to remove personal identifying information. These artifacts can then be made available to students during class by projecting them onto a screen when needed, or they can be accessed from computers via the Internet.

The components presented in Figure 1 offer many good examples of how previously developed portfolios might be used by teacher educators to help students learn specific skills related to teaching. Imagine you are a faculty member facilitating a methods class addressing important pedagogical topics, such as classroom management. Now suppose you assigned your students the task of developing a plan for improving the use of computers in the classrooms they were observing within their field experience placements. Students might include this assignment as part of their overall education portfolios, with the resulting work becoming a portfolio artifact in "Portfolio Component 2: Media as Tools of the Professional Educator" as presented in Figure 1. Specifically, the assignment might be included in "Subcomponent 2c: The One Computer Classroom." As a teacher, part of the instruction for this assignment could focus on your presentation of cooperative learning strategies that address the need for role assignments when sharing limited resources (Johnson & Johnson, 1998). If you had access to previously submitted portfolio artifacts in this category, you might be able to

Figure 1. Sample professional education ePortfolio requirements

Portfolio Component	Sub-Component	Artifacts/Criteria
1. Web-Based Portfolio Shell	a. Personal Image	Create and present a personal image digital file that includes: ▪ Personal image scanned or obtained via digital camera ▪ Converted to .gif or .jpg ▪ *Economic* use of size/colors
	b. Links	Develop, at a minimum, a Web page presenting links that include: ▪ Grade-level/subject matter professional organizations and journals ▪ Employment opportunities ▪ Grade-level/subject matter resources and references ▪ Local-state-national standards for specific grade level and/or content area
	c. Instructional Web Site Reviews	Develop a Web page that presents an overview of at least three existing educational Web sites, including a description of how they might be useful in facilitating specific standards related to your future professional practice
	d. Personal Philosophy and "Best Practice" Showcase	Present clearly articulated personal educational philosophies (before *and* after field experience) Present a sample of work representing area of personal, professional "Best Practice"
	e. Résumé	Create a professionally formatted Word document including, at a minimum: ▪ Educational background ▪ Technological competencies ▪ Community service experiences ▪ Previous work experiences ▪ Personal and career goals
2. Media as Tools of the Professional Educator	a. Instructional Management Tools	Communicate strategies and examples illustrating successful use of electronic media to improve instructional management skills and procedures (grades, record-keeping, resource management, etc.)
	b. Communication Tools	Present strategies and examples illustrating successful use of electronic media to increase classroom communication with the outside (real) world
	c. The One-Computer Classroom	Present a clearly articulated description and examples of the effective use of a single or small number of computers in your specific grade level or content-area classroom (if applicable)
	d. Resource Access and Use	Present descriptions of how the following education-related resources were obtained from the Internet and used (legally and ethically) within your professional practice: ▪ Freeware/shareware ▪ Lesson planning resources ▪ Images/sound/video files
	e. Media as Context	Present specific ways in which you have used electronic media to increase the meaning and/or purpose of instructional experiences in your classroom
	f. Media in the Content Area	Present unique ways in which electronic media, particularly computers, are being utilized to improve the quality and effectiveness of specific content-area and/or grade-level instructional methods and strategies

continued on following page

Figure 1. continued

3. Educational Research and Evaluation	Develop a well-constructed narrative presenting educational research, evaluation, and/or assessment efforts; this *may* be a project and/or report successfully completed within an approved evaluation or research course Generate effective graphic data presentation where appropriate	
4. Professional Presentations	Create electronically projected material (such as PowerPoint) conforming to appropriate projected message design criteria of a presentation you have made to a group of students or professionals (building or district meeting, conference, etc.)	
5. Educational Material Evaluations	Evaluate instructional material (print, software, Web site, etc.) used to facilitate the learning of specific outcomes; evaluation report should include (but is *not* limited to addressing): ▪ *Context:* Critical analysis of the learning context established ▪ *Components:* Identification and critique of instructional design components presented within the instructional material ▪ *Conditions:* Identification of outcomes addressed within the instruction, description of conditions and strategies implemented, critique of relationship between conditions/strategies and outcomes ▪ Evaluation of message display characteristics employed	
6. Content Area Conceptual "Big Pictures"	Create graphic concept map(s) depicting the relationships between distinct key ideas, skills, knowledge, concepts, and/or other important aspects of grade levels and/or content-area domains	
7. Problem-Based Learning Instructional Material	Plan, develop (author), implement, and evaluate instruction designed to facilitate the learning of specific standards/outcomes within a problem-based learning context. This learning experience should include, but is not limited to, the following elements: ▪ Outcome(s) the program is designed to facilitate must be clearly stated and well written ▪ *Context:* Meaningful, purposeful problem-based learning context must be established ▪ *Components:* Appropriate instructional design components must be developed for context type ▪ *Conditions:* Appropriate strategies and conditions must be developed for outcome type(s) ▪ *Message Display:* Instructional messages and program usability must conform to appropriate standards Evidence of student achievement must be included in the final evaluation of the material	
8. Instructional Design Project Management	Provide a record of design documents for one or more lesson-planning or instructional design projects: storyboards, instructional analyses, instructional strategy descriptions, formative evaluation procedures, summaries of any client/designer interactions, and functional specifications for the use of tools/media to solve particular lesson planning and instructional materials development problems	
9. Formative Evaluation Practices	Present plans and results from formative evaluation experiences conducted during your field experiences, including one-to-one evaluations, expert reviews, and field trials	
10. Strategies for Cultivating a Learner-Centered Classroom	a. Meaningful Learning Contexts	Provide evidence that lessons presented within meaningful contexts enable learners to set their own personal goals and relate to the learners' personal lives
	b. Differentiated Instruction	Provide evidence of enrichment, remediation, and alternate means of implementing instructional strategies to facilitate the learning of specific outcomes
	c. Time Management	Provide evidence that specific lessons (particularly large project- or problem-based experiences) allow learners to schedule their time (day, week)
	d. Physical Classroom Arrangement	Provide evidence that the physical arrangement of the classroom in which you facilitated learning: (1) ensured that necessary classroom resources were readily available to the learners; and (2) accommodated all *learner-centered classroom* strategies

continued on following page

Figure 1. continued

	e. Adequate Instructional Scaffolds	Present adequate scaffolds for specific instructional experiences; such scaffolds might include procedural, conceptual, metacognitive, strategic, and/or interpersonal support mechanisms for individual learners
	f. Self-Assessment	Present evidence that you structured self-assessment experiences for your learners and provided analytic rubrics at the beginning of a problem or project-based learning experience
	g. Roles	Provide evidence that you assign specific roles to each member of learning teams and implement other appropriate forms of positive interdependence when grouping students
11. Multicultural Classroom Environment	Provide evidence that you: (1) identified biases in the instructional material used to facilitate learning and you communicated these to your learners; and (2) developed instructional experiences that foster positive attitudes toward human diversity	
12. Field Experience Reflections	Present a variety of narratives documenting your personal insight and growth as you journey through your field experiences; these reflections should reference the feedback received from formal as well as informal evaluations conducted by cooperating teachers and university supervisors	

present actual digital pictures of students in local classrooms working in small groups around a single computer. Such examples might depict one student in a group recording information by using the computer keyboard, another group member reading aloud from a text-based resource, another student leaving the group as the designated "runner" to obtain additional resources, and another student (clipboard in hand) monitoring group activity to provide feedback over group member behaviors. Having such clear examples of role assignments would certainly help those students who were learning about incorporating formal cooperative learning strategies into the lesson planning process.

Role 5: Assessment

As previously discussed, ePortfolios are often used as a platform for the presentation of "best practice" examples, and they are also commonly used as a means of collecting and organizing artifacts that represent evidence of achievement aligning with specific learning outcomes. In both cases, learners can use detailed portfolio requirement criteria (as well as examples of artifacts developed by other learners) to help them regulate their learning and assess their progress as they develop their own artifacts. More directly, portfolio artifacts can be used to measure the learning of outcomes that would be difficult to assess using more traditional testing procedures.

Once again, a good example of how an ePortfolio artifact could be used to measure the learning of a specific outcome is found within the portfolio requirements presented in Figure 1. The details of "Portfolio Component 6: Content Area Conceptual 'Big Picture'" include the following:

Create graphic concept map[s] depicting the relationships between distinct key ideas, skills, knowledge, concepts, and/or other important aspects of grade levels and/or content-area domains.

Successfully accomplishing this task would involve, at a minimum, the application of skills in the areas of developmentally specific content

Figure 2. Assessment criteria for designing projected message displays (visual literacy principles)

Assessment Category	Assessment Criteria*
General Message Display	Screen display should follow the horizontal-vertical and left-right organization that is common to the culture of the intended audience: typically left-to-right, up-to-down in American public school culture.
	Attention should be drawn to those parts of a message intended to stand in contrast to other screen elements. Contrasts used to draw attention should be abrupt, using one or more of the following display characteristics: ▪ Brightness (regular versus dimmed text and pictures) ▪ Volume (i.e., bolded font, larger font size, etc.) ▪ Color ▪ Use of graphic devices such as lines and arrows ▪ Animation
	Messages should not be obscured by too much non-critical detail. The universal rule of design should generally apply: KEEP IT SIMPLE. One strategy for "keeping it simple" is to limit the amount of text on the screen. This can be accomplished by bulleting key ideas, not entire sentences.
	Avoid backgrounds that fade from dark to light across the entire slide *or* present a picture or pattern with very distinct light and dark regions.
Text Use	Text and background contrast should be clear (i.e., black text on a white background, white text on a blue background, etc.).
	Use a plain, light-colored background with dark text, or a plain dark background with light-colored text.
	Standard text formatting (mixed upper and lower case letters following standard grammar) should be used throughout, even for titles, headings, etc.
	Limit the amount of text per slide! A good rule of thumb is the 6 X 6 rule: Six words per line, six lines per slide MAX.
	Usually, complete sentences use too many words. Consider presenting the key ideas as bulleted points.
	Sans serif fonts are generally easier to read than serif fonts when projected. Serif fonts have little hooks or "feet" along the edges of each character; sans serif fonts do not.
	Try not to use a font size smaller than 16 point. Generally, the bigger the better.
	Use consistent fonts throughout (do not mix too many font types).
	Keep text away from side edges and borders.

continued on following page

knowledge, concept mapping, and the use of software enabling the visual creation or representation of a concept map. Now consider an elementary education student who is expected to learn the skills indicated within the National Council for Accreditation of Teacher Education's (NCATE) program standards for elementary teacher preparation, based on the standards developed by the Association for Childhood Education International (AECI). One of the standards in the "Connections Across the Curriculum" category states:

Candidates know and understand the connections among concepts, procedures, and applications from content areas.

Assessing this outcome might be easily accomplished through exams within specific content-area courses, though many higher

Figure 2. continued

Pictures and Illustrations	A picture's function on the slide should be clear (conceptual support, graphic organizer, lucid example, etc.).
	Pictures and illustrations should be closely related to the context of the text.
	Pictures designed to organize concepts and ideas should incorporate devices stressing temporal (time), conceptual, and/or spatial relationships: ▪ Storyboard layout ▪ Sequence emphasized by arrows, numbers, or labels ▪ Pictures in sequence presented one at a time in correct sequence (or video used to achieve same result) ▪ Spatial organization utilizes 3D diagrams or superimposition of features
	Pad the space around graphics (do not let text get too close to your pictures).
	Make the picture background transparent if it is different from slide background (or place a border around picture).
Diagrams, Charts, and Graphs	Diagrams and charts should be used to concisely communicate the relationship between related variables, especially variables that have numeric data presented in tables…
	…BUT concrete ideas might end up too abstract when presented in graphic form.
	Attention should be drawn to captions.
	The relative importance of elements should be represented by relative sizes in the diagram, thicker lines for stronger relationships, and so forth.
	Graphs depicting more precise amounts should utilize a Cartesian graph (x and y axis).
	Graphs depicting comparative amounts where precision is not important may utilize pie charts.
	Trends should generally be illustrated by line graphs.
	Comparisons may be illustrated by bar graphs or pie charts.
	Because chart labels are often presented in smaller font, it is usually best to place graphs and charts on individual slides with completely white backgrounds.

Note: Many of these visual design guidelines were adapted from Fleming and Levie (1993)

education subject matter courses do not necessarily address content as it relates to specific grade levels. But even if exam results were obtained for individual students, a relationship would need to be established between specific test items and " ... connections among concepts, procedures, and applications." Compare this option with using the corresponding ePortfolio artifact requirement for the development of a conceptual "Big Picture" (Figure 1, Component 6). In this case, the portfolio artifact reflects a means of assessment that is easier to access and communicate among and between faculty, and it represents a very effective way to measure the performance of those concepts indicated within the standard.

Role 6: Reflection

A very effective instructional strategy that applies to the learning of most types of skills is the facilitation of a review or closure experience within the instructional element. Particularly for adult learners, some of the more effective review activities include ensuring that individual learners reflect on what they learned, and examine the strengths and areas for improvement regarding *how* they learned these new skills (Knowles, 1984).

Most ePortfolio environments include the ability to easily add comments and/or notes to works-in-progress as well as completed artifacts. This capability of ePortfolio systems makes it easy to include opportunities for reflection and self-evaluation in the portfolio requirements. Figure 1 includes an example of a formal reflection requirement for a teacher education portfolio ("Portfolio Component 12: Field Experience Reflections"). Additionally, artifact creation often involves the development of many different versions or drafts before a permanent portfolio fixture is produced. These drafts can help learners reflect on the process they personally engaged in as they developed a complete and acceptable artifact.

Role 7: Communication

Many ePortfolio development programs and service (such as LiveText or TaskStream) include Web-based communication features. In addition to easily sharing electronic artifacts with others by displaying the material in Web pages, most of these popular Web-based ePortfolio environments integrate e-mail features, the ability to post comments within an electronic bulletin board, and even the ability to communicate in real time within Web-based chat windows.

There are a variety of ways in which e-mail, bulletin boards, and chat capabilities can improve the overall efficacy of an instructional experience. First and foremost, these methods of communication can provide feedback for students who are trying to learn specific skills. Feedback can come from teachers, peers, or even outside experts who might be invited to participate in a review of material. Likewise, additional examples and non-examples can be provided by various members of a learning community when a request for such support is made. This type of communication could also provide encouragement and motivation for learners as they engage in dialogue with others interested in their projects. And speaking of motivation, knowing that finished projects could be accessible to parents, peers, and/or potential employers can motivate some students to learn and perform at their best.

The ability to communicate with others also makes it possible to work on group projects more effectively. Today, computer users on a network can share files, work on the same file simultaneously, and communicate in real time with members of a learning community regardless of their physical location. These resources might encourage educators to include more collaborative exercises within a course, which could lead to more effective learning experiences for those students who flourish in socially rich learning environments.

Role 8: Instructor Planning and Management Tool

Perhaps one of the most overlooked roles that ePortfolios can play in the teaching and learning process is the support that portfolios provide in the planning and management of instructional experiences. ePortfolios can help teachers manage the instructional process by enabling them to view, track, and evaluate learner progress from a single networked computer. And the built-in communication features within many ePortfolio environments can simplify the process of informing students about various aspects of their project development.

In addition to helping manage the instructional process, all the decisions that educators must make about the type of artifacts to be included within student portfolios as well as the development of assessment rubrics and/or grading criteria to help guide student portfolio creation constitute very effective planning practices. For example, consider the thought processes that most likely went into developing just one of the portfolio requirements presented in Figure 1. Portfolio Component 10, for example, includes the artifact requirements for teacher education students in the area of cultivating a learner-centered classroom. These learner-centered strategy categories include: (a) meaningful learning contexts, (b) differentiated instruction, (c) time management, (d) physical classroom arrangement, (e) adequate instructional scaffolds, (f) self-assessment, and (g) roles. The descriptions included for each of these categories needed to be developed in an organized and clearly worded fashion. In fact, the wording of the descriptions could be regarded as instructional goals. And these goals were most likely formulated in accordance with a broader set of standards to which all teacher education students would be held accountable.

Examining one of the ACEI standards for elementary educators illustrates this point. The following represents one of ACEI's "Instruction" standards:

3d. Active engagement in learning—Candidates use their knowledge and understanding of individual and group motivation and behavior among students at the K-6 level to foster active engagement in learning, self- motivation, and positive social interaction and to create supportive learning environments.

The connection between this standard and the individual strategy categories included in Portfolio Component 10 appears fairly direct. Education faculty members who might be responsible for ensuring that students involved in field experience activities develop portfolio artifacts in compliance with Portfolio Component 10 already have their instructional goals established, and these goals are already aligned with national professional standards. In addition to established goals, education faculty members may also have easy access to Portfolio Component 10 artifacts from previous students. As indicated earlier in this chapter, such resources can be invaluable in the development and implementation of effective instruction.

Role 9: Learner Organization Tool

In addition to helping educators plan and manage the instructional process, ePortfolios can also play an important role in organizing the learning process for students. Portfolio requirements can be used as a conceptual "Big Picture" throughout students' courses and projects. This can help learners make connections between new skills they are learning and those skills they have already learned. Likewise, this "Big Picture" can be a constant reminder of the overall instructional goals that learners would be expected to achieve within a course, grade level, or program. And access to portfolio components and artifacts that have been developed by other learners can be used as a means of ensuring that the instructional goals are clearly understood by each learner.

Clearly defined goals can help learners mentally organize many aspects of an instructional experience. But portfolios can also help learners remain organized in other, more concrete ways. Because ePortfolios include a variety of computer file types that comprise the resources used to develop a particular artifact, learners must organize their work according to the conventions of typical computer environments. Figure 3 presents an example of the types of folders and files that might be included in a computer workspace used by individual students in the process of developing ePortfolio artifacts. Generally speaking, experienced computer users learn that complex projects involv-

Figure 3. Typical computer file structure for supporting the development of electronic portfolio artifacts

Folder	Sub Folders	File Descriptions
Assignments	Portfolio Requirements	This folder might include a document that details the requirements for the overall portfolio (similar to Figure 1).
	Artifact Rubrics	Rubrics or assessment criteria for each artifact could be included in this folder (documents similar to Figure 2).
	Calendars and Timelines	Project management information, such as calendars, timelines, task lists, and so forth, could be included in this folder.
In Progress	Project 1 Folder	This folder would include documents related to one specific project/artifact. Word processing documents, Web page files, video clips, and so forth could be included in this folder.
	Project 2 Folder	A separate folder for each project could be developed to organize the files that will contribute to the final product for each artifact or project.
	Images	Image files to be used throughout the various projects could be stored in one folder in order to make it easier to keep track of them. This folder might include two sub-folders, one for the images in their pre-edit phase, and the other with images that are ready to be used in Web pages.
	Resource Files	Additional resource files that might be used throughout the portfolio development process could be included in this folder, including a file that keeps track of all references used throughout the different projects, files that include resource information obtained from various sources, and raw artifacts such as course research papers that might be used in other projects.
Completed	Project 1 Folder	This folder might include all the files constituting a completed artifact, including Web pages, images, video clips, and so forth.
	Project 2 Folder	Separate folders for each completed project should be established. These folders could be labeled with the same numbering convention used in the overall portfolio requirements document. For example, the numbering and labels used in Figure 1 might result in a completed projects folder with the label "artifact_10c."
	Checklists	This folder would include the checklists used to keep track of the status of various projects.

ing many different types of files require an organized file structure on their computer in order to manage and keep track of everything. By encouraging learners to develop an organized structure like the presented in Figure 3, teachers can model metacognitive strategies. And for teacher education students, this type of modeling might also impact their ability to establish procedures for structuring learner-centered classrooms.

Modeling an organized way to manage the portfolio development process is an important means of helping students learn and apply project management skills. Additionaly, detailed assessment rubrics or grading criteria for each artifact can be used by students to regulate their own learning and plan the steps needed to successfully accomplish each task.

Role 10: Interdisciplinary Teaching and Learning

One thing that becomes very apparent after closely examining the requirements presented in the teacher education portfolio sample in Figure 1 is the fact that, as a whole, the portfolio is much bigger than any single course could address. Indeed, teacher education students hoping to develop all the artifacts for their portfolio would need to apply and repurpose material from a variety of courses, field experience assignments, and personal experiences. This is a prime example of interdisciplinary teaching and learning. Skills and experiences from one course might need to be directly applied to projects in another course, and assignments for specific courses might need to be directly tied to the general portfolio requirements, ensuring that a broad set of standards are learned across courses. And the challenges associated with evaluating portfolio artifacts throughout an individual student's journey in a teacher education program would necessitate the need for faculty members to work closely together in order to maintain consistency, quality, and accountability.

Role 11: Historical Records and Stories as Role Models

The final ePortfolio role addressed is a very good role on which to end this chapter. When comprehensive, programmatic portfolios like the one presented in Figure 1 are completed, the learners leave behind an official, historic record of their experiences within the program. Collectively, the portfolio tells a detailed story of personal achievement. Portfolios can also provide the opportunity to get inside the mind of learners as they faced the many challenges associated with learning important things. And the personal nature of these stories can be used by educators to help novice learners acquire positive attitudes about learning those skills that other students have learned before them.

CONCLUSION

ePortfolios are not always designed to support the instructional process. As previously indicated, portfolios can be used as a means of communicating the best practice of students, or more commonly they can be used simply as a means of assessing student achievement. But ePortfolios can also be used to support the instructional process in a number of effective and creative ways, as illustrated by the 11 different roles presented in this chapter. Today, the options available to educators in the area of ePortfolios are tremendous. There are numerous Web-based services that provide students with computer-based products and services designed to help them develop portfolio material in digital form to be organized and delivered via the Internet. Most school districts and institutions of higher education provide students with the resources needed to store digital information in a variety of formats. And as more homes become networked, the opportunities for learners to extend their portfolio development efforts into their lives outside school expands the possibilities of using ePortfolios to establish meaning, purpose, and personal relevance to the activities that occur within the classroom. Also, when students graduate and move on to bigger and better things, they leave behind stories and examples that can be used to support instruction for future learners.

Setting an example is not the main means of influencing another; it is the only means.
—Albert Einstein

REFERENCES

Dick, W., & Carey, L. (1996). *The systematic design of instruction* (4th ed.). New York: HarperCollins.

Fleming, M., & Levie, W. H. (Eds.). (1993). *Instructional message design: Principles from the behavioral and cognitive sciences*. Englewood Cliffs, NJ: Educational Technology Publications.

Gagné, R., & Driscoll, M. (1988). *Essentials of learning for instruction*. Englewood Cliffs, NJ: Prentice-Hall.

Hunter, M. (1982). *Mastery teaching*. Thousand Oaks, CA: Corwin Press.

Johnson, D., & Johnson, R. (1998). *Learning together and alone: Cooperative, competi-*

tive and individualistic learning (5th ed.). Boston: Allyn and Bacon.

Jonassen, D., Peck, K., & Wilson, B. (1999). *Learning with technology: A constructivist perspective*. Upper Saddle River, NJ: Prentice-Hall.

Knowles, M. (1984). *The adult learner: A neglected species* (3rd ed.). Houston: Gulf Publishing.

Merrill, M. D., & Tennyson, R. (1994). *Teaching concepts: An instructional design*. Englewood Cliffs, NJ: Educational Technology Publications.

KEY TERMS

Assessment: Measurement of the degree to which a learner acquired the skills, knowledge, and/or attitudes that a learning experience was designed to facilitate.

Instructional Context: All the factors external to learners within an instructional environment that provide meaning for the messages they receive. These are the factors that influence and define what, when, where, how, why, and with whom individual learners learn from instruction.

Instructional Design: Process of deciding how a learning environment should be arranged (specifying specific instructional events and learning conditions) in order to maximize the probability that targeted learners will acquire specified skills, knowledge, and/or attitudes.

Instructional Scaffolding: Support mechanisms included within a learning environment designed to help individual learners successfully accomplish their learning goals.

Instructional Strategies: Activities specifically designed to achieve instructional goals. Generally, the most effective strategies used within an instructional experience depend on the types of skills, knowledge, and/or attitudes facilitated.

Media: Physical elements within a person's environment that communicate messages.

Metacognitive Strategies: Plans or approaches learners use to accomplish difficult cognitive tasks such as problem solving.

Reflection: Activities related to specific learning experiences in which learners think about what they are learning, how new things being learned relate to their preexisting knowledge, and how they are personally learning the new skills, knowledge, and/or attitudes.

Chapter II
ePortfolios:
Beyond Assessment

Teresa Acosta
University of Houston, USA

Youmei Liu
University of Houston, USA

ABSTRACT

This chapter focuses on how ePortfolios: (1) shift the locus of control from instructor to student, (2) change curriculum design, and (3) develop social capital. Our contention is that as ePortfolio use gains momentum, the curricula will be scrutinized by persons both in and out of academia, and will evolve to adapt. As business, industry, the arts, government, and so forth influence and shape what is to be assessed, social capital (Bourdieu, 1986) is created, thus opening doors for new graduates entering their profession. Therefore, ePortfolios are not only tools for assessing learning and teaching, but more importantly they promote reform of the traditional educational system, bridge the divide between the academy and society, and develop social capital for the best interest of the global community.

INTRODUCTION

The advent of Web technology has brought about the ePortfolio, which is not only an effective way to assess student learning, but it is also a vehicle for knowledge transmission for career building (Napper & Barrett, 2004). This chapter focuses on three main areas: (1) how ePortfolios shift the locus of control—explaining the transfer of learning from being teacher-centric to student-centric; (2) how ePortfolios change curriculum design—covering the changes in the curriculum and instruction that will take place to match the collaborative learning promoted through ePortfolios; and (3) how ePortfolios develop social capital—addressing the important impact of ePortfolios on students' social awareness and development of social capital, defined by Bourdieu (1986) as "the aggregate of the actual or potential resources which are linked to possession of a durable network of more or less institutionalized relationships of mutual acquaintance and recognition" (pp. 248-249).

In her review of the literature on portfolio assessment, Brown (2002) classifies portfolios as either "capstone experience" portfolios, considered the student's best work, or "process or learning" portfolios, which document cognitive growth and transference of learning to the workplace. This chapter will concentrate on the latter type, the process or learning portfolio, and the potential it has in its modern form, the ePortfolio.

ePORTFOLIOS SHIFTING THE LOCUS OF CONTROL

Dynamic Student Body

For traditional-age students (those in the 18- to 24-year-old range), ePortfolios can help them make professional connections, allow them to gain experience and understand societal needs, and encourage their lifelong learning. As society moves from the "Second Wave," the Industrial Revolution, and enters the "Third Wave," the Information Age, traditional-age students will more than likely experience many careers and will have to constantly learn new information and translate that information into knowledge (Toffler, 1980). Using ePortfolios will help these students document their career and learning experiences.

The second group of students to benefit is full-time working students. Aslanian (2001) has found that approximately "42% of all students at both private and public institutions are age 25 or older" (p. 4). Factors that contribute to older students returning to higher education are "the growth of continuing education programs, economic necessity, the rapidly changing job market, changes in the economy, and the simple aging of student populations" (Bishop & Spake, 2003, p. 374). ePortfolios can better assess students with work and life experiences.

Another group returning to college and university are baby boomer (persons born in the United States between 1946 and 1964) retirees who are living longer due to advancements in health and medicine. Second (or even third) careers, soft-skills (computer/technical) training, or education-for-enjoyment will draw pensioners back to higher education, and their life and work experiences will require a different type of assessment. Given these demographic changes, ePortfolios appropriately demonstrate the learning of these non-traditional students and offer them the opportunity to reflect on their life and work.

Adult Learners' Characteristics

How will institutions of higher education be able to address the learning needs of traditional-age students, working students, and retired students? In his andragogical theory, Knowles (1980) summarizes four crucial assumptions about the characteristics of adult learners that are different from the assumptions on which traditional pedagogy is premised. He states that as individuals mature:

1. their self-concept moves from one of being a dependent personality toward being a self-directed human being;
2. they accumulate a growing reservoir of experience that becomes an increasingly rich resource for learning;
3. their readiness to learn becomes oriented to the development tasks of their social roles; and
4. their time perspective changes from one of postponed application of knowledge to immediacy of application, and accordingly,

> their orientation toward learning shifts from one of subject-centeredness to one of performance-centeredness. (pp. 44-45)

The assumptions of this learning model call for individualized and more personalized pedagogy. Commercial course management systems (CMSs), such as those developed by WebCT and Blackboard, are playing a dominant role in higher education in transferring education online. These systems are moving instruction from being teacher-centric to student-centric by opening up communication between students and instructors, allowing for synchronous and asynchronous interactions, as well as giving students access to course materials, which was not possible a decade ago. At present, it is technically conceivable to customize the curriculum to the student's individual learning needs; however, a CMS cannot accomplish true learner-centeredness without an assessment model, such as an ePortfolio, that allows for the possibility of student, instructor, teaching assistant, advisor, mentor, and even peer reflection on the student's coursework and learning.

ePortfolios for Student-Centeredness

Traditional portfolio work has focused on the passive collection of artifacts to create a polished product. The instructor typically would determine the type of content in the portfolio and how it would be evaluated; thus, the traditional portfolio falls in the teacher-centric category. On the other hand, ePortfolios emphasize analysis and reflection, and the process, not the product. Emphasizing the process not only raises the cognitive bar, but it also shifts the locus of control to the student. With an ePortfolio model in place, it is not so much what the instructor is doing, but what the student is doing to meet learning objectives. In addition, the student can reflect on her learning and can demonstrate learning to persons outside of the immediate learning environment with electronic artifacts. For example, interested employers could review a senior-level student's résumé, sample writings, examples of spreadsheet work, group project contributions, and a number of other items that the student wants to make accessible. If the same student is also applying to graduate school, then she can make available to the admissions committee her transcript, letters of recommendation, as well as her sample writings.

ePortfolios and New Learning Models

Collaborative learning, inside and outside of the academy, is another feature of the new portfolio model. Peer-to-peer, student-mentor, and student-community collaborative efforts can be documented in ePortfolios. Peer-to-peer projects promote teamwork and organizational and communication skills. Student-mentor projects, internships, and so forth give students the opportunity to enter the world of work for better understanding of their future profession and workplace culture. Student-community projects offer the student first-hand understanding of societal issues and problems. Regardless of the type of project, the student should maintain control of his or her ePortfolio and allow peers, mentors, and the community to give input, while the instructor provides the opportunity for the interactions and assesses final outcomes.

ePORTFOLIOS CHANGING CURRICULUM DESIGN

"The institution of education is activated by a curriculum that itself changes in response to forces affecting it" (Oliva, 2001, p. 20). The ePortfolio, a product of modern computer and Internet technology, is a catalyst for curriculum change as a new model of assessment. It connects the educational mission and objectives with the needs of society, it brings students closer to their future profession, and it carries learning into graduates' careers and possibly into their retirement.

Specifically, student-mentor and student-community ePortfolio projects open a dialogue between the academy and society. This creates a feedback loop that serves to update the academy on the skills required by students as they enter society. It is anticipated that faculty members will be in discussions with interested parties in the community and professional market to determine student outcomes; therefore, the assessment of a course, program, discipline, and so forth will be more and more influenced by persons outside of the academy. Hence, the ePortfolio, as a tool to assess the teaching and learning, changes traditional teaching mentality, promotes collaborative learning, and develops curriculum standards.

ePortfolio and Curriculum Development

ePortfolios promulgate extensive collaborative learning that incorporates societal issues and student internships in the process of education, and moves the curriculum from being edu-centric to social-centric. If students are immersed in projects that extend into the dynamic workplace and community (rather than the limitations of the campus), then they must demonstrate not only applicability of knowledge, but also flexibility and adaptability. The pedagogical challenge then is to set up connections between academic objectives and societal needs that will update the curriculum by incorporating current global perspectives.

Seven general skill areas have been outlined by Carnevale, Gainer, and Meltzer (1990) that are appropriate for the Third Wave of students: (1) learning to learn, (2) basic competency, (3) communication skills, (4) developmental skills, (5) adaptability skills, (6) group effectiveness skills, and (7) influencing skills. In addition to this skills set, the curriculum should address the following aspects: (1) incorporating societal needs as a foundation of curriculum planning and developing, (2) using the ePortfolio as an evaluation tool to analyze the quality of the curriculum implementation, and (3) developing student competency based on societal needs. It is very important to develop a curriculum that can help students succeed in a collaborative learning environment, as well as build a valuable electronic repository that benefits students and society.

ePortfolio and Instruction

As recommended by Oliva (2001), the cyclical model of curriculum-instruction relationship is that the "curriculum makes a continuous impact on instruction and, vice versa, instruction has impact on curriculum" (p. 10). In other words, the relationship between curriculum development and instructional design is interdependent. New teaching methods and learning models will spin off as a result of these changes to the curriculum. The traditional college lecture format and rote learning cannot adequately address the needs of students taking on community projects and entering the workplace for the first time, much less the needs of working students. Lifelong learning and continuing education endeavors also call for new instructional models. Instructors will have to step away from lecture notes, textbooks, and laboratories, to some extent, and engage with the community to create a community of learners. For example, online interviews, discussions, or group projects with subject matter experts or community leaders are some ways to build this sense of community.

The diverse interactions, collaborations, and communications should be integrated in daily teaching activities. The research study conducted by Veenman, Denessen, Akker, and Rijt (2005) indicates that "students do not naturally develop constructive interactional patterns without instruction" (p. 120). Teachers must provide explicit instructions on how to conduct collaborative and community learning, as well as create an environment to develop and practice the skills required for effective communication and collaborations to positively affect the quality of the ePortfolio.

Instructor's Role

While online teaching and course management systems offer instructors the opportunities to be more creative, include more real-world issues in the curriculum, push out more content, and communicate more with students, more is not necessarily better for either party. Cyber classroom management is the key. Therefore, developing strategic approaches to enhance teaching and learning while still maintaining the integrity of the curriculum is a challenge to be faced if ePortfolios are adopted. In fact, class management in the new curriculum model will play an even greater role than in the traditional model, with the instructor acting as a project manager for various projects and activities.

As project manager, responsibilities would include, but are not limited to: (1) coordinating with other faculty as well as members outside of the academy to align course and program standards with those of a particular industry or other relevant outside agency; (2) teaching students requisite concepts and skills, perhaps even developing tutorials for basic competencies and remediation; (3) confirming that student projects meet pre-determined standards and objectives; (4) setting up contacts between the persons or groups outside of the academy and students; (5) meeting with students and mentors for formative and summative assessment purposes; (6) assessing the ePortfolio artifacts, which more than likely means working in conjunction with other evaluators; and (7) conducting a formal course evaluation at semester's end. It goes without saying that such discernible changes in the instructor role and responsibilities will call for training of the faculty and leadership, and support on the part of the administration.

ePORTFOLIOS DEVELOPING SOCIAL CAPITAL

ePortfolio Community

In traditional academic learning environments, it is difficult for students to make meaningful reflections of the knowledge they have learned and the contribution they can make to society because of their lack of connection with society and the understanding of societal needs. ePortfolios can extend learning beyond the campus and foster learning community. Tosh (2004) summarized three benefits of ePortfolio: a learning tool for students, a monitoring tool for institutions, and a mechanism for employment opportunities. The social functions of these benefits define a special relationship of students, instructors, advisors, peers, and potential employers, and create a varied learning community. The ePortfolio community will promote new and authentic collaborations, and provide the means to foster learning, accountability, and reflections across the spectrum of academia and society.

ePortfolio communities can be successfully established through three channels. First, schools can develop a special relationship with local communities, industries, research institutions, professional associations, and non-profit organizations to create diverse activities and projects that are related to students' majors, so that students will have an opportunity to validate their school knowledge in reality. Second, faculty members, especially adjunct faculty members, who are providing professional consultation or working in the areas that are related to the subject areas they are teaching, can build a connection for students. They can help students arrange a learning community in which they work with professionals on special projects and experiments. Third, non-traditional working and retired students already have formed a social bond. They can help classmates to create learning communities in their working environments. In ePortfolio communities, students will be able to learn to interact with members in the community and creatively merge their learning with reality. They can get feedback through effective communication with community members and other learners, and have a better and deeper understanding of social needs so that they can revitalize their ePortfolios with rich life experiences that increase their value and applicability to society.

ePortfolio and Social Awareness

ePortfolio communities not only benefit students in making meaningful connections between schools and society for their careers, but more importantly, the process will help them raise their awareness of being active members of the society, increase their sense of social responsibilities, and develop their competencies to contribute to society. According to Selman's (2003) definition of social awareness, it includes both the awareness of social relationships and the awareness of risks a student faces during the growth. The ePortfolio community interactions can help students improve the skills of coordinating diverse social perspectives, and it will also help them to understand one's own point of view in relation to the point of view of others (Selman, 2003). The cooperation will make students more aware of the needs of others in the group (Veenman et al., 2005).

It takes time and effort for both students and teachers to become socially aware and develop social competencies. Teachers should foster a culture and environment conducive to the promotion of social awareness. Besides the ePortfolio community, there are other class activities that can be organized to promote student social awareness and help students develop social competence. These activities should be integrated into daily teaching and learning, such as group projects, collaborative learning experiments, student self-organized activities, discussion topics on how students can relate their learning and experiences to societal needs, project-based homework assignments, and so forth. As Selman (2003) stresses, "Social competence must be constantly practiced, or those skills will not be there when we most need them" (para. 3). Social awareness is easier to develop in a group or community in a shared environment (Divitini, 2003). It is very important that students are able to reflect their comprehensive understanding of social relationships and their social competence in their ePortfolios to demonstrate their readiness to make contributions to society.

ePortfolio and Social Change

ePortfolios will impact positive social change in that they promote community and lifelong learning, as well as create a bridge between academia and society. "The ePortfolio is the expression of learning as social activity" (Ravet & Layte, 2004, para. 7). The value of community learning lies in that it provides a learning context in which students can effectively relate what they have learned in school with how the knowledge can be applied in reality. Students will have opportunities to interact with professionals and other learners to share knowledge through communities and further improve social competency. They will also develop new knowledge and perspectives from cognitive learning through neutralizing the discrepancy of school knowledge (Kourilsky & Wittrock, 1992). The ePortfolio should reflect the student's ability to learn and share knowledge in the community.

Developing an ePortfolio should be a lifelong process. With the accumulation of education, life, and work experiences, students can consistently add value to improve the quality of the ePortfolio in their life span. Students can learn purposefully and build an objective-focused ePortfolio to meet the standards and needs of society. Besides career-seeking function, ePortfolios can enable students to look back at their own life experiences and reflect on the weaknesses and strengths for developmental needs. What makes an ePortfolio a powerful tool is its dynamic nature, it is a process of constant building and learning. Students can significantly benefit from this tool by accessing "their records, digital repository, reflections to achieve a greater understanding of their individual growth" (Tosh, 2004, para. 4).

The networked ePortfolio is a tool that can transform social interaction (Ravet & Layte, 2004). By bridging the divide between academia and society, the special relationships between students and employers, and between students and community members will help students understand the professions they are entering, improve their interpersonal skills, and engage students in a wider public sphere. Students will have opportunities to make career connections and prepare for dynamic work environments. They can take proactive roles in creating an ePortfolio that can differentiate multiple career paths based on the inter-relatedness of knowledge and potential occupations.

ePortfolio and Social Capital

ePortfolios help students set up social norms and connections that will contribute to social capital. Social capital has been defined from different perspectives; the central meaning of it is clear—using collective power and resources to improve and benefit society and the individual through strong relationships and active interactions. This is exactly the objective of developing solid and well-grounded ePortfolios. Internet technology has further expanded the ability for ePortfolios to contribute to social capital worldwide. The successful establishment of social network and infrastructure through the ePortfolio community will maximize the benefit of social capital to the global community.

The four major components of social capital, as delineated by Nahapiet and Ghoshal (1998), are: trust, norms, obligations, and identification. ePortfolio community interactions help members develop social norms and mutual trust. In such an environment, community members are likely to share values, information, and knowledge that promote the exploration and utilization of social resources in benefiting communities in the most efficient ways. ePortfolios can contribute to the development of social capital by: (1) building trust relationships between parties to promote social interactions and engagement; (2) sharing information, personal experiences, and knowledge to contribute to social capital inventory; (3) improving students' sense of responsibility, accountability, and commitment; and (4) increasing the efficient use of resources worldwide. ePortfolios are becoming more and more important to the development of social capital and improvement of intellectual resource management.

Developing social capital directly involves the relationship and interaction of students in the ePortfolio community. The vital elements to build a strong ePortfolio community are all related to an individual's personal qualities; understanding of shared trust, norms, and values; and commitment and accountability to the community. Bourdieu (1996) considers social capital to be an attribute of an individual in a social context. Students should learn to trust others and learn to understand different value systems. The more comprehensive value systems students can build into their ePortfolio, the more valuable it will be to the social capital.

CONCLUSION

ePortfolios must be integrated into the curriculum in consideration of societal needs, otherwise "they may never fulfill their potential and become a tool that alters learning pedagogy" (Tosh, 2004). The development and implementation of ePortfolios imposes challenges to the traditional educational system, which has been confined for centuries in the ivory tower. Walking out of campus into the society, stepping down from the lecture podium, learning from the populace, and sharing resources with the global community will become common practice in the process of education. The ePortfolio is also an effective tool to evaluate the curriculum planning and implementation to make certain that education is incorporating societal needs and nurturing students who can make contributions to the global community.

REFERENCES

Aslanian, C. B. (2001). *Adult students today*. New York: The College Board.

Bishop, J. S., & Spake, D. F. (2003). Distance education: A bibliographic review for educational planners and policymakers 1992-2002. *Journal of Planning Literature, 17*(3).

Bolender, R. K. (1996). *The development of portfolio assessment process for the Bachelor of Business Administration program at Mount Vernon Nazarene College*. Fort Lauderdale, FL: Nova Southeastern University. (ERIC Document Reproduction Service No. ED406914)

Bourdieu, P. (1986). The forms of capital (R. Nice, Trans.). In J. Richardson (Ed.), *Handbook of theory and research for the sociology of education* (pp. 241-258). New York: Greenwood Press.

Bourdieu, P. (1996). On the family as a realized category. *Theory, Culture & Society 13*(1), 19-26.

Brown, C. A. (2002). *Portfolio assessment: How far have we come?* (ERIC Document Reproduction Service No. ED477941)

Bucuvalas, A. (2003). *Teaching social awareness—an interview with Larsen Professor Robert Selman*. Retrieved May 14, 2005, from http://gseweb.harvard.edu/news/features/selman02012003.html

Carnevale, A. P., Gainer, L. J., & Meltzer, A. S. (1990). *Workplace basics: The essential skills employers want*. San Francisco: Jossey-Bass.

Divitini, M. (2003). *Supporting social awareness: Requirements for educational CVE*. Retrieved May 14, 2005, from http://www.idi.ntnu.no/grupper/su/publ/ekaterina/prasolova-divitini-icalt2003.pdf

Knowles, M. S. (1990). *The adult learner: A neglected species* (4th ed.). Houston: Gulf.

Kourilsky, M., & Wittrock, M. C. (1992). Generative teaching: An enhancement strategy for the learning of economics in cooperative groups. *American Educational Research Journal, 29*, 861-876.

Nahapiet, J., & Ghoshal, S. (1998). Social capital, intellectual capital and the organizational advantage. *Academy of Management Review, 23*(2), 242-266.

Napper, V. S., & Barrett, H. C. (2004). Information and technology: Assessment and e-folio. *Proceedings of the Society for Information Technology & Teacher Education Conference* (pp. 39-40).

Oliva, P. F. (2001). *Developing the curriculum*. New York: Priscilla McGeehon.

Ravet, S., & Layte, M. (2004). *E-portfolio: Revolutionizing e-learning*. Retrieved May 15, 2005, from http://www.learningcitizen.net/articles/e-portfoliosRevolutio.shtml

Selman, R. (2003). *The promotion of social awareness*. New York: Russell Sage Foundation.

Toffler, A. (1980). *The third wave*. New York: Bantam.

Tosh, D. (2004). *E-portfolios and Weblogs: One vision for e-portfolio development*. Retrieved May 11, 2005, from http://www.eradc.org/papers/e-portfolio_Weblog.pdf

Veenman, S., Denessen, E., Akker, A., & Rijt, J. (2005). Effects of a cooperative learning program on the elaborations of students during help seeking and help giving. *American Educational Research Journal, 42*, 115-151.

KEY TERMS

Assessment: Student assessment is the process of documenting knowledge, skills, attitudes, and beliefs, usually in measurable terms. Assessment of a learning system includes the process of collecting and interpreting information to evaluate the curriculum.

Curriculum Design: The process of designing and organizing the curriculum to include content, teaching and learning strategies, learning activities and experiences, as well as assessments and evaluations to meet educational goals and purposes.

Curriculum Development: The determination of the purposes, goals, content, and standards of measurement for an educational institution or program. Curriculum development is seen as "the process for making programmatic decisions and for revising the products of those decisions on the basis of continuous and subsequent evaluation" (Oliva, 2001, p. 139).

Higher Education: Education beyond the secondary level; usually considered education at the college or university level.

Learning Communities: A group of individuals who engage in the acquisition, transformation, or creation of knowledge.

Pedagogy: The act, process, or art of transmitting knowledge and skills.

Chapter III
The Learning Landscape:
A Conceptual Framework for ePortfolios

David Tosh
University of Edinburgh, UK

Ben Werdmuller
Curverider LTD, UK

Helen L. Chen
Stanford Center for Innovations in Learning, USA

Tracy Penny Light
University of Waterloo, Canada

Jeff Haywood
University of Edinburgh, UK

ABSTRACT

Adoption of ePortfolio tools in higher education has been implemented in individual courses, departments, schools, and across institutions to demonstrate evidence of more authentic student work, show student progress over time, and represent collections of best work. New technologies have enhanced the learning affordances of ePortfolios to include its usefulness as a tool to support integration, synthesis, and re-use of formal and informal learning experiences. The challenge for educators is to develop new pedagogical approaches to encourage students to recognize and extend the value of ePortfolio software beyond simple course applications and outside the context of their undergraduate education. This chapter describes the learning landscape model, a conceptual framework which promotes a view of "learning" that supersedes the rigid structure of degree outlines and requirements by taking advantage of a variety of technologies to incorporate overlapping experiences through social networking among faculty, mentors, peers, and employers and resources.

INTRODUCTION

Portfolios have been commonly used to demonstrate progress over time (i.e., multiple essay drafts in a writing course portfolio), represent samples of best work (i.e., showcasing projects in art or architecture portfolios), and prepare for job or career searches (i.e., updating résumés, compiling artifacts such as writing samples, awards, and transcripts). For many of these kinds of portfolios, there is a specific objective or purpose in mind.

More recently, advances in Web-based technologies as well as the availability of lower cost, higher capacity memory storage have increased the opportunity and potential of *electronic* portfolios (ePortfolios) to support student learning in a variety of courses, environments, and experiences, both inside and outside the classroom.[1] This development parallels a growing interest in higher education, both nationally and internationally, to foster *intentional* learners who are able to adapt to new environments and situations, synthesize knowledge and experiences from a variety of sources, and seek out opportunities for continued learning throughout their lives (AAC&U, 2002; Huber & Hutchings, 2004).

This interest stems from the potential of electronic portfolios to contribute and support the work of integrative learning. For example, in the U.S., through a partnership between the Carnegie Foundation for the Advancement of Teaching and the Association of American Colleges and Universities (AAC&U), Portland State University, LaGuardia Community College, and Salve Regina University have experimented with the use of ePortfolios to strengthen community-based learning across the curriculum, assessment efforts, and curricular and co-curricular partnerships. In the UK, the personal development and planning (PDP) movement emphasizing reflections, action plans, and self-assessments and their relationship to ePortfolios have caught the attention of the Centre for Recording Achievement and the Joint Information Systems Committee (JISC) (Beetham, 2005).

ePortfolios support deep learning by facilitating the making of connections among learning experiences that occur in various contexts and environments. Research on student engagement with learning suggests that when students perceive that they have choices in how to learn subject matter, they are more motivated to move beyond just information acquisition to gaining a deeper understanding of the subject (Ramsden, 2003; Marton & Saljo, 1984; LaSere Erickson & Weltner-Strommer, 1991; Entwistle, 1998). ePortfolio tools are characterized by a focus on learner control, a customized learning environment, and the ability to digitally represent and share formal and informal learning experiences with others. These features can be used to enhance both social and intellectual interactions in various learning contexts (academic, workplace, community).

Another influential factor in evaluating the potential benefits of ePortfolios in higher education is to consider the characteristics of the students who are entering today's colleges and universities. Today's learners are more engaged than ever with communities that live beyond the classroom. Digital chat rooms, online games, and cellular phones all provide greater access to networks that are not constrained by a physical classroom or geographical boundaries. Current research that examines educational gaming, for instance, identify a range of learning opportunities available in such non-traditional learning contexts (Gee, 2003; Herz, 2002; Jones, 2003; Prensky, 2000; Squire, 2004).

As we consider the growing number of thriving online communities across the Internet, there is evidence of 'learners' actively contributing to shared knowledge bases through various Web technologies and services. However, it cannot be assumed that the mere existence of these communities can provide a richer learning experience for students. Students do not automatically and readily connect and value the skills and learning acquired in their social networks—out-of-class learning experiences are not necessarily connected with those which occur in more traditional learning environments.

Oblinger and Oblinger (2005) point to the need to harness the new learners' knowledge of technology. They suggest:

Multi-user virtual environments and ubiquitous computing will allow users to move beyond the desktop interface to much more immersive environments that enhance learning. In turn, learning styles will evolve based on mediated immersion and distributed learning communities.

The learning landscape framework seeks to conceptualize how these new learning styles might develop with the emergence of ePortfolio-related technologies.

THE LEARNING LANDSCAPE FRAMEWORK

At the core of the learning landscape framework is an emphasis on integration and synthesis of learning, irrespective of where that learning occurs (inside or outside the classroom, on campus or off campus, during an undergraduate career or beyond, face to face or virtually). The learning landscape model and accompanying ePortfolio tools are characterized by three elements.

- **Reflection:** The learner maps out his or her thoughts on a course, a piece of work, or more general experiences.
- **Communication:** The learner communicates his or her reflections to other students, staff, tutors, and lecturers.
- **Sharing:** The learner gives selected other users access to his or her material—reflections, artifacts, resources.

The sources and opportunities for learning are all broadly defined, and similarly, the definition of an ePortfolio is expanded to encompass a wider range of tools and media that students regularly interact with such as Weblogs, e-mail, instant messaging, and other Web-based programs. As illustrated in Figure 1, the overlapping domains of academic, workplace, and community are linked by the transfer and reuse of skills, knowledge, and experiences through reflective thinking and self-assessment.

Building upon models of social constructivism and active learning, Batson (2002) describes how ePortfolios can alter the dynamics of learning pedagogy where students are active participants in their learning and not just the passive recipients of information. Yancey (2001, p. 83) reiterates that "the engaged learner, one who records and interprets and evaluates his or her own learning, is the best learner." The tools and practices that comprise an ePortfolio support these activities on a personal level but also through social networking. The added value of social interaction to facilitate self-awareness and heightened intentionality as enabled by this expanded ePortfolio tool set is the main focus and primary contribution of the learning landscape model.

THE OUTCOME: CREATING A SENSE OF COMMUNITY

Social networking enables learners to create their own learning or social communities in an engaging environment such as keeping in touch

Figure 1. The learning landscape

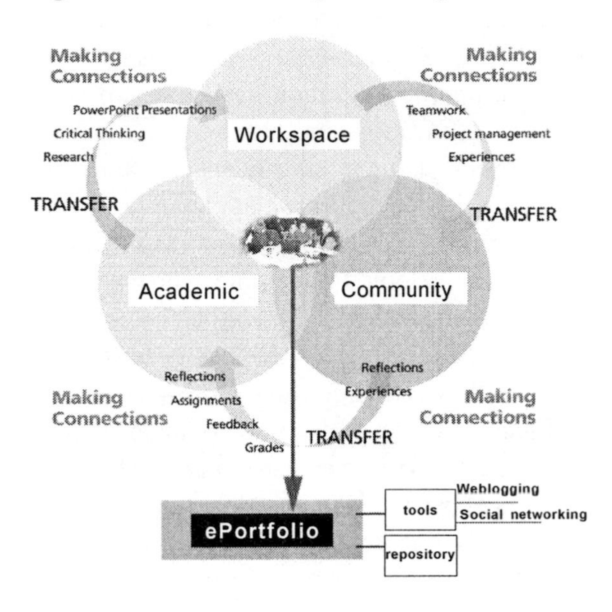

with each other or finding the latest resources and sharing their own experiences. The sense of belonging to a community and fostering an ability to share problems, experiences, resources, and so forth with other learners can harbor a sense of confidence. Learners who participate in this process will gradually develop a trusted support system, a network of knowledge transfer and exchange.

DEEP LEARNING THROUGH ENGAGEMENT

[Deep learning] ... learning that promotes the development of conditionalized knowledge and metacognition through communities of inquiry, this can further enhance with the advent of 'knowledge rooms', areas of cyberspace that allow students to collaborate.[2]

The use of ePortfolio tools to promote deep learning is intriguing—deep learning reflects a greater, more complex understanding of a subject. Some argue:

The experience of deep learning better equips the learner to excel in future learning opportunities because the learner can discern both familiar patterns and critical variations in entirely new surface conditions. Thus, learning at both the individual and collective level involves coming to see familiar phenomena in new ways, "thereby widening the world we experience.[3]

From this perspective, the combination of ePortfolios and social networks within the learning landscape framework may have immense benefits for the learner. These tools and the ethos behind them enhance the prospect for deep learning. The ability to engage with other learners, pull in information from various resource sources, share thoughts and feelings, form communities of learning or social activity, interact with peers and tutors within one or more institutions, creates a milieu which pro motes user engagement and, in turn, a level of deeper learning.

EXPANDING THE ePORTFOLIO MODEL: CURRENT WEB TECHNOLOGIES

ePortfolios are one component of the digital learning landscape that learners inhabit. It is worth noting that the technology does not define the learning landscape, and the framework allows substitution of emerging technologies as and when they become available.

The ePortfolio is meant to enhance a learner-centric approach, encouraging learners to look holistically at their learning instead of arbitrarily compartmentalizing these experiences. ePortfolios facilitate the promotion of conceptual thinking about learning as an ongoing process—a process that does not start or stop with the traditional classroom experience.

Weblogging

A Weblog (commonly referred to as a "blog") is a frequently updated Web site consisting of chronologically ordered text or photographs, most often displayed in a diary form. Due to the high quality and ease of use of the underlying technology, this has been incredibly popular; updating a Web site no longer requires technology-specific skills such as HTML or server maintenance. Some adherents have nicknamed the Weblogging culture "Web 2.0," which references the original concept of the World Wide Web as a medium to share information.

Folksonomy and Social Networking

In a 'folksonomy', a Weblog post or an uploaded file will be marked by a number of keywords (or "tags"), which the user creates by typing free text. If anyone else has also marked posts or uploads with those keywords, the user will be able to see an aggregated list. Because an infinite number of keywords are theoretically possible, and all keywords have at least one attached object, the classification system is constantly adapting to the content on the site. This means the categorization system is efficient: a user clicking a keyword is always sure to find at least one object. Often there will be a page displaying either a set of random keywords or the most popular keywords, with the individual popularity of each indicated by that keyword's font size. Probably the most popular of these sites is the photography site Flickr (http://www.flickr.com/), which allows users to sort both their own and other peoples' pictures through tags.

Social networking is a Web technology which allows users to discover new business or personal contacts by traversing relationship links between people, and then keep track of their activity within a system. It is common for users to be found using a simple search function; alternatively, each user may have a profile containing embedded folksonomy tags. Someone can then look for anyone who has self-tagged themselves as having an interest in eLearning, for example. This can be combined with top-down categorization, allowing for hybrid searches such as "people in Canada [a top-down category] interested in eLearning [a tag]." Flickr is also a social networking site: you can mark particular users as being contacts, and then keep track of their new photographs as they upload them into the system.

During 2004 and 2005 the use of social software exploded; at last count (April 2005) there were around 380 different Web services offering social networking (Social Software, 2005). Their importance has been underlined by high-profile purchases of social software by both Yahoo! and Google.

The combination of a digital repository with Weblogging, folksonomies and social is powerful; these features provide the mechanism by which the artifacts can be shared. A user can upload an artifact and then mark it with folksonomy tags so it can be found by category; they can also choose which of their contacts they would like to have access to it. Finally, they can make a Weblog post and embed the artifact. This might provide context and possibly allow for discussion regarding its contents.

Distributed Systems

So far we have painted an image of a learning landscape with integrated Weblogging (complete with a "friends page," comments, and trackbacks), social networking, a folksonomy-based classification system, and digital artifacts. However, what if a user wants to discover resources outside his or her institution? A distributed learning landscape would allow users to not just discover all the users interested in eLearning at their institution, but also throughout *every* learning landscape system. A user at Edinburgh could add a user at Stanford to his or her friends page, or allow them access to an uploaded repository artifact. In less ambitious terms, a user at a university's medical school could add a user in the humanities system as a friend.

Standards

The need for standards then becomes clear. A global, distributed learning landscape can only be effective if it is not limited to a single piece of software installed on multiple servers; rather, *all* software using the same standards would be able to interact with each other. Additionally, this interaction should not be reliant on a centralized set of servers, in case these should be external to a particular system and one day disappear. "Peer-to-peer" is a technology that allows a global search to occur by passing requests to a server's neighbors and aggregating the results. This methodology ensures that no school or institution is reliant on any other school or institution to remain part of the global learning landscape network.

SYNDICATION

XML

XML—the eXtensible Markup Language—is an industry-standard, extensible format for self-describing data which allows for easy data transfer between computers, whatever the operating system or model. Due to its widespread use, it can be very easily written and read by a wide variety of clients. For compatibility reasons, it is therefore sensible to use standards based on this format whenever transferring data between servers on the Web. The following standards are all XML-based.

Friend of a Friend

Friend of a Friend (FOAF) is an XML standard that allows Web site owners to define who they are as well as their relationships with other Web site owners—effectively creating a wide area social network. Unlike traditional social networking software, FOAF does not require relationships to be within a single system; resources can be associated with each relationship within the XML, so while one relationship link might lead to a Weblog, another might lead to a photo album or a portfolio page. Relationship links can also be made to individual objects.

While the programming overhead including FOAF capabilities in software is very small, the benefits can be large; following the links in FOAF files and merging the data can result in a large, continually updated directory of users.

RSS and Atom

Really simple syndication (RSS) is an XML format for summarizing Web content (usually of the chronologically ordered kind, such as Weblogs and newspaper articles). A site's posts or content items are expressed using XML markup, and can then be imported into specialized RSS readers or themselves added to a user's "friends page." LiveJournal, for example, allows RSS feeds to be viewed and commented on as if they were just another user Weblog within the system.

Atom is a more advanced XML-based technology that also allows users to syndicate and aggregate Web content. However, it also allows users to post to the Web using third-party client software. As there is a significant base of software growing, supporting Atom allows users to read, create, and upload content using software they are already familiar with.

HOW THIS APPLIES TO ePORTFOLIOS

A Redesign of Syndication Standards for Portfolios

Rather than an XML file that stores summaries of Weblog posts, the ePortfolio system might maintain a file containing identifying information about the user. XML files generally have a main tag, with all the other tags as children; this could simply be called "portfolio," which might have the attribute "name," containing the portfolio owner's name. Another possibility may be a "portfolio-info" tag, which would contain subtags with the date the portfolio was created, the date it was last edited, the establishment it was last edited within, and the software platform used. There would be another tag with "user-info" (or a similar name), containing contact details and so on. A sample portion of this part of the portfolio file might look something like the following, although the final XML schema would be significantly more sophisticated.

```
<portfolio name="John Smith">
        <portfolio-info>
        <date-created>March 07, 2004 20:45 +00:00</date-created>
        <date-last-edited>March 07, 2004 21:09 +00:00</date-last-edited>
        <establishment>University of Edinburgh</establishment>
        <software>Edinburgh E-Portfolio System</software>
<portfolio-info>
<user-info>
        <born>January 07, 1979</born>
        <address>
                Moray House School of Education
                Holyrood Rd
                Edinburgh, EH8 8AQ
        </address>
        <country>UK</country>
</user-info>
</portfolio>
```

XML allows for binary data to be stored within its tags: this allows for artifacts to be stored as embedded objects within an XML file. There could be a tag called "objects" (or similar), with sub-tags containing particular pieces of work that the portfolio owner might want to make available. Word documents, pieces of art—the type of file would not matter.

CONCLUSION

The chapter describes the learning landscape framework where student motivation and engagement in learning are the primary emphases. Creating an environment where learners engage in the process because they *want* to rather than *have* to is a powerful way to tap into the enormous potential of ePortfolios.

With the expansion of the ePortfolio tool set, the technical and pedagogical affordances of the learning landscape have been strengthened. However, the challenges of implementing such a model will always rest on the side of the pedagogy behind the use of the tool. Therefore, before any choice of tools, communicative or otherwise, can be decided upon, it is necessary to clarify to all potential stakeholders the purpose of the ePortfolio tools and activities, and to give careful thought to how these ideas are presented to the learners. In the right environment, the social networking potential of the learning landscape and ePortfolio-related tools are features that facilitate and enhance the making of connections and the linking together of people, ideas, resources, and learning domains.

REFERENCES

AAC&U (Association of American Colleges and Universities). (2002). *Greater expectations: A new vision for learning as a nation goes to college*. Washington, DC: Association of American Colleges and Universities.

Barrett, H. (2004). *Electronic portfolios as digital stories of deep learning—emerging digital tools to support reflection in learner-centered portfolios*. Retrieved October 1, 2005, from http://electronicportfolios.org/digistory/epstory.html

Batson, T. (2002). *Electronic portfolio boom: What's it all about?* Retrieved October 1, 2005, from http://www.syllabus.com/article.asp?id=6984

Beetham, H. (2005). *E-portfolios in post-16 learning in the UK: Developments, issues and opportunities*. Report prepared for the JISC e-Learning and Pedagogy strand of the JISC e-Learning Program. Retrieved October 1, 2005, from http://www.jisc.ac.uk/uploaded_documents/e-portfolio_ped.doc

Entwistle, N. (1998). Approaches to learning and forms of understanding. In B. Dart & Boulton-Lewis (Eds.), *Teaching and learning in higher education.* Melbourne: ACER.

Gee, J. P. (2003). *What video games have to teach us about learning and literacy.* New York: Palgrave Macmillan.

Hebert, E. (2001). *The power of portfolios*. San Francisco: Jossey-Bass

Herz, J. C. (2002). gaming the system: what higher education can learn from multiplayer online worlds. In M. Devlin, R. Larson, & J. Myerson (Eds.), *The Internet and the university: Forum 2001* (pp. 169-191). Boulder, CO: EDUCAUSE.

Huber, M. T., & Hutchings, P. (2004). *Integrative learning: Mapping the terrain.* Washington, DC: Association of American Colleges & Universities.

Jonassen, D. H. (1991). Objectivism vs. constructivism: Do we need a new philosophical paradigm? *Educational Technology: Research and Development*, *39*(3), 5-14.

Jones, S. (2003). *Let the games begin: Gaming technology and entertainment among college students*. Washington, DC: Pew Internet & American Life Project.

LaSere Erickson, B., & D. Weltner-Strommer. (1991). Knowing, understanding, and thinking: The golas of freshman instruction. In *Teaching college freshmen.* San Francisco: Jossey-Bass.

Leinonen, T. (n.d.). Retrieved from http://flosse.dicole.org/?item=critical-history-of-ict-in-education-and-where-we-are-heading

Love, D., McKean, G., & Gathercoal, P. (2004). Portfolios to Webfolios and beyond: Levels of maturation. *Educause Quarterly, 27*(2). Retrieved October 1, 2005, from http://www.educause.edu/pub/eq/eqm04/eqm0423.asp?print=yes]

Marton, F., & Saljo, R. (1984). Approaches to learning. In F. Marton, D. Hounsell, & N. Entwistle (Eds.), *The experience of learning.* Edinburgh: Scottish Academic Press.

Oblinger, D., & Oblinger, J. (Eds.). (2005). *Educating the Net generation*. Retrieved October 1, 2005, from http://www.educause.edu/educatingthenetgen/

Prensky, M. (2000). *Digital game-based learning.* New York: McGraw-Hill.

Ramsdon, P. (2003). *Learning to teach in higher education* (2nd ed.) London: Routledge Falmer.

Social Software. (2005). *Home of the social networking services meta list.* Retrieved May 18, 2004, from http://socialsoftware.

Weblogsinc.com/entry/9817137581524458/

Squire, K. (2004). *Video games in education.* Retrieved October 1, 2005, from http://www.educationarcade.org/gtt/pubs/IJIS.doc

Tosh, D., & Werdmuller, B. (2004). *E-portfolios and Weblogs: One vision for e-portfolio development.* Retrieved July 14, 2005, from http://www.eradc.org/papers/e-portfolio_Weblog.pdf"]

Weigel, V. B. (2002). *Deep learning for a digital age: Technology's untapped potential to enrich higher education.* San Francisco: Jossey-Bass

Yancey, K. B. (2001). General patterns and the future. In B. Cambridge et al. (Eds.), *Electronic portfolios: Emerging practices in student, faculty, and institutional learning* (pp. 83-87). Washington, DC: American Association of Higher Education.

KEY TERMS

Deep Learning: Learning that goes beyond a surface level and promotes the development of metacognition through communities of inquiry.

ePortfolio: My ePortfolio is my digital identity—a place to reflect upon my experiences and store artifacts that relate to them; it is a means to interact with others, resources, and so forth. Most importantly, it is mine.

FOAF: Friend of a Friend is an XML standard that allows Web site owners to define who they are as well as their relationships with other Web site owners.

Folksonomy: A bottom-up user-defined classification system.

RSS: Really simple syndication (RSS) is an XML format for summarizing Web content (usually of the chronologically ordered kind, such as Weblogs).

Social Networking: A Web technology which allows users to discover new business or personal contacts by traversing relationship links between people and resources.

Weblog: A technology which allows users to post text-based content onto the Web quickly and easily.

XML: The eXtensible Markup Language is an industry-standard, extensible format for self-describing data which allows for easy data transfer between computers, whatever the operating system or model.

ENDNOTES

1. George Siemens (http://www.elearnspace.org/blog/) and Stephen Downes (http://www.downes.ca/)
2. http://teachopolis.org/library/deep_learning.htm
3. http://www.unca.edu/et/br110698.html

Chapter IV
ePortfolios:
Constructing Meaning Across Time, Space, and Curriculum

Colleen Carmean
Arizona State University, USA

Alice Christie
Arizona State University, USA

ABSTRACT

This chapter explores research on ePortfolios from the perspective of defining, evaluating, and demonstrating value to enduring learning. It makes a case for the public/private container and the value to the learner of digital artifact creation, self-reflection, and presentation. It explores the use and challenges of ePortfolios in instruction and makes a case for the ePortfolio as an effective tool for knowledge creation. Finally, the authors examine the question of assessment in implementation of an enterprise ePortfolio: the value of learner assessment, peer and public assessment, and the need for institutional assessment of the ePortfolio.

SCENARIO

Reggie rushes onto campus 35 minutes before class and heads for the University Commons, seeking a double mocha and a quiet seat in the shade. She has worked much of the night on the first draft of her Communications 200 ePortfolio section, and despite the initial proposal review and go-ahead by Professor Harrison, she has some doubts regarding how her performance team members will critique it. Sure, it meets the learning goals she had proposed, but does her project really work for an external audience? Do the pages have good navigation? Are the timings on the Flash module she (crazily) decided to use paced right? What about the pictures she loaded into the "nonverbal behavior" analysis? Should she have checked them on multiple browsers?

It may be last minute jitters, too little sleep, or simple insecurity, but Reggie decides to make one more pass on her project reflection narrative. She should also make sure that the permissions are set for her team to review. Reggie would not want her mother wandering into her public "giving speeches" module and asking a lot of questions about her learning process material. Mom already asks too many who-what-when-where-and-why questions.

Reggie pops open her laptop, gulps hot mocha, and signs into the campus wireless network. First she brings up her public page as an anonymous Web viewer, and navigates to the COMM200 site. Looks good in Firefox®. She then logs in, checks the COMM200 folder permissions, verifies her team member rights, and opens her reflection narrative.

She tries to ignore the semester of work, thought, and knowledge creation she has put into understanding effective speaking and imagines it from the perspective of her team of fellow learners. She reads over her explanation of why she made some of the choices she did. Would her team members have made similar choices? Josh, whose final project was to create a resource site of jokes and stories for speeches, will probably be the worst critic of her Flash piece. It would not be the first time he jumped on style, ignoring the content. She decides to add a reminder that this was her first foray into Flash, and the simple design she chose was to help the viewer better understand the 10 ways to ensure audience understanding of meaning—not to wow Josh with fancy, 'flashy' moving objects.

Checking her watch, Reggie sighs, saves, then enters the course area and checks Professor Harrison's latest announcements, glances at the number of unread messages for all her courses, and with 13 minutes to deadline, posts her personal MyPort address in the COMM 200 assignments area, and sets her laptop to sleep. Would that she could do the same (sleep), but she has two more back-to-back classes, dinner with Jeremy (wouldn't Mom love to know), and three site reviews of her COMM team members to begin. Maybe another mocha wouldn't hurt? No time. Off to class.

THE ePORTFOLIO

What Is It?

A quietly growing response to a variety of demands being made of higher education is the use of the ePortfolio to assess student learning, document learner progress, and provide the graduate with a functional tool for selecting and presenting their achievements and records. Across the academy, pockets of innovation are occurring that ask the learner to create a "personal digital record containing information such as personal profile and collection of achievements" (Wikipedia, n.d), as well as information, artifacts, links, tools, and records that can selectively be provided to the owner of the ePortfolio and to the faculty, peers, friends, prospective employers, or public to whom the owner has chosen to grant permission.

A portfolio can be as simple as a collection of a student's best work or as complex as an alternative assessment procedure. It can be a learning strategy or an elaborate assessment. Graves (1994) says a portfolio "is a place where a student's selected work is kept, ... [any] container designed or created by the student to hold his or her artifacts" (p. 171). What goes into the portfolio depends on the purposes of student and teacher (Graves, 1994). Barrett (1998) explains that a portfolio is "a purposeful collection of student's work that illustrates efforts, progress and achievement" (p. 7). It is a means of communicating growth made by a student, and is much more than a form of assessment (Barrett, 1998; Dudley, 2001). It is also more than a collection of artifacts haphazardly connected together in a multimedia program or document. The collection must include student participation in selecting contents, the criteria for selection, the criteria for judging merit, and evidence of student self-reflection. Moritz and Christie (2005) draw on other researchers to define ePortfolios as:

1. tools to motivate, encourage, and instruct students in the classroom: students become reflective learners as portfolio use is expected to foster self-analysis, goal setting, and a sense of self-motivation by the learner (Barrett, 2000; Galley, 2000; Graves, 1992); and
2. mechanisms to monitor and improve teacher's instruction in the classroom (Benson & Smith, 1998; Galley, 2000; Graves, 1992).

The effective ePortfolio is a purposeful collection of student work that exhibits a learner's efforts, progress, and achievements in one or more areas. Students participating in a study reported by Danielson and Abrutyn (1997) engaged in a five-stage process of portfolio creation to achieve this purpose. Each stage is outlined below:

1. The **conception** stage of the process involved planning the portfolio. At this point decisions were made to determine the central focus and general direction of the learning path the teacher would take. Growth goals were developed around available standards.
2. The **collection** stage of the process involved the collection of all potential artifacts relating to their growth goal. This component took the greatest amount of time, as the collection of artifacts required the entire length of the course to gather, and potentially involved collecting all coursework for consideration for inclusion in the digital portfolio.
3. The **selection** stage involved the selection of representative artifacts for inclusion in the digital portfolio. Work in this stage required waiting for the "collection" to become large enough to support a winnowing process for selecting high-quality artifacts.
4. The **reflection** stage involved reflecting on one's progress toward a growth goal and how each of the "selected" artifacts affected student learning. These reflections were to be included in the digital portfolio along with the artifact.
5. The **connection** stage involved connecting the "selected" artifacts and reflections using PowerPoint™ as the medium for displaying digital teaching portfolios. This stage also involved connecting the artifacts back to the growth goal.

Who's Doing It?

Across the academy, pockets of innovation are occurring that ask learners to document their learning experience and understanding that pull together their education, and make available artifacts of their achievement, skills, interests, and understandings. The success of this movement will depend on the usability of the software, implementation in the curriculum, and widespread understanding and acceptance of the medium (Jafari & Greenberg, 2003).

Certainly the concept of "portfolio" is easy to grasp for educational use. It has long been used in the arts and architecture to track the body of student work. It has not been used extensively in other disciplines, often due to the lack of self-direction or reflection in traditional education models. Learners had no interest or incentive to save their test scores or assigned papers.

A culture of personally owned Web pages, course management system discussions, and personal knowledge digitally captured has created a new understanding on the part of instructors and learners of the value of digital artifacts of the learner experience and the value of using an ePortfolio system to track and contain artifacts of student learning (Jafari et al., n.d.).

Although shifting, the strongest movement in ePortfolio implementation within higher education has been within the colleges of teacher education, where emphasis is being placed on the need for students to express their understanding at a higher level within Bloom's taxonomy (Bloom, Englehart, Furst, Hill, & Krathwohl, 1956), and to create outcomes that demonstrate the creation, integration, and critique (Bloom's synthesis and evaluation) of what they have learned.

One tool that offers opportunities for connection, collaboration, reflection, and evaluation is the digital teaching portfolio. For many years, educators have successfully used teaching portfolios as a professional development tool to examine their professional practice and reflect on their growth over time (Doolittle, 1994). With new technologies available, portfolios can utilize digital formats that allow for greater portability and sharing (Gibson & Barrett, 2002). The portfolio development process provides an avenue for teachers to reflect on their practice and to align it to theory, research, and best practices while being supported by their colleagues (Doolittle, 1994; Heath, 2002; Holbein & Jackson, 1999). Through the creation of and reflection on portfolios for professional development, teachers grow in their skill and practice (Barrett, 2000; Gatlin & Jacob, 2002; Heath, 2002; Holbein & Jackson, 1999). These authors also indicate that teachers involved in creating reflective digital portfolios develop technology-related skills that have a transfer to the classroom (Gatlin & Jacob, 2002; Heath, 2002; Holbein & Jackson, 1999). Through the collaborative and reflective experiences in the digital portfolio process, teachers become facilitators, helping students discover what they must know and be able to do to meet state and national standards (King, 2002).

Baker and Christie (2005) found that teachers completing ePortfolios during a graduate class on using technology to enhance learning reported that creating digital teaching portfolios helps them become better teachers. There was evidence that the digital portfolio process engaged teachers in the process of reflection when they reported that:

1. [The digital portfolio process] uncovers strengths and weaknesses for growth and development.
2. Completing electronic portfolios helps a teacher reflect on learning.
3. [Teachers] can model lifelong learning for their students and other teachers.
4. [The digital portfolio process] allows for a wide range of learning styles to be addressed and shared.

Why Is It Significant?

As higher education begins to prepare its students for the information age and knowledge economy, it wrestles with new ways of teaching and learning, with the definition of an educated person, and with the changes it must make to serve a society that wants universal access to a college education. Students, their parents, and employers are now demanding a different kind of education than colleges and universities have offered in the past. Accountability, assessment, and educated workers are now the outcomes asked of higher education (AAC&U, 2002).

The explosion of information available has also created a change in the definition of knowledge. It is no longer what the educated person knows that makes him or her smart; it is the just-in-time ability to find out what one needs to know when it is needed that redefines knowledge (Siemens, 2005).

Research in cognitive science, psychology, and educational theory also currently provides us with a better understanding of enduring, meaningful learning (Bransford, Brown, & Cocking, 2000). Passive learning can no longer provide the critical skills needed in the educated workforce of the information economy. Deep, meaningful learning takes place when a number of conditions, delivered through any mode and in place in any combination, are present. A summary of the research suggests that these conditions include: (1) social, (2) contextual, (3) active experiences that (4) demand ownership by the learner and (5) encourages engagement and curiosity (Carmean & Haefner, 2002). Regardless of age, the next generation of higher-education learners has to seek out knowledge in new, independent, and instantaneous ways (Oblinger, 2003). The nature of learning becomes more self-directed and independent in the wake of the information explosion. Instructors lose control of information when "to google" becomes a verb (Word Spy, n.d) and learners begin choosing their own content and sources for learning and verifying knowledge.

The goal of faculty is to get students to collect artifacts, select the key pieces, reflect on their growth over time, project their future goals, and respect their work through sharing with a wider audience (Barrett, 2005). To give the portfolio purpose and structure, it should be organized around standards or benchmarks and reflect the learner's growth toward those standards. It should include the learner's focused goals for future growth based on his or her evaluation of past performances and current strengths as detailed by the included artifacts. These goals and evaluation of growth toward these goals make up the most important aspect of the portfolio: reflection. The reflections become the identifying character or unique expression of the individual creating the portfolio (Heath, 2002). Through these reflections, the audience (self, professor, mentor, student, administrator, professional developer, and/or licensure board) is able to form a deeper understanding of the creator's growth as he or she analyzes, evaluates, and synthesizes his or her own work (Kilbane & Milman, 2003). As Barrett (2005) reminds us, "reflection is not a mirror, it's a lens."

CHALLENGES

Faculty members face both intellectual and practical challenges as they adjust their roles to this more collaborative assessment strategy. Intellectual challenges for faculty include the need to re-examine the nature and purpose of learning and assessment, understand that both are redefined continually as society's demands for educated citizens change, and acknowledge that multiple assessment strategies are preferable for students, faculty, and society. Practical challenges include restructuring the learning process, learning how to move from knowledge dispenser to facilitator of personally relevant learning, viewing assessment as an integral part of learning, and learning to collaborate with students in the assessment process. In addition, they need to use many information sources and media types rather than a single printed text, honor multiple ways of knowing/learning, and evaluate learning authentically/critically.

Students face their own set of challenges. Rather than relying on faculty members to prescribe the learning and assess student progress using traditional assessment methods, they must take more responsibility for their learning, including learning from numerous people and using a wide array of learning tools; and they must be more reflective about their own learning and learning paths, and collaborate fully in the assessment process.

Administration, those responsible for long-term planning, are challenged to embrace the call for change being asked of them by students, parents, politicians, and society (Ramaley & Leske, 2002). Long removed from teaching and learning, administrators are often hard-pressed to understand the shift in learning styles, knowledge management, and competencies being asked of the new educated graduate (Brown, 2000). When pressed to implement change, they can find it difficult to determine and execute the meaningful leadership that creates incentives to facilitate a new, formative assessment system such as an ePortfolio-based system.

ASSESSMENT

The Value of Reflection

There are two important components that need be a part of a classroom's environment for portfolios to be effective assessment tools: *involving learners in the assessment and review of their work* (Graves, 1992), and *teacher's authentic planning based on assessments of learners' performance* (Galley, 2000). Involving learners in assessment is important because the goal of evaluation is to have students be self-evaluative. Self-awareness of the learning process is developed through modeling, discussion, and instruction on reflection and evaluation of students' work and process (Adodeeb & Courtney, 1999; Goodman, 1989). By looking through students' portfolios and the teacher's assessment folders, the teacher directs the instruction to the needs of each learner (Adodeeb & Courtney, 1999; Benson & Smith, 1998).

Student growth through the creation and use of portfolios relies on students' involvement in the assessment process and authentic planning by the teacher. Growth can be expected through instruction and the practice of reflection. Student choice and shared control on what is included in the portfolio are important as well. Reflection and self-analysis processes that students go through heighten their ability to think critically, be self-reflective, and set goals for themselves (Moritz & Christie, 2005). Assessment and evaluation differ. Assessment is the collection of relevant information that is used to make decisions. Evaluation is the application of a decision-making system to assess data and make judgments about the adequacy of learning. Portfolio assessment:

1. Transfers responsibility for learning to the student, who then establishes individual learning goals
2. Encourages a learner-centered environment that connects learning and assessment
3. Uses samples of student work and reflections collected over an entire semester/year/college career
4. Provides guidelines for selection of representative materials (not all work completed in a course)
5. Requires student-reflection, peer feedback, and instructor feedback and guidance
6. References standards, benchmarks, or exemplars of excellence
7. Provides clear and appropriate criteria that allow students and teachers to evaluate student learning

Portfolio assessment benefits both students and teachers. Students involved in portfolio assessment are actively involved in self-directed learning, are continually assessing their own learning, and are valuing themselves as learners, thereby enhancing their success as learners. Teachers, by reflecting on their own practice, are more likely to become better teachers; in addition, teachers gain a better understanding of assessment, evaluation, and the learning–assessment connection. Communication between students and teachers improves, and the classroom environment becomes more learner centered and less teacher directed. Further research in best practices and effective assessment is needed in this relatively new implementation that combines software, services, selective access to materials, and a framework of tools that are still to be determined.

A Lifelong Tool for Evaluation

As ePortfolio adoption continues to grow in higher education, lifelong ePortfolios are gaining attention in a variety of settings. One leading example is the innovative State of Indiana initiative, Indiana@Work, that offers lifelong personal ePortfolio accounts and services to individual "Hoosiers" (Indiana@Work, n.d). The need for educated citizens and workers to update and synthesize their knowledge, skills, interests, and understandings will continue to be an issue for a society coping with the demands of the information age.

Many are beginning to see value in the ePortfolio's ability to create and deliver information. For the owner and the viewer, it presents an intuitive and easy-to-access umbrella of services. The conceptual framework, levels of permission, and integrated tools provide a narrower, but more functional interface than previous uses of online Web pages, databanks, or résumés to "make career decisions, demonstrate that one has met program or certification requirements, present skills and accomplishments for employment, and review professional development for career advancement" (Jafari & Greenberg, 2003).

Institutional Assessment

Assessment does not end with an evaluation of the student's learning. Hard questions will need to be asked of the institution before implementing an ePortfolio system. Similar to the rush to solution seen in the adoption of Course/Learning Management Systems (Carmean & Brown, 2005), the institution can ill afford the resources of time, money, and disruption that can be brought about by not being able to make explicit value of a new enterprise service to students, faculty, administrators, or instructional and technology support services. Difficult assessment questions to be asked might include:

1. What are the teaching and learning implications associated with ePortfolios in higher education? What are the pedagogical benefits and how does one assess them? What content standards should be used for ePortfolios?
2. What are the implications associated with ePortfolios in higher education? What policy implications must be considered and resolved? Do institutions of higher education need new intellectual property policies for retained student work? How does the institution build faculty and student buy-in?
3. What are the technical issues associated with ePortfolios in higher education? Who should be responsible for choosing and maintaining the institutional system? What are the support issues and implications for IT regarding enterprise software not previously on their radar? What are the ongoing training and usage issues for faculty and students? What are the costs and choices in short- and long-term maintenance?

As valuable as the evidence may be for the use of ePortfolios in authentic teaching, learning, and assessment, the adoption of a new pedagogical tool in a meaningful way is a transformational change. Institutional commitment must be in place, understanding of the value must be clear, and the faculty rewards for undertaking difficult change must be rewarded.

CONCLUSION

The ePortfolio is a promising framework for enduring learning, self-assessment, and construction of value across a student's educational path. Learners learn by doing, and by constructing knowledge, meaning, ownership, and value from the act of learning. Initial evidence demonstrates that ePortfolios provide an effective environment for storing artifacts, creating reflections, demonstrating knowledge, and reflecting on self and other's learning.

Although evidence for the value of the ePortfolio is strong, careful consideration of the implications must be considered and uniquely dealt with by each institution looking to adopt an ePortfolio system in a systematic way. Assessment of learning, faculty adoption, and institutional resources needed to implement are necessary for meaningful and lasting implementation of the ePortfolio across the institution.

REFERENCES

AAC&U (American Association of Colleges & Universities). (2002). *Greater expectations: A new vision for learning as a nation goes to college.* Retrieved from http://www.greaterexpectations.org/

Adodeeb, T. L., & Courtney, A. M. (1999). Diagnostic-reflective portfolios. *The Reading Teacher, 52*(7), 708-714.

Baker, R., & Christie, A. (2005). Can digital teaching portfolios become tools for technology integration? In C. Crawford, D. Willis, R. Carlsen, I. Gibson, K. McFerrin, & J. Price (Eds.), *Proceedings of the 16th International Society for Information Technology & Teacher Education Conference* (pp. 15-20). Norfolk, VA: Association for the Advancement of Computing in Education (AACE).

Barrett, H. C. (1998). Strategic questions to consider when planning for electronic portfolios. *Learning & Leading with Technology, 26*(2), 6-13.

Barrett, H. (2000). Electronic teaching portfolios: Multimedia skills + portfolio development = powerful professional development. *Proceedings of the Society for Information Technology & Teacher Education International Conference,* Seattle, WA (ERIC Document Reproduction Service No. ED 444514).

Barrett, H. (2005). Personal correspondence.

Benson, T. R., & Smith, L. J. (1998). Portfolios in first grade: Four teachers learn to use alternative assessment. *Early Childhood Education Journal, 25*(3), 173-179.

Bloom, B., Englehart, M., Furst, E., Hill, W., & Krathwohl, D. (1956). *Taxonomy of educational objectives: The classification of educational goals. Handbook I: Cognitive domain.* New York; Toronto: Longmans, Green.

Bransford, J., Brown, A., & Cocking, R. (2000). *How people learn: Brain, mind, experience and school.* Washington, DC: National Research Council.

Brown, J. S. (2000). Growing up digital: How the Web changes work, education, and the ways people learn. *Change, 32*(2662), 10-11.

Carmean, C., & Brown, G. (2005). Measure for measure: Assessing course management systems. In P. McGee, C. Carmean, & A. Jafari (Eds.), *Course management systems for learning: Beyond accidental pedagogy* (pp. 1-13). Hershey, PA: Information Science Publishing.

Carmean, C., & Haefner, J. (2002). Mind over Matter. *Educause Review, 37*(6), 26-34.

Danielson, C., & Abrutyn, L. (1997). *An introduction to using portfolios in the classroom*. Alexandria, VA: Association for Supervision and Curriculum Development.

Doolittle, P. (1994). *Teacher portfolio assessment*. Washington, DC: Eric Clearinghouse on Assessment and Evaluation. (ERIC Document Reproduction Service No. ED385608)

Dudley, M. (2001). Portfolio assessment: When bad things happen to good ideas. *English Journal, 90*(6), 19-20.

Galley, S. (2000). Portfolio as mirror: Student and teacher learning reflected through the standards. *Language Arts, 78*(2), 121-127.

Gatlin, L., & Jacob, S. (2002). Standards-based digital portfolios: A component of authentic assessment for preservice teachers. *Action in Teacher Education, 23*(4), 35-42.

Gibson, D., & Barrett, H. (2002, November). *Directions in electronic portfolio development*. Retrieved October 19, 2003, from http://electronicportfolios.com/ITFOURM66.html

Goodman, K. (1989). Theory and general principals. In K. S. Goodman, Y. M. Goodman, & W. J. Hood (Eds.), *The whole language evaluation book*. Portsmouth, NH: Heinemann.

Graves, D. (1992). Portfolios: Keep a good idea growing. In D. H. Graves & B. S. Sunstein (Eds.), *Portfolio portraits*. Portsmouth, NH: Heinemann.

Graves, D. (1994). Help children to revise their work. In D. H. Graves (Ed.), *A fresh look at writing*. Portsmouth, NH: Heinemann.

Heath, M. (2002). Electronic portfolios for reflective self-assessment. *Teacher Librarian, 30*(1), 19-23.

Holbein, M. F. D., & Jackson, K. (1999). Study groups and electronic portfolios: A professional development school in-service project. *Journal of Technology and Teacher Education, 7*(3), 205-217.

Indiana@Work. (n.d). *E-portfolios*. Retrieved May 14, 2005, from http://in.ePortfolio.us/Content/Root/Home.aspx

Jafari, A., & Greenberg, G.(2003). *Electronic portfolio white paper*. Retrieved May 12, 2005, from http://www.eportconsortium.org/Uploads/whitepaperV1_0.pdf

Kilbane, C. R., & Milman, N. B. (2003). *The digital teaching portfolio handbook: A how-to guide for educators*. Boston: Allyn and Bacon

King, K. P. (2002). Educational technology professional development as transformative learning opportunities. *Computers & Education, 39*(3), 283-297.

Moritz, J., & Christie, A. (2005). It's elementary! Using electronic portfolios with young students. In C. Crawford, D. Willis, R. Carlsen, I. Gibson, K. McFerrin, & J. Price (Eds.), *Proceedings of the 16th International Society for Information Technology & Teacher Education Conference* (pp. 1905-1909). Norfolk, VA: Association for the Advancement of Computing in Education (AACE).

Oblinger, D. (2003, July/August). Boomers, gen-Xers and millennials: Understanding the new students. *Educause Review,* 37-47.

Ramaley, J., & Leskes, A. (2002). *Greater expectations: A new vision for learning as a nation goes to college*. Washington, DC: Association of American Colleges & Universities. Retrieved September 1, 2005, from http://www.greaterexpectations.org/

Siemens, G. (2005). Connectivism: A learning theory for the digital age. *International Journal of Instructional Technology and Distance Learning, 2*(1), 8.

Wikipedia. (n.d). *E-portfolio*. Retrieved May 13, 2005, from http://en.wikipedia.org/wiki/E-portfolio

Word Spy. (n.d). *Google*. Retrieved May 14, 2005, from http://www.wordspy.com/words/google.asp

KEY TERMS

Benchmark: A clear, specific description of knowledge or skills that students should acquire by a particular point in their schooling. Benchmarks are often defined locally, while standards are defined statewide or by professional organizations. Benchmarks are often more specific than content standards. Other terms for benchmark include indicator or learning expectation. *See Content Standards.*

Content Standards: Summary descriptions of what students should know and/or be able to do within a particular discipline or educational level. Content standards primarily serve to organize an academic subject through a manageable number of generally stated goals for student learning. *See Benchmark.*

Digital Artifact: Materials having significance or meaning to learners that have been digitized for inclusion in an ePortfolio. As learners collect artifacts, they reflect on their learning experiences and record these reflections to show how each artifact meets specific professional standards, goals, or benchmarks.

Digital Teaching Portfolio: A goal-driven, professional development tool used by in-service teachers to examine their professional practice and reflect on their growth over time. This portfolio development process provides an avenue for teachers to reflect on their practice and to align it to theory, research, or best practices.

Educated Person: A term that has changed extensively in the last decade. The twenty-first-century definition no longer addresses what a person knows; rather, it focuses on the ability to find out what one needs to know in a timely way. By implication, a twenty-first-century-educated person is an independent lifelong learner, an informed decision maker, a reflective learner, a resource-based learner, a problem solver, and often a collaborator.

Institutional Assessment: A broad category of measurement strategies done at universities to inform campus decision making and planning in areas such as admissions, financial aid, curriculum, enrollment, staffing, student life, finance, facilities, athletics, and alumni relations. In this chapter, institutional assessment refers to examining how and why ePortfolios can be used to improve teaching and learning in higher education.

Knowledge Creation: A term historically centered on the acquisition, accumulation, and utilization of existing knowledge, but used in this chapter to mean the dynamic knowledge generated by learners, as well as the social processes within which this knowledge is created. Unlike most resources that are depleted when used, information and knowledge can be shared, and actually grow through application and collaboration.

Learner Assessment: A strategy for measuring and documenting student learning.

In this chapter, learner assessment is a collaborative process involving student and instructor/mentor that examines student learning by selecting artifacts from a student's work over time to demonstrate that learning has occurred. Sometimes called alternative assessment or portfolio assessment, it is in direct contrast to what is commonly known as performance evaluation, traditional assessment, or summative assessment.

Learner-Centered Environment: An environment that accommodates a variety of learning styles; features knowledge creation, collaboration, and discussion among and by learners; focuses on student needs; and places the responsibility for learning on the student¾with the instructor assuming responsibility for facilitating students' learning. Such pedagogy often leads to collaborative partnerships between university faculty and students.

Reflection/Self-Reflection: Thoughtful consideration by the learner on one's progress toward goals. Reflection is a process by which learners explore their work, assess their strengths and weaknesses, describe their learning processes, and consider implications for future learning. In addition, reflection or discussion of how selected artifacts affect and indicate student learning is what distinguishes an ePortfolio from a scrapbook or mere collection of artifacts. *See Reflective Learners.*

Reflective Learners: A term often referred to as *learning to learn.* Reflective learners explore learning experiences to better understand how they learn, improve their further learning, develop critical thinking skills, increase their autonomy as learners, and observe and reflect on their learning over time. Based on Dewey's 1933 conceptualization of reflective learning as active, persistent, and careful consideration of beliefs and knowledge. *See Reflection.*

Self-Directed Learning: Best described by the old adage, "Give me a fish and I will eat for a day. Teach me to fish and I eat for a lifetime." The reflection required in ePortfolio creation is facilitated when learners are self-directed and take responsibility in the learning-assessment process. *See Reflection.*

Chapter V
Perspectives on a Visual Map-Based Electronic Portfolio System

Paul Kim
Stanford University, USA

ABSTRACT

This chapter introduces portfolio system design perspectives that incorporate concept mapping and the map-based user interface. It also presents a prototype of a portfolio system that has been developed based on the discussed perspectives, along with its capacities and the lessons learned in the design and pilot-testing processes. The author argues that a concept map-based design can enhance a portfolio system, and a concept map as a visual aid can be an efficient user interface for students to better organize, present, archive, and retrieve multimedia contents. This chapter will help educators understand the benefits of incorporating the principles of concept mapping in the design of portfolio systems, and how the system capacities may support constructivist learning environments and qualitative assessment strategies linked to curriculum standards.

INTRODUCTION

Advantages of adopting portfolio-based learning and assessment have been reported by researchers (Cole, Ryan, & Kirk, 1995; Frey, 1995; Kim, 2004; Lehman & Richardson, 2003; Russell & Butcher, 1999) and acknowledged enough by accreditation agencies (e.g., NCATE) to consider the criterion-based portfolio assessment as one of standard assessment methods. While portfolios are being adopted in various educational settings, the rapid advancement of digital and communication technologies are making it possible for the innovative designs, implementations, and applications of portfolios and portfolio systems. Two emerging areas of educational research studies and investigation attempts that are supporting, if not shaping, today's evolution of portfolio systems are: (1) collaborative learning and qualitative assessment through concept-mapping, and (2) interactive visual interface-based multimedia storage and information retrieval. These two areas are particularly relevant and important to portfolio system designs, because concept mapping through collaboration may fit nicely into the role of promoting and supporting constructivist learning while enabling both formative and summative evaluations of students' progressive development processes, competencies, and the integrity of the purposefully organized portfolios.

The interactive visual interface aspect of concept map approaches are also relevant in the portfolio design discussions because the visual interface may assist the metacognition processes of creating, collecting, organizing, distributing, sharing, and archiving learning objects and student works of the digital age.

In regards to the terms used in the discussion, one can expect to find numerous terms such as "knowledge map," "mind map," "semantic map," "cognitive map," "Web map," "hyper map," along with "concept map" in various studies, and they are often interchangeably used and in some cases they mean different things. In this chapter when the term "visual map" appears, it means more of a freestyle graphical representation over the Web, which does not strictly require a proposition or semantic path, but does incorporate various multimedia components.

Assessment and Cognitive Development with Concept Mapping

The cognitive structure assessment through concept mapping has been considered as one of valuable qualitative assessment methods (Biggs, 1999; Kinchin, 2000) and an emerging pedagogy linked to the constructivist view of learning (Kinchin, 1998; Marshall, Zhang, Shen, Fox, & Cassel, 2003; Novak, 1998; Shen, Richardson, & Fox, 2003). The last several decades of research studies support that there are notable advantages of adopting concept mapping activity in various educational settings. As an assessment technique, exploring students' cognitive structure using concept maps can be an important part of pedagogy when evaluating student learning (Tsai & Huang, 2002), because the assessment of the cognitive structure can make explicit the thoughts and understandings, or even misconceptions and biased beliefs, of the student (Kinchin, 1998) as if conducting in-depth individual interviews (Edwards & Fraser, 1983).

As a metacognitive strategy for learners, elaborating cognitive structures can facilitate conceptual development and conceptual change over time (Tsai & Huang, 2002). This is due to the fact that "identifying" new meanings or relationships that they may not have recognized or grasped consciously before explicitly constructing the maps can lead to progressive conceptual development (Novak & Gowin, 1984). The guided concept mapping process plays an important role in facilitating constant and progressive conceptual development over time by students' repetitive comparisons and analyses of their own cognitive structures at multiple stages (Freeman & Urbaczewski, 2002). In the Vygotskian view, this process may help identify the dimensions of a student's zone of proximal development (Brown & Ferrara, 1985).

Concept Map as Visual Interface

The graphical representation of concept maps serves not only as an effective visual aid to learning processes (Nuutinen & Sutinen, 2003), but also as an efficient user interface to manipulate multimedia materials. For example, a concept map-based visual interface leads to higher accuracy in search performance than a typical Web page-based browser (Carnot, Dunn,

Cañas, Graham, & Muldoon, 2003). In a comparison study with knowledge maps and conventional hypertext, users reported less frustration and confusion when using a knowledge map-based interface rather than a hypertext interface (Reynolds & Dansereau, 1990). Furthermore, Shen et al. (2003) assert that concept maps as knowledge visualization tools have great potential for digital library applications, because concept maps constructed by learners can serve as summarization of domain and concept maps that take advantage of digital libraries to further engage both learners and instructors in an active learning approach and collaboration setting.

Weideman and Kritzinger (2003) suggest concept mapping as an alternative visual interface for knowledge repository and retrieval, and Alpert (2003) has incorporated the very same perspective into a visual interface embedded in a standard Web browser to help the user construct concept maps with multimedia components. In supporting multimedia integrated concept map design, Alpert and Grueneberg (2001) state:

> *Incorporating multimedia in concept mapping software should (1) offer the illustrative advantages of dynamic visual imagery and audio to students learning new concepts and domains, (2) provide the capability of reifying concepts with concrete instances that can be seen and heard, (3) offer richer expressive power for concept map authors, (4) provide for a more engaging student experience, and (5) better capitalize on the functionality available in modern personal computers.* (p. 3)

Design Principles of a Digital Portfolio System

As noted in the literature review, various studies report the positive educational effects of concept mapping and possible performance efficiencies with the concept map as a visual interface. This section will focus on the concept of applying the emerging perspectives into the design of a digital portfolio system.

If a digital portfolio system is to be designed to incorporate the principles of concept mapping, such a system should enable students to recognize and reflect their own learning processes using both effective and ineffective strategies, understandings and misunderstandings, and progressively developing their own competencies by constant comparisons with peers' learning processes. From the repetitive comparisons, students can understand more about their own work in progress, along with enhancing strategies over time, and continuously refine their representations for a purposeful length or event. The collaboration efforts in such an interactive environment would enable students to perform at their highest potential, which could not be achieved independently. Therefore, such a digital portfolio system would be in the same vein as concept map-based learning to support a constructivist learning environment.

However, conventional concept mapping mainly involves textual information. The primary difference between a digital portfolio and concept map is that concept maps incorporate mostly propositions, indicated by connecting lines between concepts and labels on the line specifying the relationship between the concepts, whereas a digital portfolio integrates not only textual information but also various multimedia materials based on the learning objective criteria to demonstrate required competencies.

In order for a digital portfolio system to effectively support the learning processes with concept mapping, the user interface must be able to integrate various media including, but not limited to, video, sound, graphic images, drawing, concept maps, Web pages, and any imaginable material in a digital format. In addition, the interface must allow users to organize and present materials in a free visual structure that could be edited repeatedly and conveniently as needed (e.g., a process similar to using a scratch pad or word processor).

The advantage of using a visual interface coupled with concept mapping as a learning technique lies in the possibility of having a freestyle visual representation of information which is highly useful for learners who can memorize information contained in a picture, and for learners who have good synthesis skills (Cicognani, 2000). Navigating through the visual mapping, reviewers can obtain visual displays of a student's cognitive structures (Freeman & Urbaczewski, 2002; Tsai & Huang, 2002), and the same process itself often helps students to understand their curricula and the structure behind them (Nuutinen & Sutinen, 2003). For example, students should be able to represent their conceptual understandings of a domain (e.g., educational technology) with a visual map and integrate learning evidences (e.g., sample curriculum integrating technology), course projects (e.g., literature reviews in MS Word or presentations in PowerPoint format), or videos with annotations (e.g., qualitative assessment data) to support their conceptual representations. If needed, students should be able to synthesize different conceptual understandings of multiple domains into one master visual map to present how a student integrates previous learning or experiences with a current program (e.g., MA in educational technology), what artifacts they have produced during the program (e.g., course works in different classes), and possibly what reflections they have for their practicum experiences or ongoing learning experiences.

The capacity to construct a conceptual representation and the ability to integrate justifications for such visual representation and various supporting evidences to the curriculum requirements may give the reviewers the opportunity to assess not only students' overall cognitive structure in relevant domains linked to the competency standards, but also the progressive development over time through collaboration efforts. This capacity is often missing in conventional portfolio systems that incorporate hierarchical folders or fixed template-based structures.

In regards to the evaluation of completed portfolios, Russell & Butcher (1999) state:

At the end of the course, the complete portfolio is evaluated in terms of how well the portfolio 'hangs together' as an integrated product. How well do the pieces fit together to support a user's understanding of the selected topic? Is the portfolio well organized, making it easy to locate specific items? Is the work neatly arranged and attractively presented? A well-organized portfolio is helpful in demonstrating [a] student's skills and abilities to current and/ or future employers. (p. 3)

If a portfolio system is to evolve to something beyond a simple checklist-based system—more of a learning space where students can visually express not only conceptual understandings, but also demonstrate the integrity of their mental cognitive structure with supporting evidence while collaborating with peers, continuously enhancing strategies, refining their presentations, recognizing and reflecting their own progressive development over time, and ultimately building competencies with the help of peers and the instructor—a new design perspective is worth exploring.

Development of a Prototype of a Visual Map-Based Portfolio System

Considering the perspectives discussed, this section will present a developed prototype of a portfolio system which employs a concept map-

Figure 1. Visual map construction in progress

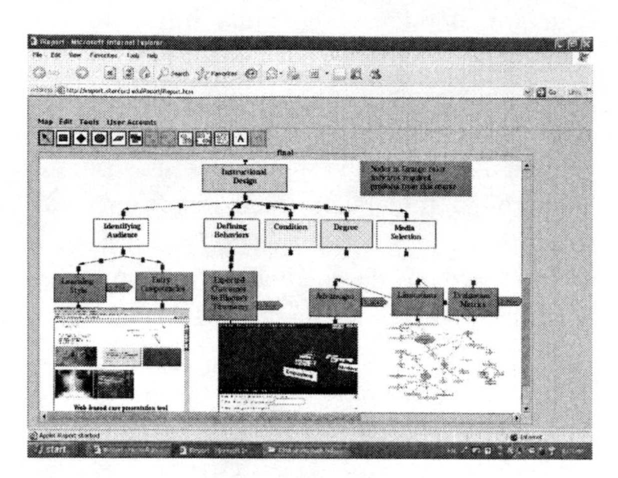

Figure 2. Node attributes

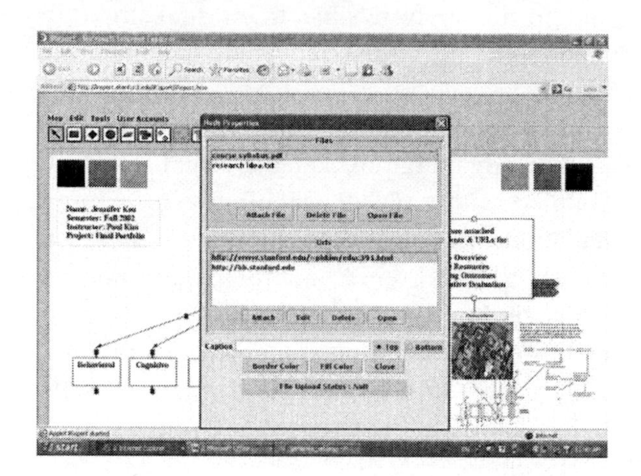

ping approach in the process of creating, collecting, organizing, distributing, sharing, and archiving learning objects and student works.

In this design, as shown in Figure 1, all portfolio objects are stored in a relational database in the back-end and represented with visual maps (i.e., with nodes, relationship notes, etc.) through a conventional Web browser in the front-end. Each map gets a unique URL which can be used by designated users to access maps for modification, addition, and exchange of objects.

These graphical representations, coupled with supporting materials (e.g., sound and video clips, Web pages, documents, scanned images, links to other visual maps, etc.), provide a "big picture" or contextual "overview" for their collection of ideas and the underlying principles they are attempting to express with their portfolio.

Unlike hierarchical-directory structured portfolio systems, a visual mapping space enables students to freely express visual drawings or add components in their portfolio, while brainstorming, collaborating, or presenting their ideas. Therefore, visual maps can also serve as stimulants for ongoing interactions while they are engaged in a "portfolioing" activity.

With this design concept, the management strategy of a reservoir of such portfolio maps or interconnected visual schema leads to a new way of systematically archiving and searching portfolios and objects that integrate complex multimedia components. As shown in Figure 2, all objects used in a map can have "node attributes" that allow students to attach various

Figure 3. Recording of the portfolio construction process

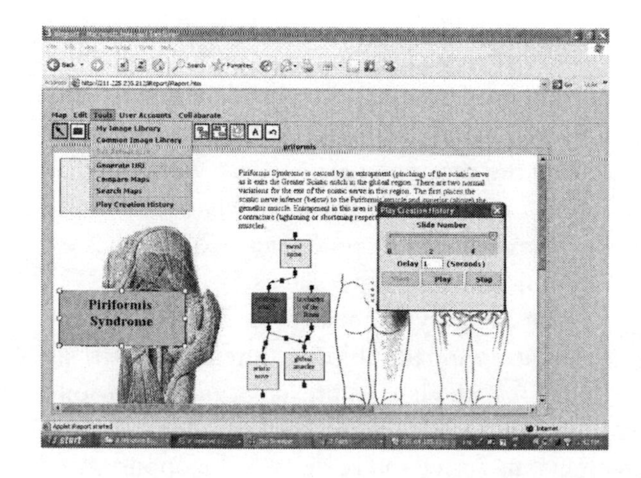

types of multimedia components. Also, objects can be maintained at both the personal and public object library level.

In the visual map environment, various learning activities can be rapidly developed without the use of any additional authoring tools. Also, "required performance" for a course can be pre-defined as expected outcomes for a planned learning session. For example, ill-structured schema can be presented for students to correct, modify, or improve by reorganizing layouts, attaching justifications, supplying reflections, or incorporating research findings on top of the visual template. As shown in Figure 3, a visual map can be linked to other presentations via URLs for more detailed explanations of a certain object or topic in the master map. In addition, the entire portfolio construction process can be recorded and replayed to examine every step a student has taken to organize materials and construct a portfolio.

Learning Experiences from the Designing Process of the Prototype

There was much learning as various issues surfaced and resolutions had to be devised accordingly to keep meeting the needs identified in the needs analysis process. As the concept mapping and visual interface perspectives constituted the design foundation, the needs analysis rendered 12 required technical capacities which were used as guidelines throughout the design and development of the prototype system. The 12 defined capacities are as follows:

1. **Accessibility:** Users are to access the portfolio system with a simple conventional Web browser on major OS platforms without much preparation (e.g., downloading and installing multiple drivers, extensive configuration, or high-end hardware specification). In this design, the system was built with JAVA and runs on most standard Web browsers on platforms such as Windows, Mac OS X, and UNIX families.
2. **Collaborability:** Users can collaborate on creating and organizing portfolios from scratch to completion. Users will need to review and augment peers' work while exchanging comments, and sharing objects and maps based on assigned access privileges. The prototype provided a unique URL for each portfolio map so they can be e-mailed to reviewers. Also, the earlier version of the prototype provided a real-time collaboration feature which allowed multiple users to login to the system at the same to construct maps together while discussing through instant messaging. This feature was conceived as researchers have indicated that synchronous feedback exchange is superior to asynchronous mode in concept mapping (e.g., De Simone, 2001).
3. **Exportability:** Users can export the partial or completed portfolios to conventional formats including HTML, XML, ZIP, and so forth. Screenshots of visual maps may be exported to GIF or JPG images.
4. **Flexibility:** Users can express concepts or draw visual representations in flexible styles and formats so that the overall presentation or the organization of portfolio components is not confined in linear or hierarchical structures.
5. **Interoperability:** The portfolio system can work with other systems such as a course management system or connect to LDAP server for authentication, and so on. The portfolio system can be pluggable to other systems as a component. The system structure should support major relational database engines without much effort in porting.

6. **Maintainability:** The portfolio system should not require increasing resources over time to maintain the daily operation and minor refinements.
7. **Reliability:** The system features should perform consistently and provide services under the stated normal condition for a defined time.
8. **Retrievability:** Users should be able to quickly search and retrieve part or full portfolio materials as needed using URL, keyword, owner information, portfolio name, or an attached file name.
9. **Reusability:** Partial or complete portfolios, along with attached videos or images, should be reusable in more than one condition or session. Portfolios, along with multimedia components that are attached, should be transferable to other users or locations within the system for later reuse.
10. **Scalability:** The portfolio system should be able to easily scale up as more contents are stored and more concurrent sessions with an increasing number of users access the system. Storage units, along with processing power, need to be easily expandable with minimum downtime.
11. **Trainability:** It should be easy to train users to access and operate the system. Any user with minimum computer literacy (i.e., knows how to start a browser or attach files to e-mails) should be able to start using the system within a few minutes of training. In this design, most of the features followed standard user interface approaches found in commonly used software packages, although some inherent JAVA characteristics were also apparent.
12. **Usability:** Operation should be intuitive and efficient in the processes of creating, collecting, organizing, distributing, sharing, and archiving objects and portfolios.

Pilot-Testing

Developing a prototype and conducting pilot tests in various educational situations helped the developers understand the potential problems as well as merits that may be realized when the actual system is implemented. For example, a pilot test at an elementary school which had only Macintosh computers helped the developers understand how different characteristics of computer platforms played a significant role in student performance. In a different case, the developers also learned how graduate students had become more expressive when they were given a tool to freely put together their ideas and share externalized internal cognitive structures among peers. Also a pilot test at an overseas site helped the developers understand multiple language requirements and network lag issues. In some cases, administrators of a school pointed out copyright and identity issues with portfolio activities.

The learning process will continue, as the development and enhancement will also continue as needs, requirements, and standards may change. Some of the existing capabilities may be dropped or new features may be added. Currently, more pilot tests are being conducted to enhance the system, and new development techniques and solutions are being examined to keep up with the trends of information technology.

CONCLUSION

Research studies relevant to concept map-based qualitative assessment and constructivist learning, and the concept map as a visual interface, have been reviewed, and these perspectives have been applied to develop a prototype of a visual map-based portfolio system. This prototype, designed with 12 defined capacities which were identified in the needs analysis, has been presented.

In any portfolio system development case, curriculum standards must drive the design of a portfolio system with necessary features and capabilities. However, it is still the student who pulls together information and artifacts to present expected understandings and competencies along with idiosyncrasies and creativity. Therefore, technology must be able to support such a learning experience and ease the use of necessary tools.

The advantage of using a visual map-based portfolio as a learning and assessment technique lies in the possibility to engage students in explicitly elaborating freestyle visual representations of multimedia in active collaboration settings, while demonstrating specifically required individual learning outcomes and achievements. At the same time, the system helps metacognition in the overall "portfolioing" experience, and allows peers and reviewers to observe and analyze the student's progressive cognitive development in various stages where active exchanges of feedback and scaffolding and learning may take place.

REFERENCES

Alpert, S. (2003). Abstraction in concept map and coupled outline knowledge representations. *Journal of Interactive Learning Research, 14*(1), 31-49.

Alpert, S. R., & Grueneberg, K. (2001). Multimedia in concept maps: A design rationale and Web-based application. In C. Montgomerie & J. Viteli (Eds.), *Proceedings of Ed-Media 2001, World Conference on Educational Multimedia Hypermedia and Telecommunications* (pp. 31-36). Charlottesville, VA: Association for the Advancement of Computing in Education.

Biggs, J. B. (1999). *Teaching for quality learning at university.* Buckingham: Open University Press.

Brown, A. L., & Ferrara, R. A. (1985). *Diagnosing zones of proximal development.* Cambridge: Cambridge University Press.

Carnot, M. J., Dunn, B., Cañas, A. J., Graham, P., & Muldoon, J. (2001). *Concept maps vs. Web pages for information searching and browsing.* Retrieved from http://www.ihmc.us/users/acanas/Publications/CMapsVSWebPagesExp1/CMapsVSWebPagesExp1.htm

Cicognani, A. (2000). Concept mapping as a collaborative tool for enhanced online learning. *Educational Technology & Society, 3*(3), 150-158.

Cole, D. J., Ryan, C. W., & Kirk, F. (1995). *Portfolios across the curriculum and beyond.* Thousand Oaks, CA: Corwin Press.

De Simone, C. (2001). Supporting the learning process with collaborative concept mapping using computer-based communication tools and processes. *Educational Research and Evaluation, 7*(2-3), 263-283.

Edwards, J., & Fraser, K. (1983). Concept maps as reflectors of conceptual understanding. *Research in Science Education, 13,* 19-26.

Freeman, L. A., & Urbaczewski, A. (2002). Concept maps as an alternative technique for assessing students' understanding of telecommunications. In *Proceedings of the 2002 International Conference on Informatics Education and Research* (pp. 135-145). Barcelona, Spain: International Academy for Information Management.

Frey, B. D. (1995). *Portfolio assessment* (Report No. CE-073-452). Lewistown, PA: TIU Adult Education and Job Training Center. (ERIC

Document Reproduction Service No. ED 404 503)

Kim, P. (2004). iReport: A Web-based digital portfolio system. In Y. Saito-Abott (Ed.), *Digital stream: Emerging technologies in teaching languages and cultures* (pp. 401-412). San Diego: LARC Press.

Kinchin, I. M. (1998, August). Constructivism in the classroom: Mapping your way through. In *Proceedings of the Annual Student Conference of the British Educational Research Association,* Belfast. Retrieved August 25, 2004, from http://www.leeds.ac.uk/educol/documents/000000811.htm

Kinchin, I. M. (2000). How a qualitative approach to concept map analysis can be used to aid learning by illustrating patterns of conceptual development. *Educational Research, 42*(1), 43-57.

Lehman, J., & Richardson, J. (2003, January). Creating a Web-based electronic portfolio system: Lessons from one teacher education program. In *Proceedings of the Annual Meeting of the American Association of Colleges of Teacher Education,* New Orleans, LA. Retrieved January 11, 2003, from http://p3t3.soe.purdue.edu/AACTE2003Portfolio.pdf

Marshall, B., Zhang, Y., Shen, R., Fox, E., & Cassel, L. (2003). Convergence of knowledge management and e-learning: The GetSmart experience. In *Proceedings of the 2003 Joint Conference on Digital Libraries.*

Novak, J. D. (1998). *Creating, and using knowledge: Concept maps as facilitative tools in schools and corporations.* Mahwah, NJ: Lawrence Erlbaum.

Novak, J. D., & Gowin, D. B. (1984). *Learning how to learn.* Cambridge: Cambridge University Press.

Nuutinen, J. A., & Sutinen, E. (2003). Visualization of the learning process using concept mapping. In *Proceedings of the 3rd IEEE International Conference on Advanced Learning Technologies* (pp. 348-349). Washington, DC: IEEE Computer Society.

Reynolds, S., & Dansereau, D. (1990). The knowledge hypermap: An alternative to hypertext. *Computers in Education, 14*(5), 409-416.

Russell, J. D., & Butcher, C. (1999). Using portfolios in educational technology courses. *Journal of Technology and Teacher Education, 7*(4), 279-289.

Shen, R., Richardson, R., & Fox, E. (2004). *Concept maps as visual interfaces to digital libraries: Summarization, collaboration, and automatic generation.* Retrieved January 20, 2004, from http://vw.indiana.edu/ivira03/shen-et-al.pdf

Tsai, C. C., & Huang, C. M. (2002). Exploring students' cognitive structures in learning science: A review of relevant methods. *Journal of Biological Education, 36,* 163-169.

KEY TERMS

Conceptual Development: A mental activity in acquisition and augmentation of information or knowledge. This term is often interchangeable with "cognitive development."

Concept Map: A visual representation of ideas, concepts, and principles often laid out with propositions and labels.

Cognitive Structure: An internal knowledge structure or schema.

Digital Portfolio: A collection of purposefully organized digital artifacts. This term is interchangeable with "ePortfolio."

Visual Interface: A concept map-like user interface a user can control to organize, present, archive, and search digital contents where the user may graphically lay out concepts and attach digital artifacts to concepts.

Visual Map: A freestyle graphical representation over the Web which does not "strictly require" a proposition or semantic path as found in semantic maps, but does incorporate various multimedia components.

Chapter VI
ePortfolio Thinking:
A Provost Perspective

Ronald J. Henry
Georgia State University, USA

ABSTRACT

This chapter introduces an electronic portfolio (ePortfolio) that includes student work, student reflection, and faculty comments as a means of capturing student progress through a program of study. It argues that with an ePortfolio, a student could record progress through a program of study and then graduate on demonstrated mastery of learning outcomes rather than on credits earned and hours in class. Alternatively, it could contain evidence of mastery of a particular literacy or skill that might give a student a credential that is more than a course but less than a degree. Further, an ePortfolio has the potential to enhance advising and admissions practices for students transferring from one institution to another. Once in an institution, an ePortfolio has the potential to be linked to a student tracking system, where advisers could be automatically alerted about student progress on development towards program learning outcomes and could intervene as necessary.

SCENARIO

August 2008: Andrea is in her eighth semester out of high school. She transferred to her current university after three semesters in a community college. She was immediately well placed in a program of study through use of an ePortfolio that she learned to develop at her community college. This structured ePortfolio was organized around eight dimensions of general learning. Documents on Andrea's progress towards these learning outcomes included some of her student work, her reflections on the work and its relevance to the learning outcomes, and comments from her instructors and advisers on her progress towards each learning outcome. This ePortfolio allowed her new university to place Andrea in a program towards her chosen major. She was advised of the courses to take over the subsequent five semesters assuming that she would be a full-time student. Further, she was given the set of learning outcomes for the major that complement the general learning outcomes. A software program at the university provides automatic monitoring of Andrea's progress on her chosen path towards a degree, with e-mail to her adviser if she deviates from the path. Also, the software prompts her instructors and advisers to examine her ePortfolio at set milestones and to add comments on her progress towards each outcome. In her third semester at the university, as a result of discussion with her adviser who had been prompted by the software that Andrea was not making satisfactory progress towards her chosen degree, Andrea decided to change her major. She was given a set of learning outcomes for this new major and her ePortfolio was restructured to reflect her new path. Andrea is currently anticipating graduation next semester.

INTRODUCTION

The above hypothetical scenario might someday be a reality for all students. I am interested in the development of an electronic portfolio (ePortfolio) as a vehicle to trace student progress as she or he journeys through the curriculum. From my perspective, an ePortfolio has the potential to provide an environment with tools to demonstrate and assess student learning so that a student can demonstrate mastery learning with deep understanding. Learning is the centerpiece of any ePortfolio.

I have been interested for a number of years in trying to change our culture to judge students' progress based on results, rather than hours in class; that is, in graduating students who have demonstrated mastery of learning outcomes—results—rather than on credits earned and the hours they sit in class. Working smarter rather than harder can sometimes produce results. We must reward students who get their results quicker by allowing them to graduate when they demonstrate proficiency in all learning outcomes.

For the last seven years, I have been involved with Quality in Undergraduate Education (QUE) (Albertine & Henry, 2004), a national project of higher education faculty at selected four-year public institutions and partner two-year colleges who are establishing draft, voluntary discipline-based learning outcomes in the undergraduate majors for biology, chemistry, English, history, and mathematics. We have learned to approach assessment as a register of each student's progress through the curriculum, not just in a particular course. Some participants in QUE have found that conceptual mapping of the curriculum helps to locate courses within the program and begins to suggest how skill development or higher-order thinking ought to emerge in students' performance at certain points. We have been challenged to understand and document what students learn when they take courses randomly, as is frequently the case for transfer, working, and part-time students. For many participants in QUE, an ePortfolio appears to be an essential feature of a student-centered learning curriculum.

The number of transfer students will continue to increase rapidly, since two-year college tuition is generally significantly less than that of four-year colleges. However, to reach the goal of a bachelor's degree, these students need to transfer. Agreement between two- and four-year institutions on learning outcomes will lead to better alignment of curricula, assuring more timely progress towards a degree for both the native and the transfer student. Although many two- and four-year institutions forge articulation agreements that govern transfer of credits, true seamless transfer from a two-year to a four-year institution occurs when the institutions agree on learning outcomes for students as they move through the curriculum. An ePortfolio would provide a supplement to the traditional transcript and assist in better advisement and placement of the transfer student.

As an offshoot of QUE, some institutions are involved in a Fund for the Improvement of Postsecondary Education (FIPSE)-supported project, Seamless Learning and Transfer Consortium (SLTC)[1]. Our premise is that the current system, based solely upon course completion and appropriate organization of credits, does not provide clear evidence of what students have actually learned, nor does this system contribute to the continuity and coherence of that learning. There are three major principles that underlie our approach to the development and implementation of systems to document student learning: (1) the best evidence of student learning is found in actual student work that is appropriately analyzed and documented; (2) the process of documenting student learning must also contribute to that learning; and (3) the system must be credible, validated, and portable so that as students move from one institution to another, they can demonstrate their accomplishments in ways that are accepted by the receiving institution.

The system envisioned by SLTC is an ePortfolio constructed by students in collaboration with faculty. The ePortfolio will at a minimum include student work submitted to indicate progress toward defined learning goals at different points in a student's career. This student work is evaluated by faculty and linked to scoring systems that are developmental as students progress from their entry into higher education to their completion of the learning expected for the baccalaureate.

There is the promise that the evidence provided in assessed student work might be viewed from two orthogonal perspectives—disciplinary knowledge and skills, and general learning knowledge and skills. Learning outcomes for disciplinary knowledge (facts, concepts, principles) and skills (processes, strategies, methods) can be delineated for graduation and at intermediate points along a program trajectory such as at entrance into the major—a gateway course. Learning outcomes for general learning can similarly be delineated. While this general learning will vary slightly from institution to institution, nationally there is consensus about categories such as those delineated by the American Association of Colleges & Universities (AAC&U, 2004). At Georgia State, such learning includes oral and written communication skills; inquiry/analysis/critical thinking; collaboration; quantitative skills; contemporary issues: multicultural and diversity understanding, and global/international perspectives; and technology.

ePORTFOLIOS

Greenberg (2004) describes three types of ePortfolios: (1) a showcase ePortfolio allows organization after work has been created; (2) a structured ePortfolio gives a predefined organization for work that is yet to be created; and (3) a learning ePortfolio provides organization for work and evolves as work is created. From a provost's perspective, a structured ePortfolio has significant potential for native and transfer students. As students mature, the structured ePortfolio might be transformed into a learning ePortfolio. Also, the student would be able to select parts of the structured ePortfolio to create a showcase ePortfolio.

Why would students be interested in an ePortfolio? Zemsky and Massy (2004) note that while the promise of eLearning has mostly yet to be fulfilled, most early promoters of eLearning simply missed the students' devotion to complex presentations of self.

Student fascination with computers and software has three major components. They want to be connected, principally to one another. They want to be entertained, principally by games, music, and movies. And they want to present themselves and their work. (p. 51)

It is this last fascination that will probably provide the hook for students and ePortfolios. It will allow students an opportunity to develop a showcase ePortfolio. An example of an institution with a showcase portfolio is Florida State University (2005). Florida State suggests nine marketable, transferable skills—or general learning knowledge and skills—that employers and graduate schools look for in graduates. They provide a "Skills Development Matrix" where students can document their experiences with examples of work done in courses, jobs or internships, service or volunteer work, extracurricular activities, and personal interests. So, not only would students end up with a showcase ePortfolio, but students could also maintain their learning ePortfolios if proficiencies acquired were made explicit.

While students can choose their best work to include in a showcase ePortfolio, faculty and students can use structured or learning ePortfolios to determine progress towards a degree. From a provost perspective, institutional effectiveness can be demonstrated more readily by using samples of learning ePortfolios as direct evidence of student learning.

LEARNING OUTCOMES

What are some functional requirements for faculty? As we have learned through the QUE project, faculty need to develop learning outcomes for each course, learning outcomes for the program of study, and then map the course learning outcomes on to the program learning outcomes. Establishing learning goals of necessity involves discussions of curricula, teaching, and assessment for learning.

A gap analysis or super-matrix provides a visual means of charting learning outcomes for a program in relationship to learning outcomes for various courses. The key is that a student should have opportunity for mastery of each program learning outcome, regardless of which path is used to navigate through the program of study. In particular, when there are choices of electives, only the learning outcomes common to the elective group should be used in the gap analysis. An ePortfolio should be of particular importance for students who take a random path rather than a prescribed or preferred trajectory through the curriculum.

For example, to conduct a gap analysis, departmental faculty need to describe each program learning outcome in a sentence or short paragraph. Then, for each course, use a numeric rubric (0-4) to indicate level of contribution to a learning outcome. Contributions can be depth by which outcome is introduced, developed, and reinforced throughout the course and/or by degree to which outcome is assessed in the course. On adding up the score for each programmatic outcome, faculty would determine if there is sufficient opportunity for students to gain mastery of each program outcome through their courses of study. When there are courses taken outside the department for the major, analysis promotes discussion between departments.

The super-matrix is a means to an end, not an end in itself. Its completion is the beginning of a dialog at the departmental level about curriculum and the essential elements in relationship to the learning outcomes. It provides guidelines on modifications to courses and/or assessments. It should be regarded as a template for the design of the appropriate assessments in key courses and potential milestones. An ePortfolio has the potential to provide a mechanism to trace student growth as a journey through the curriculum.

How can we demonstrate that students have met at least proficient levels on learning outcomes? What are the intermediate stages one passes through in the course of moving from being a beginner to being an expert? What are the intermediate groupings of experience between novice and accomplished learner? What matters is that a sequence is useful in moving the learner toward greater mastery, and that a sequence will not necessarily be the same for all learners. But what we can see falling out in a semi-predictable order is the increasing complexity of performances to which the student can apply the learning.

For example, at Georgia State University, the University Senate passed a policy that all course syllabi must describe measurable learning outcomes. Further, the Academic Program Review process requires a department to give measurable learning outcomes for each academic program. Thus faculty and students have an opportunity to recognize relationships between and among courses, and how courses contribute collectively to a more coherent curriculum. In part, such an approach has the potential to answer the perennial question, "Why do I have to take this course?"

ENHANCED ADVISING AND LEARNING

An additional benefit of a well-constructed curriculum is a potential for being able to develop a robust student tracking system that might lead to significantly enhanced graduation rates. For example, the University of Florida initiated a tracking system in 1995 and has continued to refine it. Their resulting six-year graduation rates improved from 64% in 1997 to 77% in 2002 (Carey, 2004). In its tracking system, students are required to immediately declare a major, although students can certainly change it. From the beginning of their experience in college, students are prompted to begin thinking about what shape their college career will take. Departments are expected to be very clear about what specific courses students should take and when to be considered making minimum progress toward that degree. Students are tracked and notified when they are not making progress toward a degree within that major. Students who are not taking the classes when they need to be are called in during the semester by their advisers. Advisers discuss what is going on with the students and remind students about the importance of making progress towards their degrees. And if students seem to be struggling in the courses, the adviser works to get them help and remind them about the many academic support services offered. The second time a student is flagged for not seeming to make minimum progress, the discussion is about the appropriateness of that major. Is this a really good fit for the student? The other side of the equation is a commitment from the university to make sure the courses students need to make progress are available to them and that they will be able to get seats in the classes. While this tracking system is not tied to an ePortfolio, combination of the two could provide a more powerful learning experience for the student, as progress could be tied to student development towards program learning outcomes and not just to success in distinct courses.

In addition to establishing learning goals, we need to identify what types of evidence should be captured in an ePortfolio. This is of particular importance if an ePortfolio is to be used by a student transferring from one institution to another. As a start, can institutions that have a large number of students transferring from one to the other agree on contents of an ePortfolio? For example, about 900 students transfer annually from Georgia Perimeter College to Georgia State. Then, an ePortfolio will have the potential to enhance advising and admissions practices, and will also contribute to the coherence and ongoing development of student learning.

The classroom works best when it is participatory. Students become effective problem solvers only when they have mastered the art of critical thinking and have acquired the discipline necessary to be self-paced learners. Constant assessment and feedback are critical, so that both student and instructor can determine, before it is too late, whether the student is mastering the necessary material. Attending classes and taking tests are not enough to help a student become engaged in learning. Also, simply collecting work without getting feedback is unlikely to offer new perspectives that will help the student develop and evolve as a professional. Mentkowski and Associates (2000) define learning that lasts as "an integration of learning, development, and performance" (p. 4). Reflection and self-assessment are integral to learning that lasts. The ePortfolio is a catalyst for this feedback—for communication and interaction with teachers, mentors, and peers. It provokes new ideas and new directions, and facilitates reflection on and reevaluation of accomplishments. Feedback from faculty might signal that the student needs more evidence of achievement and understanding of the learning outcome or that the student can move on to the next level of progress. The reflection is as important as the evidence because it indicates that the student understands the significance of the learning outcome and of the evidence. Further, an ePortfolio, with an emphasis on learning, reinforces the paradigm shift of Barr and Tagg (1995) to redefine the role of faculty away from the 'sage on the stage' to 'guide on the side'.

In addition to students who come to college seeking a degree, many students are now interested in discrete clustering of experiences such as those that lead to certificates. The certificate is a "standalone" award, and its completion has meaning for students and adds value to their experience. An ePortfolio could be a convenient way to demonstrate attainment of proficiencies that relate to the certificate.

An ePortfolio would also be a convenient way to capture knowledge and skills from life/work experience and formal learning assessed for assignment of credit such as performed by the Council on Adult and Experiential Learning (CAEL). CAEL has been a pioneer in developing many of the basic concepts and techniques of prior learning assessment. Such an ePortfolio would give a student a solid basis from which to move towards a degree or certificate.

CHALLENGES FACING PROVOSTS IMPLEMENTING ePORTFOLIO SYSTEMS

As part of the SLTC project, Georgia State University and Georgia Perimeter College have piloted use of an electronic portfolio in some of the freshman learning communities (FLCs) that are designed around clusters of freshmen-level courses, including the first-year seminar course GSU 1010. In the pilot, students are introduced to an ePortfolio in GSU1010, and they include materials from their mathematics and English courses. One unanticipated value for students at the two-year college was an increase in confidence to compete with native four-year students.

Several faculty were willing to be involved in the initial pilot—it is normally the situation that some faculty will be pioneers or early adopters. There are at least two challenges going forward: expanding to incorporate a larger number of FLCs—Georgia State had 50 FLCs in fall 2005; and continuing the use of ePortfolios in classes beyond the freshman-level courses. Training of faculty and students in the use of ePortfolios is one key to successful implementation. The vendor which provides our platform has partnered with our educational technology services group in providing training. Convincing faculty of the value of using ePortfolios is another key: Is student learning enhanced through use of ePortfolios? As a stimulus to faculty and students to use ePortfolios, we are connecting their use to assessment of general education outcomes of oral and written communication. If this is a successful strategy, then we will extend use of ePortfolios to demonstrating assessment of all general education outcomes.

The overall challenge is one of bringing a reform initiative such as use of ePortfolios to scale. We need to include four interrelated dimensions (Coburn, 2003): depth, sustainability, spread, and shift in ownership. For example, if we find that use of ePortfolios by faculty leads to deeper student understanding, then how do we measure that such changes in instructional practices are brought to scale? For depth: Are underlying pedagogical principles embodied in a way that faculty engage students in using materials and tasks? For sustainability: Do changes persist over time? Is use of ePortfolios becoming the norm for the involved faculty in all their courses? Have faculty moved progressively from including ePortfolios in a single course to using the same approach to all their courses? For spread: Does the practice spread to other faculty in the department? Has a department moved from one or a few instructors to all instructors using ePortfolios? Is there an impact on reward, recognition, and incentive policies in the department?

For shift in reform ownership: Is use of ePortfolios adopted more widely in other partner institutions, especially those that send a large number of transfer students?

CONCLUSION

From a provost perspective, many of the elements necessary to construct an ePortfolio that is useful to student, faculty, and institution are now in place. Faculty have worked together in projects such as QUE to determine learning outcomes for a program that comprise meaningful and coherent sets of experiences in courses. Faculty in projects such as SLTC have piloted electronic portfolios where student work is captured and students and faculty provide reflections on the work. Whether students are interested in certificate or degree programs, it is possible to design an ePortfolio for the situation. Further, student progress towards learning goals can be determined from an ePortfolio by faculty, and native or transfer students can be advised appropriately on their course of study. The possibility exists that this process can be automated through a tracking system. Institutions can use random samples of ePortfolios to monitor the quality of their academic programs and determine areas for improvement. The above suggests that with ePortfolios, it is possible to progress from our present state of awarding degrees based on credits and seat time to the scenario depicted in the opening paragraph.

REFERENCES

AAC&U. (2004). *Taking responsibility for the quality of the baccalaureate degree.* Washington, DC: AAC&U.

Albertine, S., & Henry, R. J. (2004). Quality in undergraduate education—a collaborative project. *AAC&U Liberal Education, 90*(3), 46-53.

Barr, R. B., & Tagg, J. (1995). From teaching to learning: A new paradigm for undergraduate education. *Change, 27*(6), 13-25.

Carey, K. (2004). *A matter of degrees: Improving graduation rates in four-year universities and colleges.* Washington, DC: The Education Trust.

Coburn, C. E. (2003). Rethinking scale: Moving beyond numbers to deep and lasting change. *Educational Researcher, 32*(6) 3-12.

Florida State University. (2005). *The Career Center.* Retrieved May 25, 2005, from http://www.career-recruit.fsu.edu/careerportfolio/enter/login.html

Greenberg, G. (2004). The digital convergence: Extending the portfolio model. *Educause Review, 39*(4), 28-36.

Mentkowski, M., & Associates. (2000). *Learning that lasts: Integrating learning, development, and performance in college and beyond.* San Francisco: Jossey-Bass.

Zemsky, R., & Massy, W. F. (2004). *Thwarted innovation: What happened to e-learning and why.* Philadelphia: The Learning Alliance at the University of Pennsylvania.

KEY TERMS

Assessment: The primary aim of assessment is to foster learning of worthwhile academic content for all students. College communities use assessment results in a formative way to determine how well they are meeting instructional goals and how to alter curriculum and instruction so that goals can be better met.

Higher Education: Education at a level beyond high school. Sometimes referred to as 'post-secondary education' or 'tertiary education'.

Learning Outcomes: Explicit identification of learning expectations facilitates coherence about goals. Sharing those expectations explicitly with students can provide an effective learning scaffold on which students can build their experiences and render effective performance. Outcomes can be specified in a developmental hierarchy.

Student-Centered Learning: In student-centered learning, the planning, teaching, and assessment are around the needs and abilities of the students. The main idea behind the practice is that learning is most meaningful when topics are relevant to the students' lives, needs, and interests, and when the students themselves are actively engaged in creating, understanding, and connecting to knowledge.

Undergraduate Education: Period of education beyond high school up to first bachelor's degree.

ENDNOTE

1 Georgia Perimeter College and Georgia State University are partnering with Alverno College and Waukesha County Technical College in a FIPSE grant to Portland State University and Clackamas Community College.

Chapter VII
The Promise of the Student Electronic Portfolio: A Provost's Perspective

William M. Plater
Indiana University-Purdue University Indianapolis, USA

ABSTRACT

The development and pervasive adoption of student electronic portfolios have the potential to transform higher education at both the institutional and national sector levels. While much depends on the continued expansion of the ePortfolio's technological capabilities, its transformative power derives from allowing students, faculty, and institutions to actually do what heretofore they have only imagined: enable each student to have a personally managed, meaningful, coherent, integrated lifelong record of learning that demonstrates competence, transcends educational levels, and is portable across institutions of learning—formal and informal. The ePortfolio is lifelong learning co-owned and co-managed by the individual student.

PROVOSTS, PORTFOLIOS, AND THE PROMISE

An institution's chief academic officer—a provost by whatever name—has a vested responsibility for providing a meaningful connection between institutional mission, values, and integrity, on the one hand, and the credentials it awards to individual students, on the other. While most colleges and universities explicitly assign to faculty the responsibility for recommending degree recipients to the trustees who formally confer the degrees through the actions of the president or chancellor, the chief academic officer is the one person solely responsible for attending to the relationship between abstract—occasionally rhetorical—principles of learning and their realization in course credit, certificates, or degrees. Degrees and certificates have value only because of this closely linked relationship of institutional integrity and the record of attendance—not because a degree or a transcript actually proves that a recipient has attained certifiable knowledge or can *do* anything.

How many provosts have wondered quietly to themselves about that intersection of principle and performance when, at faculty meetings, a registrar or recorder announces that she has in hand a list of students who have met all of the requirements for a degree—and the faculty vote to accept the list without reflecting on the degree requirements, the meaning of the degree, or the specific individual and personal experiences of the students themselves. We often certify graduates—not only the courses they have taken and their grades, but what they know, understand, accept, or can actually *do*—without making a meaningful connection between a list of courses and competence.

After a century of prevailing practice, most provosts accept at face value the record of attendance and grades matched against a list of degree requirements as a proxy for demonstrated learning—as do the faculty, the trustees, and the public, including graduate schools, employers, and the students themselves. This is not unreasonable given the history of most accredited institutions. They produce graduates who succeed and are largely satisfied with their experiences. We just "know" that they must be meeting the expectations we have for various degree programs—but only in those instances of state or nationally normed licensure do we ordinarily have any third-party validation.

Most provosts also wonder if this time-honored process is still sufficient. At a time when both information and knowledge have expanded at accelerating rates, it is no longer sufficient to have been exposed to learning. Now individuals must actually know enough to be able to assemble and reassemble knowledge and experience in meaningful ways and be able to continue to learn. Based on their knowledge of the classroom and their understanding of the public's trust, provosts are in the unique position to align expectation with performance ... and to wonder if there is not a better way.

The emergence of the student ePortfolio provides a better way. The electronic portfolio has capacities far beyond paper records to be interactive and dynamic—presenting information in ways that are both certifiable and practically useful. The burden of responsibility for provosts can then shift from critical self-appraisal to the means to act. Provosts now have the capacity to enable their faculties to address individual student performance and to empower students to assume real responsibility for their own learning. If the ePortfolio delivers on its promise, then most provosts will have to lead their institutions to adopt some version of the student ePortfolio, to develop an equivalent, or to reconcile their knowledge of what is possible with their failure to act—a matter of personal conscience.

Consequently, the perspective of provosts on the development of student ePortfolios is critical if not determinative. It is the opportunity, role, responsibility, and even burden of the provost to help guide the faculty of an institution to accept the singular change that the student ePortfolio represents in their institution's ability to graduate students who can actually *do* what their degrees announce that they *should* be able to do.

While the technology is not yet proven, the stakes are high. If the ePortfolio can become a performance record, it will supplant the traditional transcript and replace the degree. Attending and graduating from an institution with a good reputation may no longer be sufficient. This is especially true in the environment of a growing array of for-profit but accredited colleges, universities, and specialized institutions. Moreover, in the global marketplace, students educated abroad—especially in technical fields as diverse as engineering, biology, computer science, or nursing—may have learning records from places that are unfamiliar or unknown.

The development and wise use of human potential deserves a more rigorous and equitable means of determining who can actually do the things their credentials represent. In his new book *The World is Flat* (2005), New York Times columnist Thomas Friedman makes this point so convincingly that institutions failing to heed this warning do so at risk to their own continued relevance. Computer scientists trained in India, geneticists educated in Great Britain, international lawyers prepared in Australia, or electrical engineers developed in China may soon surpass those educated in the U.S. as determined by performance and as recognized by the marketplaces of ideas, commerce, discovery, and networks.

TRANSFORMATION

What is transformative about the student ePortfolio? The change, the transformation, is that *a student becomes the co-owner of her own learning record* with the successful implementation of the ePortfolio. Until now, the record belonged solely to the institution—and to each institution separately. If the student moved from high school to college, from community college to four-year college, from university to graduate school, or from professional school to national certification, the record is transferred from place to place along with credits and equivalencies. Each institution owns its own record and the student as supplicant asks to have it transferred from place to place that accepts, rejects, or translates that record into its own.

A guild of registrars—with a history that pre-dates the medieval guilds—protects the integrity of the record of attendance and the grades for each course with a fervor that could inspire Umberto Ecco (*The Name of the Rose*, 1984) or Dan Brown (*The Da Vinci Code*, 2003) to write a novel. Under the watchful eye of faculty committees, the registrars (with their allies in admissions offices) translate one set of educational experiences into another set, adapting some other institution's credits into their own.

When colleges or universities transfer—accept—credits from another institution but not the grades, what are they accepting? Are they accepting performance or attendance of the individual student? Or are they accepting the reputation and accreditation of the institution? What is presumed by allowing transferred credits (or credits earned through demonstrated competence for life experiences or equivalent credit from para-educational institutions such as the military or professional training academies) to apply to a degree at the receiving institution? Is competence or demonstrated learning required?

In brief, where is the student in this process of transferred meaning? Until collected into a certificate or degree, individual courses or experiences rarely "mean" anything—that is, they have no real commercial or social value. And students' own perceptions of their learning are not only inconsequential, but they are suspect. Why?

Until now, students have been the messenger—carrying a record from one place to another. Their own understanding of what their course titles and their actual content, their individual attendance and attentiveness, their grades and personal achievement might mean are largely incidental and even ignored. Rarely are students asked to provide any evidence of their having met course or program goals unless credit is withheld pending satisfactory completion of a course at a higher level, as often is the case in mathematics or language study. What if the student actually played a direct role in certifying credits or programs or certificates or degrees?

This concept of co-ownership is the radical, the unexpected, the catalyst for change. If the student co-owns the record of learning and can affect its shape, content, meaning, and use, then the role of the institution is changed—even if not diminished. There is risk in this new capacity. If we believe *the record* is what learning is all about, then change is likely to be a calculus of loss, and institutions may not be as important as we once thought. On the other hand, if *learning* is our end and we can enable, facilitate, or support learners in accepting responsibility for their own learning and its *performance*, then we may have succeeded beyond our own imaginations when we created degrees—which we did long before there were courses.

And registrars worthy of their role as the guarantors of integrity would welcome this change because it elevates them from the agents of security to the ringmasters of performance. Education is not a circus, but learning is nothing if it is not performance. Orchestrating the demonstration of learning as the ringmaster presents the act to the audience gives the registrar a new, expanded capacity to define and show institutional quality in ways that can be validated by others. Beyond trust and reputation, there is performance—and the student is a necessary partner.

CO-OWNERSHIP OF THE LEARNING RECORD

The ePortfolio goes beyond the concept of a certified record to become a process—a means of performance and action. Because it is dynamic, flexible, and adaptable, the portfolio itself becomes the act of "doing learning" as students and the institutions that have provided the educational experiences collaborate to present both a record and a demonstration of learning. Co-ownership is critical, because one partner alone cannot provide all that is needed to a third party—an employer, a license grantor, a graduate school, or a transfer institution—to ensure that the student can actually do the things a university says its degree graduates or course completers can.

Universities—through their registrars—must continue to provide a *record of attendance* that includes both defined learning experiences (the *course* with its title on the transcript and its full description or even syllabus in accessible storage) and assessment of learning (the *grade*). The integrity of the record guarded by the registrar properly does not allow for performance. It is a static record of fact, a history, that forms the solid, immutable stage on which learning can be enacted and demonstrated. As long as that record cannot be modified by the student and is controlled solely by the institution, there is a solid foundation and framework that will always ground and even constrain the claims that students may make in performing their learning. But students need to be able to use that record and adapt it to their own ends.

While the most important and stable co-owner of the learning record will continue to be accredited colleges and universities whose reputations are based on more than their own self-proclamations or advertising, there is room for others to contribute to the record. Corporations, unions, governmental agencies, non-profit organizations, military branches and others that provide certified training programs could also make their records of participation and achievement available in the portfolio along with colleges and universities. Colleges and universities can even give themselves more of a role by incorporating internships, co-curricular programs, and voluntary activities that traditionally have not been included as a part of the formal transcript—noting leadership in social settings or participation in athletics or the arts, for example.

In some instances, colleges and universities might also collaborate with independent third parties to co-validate their records and to provide even higher degrees of certification than implied by attendance and course-level assessment. Already, governmental agencies and professional societies provide independent and typically cumulative assessments of student achievement through examinations, portfolio reviews, and other means. They verify the claims made by both the student and the institution. The electronic portfolio makes it possible to have separate institutional owners of records and to allow the student to integrate these components into a personal record.

The learner's role as the co-owner of the portfolio is to give experiences coherence and meaning and to give historical records life. By showing authentic work completed in courses or in degree programs spanning several courses, students cannot only offer evidence of achievement, but provide a reflective context that is itself further evidence of understanding and critical thinking. Students can repurpose their learning portfolio as a career portfolio on one day and restore it as an educational record on the next.

The most immediate forms of evidence are products such as written reports or papers, videos of speeches or performances, software programs or simulations—each of which can be linked to one or more courses or a degree program, each of which can have assessments from one or more faculty members. Students can select the evidence that they believe best represents them for a specific context—a job interview, a graduate school application, a nomination for a community service board, a proposal for funding from a foundation. They can rearrange the evidence for different needs at different times. They continuously update their record by adding additional learning experiences and further personal reflections on the meaning of their learning and its relevance to any particular situation.

As the technical capacities of the ePortfolio mature and as the social uses of the ePortfolio grow, the concept of co-ownership will likewise develop. Ill-defined issues such as whether an institution or the student owns a paper or an examination or a project can be clarified through co-ownership. Most faculty return papers or projects to students at the end of the term, but they retain their right to their own assessment, whether in the form of a critique or merely a grade—in the instructional record if in no other form. Some professors would not mind if a student quoted from their concluding comments on a paper, using it as part of a job application—but others might, especially if the context were not made clear. The ePortfolio makes it possible for the faculty member (or institution) and the student to co-own such assessments.

The institution can maintain as part of its records the assessments of individual faculty or committees in a secure form, but allow students to have access to the assessments for purposes of representing themselves to others. Evidence of learning and competence can thus be certified in multiple dimensions—by the students presenting their own work products and explaining their value or relevance, calling upon stored assessments of the specific products, and adding third-party assessments from noncredit but certified training or licensure. By the very act of arranging the information and the evidence, the students are able to recreate and enact their own learning in a form that itself shows ability, competence, and mastery.

Co-ownership depends on conceiving the record of learning as shared workspace that is dynamic, ever-changing, always expanding as the learner's own experiences grow. The elements within the workspace may be uniquely the property of one party or another and thus unchanging, but their combination and perpetual reuse change purposefully. As already noted, the institution owns the record of attendance, defined course and degree experiences, and course-level assessment. The faculty own their own commentaries and discursive assessments. Students own their own reflections on meaning and application to particular circumstances.

Students and the institutions may co-own or determine assignment of ownership for work products and intellectual property created in the learning process. And almost anyone can own the machinery for presenting the learning record—the colleges and universities, the various levels of government, corporations, nonprofit organizations, or even the student herself. These service providers need only provide the tools that make the presentations effective, secure, and reliable.

LIFELONG LEARNING AND COMMUNITIES OF PRACTICE

At Indiana University-Purdue University Indianapolis (IUPUI), the student ePortfolio (ePort) is being developed with all of these possibilities for transformation and ownership in mind. In partnership with the Indiana University Information Technology Services (UITS), the IUPUI Center on Integrating Learning is leading an effort to create a co-owned student record based on institutional-level learning objectives for all undergraduates—six Principles of Undergraduate Learning that can be documented with authentic work products and faculty assessments at three levels of competence—introductory, intermediate, and advanced—with a fourth optional assessment of experiential learning (not itself a "level"). While the learning goals are specific to IUPUI and will stand as the unifying representative of what a baccalaureate from IUPUI means, the portfolio apparatus itself is being built as part of a multi-institutional consortium to ensure its ease of use and its portability from place to place.

Each of these six principles—composed of (1) core skills in writing, interpretation and analysis, oral communication, analytical reasoning, and information literacy; (2) critical thinking; (3) intellectual depth, breadth, and adaptiveness; (4) integration and application of knowledge; (5) understanding culture and society; and (6) values and ethics—is the responsibility of a group of faculty drawn from across all the disciplines of the campus who have established a community of practice for each of the six principles to complement their disciplinary work. These faculty share an interest in ensuring that all graduates have demonstrated their abilities to actually perform in satisfactory ways in each of the principles. The record of demonstrated performance at the baccalaureate level provides the foundation for lifelong learning, in turn shaping expectations for K-12 learning and providing the means for continuing learning.

The community of practice is based on knowledge, experience, and reflection. Each of the six communities of practice provides the means for unifying and assigning meaning to learning growing out of action, out of practice. The faculty role in belonging to a community of practice is to consider constantly what the learning outcomes for each level of competence in each principle are and to assess individual student performance within each of the principles at each level.

The community of practice may well include alumni, other community members, emeriti faculty, or even advanced students who have demonstrated their competence at the level of review. As members of the community of practice, the participants are actively using—practicing—the knowledge they are assessing, and in the process they are defining what the baccalaureate awarded by IUPUI means. It is this record of enacted learning instead of an accumulation of credit hours or a pattern of specific courses that makes a graduate of IUPUI.

With the baccalaureate as the template, it is possible to conceive of a record of continuous learning, stretching from kindergarten through post-baccalaureate education to lifelong learning, with continuity and purpose, yet with infinite flexibility. If we know what the baccalaureate means and if we align K-12 learning objectives with both the matriculation expectations of colleges and their graduation requirements, it is possible to develop a learning record that follows students throughout their formal learning.

Schools, community colleges, and a variety of learning intermediaries can each have their own records but permit students to share in the communication and transfer of these records through successive and cumulative levels to the baccalaureate level. As a continuum that can be refreshed and updated, earlier experiences can be amplified, reinforced, or even corrected in a record of progressive achievement. It is a record of hope and promise.

As students mature as learners and move beyond certificates and degrees, they will continue to learn and to reflect upon their experiences—reassembling prior knowledge and experience into yet some new purpose and form. The ePortfolio becomes the basis for vocation and the integration of separate jobs into a pathway of personal and professional development with its own logic and reflective meaning, interweaving schooling, work, and civic engagement into a record of performance and a plan for future growth. The opportunity for colleges and universities to play a role in this ever-expanding personal transformation is unlimited. Faculty can take advantage of emerging technologies to provide updates and validations for specialized knowledge or professional training, to offer a range of learning services far beyond the component courses of degrees.

TRANSFORMING TEACHING

In most respects, the emergence of the student ePortfolio can take place with only minimal faculty involvement because the portfolio itself can adapt to conventional artifacts and procedures. Courses and their learning objectives, student works and their assessment, and records of attendance can all be incorporated into the portfolio without modification, at least to the extent that they exist in electronic form. The restructuring and repurposing of these artifacts and elements can occur by moving them around and creating an explanatory context.

The emergence of the ePortfolio as a transformative record will depend solely on its value in representing the experiences and knowledge of students, and this value is likely to be determined by the marketplace instead of colleges and universities. If employers, graduate programs, and other institutions that depend on education as performance begin to expect the kind of dynamic record of authentic accomplishment that the ePortfolio promises, then this demand-side force will transform higher education.

One of the most immediate consequences of market-driven forces will be to expand the range and variety of educational providers and facilitators. Already certifications awarded by corporations and professional associations for co-curricular competencies attained in credit-bearing courses that rely on externally produced and nationally normed learning tools (e.g., a computer programming language, a piece of simulation software, using laboratory techniques) add real value to the credit and to the record of course attendance. There may well be significant changes in our understanding of who the teachers are, the differentiated roles they play, and the interrelationship of divergent learning objectives within the same social experience we used to call "a course."

However, some innovative institutions may also decide to transform themselves from the inside out instead of waiting for the external pressures. Those institutions that recognize the transformative capacity of the ePortfolio may well begin adapting their teaching to a more learning-centered model, reconceiving the role of faculty to be supportive of students in finding their own ways to meet the learning objectives at the course, program, and degree or certificate levels. They may readily embrace the teaching role of others outside the academy—in community-based learning, in prior life experiences, and in work. The student ePortfolio as a record of documented learning has the capacity to change the fundamental interaction between teacher and student, to replace classroom practices that emphasize transmission of information with goals and multiple pathways to meet these goals, and to accept as valid knowledge and competence gain outside the course.

As faculty discover the flexibility and freedom that teaching outcomes afford, they will also discover that they can customize student learning processes, using different strategies to accommodate different learning styles, allowing varying timeframes for mastery of goals, and incorporating new learning resources. Instead of designing a course and its pedagogy to address the needs of a hypothetical (and totally unrealistic) normative student, faculty can have several pedagogies with one set of expectations for demonstrated performance, thus accommodating in one class a range of student learning styles, levels of preparation, and degrees of life experience.

One of the most important transformations will be making students partners in their learning by having them understand the goals and objectives of courses as well as degrees, and giving them the means not only to relate component parts into meaningful wholes but to reflect on what education experiences mean in their lives. The ePortfolio has the potential of students' also sharing the responsibility for their own learning in a pragmatic and assessable way. Through shared ownership, the portfolio provides the means for lifelong learning that is continuously reformed and reshaped to take full advantage of life's uncertain opportunities and challenges.

As noted, the ePortfolio can actually be implemented with only minimal changes in the individual behaviors and practices of faculty. But transformation will come with realization that the classroom is about learning, not teaching, and by a recognition that "the course" is not the most meaningful unit of learning. When faculty acting together as a department with shared understandings about the meaning of a degree in a particular discipline—as many professions have already done—structure courses into a cumulative record of meaningfully connected parts, then they will have begun the transformation. In the transformed college, the student will play a role in constructing—and in assuming responsibility for—the meaning of the learning and its performance.

PERSPECTIVE AND PROMISE

Fundamental social changes are already underway that will undoubtedly affect learning to the same extent they are health care and the management of retirement benefits. As the costs of health care increase along with the recognition that individual decisions and conditions make management of health care intensely personal, health practitioners, hospitals, insurance companies, and governmental agencies are realizing that the "patients" must co-own and accept co-responsibility for their health records and their actual health—not just the transcripted facts of ailments, test results, prescriptions, treatments, and prognoses.

Inevitably, the record of health activity and health care must be personalized and unified in the experience of the individual—not in the separate records of clinics visited, surgical procedures performed, or therapies tried. If health care is changing in such a profound way, how long can education remain immune to questions about how high school performance relates to college matriculation, how degrees relate to competence, and how learning extends beyond graduation?

A similarly profound transformation is underway with the management of retirement benefits. As the defined pension plans of stable, lifelong employers give way to individually managed contribution programs, and as changes in Social Security raise questions about who should own the responsibility for investment decisions, the role of the worker as a co-owner of the assets and their management signals a major shift in society's thinking about social benefits. The fact that most workers will change employers many times over a career demands a new structure of portability of benefits, just as learning in different settings requires a mechanism to accumulate and integrate experiences so they can be applied in different ways as circumstances change, as markets go up and down.

But the most likely stimulus for change will be international competition. As anyone who has read Friedman's book understands, global change because of technology will have some of its most telling impacts on education and the corporations, institutions, and governments that depend on an educated workforce. Already European nations have agreed to develop common standards for learning outcomes across national borders through a voluntary program called the "Bologna Process," following protocols adopted by the European Credit Transfer and Accumulation System. Regional groups in Asia and South America are developing similar agreements to permit the portability of learning across national and geographic borders to expand trade and take advantage of global supplies of highly educated workers. Electronic student portfolios are being developed to allow students, as co-owners of their own learning and competence, to move freely around cooperating countries, certain that their achievements can be recognized by other institutions and valued by employers.

Provosts who understand the nature of such global social forces as health care, retirement benefits, and international cartels of learning can prepare their faculties and administrators for parallel changes that are certain to affect higher education in the next decade. When co-responsibility and co-ownership, portability, and adaptability are applied to evidence of performance, the learning record is no longer merely a transcript. It is a means of learning. And provosts—more than anyone else—can help their colleagues adapt to the world's changed expectations.

CHALLENGES FOR PROVOSTS

For the individual provost who wishes to address the challenges and opportunities presented by the electronic student portfolio, what are some of the key issues to consider? The answer, of course, depends entirely on the circumstances of the provost's own institution and its degree of readiness—both in terms of technological capacity and faculty receptivity. An institution with the finest in technology capacity and support can proceed no more quickly than the faculty are willing to adapt pedagogy and to refine degree requirements in support of measures of learning that go beyond records of attendance and course grades. If there is not a collective will to understand and certify learning at levels beyond the course, the provost's path is certain to be lonely and uncertain. But the provost can help create the collective will for institutional change.

The provost's role is to lead, even when leadership takes the form of provocation. Here are some strategies to consider:

- Articulate a clear rationale for documenting and certifying learning at the certificate and degree levels apart from the means of doing so. The principle is more important than the means, but the electronic student portfolio in most instances will quickly become the most preferred means. The provost has special status for speaking on behalf of the institution as a whole—at levels beyond the college or school, at the level of the degree. Talking about the portfolio in informed, consistent, confident ways at every appropriate opportunity may have the greatest impact.
- Outline what the electronic portfolio can do that paper records cannot—including the principles of co-ownership and portability. Other advantages, such as cost-efficient storage and file management, have less appeal to faculty than the value-added dimensions of the portfolio with regard to the uses and applications of learning. In most professional fields, the value of documented learning and competencies fits well with emerging accreditation standards and standards of professional practice—including continuing professional education and certification. The ability to leverage professional education in the arts, sciences, and related disciplines can be powerful, because often the most difficult achievements to document are in the arts and sciences and professional school colleagues may become advocates of the portfolio.
- Create opportunities to demonstrate that the electronic portfolio offers solutions to intermediate or short-range objectives of immediate value to faculty, students, and administrators. For students, the portfolio is of immediate value in seeking employment or admission to graduate school; demand-driven development of the electronic student portfolio is a powerful force. For faculty, the portfolio offers a supplement to grades, a means to extend the learning experience, and a convenient means to collect and organize a term's set of papers, tests, and reports. For administrators, the electronic portfolio permits aggregation of data and information at the discipline, college, and campus levels for accreditation, annual reports, or marketing. By offering solutions to specific issues, the portfolio's aggregate power may be best discovered after the fact—when its utility has been demonstrated in more immediate and localized ways.
- Being realistic about any administrator's time in office, the prudent provost will define phases of implementation that will allow clear progress over a period of several years. By having clear benchmarks developed jointly with the technologists and the pedagogical leadership, the provost can ensure progress on the institutional adoption of the electronic student portfolio even beyond her term in office.
- Recognize the value of external pressures to create demand, including external ac-

crediting bodies, employers' needs, and local economic development opportunities, threats from for-profit competitors, or external funding for demonstration projects.

- Invest resources strategically in small amounts to sustain the timeline and support the benchmarked goals.
- Most importantly, develop champions among several of the key faculty constituencies—whether these are defined by disciplines or by forms of faculty engagement in campus life through governance or hierarchies of authority. Having informed, key advocates within the technology support group and administrative offices (especially the registrar, admissions officer, and career center director) is essential. No provost can overcome the indifference or intransigence of unwilling administrative colleagues.

There is much a provost can do once she accepts the electronic student portfolio as a necessary step to empower students to share an equal responsibility for their own learning. But nothing is more important than the provost's own conviction that the portfolio gives us a practical means—for the first time in modern, mass education—to actually document and certify learning at the level of the degree with goals that are greater than the course.

REFERENCES

Center on Integrating Learning. (2005). *Homepage.* Retrieved March 19, 2006, from http://www. opd.iupui.edu/coil/

ePort. (2005). *The IUPUI student electronic portfolio.* Retrieved March 19, 2006, from http://www.opd. iupui.edu/coil/eport.htm

European Commission for Education and Training. (2005). *Bologna process.* Retrieved March 19, 2006, from http://europa.eu.int/comm/education/policies/educ/bologna/bologna_en.html

European Commission for Education and Training. (2005). *European credit transfer and accumulation system.* Retrieved March 19, 2006, from http://europa.eu.int/comm/education/programmes/socrates/ects/index_en.html

Freidman, T.L. (2005). *The world is flat: A brief history of the twenty-first century.* New York: Farrar, Straus, and Giroux.

IUPUI. (2005). *Homepage.* Retrieved from http://www.iupui.edu/

IUPUI. (2005). *IUPUI institutional portfolio.* Retrieved March 19, 2006, from http://www.iport.iupui.edu/

IUPUI. (2005). *Principles of Undergraduate Learning of IUPUI.* Retrieved March 19, 2006, from http://www.iupui.edu/academic/undergrad_principles.html

KEY TERMS

Certificate: A specific, focused record of learning defined by levels of participation, competence, achievement, or understanding unique to an institution that can be assessed against stipulated objectives, ordinarily to an extent that is less than those required for a degree.

Co-Ownership: In the academic section, formal records of learning (i.e., transcripts) are owned by the issuing institution. Only the institution may set the form, format, and content or make changes in the record. Co-ownership by the student would permit the student to add to or to select content, set format, and create multiple forms while still ensuring that some components or data elements (e.g., grades, course titles, period of attendance) are controlled and certified by the institution.

Course Credit: A flexible convention used to assign quantitative value to assessed learning, typically correlated to time spent in class so that one hour of class meeting equals one credit, but also used to assign value to achievement demonstrated by other means and to transfer "credit" from one institution to another.

Degree: A specific, focused record of learning defined by course attendance and credits that complete defined learning objectives generally recognized by other colleges and universities and that are subject to review and approval by accrediting associations and/or state agencies.

Principles of Learning: The educational objectives set forth by a college or university faculty for *all* students who are receiving a degree from the institution to have learned regardless of their majors or specializations—often referred to as general education or liberal education.

Provost: The chief academic officer of a college or university, often called a vice chancellor or vice president for academic affairs or a dean of faculties, whose duties typically include responsibility for hiring and assessing faculty, approving and reviewing degree programs, and resource management related to the academic mission of the institution.

Record of Learning: Ordinarily a transcript issued by an accredited school, college, or university that includes name of the learning experience (course), period of attendance, and grade, but which can be expanded to include actual products or artifacts of learning (e.g., papers, tests, projects, videos) as well as assessments of these products.

Student Electronic Portfolios (ePortfolios): A record of learning maintained in electronic form that consists of conventional records of attendance as indicated by course completion, credits, and grades, but also including actual artifacts of learning achievement, such as papers, projects, videos, and other artifacts which have been assessed or evaluated.

Chapter VIII
ePortfolios as Learning Construction Zones:
Provost's Perspective

Kathleen O'Brien
Alverno College, USA

ABSTRACT

ePortfolios can be more than storage devices of the learner's best work when faculty develop a curriculum that integrates them across each student's academic career. This chapter describes how one version of an ePortfolio, designed using faculty-held learning principles and assumptions, helps students explore and extend their learning in a developmental manner. It also describes how a provost sees the ePortfolio system fulfilling an often neglected CAO responsibility: improving the educational effectiveness of faculty. The author also outlines other educational goals that can be met with a developmental ePortfolio system. Finally, the author comments on the downside of using such a system, but suggests that the benefits outweigh the deficits.

INTRODUCTION

Of the many uses of ePortfolios, optimizing and making available in an anytime, anywhere format faculty judgment and student self-assessment—critical elements of the teaching, learning, and assessment equation—are among the most useful, efficacious, and cost-effective purposes of these Web-enabled tools. Despite current and potential limitations, ePortfolios configured to capture the content, process, and expert judgments of faculty assessors and the reflections of students across the boundaries of the disciplines and their learning experiences hold promise for a new era of teaching, student-directed learning, and curriculum development.

TYPES AND USES OF ePORTFOLIOS

ePortfolios, as this volume attests, are blossoming throughout K-16 education. As Ehley (2004) points out however, most are showcase portfolios in which students select evidence they believe demonstrates how they meet specific learning outcomes, outcomes that at times they themselves design rather than those the institution requires as part of the baccalaureate. As worthy and creative as these are, they are often supplements to the educational process, adding a new dimension to faculty pedagogical and student reflective practice, but adding costs as well. Integration into the everyday teaching-learning process is achieved in only a few variants of this type of ePortfolio.

Love, McKean, and Gathercoal (2004) have described five levels of maturation of portfolio development in educational institutions, citing the following as key qualities: type of portfolio, its organization, whether the portfolio must include student artifacts, feedback and standards, nature of content, heuristics involved, context, and delivery mode. Using these qualities, they have developed a five-level taxonomy in which portfolios are described as moving from scrapbook (level 1), curriculum vitae (level 2), curriculum collaboration between student and faculty (level 3), mentoring leading to mastery (level 4), and authentic evidence as the authoritative evidence for assessment and reporting (level 5). The authors point out that Web-enabled portfolios are the only type that are robust enough to support all five levels of the taxonomy, weaving all the qualities identified into their structure in a dynamic way. But being Web-enabled is not enough.

One of the reasons for the number of ePortfolios at the showcase, scrapbook, or curriculum vitae levels is that as educators we have failed to infuse into the portfolio design process explicit educational principles that we know should undergird any effective teaching, learning, and assessment process. Failure to do so relegates many of these otherwise creative uses of technology to be mostly add-ons to the educational process that also add costs over and above the necessary technology infrastructure. At my institution, we have attempted to integrate ePortfolios into the teaching and learning process across the college in a way that is integral to every course and that supports our core educational beliefs, helping realize them more effectively and efficiently. What follows is one example of a tool that though still in its infancy, may come to be a major educational lever, poised to ratchet up both student and faculty learning. I set it forth here, not as *the* example of a student learning-centered ePortfolio, but an example of its potential.

AN EXAMPLE OF A LEARNING-CENTERED ePORTFOLIO: THE DIAGNOSTIC DIGITAL PORTFOLIO

Technology use is not new to my college. Over 25 years ago Alverno faculty began to record the development of each student's speaking and interaction abilities, creating what we call a video portfolio, containing samples of each student's growing communication and team skills. Similarly, faculty created a writing portfolio for each student that contains samples of each student's writing from first semester through last. Since samples of speaking, group work, and writing are kept from general education courses and the student's major and minor, each graduate can take to his or her employer or graduate school a developmental profile of what he or she had achieved. Selection of samples for the video and paper portfolios is guided by Alverno College faculty's educational philosophy of *assessment-as-learning* (Mentkowski & Associates, 2000) which will be described more fully later.

With the advent of the World Wide Web and the Internet, it was not much of a stretch for the faculty to use the power of the Web and digital technology to expand and enhance speaking, interaction, and written portfolios for each student. So in the late 1990s we created the Diagnostic Digital Portfolio (DDP), a Web-based system that enables each Alverno student—anyplace, anytime—to follow his or her learning progress throughout his or her years of study. It helps the student process the feedback he or she receives from faculty, external assessors, and peers. It also enables her to look for patterns in her academic work so she can take more control of her own development and become a more autonomous learner. Alverno's DDP can be viewed as providing the student with a kind of learning construction zone in which the student can build a sense of her growing ability in multiple learning domains and make plans for improvement and enhancement. She does so by reviewing, both independently and with the guidance of her faculty, selected performances from her courses, internships, her own self-assessments, and faculty feedback on each of the key performances.

Figure 1. Example of Alverno College student homepage

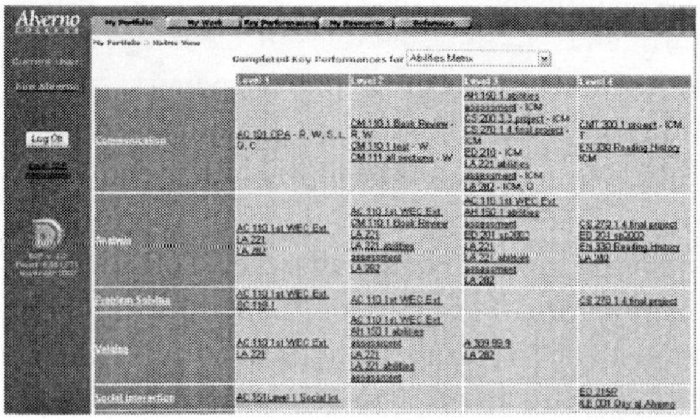

The DDP combines a relational database engine with a structured, *outcomes-based approach to learning*, managing performance information about learning within and across courses and departments throughout the duration of a student's enrollment. For more specific information on the DDP, readers are directed to a presentation at http://www.ddp.alverno.edu. Figure 1 provides a glimpse of the student homepage and how both student work and abilities are organized. Click on any "key performance"—another name for an uploaded videotape of a speech, written assignment, interaction, and so forth—and the student or faculty member will find a written (sometimes audio) statement of faculty judgment on the performance, a list of the criteria used to make the judgment, and the student's self-assessment based on the criteria. We selected these elements to include in the DDP specifically because of what our longitudinal research said about patterns of student learning (Mentkowski & Associates, 2000). We found that students need to review their previous performances in a variety of disciplinary contexts, and revisit their self-assessments and faculty feedback, in order to optimize their learning progress.

EDUCATIONAL PRINCIPLES THAT INFORM THE DIAGNOSTIC DIGITAL PORTFOLIO

Being able to do what one knows, demonstrating one's learning in a performance related to the discipline or profession's practice, is a key educational principle of Alverno's curriculum (Alverno College Faculty, 1979/1994). When students enact their learning in multidimensional and complex performance, their learning can become securely grounded in their frameworks for action. Another key principle is that assessment is integral to learning. Effective student assessment involves observing performances of an individual learner in action and judging him or her on the basis of explicit developmental criteria, with resulting feedback to the learner. When performance and the criteria for judging it are made public and linked to multidimensional and complex abilities, performance becomes accessible to the learning dynamic of self-assessment and feedback, assisting the learner to new insights into his or her performance. A comprehensive and in-depth program of longitudinal research shows that these insights become secured by habit and understanding as the learner repeatedly grapples with what it means to extend and transfer learning into new and diverse contexts (Mentkowski & Associates, 2000). Broad and common definitions of abilities that cross a range of learning experiences and that are assessed in a disciplinary or interdisciplinary context over a sustained program of study assist students to develop an understanding of these abilities as frameworks for constructing role performance.

Such learning is deep and durable. Three transformative learning processes make it so:

1. When students learn to **use metacognitive strategies**, performance itself becomes self-aware so that learners become conscious of selecting and applying frameworks for performance.
2. Through supported **self-assessment of role performance**, learners develop in their capacity to independently self-assess the relationship between what a situation requires and their abilities. Their sustained and supported self-reflection on how they are continuously improving and transferring their learning and performance across contexts consolidates into durable and guiding identities. They identify with being a learner, performer, and contributor, valuing their capacity to rise to the challenge of the occasion. These identities carry their learning into their civic, work, and personal lives.
3. Through **engagement of diverse approaches, views, and activities**, learners develop and deepen their commitment to independently and collaboratively pursue broader ideals. These ideals include contributing to civic, work, and family settings, but are also imbued with more specific and deeper personal meaning and significance. Diverse approaches to learning, diverse views on social issues, and diverse activities enable students to better see their own ideals and their need to commit to them. They hear within themselves their own personal calling to become the person they can be.

The DDP uniquely builds on these empirically confirmed insights into the nature of deep and durable learning. Its key performance templates call attention to the key design features of assessment-as-learning by explicitly including the public criteria for judging performance, the potential variation in the mode of student performance, assessment elements that promote integration and transfer, and the developmental sequencing of performance expectations. Of critical significance, it provides a common framework for displaying and organizing not only student work, but also faculty feedback and student self-assessment on diverse, developmentally sequenced performances across a curriculum.

Alverno's overall approach epitomizes the recommendations presented in How People Learn: Brain, Mind, Experience, and School (Bransford, Brown, & Cocking, 1999). Moreover, the DDP provides capabilities for longitudinal performance assessment that are consistent with the recommendations presented in

Knowing What Students Know: The Science and Design of Educational Assessments (Pellegrino, Chudowsky, & Glaser, 2001).

PROVOST'S PERSPECTIVE ON THE DDP: CREATING A MEANINGFUL AND DYNAMIC MEMORY OF FACULTY JUDGMENT ON EACH STUDENT'S LEARNING

What is particularly significant from a provost's perspective is the power of the DDP system to assist in an often neglected aspect of the chief academic role: enhancing the *educational effectiveness of faculty*. Many CAOs see their role as helping faculty continue to build disciplinary expertise and research capability. Clearly these are significant functions, particularly in Research I universities. Yet almost all of us are also responsible for undergraduate education and the development of the faculty to meet the challenges of teaching each generation of students. Reflecting our college or university missions, we place a high priority on producing liberally educated graduates capable of meeting the needs of the civic, business, and government sectors. Faculty research to support these sectors is clearly one way our institutions contribute to meeting these needs. Another, and for most institutions the primary way, is to produce capable graduates who think critically, know how to solve problems, communicate well, are able to be effective on teams, act ethically, and numerous other qualities that help society function effectively. Consequently, as a CAO, my focus must be on student learning and assisting faculty to continue their scholarly efforts to improve their teaching practice. Here is where I see the potential of digital portfolios: they keep before students and faculty the learning progress of each student in a concrete, available, timely, and cost-effective manner. Digital portfolios can provide a space where learners can reflect on their development and where faculty can study their practice. In this sense ePortfolios are construction zones for both student and faculty learning.

The Power of ePortfolios to Improve Student Learning

Many faculty experience the challenge of facing a new group of students on the first day of class, wondering what each has learned from previous courses in the curriculum, not in general, but what each learner has uniquely developed. Most college catalogs provide a list of required courses in a major which may tell the instructor what was "covered" in prior courses, but not what was learned. In most institutions the only guide to what students may have developed is faculty judgment of student achievement in previous course work in the form of grades and grade point averages. But grades tell only a small part of the story of each student's learning. What has been discarded, in effect, is the professional judgment of faculty, usually in the form of feedback on student work that would provide a picture of the unique learning progress of each student. What is also lost is any documentation of the student's own awareness of his or her own learning development. This is a waste of the expertise of experienced teachers and a waste of a rich source of information on each student's achievements and learning needs—information that is vital for instructors to use in creating teaching and assessment strategies.

An ePortfolio system designed to capture important information about each student's learning across his or her academic career is one way to harness what happens in every classroom, with the potential for transforming how students learn and how faculty teach.

Because I have seen what a fairly rudimentary ePortfolio system can do to provide important student information with efficiency and depth, I believe we have an important new tool for both enhancing student learning and helping faculty develop as scholars of their own teaching. Here are a few examples from my institution's experience in using the diagnostic digital portfolio that I hope will illustrate these points.

1. Our ePortfolio system stores and saves not only the final outcomes of faculty evaluations of students, but also provides information on the context for each summary judgment; the processes undertaken; often the student's work whether in text, audio, or video format; and faculty-selected evidence from the student's work that supports each judgment. These then can be retrieved, not only in a linear fashion, but when linked to specific learning outcomes and levels, in a mode that enables patterns of each student's learning to emerge. Because the DDP allows sorting student records by abilities and outcomes demonstrated, faculty can retrieve this information on students coming into a course, enabling them to more carefully target teaching strategies.
2. Another feature of the DDP system is that it allows faculty creative multiple and different uses across the disciplines. For example, the English Department now requires each of its majors, in the first course they take in the department, to draw up a bibliography of books related to their choice of career. A student planning a teaching career in middle schools might select a number of novels and poetry suitable for adolescents. A major planning to go on to graduate school might select literature from a period in American or British cultural history. Whatever the professional or personal aim of each English major, his or her bibliography is entered into the DDP, and as each student continues on in his or her major courses, he or she not only reads the selected texts, but annotates each book read, noting how he or she thinks the text will be of significance to his or her future career. The student then enters his or her comments into the DDP. As each semester begins, each English major is expected to add new texts to the original bibliography, continuing to reinterpret them in light of new knowledge. Once a year, the department faculty review the growing bibliography and annotations, and write feedback to each student. This practice helps students become more intentional about their reading choices and helps faculty monitor how well their majors are growing in their understanding of the discipline.
3. The biology and chemistry departments are using the DDP as an inquiry tool that will help them find patterns in how students in each of these majors develop problem-solving ability. Since each student enters work samples of her growing ability to use the scientific method in a variety of courses, the faculty are using the DPP to track underlying learning patterns and discern particular pedagogical challenges students face in developing this ability in the sciences.
4. In the beginning semester of the business and management major, students select a for-profit company they will revisit and study in each course of the major using the frameworks, concepts, and principles they have learned in courses on finance, accounting, marketing, and organizational behavior. At the end of each course completed, each student analyzes her selected

company using what she has learned from the course, entering her analysis and her observations into the DDP. Again, instructors are able to see, in a connected, developmental way, how the student is building on what she has learned in previous courses, and applying her synthesis to her analysis of the company.

These are but a few examples of how the DDP serves as a pedagogical tool, helping students connect learning across courses, assisting faculty to extend the learning terrain of their majors, and helping both students and faculty to discover each student's learning patterns.

The Power of ePortfolios to Assist in Faculty Development

Not only does the DDP allow faculty to provide students feedback on assessments, but because it stores criteria and feedback by courses and major outcomes, faculty can study their own assessment practice over time by specific courses and outcomes. It also allows faculty to explore the kind and quality of their feedback for students at beginning, intermediate, and advanced stages of their majors. For instance, one outcome of our English major is that the student will be able to read and interpret diverse cultural expressions in works of literature, film, and other media. An English professor can use the DDP as an inquiry tool, asking whether his or her criteria related to this outcome become increasingly sophisticated on assignments and assessments from early to more advanced courses in the major. The DDP allows the professor to search feedback samples by outcome and display these samples for beginning to advanced courses. This same professor can also search and compile feedback he or she has given to students in a particular course over the past several years to find examples of particularly high-quality feedback or feedback that has been found to be particularly effective. The DDP also allows the entire English Department to study how their majors have performed on key assessments related to all their major outcomes to determine whether their courses are helping students adequately develop these outcomes.

From a provost's perspective, having a tool that enables faculty to more directly and efficiently assess their own work is a major enhancement to faculty development programs. If one major mark of a profession is that it is self-evaluating, a tool such as the DDP provides a new, more powerful way to diagnose one's teaching and assessment practice.

DANGERS AND OBSTACLES IN THE DIGITAL CONSTRUCTION ZONE

Despite its many promising features and power as a learning tool, the DDP, like most new technology, has its drawbacks and concerns. From a provost's perspective, the ongoing training and technology upgrades are the most vexing, yet there are many other challenges to be faced.

Designing and Implementing the System

At my institution, the first major obstacle was the process of designing and implementing an ePortfolio system that would be cost effective, user friendly, and accepted and used by faculty and students. Having won several major grants that helped underwrite the initial development of the system, we outsourced the technical work, but involved our own faculty, staff, and students on the initial design team. Once the system was up and running, we then faced the ongoing challenge of keeping the system updated and monitored for the usual technical problems. Now in its fifth year of operation, the most common problem related to the technical system is how to provide sufficient funding to upgrade the software based on user feedback and new uses.

Acceptance by Users

Students are by far the most satisfied users of the system with some exceptions. They report that they like the accessibility of important assessment feedback, the ability to see their learning progress over time, and the efficiency of working on their assessments/self-assessments and receiving faculty feedback in an anytime, anywhere mode. They also like the ability to download their personal DDP to disk once they graduate. On the other hand, though faculty report creative and meaningful uses of the system, many are far less satisfied than students. Though we have only recently begun more systematic study of faculty attitudes and uses of the DDP, early findings indicate that discomfort with fairly simple technical skills such as uploading files is one major source of dissatisfaction. There is also a confidentiality concern that is common to users of any Web-based tool, no matter how secure our technical personnel have made the system. Finally, since we regularly videotape student speeches and group interactions, determining more efficient and user-friendly approaches to digitizing and uploading video samples is a major obstacle to faculty use.

Training

Probably the most difficult challenge for the provost's office is the need to provide just-in-time training to full-time and part-time faculty. We have many more questions than answers. To what level of proficiency should we expect all full- and part-time faculty? When should we provide training so that it is timed to faculty actual use in the classroom? How much staff support should we continue to budget? Should we expect faculty technology skills to mirror those of the students? Though we have offered numerous workshops and provide staff support, we know these questions are not completely answered and will continue to challenge us in the coming decade.

A PROVOST'S HOPE

As a chief academic officer, I continue to be amazed by the exciting possibilities of this dynamic new technology, and the creative work faculty have done to employ the DDP to enhance student learning. I see my work as removing obstacles so that faculty can serve as innovators, harnessing digital technologies to improve, if not transform, the experience of each learner.

For those of us charged with the responsibility of ensuring that what we set forth in our college catalogs and state as our mission as educational institutions actually happens, ePortfolios such as Alverno's Diagnostic Digital Portfolio provide a promising practice for enhancing the teaching, learning, and assessment enterprise in ways we have never imagined before.

REFERENCES

Alverno College Faculty. (1979/1994). *Student assessment-as-learning at Alverno College.* Milwaukee, WI: Alverno College Institute. (Original work published 1979, revised 1985 and 1994.)

Alverno College Faculty. (2000). *Student self-assessment at Alverno College.* Milwaukee, WI: Alverno College Institute.

Bransford, J., Brown, A., & Cocking, R. (1999). *How people learn: Brain, mind, experience, and schooling.* Washington, DC: NAS Press.

Ehley, L. (2004). *Student use of the diagnostic digital portfolio.* Paper submitted as part of doctoral work.

Graesser, A. C., Person, N. K., & Hu, X. (2002). Improving comprehension through discourse processing. In D. Halpern & M. D. Hakel (Eds.), Applying the science of learning to university teaching and beyond. *New Directions in Teaching and Learning, 89,* 33-44.

Hunt, E., & Pellegrino, J. W. (2002). Issues, examples, and challenges in formative assessment. In D. Halpern & M.D. Hakel (Eds.), Applying the science of learning to university teaching and beyond. *New Directions in Teaching and Learning, 89,* 73-86.

Love, D., McKean, G., & Gathercoal, P. (2004). Portfolios to Webfolios and beyond: Levels of maturation. *Educause Quarterly,* (2).

Mentkowski, M., & Associates. (2000). *Learning that lasts: Integrating learning, development, and performance in college and beyond.* San Francisco: Jossey-Bass.

National Center for Public Policy and Higher Education. (2000). *Measuring up 2000: The state-by-state report card for higher education.* Washington, DC: Author.

Pellegrino, J., Chudowsky, N., & Glaser, R. (2001). *Knowing what students know: The Science and design of educational assessments.* Washington, DC: NAS Press.

KEY TERMS

Abilities: An integrated combination of multiple components including skills, behaviors, knowledge, values, attitudes, motives, dispositions, and self-perceptions.

Diagnostic Digital Portfolio: A Web-based, relational, searchable database of selected assessments and assignments from each student that can be accessed anytime and anyplace, primarily designed to assist students to reflect upon and monitor their learning achievement over time.

Feedback: Evaluative information from an instructor to a student based on student performance.

Key Performance: A description of an assignment or assessment, associated criteria, the student's self-assessment, and instructor's/assessor's feedback.

Program Assessment: A process that provides meaningful feedback to faculty, staff, and various publics about patterns of student and alumni performance on a range of curriculum outcomes.

Self-Assessment: Ability of a student to observe, analyze, and judge his or her performance on the basis of criteria and determine how to improve it.

Student Assessment as Learning: Process of observing performances of an individual learner in action and judging them on the basis of explicit criteria with resulting feedback to the student.

Chapter IX
Enhancing Self-Regulation and Goal Orientation with ePortfolios

Jessica L. Blackburn
Bowling Green State University, USA

Milton D. Hakel
Bowling Green State University, USA

ABSTRACT

This chapter reviews the self-regulatory learning and goal orientation literatures. Findings from these literatures are used to make specific recommendations for the effective design and use of electronic portfolios in order to increase academic learning. Specifically, the authors recommend that electronic portfolios provide the means for students to set learning goals, monitor and regulate their progress toward these goals, as well as develop their self-assessment skills. Additionally, they suggest that these goals be focused on learning objectives rather than performance objectives.

INTRODUCTION

Portfolios have many uses. They are often used as a tool for assessing classroom learning. Portfolios are also used as a tool for job applicants to demonstrate their experience, skills, and abilities to prospective employers. Additionally, portfolios may serve as a tool for facilitating learning. Electronic portfolios are advantageous because they allow students to simultaneously use the same source files for *all* of the above listed purposes. The technology associated with ePortfolios makes it possible for students to store all of their academic work, while allowing prospective employers access only to the work that best demonstrates their abilities. Additionally, ePortfolios allow professors and teachers to see and evaluate student progress. ePortfolios have many uses, but this chapter will focus on the ePortfolio as a tool to promote development and learning. Specifically, we will examine two streams of research to discern what they imply for effective practice in using ePortfolios. ePortfolios can foster self-regulated learning and also can serve as a framework for inducing a more effective goal orientation. This chapter reviews the research literature, examining findings pertaining to self-regulatory learning and goal orientation. The chapter also offers recommendations for improving the design and use of ePortfolios in a manner that is consistent with the research findings.

SELF-REGULATED LEARNING

Self-regulated learning serves as an effective tool for increasing metacognition, motivation, and task engagement—all of which are associated with increased learning and improved academic performance (Paris & Paris, 2001). Self-regulated learning refers to the process by which people manage and control their thoughts, motivation, and behaviors in order to pursue learning goals (Paris & Paris, 2001; Pintrich, 2004). According to Boekaerts and Corno (2005), self-regulatory learning theorists " ... assume that students who self-regulate their learning are engaged actively and constructively in a process of meaning generation and that they adapt their thoughts, feelings, and actions as needed to affect their learning and motivation" (p. 201).

Pintrich (2004) outlines four stages of self-regulated learning: goal setting, monitoring, regulation, and reflection. Often, these stages occur implicitly, rather than explicitly. Additionally, these processes may co-occur. Applications and recommendations for ePortfolios will be discussed as they pertain to each of the above-listed stages.

Goal Setting

There is an extensive body of research in both academic and workplace settings demonstrating the positive effects of goal setting. Performance is higher for students who "set specific goals, effectively use feedback, and make appropriate strategy attributions" (Boekaerts & Corno, 2005, p. 215). Locke and Latham (2002) describe four mechanisms through which goals increase performance. Goals increase performance because they enable a person to focus on the goal, lead to increased effort and time directed toward the goal, and cause people to use prior knowledge, skills, and abilities as well as develop strategies for goal attainment. Previous research findings have demonstrated that goals that are both specific and difficult lead to higher levels of performance (Locke & Latham, 1990, 2002). In addition, findings have shown that goal commitment and feedback moderate the effectiveness of goal setting such that performance is higher when people are committed to goals and receive feedback as to their progress toward goals (Locke & Latham, 1990, 2002).

Based on the findings from research on goal setting, we suggest that ePortfolio software should provide space and prompt students to outline their learning and developmental goals. Additionally, the design of the ePortfolios should encourage students to set specific and challenging goals.

Monitoring

Monitoring refers to the process by which people assess their progress toward their goals. Bell and Kozlowski (2002) give prescriptive information about what types of feedback are most effective. They studied the effects of adaptive guidance on learning and performance on a learner-controlled training task. In a learner-controlled environment, people control how, when, what, and how often they study. Adaptive guidance goes beyond the typical feedback that is provided to individuals in training. Adaptive guidance provides individuals with suggestions on which content areas to focus on and suggestions for strategies to improve those areas. Adaptive guidance was positively related to learning and learning transfer for participants undergoing radar-tracking training (Bell & Kozlowski, 2002). The use of ePortfolios can be improved by providing users with more guidance on which skills and knowledge areas to improve on and suggestions for how to improve those areas.

Previous research has demonstrated the effectiveness of self-monitoring on learning and performance. Kauffman (2004) found that when college students were prompted to monitor their learning (in the form of making confidence judgments about their learning), students performed higher on the quizzes. Veenman, Elshout, and Busato (1994) demonstrated that students who were prompted to self-monitor had better learning strategies and were more knowledgeable after completing a computer-based educational unit on electricity.

Based on these findings, we recommend that instructors incorporate self-monitoring with their use of ePortfolios. Instructors should encourage and perhaps require that students regularly assess their progress toward their learning goals. The monitoring process may be further enhanced through the process of reflection or self-assessments. Reflection and self-assessments are discussed further below.

Ideally, the space for setting goals should be electronically linked to spaces for instructors and advisors to provide students with feedback about their progress toward these goals.

Regulation

Gollwitzer's work on implementation intentions provides further insights into effective strategies for setting goals as a means for learning and development. According to Gollwitzer (1999): "Implementation intentions are subordinate to goal intentions and specify the when, where, and how of responses leading to goal attainment" (p. 494). Thus, in a sense, implementation intentions are specific strategies that assist people in attaining goals. Gollwitzer and Brandstätter (1997) found that implementation intentions increased the probability of a person attaining a goal.

Thus, ePortfolios should provide space, and students should be prompted to outline strategies (the when, where, and how) for attaining each of their goals.

Reflection

In order to effectively set and pursue goals, people must be able to accurately assess their knowledge and abilities. This process of self-assessment primarily occurs through metacognition. According to Schmidt and Ford, "Individuals engaged in metacognitive activities actively monitor their progress, determine where problems exist, and adjust their learning strategies accordingly" (2003, p. 406). Previous research demonstrates that interventions aimed at increasing metacognitive activity are related to increases in performance on learning outcomes (Schmidt & Ford, 2003).

Self-assessment, as a form of metacognition, is effective because it causes students to evaluate the causes of their performance. Understanding and identifying the causes of success and failure may further assist students in developing strategies for success (Olina & Sullivan, 2004). The construction of portfolios increases metacognition by providing students with natural opportunities for self-assessment and self-reflection (Commander & Valeri-Gold, 2001; Hamm & Adams, 1992).

The potential of ePortfolios to increase learning can be enhanced if students are prompted to assess and reflect upon the work they include in their portfolios. Previous research demonstrates that students are not always accurate at self-assessment, and this can decrease the potential of self-assessments to improve performance

(Olina & Sullivan, 2004). Therefore, any inclusion of self-assessment and self-evaluation in ePortfolios should provide students with guidelines for self-assessment. This should increase the quality of student self-assessments and, as a result, the potential for self-evaluations to improve performance.

Guidelines for reflections should encourage students to relate classroom work to their goals. Students should explain how the work demonstrates progress toward goals. Additionally, students should be encouraged to evaluate the strategies they used to complete the assignment. This evaluation of strategies should allow students to determine what sorts of strategies are effective and how they might be modified to improve performance.

ePortfolios should also allow students to link their self-assessment with feedback provided by instructors (see above). This will allow students the opportunity to compare one's self-assessment with the assessment completed by someone else. Discrepancies between the assessments can be observed, and students have the opportunity to recalibrate their self-assessment.

The research literature shows that ePortfolios that include the features listed above are likely to be more effective in promoting student success and improving academic performance.

GOAL ORIENTATION

Research has identified two general categories of achievement goals: learning goals and performance goals (Grant & Dweck, 2003). Learning goals are aimed at growth and improvement, whereas performance goals are related to achieving some specific level or quantity of performance. Learning goals, in comparison to performance goals, are associated with higher levels of challenge seeking behaviors, task persistence, learning transfer (Dweck, 1986), classroom performance and improvement, and intrinsic motivation (Bell & Kozlowski, 2002; Grant & Dweck, 2003). Bell and Kozlowski (2002) found that a learning goal orientation is associated with higher levels of self-efficacy. Additionally, Bouffard, Boisvert, Vezeau, and Larouche (1995) found that a learning goal orientation is positively related to self-regulatory activities (including cognitive strategies, metacognitive strategies, and motivation) among college students. Other research has also found a positive relationship between a learning orientation and metacognitive activity (e.g., Ford, Smith, Weissbein, Gully, & Salas, 1998; Schmidt & Ford, 2003).

Although much of the goal orientation literature characterizes goal orientation as an individual characteristic, there is also evidence that specific goal orientations can be induced by situational characteristics (Grant & Dweck, 2003; Kozlowski et al., 2001).

> *Classroom settings that emphasize learning, effort, challenge, and errors as diagnostic feedback induce learning or mastery orientation, whereas settings that emphasize the achievement of high grades and minimization of mistakes induce a performance orientation.* (Kozlowski et al., 2001, p. 5)

A learning orientation can also be induced by having people focus on strategies for learning rather than performance outcomes (Winters & Latham, 1996). Additionally, researchers have found that an induced learning goal orientation can improve performance on learning outcomes above those effects caused by trait-like learning orientation (Kozlowski et al., 2001).

ePortfolios can provide a means for inducing a learning orientation because they can direct the student's attention to goals focused on learning rather than on goals strictly associated with performance. By focusing students' attention on goals associated with learning, rather than simply grades, ePortfolios have the potential to encourage students to challenge themselves as well as to more effectively develop their skills and abilities.

Additionally, ePortfolios can affect the way that feedback is given to and processed by ePortfolio users. When feedback is perceived as a tool for determining areas that need improvement, rather than as an evaluation of ability, this feedback has a greater potential to be used for developmental growth (Kozlowski et al., 2001). Therefore, ePortfolios should be designed in such a way that feedback given to students is independent of course performance evaluations. Students should be cued and encouraged to use the feedback to set developmental goals.

ADDITIONAL RESEARCH

Wade and Yarbrough (1996) conducted a study to examine the effectiveness of portfolios for increasing reflective thinking among education students. Although the researchers found that portfolios were effective for increasing reflective thinking, they also found that many students struggled with understanding the portfolio process. More effort needs to be placed on educating students about the purpose of portfolios. Furthermore, institutions should provide guidance on how to best use ePortfolios so that the potential for ePortfolios as a learning tool can be more fully realized.

Tillema (2001) compared three types of portfolios (showcase, course-based, and reflective) and found that people using a reflective portfolio were more receptive to feedback and demonstrated the greatest improvement in performance. This study highlights the need to clarify the objectives of the portfolio. Developers of ePortfolios are challenged, then, to develop ePortfolios in such a way as to emphasize the developmental purpose of the portfolio and make them useful for showcase purposes.

CONCLUSION

In summary, ePortfolios can be an effective learning tool because they provide students with the opportunity to collect their work and reflect on their learning progress. In order to improve the use of ePortfolios, we recommend that the design of ePortfolios explicitly include a goal-setting element. This goal-setting element should provide students with the opportunity to set learning and developmental goals. Students should be discouraged from setting strictly performance type goals. Furthermore, we recommend that students be encouraged to set specific and challenging goals, and develop specific strategies for attaining those goals. Additionally, ePortfolios should provide the space for instructors and advisors to provide feedback to students about their progress toward those goals. This feedback should include specific recommendations to students about how to best attain their goals.

Students should also be encouraged to regularly monitor their progress toward their learning goals. Students should also be encouraged to assess and reflect upon their work. This reflection process should require that students relate their work to their goals and evaluate the strategies they used to complete the work. Self-assessment can be improved if students have the opportunity to compare their self-assessments with the assessments made by others.

REFERENCES

Bell, B. S., & Kozlowski, S. W. J. (2002). Adaptive guidance: Enhancing self-regulation, knowledge, and performance in technology-based training. *Personnel Psychology, 55,* 267-306.

Boekaerts, M., & Corno, L. (2005). Self-regulation in the classroom: A perspective on assessment and intervention. *Applied Psychology: An International Review, 54,* 199-231.

Bouffard, T., Boisvert, J., Vezeau, C., & Larouche, C. (1995). The impact of goal orientation on self-regulation and performance among college students. *British Journal of Educational Psychology, 65,* 317-329.

Commander, N. E., & Valeri-Gold, M. (2001). The learning portfolio: A valuable tool for increasing metacognitive awareness. *The Learning Assistance Review, 6,* 5-18.

Dweck, C. S. (1986). Motivational processes affecting learning. *American Psychologist, 41,* 1040-1048.

Ford, J. K., Smith, E. M., Weissbein, D. A., Gully, S. M., & Salas, E. (1998). Relationships of goal orientation, metacognitive activity, and practice strategies with learning outcomes and transfer. *Journal of Applied Psychology, 83,* 218-233.

Gollwitzer, P. M. (1999) Implementation intentions: Strong effects of simple plans. *American Psychologist, 54,* 493-503

Gollwitzer, P. M., & Brandstätter, V. (1997). Implementation intentions and effective goal pursuit. *Journal of Personality and Social Psychology, 73,* 186-199.

Grant, H., & Dweck, C.S. (2003). Clarifying achievement goals and their impact. *Journal of Personality and Social Psychology, 85,* 541-553.

Hamm, M., & Adams, D. (1992). Portfolios: A valuable tool for reflection and assessment. *The Journal of Experiential Education, 15,* 48-50.

Kauffman, D. F. (2004). Self-regulated learning in Web-based environments: Instructional tools designed to facilitate cognitive strategy use, metacognitive processing, and motivational beliefs. *Journal of Educational Computing Research, 30,* 139-161.

Kozlowski, S. W. J., Gully, S. M., Brown, K. G., Salas, E., Smith, E. M., & Nason, E. R. (2001). Effects of training goals and goal orientation traits on multidimensional training outcomes and performance adaptability. *Organizational Behavior and Human Decision Processes, 85,* 1-21.

Locke, E. A., & Latham, G. P. (1990). *A theory of goal setting and task performance.* Englewood Cliffs, NJ: Prentice-Hall.

Locke, E. A., & Latham, G. P. (2002). Building a practically useful theory of goal setting and task motivation. *American Psychologist, 57,* 705-717.

Olina, Z., & Sullivan, H. J. (2004). Student self-evaluation, teacher evaluation, and learner performance. *Journal of Educational Technology Research and Development, 52,* 5-22.

Paris, S. G., & Paris, A. H. (2001). Classroom applications of research on self-regulated learning. *Educational Psychologist, 36,* 89-101.

Pintrich, P. R. (2004). A conceptual framework for assessing motivation and self-regulated learning in college students. *Educational Psychology Review, 16,* 385-407.

Schmidt, A. M., & Ford, J. K. (2003). Learning within a learner control training environment: The interactive effects of goal orientation and metacognitive instruction on learning outcomes. *Personnel Psychology, 56,* 405-429.

Tillema, H. H. (2001). Portfolios as developmental assessment tools. *International Journal of Training and Development, 5,* 126-135.

Veenman, M., Elshout, J., & Busato, V. (1994). Metacognitive mediation in learning with computer-based simulations. *Computers and Human Behavior, 30,* 139-161.

Wade, R. C., & Yarbrough, D. B. (1996). Portfolios: A tool for reflective thinking in teacher education? *Teaching and Teacher Education, 12,* 63-79.

Winters, D., & Latham, G. P. (1996). The effect of learning versus outcome goals on a simple versus complex task. *Group and Organization Management, 21,* 236-250.

KEY TERMS

Critical Thinking: Cognitive skills or strategies that increase the probability of a desirable outcome; used to describe thinking that is purposeful, reasoned, and goal directed—the kind of thinking involved in solving problems, formulating inferences, calculating likelihoods, and making decisions when the thinker is using skills that are thoughtful and effective for the particular context and type of thinking task. Critical thinking also involves evaluating the thinking process. *See Reflection and Metacognition.*

Goal Orientation: Distinguishes between goals that either focus on learning as the outcome or performance as the outcome.

Metacognition: Process by which a person thinks about his/her own thought process.

Reflection: A key strategy for becoming an outstanding performer is to ask yourself, after each and every performance, "What did I learn from doing this?" The practice of thinking about and analyzing your performance is called "reflection." It might also be called "self-assessment," "metacognition," "do differents," or "an after-action review."

Self-Assessment: Process by which a person evaluates his/her skills, abilities, learning progress, and performance.

Self-Efficacy: A person's evaluation of his/her ability to behave and perform in desired ways.

Self-Regulated Learning: Process by which a learner sets his/her own learning goal(s), assesses and monitors progress toward those learning goals, and makes modifications in order to increase progress toward the learning goal(s).

Chapter X
Mining for Meaning: Teaching Students How to Reflect

Bonnie Riedinger
FacultyMentor, LLC, USA

ABSTRACT

This chapter examines the challenges and benefits of using reflection in ePortfolios, and reviews strategies for teaching and encouraging deep reflection. It includes a brief history of the use of reflection in portfolios, summaries of the main types of reflection, and general approaches for the development of student reflection. Barriers to successful reflection, such as inexperienced students and faculty, student fear and distrust of reflection, formulaic responses, and time constraints will be examined, and solutions will be proposed. The effects of the ePortfolio on reflection and the possibilities offered by technological advances and new software also will be reviewed. The chapter argues that faculty must carefully construct reflection learning objectives if they expect meaningful summative or formative assessment to take place. The author hopes that the discussion of prompts, scaffolding, cycling, and other mining techniques will help instructors transform reflection theory into practice.

INTRODUCTION

As any parent of a toddler knows, one of a young child's favorite words is "why." Children need to know and understand the new world they are exploring, and they have no inhibitions about asking probing and at times unsettling questions. That same quest for answers lies at the heart of adult reflection as well. Although the questions reflected upon become more complex, the same drive for understanding underlies the process. Unfortunately, for many, that quest seems to become less natural with maturity.

Development of the ability to understand and engage in higher-order thinking—to reflect deeply and analyze critically—has been implicit in the definition of higher education. For many years, reflection has been a teaching and learning cornerstone in diverse disciplines, ranging from creative writing and teacher education to engineering, health, and the sciences. These disciplines also often use portfolios for formative and summative evaluation of student work and rely heavily on reflection for these assessments.

In the last decade, a number of universities, programs, and courses have moved from paper to electronic portfolios. Reflection is a vital component of a successful ePortfolio. Without reflection, the ePortfolio is merely *storage*. With reflection, it becomes, as numerous researchers and instructors have pointed out, a *story*—a narrative of exploration and learning that ideally would build recursively throughout the author's lifetime. As more institutions offer graduates lifetime access to their ePortfolios, the potential of reflective portfolios for truly lifelong learning could be realized as graduates add material to their ePortfolios and reflect upon their studies, careers, and lives using each "chapter" of their lives to plan for the unfolding chapters.

This is a powerful tool for student development as well as for more traditional academic assessment, but translating theory about reflection into practical classroom experience often is frustrating for students and faculty alike. This chapter examines the challenges and benefits of using reflection in ePortfolios and reviews best practices for teaching and encouraging deep reflection. It includes a brief history of the use of reflection in portfolios, summaries of the main types of reflection, and general strategies for the development of student reflection. Barriers to successful reflection, such as inexperienced students and faculty, student fear and distrust of reflection, formulaic responses, and time constraints will be examined. Faculty must carefully construct reflection course objectives if they expect meaningful summative or formative assessment to take place. Although each discipline, course, and group of students will require its own goals and approach to reflection, this review of prompts, scaffolding, cycling, and other mining techniques can be used and adapted by instructors across the curriculum to help transform reflection theory into practice. Instructors seeking specific prompts or discipline-specific articles about reflection will have no difficulty finding sources and are advised to do this research before using reflection in ePortfolio assignments.

This chapter will reflect on why and how to use reflection. May the author's reflections inspire the readers'.

BACKGROUND

Like most academic subjects, reflection can be slippery to define. Reflection's definitions, discourses, and practical applications are as wide ranging as the disciplines encompassed by higher education.

Human beings like to think of themselves as reflective creatures, and at some level we all are reflective. The saints confess, the monks contemplate, the great authors keep journals, the scholars write treatises, and high school girls scribble in diaries—all in pursuit of understanding ideas, themselves, and the world. We have a history of thought about thought. But not all reflection is equal, and in the fractured academic world, each discipline privileges different definitions and approaches.

Although this chapter will review several definitions, a general working definition can perhaps be agreed upon, at least insofar as it will serve as a useful starting point for students as well as faculty. Reflection can be defined as much by what it is not as what it is. Reflection is not summary. A reflective journal is not a laundry list of the quotidian. A reflective story is not a plot without a theme. A reflection is not a generalization. A reflection is not superficial. A reflection is not a cliché. A reflection is not what the author thinks others want to read or hear. Yet, these are often the results when instructors ask students to reflect.

Reflection was introduced to the modern academy primarily by Dewey, who in 1933 defined reflection as: "Active, persistent and careful consideration of any belief or supposed form of knowledge ... " (p. 118). A practical educator, Dewey advocated the importance of experience in learning, emphasizing that learning is a participatory activity through which theory is made tangible to the learner. Of course, Dewey wrote extensively about reflection, thinking, and learning, but this succinct definition serves as a good starting point for any reflective discussions or exercises, regardless of discipline.

Since Dewey, various educators and scholars have expanded on his concepts. Nearly every discipline has added such trimmings as their scholars found useful, academically or politically. Although each instructor must decide which learning theories she/he wants to embrace and which approaches to use when designing reflection assignments, the search for deep understanding should be the basis for such assignments. Two of the most well-known reflection scholars and writers are Kolb, developer of the Kolb cycle of experiential learning, and Schon, who in the 1980s coined the phrases "reflection-on-action" and "reflection-in-action." Much subsequent research on reflection has its genesis in the theories of Dewey, Schon, and Kolb, and expands the field by examining the links between reflection and learning, the timing of reflection, and the context of reflections. Useful summaries and discussions of the evolution and application of reflection theory in higher education are provided in *The Development of Student Skills in Reflective Writing* by Terry King of the University of Portsmouth in the United Kingdom and in several papers by Jenny Moon of the University of Exeter.

Schon's division of reflection by time has become part of mainstream reflection practice in higher education and is closely related to formative and summative assessment. Even those who are not familiar with Schon probably intuitively make these distinctions.

Like summative assessment, reflection-on-action is used in higher education to help students sum up what they have learned, how they learned it, and to determine what they might have done differently. Reflection-on-action questions for a first-year student might include: What did I learn during my first semester? How did my classes contribute to my academic, personal, and social development? What could I have done differently last semester to improve my grades? What can I use from this semester's experience to improve my performance during the next semester?

Although this exploration of past actions and lessons learned is completed at the end of a course or semester, it still can be used for further planning and learning if incorporated into a graduation or lifelong learning portfolio. Digitally preserved, electronic reflections can forever be consulted, reviewed, and re-reflected upon.

Like formative assessment, reflection-in-action, as practiced in higher education today, takes place in progress. It is a process rather than an end product and may or may not be graded by the instructor. Students reflect on and evaluate what they are doing as they are doing it, usually with the goal of improving their performance, end product, or understanding of the process. In the writing classroom, for example, reflection-in-action takes the form of multiple drafts, peer review, and coaching. In service learning or teacher education, reflection-in-action could consist of journals, coaching sessions with peers or instructors, and drafts of reflective papers. Campus Compact, which provides extensive information on service learning and reflection, recommends Schon's "ladder of reflection" to help structure reflection.

Under coaching, an experienced individual uses a combination of tips, advice, and examples to help students achieve success ... Schon visualizes the coaching process as a ladder of reflection where students and faculty reflect on their actions or prior reflections as well as on each other's actions/ reflections. This type of a coaching process calls for frequent reflection and timely feedback. (Campus Compact, n.d.)

Reflection at any point in time requires introspection, but unlike the contemplative monks, students are, in most cases, expected to incorporate the views of others in their reflection. Whether through peer review or one-on-one consultations with an adviser or instructor, students in most disciplines must consider outside views and feedback in their reflection, particularly when the focus is reflection-in-action. The ePortfolio offers many opportunities for such communication. Some ePortfolios offer internal e-mail communication or messaging so instructors, peers, and coaches can provide a stream of feedback. These communications also can be archived by many ePortfolio platforms so that students can reflect on the cycle of drafting, critique, reflection, and re-drafting. Listservs, discussion forums, and e-mail messages from course work also can be included and reflected upon in ePortfolios. Reviewing and annotation features in word processing programs also provide electronic records of peer comments as well as student revisions, which can be valuable artifacts for reflection.

Reflection that focuses on personal experience is often used in first-year-orientation courses, writing courses, and in teacher, nursing, and other medical training courses. Although journals and similar reflective assignments are inherently personal, they are not necessarily private either in their creation or their results. Darell, in a 2003 conference paper, describes the reflective journals used in her PhD research on teaching, wherein teachers were asked to reflect on their experiences "inwardly, outwardly, backwards and forwards" and to explore "internal feelings, the environment and nature of reality, as well as the relationship of the past, present and future as well as the temporal."

Feldman and Rearick (1999) break reflection into three categories: autobiographical, collaborative, and communal. They define autobiographical reflection as the first stage wherein the "researcher is the main focus of the research," examines the literal meaning of his or her stories, and probes into the metaphorical meanings as they relate to common usage. The aim is to understand, then explain." Feldman and Rearick state that collaborative reflection requires the researcher to seek answers that cannot be found through introspection. "Whereas autobiographical reflection preserves the significance of particularity, collaborative reflection involves reflecting on the social construction of the self and the system within a larger interpersonal context and may consider interpretive, scientific, artistic and poetic works," the authors explain. The final stage of reflection, communal, "involves reflecting on the self in interaction with others in even larger contexts—cultural, historical, and institutional," Feldman and Rearick write. Reflection is not simply navel gazing. However, the degree to which it should be social must be determined by the goals of each course and its learning objectives.

Reflection as a central component of ePortfolios is incorporated into what Chen and Mazow (2002) have termed "folio thinking," which "aims to:

- Encourage students to integrate discrete learning experiences
- Enhance students' self-understanding
- Promote students' taking responsibility for their own learning
- Support students in developing an intellectual identity."

Because ePortfolios offer such ease of storage and accessibility, they open wide the possibilities for reflections of all types: in action, before action, after action, in solitude, in consultation with peers, in consultation with instructors, coaches, and advisers, written, spoken, videotaped, or graphically represented.

MAIN THRUST

Although reflection can be an effective learning tool, its use, whether on paper or electronically, presents challenges. These include:

1. **Defining Reflection:** Faculty must understand the type of reflection in which students are to engage and define what they hope to accomplish.
2. **Teaching Students How to Reflect:** As a number of researchers have pointed out, reflection does not necessarily flow naturally from all students. Although some may learn quickly, others may require more training and feedback. Simply telling students to reflect on a subject or even asking open-ended questions may still result in simple description or superficial responses. Instructors must develop training that will help students learn to think deeply and continue to probe beneath the surface for answers.
3. **Resistance to Reflection:** Even when students understand how to reflect, they may resist it. Even adults and educators may be uncomfortable with reflection. The causes for this resistance may include: not understanding the benefits of reflection and believing it is busy work, reluctance to invest the time and work necessary for deep reflection, fear of criticism, fear of making mistakes, fear that admission of a weakness or mistake will lead to a poor grade, and fear of disclosure.
4. **Clichéd Responses:** As anyone who has taught knows, some students believe that in order to succeed, they must discover what the teacher wants and say/write that. Writing teacher O'Neill (2004) notes that some of her students' portfolio cover letters contained "stereotypical lines" designed to project an image of a student who is "hard working, that has been converted to process pedagogy, that now enjoys writing, and that has learned a lot." O'Neill wonders:

   How do I know if what they say in the reflective text is authentic, said to please me, or fabricated because they need to fill up space? Are they using the language from the syllabus and class work because it is now part of their vocabulary for talking about writing or because they think that is what I want to hear?

SOLUTIONS AND RECOMMENDATIONS

Defining and Preparing for Reflection

Institutions, departments, and individual faculty members should be discouraged from using reflection as part of the curriculum until they have decided what type of reflection will be required of students; how that reflection serves the learning objectives of the course, program, or institution; and how the reflection will be assessed. The temptation to use reflections or ePortfolios because they are the latest educational trend should be resisted until a well-considered plan is in place. Learning objectives and assignments should be tailored to the needs of the students and the institution, and reflection should be an integral part of the curriculum rather than an afterthought. Instructors should then be trained to teach and assess reflection and portfolios. Students who are given vague instructions about the goals and objectives of portfolios and reflection may become confused, frustrated, and resistant to further reflection. Without clear guidelines, students may fill their ePortfolios with journal entries or "reflective" papers that accomplish little or no learning, and poison the well for future reflection. As O'Neill points out:

Incorporating reflection ethically requires more than just adding a cover letter or a reflective essay because students need to be taught what we mean by reflection, how to generate reflective texts, and how to evaluate them as processes and products.

The power of ePortfolios and reflection can be squandered if their purposes are not clearly defined.

Noting the "need to make the process of reflection intentional," the University of Portsmouth has developed reflection workshops for staff and students that explore the "stages of reflection and how to get the best results from good reflective writing" (King, n.d.). King describes the staff workshop as follows: The workshop included discussions of the definitions and importance of reflection as well as exercises such as grading of various types of student reflective writing. Workshop participants then discussed the necessity of making the reflection "process explicit to students," by defining "criteria, depth and range" before beginning the assignment. Participants graded the student writing samples before they were introduced to the stages of reflection based on Moon's model. This model includes seven stages: "Purpose—an understanding of the purpose of the reflective activity; basic observations; additional information—the addition of further observations, new information, etc."—revisiting; standing back; moving on; and finally further reflection. King suggests that the model can be used as the basis for grading, with evidence of higher reflection stages resulting in higher grades. After viewing the model, participants were then asked to form small grading groups to "reconsider the initial reflective writing examples in light of the stages of reflection," King writes. This combination of examples, discussions, and hands-on work is a good training model that can be readily customized to meet the needs of various disciplines.

According to King, the student workshop, which lasted two hours, followed a similar model but included more time for hands-on exercises. After a discussion of the importance of reflection, King writes that the students spent 20 minutes writing a reflection about "their experiences of student induction at the University over the previous week," which they then exchanged with another student. The first three stages of reflection (purpose, basic observations, and additional information) and examples of each stage were introduced and the students were then asked to "find examples of the three basic levels of reflection" in their peer's writing sample, King writes. Students then learned about the higher stages of reflection and grading based on these stages, and were asked to reread and grade their peer's reflection and discuss the paper with the peer, King writes.

As in the design of the staff workshop, the University of Portsmouth student workshop provides clear definitions, examples, and the time for students to practice and discuss reflection. The peer work and general discussions can be particularly helpful as they bring reflection from the purely personal to the communal, showing students different perspectives on the same subject.

Teaching Students to Reflect

Once program and course goals for reflection have been established, instructors must be certain that students understand the basics of reflection. Upper-division students as well as first-year students may need help to become proficient at reflection. Although the level of discourse should be adjusted according to the level of student, practical, down-to-earth explanations and examples should accompany any discussions of reflection theory. Illustrations of the stages or cycles of reflection, such as those developed by Kolb, Moon, and others, may also help students understand the process. Feedback throughout the process also is essential to keep students on track as they learn to reflect.

A review of some of the common definitions of reflection, beginning with Dewey's, can serve as a good introduction for any course or student. An introductory reflective assignment could focus on group or peer discussions of what makes a good reflection. Institutions and instructors may also develop their own definitions to suit institutional and pedagogical goals. Penn State, Albion College, and Kalamazoo College all have established ePortfolio programs, and their Web sites contain much useful advice about reflection, reflective questions, and assignments. Campus Compact's Web site also offers many insights into using reflection in service learning that can be applied to other reflective activities.

First-year students, particularly those who are under-prepared for college, may need a great deal of coaching and modeling before they understand the value of reflection or how to reflect deeply. Most first-year programs that incorporate reflective writing focus on developing students as self-directed learners who can be analytical about their academic and career goals. But reflection in a first-year program can be more emotionally challenging for students and instructors than reflection in a mathematics or physics class that focuses more on scientific reasoning than feelings.

Many first-year instructors are drawn from various disciplines with divergent pedagogies and levels of comfort when dealing with the more personal writing that emerges when students reflect about their lives and aspirations. Although first-year programs can incorporate more impersonal assessments such as computerized skills assessments, many first-year programs ask students to reflect on their goals and dreams, strengths and weaknesses, study and social habits. The first-year student is adjusting to a new and sometimes frightening world fraught with academic challenges, the temptations of drugs and alcohol, peer pressure, depression, homesickness, dating woes, and often financial pressures. Reflective questions that ask students how they *feel* about their first semester at college often prompt a flood of pent-up emotions. Instructors must decide if they are willing and able to play Virgil to a student Dante who may need to travel a hellish route to self-realization.

On a more positive note, first-year students can also be the most open and willing to truly reflect once they understand the process. The technology of ePortfolios often attracts students who enjoy incorporating graphics, audio, and video to illustrate their first-year experience. In my first-year course, I introduced the technology by showing students how to post autobiographies and jpegs of themselves, and encouraging them to create non-academic sections that showcased hobbies. This created a sense of ownership and interest in the ePortfolios that eased the transition to more analytical thinking about the "stories" they were learning to write about themselves. If the academic goal is to cultivate in students a habit of lifelong reflection, the portfolio and the value of reflection should be presented within the context of the student's life and interests to avoid the perception that reflection is "just another hoop to jump through." All the modeling, examples, and explanations of reflection will be for naught if there is no student buy-in. That initial buy-in may be best achieved when students see tangible results that relate to their experiences. Although one semester may not provide sufficient time and distance for students to see, revisit, and reflect upon changes in their lives, a four-year portfolio program generally provides ample opportunities for recursive reflection and strikingly illustrates changes in students' views and goals.

Mining Exercise

Another common way to introduce reflection is use of the five Ws of journalism: *who, what, where, when,* and *why.* This model has also been expanded by many schools to include *how, so what,* and *now what,* and serves as the foundation for instructor-developed prompts and as a mining model for students to develop their own questions as they reflect on their portfolios.

In my writing classes, I explain to students that summary explains who, what, where, and when, and that reflection and analysis explore why and how. In an exercise to help students make these distinctions, they are told to mark up their own or their peers' journal entries or essay drafts, noting in the margins which types of questions are being answered. Sentences and paragraphs can then be highlighted in different colors—yellow for summary and green for reflection or analysis, for example. If the yellow outweighs the green, students are then instructed to develop their own mining questions (using *why, how, so what,* or *now what* and the five Ws as appropriate) about the summary statements in the essay or journal entry. Subsequent drafts of an essay or journal can be enriched as students formulate and provide answers to these questions. This mining technique also can be used to elicit more and richer details and reflection when a student's writing exceeds summary, but remains superficial.

Mining questions could be applied to some of the "stereotypical lines" O'Neill suspects students may have written to create the image they think she wants.

Student:
I never considered myself a writer before but now I do. (O'Neill, 2004)

Mining questions:
Why didn't you consider yourself a writer? How did you come to that conclusion? What do you think are the characteristics of a good writer? Why? How have you changed? What are some examples of the changes in your writing?

ePortfolios can enhance these types of exercises. Using standard Web page creation software such as FrontPage, students can easily create hyperlinks in a first draft that drill down to provide more details and analysis as they create and answer mining questions and respond to peer and instructor comments. This graphically illustrates the layers of meaning that are created as students reflect.

A standard creative writing technique also can help students open up new perspectives when writing personal development reflections or reflections about highly charged emotions or controversial issues. Ask students to write from the perspective of someone who is a polar opposite, taking into account that person's emotions and background. Even switching from first person to third person can change perspectives. Although journal entries have been one area where academic prohibitions against use of the first person have been eased, writing in the third person may actually result in deeper understanding. According to a 2005 study at Ohio State University, students who reflect in the third person can perceive more change in themselves. Libby, the assistant professor of psychology who co-authored the study, asked college students who had been in psychotherapy to visualize their first appointment and rate how much they had changed since then. The half who visualized from the third person perspective perceived more change. According to Libby, "Other studies have shown that if you remember an incident in the first person, you tend to re-experience the event, how everything unfolded. You're wrapped up in the emotions, so you don't reflect on the event and the overall meaning" (Libby, 2005, pp. 8-9).

Most research supports the use of scaffolding to support reflection, but there is some dissent over how directive prompts and coaching should be. Some process learning includes the use of structured journals. Apple, Beyerlein, Carroll, and Ford (n.d.) write that "by asking students to respond to a predetermined set of fill-in-the-blanks and guided discovery questions[,] it is possible to increase both the quantity and the quality of their writing."

Others, particularly in the composition field, are often wary of providing overly directive prompts or feedback for fear of taking "ownership" of the writing and learning away from the student. Each instructor will have to balance the advantages and constraints of these approaches with her/his learning objectives for the course. Although rote answers prompted by overly specific questions are not desirable, neither are the vague and meandering responses produced by students who have received no training or coaching in the reflective process. To allow such students to flounder also defeats the learning process. This should not, however, be interpreted to mean that reflections should be perfect, polished products. Reflection is growth, and growth is incremental and often messy.

Training students in mining techniques may go far in alleviating this conflict between undirected self-discovery and narrow directive instruction. Once students understand the tools necessary for reflection and are trained in their use, they can formulate their own questions.

RESISTANCE TO REFLECTION

Learning can be enjoyable, but at its best it can also be somewhat frightening, particularly when students are engaged in personal development reflection. This can create what Belanoff calls in a 2005 paper "dis-ease," wherein "... reflection often grows out of discomfort even though it may afford delight and thrive in mystery and paradox" (p. 420). The uncertainty of the unknown and the fears of what may be discovered can be daunting to anyone, but may be particularly so for students trying to find their place in the world. Reflection can help students in that search, but only with the proper guidance. This also is a world where spin and appearances are part of competitive daily life. How can students who constantly receive reminders about the importance of good grades and effective presentation be encouraged to look honestly at the areas in which they need improvement? How can instructors create an atmosphere of trust that will enable students to feel comfortable with self- and peer assessment? When instructors assess reflection, how heavily should they weigh process versus product? How can instructors deal with the often raw emotions that appear in students' reflective journals? What is too personal for academic writing? How does the transactional distance of communication through a courseware management system or ePortfolio affect instructor/student communication? How can the time necessary for reflection be accommodated in a course already crammed with learning objectives and assignments?

Preparation and the willingness of instructors to continually reflect and revise their pedagogy are key. A thorough exploration of the use and goals of reflection in each instructor's discipline should be undertaken before reflection is incorporated into the curriculum. Familiarity with the technology used in an ePortfolio also is necessary, as is an understanding of how the technology will affect learning objectives and time management.

Less traditional campuses that have long used reflection, and graduation portfolios may be better equipped to make the transition to reflective ePortfolios. Institutional commitment to reflection, student-centered learning, and constructivist pedagogy also certainly ease the way for instructors who may be offered formal training as well as access to experienced peers. Formal portfolio programs also set student expectations for learning and provide structured reinforcement of reflective practices. Institutions or individuals interested in reflection can benefit from the lessons learned by experienced practitioners via institution Web sites, journal articles, or networking.

Much research has gone into these questions and they certainly merit further study, but ultimately each instructor must negotiate her/his own level of comfort with students' discomfort, decide how his/her communication style and personality will aid or inhibit student reflection, and determine how much of a priority reflection will have in the classroom. These pedagogical questions are worthy of sustained reflection.

FUTURE TRENDS

As ePortfolio use increases, questions about their integration with standard curricula and new software and courseware management systems must be confronted. New software to support electronic reflection is under development, and older software such as If Monks Had Macs and Daedalus can ease the way to reflection for novice instructors as well as students. Additions to ePortfolio reflections could include hypertext reflections such as those developed by the Webfolio Project and scaffolding software such as Mildred, a joint project of the University of Washington and the University of Michigan, which supports science education. Effective integration of new software as well as video, audio, graphics, MUDs, MOOs, wikis, Weblogs, asynchronous discussion forums, and listservs into ePortfolios may expand the definitions of reflection well beyond text.

CONCLUSION

Reflection is not simple, but for those who chose to teach and learn with ePortfolios, it is a necessity. ePortfolios offer great potential for deep learning, and advances in technology raise the hope of even greater dimensions for reflection. The instructor or institution embarking on a reflective project must do the necessary homework: research, network, and develop clear goals for teaching and learning. Once those goals are established, continue to reflect on the process at all levels from administration to student. What works in one academic culture or discipline, or even course, will not necessarily be effective in another. Constant and consistent reflection and re-reflection is not just for students. Effective reflection will depend on the willingness of all to take risks, think outside of their disciplines, and relearn childhood curiosity—the art of asking why.

REFERENCES

Apple, D., Beyerlein. S., Carroll, S., & Ford, M. (n.d.). *The learning assessment journal as a tool for structured reflection in process education.* Retrieved April 15, 2005, from http://fie.engrng.pitt.edu/fie96/papers/169.pdf

Belanoff, P. (2001, February). Silence: Reflection, literacy, learning, and teaching. *CCC, 52*(3), 420. Retrieved April 15, 2005, from http://www.paulofreireinstitute.org/Documents/reflection_and_literacy_by_Pat.pdf

Campus Compact. (n.d.). *Structuring the reflective process.* Retrieved April 15, 2005, from http://www.compact.org/disciplines/reflection/structuring/coaching.html

Chen, H. L., & Mazo, C. (2002, October 28). *Electronic learning portfolios and student affairs.* Retrieved April 21, 2004, from http://www.naspa.org/netresults/PrinterFriendly.cfm?ID=825

Darell, R. (2003, November 29-December 3). *Working with teachers: Beliefs, experiences and the creative arts (drama).* Retrieved April 15, 2005, from http://www.aare.edu.au/03pap/dar03394.pdf

Dewey, J. (1933). *How we think* (p. 118). New York: D.C. Heath.

Feldman, A., & Rearick, M. L. (1999). Orientations, purposes and reflection: A framework for understanding action research. *Teaching and Teacher Education, 15,* 335-336. Retrieved April 15, 2005, from http://www.ece.uncc.edu/succeed/journals/PDF-files/tte-18.pdf

King, T. (n.d.). *Development of student skills in reflective writing.* Retrieved April 15, 2005, from http://www.csd.uwa.edu.au/iced2002/publication/Terry_King.pdf

Libby, L. (2005). Change your perspective to see changes in yourself. *Ohio State Alumni Magazine,* (May/June), 8-9.

O'Neill, P. (2004, January 4). *Reflection and self-assessment: Resisting ritualistic discourse.* Retrieved from http://www.writinginstructor.com/essays/oneill1.html

Schön, D. (1983). *The reflective practitioner. How professionals think in action.* London: Temple Smith.

Schön, D. (1987). *Educating the reflective practitioner.* San Francisco: Jossey-Bass.

KEY TERMS

Electronic Portfolio (ePortfolio): Digital storage area where the author can collect, assess, and reflect upon work, processes, and goals. ePortfolios may be shared with others as part of assessment or as a showcase for work.

Formative Evaluation: Assessment of work in progress to provide feedback and direction.

Reflection: Defined by Dewey (1993) as "active, persistent and careful consideration of any belief or supposed form of knowledge ..."

Reflection-in-Action: Term used initially by Schön to describe on the process of reflecting on and evaluating work in progress. Examples of this in the writing classroom would be multiple drafts, peer review, and coaching.

Reflection-on-Action: Term used initially by Schön to describe how students can look back at completed work to see what and how they learned, and to determine what they might have done differently.

Service Learning: A type of experiential learning that links community projects to academic work, providing real-world lessons.

Summative Evaluation: Assessment of completed work.

Chapter XI
ePortfolios:
Pathway from Classroom to Career

Eleanor J. Flanigan
Montclair State University, USA

Susan Amirian
East Stroudsburg University, USA

ABSTRACT

This chapter includes three main themes, answering basic questions of "Why," "Where," and "How" that are asked when discussing the development of career portfolios during a student's academic program. The reasons why portfolios in general should be created are discussed primarily in the Rationale section. Following this is a description of ongoing programs at two universities where portfolios are an integral part of the curriculum for students in two diverse departments: Media Communications in a School of Professional Studies, and Management Information Systems in a School of Business. Finally, there is an outline of the portfolio development process with concrete suggestions on the steps to follow, the design process, and modes of distribution. The authors hope that their experiences in helping students to compile their electronic portfolios will encourage other educators to engage in this creative process, smoothing the pathway from classroom to career.

RATIONALE FOR DEVELOPING ePORTFOLIOS

One of the greatest challenges faced by educators on all levels from pre-K through adult education programs is the attempt to ensure that students gather the knowledge building blocks they need in order to provide a solid base for new learning. This accretion may be compared to the construction of the great pyramids of Egypt. A huge base of separate blocks provided the foundation, and the structures gradually rose with one layer of block at a time. Students build their knowledge by attaching new learning to old. In the process, relationships are made and links are connected. Or at least that is what is supposed to happen!

Students are sometimes oblivious of the structured paths that lead them from one level of knowledge to another. Unless they are unusually reflective and deliberately trace their intellectual growth, most students, particularly in higher education, move ahead according to the required curriculum, taking prescribed courses as directed. Somehow the parts are supposed to congeal into the whole, and students are expected to emerge as educated people able to do self-appraisal, having absorbed and connected all of those separate learning experiences.

Rather than waiting until the end of their academic careers, it may increase the students' ability to comprehend the path of learning if they had to do a continual formal assessment of their work. Developing portfolios serves this purpose and can be started at any point along the educational continuum. Students are directed to collect and preserve their work in creative accumulative projects, reflecting and assessing their learning during the process. The more traditional paper-based portfolios have given way to digital portfolios, using students' technological skills to gather and preserve artifacts in more permanent forms. Students may create individual course portfolios as well as an academic career portfolio as they move through their educational programs.

Digital portfolios provide a connection or a pathway, moving the student along from the classroom environment into chosen careers. According to Confucian teaching, learning without thought is labor lost. Developing an innovative and original professional digital business portfolio constitutes a lasting comprehensive experience for the students, adding to their professional development. Continual reflection upon their work arms them with more confidence in their own competence and worth as they embark on their professional careers. Business schools in particular strive to develop students into sophisticated knowledge workers, able to analyze processes. Examination of their work in the portfolio enables students to "recalibrate" (Poore, 2001) and to enhance their growth by analyzing their work objectively.

As university graduation nears, students find that preparing a comprehensive career résumé summing up their achievements and experiences is not an onerous task, as they are prepared to show concrete examples of their competencies in their electronic portfolios. According to Williams and Hall (2001), students can start "interesting conversations" in employment interviews that would not be possible without a portfolio in hand.

Digital career portfolios are basically collections of artifacts used to validate claims made by the creator. These artifacts are in a creative variety of formats: text documents, Web pages, presentations, research papers, assessment instruments, original projects, academic or external teamwork, internships, presentation videos, certificates of achievement, spreadsheets, databases, digital images, and multimedia demonstrations. These digital portfolios serve the career student population, particularly information technology (IT) professionals, encouraging them to develop technologically creative résumés. The artifacts support the students' statements of proficiency in their chosen fields. Prospective employers, especially those in information systems (IS) recruiting, look for technical knowledge and proof of technical competence. Portfolios in digital form showing creative technical projects aid the student-interviewee to both tell about and show competencies.

In short, a portfolio is a demonstration of skills and abilities, containing evidence of growth and competence. Satterthwaite and D'Orsi (2003) state that a portfolio is a collection of easily portable artifacts that serve to validate claims people make about themselves. Portfolios can be learning tools, job search tools, and career growth tools. The purpose of the portfolio to some degree dictates the artifacts collected as well as the format of the presentation design.

This chapter will give a description of the process used in two ongoing programs at two universities where portfolios as learning tools and job search tools are an integral part of the curriculum for students in two diverse departments: Media Communications in a School of Professional Studies, and Management Information Systems in a School of Business. Also in this chapter is an outline of the portfolio development process with concrete suggestions on the steps to follow, the design process, and modes of distribution.

PROGRAM DESCRIPTION

Digital portfolios were implemented in the courses of two professors at Montclair State University in New Jersey and East Stroudsburg University in Pennsylvania. The programs in which portfolios were created were in the Department of Management and Information Systems (MIS) in the School of Business and the Department of Media Communication & Technology (MCOM) in the School of Professional Studies. Although teaching at separate universities and in very different programs, the two authors collaborated on their portfolio strategies, processes, and results over a two-year period.

In total to date, 135 students have participated in the creation of digital portfolios in three courses at the two universities. One course was required for the Master of Communication (MCOM) degree and focused on advanced use of imaging technologies, while the second was an advanced MCOM elective concentrating on interactive media production. The School of Business course was an independent study course in MIS, designed to support the creation of career portfolios. In each course students created digital portfolios as an integral part of their learning experience, in addition to contributing to their preparation for internships, cooperative work experience, or job searches upon graduation.

Two types of digital portfolios were implemented in these courses—course portfolios and career portfolios. Students in the MCOM major course created course portfolios as part of the learning design, collecting an artifact of each assignment to display in their course portfolio. Students were required to include a short reflective text with each assignment display. Those in the MIS course created career portfolios as ancillary projects to strengthen their job searches and interviews with prospective employers or human resource offices. They were required to keep a journal of their progress and submit this weekly to the professor along with the portfolio segment assigned for the week. These types of activities aided in both teacher and student assessment of course work.

DESCRIPTION OF PORTFOLIO DEVELOPMENT PROCESS

Step-by-Step Process

While the specific steps followed for each course were sometimes different, depending on the purpose and design of the portfolios, there were commonalities among all courses and types of portfolios.

a. **Introducing the Process:** Initially students were introduced to the concept and purpose of portfolios for each course. General procedures and calendars were presented to guide students when building their portfolios. Whether course or career portfolio, each type had different steps to create it. Examples of completed portfolios were shown to enhance students' understanding, to spark their ideas, and to generate questions regarding the process.

b. **Metaphors and Navigation:** Students developed the concept of their portfolio designs and presented them for brainstorming and approval. These concepts included defining the visual metaphor the portfolio would follow graphically and describing the structure the portfolio would adhere to. Visualizing a graphic metaphor such as a book or a Web site aided students in creating the organization, storyboard, behavior, look, and graphic feel of their portfolio pages, as well as designing effective navigation. A linear portfolio would be viewed in a sequential way, one page at a time. There might be a cover, table of contents, chapters, and an order to the portfolio contents like a book. A portfolio using a Web structure could be viewed in any order the user chose, having the ability through navigation to jump from one content area to another.

c. **Templates:** Students built templates for their portfolio cover and pages in the software in which they had expertise, such as Microsoft PowerPoint, Adobe Photoshop, or Microsoft Word. These templates became the pages of their portfolios on which they would place the text, video, images, and links to document that comprised their portfolio content. Special attention was given to using color creatively, creating intuitive navigation, and ensuring a professional appearance. Since the portfolios were designed as primary digital documents to be viewed on the computer, screen design, resolution, and legibility issues were introduced. Web-safe colors and system fonts were selected as universal design elements for consistent viewing across platforms. Graphics were created or optimized for screen viewing at 72 pixels per inch (ppi). The dimension of the portfolio pages was designed for computers with a resolution of 800 by 600 pixels.

d. **Artifacts:** Documents, projects, and video that students felt represented their best works and abilities were collected as artifacts for the portfolios; then they were stored. In the case of course portfolios, this stage was repeated throughout the course to the completion. The instructor reviewed students' selections periodically, and students were prompted to select or create effective artifacts. In addition to collecting and storing the original files, paper artifacts were digitized by scanning and all digital files were optimized so that two files for each artifact were saved. Optimization included sizing and using image compression to create files that would view efficiently on screen in the portfolio presentation.

e. **Tutorials:** Element K (2005) online tutorials were made available to the students in the computer labs. One-to-one support with software was provided where required. Students needed special help in evaluating their academic experiences to edit their artifacts or create their résumés. Step-by-step guides were given to help students prepare their multimedia (i.e., digital video, audio, and animation) artifacts for inclusion in their portfolios.

f. **Incorporation and Reflection:** Students arranged their prepared artifacts in their portfolio templates to construct the portfolio. In course portfolios, students added reflective text with each artifact to recall their experience in fulfilling each assignment.

g. **Grading and Presentations:** Students handed in their portfolios at mid-term for grading as well as giving a presentation of their concepts and progress to their classmates for critique.
h. **Ongoing Evaluation Methods:** Portfolio evaluation was ongoing by both peers and faculty, while students continued to collect, create, and prepare their artifacts throughout the semester. Using set rubrics allowed instructors to give formal evaluation to these portfolios.
i. **Distribution:** When completed, students created a final CD or DVD for distribution.
j. **CD/DVD Enhancement:** Students designed CD labels, jewel case inserts, and collateral pieces delivered on paper toward their final presentation of the portfolio and for grading.

Design Considerations

a. **Software:** The software chosen for the creation of the digital portfolios was different for each course. The common challenges were that the resulting portfolios had to meet the criteria of being cross-platform, easily distributed, and in a common format that most viewers would be likely to open successfully. In some cases the software was part of the course design, where all students used a common program, Macromedia Director, to build their interactive portfolios. In other cases the students were encouraged to build their portfolio templates in software in which they already had competency, such as PowerPoint or Microsoft Word. In these courses students constructed their final portfolios in the portable document format (PDF) using Adobe Acrobat. The completed page templates were exported, saved, or printed to PDF. They were then assembled into a single PDF portfolio document for insertion of hyperlinking navigation controls and appropriate placement of multimedia files.
b. **Effective Formats:** The digital portfolios were designed to be viewed primarily on the computer screen. This meant that the artifacts were prepared to the monitor resolution of 72 ppi. Also the dimensions of the templates were designed to view completely on a standard screen without scrolling using 800 by 600 pixels. Documents or artifacts that could not be presented effectively in this format were prepared and linked to the electronic document to download for viewing outside of the portfolio environment.
c. **Use of Multimedia:** The ability of students to demonstrate their skills and experiences through motion media was one thing that made digital portfolios more functional than traditional paper portfolios as both a course and a career tool. Multimedia added an important dimension to the digital portfolios. It was relatively easy to prepare, incorporate, and present multimedia in the portfolio environment. Students who were not familiar with the creation or preparation of multimedia required more support and instruction in creating this type of artifact. The types of multimedia used included video, animation, Flash documents, and audio. Adobe Acrobat and Director, two programs used to create the portfolios, both support multimedia. Audio and video were edited and formatted using Final Cut, iMovie, Premiere, or Pinnacle Studio. Animation was created in ImageReady or Flash and formatted in a video program or QuickTime Pro.

Digital File Storage

a. **Suggested Storage Media:** Digital portfolios and the collection of full resolution digital artifacts can make the planning and selection of storage media one of the first decisions required to implement digital portfolios in a course. Storage media needs to be portable, easily accessible, and affordable, whether purchased by the student or the school. Storage for artifacts should be permanent and redundant so that if one drive or disk fails, students will have a backup and not lose any of their artifacts. Moving files back and forth among class, computer labs, and desktop was done effectively with CDs and USB flash drives. Some students used 100-750 MB Zip disks, while some had file sizes that required DVDs. Neither of the authors' schools at the time had large network storage to prepare and save students' work, though they had limited local network drive space for temporary storage of student work in the labs.

b. **Final Portfolio Storage**: The finished portfolios were planned to fit on a standard CD with a 700 MB capacity, although some students with large motion files prepared their portfolios for DVDs. Students exercised further creativity by designing CD labels and jewel case inserts. The size of the storage media depended on the artifacts the students collected. If there was heavy use of video or other multimedia, more storage space was required than for primarily text documents.

Problems, Glitches, and Suggestions

a. **Software Availability:** Chances are that students have access to the software that they used to create their artifacts originally. The problem may come when they have to edit artifacts in software they have not used, such as audio or video editing programs or PDF creation tools. Seeing portfolios as a cross-curriculum activity and Adobe Acrobat as a business standard, we sought campus-wide licenses to be purchased by the universities. At first we purchased department licenses for our labs to demonstrate proof of concept to support this request.

b. **Adequate Hardware Storage:** Students in our programs were not required to purchase portable external hard drives, and the university did not provide large network storage, so we encouraged students to use the least expensive alternatives, disk storage. This included CDs, DVDs, and Zip disks. Students frequently chose to use high-capacity USB flash drives to move files from the lab computers to their home computers, but did not use these devices for long-term storage.

c. **Training Resources:** Students come to portfolio creation with all levels of skills with the broad variety of software that they may want to use to produce their portfolios. To support a large group of students in software training individually or even in small groups might pose too great a burden on the teacher, so other resources were sought. Two were used successfully. Element K online tutorial subscriptions were purchased for the department computer lab for student use. Safari Tech (2005) book subscriptions were purchased through the library for the software titles most used by the project.

d. **Student-Teacher Interaction Time:** In the media courses, building portfolios was part of the regularly scheduled and conducted curriculum. Contrasted to that was the independent study approach used by the business MIS course. The instructor scheduled one hour twice a week for any or all of the students to meet as a group to discuss their progress. Many frequently asked questions (FAQs) were assembled by the students, and they made up FAQ sheets for distribution and for posting in Blackboard, the course management system used by the university. Informal peer-to-peer instruction was most evident during students' lab time. Other interaction was through Blackboard discussion boards, e-mail, faculty office hours, and informal chance meetings. Students had to be reminded to exhaust the software training resources as well as the above-mentioned Blackboard features before bringing questions to the instructor. Emphasis was on the quest for independent learning as a secondary goal in the portfolio development process.

e. **Lost Data:** It is an inevitable trait of computer creation that data is occasionally lost. For us, this most commonly occurred when disks failed or were lost. Sometimes students accidentally overwrote original files. Drives failed. The only solution is to make sure that all work, all artifacts, all prepared files are backed up at least to one other source as mentioned above in the discussion on storage. For critical files, it is not unreasonable to back it up twice.

Figure 1. Course portfolio using notebook metaphor

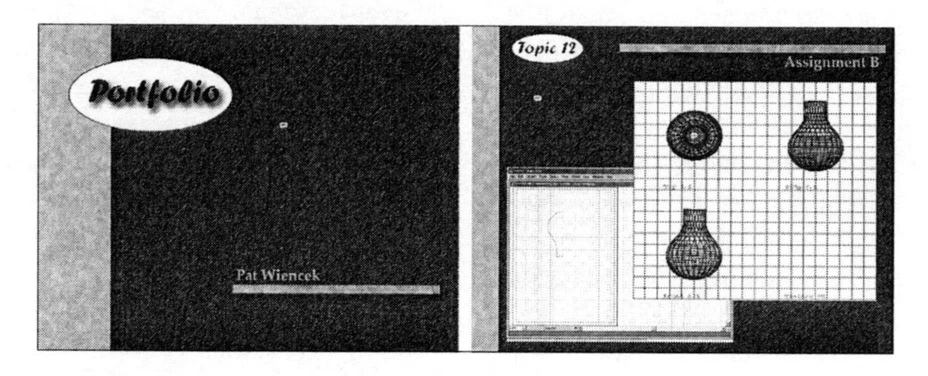

Figure 2. Course portfolio using book metaphor

Figure 3. Course portfolio using scrapbook metaphor

Figure 4. Career portfolio using Web site metaphor

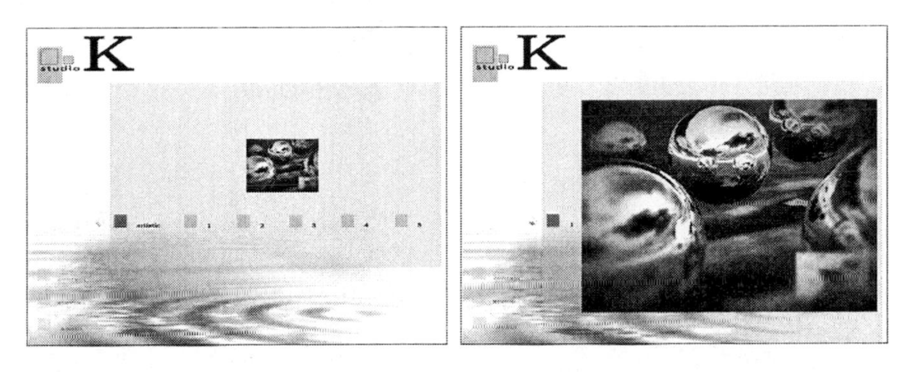

Figure 5. Career portfolio using PowerPoint metaphor

Figure 6. Career portfolio using art gallery metaphor

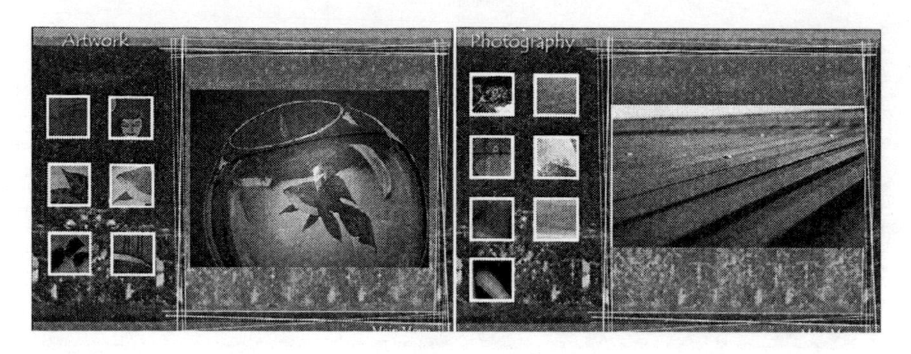

CONCLUSION

Compiling their digital portfolios was a strong asset in the students' learning paths. It served not only as an archive for precious material that may be otherwise lost over the years but it also served as an organizing principle. Students remember what they do and what they produce. Their portfolios captured a moment in time when the students were acquiring the skills and competencies needed for their careers. The reflections they made when collecting and archiving their projects allowed them to make cohesive connections between concepts learned in various courses. The authors hope that sharing their experiences in helping students to compile their electronic portfolios will encourage other educators to engage in this creative process, smoothing the students' pathways from classroom to career.

REFERENCES

Element K Online. (n.d.). *E-learning*. Retrieved May 25, 2005, from http://www.elementk.com

Poore, C. (2001). *Building your career portfolio*. Franklin Lakes, NJ: Career Press.

Safari Books Online, LLCS. (n.d.). Retrieved May 25, 2005, from http://www.safaribooksonline.com

Satterthwaite, F., & D'Orsi, G. (2003). *The career portfolio workbook*. New York: McGraw-Hill.

Williams, A., & Hall, K. (2001). *Creating your career portfolio*. Upper Saddle River, NJ: Prentice-Hall.

KEY TERMS

Artifact: An object created or designed for presentation. Examples of portfolio artifacts are text documents, Web pages, presentations, research papers, assessment instruments, original projects, academic or external teamwork projects, internships, presentation videos, certificates of achievement, spreadsheets, databases, digital images, and multimedia demonstrations.

Career Portfolios: Collections of artifacts used to validate claims of professional expertise made by prospective employees or for promotional justification.

Image Compression: A technique based on fractal mathematics for reducing the amount of digitized information needed to store electronically a visual image such as a movie.

Knowledge Worker: One who works in an industry that produces information rather than goods, such as management consultancy and computer programming.

PDF: An acronym for portable document format, which is a universal file format that preserves all the fonts, formatting, images, and color of a source file, regardless of the application or platform used to create it. Compacted PDF files can be exchanged, viewed, navigated, and printed with free Adobe Reader software.

Rubrics: A set of printed rules or instructions for performing a certain task. Used for evaluation or assessment by instructors and self-evaluation by students.

Storyboard: A set of sketches or slides, arranged in sequence on panels, outlining the progression of artifacts that make up the portfolio.

Templates: A master or pattern from which other similar things can be made. Can be built in any software and become portfolio pages containing text, video, images, and links.

Chapter XII
Using ePortfolios to Foster Peer Assessment, Critical Thinking, and Collaboration

Heidi J. Stevenson
University of the Pacific, USA

ABSTRACT

An ePortfolio is frequently seen as a space for electronically compiling and storing student work. After completing assignments, students generally submit their ePortfolio to an instructor, prospective employer, or other assessor. This chapter questions if the typical use of ePortfolios could be modified to create opportunities to encourage students (elementary school through graduate school) to engage in critical thinking, and provide feedback to their peers.

INTRODUCTION

In this chapter a model for computer-mediated anonymous peer assessment of ePortfolios is described in which students review each other's work and provide feedback electronically. This model results in increased opportunities for students to develop reflective and critical thinking skills, the ability to evaluate and provide thoughtful responses to different points of view, and techniques they can use to encourage and support the work of other students.

An ePortfolio is frequently seen as a space for electronically compiling and storing student work. After completing assignments, students generally submit their ePortfolio to an instructor, prospective employer, or other assessor. This chapter questions if the typical use of ePortfolios could be modified to create opportunities to encourage students (elementary school through graduate school) to engage in critical thinking, and provide feedback to their peers.

In this chapter a model for computer-mediated anonymous peer assessment of ePortfolios is described in which students review each other's work and provide feedback electronically. This model results in increased opportunities for students to develop reflective and critical thinking skills, the ability to evaluate and provide thoughtful responses to different points of view, and techniques they can use to encourage and support the work of other students.

REVIEW OF RESEARCH ON ePORTFOLIOS

The use of paper portfolios for assessment in education began in the 1980s primarily in college writing classes to address the need for more effective assessment and accountability measures in higher education (Belanoff, Elbow, & Fontaine, 1991, in Barnett, 2005). The practice of using portfolios was also implemented in K-12 classrooms, in response to high-stakes testing. K-12 schools used portfolios as a medium for students to showcase skills that could not be measured by standardized forms of assessment. Recently, universities have begun to explore numerous options for the use of the electronic version of portfolios.

Initially, each student had one portfolio serving the purpose of showcasing student work over time. The students collected examples of their work (sometimes referred to as artifacts), then they ideally reflected on their learning process, and afterwards provided their portfolio to an instructor, institution, or employer for evaluation. This process was restricted to a fairly small audience and provided limited opportunities to enhance the learning process.

With the advent of the electronic portfolio and the ease in which it may be presented to multiple audiences, the ePortfolio requirements began to serve many purposes that sometimes conflicted. Barnett (2005) observes that there are philosophical differences (e.g., constructivist and positivist) in the goals and purposes related to ePortfolios, and points to the need for a student to have more than one portfolio to address the requirements of varied content and objectives.

Greenberg (2004) refers to three different types of ePortfolios addressing various goals, including: (1) the showcase ePortfolio, which is generally designed to show work to future employers and usually entails the organization of materials after the work has been created; (2) a structured ePortfolio, which is typically created in response to standardized expectations, and therefore the organization meets predefined expectations for work that has yet to be created (e.g., ePortfolios used for the licensing of instructors); and (3) a learning ePortfolio provides students with the opportunity to tell the story of their learning (Barnett, 2005), and the organization evolves as the work is created (Greenburg, 2004).

There are currently no standardized terms associated with the various types of ePortfolios. The ePortConsortium (2003) and Barnett (2005) make reference to ePortfolios with similar characteristics, but use alternative terminology. The current chapter will use the terminology and definitions associated with the three types of ePortfolios as outlined by Greenberg (2004).

REVIEW OF RESEARCH ON PEER REVIEW

Vygotsky (1978) states that people learn by making meaning through their social dialogue and interactions with their environment. Peer assessment offers opportunities for students to develop as reflective learners as they construct knowledge from critically reading and evaluating the work of others (Sambell & McDowell, 1998; Rowland, 2000; Bostock, 2000b). Through providing evaluations to their peers, students are able to develop important skills as critical thinkers (Juwah, 2003; Dochy, Segers, & Slujismans, 1999; Bostock, 2000; Heywood, 2000; Topping, 1998; Boud, Cohen, & Sampson, 1999). Developing the ability to provide meaningful feedback can be an important skill for students throughout their education and professional lives (Brown, Rust, & Gibbs, 1994).

Peer assessment provides opportunities for students to see their work from multiple perspectives, and these points of view can provide valuable feedback as to how the reviewed students' work can be improved (Bostock, 2000; Robinson, 1999; Topping, 1998; Perry, 1988). Peer assessment (Topping, 1998), and computer-mediated assessment in particular, can also offer multiple perspectives in a more immediate fashion than that from one instructor.

The quality of peer assessment relies heavily on invested peers who feel confident in their ability to provide meaningful feedback. Shen, Bieber, and Hiltz (2004) and Svinicki (2001) found that students might not perceive that they are adequately capable of offering meaningful feedback to a peer and therefore are reluctant to participate in peer review. To develop feelings of competence and confidence in evaluating others' work, students must be made aware of: (1) the expectations of the assignment, (2) criteria used to assess that assignment, and (3) examples of quality constructive feedback on this particular assignment using the specified assessment criteria.

Some researchers have purported that peer review may reduce the time instructors invest in evaluating students' work (Boud, 2002; Juwah, 2003; Bhalerao & Ward, 2001). While this may be true for some instructors, the author and others (e.g., Bostock, 2000) believe that when used as intended, peer review may actually take more instructor evaluation time. Regardless, to effectively implement a productive computer-mediated anonymous peer assessment program that fosters critical thinking, the instructor must offer supports at many junctures throughout the process.

THE ROLE OF THE INSTRUCTOR IN PEER REVIEW

The participation of the instructor in peer review is essential for student success. The instructor needs to provide clear objectives, assessment criteria, modeling, monitoring, and feedback to facilitate the process of effective peer review.

Clear Assignment Objectives and Expectations

Designing any form of assessment begins with the end in mind. Ramsden (1992) asserts that assessment guides instruction, and Boud (1990) stresses the importance of aligning assessment practices with curricular goals. One must take stock of the philosophical underpinnings and goals that guide the assignment and assessment method chosen.

Clear Assessment Criteria

Many researchers have heralded the importance of providing clear expectations to students regarding their assignment requirements and the manner in which assignments will be assessed (Race, 1999; Issacs, 1999; Topping, 1998). Rubrics or checklists are commonly used tools to facilitate assessment. In certain cases, and particularly with structured ePortfolios, there are existing assessment criteria established by an institution or credentialing agency. In other instances where criteria are not established by a source outside the classroom (e.g., most showcase and learning ePortfolios), an instructor may choose to co-create criteria for the assessment with students. Student involvement in the assessment process appears to increase their motivation to participate and their understanding of assessment criteria (Baume, 2001; Biggs, 1999; Race, 1995).

Training in and Modeling of Assessment

Clear criteria are the first step in assisting students with peer assessment, and as stated by Bostock (2000) and Murphy (2001), the ability to provide quality peer feedback is developed by offering guidance to students. Nilson (2002) observes that instructors need to create assessment tools and activities, which encourage students to use higher-level thinking skills, by asking thought-provoking questions, and providing guidance as to the most effective method of evaluating a particular assignment.

Monitoring Feedback

To insure that peers are providing meaningful feedback, Bostock (2000) among others (e.g. Topping, 1998), maintain that monitoring the quality of the peer review process and providing ongoing feedback are essential. This may be a difficult and somewhat time-consuming process for the instructor, but computer-mediated environments serve to economize this procedure.

Working in a computer-mediated environment provides various ways in which an instructor can monitor student feedback. In an effort to support students in becoming critical thinkers and having the capacity to provide constructive feedback, the instructor must scaffold students (Whipp, 2003). Nilson (2002) proposes providing guiding questions or other activities that assist students in critically evaluating peer assignments. Another way to assist students is for the instructor to provide comments on peer feedback so that both the assessor and the assessed may view it and benefit from the instructor's comments. Also instructors can provide examples of student feedback to the class (face-to-face or via a discussion board) and have students analyze the quality of the evaluation, offer suggestions as to how the feedback can be improved, present alternative feedback, and post their views on a discussion board.

The feedback and discussion may be more effective if students' comments are contributed anonymously. The instructor may need to carefully monitor proper use of feedback, because in an anonymous environment there are added risks that students may engage in flaming (using abusive language) and/or providing overly critical feedback. These concerns will be addressed in a later section concerning anonymity.

Provide Opportunities for Multiple Reviewers

Employing multiple peer reviewing (more than one peer providing feedback on an assignment), students are able to receive several points of view regarding their work (Nilson, 2002). If they receive similar feedback after a number of reviews, students may be able to identify areas in need of change. Multiple reviewers not only provide feedback on areas that need to be improved (Race, 1995), but also help with insuring the reliability and validity of feedback (Bostock, 2000).

Computer-Mediated Reviewing

Computers and the use of the Internet or intranet can vastly increase the efficiency of peer review of ePortfolios because they can store and share various forms of work (e.g., word processing documents, movies, Web sites, blogs). The computer also affords the opportunity for peers to submit work and provide feedback anonymously (Bostock, 2000; Bahlerao & Ward, 2001; Chapman, 2001).

Online communities can be fostered and developed through the use of a computer-mediated peer review system. This is particularly valuable in situations where students may have limited face-to-face time together (such as in some student teaching programs or online courses). Walther (1992, 1996) found that over time, an online community may also allow people to experience interpersonal levels that surpass those of face-to-face interactions.

ROLE OF ANONYMITY IN COMPUTER-MEDIATED COMMUNICATION (CMC)

Due to the history of education as being conducted in a context of face-to-face interactions, anonymity was not regarded as a relevant avenue of educational research. Due to the recent popularity of computer-mediated communication through e-mail, the Internet, and online classes, anonymity has become a more pertinent, although sparsely investigated, area of research.

Much of the research that exists on anonymity was conducted in the mid- to late 1990s in response to people's behavior in chat rooms. During that time, many people would abuse their anonymity and "flame" other people by addressing them through using rude words or ideas, generally acting differently from how they would behave if their identity were included with their comments (Bloch, 2002; Debard & Guidara, 1999; Rheingold, 1994). Even if a person's identity is known, there are still risks that misunderstandings may ensue in the absence of face-to-face context (Bloch, 2002).

In an educational setting it was found that online anonymity had many advantages. Students reported an increased sense of equity (Collins & Berge, 1995; McComb, 1994) and an expectation that they would be treated with less prejudice (Rheingold, 1994). Many students feel less social pressure in an anonymous environment and therefore are more willing to openly express their opinions (Zhao, 1998; Atkinson, 1999). Thus, participation in peer review may increase.

A risk associated with complete anonymity is that if students feel that their identity is anonymous to all parties involved, including the instructor, they may engage in social loafing (Zhao, 1998). Social loafing is a situation in which people feel comfortable performing at a lower level or completing less work because they are not held accountable for their performance.

To control for any flaming, avoid social loafing, and provide students with the opportunity to receive appraisals of their feedback by the instructors, the author recommends the use of mutual anonymity. Mutual anonymity necessitates that the instructor is aware of the identities of all parties engaging in peer review, while the peers are unaware of each other's identities. Further, the author supposes that this form of anonymity will foster quality feedback and optimal participation among students. Anonymity may free students from incurring risks of social constraints, allowing them to feel comfortable to express their opinions without social conflict (Atkinson, 1999).

VARIATIONS ON A THEME: DIFFERENT ePORTFOLIOS WITH DIFFERENT GOALS REQUIRE DIFFERENT PEER FEEDBACK

There are three forms of ePortfolios referred to in this chapter—showcase, structured, and learning. Each of these ePortfolios has particular goals and a certain audience associated with its assessment. Therefore, all three portfolios require a somewhat different form of peer feedback and support from the instructor, which will be outlined below.

Showcase ePortfolio

The showcase ePortfolio is generally used to display work to prospective employers or clients. There are typically no set criteria by which this work will be assessed. Furthermore, the most meaningful feedback that can be provided on the work in this ePortfolio is likely specific to an area of expertise.

Peer Assessment for Showcase ePortfolio. Showcase ePortfolios can provide an opportunity for students to contribute to the criteria by which work will be assessed. It may be advantageous to engage students in researching assessment criteria via the Internet, and possibly interviewing employers or leaders in their field, to determine the most appropriate content and criteria to assess their showcase ePortfolios. After determining appropriate criteria for assessment, students (individually or as a group) can develop a rubric specific to their area of expertise.

Role of Anonymity for the Showcase ePortfolio. Mutual anonymity (where both the party submitting work and the assessing party are anonymous to each other with the instructor knowing both their identities) might be difficult to accomplish in regards to showcase ePortfolios. Since each student may be an expert in his or her area, have a personalized rubric, and possibly have conferred with others in the class or made an expert presentation, it may be difficult to protect the anonymity of the person being reviewed. This student's name does not need to be revealed, but classmates may be aware of each other's area of expertise. Regardless, the reviewer's identity may technically remain anonymous.

Role of Instructor for the Showcase ePortfolio. The role of the instructor may be to guide students not only through assessing each other's work and providing feedback, but also in determining the criteria by which their work should be assessed. The instructor, therefore, most likely needs to be informed on a variety of specialty areas. Ideally, the students will become experts in their area of interest and they will be able to adequately construct an appropriate rubric that the instructor will need to assess and provide suggestions for improvements. These rubrics could be shared with each other and possibly posted on the World Wide Web for future use by students in the course or others entering a similar field. Due to the students' development of expertise in a specific area, a great deal of consideration needs to be devoted to the pairings of multiple reviewers.

Structured ePortfolio

The structured ePortfolio is usually designed to meet preset requirements by an accrediting agency or institution of higher education. Therefore, criteria should be readily available outlining requirements for the components of the ePortfolio and the tool used for assessment.

Role of Peer Assessment in Structured ePortfolios. Due to the preset requirements and assessment tools made available to students, with the proper training they should be able to adequately assess each other's work and make constructive suggestions for improvement. Structured ePortfolios are generally directly related to receiving a certificate, degree, or credential. Therefore, students are usually invested in doing well.

Through engaging in discussion and the peer review process, students can interpret the requirements of the assignment and determine the best methods to demonstrate, in their structured ePortfolios, that they have met or exceeded these requirements. Having multiple invested reviewers using the established rubric or other assessment tool may not only contribute to the quality of work of the person being assessed, but may also assist the student assessor to better understand the requirements of the assignment (possibly improving the assessor's future drafts of this assignment). Furthermore, reading the assignments and critically evaluating the work of their peers may afford opportunities for students to construct new knowledge and gain an overall deeper understanding of the area being assessed.

Role of Instructor in Structured ePortfolios. Many times official assessors are extensively trained in the expectations related to the components of the structured ePortfolio and assessment system. Students are generally trained in the expectations of the assignment, but may not receive training in how to utilize the associated rubric or other assessment criteria. To fully understand how to adequately complete the assignment, students may need to have the use of the assessment tool modeled for them.

Some believe that it would be prudent to provide students with examples of work that have scored at different levels, from excellent to poor, on the assessment tool (typically a rubric) provided, whereas others believe that students should be exposed to only the highest scoring work. This decision is one that should be considered carefully by the assessing institution and instructor.

As discussed earlier in this chapter, the instructor needs to support the reflective process through modeling and scaffolding (Whipp, 2003). Through this process the instructor should also specify the type of language and associated vocabulary with reflection. Requirements for a structured ePortfolio may allow for affective language, but are most likely referring to the use of analytical language to reflect on one's work. To assist in the scaffolding process, the instructor may even choose to limit the use of words that seem cliché or do not reflect a deeper level of thinking (Chen, 2005).

Ideally, the instructor facilitates reflection and evaluation concerning what one learned from the process of evaluating others' work, and how that work compared to their own. Also, students reflect on how the process of assessing another person's work factored into improvements that they made to their own structured ePortfolios or their practice. The instructor needs to encourage students to analyze what they learned through participating in the peer review process and support the reflective process through scaffolding.

Learning ePortfolio

Learning ePortfolios exhibit what students have learned, but are more student-directed and less rigid in their makeup. Compared to the structured and showcase ePortfolios, the learning ePortfolios are more student driven in their goals and content. Due to this student-centered nature of the learning ePortfolio, students are able to construct their own knowledge, and the author believes that this format offers the richest arena for developing reflective and critical thinking skills.

The learning ePortfolios are usually shown to the instructor to demonstrate evidence of learning and growth in a particular area. Samples of work and reflections are included that do not have a right or wrong answer. As a result of the student-centered nature of these portfolios, there is more flexibility for directions regarding the goals the instructor has and the learning ePortfolio's contents.

Co-Creating Assessment Criteria. One way in which instructors may choose to use the learning ePortfolio is to request that students identify specific learning objectives (related to a particular course or subject area) by which their learning ePortfolio would be assessed. The students would then provide evidence, through samples of their work and reflections on what they have learned, that show confirmation that they have met these learning objectives. Allowing students to choose goals and the samples of their work supports students in having ownership of their learning, and the opportunity to construct their own meaning.

Student Reflection. Reflection is important to show evidence of learning. This is true with all three ePortfolios, but even more so with learning ePortfolios because it demonstrates students' ability to think critically about their learning. Through the process of sharing evidence of learning through reflections, others become cognizant of the knowledge gained by the learning ePortfolio author.

Online Community of Practice Through Learning ePortfolios. Another objective an instructor may choose for a portion of the learning ePortfolio is to create an online community of practice (Cambridge, Kaplan, & Sutter, 2005). This would be a community in which students could share their knowledge and emotions with their peers.

One way to create a community of practice through the peer review of learning ePortfolios is to have students include a blog (an acronym for a Web log), which is similar to an online diary. Through their blogs students may chronicle their life experiences in general or focus on a particular topic related to course work or training.

Online interactive journal writing can provide many opportunities for student learning (Whipp, 2003; Chen, 2005; Andrusyszyn & Davie, 1997). Keeping blogs provides students with a record of their growth over time in regards to their experiences, and therefore, students will be able to reflect on the lessons they have learned. Interactive blogs can also allow students to request assistance from others about various situations or challenges they may be facing. In addition, students may choose to read each others' blogs and get a sense that they are not the only person who is having challenges or successes in certain areas. All these avenues can support students in developing a community of practice on a certain topic or area.

Anonymity and Community of Practice. Sharing blogs anonymously may encourage students to reveal more personal information and assist them in feeling as if they can write and share without being judged. With anonymity they are also free of racial or other stereotypes as they write and have others read their work (Rheingold, 1994). In addition to posting in their blogs anonymously, students could also provide advice or feedback in an anonymous fashion. Shy students (Atkinson, 1999), English learners (ELs), non-auditory learners, or any students that may be hesitant to participate in class discussions may feel more inclined to participate in a computer-mediated discussion. Increased opportunities for participation may be afforded to the additional time students have to consider the construction of their feedback (e.g., philosophically, logically, grammatically, etc.), compared to the fast pace of conversations in a face-to-face classroom environment.

Again, the instructor would need to closely monitor anonymous feedback to control for flaming. In the case of using blogs in learning ePortfolios, instructors may even choose to act as moderators. In this case, feedback would not be provided to peers until the instructor was able to review it. This could hopefully assist in assuring that all feedback was constructive in nature.

Sharing Resources. For certain courses it may be advantageous for students to share resources included in their learning ePortfolios. The instructor may choose to create an organizational system specific to the course content and goals to facilitate this process. For example, students studying to become teachers (student teachers) may benefit from a system that allows them to view, and in effect, exchange lesson plans for certain subjects or grade levels.

The course instructor may choose to create a system in which peers give feedback on the exchanged resources. In the example of the lesson plan exchange above, student teachers may give feedback on modifications they successfully made to a lesson plan, suggestions they have for its improvement, or feedback on their experience teaching the lesson plan. In addition, student teachers may opt to share videos of their teaching or blogs of their experiences in classrooms.

Learning ePortfolio authors at any stage in their education may want to share writing, artwork, video projects, and so forth with their peers to receive feedback for projects in which the instructor does not require peer review. Their experience sharing resources and experiences through their learning ePortfolio may even encourage students to create an informal peer review system or online community of practice separate from the course in which they may be enrolled.

CHALLENGES

Despite the numerous advantages of supporting critical thinking and constructivism associated with the use of a computer-mediated anonymous peer assessment system, there are also many challenges. The author has been able to find software that promotes complete anonymity, but has had difficulties finding software that easily promotes mutually anonymous peer review (instructors are able to monitor peer review feedback, but the students are anonymous to each other).

In addition to having the necessary requirements of computer-mediated mutual anonymity, the model also necessitates ease of use by the students and instructors. Instructors require the ability to pair groups of anonymous peers for reviewing work and providing feedback. The capabilities to provide feedback to and monitor the responses of students also need to be readily available to instructors. Students need to easily be able to identify which work is being submitted for peer review and also require the ability to provide password access to certain portions of the ePortfolios (such as in the case of the showcase ePortfolio).

This model relies not only on the operation of functional software, but also depends heavily on instructor involvement. Instructors need to invest a great deal of time in pairing peer reviewers, monitoring feedback, and providing advice. It is important that instructors continually monitor feedback to control for flaming, and also to encourage student participation. Feedback must be frequently given to scaffold students, through the instructors' modeling of effective constructive feedback. This scaffolding may be achieved by offering opportunities to evaluate and improve the feedback provided both as a class and with individual students.

FUTURE RESEARCH

There is a great deal of research that could be conducted on a model of computer-mediated anonymous peer review. One could determine the best software and organizational methods to effectively and easily facilitate the process of exchanging materials and instructor monitoring. Additional work is required in the area of anonymity, including which form of anonymity, if any, appears the most advantageous to student learning, and how this can best be achieved. Also, it would be quite interesting to determine what value students receive from giving and receiving feedback in an anonymous environment. Do they feel a part of a community of practice? Is peer feedback viewed as valuable information that contributes to student learning? Does the process of providing peer feedback increase students' levels of understanding and quality of their own work?

CONCLUSION

As one can see, there are numerous opportunities for research on this proposed model. Using an ePortfolio, the instructor may choose to implement a system in which peers are able to review each other's work. This will require effort on the instructor's part to set objectives for the assignment, establish criteria for the assessment of assignments, determine how peers should be matched for evaluation, and decide how to best facilitate the exchange of peer feedback. Despite the work involved in this endeavor, computer-mediated anonymous peer assessment appears to offer extensive opportunities for developing reflective, empathetic learners that are able to think critically and provide constructive feedback.

REFERENCES

Andrusyszyn, M. A., & Davie, L. (1997). Facilitating reflection through interactive journal writing in an online graduate course. *Journal of Distance Education, 12*(1-2), 103-126.

Atkinson, D. (1999). Student feedback collected using groupware. In K. Martin, N. Stanley, & N. Davison (Eds.), *Teaching in the Disciplines/Learning in Context—Proceedings of the 8th Annual Teaching Learning Forum,* The University of Western Australia.

Barnett, H. (2005). *White paper: Researching electronic portfolios and learner engagement.* Retrieved May 10, 2005, from http://electronicportfolios.com/reflect/whitepaper.pdf

Baume, D. (2001). *Briefing on assessment of portfolios.* Retrieved May 15, 2005, from http://www.ltsn.ac.uk/genericcentre/projects/assessment/assess_series/06Portfolios.rtf

Belanoff, P., Elbow, P., & Fontaine, S. I. (Eds.). (1991). *Nothing begins with n: New investigations of freewriting.* Carbondale, IL: Southern Illinois University Press.

Bhalerao, A., & Ward, A. (2001). Towards electronically assisted peer assessment. A case study. *ALT-J, 9*(1), 26-37.

Biggs, J. (1999). *Teaching for quality learning at university.* Buckingham: Society for Research into Higher Education & Open University Press.

Bloch, J. (2002). Student/teacher interaction via email: The social context of Internet discourse. *Journal of Second Language Writing, 11*(2), 117-134.

Bostock, S. (2000). *Student peer assessment, learning technology*. Retrieved May 19, 2005, from http://www.keele.ac.uk/depts/cs/Stephen_Bostock/doc/bostock_ peer_assessment.htm

Bostock, S. (2000b). *Computer assisted assessment: Experiments in three courses.* Retrieved May 19, 2005, from http://www.keele.ac.uk/depts/aa/landt/lt/docs/caa-ktn.htm

Boud, D. (1990). Assessment and the promotion of academic values. *Studies in Higher Education, 15*(1), 101-111.

Boud, D., Cohen, R., & Sampson, J. (1999). Peer learning and assessment. *Assessment and Evaluation in Higher Education, 24*(4), 413-426.

Brown, S., Rust C., & Gibbs, G. (1994). *Strategies for diversifying assessment in higher education.* Oxford: Oxford Centre for Staff Development.

Brown, S., Sambell, K., & McDowell, L. (1998). What do students think about assessment? In S. Brown (Ed.), *Peer assessment in practice* (pp. 107-112). Birmingham: SEDA.

Cambridge, D., Kaplan, S., & Sutter, V. (2005). *Community of practice design guide: A step-by-step for designing & cultivating communities of practice in higher education.* Retrieved May 15, 2005, from http://www.educause.edu/LibraryDetailPage/666?ID=NLI0531

Chapman, O.L. (2001). *The white paper: A description of CPR.* Retrieved June 19, 2002, from http://cpr.molsci.ucla.edu

Chen, H. (2005, April 26). Electronic portfolio workshop. In *Proceedings of the Educause Meeting,* San Francisco.

Collins, M. P., & Berge, Z. L. (1995). Introduction: Computer mediated communications and the online classroom in higher education. In Z. L. Berge & M. P. Collins (Eds.), *Computer mediated communication and the online classroom: Vol. 2: Higher education* (pp. 1-10). Cresskill, NJ: Hampton Press.

DeBard, R., & Guidera, S. (1999). Adapting asynchronous communication to meet the seven principles of effective teaching. *Journal of Educational Technology Systems, 28*(3), 219-239.

Dochy, F., Segers, M., & Sluijsmans, D. M. A. (1999). The use of self, peer and co-assessment in higher education: A review. *Studies in Higher Education, 24*(3), 331-350.

Greenberg, G. (2004). The digital convergence: Extending the portfolio model [electronic version]. *Educause Review, 39*(4), 28-37.

Heywood, J. (2000). *Assessment in higher education.* London: Jessica Kingsley.

Issacs, G. (1999). *Brief briefing: Peer and self assessment.* Retrieved May 15, 2005, from http://www.tedi.uq.edu.au/conferences/A_conf/papers/Isaacs.html

Juwah, C. (2003). Using peer assessment to develop skills and capabilities. *USDLA Journal, 17*(1).

McComb, M. (1994). Benefits of computer-mediated communication in college courses. *Communication Education, 43*(2), 159-170.

Murphy, R. (2001). *A briefing on key skills in higher education: Assessment series No. 5.* York: Learning and Teaching Support Network.

Perry, G. (1988). Different worlds in the same classroom. In P. Ramsden (Ed.), *Improving learning: New perspectives* (pp. 145-161). London: Kogan Page.

Race, P. (1995). The art of assessing. *The New Academic, 4*(3), 3-6.

Race, P. (1999). *How to get a good degree.* Buckingham: Open University Press.

Ramsden, P. (1992). *Learning to teach in higher education.* London: Routledge.

Rheingold, H. (1994). *The virtual community: Finding connection in a computerized world.* London: Secker & Warburg.

Robinson, J. (1999). Electronically assisted peer review. In S. Brown, P. Race, & J. Bull (Eds.), *Computer-assisted assessment in higher education. Staff and educational development series.* Birmingham: SEDA.

Rowland, S. (2000). *The enquiring university teacher*. Buckingham: SRHE & Open University Press.

Shen, J. K. E., Bieber, M., & Hiltz, S. R. (2004). Traditional in-class examination vs. collaborative online examination in asynchronous learning networks: Field evaluation results. In *Proceedings of the 2004 Americas Conference on Information Systems,* New York.

Svinicki, M. D. (2001). Encouraging your students to give feedback. In K. G. Lewis (Ed.), *Techniques and strategies for interpreting student evaluations. New directions in teaching and learning 87* (pp. 17-24). San Francisco: Jossey-Bass.

Topping, K. (1998). Peer assessment between students and colleges and universities. *Review of Educational Research, 68*(3), 249-276.

Vygotsky, L. S. (1978). *Mind and society: The development of higher mental processes.* Cambridge: Harvard University Press.

Walther, J. B. (1992). Relational aspects of computer-mediated communication: Experimental observations over time. *Organization Science, 6*(2), 186-203.

Walther, J. B. (1996). Computer-mediated communication: Impersonal, interpersonal, and hyperpersonal interaction. *Communication Research, 23*(1), 3-43.

Whipp, J. (2003). Scaffolding critical reflection in online discussions: Helping prospective teachers think deeply about field experiences in urban schools. *Journal of Teacher Education, 54*(4), 321-333.

Zhao, Y. (1998) The effects of anonymity on computer-mediated peer review. *International Journal of Educational Telecommunications, 4*(4), 311-345.

KEY TERMS

All definitions are taken from dictionary.com.

Assessment: A procedure for critical evaluation; a means of determining the presence, quality, or truth of something; a trial: a test of one's eyesight; subjecting a hypothesis to a test; a test of an athlete's endurance.

BLOG: An online diary; a personal chronological log of thoughts published on a Web page; also called Weblog, Web log.

Collaborative Learning: The act, process, or experience of gaining knowledge or skill through working together, especially in a joint intellectual effort.

Educational Technology: Electronic or digital products and systems used for the act, process, or experience of gaining knowledge or skill.

Online Learning Community: The act, process, or experience of gaining knowledge or skill through working together via a computer or computer network, especially in a joint intellectual effort.

Peer Review: A person who has equal standing with another or others, as in rank, class, or age who does the following: (1) to look over, study, or examine again; (2) to consider retrospectively, look back on; (3) to examine with an eye to criticism or correction: reviewed the research findings; (4) to write or give a critical report on (a new work or performance, for example).

Technology-Mediated Learning: The act, process, or experience of gaining knowledge or skill through electronic or digital products and systems.

Chapter XIII
ePortfolios for Knowledge and Learning

Elizabeth Hartnell-Young
The University of Nottingham, UK

ABSTRACT

In the 21st century, we talk of knowledge as the new currency, and knowledge building as the work to be done in learning organizations. While knowledge building is activity directed outward towards the creation of knowledge itself, learning is a personal consequence of this process, the aspect that is directed to enhancing individual abilities and dispositions. This chapter considers how ePortfolios can support four aspects of lifelong learning in the knowledge economy: engagement with technology, representations of identity, developing critical multiliteracies, and global and local mobility. It argues that the focus should be on lifelong learners' capacity to create and communicate with digital technologies, rather than on rigid frameworks that reduce ePortfolio development to a series of pre-packaged choices.

LIVING IN THE KNOWLEDGE ECONOMY

In the knowledge economy—where knowledge is capital—new ways of working have arisen, often promoted by business and government to ensure a more flexible labour market. These include part-time employment for women and men, short-term contracts rather than lifetime security, and industrial legislation that encourages individual, rather than collective, approaches. People are told that they must take charge of their own career, be their own small business, create their own work (Bridges, 1997). Reflecting on these trends, Handy (1989) predicted the rise of portfolio workers: people who know what they offer and build up a portfolio of work rather than a regular job. However, not everyone who finds themselves in the position of portfolio worker has the self-knowledge or access to the tools required to present what they offer to the employment market (Hargreaves, 2004). Portfolio workers must be flexible and mobile, and they must be lifelong learners. It makes sense to argue that these portfolio workers need ePortfolios to chart their history and communicate their offerings.

Essentially, ePortfolios are containers for a selection of artefacts in the form of digital files—whether they be in audio, visual, or textual form, or a combination of these—with a focus on purpose: employment, family history, assessment, for example. This selection should not be confused with the *archive:* the collection from which the selection is made (Hartnell-Young & Morriss, 1999a). Love, McKean, and Gathercoal (2004) make a distinction between 'ePortfolios' and 'Webfolios', suggesting that the former are stored on transportable media such as CD-ROM and not accessible from the Web, but in this chapter the term ePortfolio includes all digital forms of representation.

Well-constructed ePortfolios could be expected to support portfolio workers' claims of employability, by providing an inventory of acquired knowledge and skills. They should, however, have a richer purpose: they should facilitate lifelong learning. Lifelong learners are said to be reflective and self-directed, active investigators and problem solvers, and effective communicators, among other things. ePortfolios have the potential to meet these needs too: they should encourage reflection on life and learning, suggest opportunities for action, raise problems to solve, and offer flexibility of presentation to communicate to a range of audiences. The absolute essentials of ePortfolios are purpose, reflection, and communication.

Lifelong learners, suggests Hargreaves (2004), know what they know, what they have to learn, and what they can do for an employer. This self-knowledge comes from spending some time in reflection on one's beliefs, values, and achievements: situating oneself in society. While Hargreaves notes that lifelong learning is sometimes thought of as referring only to post-compulsory schooling, the term clearly has the potential to be inclusive of all from the cradle to the grave. There is increasing evidence that lifelong learning does not start after schooling ends. Like the concept of mobile learning, it is a mindset that we carry with us from birth, as we explore our environment and learn from it and the people around us at every moment.

THE RELATIONSHIP BETWEEN KNOWLEDGE AND LEARNING IN A KNOWLEDGE SOCIETY

Dewey (1910) regarded knowledge as a product constructed by people and containing the meaning of objects and events. Learning is the process by which knowledge is created. Knowledge itself is in the form of objects (including principles and theories) to be considered, criticized, and improved by the learners (Bereiter & Scardamalia, 1998). Knowledge building is activity directed outward towards the creation of knowledge itself, while learning is a personal consequence of this process, the aspect that is directed to enhancing one's own abilities and dispositions. As Scardamalia and Bereiter (1999) put it, knowledge itself must be in the world, rather than in the mind. ePortfolios have the potential to present the collective store of knowledge of a group or organization to a wider audience, and to support corporate memory in times of change.

In a constructivist learning relationship, teachers require students to take responsibility for making their own meaning, rather than accepting prefabricated meanings of information or instruction. It is therefore seen as substantially different from a relationship where teachers as experts transfer knowledge to students. Attributes of constructivism are said to include student initiative, higher-level thinking, social discourse between students and with teachers, and the use of raw data, primary sources, and interactive materials to encourage multiple perspectives on an issue (Brooks & Brooks, 1993). Learners are expected to work towards autonomy and self-regulated learning, and to achieve greater understanding of the processes of learning itself. They become the observers of their own behaviour, and through reflection gauge their own progress, judge the extent to which their knowledge is effective action, and gain the insight necessary to improve their own learning (Brown & Palincsar, 1989). Teachers are expected to develop knowledge of the different learning styles of their students, thus enabling them to personalize learning.

Where learners are making meaning for themselves, and reflecting on their learning to become better at it, new assessment methods are required. Building on constructivism, those who promote situated learning argue that meaning is a product of activity and the culture and context in which that activity occurs (Brown & Palincsar, 1989; Brown, Collins, & Duguid, 1989; Lave & Wenger, 1994). Students in a situated learning environment, they also say, are engaged in *authentic* learning activities, which have a purpose that goes beyond demonstrating mastery of tasks, allowing students to learn and practise skills in real contexts where they are applicable, such as writing for publication in the press or designing Web sites for real clients. The collection of products into archives and ePortfolios is seen as a means of supporting the assessment of such authentic learning activities.

Reflection is an essential element that differentiates an ePortfolio from a simple repository of artefacts. It can be difficult for many learners to find the time and the skills for serious reflection, and rendered more difficult, as Barrett (2005) argues, by many of the assessment portfolio solutions that focus on the administrators' needs for assessment data rather than the individual's deep learning. She suggests a possible solution:

> *Portfolios should support an environment of reflection and collaboration. It is a rare system that supports those multiple needs. That is why I often advocate for three interconnected systems: an archive of student work, an assessment management system to document achievement of standards, and an authoring environment where students can construct their own electronic portfolios and reflective, digital stories of learning.* (Barrett, 2005, p. 14)

If the knowledge economy depends on access to and sharing of knowledge, ePortfolios have a purpose as containers of knowledge products that reflect the learning processes required to construct them. Their purpose then becomes broader than showcasing achievements or employability: for the individual creator they can capture a learning journey, while for society they can contribute to knowledge building by communicating knowledge from the mind into the world. In this chapter, ePortfolios are considered in light of four aspects of learning common in the twenty-first century: engaging with technology, representing identity, developing critical multiliteracies, and local and global mobility. From the stance of learners, ePortfolios can both support and be enhanced by consideration of these aspects.

ENGAGEMENT WITH TECHNOLOGY

A feature of the knowledge society is its capacity to use technology to build, store, and disseminate knowledge. However, as Castells (1999) noted, some uses of technology tend to place people in passive relationships, as if they have no power to control it for their learning. In contrast, a social-constructivist interpretation of technology places users in a position to claim back technology for the purpose of knowledge building. This is particularly relevant to the current work being done on ePortfolios around the world. In one sense, the notion of ePortfolios developed because it could. Print-based artefacts could be converted into digital format and with HTML, and users were able to make links between copious amounts of data, leading to a growing interest in creating personal digital archives, such as the Microsoft LifeBits project (Fontana, 2003). However, with massive databases underlying ePortfolio systems, the technology issues have become large scale, largely hidden from the users, and, as noted above, in some cases people are limited in reflecting on and learning from their work.

Among those favouring a user-centred approach, Leask and Pachler (2001) argue that software that helps users to process information, engage in abstract thinking, make knowledge construction processes apparent, and build classification systems is liberating and empowering because it allows for cognitive and creative thinking. It is in essence *empty*, allowing space for thinking and learning. This *creators-not-consumers* approach underpins the work of van Eeden and Thompson and the Student Youth Network (syn.fm), winners of a fully fledged community radio license in Melbourne (van Eeden, 2001). Computers are a medium for making other media. ePortfolio systems that take away this creativity by providing rigid structures and little freedom of choice are limiting the learning potential of the ePortfolio development process. Even the use of Web authoring programs can be disempowering, in that they hide the underlying HyperText Markup Language (HTML) from the gaze of the creator.

These concerns underpinned the *women@the cutting edge* project developed in Australia in the late 1990s. A group of women teachers and administrators in education came together to conceptualize, design, and create a collaborative digital portfolio showing evidence of their professional achievements (Hartnell-Young, 2001; Hartnell-Young & Morriss, 1999b). However the purposes were manifold. A constructivist approach to teachers' learning meant that the group collaborated in all aspects of the task: collecting evidence, reflecting on its value, selecting appropriate artefacts for a portfolio, and learning the necessary technical skills in a just-in-time way. Risk-taking, play, and loosely structured activities were encouraged, as well as extensive recording and reflection as a means of tracking learning and development, and celebration of milestones along the way. Participants gained a sense of shaping technology to their own purposes. This successful grassroots project was later supported by the telecommunications company, AT&T, and has underpinned further work with students and teachers.

ePortfolios have the potential to encourage engagement with technology, but this will not occur merely though their availability or the promise they offer. Pachler (2001) agrees that enabling users to create and distribute their own work makes them active participants in the culture creation process, but argues that they need to be taught basic and higher-order skills, such as informatic, visual, and critical media literacies, to avoid being exploited by software producers and distributors. This aspect is discussed later in the chapter.

REPRESENTATIONS OF IDENTITY

Much of the literature on identity is based on the notion of individual choice in identity creation. For Giddens (1991), individual lifestyle choices are a key to creating self-identity. Whether the choices are limited or abundant, a person engages in what Giddens terms the *reflexive project of the self.* One can see how ePortfolios have a part to play in the project, given their focus on the individual's life achievement and personal reflection. A schoolteacher engaged in ePortfolio development observed this, and wrote:

Identifying skills such as teamwork, listening with empathy and understanding, interacting within the community, and being persistent, requires us to value and acknowledge diverse aspects of students' lives and interests. Students are encouraged to draw upon wider experiences that may well be found outside the school context, to create a richer picture of who they are *[unitalicized emphasis added].* (Kane, 2004)

Similarly, in a research project using camera phones to capture evidence, it became apparent that even at a young age, people have a sense that it is useful to record some aspects that will go towards creating an identity. An eight-year-old made a video of his first ride on a horse "because you can keep it all your life," while others captured first occurrences of achieving learning outcomes and personal events. At the Queensland University of Technology, 40,000 students now have the opportunity to create an online ePortfolio. They are encouraged to record, reflect on, catalogue, and retrieve artefacts representing their identities within and outside the university. However, many authors, such as Strauss (1997), recognize that individuals create multiple identities, depending on context and purpose, in a social setting. This is a consideration for ePortfolios as communication tools for differing purposes: Which identity does one want to present to this employer or this teacher?

Most discussion around ePortfolios assumes an individualized approach to their production, with very little focus on creating collective ePortfolios in a collaborative manner. Yet this would seem to be a legitimate social constructivist activity, depending of course on the purpose of the task. In his book on communities of practice, Wenger (1998) argues that the purpose of education is to create identities, and Cope and Kalantzis (2000) state that the presentation of self and culture across a range of media are central elements in the new economy. "Who are we?" is perhaps a more complicated question than "Who am I?" The collective *project of selves* could have even greater potential than the individual ePortfolio movement.

ePortfolio development that encourages interaction through feedback mechanisms has the capacity to support identity formation as well as representation. In the symbolic interactionist perspective (Blumer, 1962), the processes by which definitions of self are constructed and negotiated are supported by symbols: mental representations of objects and events with agreed-upon social meanings. The communicative potential of ePortfolios as symbol-holders during the development phase, that is, as containers of negotiated content, is an area for further exploration. On the other hand, with the increasing numbers of relationships available through communication technologies, Gergen (2001) suggests that people are engaged in populating the self, leading to social saturation, and as this proceeds, the multiple identities can lead to increasing self-doubt. Perhaps the ePortfolio process, with its underpinning archive and the possibility of clarification and self-knowledge, will provide an anchor in this situation.

If constructing identities is an outcome of portfolio development, we need to consider to what extent the systems we devise are able to fulfil that purpose. If people are to be creators, rather than consumers, they need to attend to recording, selecting, and publishing material that presents individual and collective identities to others. While some systems allow for the 'academic me', the 'social me', and so on, it sometimes appears that software developers expect a definitive identity. And some ePortfolio systems even hide individuality or personality because of their dense and rigid structures. A more loosely coupled approach might allow greater creativity and foster the development of the many literacies that are required in the digital environment.

DEVELOPING CRITICAL MULTILITERACIES

"Multiliteracies" is a term that acknowledges cultural and linguistic diversity and the communication opportunities of new media. Those who are multiliterate can express themselves and make sense of the world through multiple modes: linguistic, visual, audio, gestural, and so on (Cope & Kalantzis, 2000). Similarly Unsworth (2001) argues that the notion of literacy needs to be reconceived as a plurality of literacies, and *becoming* literate is a more apt term than *being* literate.

What role can ePortfolios play in becoming literate? Where they are seen as communicating devices, looking outward, they embrace the broad range of literacies. Unsworth (2001) argues that, to become effective participants in emerging multiliteracies, people need to develop knowledge about linguistic, visual, and digital meaning-making systems. Cope and Kalantzis (2001) suggest that learning of multiliteracies must be situated in learners' own experience, and includes explicit teaching of a meta-language that describes design in the broadest sense, investigates the cultural context, and applies the designs in a new context. To transfer this thinking to ePortfolio development, one would start with a purpose owned by the users, and provide explicit information about the tools, learning processes, or other relevant needs. Then some critical appraisal by the users would establish which tools best suit the situation, and reflect on the communicated meanings of the content. Finally, transformed practice would see users contributing to the form and purposes as well as to the content of ePortfolios in an ongoing project of transformation. Where are the designers who can create such a fluid ePortfolio system at a large scale?

The concept of multiliteracies should accommodate the needs for accessibility to ePortfolio tools and products. The ability to be "critical" requires that people understand and control the media themselves so they can make informed decisions. Critical literacies for ePortfolio creators include judging the effectiveness of the various communication modes, and their appropriateness for particular audiences. They can "read the world" (Cope & Kalantzis, 2001). In a potential precursor to ePortfolio development, a group of students in regular schools in Melbourne created bilingual digital stories using AUSLAN, the Australian Sign Language, which is completely visual, and English, which is in this case the second language for the audience of hearing-impaired students. A narration recorded and played in English accompanies subtitles and signing through a split-screen technique. Although resource intensive, this project clearly bridges social and linguistic divides.

All those interested in successful ePortfolio development must also consider how we help potential audiences to learn more about ePortfolios as expressions of identity and how to make judgements about them. This means those who will view and assess ePortfolios, as well as their creators, need the skills of critical literacies. It is not yet clear whether many audiences are equipped to make judgements, yet it is a concern for career advisors, assessors, educators, and employers alike. While many believe that employers will value ePortfolios (Love et al., 2004), a recent Australian research study (Leece, 2004) found that only 10% of employers had heard of portfolios, 28% would consider using them for graduate recruitment, and most had not noticed any increase in their use.

LOCAL AND GLOBAL MOBILITY

Globalization describes the process of joining up the world's economic systems, enabling the flow of capital (including knowledge) across national and continental boundaries, and, it seems, increasing the hegemony of the English language through the Internet and the influence of powerful English-speaking nations. Knowledge building implies a flow of knowledge both locally and at a wider scale: indeed, it is people who mobilize knowledge. As knowledge travels rapidly, so do many people, whether portfolio workers offering employment, or others enjoying recreation or seeking self-understanding in various parts of the world. In the employment market it makes sense to have a means of communicating rich information about skills and achievements around the world. Since ePortfolios, as the name suggests, are mobile containers (porter = to carry; portable = movable) for artefacts in a range of media, they can support the employability and the digital stories of these boundary-crossing adventurers. Increasingly, young Australians are taking the initiative to use digital or ePortfolios as a "cold calling" and job application tool, leading to employment in a range of countries. The considerations in using ePortfolios as communication tools in a global sense are many: choice of language and style (within English there are variants of spelling and meaning), interoperability across technical systems and institutions, and fit with systems of competency and knowledge assessment.

At the local level, mobility takes many forms. Mobile devices including video cameras, voice recorders, phones, and a range of software are a new form of computer. Already there are many projects where chunks of learning materials are available on mobile devices. Attewell (2005) describes a project where learners were able to create and edit mini-Web pages for viewing on mobile and desktop devices. Pages included text, images, animations, audio, blogs, and links to Web pages. One of my own projects uses proprietary software (Nokia's Lifeblog) on a mobile camera phone in a similar way. In one context, the handset was used by building apprentices as a tool for onsite assessment. Their teacher collected their evidence of competence and used digital storage to reduce paperwork. An employer used the video feature to capture the house framing completed by his apprentice, and reported that he preferred the digital device for several reasons. First, his mobile device was always to hand. Second, it was easy to use, and third, it increased his literacy options. As he was not confident with written English, he felt that making a video clip was simpler than writing. He approached multiliteracies from his most comfortable direction.

In line with the *creation-not-consumption* view, the ability to instantly record events, evidence of achievement, and reflections with 'devices to hand' means that ePortfolio developers will have an increasingly rich and dynamic archive from which to select. As Stephen Heppell says, mobile phone technology is important, but what matters most is what students and teachers can do with it (Cole, 2003). One such project in England asked students to contribute a narrative describing their journey in creating knowledge products in order to develop an online portfolio where they annotated evidence of their learning in ICT. They then took part in a telephone survey in which they answered a number of pre-selected questions, designed to encourage a dialogue, which would better enable the assessment of higher levels of attainment and understanding, rather than simply testing a body of knowledge (Worthmedia, 2004).

Both new ways of learning and the elements of ePortfolio development are emerging from these explorations. Individual, portable 'devices to hand' (phones, PDAs, iPods, and so on) could be the new pen and paper for a multiliterate society. Situated learning and authentic assessment are integrated into daily work. Archiving evidence of experiences, selecting products and artefacts, and reflecting on the learning journey anytime, anywhere all support lifelong learning.

CONCLUSION

Living in the knowledge society brings opportunities and challenges, not least in the area of ePortfolios. Using as our underpinning Dewey's (1910) view of knowledge as the construction of people and learning as the process of creating knowledge, and Bereiter and Scardamalia's (1998) exhortation that knowledge must be in the world, rather than in the mind, we should focus on developing ePortfolio systems that support individual and collaborative learning through the very creation of ePortfolios, leading to containers of knowledge that can be shared globally. As well as focusing on individual notions of identity and employability, we should aim for "sociable ePortfolios"—those that cross boundaries, informing others, with the purpose of adding to global understanding. Castells (1999) suggests that the multimedia world will be populated by the *interacting* (those who can select their circuits of communication) and the *interacted* (those who are provided with a restricted number of pre-packaged choices). Lifelong learners need lifelong access to the tools that enable them to create and share ePortfolios. Let us make sure that their identities are represented, and their creativity encouraged, in order to cross this digital divide.

REFERENCES

Attewell, J. (2005). *Mobile technologies and learning*. London: Learning and Skills Development Agency.

Barrett, H. (2005). Researching electronic portfolios and learner engagement. *The REFLECT initiative researching electronic portfolios: Learning, engagement and collaboration through technology*. Retrieved May 31, 2005, from http://electronicportfolios.com/reflect/whitepaper.pdf

Bereiter, C., & Scardamalia, M. (1998). Rethinking learning. In D. Olson & N. Torrance (Eds.), *The handbook of education and human development: New models of learning, teaching and schooling* (pp. 485-514). Cambridge, MA: Blackwell.

Blumer, H. (1962). *Symbolic interactionism: Perspective and method*. Berkeley, CA: University of California Press.

Bridges, W. (1997). *Jobshift*. New York: Addison-Wesley.

Brooks, J., & Brooks, M. (1993). *In search of understanding: The case for constructivist classrooms*. Alexandria, VA: Association for Supervision and Curriculum Development.

Brown, J., Collins, A., & Duguid, P. (1989). Situated cognition and the culture of learning. *Educational Researcher, 18*(1), 32-42.

Brown, A., & Palincsar, A. (1989). Guided, cooperative learning and individual knowledge acquisition. In L. Resnick (Ed.), *Knowing, learning and instruction* (pp. 393-452). Hillside, NJ: Lawrence Erlbaum.

Castells, M. (1999). *The rise of the network society* (vol. 1). Malden, MA: Blackwell.

Cole, G. (2003, January 7). Ring tone revolution. *The Guardian*. Retrieved May 31, 2005, from http://education.guardian.co.uk/elearning/story/0,10577,869659,00.html

Cope, B., & Kalantzis, M. (Eds.). (2000). *Multiliteracies: Literacy learning and the design of social futures*. London: Routledge.

Dewey, J. (1910). *How we think*. Boston: Heath and Co.

Fontana, J. (2003, June 30). Microsoft taking on identity management. Retrieved July 16, 2003, from http://www.nwfusion.com/news/2003/0630microsoft.html

Gergen, K. (2001). The saturated self. In A. Branaman (Ed.), *Self and society* (pp. 265-280). Malden, MA: Blackwell.

Giddens, A. (1991). *Modernity and self-identity: Self and society in the late modern age*. Stanford, CA: Stanford University Press.

Handy, C. (1989). *The age of unreason*. Boston: Harvard Business School Press.

Hargreaves, D. (2004). *Learning for life: The foundations of lifelong learning*. Bristol: The Policy Press.

Hartnell-Young, E. (2001). Women@the cutting edge: Developing professional portfolios. In A. Kinnear & L. Green (Eds.), *Commemorative issue selected conference papers 1998-2000* (pp. 99-104). Perth: Edith Cowan University.

Hartnell-Young, E., & Morriss, M. (1999a). *Digital professional portfolios for change*. Arlington Heights, IL: Skylight Training and Publishing.

Hartnell-Young, E., & Morriss, M. (1999b). Using portfolios as a vehicle for teacher professional development in technology: women@the cutting edge. In P. Linnakylä, M. Kankaanranta, & J. Bopry (Eds.), *Portfolioita verkossa/Portfolios on the Web* (pp. 194-208). Jyväskylä, Finland: The Institute for Educational Research at the University of Jyväskylä.

Kane, Y. (2004). Digital portfolios: Showcasing students as learners. In *Proceedings of the E-Portfolio Australia Conference,* Melbourne, Australia.

Lave, J., & Wenger, E. (1994). *Situated learning: Legitimate peripheral participation*. Cambridge: Cambridge University Press.

Leask, M., & Pachler, N. (2001). *Learning to teach using ICT in the secondary school*. London: Routledge Falmer.

Leece, R. (2004). E-portfolios: Know your audience and give 'em what they want! In *Proceedings of the National Association of Graduate Careers Advisory Services Conference,* Perth, Western Australia.

Love, D., McKean, G., & Gathercoal, P. (2004). Portfolios to Webfolios and beyond: Levels of maturation. *Educause Quarterly, 27*(2), 24-37.

Pachler, N. (2001). Connecting schools and pupils: To what end? In M. Leask (Ed.), *Issues in teaching using ICT* (pp. 15-30). London: Routledge Falmer.

Scardamalia, M., & Bereiter, C. (1999). Schools as knowledge building organizations. In D. Keating & C. Hertzman (Eds.), *Developmental health and the wealth of nations: Social, biological and educational dynamics* (pp. 274-289). New York: The Guildford Press.

Strauss, A. (1997). *Mirrors and masks: The search for identity*. New Brunswick: Transaction.

Unsworth, L. (2001). *Teaching multiliteracies across the curriculum*. Buckingham: Open University Press.

van Eeden, P. (2001, December 27). Why we won a license. *The Age Green Guide,* 4.

Wenger, E. (1998). *Communities of practice: Learning, meaning, identity*. Cambridge: Cambridge University Press.

Worthmedia. (2004). *QCA and the eVIVA: Aligning assessment*. London: DfES.

KEY TERMS

Archive: A collection of items in a repository that provides evidence of skills, achievements, or life events. A digital archive includes text, images, and sound.

Employability: The capacity of an individual to provide the skills and abilities needed for the labour market at the time.

Knowledge Building: When knowledge is seen as a product constructed by people and containing the meaning of objects and events, knowledge building is the process of its construction.

Lifelong Learning: Learning is what people do when constructing knowledge, while lifelong learning is a term that recognizes this process takes place throughout life, not only through formal education.

Multiliteracies: This refers to a plurality of literacies, so that individuals make meaning in many modes, including written-linguistic modes that interface with visual, audio, gestural, and spatial patterns.

Mobility: The movement of people, knowledge, capital, and so on. This is supported at large and small scales by transportation, telecommunication networks, and small electronic devices.

Situated Learning: A theory (developed by Jean Lave) stating that learning is a function of the activity, context, and culture in which it occurs, and should be authentic, such as school students building Web sites for external clients.

Chapter XIV
ePortfolio Decisions and Dilemmas

David Gibson
CurveShift, LLC, USA

ABSTRACT

This chapter combines existing ideas and metaphors from recent portfolio literature into a new framework for thinking about the decisions and dilemmas of ePortfolios. It argues that since the definition of "ePortfolio" covers a spectrum of approaches to the challenge of documenting and assessing student knowledge and skills, the wide array of differing audiences and purposes of assessment leads to many decisions about a portfolio system's mix of content and message ownership, review and validation processes, and expectations about media. In addition, the unique role of technology in the mediation of action and learning adds to the dilemmas inherent in decision making about the system's artifacts. It is hoped that the framework offers a new analytical perspective and a set of questions to guide people in building more effective ePortfolio systems.

INTRODUCTION

Electronic portfolios are increasingly seen as an important activity in education settings such as courses, schools, colleges, and employment interviews. The process of creating them is thought to be valuable for reflection and building records of achievement (Barrett, 2002; Diez, 1994). Their wide varieties of organizational possibilities provide a seemingly endless number of ways of recording and representing knowledge (Bruce & Levin, 1997). For example, their artifacts or works provide evidence for making reasoned judgments about what someone knows and can do (Pellegrino, Chudowsky, & Glaser, 2001; Almond, Steinberg, & Mislevy, 2002).

However, the word "portfolio" itself is used in a bewilderingly diverse number of ways, to represent a collection of work, a performance assessment, a learning and assessment management system, an archive of achievement, a personal or cultural story, an institutional requirement, a large-scale assessment. What exactly do we mean by "electronic portfolios?" How, with so many viewpoints, can we think about the decisions and dilemmas inherent in the processes, artifacts. and organizational options of ePortfolios?

DEFINING THE DECISIONS AND DELEMMAS OF "ePORTFOLIOS"

Portfolios—both electronic and paper based—mean different things depending upon one's point of view. This is part of their charm, but it is also a source of confusion and misunderstanding. For example, consider the purposes and expectations of a portfolio's audience. One audience is the individual. Another is a trusted advisor or teacher who is helping the individual learn. A third audience for a portfolio might be a future employer or a reviewer. These audiences are not all looking for the same things in a "portfolio." The individual might be looking for an accurate reflection of a personal message. A teacher might be looking for evidence of knowledge; an employer, for a record of experience and education.

In addition to being simply different from one another, the meanings of "portfolio" for different audiences are sometimes in conflict, which gives rise to dilemmas. For example, in a private working portfolio, an individual might want to reveal a weakness in order to receive help from a trusted advisor. But that same person might not want to not mention that weakness to a future employer through a showcase portfolio. Joanne Carney (2002) calls this the "personal revelation dilemma." A trusted advisor wants to see the course of development of ideas over time, but a program reviewer needs to see a summation of the end results. Even within a single category of audience, such as "future employers," there can be different and sometimes conflicting purposes. For example, one employer might want to see artifacts that demonstrate that the individual can write well, while another might want to see documentation of passing certain core courses, or of an ability to reflect on one's learning, and so on. Portfolios of interest to one audience that fulfill one purpose can thus be irrelevant to another, because the purposes change *along with* as well as *among* various audiences. Carney refers to this as the "multipurpose dilemma." How can educators who want to use ePortfolios decide what to do about this situation? How can we better understand the dilemmas inherent in preparing portfolios with a variety of media options for various purposes and audiences?

To address these questions, this chapter provides a framework for thinking about the decisions and dilemmas inherent in the options available for making and using ePortfolios. The framework will hopefully offer a way of clarifying the definition of portfolios and their contents for different kinds of audiences, for different kinds of purposes, under a variety of decision conditions concerning the artifact collection. The framework should also help clarify what "ePortfolio" means as both a starting point for reflection as well as an archive for communicating about our knowledge, abilities, and self-expressions.

In what follows, a review of the decisions and dilemmas inherent in creating and utilizing ePortfolios will lead to a discussion of a new feature of the "e" in ePortfolio, as a special kind of assessment artifact with both affordances and limitations. Gibson and Barrett (2003) dealt briefly with the primary added value of ePortfolios over traditional portfolios, outlining a range of options in setting up ePortfolio programs. In this chapter, those ideas and others are discussed within the new framework in an attempt to unify the main concerns inherent in the decisions and dilemmas of ePortfolios. At the end, a set of questions (see Table 1) is provided for students, program planners, and institutional portfolio leaders to further refine what they intend to create in their own ePortfolio systems.

Insoluable and Practical Dilemmas

Hampden-Turner (1990) discerns between a "pure dilemma," which is theoretical and unsolvable in principle, and "practical dilemmas," which create value when reconciled. We clearly want to work on practical dilemmas here, since

Table 1. Questions for decision making about ePortfolios

	Personal	Trusted Others	Public
Focus of the Artifact			
Sonnet	Does the structure of the portfolio support its personal focus or reveal something about the learner?	Does this collection provide an image that makes trusted others proud of their investment in the learner?	Does the portfolio provide an image of a well-prepared professional?
Mirror	Is there a primary message about or image of the learner?	Does the portfolio represent the trusted group's skill in guiding and advising me?	Does the ePortfolio do a good job of representing the learner as a professional?
Map	Does the portfolio show how its parts are connected together and how they came to be or are still in stages of development (e.g., "working portfolio")?	Does the portfolio contain a complete and sufficient linking to standards for graduation? Have the "Rubrics and Rules" (Carney, 2002) been followed and used (e.g., "working portfolio" or "graduation portfolio")?	Does the collection include proof of readiness, certification, validity as a professional? Is it suitable for gaining employment (e.g., "employment portfolio")?
Ownership of the Artifact			
Sonnet	Are the statements created by the learner and for the learner's benefit?	Do the trusted others see clear connections in the portfolio to their professional culture and to the person who had an impact on his or her advisors and teachers?	Does an appropriate public recognize the portfolio's structure? Do they "own" the validity of the structure as a professional context for a representation of teaching?
Mirror	Does the learner have the power to create and present any kind of representation?	Does the portfolio present an image that the trusted others would own or want to represent as their part of the history with this individual?	Does an appropriate public see a representation of an educator they would recognize as a peer? Is it an image they would own as professionals?
Map	Can the learner change the meanings of this collection at anytime?	Does the portfolio document the advisors' efforts to influence this person (or not) and why? Can the advisors trace their edits and influence in the portfolio?	Does the portfolio show some of the important ways in which the pubic investment in this individual has or will pay off to others?
Affordances and Constraints of the Artifact's Media			
Sonnet	Does the media enhance the content and structure of the message?	Does the choice of media enhance the assessment and feedback on the portfolio?	Does the choice of media influence the public perception of the portfolio?
Mirror	Does the choice of media enhance creativity and assist in the realization of the intentions of the learner?	Does the quality of the use of media reflect the desired level of professional technology practice maintained by trusted others?	Does the quality of the use of media reflect generally accepted professional practice?
Map	Do the affordances of the media (what the media allows) enhance the correspondence of the portfolio to reality?	Do the affordances of the media (what the media allows) enhance institutional connections to standards or other external sources of validity?	Do the affordances of the media (what the media allows) enhance association with generally accepted levels of professional representation?

unsolvable ones would not help us progress very far from where we are now. It may be that the confusion that exists now around the word "portfolio" is in part a result of its involving some pure dilemmas as well as political issues and thorny details. For example, the politics of using the latest "buzzwords" of education—like "portfolios"—include vendors who want to capture the attention of buyers, government funding agencies who want to stimulate innovation, and people who want to capitalize on those opportunities. This situation has led to the use of the word "portfolios" for a wide variety of products and processes, some of which are antithetical to each other (Gibson & Barrett, 2003).

In principle, there are indeed unsolvable dilemmas in the varying needs of the audiences for assessment of which ePortfolios are a part. For example, some assessment methods necessarily halt instruction, but others unobtrusively observe instruction and learner interactions. Some assessments are meant to select a small number of candidates from a large pool of applicants, while others are meant to develop expertise in every learner. These are some of the thorny details of the "pure dilemma" of assessment, which influences our perspective on ePortfolios as instruction and assessment tools. We will not develop these ideas further, but refer the reader to Pellegrino et al. (2001) and Bransford, Brown, and Cocking (2001) for recent overviews of learning and assessment theory. Regardless of the thorny details of the pure dilemmas, solutions to the practical dilemmas are possible if we have a framework for asking good questions and thinking about the issues as we make decisions in the process of creating and sharing ePortfolios.

THE FRAMEWORK OF AUDIENCE, PURPOSE, AND ARTIFACT

A three-dimensional model is proposed for dealing with the decisions and dilemmas of building and maintaining ePortfolio systems (see Figure 1). Its main features are three continuums of audiences, purposes, and artifacts that we argue make up portfolio work. We might envision the framework as a Rubik's Cube of stances, issues, and concerns that need to be addressed in order to situate a particular portfolio system within the larger context of the potential for all systems. A brief outline of the framework is presented next, followed by longer discussion on each of the three dimensions.

Carney (2002) argues that there are basic decisions and dilemmas in portfolio creation in three areas: Purpose/Audience, Ownership, and Focus. We have found that it makes sense to separate purposes from audiences to facilitate analysis of the ways they interact. This provides two dimensions of the proposed new framework—"Audiences" and "Reflective Purposes." We subsume the issues of ownership and focus into a new third dimension, which we have labeled the "Artifact." The idea of artifact broadly includes the concept of "affordances and constraints of the media" as indicated by Gibson (1977). The artifact dimen-

Figure 1. 3-D framework of decision making about ePortfolios

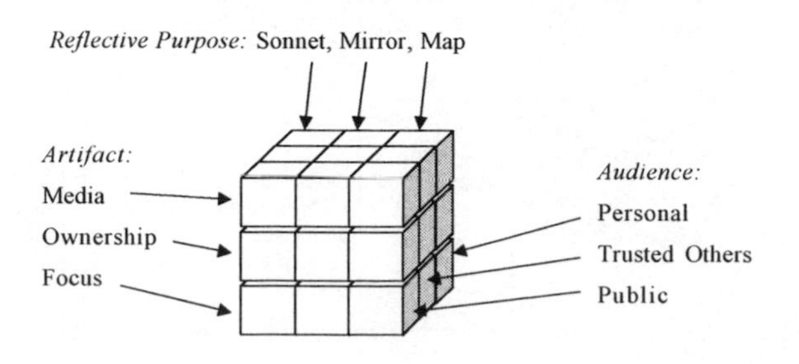

sion also includes the dilemmas inherent in the choices of media format, presentation focus and structure, and the use of generic and customizable applications (Gibson & Barrett, 2002). The three-dimensional (3D) nature of the model follows closely the activity theory ideas of Leontev (1896-1934), which depicts all purposeful human activity as interactions among subjects (audiences), artifacts (tools), and objects (purposes). The 3D framework provides a source for principled inquiry into the nature of the interaction of a portfolio's creators and users, the artifacts that stand as evidence of what people know and can do, and the inferences one might make about learners.

Reflective Purpose

Diez (1994) offers a metaphoric depiction of portfolios as a mirror, map, and sonnet, our starting point for defining the dimension of "reflective purpose."

The Mirror

A mirror is obviously a reflective tool. The metaphor aptly provides the framework with an image for the representation of self-knowledge. Carney (2002) says that the ePortfolio as an assessment device "isn't working perfectly, but it's better than any other teacher assessment method at hand ... to present a portrait of self as teacher, and then to compare that image with the ideal they had formulated in their philosophies of education." The mirror metaphor emphasizes self-reflection, central to metacognition, and thus learning itself (Bransford et al., 2000). Given the conflicts that are ahead, many decisions about how to establish and support ePortfolios have an impact on whether and to what degree this important reflective purpose is met. Any system that minimizes this aspect is missing what may be the ePortfolio's greatest potential. The set of questions in Table 1 that concern *The Mirror* must be answered affirmatively and then often revisited to ensure that this essential purpose is not lost.

The Map

A map is a representation that acts as a guide to a domain by standing in close correspondence to an underlying reality. This metaphor captures how ePortfolios can demonstrate the linkages of knowledge and ability in relation to external principles, for example in professional education, the standards for licensing and credentialing. An ePortfolio map of someone's knowledge goes beyond paper and pencil testing, and records by capturing multimedia artifacts that require and more directly represent complex skills and knowledge (Pellegrino et al., 2001). For example, a multimedia artifact in an ePortfolio can capture and represent actual performance abilities in action within natural settings. The mapping metaphor also points out that a collection of artifacts can function as a body of evidence for making a reasoned judgment about what someone knows and can do (Almond et al., 2002). This aspect of the ePortfolio is vital to assessment and evaluation of the learner.

The Sonnet

The poetic form of the sonnet is an act of expression within a recognizable form, giving us the image of the ePortfolio for conceptualizing one's knowledge and practice in artistic and metaphorical terms, but within an accepted structure of professional practice. However, as Diez (1994) points out, one cannot simply create a good sonnet by following its highly structured poetic format. A group of words in the sonnet form might contain the right number of lines and cadence in perfect iambic pentameter, but simply be a meaningless set of ideas. At the same time, words of a poet may be beautiful, but without following the established format, they would not be judged a sonnet. Likewise, the traditional structure of an expression or image within a professional practice can either be a straight jacket or a take-off point. As expertise grows, structures often become self-imposed stages from which an individual plays a role of one's own choosing. The sonnet aspect of a portfolio provides a chance for creativity within structure and forms a conceptual context for others to begin to interpret and appreciate one's expression. In professional education, the structure of ePortfolios is shaped by the growing body of professional practice in educational technology, as well as an institution's requirements and guidance to a student, which act as scaffolding for structuring one's artifacts into a valid social communication. Decisions of higher education programs that miss the portfolio's sonnet-like purpose miss the opportunity to challenge future professionals to experiment with their "fitness" for the profession. Conversely, if a future professional's ePortfolio does not meet the metaphoric purpose of the sonnet, it may be unrecognizable, underappreciated, or simply irrelevant.

Audience

A learner attempting to serve all purposes and all audiences with one portfolio faces a daunting, perhaps impossible, challenge. But at the same time, one who builds several portfolios to meet a variety of purposes and audiences also faces a plethora of decisions as they address the issues from different points of view. The 3D framework sets the issue of audience into three parts: a personal aspect; a circle of trusted advisors, friends, and others; and a larger amorphous general public.

Personal

The self as an audience brings to mind the purpose of the portfolio as a mirror, for that is one way we can see ourselves, but it is not the only one. We also see ourselves by reflecting on artifacts we have made, our intentions in creating them, and our own satisfaction with them as successes in meeting our intentions. We can be reflective about the overall meaning of our collected works by getting some distance from the work. Conversely, we can seek to find aspects of ourselves by getting much closer to the work. So it is helpful to separate the self-as-audience from the mirror-like purpose of creating a portfolio. It helps us analyze the subtleties of interaction of the purposes with the self (see Table 1). A portfolio program can support the personal audience by allowing ePortfolios to contain private areas not subject to assessment and evaluation, and by encouraging private uses of the portfolio, for example, to assemble artifacts for personal enjoyment rather than institutional requirements. Such opportunities, when prompted and provided within the institutional setting of courses and advising sessions, help establish the habits of self-reflection and the intrinsic values of self-directed work that are critical for the "mirror" to become a clear and powerful tool for reflection. Grounding the review of portfolio contents and the collection as a whole in the light of personal strengths, interests, and aspirations also underscores the fact that all learning is essentially personal progress and helps build a belief in worthiness to be and become the center of one's own education (Friedrichs & Gibson, 2002).

Trusted Others

During the educational process, it is most helpful to have trusted advisors to help us make sense of our work, to challenge us to improve to meet higher professional standards, and to recognize us when we do. Trusted others act as an inner circle, yet provide us with external input and validity. In professional education portfolio processes, trusted others might be a learner-selected group of peers, cooperating internship mentors, advisors, and professors. Learner-selection is crucial for building the trust needed for this audience to function as critical friends. In a professional education ePortfolio program, trusted others need institutional training and support in providing constructive feedback as critical advocates for the future professional. Programs that wish to take maximum advantage of the affordances of new media—for example, anytime, anywhere resources and advice, new multimedia forms of expression—face a cultural change in advising practices at both individual and organizational levels, and must undertake systemic change efforts in conjunction with specific technological training (Havelock, Sherry, & Gibson, 2002).

Public

Ultimately, in many cases, ePortfolios are made available to the public via Web sites, compact disks, or DVDs. Higher education institutions may want a permanent record that a group of candidates achieved important outcomes at a sufficiently high standard of work. Academic program reviewers want to inspect an institution's portfolios. Future employers may look at a portfolio to make selection decisions. Researchers may look into portfolios for patterns and evidence of interest. Decisions about portfolios that are dominated by a view to the public audience often conflict with decisions made from the perspective of trusted others or personal levels, and this leads to dilemmas that must be resolved by a combination of privacy controls or separation of the audiences via multiple portfolios. In higher education portfolio programs, it would be wise to consider how to support multiple portfolios so that the public purposes of one collection do not overshadow the reflective learning purposes of another.

Artifact

An ePortfolio is most often a collection of things produced to share with others: papers, videos, images, presentations, statements, audio records, poems, music, and so forth. The concept of artifacts captures the physical nature of these items. However, there is another sense of the word, meaning a record of activity that may have unconscious as well as intended meanings. For example, an artifact might literally represent a picture of a person, but unintentionally capture an essence of a culture. As a result, ePortfolios have many levels of meanings, such as individual pieces in a collection, the collection as a whole, the pieces as created, the pieces as seen through the reflective eyes of the creator or the eyes of an external evaluator. We distinguish three primary arenas for analyses of the ePortfolio as artifact: focus or practical intent of the contents, ownership or identity with the final product, and the affordances and constraints of the media.

Focus

The focus concentrates and unifies the intention of the electronic portfolio as an archival record or artifact of activity. The focus serves as a practical objective that involves its own unique dilemmas and decisions in the multiple perspectives involved in the alignment of intention with result. Making decisions about audience and purpose is a part of achieving focus, but in addition, one has to decide about content, theme, and the ends and means of representation. Encapsulating these decisions in what might be thought of as a holistic mental model of the objective of the portfolio (e.g., to get a job, to impress a friend, to experiment with self-expression) engages us in the decisions and dilemmas of achieving overall focus. Each portfolio is a unique composition of focusing decisions among all the other elements of the framework, and that composition is the portfolio's practical objective or focus.

Candidate ideas for focus include "uses" of the portfolio such as exhibition, or in assessment and evaluation processes, as well as "themes" that may appear as organizing elements of the collection or its parts. Typical focused artifact collections in the preparation of professionals are the "working portfolio" that is used to help the future professional develop the skills of planning and teaching, the "graduation portfolio" that is used to display one's achievement of the standards of teaching, and an "employment portfolio" that is designed to get a job. Notice that the audience types and the reflective purposes of portfolios are independent of these practical and intentional foci. For example, a trusted friend might also be a future employer who can be shown any of the above portfolios, or a personal artifact in a working portfolio might transform into a piece of evidence in a graduation portfolio. An important practical use of many portfolios is as an assessment tool. Portfolios can be part of a comprehensive system of assessment, in which case, the decisions and dilemmas concerning focus include balancing formative and/or summative uses and the challenges of data aggregation. We will not develop these issues here in order to continue with the broad picture being outlined.

Ownership

Who owns the ePortfolio—the individual, the institution, or the profession? The issues of ownership in professional education ePortfolios change depending on whether the portfolio is created privately, or within a competency-based licensing program, a field supervision program, or in a national certification process that validates readiness to enter the profession. While the voice (the intentions and expressions) of the individual are paramount in any individual ePortfolio, that does not mean that all ownership is therefore private. Ownership is also not completely synonymous with audience, although the categories of the personal audience, trusted others, and public are useful constructs in making ownership decisions, for example, those who control access to view the collection have some control over the audience. One way of determining ownership is by thinking about where the physical image rests—on a server, on a CD, on a Web site. Since ePortfolios can be stored in several places, it is possible to have several owners in this sense. Another dimension of ownership is: who has access to edit or select subsections for alternative representations such as a summary of artifacts found in all portfolios from a licensing program, or a graphic showing the linkages of the portfolio to external standards. Secondary editor/owners (i.e., not the creator) also need to consider how to reference the author, even when summarizing across authors, as scholars do with other published works.

Issues of ownership would be somewhat less troublesome in a professional education ePortfolio program if individuals could create and maintain multiple portfolios rather than try to resolve all of the dilemmas by making decisions about only one collection of work. As we hope we are demonstrating, the decisions about one portfolio cannot serve all audiences and purposes, nor surmount all the dilemmas. One must resolve certain sets of dilemmas by making focused decisions for a specific configuration of the elements in the framework. Luckily, having multiple portfolios is facilitated—not hampered—by the new media; it is one of its important "affordances."

Affordances and Constraints of the Media

The electronic media allows new forms of communication and expression, new ways of seeing the world, as well as some new kinds of constraints to consider (Gibson, 1977; Gibson, 2002; Vygotsky, 1978). As we interact with and express ourselves through the new media, the media acts on us in a reciprocal fashion, mediating what is known (epistemology) and how we find out what we can know (methodology). For example, before electron microscopes we had to theorize how very small things fit together, but we can now see them. Before remote sensors on spacecraft gave us images, we could only imagine a comet flying into a planet or a tide of microorganisms mediating ocean temperature, but now we can both see these things when they happen and create computer-based simulations of them for more detailed study. New tools of visualization have allowed us to simulate complex systems and bring mathematics to life in new ways. News of the day is now available in print and multimedia within minutes after an event. Documents from a century ago can be closely scrutinized from the comfort of one's home. We are just beginning to appreciate how new media is altering our perceptions of the world, and how ePortfolio artifacts are capable of capturing and representing this new knowledge in ways impossible before computers and the Internet.

Gibson (2002) outlined four broad categories of affordances of the new media, for which ePortfolios and their supportive processes are exceptionally well-suited:

1. **Access to an Abundant Multimedia Global Knowledge Storehouse:** New media resources include digital libraries (e.g., www.vlibrary.org and www.edrform.net), real-world data for analysis (e.g., nccrest.eddata.net), and connections to other people who provide information, feedback, and inspiration (e.g., in communication-oriented ePortfolios such as www.learningcentral.org), all of which can enhance learning and assessment in an ePortfolio program.
2. **A Vastly Expanded Range of Tools for Inquiry and Expression:** Digital media is more than a storage medium for information; it is a new environment for inquiry, expression, construction, and communication. Contrast a story told in writing with one relayed through film or music, and consider how all three forms of expression might work together in an ePortfolio to represent what the learner knows and can do. Gibson and Barrett (2003) discussed the use of generic technology tools (e.g., digital video, audio programs, word processors, databases, HTML editors) in an ePortfolio system, for example, for building a learner's technology skills as well as expressive capacities. That new knowledge is then encapsulated in the portfolio's artifacts, as well as in the presentation of the portfolio as a whole. For example, artifacts in a portfolio can show how the learner visualizes difficult-to-understand concepts. Other visual displays of information within and across ePortfolios in customized systems (e.g., database applications for performance assessment monitoring) can help teachers see the conceptual growth of the learner or view the structural shape of performance of a group of learners (Gibson & Barrett, 2003; Stevens, 1991). Most important, the new range of inquiry and expression changes the nature and extent of knowledge and its acquisition, with an attendant new responsibility of assessors and evaluators of portfolios to understand

and provide relevant feedback to the learner.

3. **Interactivity and Hyperlinking:** Hypermedia (digital media linked in a multiplicity of ways) allows the creation of a single archive of products and documentation that can serve the needs and purposes of many different portfolios (e.g., for different audiences, purposes, foci).
4. **New Social Networks:** Learning can be, more than ever and in ways not possible without networks, driven by the individual needs and interests of the learner in balance with the social goals of education (Friedrichs & Gibson, 2001; Bruce & Levin, 1997).

At the same time, the medium and tools we have today have limitations too. The subtleties of face-to-face interactions are not always accurately captured in videoconferences. The nuances of meetings are not captured in minutes or chat room narratives, and in fact the meeting itself is transformed when it is placed in a new setting. A phone conference, for example, is a different experience from a personal meeting. So we must recognize that an ePortfolio cannot capture all that may be important about a person for any of the audiences we have mentioned. At the same time, we can expect that the creation of an electronic portfolio will cause new types of thinking, reflection, and expression. As we face the decisions and dilemmas of electronic portfolios, it would help us to remember that we can choose to maximize various benefits in different contexts by making smart choices about the media, the ownership, and the focus.

CONCLUSION

The rich interaction of reflective purposes (the mirror, map, and sonnet metaphors) with three primary audiences (the self, trusted others, and the public) and with the dimensions of the ePortfolio as an artifact (focus, ownership, and the affordances and constraints of the media) creates a framework for considering the ePortfolio. To examine the ePortfolio system's potential to promote thinking and learning, planners, portfolio system creators, and researchers can now raise a series of principled questions based on the framework, which will hopefully be useful to help evaluate personal and institutional knowledge and practices. As scholars and practitioners develop and share answers to these questions, the field of portfolio-based assessment will continue to develop its understanding of what we know and are able to do with ePortfolios.

REFERENCES

Almond, R., Steinberg, L., & Mislevy, R. (2002). Enhancing the design and delivery of assessment systems: A four process architecture. *The Journal of Technology, Learning, and Assessment, 1*(5). Retrieved from http://www.jtla.org

Bambino, D. (2002). Critical friends. *Educational Leadership, 59*(6), 25-27.

Barrett, H. (2002, June 14). Presentation. In *Proceedings of ISTE's Forum on Assessment and Technology,* San Antonio, TX.

Bransford, J., Brown, A., & Cocking, R. (Eds.). (2000). *How people learn: Brain, mind, experience and school.* Washington: DC. National Academy Press.

Bruce, B., & Levin, J. (1997). Educational technology: Media for inquiry, communication, construction, and expression. *Journal of Educational Computing Research, 17*(1), 79-102.

Carney, J. (2002). The intimacies of electronic portfolios: Confronting preservice teachers' personal revelation dilemma. In *Proceedings of the Society for Information Technology in Teacher Education Conference,* Nashville, TN.

Diez, M. (1994). The portfolio: Sonnet, mirror and map. In K. Burke (Ed.), *Professional portfolios* (pp. 18-26). Arlington Heights, IL: Skylight Training & Publishing.

Fletcher, G. (2003). *Toward an anthropology of cyberspace.* Retrieved October 13, 2003, from http://www.spaceless.com/papers/14.htm

Friedrichs, A. (2000). *Continuous learning dialogues.* Unpublished Dissertation, University of Vermont, USA.

Friedrichs, A., & Gibson, D. (2002). Personalization and secondary school renewal. In J. DiMartino, J. Clarke, & D. Wolk, (Eds.), *Personal learning: Preparing high school students to create their future* (pp. 41-68). Lanham, MD: Scarecrow Press.

Gibson, J. (1977). The theory of affordances. In R. Shaw & J. Bransford (Eds.), *Perceiving, acting and knowing* (pp. 62-82). Hillsdale, NJ: Lawrence Erlbaum.

Gibson, D. (2003). Network-based assessment in education. *Contemporary Issues in Technology and Teacher Education, 3*(3). Retrieved from http://www.citejournal.org/vol3/iss3/general/article1.cfm

Gibson, D., & Barrett, H. (2003). Directions in electronic portfolio development. *Contemporary Issues in Technology and Teacher Education, 2*(4). Retrieved from http://www.citejournal.org/vol2/iss4/general/article3.cfm

Hampden-Turner, C. (1990). *Charting the corporate mind: Graphic solutions to business conflicts.* New York: The Free Press.

Havelock, B., Gibson, D., & Sherry, L. (2003). The personal learning planner: Collaboration through online learning and publication. In *Proceedings of the Society for Information Technology in Teacher Education (SITE) Conference,* Albuquerque, NM. Retrieved from http://www.rmcdenver.com/ten/PLPfinal.htm

Pellegrino J., Chudowsky, N., & Glaser, R. (Eds.). (2001). *Knowing what students know: The science and design of educational assessment.* Committee on the Foundations of Assessment, Board on Testing and Assessment, Center for Education, National Research Council. Washington, DC: National Academy Press.

KEY TERMS

Activity Theory: A psychological theory invented by Alexei Nikolaevich Leontyev, which has become one of the major psychological theories of sociocultural theorists. Its tenets include elements in a whole systems view of the mediation of subject, tool, and object through roles, community, and praxis.

Affordances: Refers to a physical property of something that influences how it can be used or how it influences or moderates what a user can do with an object. In ePortfolios, the affordances allowed by different media will affect the production of artifacts as well as the interpretations of those artifacts.

Artifact: Any object made, modified, or used by people. In educational assessment, artifacts provide evidence of what the person or group knows and can do.

Reflection: In ePortfolio work, means contemplation on the meaning of artifacts, ideas, expressions, and the processes that supported their creation, including a consideration of intent.

Chapter XV
Development Issues for PDP with ePortfolios: Web Services and Skills

Simon Grant
Information Strategists, UK

Adam Marshall
University of Oxford, UK

Janet Strivens
University of Liverpool, UK

Roger Clark
University of Liverpool, UK

ABSTRACT

This chapter describes approaches firstly towards a service-oriented architecture for personal development planning (PDP), and secondly towards representing skills for interoperability. We outline a personal information aggregation and distribution service (PIADS) which serves as the key concept within a distributed approach to storing information suitable for ePortfolios and PDP, and using it through Web services. Our skills "meta-framework" is outlined as a long-term practical solution to the challenge of widely diverse descriptions of skills. It uses a published specification (IMS[1] Reusable Definition of Competence or Educational Objective, RDCEO[2]), and elaborates this to distinguish between conceptual "competency" definitions and operational "educational objective" definitions. If these issues are not addressed, the practical value of ePortfolios for PDP would be limited. Thus the chapter is of particular importance to those planning and designing future ePortfolio systems and services.

INTRODUCTION

ePortfolio systems can act as repositories for personal information that has several possible uses. For example, some systems allow the kind of information that appears on résumés or application forms to be viewed by potential employers or educational institutions to which a learner is applying; some systems allow users to reflect on their experiences, and to store analyses of the skills and competencies involved, along with evidence for them; some systems store records or artefacts for assessment towards an award. ePortfolio systems could offer all of these.

It is clear that, from the perspective of an individual user, all this ePortfolio information needs to be accessible in one place to facilitate its management. Those who own or control the information need to be able to update those parts under their control, and to grant and retract permission for others to view the various parts of the information. On the other hand, some of that information is needed by institutional or corporate administration systems, and some might even be owned by such bodies (like material submitted for assessment, as well as the results of assessments). This means that ePortfolio information may naturally be spread over a number of physical and organizational locations. Some of these places are likely to be defined by the nature of the information, while others might be chosen by users and changed at their will.

One part of the work described in this chapter explores how these two requirements can be reconciled. A conceptual architecture is outlined which separates the storage of the information from the service which allows the owners of the information control over it. The service that allows this control is called a PIADS, standing for personal information aggregation and distribution service. The concept has been refined after discussions with interested parties.

One of the important functions of ePortfolio systems is to enable learners to assemble, hold, and present information and evidence about their skills and competencies. Different stakeholders may have different views, not only on what skills are relevant in a particular situation or for a particular purpose, but on how those skills are represented and grouped. This can be described under the heading of the "skills framework" that is used.

This immediately creates a challenge for ePortfolios in the context of lifelong learning: how can skills and competencies documented in terms of one skills framework be re-described or reused under a different framework? One answer to this question is to remit it to learners themselves: they have to become expert at re-describing their skills in different contexts. But this does not address the situation of the learner who lacks expertise in re-description, nor does it aid the automatic use of evidence for skills and competencies, for example, in the context of recruitment selection systems.

The other part of the work described in this chapter addresses this issue, and outlines an approach to representing skills and competencies designed to enhance the interoperability between different skills frameworks, while allowing for expected differences of view on how to learn, teach, or assess those skills.

BACKGROUND

The findings presented here are from two projects funded by the UK Joint Information Systems Committee (JISC)[3]: the Web Services for Reflective Learning (WS4RL)[4] project, and the Skills Profiling Web Service (SPWS)[5] project. Both of these projects sprang out of rich and fertile background work in the areas of personal development planning (PDP)[6], lifelong learning, and ePortfolios, from the well-established work of the Centre for Recording Achievement (CRA)[7], the work at Liverpool and Oxford on LUSID, the Liverpool University Student Interactive Database[8] (Strivens & Grant, 2000), to recent work sponsored by the JISC through their Centre for Educational Technology Interoperability Standards, their Managed Learning Environments (MLEs) for Lifelong Learning program[9], and their ELearning Framework (ELF)[10], now the EFramework for Education and Research[11].

WEB SERVICES FOR PERSONAL DEVELOPMENT PLANNING

PDP and Personal Theory Building

The UK definition of PDP still encompasses many activities[12], and in order to develop a clear position on Web services to support PDP, we had to devise a more focused concept. We called this "personal theory building," and Grant, Marshall, Strivens, & Clark (2004) have described it in more detail as part of the WS4RL project documentation. In essence, we conceive of a PDP process as supporting an individual's theory of him or herself as a learner. This happens as part of a reflective cycle which we characterize as having seven steps: noticing, documenting, recollecting, theorizing, goal setting, action planning, and acting.

The envisaged personal theory building process fits within the definition of the nature of PDP arrived at by the Evidence for Policy and Practice Information (EPPI-Centre)[13] which undertook a systematic review of research relating to the effectiveness of PDP (Gough, Kiwan, Sutcliffe, Simpson, & Houghton, 2003). This group agreed that PDP must include reflection together with at least one other process out of recording, planning, and action.

Grant et al. (2004) describe a scenario to illustrate this, involving a learner in a work situation observing presentations, and on reflection, seeking to improve their own presentation skills.

Figure 1. Components and information flows in the WS4RL architecture

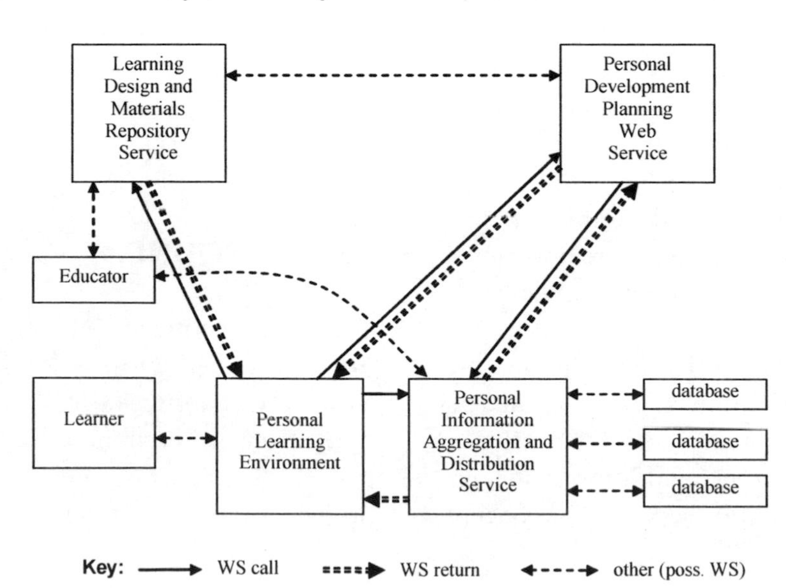

Requirements of Web Services Involving PDP

The WS4RL project aimed to enhance LUSID to offer PDP via Web services. At the outset of the project, it was not immediately clear what those Web services would be. In order to clarify this, we needed to focus on a conceptual systems architecture, which we represented in Figure 1, which is adapted from Grant et al. (2004).

As part of this exercise, we recognized that there was a need for more than one kind of Web service. One can clearly distinguish between, on the one hand, the services which are needed for storage and management of related personal information, and on the other hand, the services which actually offer guidance and support for the individual's PDP. The information handling services could be expected to be common to several potential applications, for example, LMS, ePortfolios, human resource, and student record systems. The nature of three of the key elements of the systems architecture will now be outlined.

PDP Web Service (PDPWS)

Sophisticated PDP services would ideally be customised to the learner, depending on various facts about the learner. For instance, if learners wanted to improve their presentation skills, the kind of guidance offered should ideally depend on what PDP exercises they had already done in that area, what level of competence they were aiming at, what language they wanted to learn through the medium of, and quite possibly other factors. Without this kind of customisation, PDP would be in danger of being stuck as a set of textbook exercises, with a potential for frustrating the intended beneficiary by missing the right level, in either direction.

Thus, a sophisticated PDP service should be able to make use of structured information about the learner. This kind of information may already be kept in some systems, but even so there is a long way to go before being able to use it reliably and automatically for customising PDP. A PDP service should also be able to interact with any "personal learning environment" which might be constructed, and not be limited to being usable only within large, integrated, and monolithic learning environments or learning management systems. In our view, such a PDPWS could:

- Maintain lists of authorized learners and their permissions
- Hold learners' history of interaction with the PDPWS
- Hold PDPWS-specific information about learners, e.g., PDP program signed up to
- Hold a detailed "map" of all possible "positions" of a learner's PDP progress (this "map" may include a skills/competency framework)
- Hold designed procedures for determining what to return for a user in a position (these procedures may constitute "paths" through the system)
- Offer an interface for those requesting registration
- Find and interact with the learners' PIADS

Thus, designers of the PDPWS need to design:

- The "map" defining the possible locations in their system's version of "PDP space"
- The process for each node in the map, dependent on any relevant attributes of the learner

PIADS: Personal Information Aggregation and Distribution Service

Central to the proposed architecture is the PIADS. There is no reason why personal information should be stored all in one place, and many reasons can be imagined why it should not be. Among other reasons, much information of relevance to ePortfolios and PDP may be stored anyway by the institution or other body (e.g., employer) that was responsible for its creation. This could be expected to be the case for marks, grades, reviews, appraisals, and so forth.

This leaves open the question of whether the PIADS includes local storage. But in any case, rules governing the access of third parties to the information (who could possibly be authenticated with services such as LID[14]—Lightweight IDentity—or the ideas for self-identification on the Web known as mIDm[15]) need to be stored and maintained. Identifiers for the parts of the information stored need to be organized by the owner and kept in a way that makes sense for future reference. A set of rules needs to be recorded and maintained detailing what happens when information is updated. It appears likely that the UK education sector will adopt Shibboleth[16,17] as an authentication and authorization mechanism; it could be envisaged that the location of a user's PIADS would be one of the standard Shibboleth attributes visible to eLearning systems. The locations of a user's distributed personal information stores could be listed within the PIADS system to allow it to update changed information automatically: if this could be arranged, it would hold some promise towards an often-wished-for address updating service. Authorization to access these ultimate data stores would also be controlled by Shibboleth, but there would also have to be a much finer-grained authorization mechanism applicable to third parties which would act on a per-record basis; this is comparable to the way that ePortfolios currently control access to a user's data. We concluded that a PIADS should:

- Act as a virtual database for all learner profile information and files, for everyone allowed
- Maintain identifiers for all logically distinct pieces of information—for XML documents, this involves inserting XML "id=" attributes to all nodes so that a common method of referral can be used regardless of which specification is being used
- Accept calls for information from personal learning environment (PLE) or PDP services
- Allow the owner to manage authorization to view all separate parts of the information held

Personal Learning Environment (PLE)

The concept of a PLE is currently in circulation, but as yet with no clear definition. For the purposes of this architecture, a PLE could be envisaged to:

- Provide an environment for the user to undertake supported eLearning, without necessarily being continuously online
- Manage the registrations with the different Web services for learning and PDP
- Manage the actual presentation of information to the user, whether graphical, auditory, tactile, and so forth
- Manage accessibility information which constrains the above
- Mediate dialogue on presentational styles

- Issue Web services calls to PDP and learning repository systems
- Play learning materials represented in a suitable specification (e.g., IMS Learning Design[18])
- Display related information-gathering forms, manage any data submitted, and return appropriate structures to relevant servers
- Act as a focal point for the initiation of authentication and authorization

If the PLE is going to be able to deal properly with learning design that comprises more than just one form, it would also be useful to have some means of storing intermediate results and holding the information for use on other forms, for later submission.

FURTHER WORK IN THIS AREA

The WS4RL project included an implementation of several of the Web services required for this architecture. However, as we recognized early on, it would be a large undertaking to implement the complete architecture as described, and there is much work to do before this goal could be achieved. Authentication and authorization would again probably be handled by Shibboleth, but some issues still need to be resolved.

Another issue that was beyond resolution at this stage was the plausibility of offering the kind of sophisticated PDP Web service envisaged. From a pedagogic point of view, it is easy to see the attractions of such a service. It is not so clear how much work would need to be done to implement it effectively, and how much human intervention would be necessary. LUSID has established the principle of automating many straightforward parts of PDP self-administration, but there is not yet any clear indication of the limits to this approach. How feasible is a PDP Web service employing a rule-based back-end acting like an eTutor, in the sense that it could supply suggestions for further development based upon a user's personal information?

TOWARD INTEROPERABLE SKILLS FOR PDP AND ePORTFOLIOS

The Skills Profiling Web Service (SPWS) project (Grant, 2005) logically followed on from WS4RL by recognizing that in lifelong eLearning, personal development planning (PDP), and for ePortfolio use generally, the representation and description of skills and competence play a central role. Ideally, skills developed in one context should contribute to the evidence of potential competence in a different context. Where this does not happen, one can easily imagine, for example, an employer being frustrated that a graduate or school leaver presents them with little evidence of the skills they need for employment. This may be because the relevant skills are simply not acquired; but increasingly it may be that even though they cover similar ground, it is not represented in the same way. Both the individual skills represented and the overall structure may differ between different "skills frameworks."

RDCEO

The IMS Global Learning Consortium publishes a relevant specification (Reusable Definition of Competency or Educational Objective, or RDCEO) that provides a format for declaring competency definitions so that they may be reused. However, there is no inherent provision for relating together different competency definitions. RDCEO makes no explicit distinctions between different categories of competency within it: rather, it deliberately makes no distinction between competencies and educational objectives. In our work, however, we found it helpful to distinguish, on the one side, the conceptual descriptions of skill or competency that can potentially be agreed between different stakeholders, and on the other side, the details of the way that these same skills are described—perhaps as "learning outcomes" or "educational objectives" —for the operational purposes of teaching, learning, and assessment. The latter are expected to vary between different institutions, sectors, companies, industries, or nations. Following thc terms and letters chosen for the IMS RDCEO specification, we characterized the conceptual competencies as "C" and the operational educational objectives as "EO."

Insights from LUSID

Previous work with LUSID (Strivens & Grant, 2000) in the context of transferable skills (often oriented towards employment) had already proposed that skill definitions with a finer granularity were easier to use in the context of PDP, partly because they were more readily comprehensible by learners themselves. The approach pioneered by LUSID was to find and use a finer granularity of description that could more readily be agreed upon by many stakeholders, and thus made the basis for variant groupings of these skills for use in different contexts. The finer-grained concepts are used to ask questions of the learner in analysing an experience they had. They are asked, "Did you have to…" followed by an appropriate phrase related to the particular skill in question. It is possible to formulate such questions also with a coarser grain, such as, "Did you have to work together with other people?" (covering the grouping known as "Teamwork"), but an affirmative answer is no clear guide to just what skills may have been exercised.

Why the Distinction Between "C" and "EO"

The SPWS project took undergraduate medical education as its area of application. It was clear here, even among three bodies collaborating for the project, that the way in which the skills were organized, taught, and assessed was quite different between the three institutions involved. On the other hand, there was a very clear sense that all three institutions were working towards

Figure 2. Conceptual illustration of skill relationships in SPWS

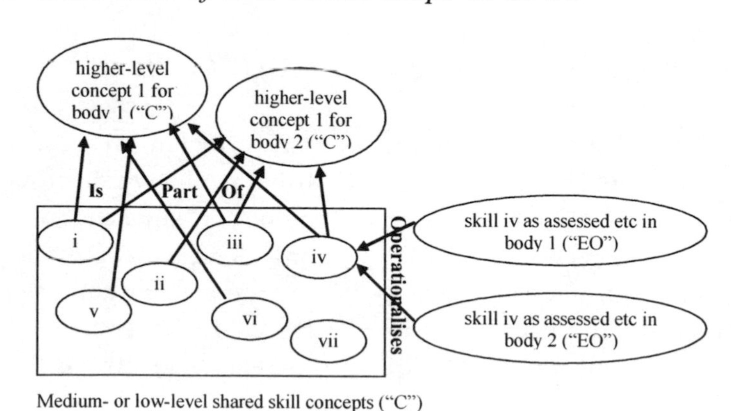

the same general set of skills. This is expressed in the UK by the document *Tomorrow's Doctors* from the General Medical Council (2003), which sets out the requirements for all undergraduate education of future doctors in the UK. This document is, however, not formally structured, nor does it always define precisely the terms and concepts used.

This pattern is repeated in other subject areas. In the last decade across all UK education and vocational training sectors, there has been a move towards specifying the intended outcomes of educational and training processes in the pursuit of comparability and accountability. The "subject benchmark" exercise in HE and the specifications for GCSEs and A levels are both good examples. However, particularly in the contexts of work or higher education, and up to a point in earlier stages of education, the way in which those outcomes are attained can be expected to vary. Indeed this is necessary to maintain innovation and improvement in learning methods.

We believed it was a useful way forward to separate, on the one hand, those things for which there was a motive for agreement, and on the other hand, those things where it made sense to allow variation. If there was no agreement, then the prospect would be lost of any kind of reliable automatic aid in relating together different instances of, say, degree programs which purported to be providing education in a similar subject area. But to insist on overall agreement would be practically infeasible, as academics could never be expected to agree.

Figure 2 is an attempt to represent these insights in diagrammatic form. The left of the figure represents the "C" side and the right the "EO" side. The lower level is a finer granularity of skill, and the upper level a coarser level. In these terms, the primary task for constructing a useful skills framework in a subject area is to find a set of reasonably fine-grained terms which can be agreed upon by all stakeholders (including the learners). These are represented inside the rectangle. When that has been done, different bodies may well have their own ways of describing higher-level groupings of skills, which may not be in a hierarchical tree structure. This is represented by the upper ovals. In practice it would be more complex. There could be different groupings within the same institution, all using the same finer-grained skills. To take a common example, different bodies may count the use of e-mail either as a constituent of computer skills, or of communication skills, or both.

On the right are shown two variant operational definitions of the same conceptual competency. The point of this arrangement is that all institutions should link their own operational skills framework to the agreed conceptual framework, with an explicit reference to the conceptual competency definition, which needs to be held publicly in an agreed location.

Detail and Facets

There is a danger in representing competencies in a very fine-grained way: that there will be an overwhelming number of individual competencies to describe, each one of which is separate because it is not identical to the others. One way of mitigating this is to use the bibliographic concept of "facets"[19] to wrap up some of the variation in a systematic way. The suggested approach here is to define any facets appropriate to the competency in question, and some facets applicable to any competency, namely those to do with the options for assessment of the competency, as the approach taken to assessment is vital to the meaning of any competency concept.

We found an example of facets in (medical) physical examination. There are four methods generally recognized (inspection, palpation, percussion, and auscultation), which together constitute one facet. A second facet proposed was the part of the body; a third was the physiological organ or system examined. Other possible medical facets include language (for communication skills), tools or equipment used, and human context. Having defined facets for a skill, any particular record of learning or assessment of that skill could have associated with it a record of the range of that facet actually used or assessed. This relates to established practice in the assessment of UK Vocational Qualifications[20].

One suggested way to represent facets is as a controlled vocabulary represented according to the specification of the IMS VDEX (Vocabulary Definition EXchange)[21].

Frameworks with Levels

Many skills and qualification frameworks have levels. This is liable to introduce rigidity into a related skills program, with the assumption that levels have to be progressed through one by one. This may be potentially useful within compulsory education and immediately afterwards, as long as there is reasonable harmony between different educational systems where systems are expected to interoperate. In contrast, it may be that developing alternative pathways helps to widen participation. This suggests that a skills framework free from fixed levels could be an advantage, particularly for lifelong learning. It is just this that is offered here: a meta-framework with which to build interoperating skills frameworks without the necessity of defining static and immutable levels, though lightweight levels can easily be superimposed on such a structure.

FURTHER WORK

If competencies are to be represented operationally as well as conceptually, there needs to be some provision for recording how a competency is assessed within a particular institution or body. Facets, as well as competency definitions, need to be made available to others. To implement the necessary changes effectively in educational institutions may need a very substantial effort from educators to document the competencies that are taught, practiced, and assessed in their courses. In many institutions, this process has already been started, with a focus on learning outcomes, but it needs to be taken much further and made more formal if the goal of skills interoperability is to be fully realised.

At that point the conditions would exist in which interoperable skills definitions could bear fruit. Learners in one context will be able to record evidence in their ePortfolios in terms of their local definitions. As they move on, they will be able to retrieve evidence of competencies based on different frameworks, through the connections mapped out by the providers.

CONCLUSION

The projects described here have identified potential ways forward for meeting some of the challenges of effective ePortfolio design and operation. We have identified a role for a personal information aggregation and distribution service (PIADS), which would act as a 'front-end' to all of an individual's records that might be relevant to an ePortfolio. The purpose of a PIADS would be to give the individual owners of information the facilities to manage the storage of and access (by themselves and others) to that ePortfolio-related information.

Individuals would be able to choose from possibilities of where particular information is to be stored, and who is allowed to access it. As PDP processes are closely linked with much of this information, it would make sense for any PDP Web service to use the same PIADS service.

Because of the close relationship between PDP and personal information, one cannot specify in general and in detail what PDP services can best be offered to a particular individual in a particular context, independently of knowing about the learner. Even in an eLearning context, the PDP interaction would need to be a dialogue, where for example the learner may ask to do some PDP, and the PDP service may ask more about the learner to determine what is appropriate. The PDP WS interface is therefore very coarse grained, as there is no universally applicable finer grain.

We have outlined the thinking of what a PDP Web service would look like and how it would integrate with both virtual learning environments and personal learning environments. The WS4RL project Web site has much more detail, with specifications of the Web services envisaged.

We have indicated how, in principle and partially in practice, skills and competencies from different frameworks could be interrelated through common reference to an agreed conceptual competency framework, and suggested how this could be used to relate evidence compiled for one set of skills drawn from one framework to be used in other contexts.

This does not—and is not intended to—remove the need for human consideration of the validity of evidence in supporting claims to any other skill than the one originally intended. But it does offer the promise of being able to guide a learner in the transfer of evidence from one skills framework to another, and of having automatic assistance in generating meaningful indications of possible evidence.

REFERENCES

General Medical Council. (2003). *Tomorrow's doctors.* Retrieved March 2006, from http://www.gmc-uk.org/education/undergraduate/tomorrows_doctors.asp

Gough, D.A., Kiwan, D., Sutcliffe, K., Simpson, D., & Houghton, N. (2003). *A systematic map and synthesis review of the effectiveness of personal development planning for improving student learning.* London: EPPI-Centre, Social Science Research Unit. Retrieved March 2006, from http://eppi.ioe.ac.uk/EPPI Web/home.aspx?page=/reel/review_groups/EPPI/LTSN/LTSN_intro.htm

Grant, S. (2005). SPWS: *Introducing the skills meta-framework.* Retrieved March 2006, from http://www.elframework.org/projects/spws/SPWS-meta-framework-final.pdf/view

Grant, S., Marshall, A., Strivens, J., & Clark, R. (2004). *Web services for reflective learning—discussion document.* Retrieved March 2006, from http://www.elframework.org/projects/ws4rl/discussion-doc-2004-11-01.pdf/view

Quality Assurance Agency. (2001). *Guidelines for HE progress files.* Retrieved March 2006, from http://www.qaa.ac.uk/academicinfrastructure/progressFiles/default.asp

Strivens, J., & Grant, S. (2000). Integrated Web-based support for learning employability skills. *Educational Technology and Society, 3*(1). Retrieved March 2006, from http://ifets.massey.ac.nz/periodical/vol_1_2000/strivens.html

KEY TERMS

Competency: A specific, identifiable, definable, and measurable skill or ability, which a person can demonstrate through performance of an activity within a specific context. The term competency is normally taken to encompass any relevant knowledge that must be applied for the activity to be carried out correctly and to the required standard.

ePortfolio Management System: A system which uses information and communication technologies to give the people the ability to use and manage their ePortfolio information. This may include the ability to record, construct, compose, store, retrieve, view, edit, or arrange that information, and to control or manage its presentation to and sharing with others.

Interoperability: (a) The ability of ePortfolio systems to export and import portable personal records so that they are usable in the receiving system. (b) The standardization of ePortfolio service definitions and interfaces, so that particular components can be replaced by others offering the same service.

Personal Development Planning (PDP): A structured and supported process undertaken by an individual to reflect upon their own learning, performance, and/or achievement, and to plan for their personal, educational, and career development.

Personal Information Aggregation and Distribution Service (PIADS): The central feature in a service-oriented architecture for systems dealing with personal information, allowing connection between multiple learner services and multiple repositories, under the control of the individual who is the subject of the information.

Personal Theory Building: A constructivist model of one aspect of personal development, designed to encompass reflection, comprising the seven stages of noticing, documenting, recollecting, theorizing, goal setting, action planning, and acting.

Service-Oriented Architecture (SOA): An architectural style whose goal is to achieve loose coupling among interacting software agents. A service is a unit of work done by a service provider to achieve desired end results for a service consumer. Both provider and consumer are roles played by software agents on behalf of their owners.

Skill/Competency Framework: A set of skills or competencies covering a particular domain, together with the relationships between them, and in particular, including the relationships between narrower or "lower-level" terms and broader or "higher-level" terms.

Web Service: Any service that is available over the Internet, uses a standardized XML messaging system, and is not tied to any operating system or programming language.

ENDNOTES

1. The IMS Global Learning Consortium: http://www.imsglobal.org/
2. http://www.imsglobal.org/competencies/
3. http://www.jisc.ac.uk/
4. http://www.elframework.org/projects/ws4rl
5. http://www.elframework.org/projects/spws
6. Personal development planning is part of a UK HE policy initiative which requires all HEIs to provide opportunities to all students at every level to develop a progress file. This includes the opportunity to engage in personal development planning,

defined as "a structured and supported process undertaken by an individual to reflect upon their own learning, performance and/or achievement and to plan for their personal, educational and career development." (Quality Assurance Agency, 2001).

[7] http://www.recordingachievement.org/

[8] http://lusid.org.uk/

[9] http://www.jisc.ac.uk/index.cfm?name=programme_buildmle_hefe

[10] http://www.elframework.org/

[11] http://www.e-framework.org/

[12] In related work also sponsored by the JISC, Simon Grant and Helen Richardson compiled a list of 33 "generic activity types" for PDP, which can be seen at http://www.cetis.ac.uk/members/PDPcontent/viewActivityTypes

[13] http://eppi.ioe.ac.uk/

[14] http://lid.netmesh.org/

[15] http://www.downes.ca/idme.htm

[16] http://shibboleth.internet2.edu/

[17] http://guanxi.sourceforge.net/

[18] http://www.imsglobal.org/learningdesign/

[19] General references to faceted classification are easy to find on the Web, for example: http://www.kmconnection.com/DOC100100.htm, http://www.archivists.org/glossary/term_details.asp?DefinitionKey=723, and http://www.iawiki.net/FacetedClassification http://www.miskatonic.org/library/facet-web-howto.html

[20] UK National Vocational Qualifications are described at http://www.qca.org.uk/610.html

[21] http://www.imsglobal.org/vdex/

Chapter XVI
Using ePortfolios to Enhance Reflective Learning and Development

Bob Doig
University of Dundee, UK

Barbara Illsley
University of Dundee, UK

Joseph McLuckie
University of Dundee, UK

Richard Parsons
University of Dundee, UK

ABSTRACT

This chapter argues that it is essential that ePortfolio development is driven by pedagogical considerations, thus ensuring the effective use of these technologies to support learning. Drawing on experience of implementing ePortfolios in an institutional context, the chapter considers how best to meet the needs of learners within a system of effective eLearning support and emphasises the key role of developing reflective writing skills if the ePortfolio is to be an effective way of learning. Creating and deploying key learning activities that effectively use ePortfolios is now a much greater constraint to the correct use of ePortfolios in learning than the technical design or capabilities of ePortfolio software.

INTRODUCTION

Professional programs within the higher education sector in the United Kingdom have used portfolios for many years, both to support learning and to provide evidence of attainment of specified professional standards. Portfolios have provided a vehicle for the collection, selection, reflection, and direction of learning (Danielson & Abrutyn, 1997). This description of purpose fits well with the concept of the reflective practitioner (Schon, 1984) and its development into the reflective professional (Light & Cox, 2001). It also links well to the concept of meta-learning: "being aware of and taking control of one's own learning" (Biggs, 1985, in Jackson, 2004). Within education, for example, the portfolio is seen as an effective vehicle to capture the complexities of learning, teaching, and learning to teach.

The teacher is capable of reflection leading to self-knowledge, the metacognitive awareness that distinguishes craftsman from architect, bookkeeper from auditor. A professional is capable not only of practicing and understanding his craft, but of communicating the reasons for professional decisions and actions to others. (Shulman & Sykes, 1983)

In other professions, such as architecture or surveying, the portfolio provides the vehicle for undertaking and recording the initial experience in the workplace, a key requirement for full membership of the professional body.

The debate surrounding the use of portfolios has widened beyond professional disciplines, however, with the emergence of the concept of personal development planning (PDP), which is defined as "a structured and supported process undertaken by an individual to reflect on their own learning performance, and/or achievement and to plan for their personal, educational and career development" (Jackson, 2001). First recommended in the United Kingdom Dearing Report (NCIHE, 1997), higher education institutions are expected to have institutionally determined policies to support PDP in place by the 2005/2006 academic session. While the PDP movement reflects a number of factors, such as a focus on quality assurance and a concern with enhancing student employability, significantly it assumes a shift towards student-cantered learning, and the emergence of the autonomous learner (O'Connell, 2003).

REFLECTIVE LEARNING

From a review of the academic literature, it is evident that there is a growing emphasis on reflective learning and practice in higher education, mainly but not exclusively associated with the education of professionals. Reflection is generally accepted to be an active and deliberative, cognitive process which, according to Reid (1993), involves "reviewing an experience of practice in order to describe, analyse, evaluate and so inform learning about practice." Moon (2004) distinguishes between a common-sense view of reflection and an academic one, with the latter involving a clearly stated purpose and an outcome "specified in terms of learning, action or clarification."

A number of authors have explored the concept of depth in reflection, resulting in the development of frameworks that distinguish between surface and deep approaches and help facilitate assessment (Van Manen, 1977; Hatton & Smith, 1995; Moon 1999). Reflection is largely absent from the surface levels, being characterised by simple recording of events, and it is most significant for approaches associated with deep learning, as the learner develops an ability to engage in a process of 'framing and reframing' their conceptions of knowledge. Deeper levels of reflection are most likely to result in quality learning outcomes.

IDENTIFICATION OF THE NEEDS OF LEARNERS

The needs of learners within higher education are rapidly changing. Traditional modes of learning, based on face-to-face contact in small groups, are increasingly being replaced by the asynchronous acquisition of knowledge using eLearning technologies. Learning is no longer fixed in space or time. The use of virtual learning environments are having an impact on distance and campus-based learners, as both sets of students have flexible access to materials, are able to engage with tutors and peers through discussion boards, and can vary their patterns of study to suit employment and personal circumstances.

For all students, however, whether they are predominantly on campus or distance learning, in professional programs or general programs, there is a common need in terms of supporting their reflection and their learning. This is the need to provide a means of collecting and organising evidence, the facility to connect and manage reflections based on collected evidence, and the ability to share their reflections with peers and tutors, with the added possibility of assessment for both formative and summative purposes. Assuming a constructivist pedagogy, reflection is vital as it not only allows learners to make sense of their experiences and values, and to develop necessary skills for action, but also to take responsibility for their own learning. This is increasingly important in the modern, higher education world.

TECHNOLOGICAL MATCH

The growth of the ePortfolio has provided a means of addressing some of the problems encountered in using traditional portfolios. The physical extent of the traditional portfolio was often seen as the critical factor by students, who would assume that a successful portfolio was a large portfolio, and thus that size was more important than quality. In addition, students could find it difficult to capture the increasing range of evidence upon which to support their reflections, and to comment on and manage reflection based on evidence. The sheer physical size of portfolios, together with the occasional geographical distance between peers, could make it difficult to use peer-supported learning in respect to these portfolios.

The development of Web-based portfolios seemed to provide an answer to some of these problems, allowing the collection of evidence of a digital nature such as electronic documents, PowerPoint presentations, digital photographs, and audio and video recordings. However, a major stumbling block to the development of Web-based portfolios was the need to develop competency in HTML and other Web skills, such as FTP transfer, and so on. While IT literacy is a vital transferable skill for many graduates, there was a danger that a major focus on technical IT-related issues would diminish the focus on the development of essential knowledge, understanding, and skills.

It is only with the development of online ePortfolio systems that a genuine solution has been found. Systems such as Blackboard and the customizable "generic" ePortfolio that has been developed at the University of Newcastle (http://www.e-portfolios.ac.uk/FDTL4?pid=54) have enabled learners' needs to be met without the major demands on time posed by the possible necessary development of Web-based skills. Effective Web-based portfolio management systems have provided a straightforward interface for users. This has allowed students to focus on their own learning needs, rather than on the skills necessary for Web-based collection and presentation that demanded additional time and effort, and detracted from the higher order skills of analysis, synthesis, and evaluation (Bloom, Mesia, & Krathwohl, 1964). The technology of Web-based portfolio management systems has allowed a continued and appropriate focus on reflection and meta-learning.

In addition to enabling collection and presentation of evidence and associated reflection, integrated Web-based portfolio software tools permit the sharing of these with both peers and tutors, thereby supporting and encouraging formative and, in some cases, summative assessment. Time and distance is no longer a problem. However, access to IT equipment is essential as is convenient and appropriate Internet access from home or study room. For institutions, this brings about increasing demands on IT infrastructure in terms of software, server space, and staff support.

Off-the-shelf systems such as Blackboard (ePortfolio) and ePortaro (Folio) provide an optimum solution for institutions that support a range of programs. However, there are examples of where *bespoke* systems have been used with effect, such as the FDTL-funded project to develop Web-based ePortfolios for undergraduates studying Medicine, based at the University of Newcastle and involving the University of Leeds, the University of Sheffield, and the University of Dundee. ePortfolio software is likely to continue to evolve at a rapid rate, but the core functionality is now stable and available.

ePORTFOLIOS IN PRACTICE

Professional education is central to the University of Dundee, which has more graduates entering the professions than any other university in Scotland (University of Dundee, 2002). Programs are offered in a range of professional disciplines, including medicine, education, engineering, and architecture, and these programs have extensive experience in the use of portfolios to support learning and to provide evidence of attainment. The University of Dundee uses Blackboard as its VLE, and despite some experience of alternative systems, in early 2004 it was decided to adopt the new Blackboard content management system including its ePortfolio facility. The ePortfolio system was piloted with two main groups of students during the 2004/2005 academic session, and the results were evaluated using questionnaires and focus groups. The experience gained throughout these pilot projects has been of central importance for planning the wider use of ePortfolios across the campus in years to come.

The first cohort was studying for a one-year post graduate diploma of Secondary Education. This is nationally accredited by the General Teaching Council (Scotland), and by the end of the course, students are expected to provide evidence that they have satisfied the Standards for Initial Teacher Education (SITE). To assist the students they were provided with an electronic template of the standards in a tabular form consisting of a two-column display, where the left-hand column listed the standards and the right-hand column provided the students with the space to evidence that they had achieved the standards.

A major aspect of the approach taken in this program was the focus on IT for learning as a means of developing appropriate skills in new teachers. Each student was issued a laptop computer to use for the duration of the one-year program. Within a short period of time, during the induction block, students were introduced to their laptop, the university e-mail system, the virtual learning environment, and the content management system, including the ePortfolio. This was a mistake. Too great a demand was made of incoming students too soon. There was a major focus on developing baseline skills associated with e-mail, VLE, and content management. As a result, students considered that portfolio construction was simply about collecting electronic evidence or artefacts. They failed uniformly to select, reflect, and direct. Time was wasted. The unfulfilled expectations placed on students generated more pressure and potential stress than was planned for, and we observed evidence of student anxiety and confusion. It was only after considerable remediation in the later stages of the one-year program that tutors helped students to develop the analytical and reflective writing skills that made the ePortfolio the successful learning vehicle that it was envisaged to be.

Tables 1 and 2 illustrate the progression made by a student as he developed his ePortfolio. In the first, we can see all he has done is to collect a series of artefacts which he has linked to his ePortfolio, whereas in the second, although he still has links to artefacts, he has initiated commentary on these artefacts and is beginning the process of greater personal reflection in trying to evidence attainment of the professional competence indicated in '1.1.1'.

The second group of students who developed ePortfolios were in the second year of an undergraduate MA (Honours) degree in Town and Regional Planning. Recognizing that planning is a varied and dynamic field of activity, the Royal Town Planning Institute (RTPI), the United Kingdom professional body, does not require accredited programs to follow a prescribed curriculum allowing planning schools to have the freedom to develop their own distinctive approaches. However, the RTPI has identified a series of indicative learning outcomes that it expects typical graduates from spatial planning programs to be able to demonstrate (RTPI, 2004).

Initially, the planning students were introduced to the concept of PDP and the relevance of the process to their future employability and careers. This was followed by a series of exercises around the creation of a portfolio using the Blackboard portfolio system. Central to the approach adopted was the use of skills templates, based on those developed for RAPID (Recording Academic, Professional, and Individual Development), a system developed at the University of Loughborough. The templates selected, which covered communication skills, working with others and self-management, were linked to the learning outcomes of the modules being studied.

Overall, the student reaction to the process was positive. The students seemed to have no preconceived ideas about PDP, or indeed much awareness of what it was about, prior to its introduction. They quickly got behind the concept and were particularly positive about the idea of being able to record how their skills would develop, adapt, and improve throughout their time at university. Having used Blackboard the previous year, the students were very positive about using an eLearning system, but the general consensus was that initially it was

Table 1. Before reflection

SITE Target	Student Comments
1.1.1 Acquire a knowledge and understanding of the relevant area(s) of pre-school, primary, or secondary school curriculum	Module assessment Module 1 feedback SE1 evaluation SE1 feedback Importance of physics 5-14 structure and balance

Table 2. After-interim reflection

SITE Target	Student Comments
1.1.1 Acquire a knowledge and understanding of the relevant area(s) of pre-school, primary, or secondary school curriculum	I have acquired knowledge and understanding of the relevant curriculum areas (physics and 5-14 science) through my school placements, in-faculty lectures, course activities, and my personal readings. My formative report (SE1), teacher mentor summative report (SE2), Module 2 assessment feedback, and SE3 PR report demonstrates my clear commitment to develop my knowledge and understanding. During my placements I have taught all years and ages covering a wide range of courses. Example lesson plans showing the range of curriculum I have taught are: S1 Science Chemistry (Gas Tests).

quite difficult to understand what ePortfolio was all about. All agreed, however, that once introduced to the system, ePortfolio was easy to use. In fact, it proved to be quite a confidence booster to those students who had been intimidated: "I found it a good learning experience. It was quite rewarding to discover being able to use it and use it quite easily." In addition, the students commented on the usefulness of a tool by which they could add data and information from their personal development planning activities into a portfolio and then potentially share with future employers or other lecturers. However, the students found the reflective dimension of the process to be challenging, with many of them focusing more on what they had learned rather than how they had learned. In this context, there was general agreement about the potential benefits of allowing peers and tutors access to their portfolio to give comments and feedback.

THE IMPORTANCE OF REFLECTION

Overall, the experience of using a professional Web-based ePortfolio system with students from different backgrounds was a positive one. Students were supportive of the concept of PDP and recognized the advantages of having an e-based framework to assist this process. Once students have become familiar with the system and have gained confidence in their IT skills, they find the process of creating portfolios relatively straightforward. The integration of the portfolio system with the wider virtual learning environment is important to users. However, as noted by Cotterill, Darby, Jones, Van Tarwijk, and Veugelers (2004), there may be a real danger that users will value ePortfolios primarily as useful and flexible repositories, containing personal details, transcripts, and examples of work, and they will not embrace the reflective dimension which is critical to the creation of the autonomous learner.

It is vitally important that IT skill development, which is needed to enable students to create portfolios, and the skills of reflection and reflective writing are kept separate early in the process. Once the necessary IT skills are in place and once reflective writing skills are developing to an acceptable extent, then the two can be brought together. Students need to access the ePortfolio system early on to collect and store the artefacts or evidence that they think they will use to support their statements of development or attainment. In an appropriately separate way, they need, through a series of tasks, to develop an understanding of reflection and the skill of writing reflectively. An important outcome of this pilot work has been the recognition that the different uses and applications of ePortfolios should be clearly introduced, and that detailed tuition of how to use an ePortfolio system to support reflective practice should be retained for a later session and deployed only when the students are comfortable with the technical basis of the ePortfolio software in use.

Reflective writing is not easy and, as Moon (2004) suggests, it is questionable whether all tutors who tell students that they must show evidence of reflective learning themselves have a clear idea of what to expect or how to guide students. Most students are unfamiliar with the process of writing in reflective mode and need an early introduction as to what is expected of them. This may become easier with successive cohorts of students, as examples of good practice can be used to give an indication of how they can acquire knowledge from both the relevant theories and placements, and then use this knowledge to analyse its impact of their own practice and development. The skill of reflective writing is more difficult than the skills necessary to construct and manage the ePortfolio, particularly when using a commercial product. The emphasis must therefore be on the skills of reflection and reflective writing.

ePortfolios can, however, be used to support and facilitate the reflective learner in a number of ways. The careful design of templates within the ePortfolio, tailored to meet the needs of a particular subject discipline or profession, can be extremely valuable in encouraging the reflective process. A good example of this is found in the RAPID (Recording Academic, Personal, and Individual Development) system, which includes a sophisticated set of templates designed for use by students within the built environment professions, such as engineering and town planning (http://rapid.lboro.ac.uk/). There are over 60 different templates, covering both generic and discipline-oriented skills, and each template describes four levels of achievement. This not only helps students to identify their competence at a specific point in time, but also to reflect on their progress in enhancing their skills.

Students can gain enormously from sharing thoughts and ideas about their learning with others, and the ePortfolio facilitates such exchanges. Students can share their portfolios with peers or tutors, and the experience of this type of collaborative learning at Dundee suggests that students welcome such interaction and dialogue. The early use of online discussion forums within the Post Graduate Diploma of Secondary Education was seen as a strength by both students and tutors, and of particular value whilst the students were on placement and in "distance learning mode."

While ePortfolios can facilitate exchange of ideas, the technology also gives students control over who has access to their material. Thus, for example, while it could be valuable to a student to write down very personal thoughts and feelings about their learning, they may not wish to share all the detail with others in their course or with their tutor. Similarly, a student may feel that reflections made at an early stage in their academic career are not relevant to a prospective employer after graduation. The ePortfolio technology allows students both to record their experiences and to be selective in their use of that material in a way not possible with traditional diaries or learning logs.

A major requirement to support reflective thought and, with it, reflective writing, is the opportunity for extended writing. It is this element of the ePortfolio that enables the student to address the four essential issues concerning reflection as identified by Hatton and Smith (1995):

- We should learn to frame and reframe complex or ambiguous problems, test out various interpretations, and then modify our actions consequently.
- Our thoughts should be extended and systematic by looking back upon our actions some time after they have taken place.
- Certain activities labelled as reflective, such as the use of journals or group discussions following practical experiences, are often not directed towards the solution of specific problems.
- We should consciously account for the wider historic, cultural, and political values or beliefs in framing practical problems to arrive at a solution. This is often identified as critical reflection. However, the term critical reflection, like reflection itself, appears to be used loosely, some taking it to mean no more than constructive self-criticism of one's actions with a view to improvement.

Using an ePortfolio as the basis for reflection provides a structured opportunity to take stock of personal development, accounted for and justified by reference to evidence. This process supports the student in the completion of the extended form of writing in which reflection is more clearly evidenced. This is illustrated by the thoughts of one student:

Throughout my teaching placements I have carefully monitored my development and how I have progressed in teaching my subject and improving my classroom management. Considering both my own personal reflections and the feedback received from my colleagues at school and the university tutors, I have ensured I have carefully taken on board observations which are being made and act on them to improve my teaching methods. During my placements, I have also listened to pupils carefully and taken on board feedback to improve my effectiveness as a teacher. Although it is particularly important to develop a style of my own, I still also recognise that I should take the advice given by those around me in the school very seriously.

And from another:

In listening to this feedback I have changed many of the initial habits I developed in order to improve my overall presence in the classroom and my general classroom management. By far my greatest achievement in doing this has been my development of effective questioning. I find in-depth questioning extremely useful in determining the understanding of the class and in defining the next steps I need to take in the following lessons. I have also been using questioning to great effect in dealing with indiscipline where I have directed my questions at those disrupting the lesson in an effort to actively engage the whole class.

CONCLUSION

ePortfolio technology can be used by students, staff, and institutions for a wide array of different purposes. This chapter has focused on the use of ePortfolios to support the development of the reflective, autonomous learner. Implementation of the technology at the University of Dundee confirms its huge potential as a vehicle for helping students to collect, record, and evidence their achievements, but it has also highlighted the fundamental importance of developing skills in reflection if students are genuinely to take responsibility for their lifelong learning. We would agree with Cotterill et al. (2004) that creating an ePortfolio should be "seen as a process, which can promote progression to independent learning and encourage a reflective approach to learning, with the learner collecting questions—not just answers."

However, to achieve an acceptable quality of reflection using ePortfolio, certain processes are required:

- Students must be introduced to the technology to build the ePortfolio and the attendant skills.
- Students must develop the skills of reflective thought and reflective writing.
- Only once both sets of skills are achieved to at least a basic level should the two be put together.
- Sharing with peers is as vital as in any other form of learning, as the process encourages clarity of thought in terms of the presentation of ideas, as well as the constructive feedback it engenders.
- In assisting the student towards the extended writing that acts as a vehicle for quality reflection, the student must be supported through a process of identifying individual aspects of development, writing

briefly about these, and linking carefully to supporting evidence or artefacts. There must also be an opportunity to identify his or her motivating philosophies or ideologies.

It is only, therefore, in the extended writing element(s) of the ePortfolio that a quality form of reflection, deep reflection, is truly encouraged to develop. Without an enhanced opportunity to 'frame and reframe' aspects, to enable opportunities to revisit events and outcomes, free of the need to solve a specific problem, the student can truly be reflective, drawing on personally held beliefs to make sense of his or her learning.

However, as Moon (2005) writes: "Generally speaking, the ability to write is treated as a 'given' that enters higher education with the student ... " We cannot expect that the mere availability or provision of an ePortfolio within a structured environment will enable all students to write reflectively. We must also support students in their writing development, and the ePortfolio provides an excellent vehicle for achieving this though the asynchronous and non-geographical dependency opportunities for sharing that it provides. What it also makes easier is the sharing with students of exemplar material produced by previous students. This "real" material can springboard students into the demands of the ePortfolio—the reflective writing, the organization of evidence, and the sharing of material. It is all of these characteristics that make the ePortfolio an incredibly powerful tool for learning.

REFERENCES

Biggs, J. B. (1985). The role of meta-learning in study processes. *British Journal of Educational Psychology, 55,* 185-212.

Bloom, B. S. Mesia, B. B., & Krathwohl, D. R. (1964). *Taxonomy of educational objectives.* New York: David McKay.

Cotterill, S., Darby, J., Jones, J.P., Van Tarwijk, G. R. J., & Veugelers, M. (2004). *E-portfolios in The Netherlands and UK.* Oxford: Association of Learning Technology. Retrieved from http://www.alt.ac.uk/docs/ALT-SURFseminar_April_2004.pdf

Danielson, C., & Abrutyn, L. (1997). *An introduction to using portfolios in the classroom.* Alexandria, VA: Association for Supervision and Curriculum Development.

Hatton, N., & Smith, D. (1995). Reflection in teacher education: Towards definition and implementation. *Teacher and Teacher Education, 11,* 33-49.

Jackson, N. (2001). *Personal development planning: What does it mean?* PDP Working Paper 1. York: LTSN Generic Centre.

Jackson, N. (2004). *Exploring the concept of meta-learning. Learning and teaching.* York: LTSN Generic Centre.

Light, G., & Cox, R. (2001). *Teaching and learning in higher education.* London: Paul Chapman.

Moon, J. A. (1999). *Reflection in learning and professional development.* London: Kogan Page.

Moon, J. A. (2004). *A handbook of reflective and experiential learning.* London: Routledge Falmer.

Moon, J. A. (2005) *ESCalate Bulletin No. 22.* London: The Higher Education Academy.

NCIHE (National Committee of Inquiry into Higher Education). (1997). *Higher education in the learning society.* London: HMSO.

O'Connell, C. (2003). The development of recording achievement in higher education: Models, methods and issues in evaluation. In D. Gosling (Ed.), *Personal development planning.* Birmingham, UK: SEDA.

Reid , B. (1993). 'But we're doing it already': Exploring a response to the concept of reflective practice in order to improve its facilitation. *Nurse Education Today, 13,* 305-309.

Royal Town Planning Institute. (2004). *Policy statement on initial planning education.* London: RTPI.

Schon, D. A. (1983). *The reflective practitioner: How professionals think in action.* London: Temple Smith.

Shulman, L. S., & Sykes, G. (Eds.). (1983). *Handbook of teaching and policy.* New York: Longman.

University of Dundee. (2002). *Vision towards 2007.* Dundee: University of Dundee.

Van Manen, M. (1977). Linking ways of knowing and ways of teaching. *Curriculum Inquiry, 6,* 205-208.

KEY TERMS

Autonomous Learner: One who solves problems or develops new ideas through a combination of divergent and convergent thinking, and functions with minimal external guidance whilst learning.

Bespoke: Custom made, developed for a specific purpose or application

Content Management System: A computer application that stores and organises a large variety of documents allowing searching capabilities, manipulation, and control over a network.

eLearning: Relates to learning and teaching that is delivered by a combination of computer, local, and wide area networks.

Personal Development Planning (PDP): A structured and supported process undertaken by an individual to reflect upon their own learning, performance, and/or achievement, and to plan for their personal, educational, and career development.

Reflective Learning: The process by which a student critically analyses his/her acquisition of knowledge and competences.

Skills Templates: Tools that facilitate the identification and recording of student achievements.

Student-Centred Learning: Where the focus is on the knowledge and skills to be gained by the student, rather than the teacher's perception of what he/she will or has taught.

Surface and Deep Approaches: Surface approaches are concerned with simple learning strategies, such as memorising facts and so forth, whereas deep approaches are concerned with seeking to understand the issues and critically interact with the content.

Virtual Learning Environments: Web server-based applications which allow the delivery of online courses utilising a variety of functions such as Web content, discussion forums, online chat, and student monitoring.

Chapter XVII
ePortfolio:
Constructing Learning

Isabelle Marcoul-Burlinson
City University, London, UK

ABSTRACT

This chapter examines the concept and the uses of electronic portfolios as pedagogical tools for adult learners, particularly in UK Higher Education, where it is part of the personal development plan (PDP) agenda on lifelong learning and widening participation. Its development relies on an environment that favours the learners' active involvement in the learning process as well as learning outcomes through reflection and collaborative participation. A better understanding of the pedagogical implications of such portfolios and their learning processes is needed and will be discussed in this chapter.

RESEARCH OBJECTIVES

This explorative study is interested in the uses of ePortfolios as pedagogical tools for adult learners. Its main objective is to investigate their potential pedagogy and innovation within the present technical context and educational changes affecting higher education in the UK. In order to do so, I will examine the relationship between ePortfolios, their contextual and technical progress in the UK, and issues of learning theories as they heavily influence the development of such portfolios.

DEFINING THE ePORTFOLIO IN ITS CONTEXT

The role of the ePortfolio is to evidence learning in general and to provide a personal digital collection of information showcasing the learning process, experience, and achievements of a learner for career purposes and for personal development. In practice the ePortfolio can be defined as a digital portfolio, dossier, digitalized box, or as a folder whose format is electronic and, when accessible through the Internet, as a Webfolio on the Web or within a virtual or managed learning environment.

In the UK the ePortfolio is a digital file of the learner's profile and development incorporated into the framework of the personal development plan (PDP), part of the widening participation and lifelong learning government agendas. E-learning technologies are helping to translate the rationale of these agendas in prompting their further development.

Through this technology and as a tool, the ePortfolio presents the learner's profile and progress, but it also brings new pedagogical approaches to learning that emphasize the construction of knowledge. Indeed the ePortfolio is an active process where the learners accept responsibility for their own learning, and draw knowledge and meaning from their experiences, reflection, as well as collaborative participation and feedback. The technology itself can promote interaction between the learners as well as prompting their independence and their locus of control. As defined by Batson (2002), the ePortfolio is the result of "the intersection of three trends": (1) the work produced by students mainly in an electronic format "based on a canonical electronic file even if it's printed out: papers, reports, proposals, simulations, solutions, experiments, renditions, graphics, or just about any other kind of student work" (para. 3); (2) the use of the Web where this work can be transferred to; and (3) the use of databases "through Web sites, allowing students to manage large volumes of their work. The 'dynamic' Web site that's database-driven, instead of HTML link-driven, has become the norm for Web developers" (para. 3).

However, the educational context in which the electronic portfolio is being used is not always favourable and supportive of the learning philosophy behind it. The learning processes of self-reflection and the construction of one's knowledge and meaning encouraged by the use of the ePortfolio may not sit well within a traditional framework of a teacher-centred approach to learning and the transmission of knowledge. This divergence between the educational context and learning theories influences the use of ePortfolios. These tensions affect the way the portfolio will be used, implemented, and understood. They make it difficult to define the ePortfolio. It can mean many things to many people in different educational sectors and countries. These difficulties reflect what is a developing tool whose uses and purposes are still in the making.

The ePortfolio terminology itself comes from North America (United States and Canada), when in the UK the electronic portfolio is mainly a digital version of the Progress Files that are part of the Personal Development Plan:

> *... a structured and supported process undertaken by an individual to reflect upon their own learning, performance and/or achievement and to plan for their personal, educational and career development.* (QAA, 2001, p. 2)

The PDP is made up of the following information:

transcript records, providing a record of assessed achievement, drawn from a[n] MIS (Managed Information System);

Personal Development Records, presenting other achievements and aspirations, provided by the learner drawn from the private personal records the learner has developed through a Personal Development Planning (PDP) Process;

a portfolio, also drawn from the learner's records, presenting evidence of assessed or non-assessed achievement such as examples of work or testimonials, identified through PDPs. (Grant, Rees Jones, & Ward, 2003, p. 3)

This portfolio may have a digital format and be stored on to a network to be assessed and commented upon by other learners or participants in the learning experience such as, for example, teacher trainees.

LIFELONG LEARNING FOR A SUPERCOMPLEX WORLD

The primary objective of the PDP is:

... to improve the capacity of individuals to understand what and how they are learning, and to review, plan and take responsibility for their own learning, helping students to:

- *become more effective, independent and confident self-directed learners;*
- *understand how they are learning and relate their learning to a wider context;*
- *improve their general skills for study and career management;*
- *articulate personal goals and evaluate progress towards their achievement;*
- *encourage a positive attitude to learning throughout life.* (QAA, 2002, p. 4)

The learners are expected to manage their learning through a PDP process. Going through this process entails that the learner understand how to learn and is aware of his or her learning needs so as to become more effective, independent, and able to adapt to a working environment perceived as ever-changing. Learning becomes an artefact itself, an object and a process in which the participants engage throughout their life. Such a construct recognizes learning, not only as part of a discipline, but as adaptable to the world of professional and work-based learning. This perception of learning is influenced by the demands made on education to provide the learners with the knowledge to live and work in what Barnett (2000) calls a world of "supercomplexity." This is a world where it is important to develop skills and understanding that implies plurality in knowledge and the ability to constantly adapt and respond to this diversity:

This is the supercomplex world that confronts graduates as they develop their careers. Professions give way to professionalism, as individual members of a profession can no longer fall back on the profession's corpus of 'knowledge' and self-understandings but, instead, have to remake themselves anew with the dawning of each day. (Barnett, 2000, p. 157)

In that respect the role of the ePortfolio is to represent the student's own voice through his or her ongoing learning cycle to face the demands made by this complex world. Gibbons (1994) talks about the shift from a subject-based learning to a more holistic learning experience. He describes two modes of knowledge: mode 1 is discipline based; mode 2 is "transdisciplinary"; and:

This dispersed and transient way of knowledge production leads to results which are also highly contextualised. Due to their inherent transdisciplinarity, they greatly enhance further diffusion and production of new knowledge through techniques, instrumentation and the tacit knowledge which move to new contexts of application and use. (p. 17)

Knowledge is accepted as constantly evolving, and learning takes place through experience and reflection that engage with its process. As Gibbons mentions, the transdisciplinary mode 2 "consists in a continuous linking and relinking, in specific clustering and configurations of knowledge which is brought together on a temporary basis in specific contexts of application" (p. 29).

The ePortfolio helps this process of building meanings by configuring this continuous clustering of knowledge. As part of the PDP, or as a stand-alone tool, the electronic portfolio contributes to the development of behaviours necessary for learning within a framework that goes beyond the limit of a specific learning discipline. These behaviours also favour a response to the chaotic and "supercomplex" world described by Barnett where the person needs to become an independent learner—"self-directed" learning for purposeful knowledge construction. To meet the demands made on higher education, a favourable context which evidences learning and its process to prepare the learners for lifelong learning is essential. Thus the efforts of standardization for the ePortfolio have taken place both at national and international levels. The initiatives by EIfEL and the ePortConsortium spring to mind. The efforts made for this homogeny reflect the preoccupation in higher education with learning within the professional world.

The use of portfolios for these purposes is far from being a new idea. Portfolios have been used for many years to provide proof of expertise and showcase of work by some professions for accreditation structures, yet technology has introduced another dimension.

THE TECHNICAL INFLUENCE ON ePORFOLIO DEVELOPMENT

Network and Web-based technology, through digitalized formats and frameworks, has made possible the development of portfolios with a wide range of contents and interactions between users, institutions, and educators. Through technology, the ePortfolio has become a multi-level artefact that can exist as a stand-alone tool or as part of a network. It can be shared, showcased, assessed, or transferred to another compatible system.

This tool brings to bear the native talents of computers-storage, management of data, retrieval, display, and communication—to challenge how to better organize student work to improve teaching and learning. (Batson, 2002, para. 8)

These technical influences, as well as the educational policies and expectations behind the ePortfolio, have led to the creation of a variety of portfolios, making it difficult to define it by one single model only. It is actually its purpose in specific contexts that describes it better. In general, their uses can be reflected in two types of ePortfolios: formative and showcasing.

Formative Portfolio

This portfolio is mainly used as a tool for the learner whilst learning as it allows its user to see his or her progress, the learning process, as well as the outcome of the learning that is taking place. This type of portfolio can also be used by teachers to assess the students in a formative manner.

Showcasing Portfolio

This type of portfolio is more directed at showcasing the evidence of the learning. It can be used for employment or professional development. Examples of such ePortfolios can be found amongst continuing professional development programs or in the health professions. This use of ePortfolios does not usually look into the process of learning, but more at its outcome. It is similar to the paper-based or traditional portfolios found in the professions such as fashion, journalism, engineering, and building where the product of knowledge or expertise is illustrated and showcased.

These types are not strictly exclusive of one another, for in practice, the purposes are blurred and one artefact may have several different functions with highlighted sections in a variety of formats. It is, however, the mapping and recurrent learning cycle that makes the ePortfolio an interesting pedagogical tool translating learning into an active process. As seen before, the ePortfolio addresses the needs of the learners to adapt to a world which emphasizes the representation and the evidence of learning, as it stands at a certain moment in time, but it can also act as a learning device in its own right.

THE ePORTFOLIO AS A PEDAGOGICAL TOOL

From a pedagogical point of view, the learning taking place adds the process to the outcome so that the learners engage in a continuous learning cycle which is then recorded in the ePortfolio. This process can be compared to the learning cycle offered by Kolb (1984) which describes the four stages of the learning process: concrete experience, observation and reflection, formation of abstraction and concepts, and testing in new situations. Learning is achieved through a process that often begins when a learner acts and then is able to see the effect of his or her action in the situation.

The next step is for the learner to draw general principles; according to Kolb, then he or she will be able to anticipate the possible effect of the action in a new circumstance. This learning is achieved through reflection upon experience as most of us do and carry on doing throughout our lives. This describes the sort of learning undertaken by learners who are given a chance to acquire and apply knowledge and skills in the relevant context. This is not about passing knowledge from teacher to student which may lead to passive learning, but instead requires the learner and the teacher to actively engage in the development of meaning from personal understanding and experience.

With the help of network technology, the learners or participants involved in the learning can implement Kolb's second stage, the process of reflection, by giving comments and feedback to the owner of an ePortfolio. In that respect feedback and interaction help in constructing one's own meaning. The learning experience becomes a social activity where the learners' existing beliefs, attitudes, and knowledge can be tested, assessed, taken into account, and/or acknowledged by others or themselves. The interaction with other ideas and meanings from a variety of viewpoints provides a convenient medium for review, reflection, and continuation at any time and form, and in any place with the feedback made possible by network technology. An example of such socially meaningful learning environment can be seen at Johns Hopkins University. There the online portfolios are designed in such a way that the feedback process between the different types of participants, students or teachers, can easily take place to support collaborative learning. The learning evidence of one learner is accessible and can easily be gathered, manipulated, changed in a constant movement of construction. Learning is not about ingesting knowledge; instead it is about the learner approaching new knowledge as something that needs to be "digested," requiring effort to assimilate in-depth so it becomes the learner's version, his or her interpretation of that particular knowledge. I use the metaphor of digested knowledge as it illustrates learning as a transformative process where the learner is at the centre. By recording, mapping and reflecting, and going through this ongoing process over and over, the learning experience should, ideally, become a deeper one that makes learning more effective and internalized, as well as more specific to the learner who constructs his or her own version of learning. This combination between process and product, where the learner is at the centre of learning, can be seen in the PACE (Personal, Academic, Careers, and Employability) ePortfolio project at the University of Wolverhampton. This portfolio is part of a repository with a variety of CVs designed for a multitude of audiences with the opportunity to share or review this product.

The users can "input" the following: "Action Plan, Experience, Thought, Achievement, Ability and Tutorial as part of the learning process and then select several formats to showcase the product such as pictures, files, videos and transcripts" (PACE, n.d., para. 2). Sutherland (2004) shows that this combination of learning outcomes and processes creates an ongoing learning cycle and the awareness for the learners of the continuous nature of learning in the context of the ePortfolio.

This flexible type of portfolio is also called "learning ePortfolio" in which the work of the learner is being organized at the same time as the learning evolves (Greenberg, 2004).

PARADIGM SHIFT AND THE IMPLEMENTATION OF THE ePORTFOLIO

A paradigm shift is needed whereby learning is not supported by teaching as a one-way instruction, but where the discovery of knowledge is to be facilitated. Tapscott (1998) sees several shifts in learning that are linked to the exploitation of the digital media within the learning institutions. We are going from linear to hypermedia, from instruction to construction and discovery, from teacher-centred to learner-centred education where the teacher does not convey knowledge but becomes a facilitator, from school to lifelong learning, and from unified to customized learning.

In essence, the ePortfolio promotes the approach of a constructivist learning theory. This is in contrast to the more traditional view that learning is about adding more knowledge. Instead, with the use of the ePortfolio, learning is based on continuous building and amending of previous structures, as new experiences, actions, and knowledge are assimilated and accommodated to involve a process of individual transformation.

The idea of constructed knowledge is not new. In 1938, Dewey (1966) talked about how formal education had shortcomings as the students were not able to create new meanings from their past or present experiences. In his view and from this philosophical stand, everyone has the ability to construct knowledge in their own minds through a process of discovery and problem solving. From the constructivist point of view of researchers such as Papert (1993), learning is a question of motivating an individual to attach new meaning to past cognitive experiences. Although his research has been mainly with children, his ambitions for their learning can be transferred to adults too. From Papert's perspective, we need to become motivated learners, critical thinkers, problem solvers, and metacognitionists. This is learning that engages the learners to construct their knowledge through a process of experience and thinking. This thinking process allows reflection, the review of the experiences, and the deepening of knowledge in a wider sense. This is a highly personalized process and requires the learners to take charge of their learning. It should, from Papert's point of view, be achieved through reforming education so that its format provides the learner with the necessary tools to participate and to take ownership of the learning process. Such views on learning are coming closer to being put into practice as more people discover the power of the technology. They also address the new demands made on the educational system to expand its learning context.

Although the ePortfolio is the learner's ownership, it is not a matter of owning knowledge, as in having it or not having knowledge; this is a more flowing process:

Learning is seen as something to understand, it takes a wider perspective or multifaced view, a more fluid or dynamic perspective of the world. The context of learning has expanded, away from the area immediately demanded by the subject of study and toward the world as a whole. (Marton & Booth, 1997, p. 37)

As the ePortfolio has not yet been adopted widely in educational sectors, it needs to be recognized by the different agents contributing to its implementation as an important process for the learning of the students.

ePORTFOLIO PROCESS

The ePortfolio is an artefact, the provisional "black box" as described by Latour (1991), where an efficient technology is, in fact, the result of complex negotiation by a variety of actants (things or people), a black box waiting to be opened.

The actor-network school of thought looks into this process in terms of enrolment or connections between non-human and human actors to build a network. In order to be accepted, the ePortfolio needs to be integrated within such a network. This process requires negotiations between the different actors as they all have different perceptions. In that respect the ePortfolio becomes part of this Web made of socio-technical relations, which are unstable as they are constantly changing, as knowledge is being constructed and exchanged. As the artefact, the ePortfolio holds up the social network. However, to evolve, it needs to provide flexibility and meaning to its users; otherwise it will disappear. In the case of the ePortfolio, it has yet to find its place within the network of human actants. It is not a smooth process, but one that evolves in general by chance, opportunity, and experiment.

Having done various searches on the Internet to find examples of electronic portfolios and good practice for reflection and collaboration towards learning using such tools, I found few examples of these ePortfolios being updated. These sites, in which the ePortfolio has been created, have been used only for a brief period of time. They only mirror the product of students' learning over a very short time. Like a slice of life or a window into a past life, they provide a frozen moment showcasing their learning. There is little evidence of a dynamic learning process or fluidity where the learners engage in a lifelong learning path.

Some showcase portfolios, besides not being regularly updated, give the impression of just being a digital CV, sometimes with some personal pictures. Some display little vignettes or stories: they are more like digital diaries that showcase snapshots of experiences without much reflection; at worst they become a fill-the-gap type of exercise where the learners tick boxes in a mechanical way without questioning their value and the way they are learning. This shows that the main difficulty for the adoption of such a tool and its process is to sustain the momentum. A learning community that supports collaborative learning and motivates the learners needs to be in place. Support from the higher education institutions, engagement from the learning community, from the educational agendas and their implementation are therefore essential. If this support and commitment to lifelong learning is withdrawn or simply never made, then the ePortfolio is just an empty tool, a list of "I can" or "I can't" boxes to be ticked and shown to the future employer, who will certainly have no time for this type of poor electronic evidence.

It is important that the process of learning be integrated within the learning itself. By this I mean that the process should be as important to the learner as the outcome. By adopting this standpoint, learning is a lifelong commitment and not a short-term, one-time project with static "frozen evidence" of learning and no record of its evolution and update. The ePortfolio cannot just be used as a global level between modules, a mechanical process if we want to avoid the fragmentation of the students' intellectual experiences in higher education.

Education is not a commodity that can be transferred by some mechanistic process. It requires self-transformation, and often involves deep personal struggle if it is to be meaningful. It needs to be nurtured and appropriate supporting facilities need to be provided. (Britain & Liber, 2004, p. 18)

MAKING THE ePORTFOLIO WORK

When talking about the PDP, Higgins (2002) emphasizes the need for "getting the process right ... [this is] probably even more important than getting the content right." For this she suggests that to create deep learning habits, the "mapping" or the learning process should be embedded as a component of courses and schools and not seen as just another form to fill out. For this process to be implemented, it is important to avoid seeing reflective value and collaboration amongst learners as a waste of valuable time, a meaningless bureaucratic exercise.

COMMON GOALS AND INTERESTS

Developing and promoting reflection and communication with collaborations is far from being easy. As Witmer (1998) points out, it is important to use existing motivations and needs to apply a new technology. The users of ePortfolios need to be part of a community of practice or "learning." Selinger (2000) strongly advises that ownership is an important element in building learning communities as well as shared goals, aims, and interests. It is interesting to see how health and educational practitioners have taken on board the use of ePortfolios more than any other part of the population. Both these communities are specifically involved with lifelong learning, training, reflective practice, and teamwork.

It is also important to note that these communities are work based and constituted by practitioners whose work requires the updating of their skills and knowledge. This implies that as a pedagogical tool, the ePortfolio may only work within a learning structure committed to this notion of fluidity of knowledge and requires almost a constant engagement with this process. The pressure on higher education to get this process right is already mounting. In "Towards a Unified E-Learning Strategy" (DfES, 2003), where learning is "self-paced, individualized, supported, joined up across environments," the DfES has started to use the term "electronic portfolio" or "ePortfolio." It wants all education and training organizations to contribute to and support a learner's ePortfolio for lifelong learning. However, this contribution may, at present, be difficult to justify or implement for many institutions where the ePortfolio is often perceived as an administrative tool or even has hardly been heard of. Changes to this will involve reviewing existing practices within educational institutions, including teaching, learning practices, and assessment.

CONCLUSION

The greatest challenge in supporting the implementation of the ePortfolio is enabling a shift in our perception of learning. We may traditionally take into account outcomes of learning, traditional methods of assessment without looking at its process. If the ePortfolio is only used as a data retrieval tool, leaving the learners to sort out their ePortfolios on their own, its impact on learning will be very minimal. The use of ePortfolios can help to "stretch" our self-reflection on learning and a deeper approach or, more so, awareness to knowledge, but it can lead, depending on its use, to very disappointing practices which are only minimally relevant to a more expedient approach of learning. There is a need to question what is being taught and how to implement the relevant structure to facilitate the construction of knowledge.

The ePortfolio is a starting point to engage with the different approaches to learning. It is a "transdisciplinary" effort to learn from constructing one's own meaning, to facilitate the negotiation amongst the learners so that they can participate and contribute to their learning. At the institutional level the use of electronic portfolios requires commitment to learning that avoids superficial managerial practices which are not always concerned or interested in the pedagogy of learning, per se. The flexibility of virtual communities allows more universal participation, but a single environment that responds to all students does not exist. The ePortfolio needs to be grounded in existing knowledge contexts where the communities of learning understand, agree, and participate in the learning process. The black-box artefact needs its voice.

REFERENCES

Barnett, R. (2000). *Realizing the university in an age of supercomplexity*. Buckingham, UK: Open University Press.

Batson, T. (2002, January). The electronic portfolio boom: What's it all about? *Campus Syllabus*. Retrieved April 25, 2004, from http://www.syllabus.com/article.asp?id=6984

Britain, S., & Liber, O. (2004). *A framework for the pedagogical evaluation of e-learning environments*. JISC Commissioned Report. Retrieved December 22, 2002, from http://www.jisc.ac.uk/uploaded_documents/VLE%20Full%20Report%2006.doc

Dewey, J. (1966). *Lectures in the philosophy of education 1899*. New York: Random House.

DfES. (2003). *The future of higher education white paper*. Retrieved December 12, 2003, from http://www.dfes.gov.uk/hegateway/strategy/hestrategy/

DfES. (2003, July). *Towards a unified e-learning strategy: Consultation document*. Retrieved September 12, 2003, from http://www.dfes.gov.uk/consultations/downloadableDocs/towards%20a%20unified%20e-learning%20strategy.pdf

EIfEL (European Institute for E-Learning). (n.d.). Retrieved September 12, 2003, from http://www.qwiki.info/projects/Europortfolio/epicc/

ePortConsortium. (n.d.) Retrieved September 12, 2003, from http://www.ePortConsortium.org/

Gibbons, M. (1994). *New Production of knowledge: Dynamics of science and research in contemporary societies*. London: Sage.

Grant, S., Rees Jones, P., &, Wards, R. (2003). *Mapping personal development records to IMS LIP to support lifelong learning.* CRA Consultation Document. Retrieved July 13, 2004, from http://www.recordingachievement.org/downloads/UK_LP1_1B_Final.pdf

Greenberg, G. (2004). The digital convergence: Extending the portfolio model. *Educause Review, 39*(4), 28-37.

Higgins, M. (2002, July). *Personal development planning in the built environment.* Retrieved May 10, 2004, from http://cebe.cf.ac.uk/learning/pdp/docs/higgins.doc

Johns Hopkins University. (n.d.). Retrieved July 24, 2004, from http://www.cte.jhu.edu/epweb/TourStart.htm

Kolb, D. (1984). *Experiential learning.* Englewood Cliffs, NJ: Prentice-Hall.

Latour, B. (1991). Technology is society made durable. In J. Law (Ed.), *A sociology of monsters: Essays on power, technology, and dominations* (pp. 103-131). London: Routledge.

Marton, F., & Booth, S. (1997). *Learning and awareness.* Mahwah, NJ: Lawrence Erlbaum.

Oliver, M., & Harvey, J. (2002). What does impact mean in the evaluation of learning technology? *Educational Technology & Society, 5*(3). Retrieved May 2, 2003, from http://ifets.ieee.org/periodical/vol_3_2002/oliver.htm

PACE. (n.d.). *PACE e-portfolio: University of Wolverhampton.* Retrieved from http://pace.wlv.ac.uk/PACE_splash_content.html

Papert, S. (1993). *The children's machine: Rethinking school in the age of the computer.* New York: Basic Books.

QAA. (2001). *Progress files for higher education guidelines for HE progress files.* Retrieved August 12, 2004, from http://www.qaa.ac.uk/academicinfrastructure/progressFiles/guidelines/progfile2001.pdf

QAA. (2002). *Personal Development Plan: PDP.* Retrieved August 2, 2004, from http://www.qaa.ac.uk/crntwork/progfileHE/contents.htm

Selinger, M. (2000). Opening up new teaching and learning spaces. In T. Evans & D. Nation (Eds.), *Changing university teaching. Reflections on creating educational technologies.* London: Kogan Page.

Sutherland, S. (2004). *PACE e-portfolio.* Retrieved May 3, 2004, from http://www.recordingachievement.org/downloads/e-portfolio%20ProcessProduct%20v2_1.pdf

Tapscott, D. (1998). *Growing up digital: The rise of the Net generation.* New York: McGraw-Hill.

Witmer, D. F. (1998). Introduction to computer-mediated communication: A master syllabus for teaching communication technology. *Communication Education, 47,* 162-173.

KEY TERMS

Artefact ePortfolio: The ePortfolio is an artefact, the provisional "black box" as described by Latour, where an efficient technology is, in fact, the result of complex negotiation by a variety of actants (things or people), a black box waiting to be opened.

Constructivism: Learning is the result of individual mental construction, whereby the learner learns by matching new knowledge against given information and establishing meaningful connections, rather than by internalising facts to be regurgitated. In the constructivist paradigm, learning is always affected by the context, beliefs, and attitudes of the learner.

Explorative Learning Tool: A tool which helps the students to learn by exploring, being involved in the learning process, and constructing their knowledge.

Formative Portfolios: A portfolio/tool for the learner whilst learning, as it allows its user to see his or her progress, the learning process, as well as the outcome of the learning that is taking place.

Lifelong Learning: Learning undertaken throughout life, to improve knowledge and skills within a personal, as well as social and employment-related viewpoint.

Personal Development Plan (PDP): A structured and supported process undertaken by an individual to reflect upon his or her own learning, performance, and/or achievement and to plan for their personal, educational, and career development.

Showcasing Portfolio: This type of portfolio is more directed at showcasing the evidence of the learning. It can be used for employment or professional development.

UK Higher Education: This defines the education UK system where students can take degree courses, postgraduate courses, and Higher National Diplomas. This education takes place in universities and higher education colleges, and in some further education colleges.

APPENDIX

These examples are just a few ePortfolios where reflection and sometimes feedback are available to the learners. The majority of these portfolio projects have been developed in the United States where they are more commonly used. The UK is developing or testing this type of project, but is not as advanced in that field as other countries.

Health

Examples of ePortfolios can be found in UK Higher Education, especially amongst health students.

- **The University of New Castle on Tyne:** http://www.ncl.ac.uk/
- **The Royal College of Nursing:** http://www.rcn.org.uk/
  This site has a learning zone that provides resources for the development of ePortfolios and online dialogue, information on projects, news, or guidelines mainly as continuing personal and professional development.
- **The FDTL 4 ePortfolio project:** http://www.e-portfolios.ac.uk/
  This is a project for ePortfolios in medical schools involving four UK universities: New Castle, the University of Leeds, the University of Sheffield, and the University of Dundee.

United States

- **The Johns Hopkins University:** http://cte.jhu.edu/epWeb/index.htm
  In the United States, this university provides an interesting example of the learning portfolio where "The EP provides a secure online environment where educators can gather evidence, reflect, collaborate, and track progress" (para. 3).
- **The Carnegie Foundation has the Knowledge Media Laboratory (KML):** http://www.carnegiefoundation.org/kml/
  to develop "tools and resources to exchange information, share knowledge and produce innovations that can transform teaching and learning at many levels" (KML, para. 2).
- **Texas Tech University:** http://www.historians.org/teaching/aahe/welcome.htm
  This institution has an example of a portfolio created by a historian teacher with examples of feedback. The main ambition of this portfolio is to answer the question: "How does the introduction of hypermedia into a history course influence student learning in that course?"
- **Catalyst by the University of Washington Center for Teaching, Learning, and Technology (CLTL):** http.//catalyst.washington.edu/
  Has a collection of tools to support learning and collaboration encouraging responsibility for learning, promoting student collaboration, facilitating discussion, and addressing diverse learning styles.
- **The Folio Thinking Project at the Royal Institute of Technology (KTH), Uppsala University, and Stanford University:** http://scil.stanford.edu/research/projects /folio.html
  There it is strongly believed that the portfolio can be used as a reflective tool in learning.

UK

Universities involved with ePortfolio projects in the UK include:

- **University of Leeds:** http://www.leeds.ac.uk/pdp/GARTREF.HTM
- **University of Liverpool:** http://lusid.liv.ac.uk/
- **University of Manchester:** http://www.intranet.man.ac.uk/rsd/ci/ra/recorda. html
- **Oxford Brookes:** http://www.brookes.ac.uk/fdtl/projects.htm!
- **PACE E-Portfolio, University of Wolverhampton:** http://pace.wlv.ac.uk/PACE_ splash_content.html
- **PADSHE, University of Nottingham:** http://www.nottingham.ac.uk/padshe/
- **Rapid:** http://rapid.lboro.ac.uk/
- **SHELL:** http://educationaldevelopment.net/shellproject/
- **University of Sheffield:** http://www.shef.ac.uk/~dme/
- **Loughborough University**

Chapter XVIII
Electronic Portfolio Initiatives:
A Flashlight Guide to Planning and Formative Evaluation

Stephen C. Ehrmann
TLT Group, USA

ABSTRACT

The goal of this chapter is to help the reader learn to use research and evaluative data to select which activities improve an ePortfolio initiative; accelerate the pace at which people within an institution begin to use ePortfolios for those activities; and limit the cost, stress, and risk associated with carrying out those activities, including the ePortfolio infrastructure that supports them.

DEFINITIONS

An *electronic portfolio (ePortfolio)* is a collection of digital work, often accompanied by reflective commentary that one person creates (sometimes in order to learn) and then makes available to others for some purpose or purposes. Note that this is a definition of function, not of software; a word processor can be used to create files that are then posted on a Web site. And ePortfolio software can be used for purposes other than these.

Formative evaluation is defined here as any and all studies that can show how to improve a program, including studies designed to show how to reduce the effort or cost involved in carrying out the program. (In contrast, *summative evaluation* is any study designed to indicate whether a program has succeeded or failed.)

The *Flashlight Program*[1] is part of the nonprofit Teaching, Learning, and Technology Group.[2] Flashlight works on issues of scholarship of teaching, evaluation, assessment, accreditation, and other uses of data to improve learning. This chapter has been adapted and abridged from the second edition of the *Flashlight Evaluation Handbook,* a resource normally available only to institutions subscribing to TLT Group services.

PROLOGUE: BEWARE OF "RAPTURE OF THE TECHNOLOGY"

Several years ago I was buttonholed by a faculty member who complained bitterly about the pressure he had gotten from his president to use technology. "I don't know how many hours I've spent putting all my lecture notes into PowerPoint, word for word. I doubt if it's helped my students one bit! I think technology is worthless!"

Of course he *was* right to be skeptical. Educational research and common sense agree: normally if you use new technology to do old things in old ways, you will usually get the same results (sometimes at greater expense). New technology usually achieves its power when it is used to support either a major improvement in a traditional activity or an activity that was not feasible before.

What this faculty member was complaining about was "rapture of the technology": the mindless assumption that the technology itself would lead to improved outcomes. Rapture of the technology has resulted in enormous waste over the past several decades: the easiest way to frustrate or destroy technology-enabled educational improvements is to pay too much attention to the technology. (For more on 'rapture of the technology,' and how to avoid it in order to improve learning, see Ehrmann, 2002.)

Moral of the Story: Like PowerPoint, ePortfolios will be worth the effort if and only if we use them to improve important activities in academic life. To put it another way, we need to shift our focus from the ePortfolio software itself—its features, its reliability, and so on—to the activities and outcomes for which that software is to be used: activities influenced by many other factors in addition to the software. If you want to improve outcomes, do not let the software dominate your planning. The purpose of this chapter is to suggest how to use evaluative studies to accomplish that.

FOCUS ON SOFTWARE VS. FOCUS ON ACTIVITIES

Table 1 suggests the difference between these two ways of thinking about what you are doing: software focused vs. activity focused.

Row #4 of Table 1 is of special importance: many of the factors that can frustrate investments in software are not themselves technological. For example, imagine a fictional institution that adopts ePortfolios for only one reason: to make student work accessible to outside experts who would then provide special kinds of feedback. So software is acquired and hundreds of student projects are put into the ePortfolios. Then people get an unpleasant surprise. The first term, only a few outside experts are used. Next term, the number increases only slightly, and the semester after that, the number of outside experts begins to decline! What went wrong? The failure may well be due to factors other than the software's features. Perhaps the institution did not have a strategy for helping faculty and students find such experts. Perhaps the people doing the assessment did not feel appreciated or rewarded, and decided not to do it again. Note that:

a. It does not matter if, afterwards, people discover what went wrong. It is still a failure.
b. It does not matter if the champions of the technology then say, "It wasn't our fault. The technology we provided was great. The rest should have been taken care of by someone else." It is still a failure.

Table 1. Focus on software; focus on activities

	Software Focused	Activity Focused
1. Primary focus of attention during planning and implementation phases of the initiative	Focus your attention on features of ePortfolio software (choosing software with the most, best features; training users about those features)	Focus your attention on changing what people do (with the help of ePortfolio software), e.g., "Help students continue to learn from a project even after the course is over."
2. Time frame?	Remaining life of the software after it has been acquired and installed (2-5 years?)	The effort to improve this activity may have begun before this particular software was acquired. The effort will probably need to extend beyond the useful life of this software and perhaps through another software lifecycle beyond that. Therefore the planning and formative evaluation both need to have long time horizons: 4-8 years or more.
3. If, in the future, we were to conclude that this ePortfolio initiative had "failed," what would we mean by "failed"?	Software was not used much and/or many people tried the software, were dissatisfied with its features, and abandoned it.	The focal educational activities and their outcomes did not improve. (This can happen sometimes even when ePortfolio software is used frequently and with reasonable satisfaction.)
4. How can we avoid such failure?	Find or create reliable software for ePortfolio use. Assure good, widely accessible training in the use of the software's various features. Do a good job of "marketing" the availability of the software.	Be clear about the most important activities to improve and then pay attention to *any* factor that could encourage, or inhibit, change in the activity (including but not limited to software-related factors). For example, if use of ePortfolios for seeking employment is important, then study all problems employers have in using ePortfolios to screen job candidates. When you discover problems, see what can be done to reduce or eliminate them.
5. Roles for formative evaluation	Studies of reliability of software, use of software features, general satisfaction of user with software and its features	As this chapter will describe, formative evaluation can provide many kinds of guidance for assuring that activities (using the ePortfolio software) can be improved at a reasonable cost.

The goal of formative evaluation is to help avoid such failures, and increase the chances that your investment in ePortfolios produces maximum change in activities and their outcomes, with the smallest possible cost and stress.

A SERIES OF FORMATIVE EVALUATIONS: SUMMARY

This chapter describes a series of formative evaluations designed to help ePortfolios improve activities. Several of the studies below may be carried out simultaneously, if you so choose. You may also choose to do just a few of these studies.

1. **Identify Activities:** That are the primary uses of the ePortfolio system—the major reasons for the investment in this use of software. Are there particular outcomes that improved activities are supposed to foster?
2. **Assess Wants and Needs:** Of the various activities and goals that could be advanced with ePortfolios, which are needed most widely? Most deeply?
3. **Study "Recipes" for Improving Activities, without and with ePortfolios:** How are those activities carried out without ePortfolios at your institution and elsewhere? What are the forces, strategies, and factors that influence success (the "recipe")? What kinds of outcomes seem to result, good and bad, as the activity changes?
4. **Measure Key Activities Periodically:** And when appropriate, measure *their outcomes*. Such studies can help focus atten-

tion and guide investment of resources over the years. If possible, begin before the ePortfolio is implemented, so that later, you can see whether, when, and how the activities and outcomes improve.

5. **Debug the Activities:** That is, discover factors that frustrate most or all users. Discover how to increase the incentives for those activities.
6. **Develop and Use Diagnostics to Reduce Barriers to 100% Participation:** That is, discover factors that frustrate individual users, and develop a process that can assess and aid such users so that participation and success rates with ePortfolio use approach 100%.
7. **Study Use of Time and of Money:** In order to *reduce stress on staff and budgets* as portfolio use widens and deepens.
8. **Test Your Theories:** Are the activities indeed improving? Because of ePortfolio use? Is there evidence that this portfolio-aided improvement in the activity is indeed aiding the desired improvements in outcomes?

Ideally you should take steps 1-5 before your first ePortfolio pilot implementation begins, even before you select the software. However, if you have already begun, you can still begin step 1 at any time. In fact, you will probably change software in a few years, so you can look at this work as preparation for the next generation of technology while simultaneously helping you get more value from the software you are already using!

1. Identify Activities

Which activities—which projected uses of ePortfolios—should most influence your planning and your formative evaluation?

One way to begin your planning is to create a menu of activities that are candidates for 'most important uses of this ePortfolio'. Table 2 lists a few such activities, showing how each activity can also be useful for selecting features of ePortfolio software.

How can you select activities on which to focus? If that choice was not made long ago, here are a couple of considerations. Step 2 below deals with needs analysis. Step 3 below deals with the factors required to improve the activity, in addition to providing an ePortfolio (e.g., if you're considering using ePortfolios in order to engage more outside experts and peers in the assessment of student work, what 'ingredients' are required for this activity, in addition to ePortfolio software?).

Who is empowered to decide on which activities an ePortfolio initiative should focus? We have heard the following story too many times in recent months. "Our IT people (or our assessment people) acquired electronic portfolio software for our institution with almost no faculty consultation. And so faculty members are up in arms!" I suspect that reality is a bit more complicated. I know that, at some institutions, the following is what really happened:

a. A few faculty members and institutional offices each began to use an ePortfolio (often using different software). These early uses had a variety of goals: some departments were responding to accreditor pressure in their profession, other users were interested in job portfolios, and still others in fostering student reflection within a course. Early on, users might employ, or seek to employ, a half dozen or more different software packages, including such basic software as word processors and Web editing packages, as well as soft-

Table 2. List of activities and relevant software features

Activity that can be supported especially well with the proper ePortfolio (and other ingredients)	Features of the software needed to support this activity
Reflection: Improve how the work is done and improve what the author learns by thinking critically about the work, and series of works, as seen against a larger context (e.g., progress toward personal goals or goals set by an authority)	▪ Software tools to create and display extensive reflections about student work, including ability to create links and solicit further comments from others ▪ Author has options to create goals, criteria, and rubrics ▪ Author has options to select outside assessors and record their comments about individual works, achievement of specific criteria, and the portfolio as a whole
Aid planning of future work by the author	▪ Display externally imposed goals and rubrics in advance, in order to help the author decide what to learn. ▪ If the goal of the ePortfolio is "constructivist" (i.e., to challenge the author to invent personally meaningful goals, rubrics, and works), then the software should make it easy for the author to create such goals and rubrics and relate them to specific works
Shift emphasis in a degree program toward development of complex skills and away from accumulation of course credits	▪ Ability to store and organize works that can exhibit "skills-in-use" (e.g., videos of the author facilitating a meeting; materials that illustrate how the author developed and carried out a research project) ▪ Ability to attach reflective essays to those papers that describe what elements of the work illustrate a skill-in-use ▪ Rubrics easily available for assessing skills exhibited in such works and reflective papers
Help author **incorporate and relate experience gained from outside the academic program** (prior experience; job experience; electives; family experiences; other informal learning)	▪ Ability for author to include projects and reflections not assigned by faculty and not part of any one specific course in this program
Widen variety of assessors, beyond the faculty teaching the courses where the work was assigned	▪ Portfolio on the Web or otherwise available online (with password arrangements for privacy that are not too complicated to manage) so that assessors can comment regardless of their location, schedules, even when the selected assessors are not employees or students of this institution ▪ Ability for assessors to discuss author work online (e.g., threaded discussion "attached" to the portfolio or specific works within the portfolio) before and after "scoring"; ability to control how public or private such commentary is
Support learning communities and other forms of collaborative learning in which students evaluate work by students in "other" courses (e.g., learning communities that consist of two or more courses taught in a coordinated way to the same cohort of students)	▪ Ability for a project to be authored or displayed by more than one student ▪ Ability for annotations or assessments for that project to be displayed for the team, or for individual authors
Make it more likely that the student will **continue to improve the project even after the course ends,** thus increasing motivation to work on the project (it is real, not just an artifact being created to please a faculty member) and deepening learning (through revisions done later on)	▪ Easy access to and ability to change (or add new versions of) projects after the course ends
Promotions, job searches, applications for further schooling, and so forth. Help author get advancement by providing tailored, rich, well-documented record of work	▪ Portfolio available to current or potential employer, grad school, and so on ▪ If some forms can be filled out simply by providing the URL of the portfolio and if the portfolio is organized to match the requirements of that form, so much the better
Formative evaluation of the academic program served by the ePortfolio: When student ePortfolios are designed to chart student progress toward a degree or certificate, they can provide an occasion for **faculty** to **debate and agree on program goals and criteria for evaluating progress** because faculty need to (a) agree on rubrics and other procedures for assessing student progress, and (b) agree on judgment and feedback for specific student portfolios. In the process they also learn about how their colleagues are teaching (e.g., assignments and rubrics used to grade them).	▪ Ability for student and assessors to see and discuss student work in context of prior work, goals, and examples of levels of goal achievement ▪ Tools for assessment (e.g., pop-up rubrics; ability for referees to discuss student work online before final score) ▪ Ability to examine all student works, or a random sample of student works, submitted in their ePortfolios as evidence of progress toward the same level of the same goal (e.g., all works submitted as evidence of level of communications skills to be achieved by rising juniors in a four-year program), along with the assessments made of those works ▪ Ability to link meta-comments about such works to the body of ePortfolios so that, for example, one faculty member can make comments about student works at a certain level and, later, another faculty member studying those same student works in order to think about program improvement will, along with those works, see the previous faculty member's commentary; in other words, these meta-comments (made as part of a program evaluation process) can be linked to the structure of the ePortfolios and vice versa

ware designed specifically for ePortfolio use. One or two users design their own ePortfolio software from scratch.

b. The IT staff begins to support a few of the specialized ePortfolio software packages. The central staff may or may not provide support for the homegrown system (or they might be building such a system for themselves).

c. As interest grows a bit, IT encourages or requires other potential users to use one of the supported packages so IT does not have to spread itself and its budget too thinly.

d. But the needs of this second generation of users does not always match the features of the first set of packages (and technical progress has brought along more, and better options).

e. Some people start talking about using ePortfolios for assessing student progress toward a degree, as part of academic records and/or for program evaluation. These applications require far more standardization and integration with other information systems than do uses of ePortfolios within course. IT Services begins pressing for just one or two standards.

f. More faculty bitterly accuse the IT department of making arbitrary decisions affecting the curriculum.

To avoid this slow slide into damaging, demoralizing conflict, it makes sense to try, earlier in the game, to create a consensus strategy. That effort will not totally avoid this problem, but it might reduce the number of accusations that the initial decisions were made without consultation!

For institution-wide portfolio initiatives, we suggest either working through a Teaching Learning Technology Roundtable[3] or with some other entity that draws on a variety of roles and points of view. Here are some types of people who ought to be playing important roles in a planning team or oversight committee:

- Some faculty who are experienced with these activities and some who are novices
- Some faculty who are experienced with these technologies and some who are novices
- Students
- IT support staff
- Faculty development/support
- Registrar
- Institutional research
- Assessment specialists and/or committee members
- Self-study team members for upcoming accreditations
- Professional schools, distance learning, and other units that would use or support the portfolio in distinctive ways (including for staff portfolios)

This kind of collaboration is unwieldy in the short term because members of the team may not share assumptions or even the same definitions for key words. But a committee like this can be vital for assuring that, once the software becomes available, its uses are well understood and widely supported.

2. Assessing Needs

Which of these activities do people most need to improve? Many past initiatives have failed because people behind the initiative wanted to be able to do something and incorrectly assumed that most other people wanted to do that same thing, too.

One way to avoid the disaster of a big investment in ePortfolios that is then little used: design an initiative that is designed to scale up slowly and only on demand. In other words, if it starts small and stays small, it is fine. If it starts small and then grows because it gradually becomes popular, fine.

A second option: assess needs for improving activities before you design the initiative, to help assure that, when the new ePortfolio capability becomes available, it is eagerly embraced and appropriately used.

There are at least two ways to discover how important it is to people to improve an activity:

1. Observe what happens when they, or people like them, have the opportunity to improve the activity
2. Ask them (e.g., surveys, focus groups, interviews)

1. Experiments: Natural Experiments and Pilot Tests

Discover what people have actually done when offered the kinds of tools provided by ePortfolios, both at your institution and at other institutions comparable to yours. For example, look for institutions with similar cultures, students, and IT infrastructure—institutions that have already tried ePortfolio pilots of different types. Did users embrace it in large numbers? Did large numbers of users resent or ignore it? Why?

Another way to use this kind of inquiry is to get some illustrative evidence about what enthusiasm, resentment, and indifference can look like—illustrations you can use in local focus groups, interviews, and surveys (see below).

Note: one of the most common mistakes in planning technology initiatives is to begin by assuming that "no institution is like ours, and no technology is like this one." In my experience, no matter where you are, there are probably dozens and, more likely, hundreds of other institutions that are similar enough to yours, and have used technologies similar enough, to provide guidance that can help you avoid costly mistakes.

2. Asking Potential Users About Which Activities They Want to Do Better

The most basic way to ask this question is something like this: "On a scale of 1 (urgent) to 5 (not a priority), how important would it be to make this activity easier for you?"

But what if the respondent cannot imagine what it would be like for this activity to be easy? That is why it is important to gather examples from pilot experiments and full implementations elsewhere, for example, video clips of people talking about what they liked and what they did not like about the use of the ePortfolio to improve this particular activity.

Focus groups and interviews can help your design team understand needs in some depth, but it is expensive to gather data this way, so this kind of needs assessment tends to involve relatively small numbers of people.

Surveys are better for creating generalizations; you can get data from hundreds of people, but it is a bit more risky to use surveys to ask people about their need for a service or activity with which they are not yet familiar.[4]

That is why, for larger initiatives with good funding and long enough lead times, it can make sense to do both: start with surveys to get a glimpse of the kinds of activities for which there might be a major need for improvement, and then use focus groups and interviews to show people what might be possible (positive, negative) and get a richer sense of their reactions.

3. Studying "Recipes"

What other "ingredients" are needed for the chosen activities, in addition to the software that organizes the ePortfolio? Another reason that initiatives fail to change activities is that the innovators never realize that factors other than the technology are also needed to change the activities.

For example, suppose one reason for your ePortfolio is that traditional grades and transcripts do not tell graduate schools or employers much about what a student can actually do. So one activity you would like to improve is documentation of student skills, for example by using annotated digital video records of students' abilities to facilitate meetings, or to dance, or to argue a legal case.

Will that activity improve if the only change is provision of ePortfolio software? Probably not. What are the some of the other elements of the recipe? Some you will already have, but some may not yet be ready:

- A curriculum to develop these skills
- Faculty and external experts who can assess these skills—this kind of learning and assessment take time, so some other themes may need to be de-emphasized or eliminated in order to make "space" for this work
- Audiences who are prepared, substantively and technically, to see and understand this material (e.g., the employers and colleges where students might be taking these portfolios)
- Technologies and facilities for producing and editing the digital video: cameras, studios with good sound and lighting, and server space for the video
- Training to use those facilities
- Standards for creating the video, to decrease the chance that a decade from now, no one will be able to view the video or the annotations because technology has changed
- Policies for assuring that everyone has access to the technology (lending equipment for use off campus?)
- Rights agreements, including people other than the author who appear in the video or who helped create it

Studying other programs that use video records in this way can help you describe this set of ingredients—this recipe for extensive use of student video—even if they do not use the same software you are planning to use.

Whether your interest is student video or some other activity, it helps to do some research on other institutions that are already doing what you would like to do. Identify the activities you would like to improve or start with ePortfolios and then look hard for other institutions that have been doing something analogous (perhaps with different software). Use the Web, telephone, and word of mouth (you talk with someone who says, "We're not doing that, but I think X is").

Once you find your fellow pioneers, ask them to describe what is going on with the activity and what they have learned about what is necessary to make that activity work. For example, if they have been using the software to include a wider variety of assessors for student work (including assessors off campus), how do they find the assessors? What is involved in signing them up? Is there some kind of agreement? What kinds of rewards do they receive? (Pleasure? Thank-you gifts? Follow-up from the institution? Fees?) How much turnover is there among these assessors?

Discover issues that occur when a pilot "scales up" to operation across courses, across departments, and over decades. For example, Steve Acker of Ohio State (2005) has written about several challenges they discovered as more and more programs and students used ePortfolios: the students' intellectual property, student motivation, and faculty time.

4. Periodically Monitor Key Activities and Outcomes

To keep people's eyes on the prize and to guide your initiative, measure the activity from time to time. It will help you see when, where, and how the activity changes as ePortfolios become available and as people learn to use the ePortfolio for this activity. Ideally you would like to start measuring the most important activities before your new ePortfolio is implemented. That would provide the baseline so that, after the ePortfolio has gone into wide use, you could compare levels to see whether the activity has indeed improved.

Whenever you start these measurements, keep going. Check on the level and effectiveness of the activity on a regular basis: perhaps once or twice a year. There are at least three reasons for periodically measuring each of the focal activities:

1. **To Help Maintain Attention on This Activity for Enough Years That the Improvements can be Even Larger:** Higher education suffers from Attention Deficit Disorder. An annual evaluation report can keep bringing people's attention back to an issue for enough years to allow really important progress.
2. **To Spot Areas Where You Can Boast:** Activity measurement can be quite useful because activities improve earlier than do outcomes. If, for example, you are implementing ePortfolios in part to improve community, as part of a larger strategy for improving retention and graduation rates, you would see improved communications and connectedness using the portfolio a year or more before you would see any resulting change in retention, and several years before you would see changes in graduation rates.
3. **To Spot Zones of Need:** (suppose that the ePortfolio initiative is college wide, but the activity has improved a lot in some departments and not at all in others) so that you can pay more attention to them, and use the data to attract fresh resources to the problem area.

5. Debug the Activities

Discover problems that are preventing everyone, or most people, from using the ePortfolio for this activity, so that you can fix the problems. Here is an example of such a "bug" that we have already mentioned: an institution wants to use outside experts to assess student ePortfolios. But they have neglected to develop a procedure for finding, rewarding, and retaining these outside experts. So faculty and students are left on their own to find help. Worse, the work is so unrewarding that outsiders rarely volunteer twice. That is a "bug": a factor that usually prevents the activity from happening as hoped.

This step in formative evaluation is designed to find such bugs early in a pilot program so that they can be fixed before people's energy is sapped and before the program's reputation begins to suffer.

Debugging might begin with focus groups. The facilitator takes participants through each step of the activity, asking open-ended questions such as, "Is anything more difficult in this step than you anticipated? Is this step easy? Exciting? Confusing? Maddening? Impossible?"

Surveys and user response forms built into the software can also help you find bugs.

6. Diagnostics to Increase the Chance of 100% Participation

Diagnostic evaluation can help you identify the reasons why not everyone is yet using the ePortfolio for this activity. Sometimes the reasons are barriers, or lack of incentives: when you use these findings, participation rates can increase, sometimes with relatively little effort.

Example: Suppose your College of Education planned its ePortfolio initiative to help faculty work with supervising teachers in area schools as they assess student teachers. A focal activity: you are hoping faculty and supervising teachers will use these collaborations to discuss how to improve the teacher education curriculum. And suppose your tracking studies indicate uneven levels of this activity: some faculty members and supervising teachers are indeed being stimulated to discuss the curriculum as they analyze student ePortfolios. But, so far, many other faculty and supervising teachers are not having such conversations. Why is that? If you could discover the reasons, your program might be able to move toward 100% use of the ePortfolio for this activity.

Because some people are succeeding, we can guess that the theory itself is sound: ePortfolios can indeed be used effectively for this activity. The aim of 'diagnostic' studies is to identify barriers and incentives that result in uneven use of the ePortfolio for this activity. Table 3 describes a few examples of such factors.

That is the way these kinds of diagnostic studies are designed. You begin by identifying a key activity that is not proceeding as planned. Then think about the elements needed for it to succeed. Study whether those elements are in fact in use. And when you discover reasons for the problem, fix it if you can.

Table 3. Identifying and overcoming barriers to 100% use for the activity: Evaluation hints

Hypothesis about barrier to collaboration among faculty members and supervising teachers	Sources of data to test this hypothesis	If this hypothesis is supported by the data, what might you do?
It has not yet occurred to some faculty and teachers that they can use ePortfolios in this way (despite your efforts to publicize this goal). These particular faculty and teachers might love to use ePortfolios this way, but it has not occurred to them to do so.	Survey Interviews	Discover why they did not see, understand, or remember your publicity or training about this use of the ePortfolio. Use these findings to improve your outreach strategy.
Many faculty and teachers deeply distrust collaboration of this type, and see it as a waste of time.	Anonymous survey Interviews	Look for examples of programs elsewhere where this kind of collaboration has been productive and popular. Use those data to help conversations among faculty and teachers to confront their doubts and decide together how to put them to the test. Maybe this is a waste of time? How would we prove that? How might we prove that good collaboration is productive?
Perhaps some participants are having trouble with relevant features of the software.	Survey	Improve training? Change software?
Perhaps the participants are each defining a key term in different ways, leading to needless misunderstandings and arguments.	Focus groups	Focus groups and larger group discussions may be able to help people develop shared definitions. Or perhaps more carefully written materials will do the job.

Figure 1. Partial draft of a faculty survey on barriers to ePortfolio use

This university has implemented a portfolio system in order to document student progress in mastering skills required for a degree. To help us evaluate and improve the ePortfolio system, we need some information from you.

1. To what degree did this course use ePortfolios for this purpose? (check the answers that apply)

- ☐ *Student works* done in this course were submitted to the ePortfolio system, so far as I know. (If you check this answer, please sign the form below and submit—you're done.)
- ☐ *Assessments* of student work were submitted to the ePortfolio system, so far as I know. (If you check this answer, please sign the form below and submit—you're done.)
- ☐ I'm not sure whether we did or did not submit works or assessments. (If you check this answer, please sign the form below; you're done.)
- ☐ This course did *not* submit student work or assessments of the work to the ePortfolio system. (If you check this answer, please also answer #2.)

2. To what extent were each of the following reasons an important factor for the decision *not* to use the ePortfolio? (on a scale from 3= "crucial reason" to 0= "not a factor")

___ The ePortfolio system is important, but not appropriate for this particular course.

___ Due to lack of training or poor manuals, I couldn't figure out how to use the system

in the time I had available.

___ I have objections to this system and decided not to use it.

___ I couldn't find enough external assessors.

___ Students told me they didn't like the system.

___ I didn't know the system existed. Sorry!

___ I had planned to use the system but we ran out of time.

(etc.)

Suppose, for example, that one activity that is important for your program is using the ePortfolio to document student progress toward graduation competences for your degree. You might discover that 75 courses are contributing data but another 50 are not. To quickly discover the reasons, you might create a survey. Figure 1 shows a bit of such a survey.

7. Studying and Controlling Stress on People and Budgets

Another reason technology initiatives fail is that, as use grows, workload or expenses grow in ways that are unanticipated and, in crucial ways, unacceptable. Cost studies, if done early, can help anticipate and prevent such burnout.

One hazard that any pilot program faces when it is about to be scaled up is that the service might create unacceptable loads as it grows: key support staff may become overburdened, workloads that are acceptable for pioneers and early adopters are unacceptable for some of the faculty or student users, expenses may grow unacceptably, and so forth. If any of those things happens, the innovation often collapses before a cure can be found. Such failures can sometimes be avoided if the potential for burnout is discovered before people become alienated and budgets are over-spent.

Study 1: Check on comparable systems being used to support comparable activities at other institutions. Which activities might become insupportable as the system grows?

Study 2: Talk with support staff, faculty, and students during the pilot phase, once they have had some experience using the system. Do they predict that they themselves will continue to use the system? Do they think all their friends or colleagues would like it and be able to fit in their schedules and budgets?

If danger signs appear, you may want to use activity-based costing to create a model of the activity and then do some "what-if" modifications to see if there are ways to redesign key elements of the activity so that, if possible, performance can improve while costs for people and budgets are reduced.[5]

8. Developing and Testing Your Theories

A theory: your program can use ePortfolios and other ingredients to support an activity which, if successful, can lead to some further valuable outcomes. One goal of evaluation is to help you develop and test such theories.

Suppose one of your focal activities is use of ePortfolios for reflection about learning, with one ultimate goal being to help students develop as self-directed learners. Here are examples of study topics that might help you elaborate and test this theory:

- Are students improving as self-directed learners as they move through and out of our program?
- Do students who were most often assigned ePortfolio reflection also develop as self-directed learners?
- Are the students who grow the most as self-directed learners inclined to give some credit to their experience with ePortfolios?
- What about students who do not improve as self-directed learners? What do they think of their ePortfolio experiences? Do they have characteristics that might make your particular use of ePortfolios inappropriate?

SUMMARY

ePortfolio software's educational value stems only from its use to support improvements in important educational activities. You can improve the chances of your initiative's success, and help control associated stress and costs, if you focus on those activities. You can follow a procedure of formative evaluation that includes some or all of these elements:

1. **Identify Activities:** That are the primary uses of the ePortfolio system—the major reasons for the investment in this use of software. Are there particular outcomes that improved activities are supposed to foster?
2. **Assess Wants and Needs:** Of the various activities and goals that could be advanced with ePortfolios, which are needed most widely? Most deeply?
3. **Study "Recipes" for Improving Activities, without and with ePortfolios:** How are those activities carried out without an ePortfolio at your institution and elsewhere? What are the forces, strategies, and factors that influence success (the "recipe")? What kinds of outcome seem to result, good and bad, as the activity changes?
4. **Measure Key Activities Periodically:** And when appropriate, measure *their outcomes*. Such studies can help focus attention and guide investment of resources over the years. If possible, begin before

the ePortfolio is implemented so that, later, you can see whether, when, and how the activities and outcomes improve.

5. **Debug the Activities:** That is, discover factors that frustrate most or all users. Discover how to increase the incentives for those activities.
6. **Develop and Use Diagnostics to Reduce Barriers to 100% Participation:** That is, discover factors that frustrate individual users, and develop a process that can assess and aid such users so that participation and success rates with ePortfolio use approach 100%.
7. **Study Use of Time and of Money:** To reduce stress on staff and budgets as portfolio use widens and deepens.
8. **Test Your Theories:** Are the activities indeed improving? Because of ePortfolio use? Is there evidence that this portfolio-aided improvement in the activity is indeed aiding the desired improvements in outcomes?

In all these areas, starting with building your list of activities, it helps to study the experience of other programs and institutions who have walked the trail before you.

REFERENCES

Acker, S. (2005). Technology-enabled teaching/e-learning dialogue: Overcoming obstacles to authentic ePortfolio assessment. *Campus Technology.* Retrieved July 12, 2005, from http://www.campus-technology.com/news_article.asp?id=10788&typeid=155

Ehrmann, S. C. (2002). Improving the outcomes of education: Learning from past mistakes. *Educause Review,* (January-February), 54-55. A slightly different version of this article is available online at http://www.tltgroup.org/resources/Visions/Improving_Outcomes.html

Ehrmann, S. C., & Milam, J. (2003). *Flashlight cost analysis handbook: Modeling resource use in teaching and learning with technology (version 2.0).* Takoma Park, MD: TLT Group.

KEY TERMS

Activities: Patterns of action. This chapter focuses on patterns of action that are made more feasible through the use of electronic portfolios.

Activity-Focused Evaluation: An inquiry into a program that focuses on what people do with available resources (e.g., ePortfolios) and why they make those choices.

Assessor: Anyone, inside or outside an educational institution, who provides feedback to students about their work

Diagnostic: A data-gathering procedure designed to detect a problem and guide its resolution.

Flashlight: (1) The TLT Group unit that works on evaluation, assessment, action research, and the scholarship of teaching ("The Flashlight Program"). (2) Flashlight Online, a Web-based, multi-institution survey system and library developed by the Flashlight Program in collaboration with Washington State University. (3) An activity-focused approach evaluation design developed by Flashlight Program (e.g., a "Flashlight evaluation").

Formative Evaluation: Any and all studies whose findings can show how to improve a program, including studies designed to show how to reduce the effort or cost involved in carrying out the program.

Rapture of the Technology: In an educational use of technology, an overemphasis on technology per se leading to neglect of other elements (e.g., training, new curricular materials, new forms of assessment, changes in institutional marketing in order to attract students interested in new programs, etc.) needed for educational success. Another sign of rapture of the technology: assuming that the newest hardware or software is totally responsible for the success or failure of any educational program that uses that new technology. Victims of rapture of the technology assume that, when a new technology emerges, there is no reason to study the successes and failures of older technology. In fact, many uses of educational technology fail or succeed for reasons quite similar to the causes of past failures and successes. This amnesia is one reason why rapture of the technology continues, despite the waste it has caused for decades.

ENDNOTES

1. To learn more about the Flashlight Program, see http://www.tltgroup.org/programs/flashlight.html
2. The TLT Group serves over 150 subscribing colleges, universities, and schools, providing resources and services in assessment/evaluation, faculty development/support, and planning/organizational change. For more information on the TLT Group, see http://www.tltgroup.org
3. For more on TLT Roundtables, see http://www.tltgroup.org/programs/tltr/home.htm
4. Flashlight Online2 is a particularly useful survey tool for this purpose because it is a collaborative Web-based survey tool. Institutions can create templates for surveys that various staff, engaged in different ePortfolio initiatives, can all use, or adapt. The TLT Group also solicits exemplary surveys from user institutions, submits these surveys to peer review, and puts the accepted surveys into Flashlight Online, where they become templates that any user, at any Flashlight Online institution, can employ. For more on Flashlight Online, see http://www.tltgroup.org/flashlightonline.htm
5. For a instruction in how to do activity-based costing of this type plus several lengthy case studies, see Ehrmann and Milam (2003). The cases are not about ePortfolios; perhaps you can do such a study and contribute it to the next edition of the Flashlight Cost Analysis Handbook!

Chapter XIX
An Overview of Student ePortfolio Functions

Phil Walz
University of California, Berkeley, USA

ABSTRACT

The possible uses of student ePortfolios are varied, complex, and novel, making it difficult for scholars and professionals alike to capture an overall picture of this new technology. This chapter will address this concern by presenting a very straightforward overview of student ePortfolio functions, according to what have been identified as their five most basic functions: (1) storage, (2) information management, (3) connections, (4) communication, and (5) development. Each of these functions will be clarified with examples of practical applications, grounded in the real needs of undergraduate students at the University of California at Berkeley. Taken together, the functionality of student ePortfolios, if used to its full potential, could transform higher education by placing students at the center of their learning, better prepared to draw connections across subject matters and across the many realms of student life.

INTRODUCTION

Electronic portfolios (ePortfolios) have a greater potential to alter higher education at its very core than any other technology application we've known thus far.

—Trent Batson, Director, Information and Instructional Technology Services, University of Rhode Island, USA

Electronic portfolios (ePortfolios) are currently receiving significant attention in higher education, with several universities and colleges creating, implementing, and using ePortfolios as tools for learning and assessment. And yet, the true excitement surrounding ePortfolios turns out to be not so much what they can do for administrators and faculty, but what they can do for students. In fact, some believe ePortfolios have the potential to transform higher education, changing its most basic power dynamics, by placing students at the center of their education and development.

Such statements will sound all too familiar in today's high-tech, always-something-new-and-better climate. But student ePortfolios may be something more than a current vogue, and here is why: ePortfolios enable students to plan, document, assess, and improve their learning by significantly changing the manner in which their education is understood and managed. A common theme of student ePortfolios is their potential to turn information into knowledge, through what ePortfolio expert Barbara Cambridge (2001) says are two important practices: reflection and social construction (p. 3). By giving students tools to construct and reflect upon their identity over time, the ePortfolio has come to be seen as a major instrument in the pedagogy of student-centered learning and student-directed development. Even more, ePortfolios allow students to link fragmented pieces of their academic and personal activities into a trajectory of their educational and professional development. The next question, of course, is how? What are student ePortfolios, practically speaking, and how can they provide such qualitative guidance to students?

The University of California at Berkeley (Berkeley) Leadership Development Program (LDP) assigned a group of eight staff from diverse areas on campus to clarify what ePortfolios are and to assess their value to Berkeley undergraduate students. Sponsored by J.R. Schulden, Director of Information Systems and Technology, and Tom Devlin, Director of the Career Center, the group spent four months investigating ePortfolios and writing a broad-based report (Bearlink, n.d.) covering a variety of different areas, including functions and benefits, current technologies, faculty uses, and policy. This chapter is based upon a section of the LDP report.

The LDP group defined ePortfolios as follows:

An ePortfolio is a highly personalized, customizable, Web-based information management system, which allows students to reflect upon and demonstrate individual and collaborative growth, achievement, and learning over time.

General definitions are helpful to a certain extent, and the group uncovered a number of similar definitions throughout the course of its research. The group did not find, however, a straightforward overview of ePortfolio functions grounded in practical applications and

Table 1. Primary and secondary purposes of ePortfolios

Primary Purposes*	
Reflection	**38%**
Student Evaluation and Grading	25%
Career and Resume Planning	17%
Program Evaluation	8%
Academic Planning and Advising	4%
Faculty Evaluation and Tenure	4%
Integration	2%
Other	2%
Institutional Assessment	0
Teaching Portfolio	0
Secondary Purposes**	
Career and Resume Planning	**23%**
Academic Planning and Advising	15%
Reflection	14%
Institutional Assessment	12%
Program Evaluation	12%
Integration	7%
Student Evaluation and Grading	6%
Faculty Evaluation and Tenure	3%
Other	3%
Teaching Portfolio	0

** Based upon the AAHE self-reported survey of 51 universities and colleges with currently implemented ePortfolios*

*** Percent of respondents listing each purpose as a secondary purpose (could have chosen more than one)*

student needs. The possible uses of student ePortfolios are varied, complex, and novel, making it difficult for scholars and professionals alike to capture the overall picture of this new technology. And yet, if the functionality of a new technology remains unclear or too general, it will not be successfully implemented, no matter how high its potential value. To address this need, the following chapter presents a very clear-cut and practical overview of student ePortfolio functions.

Before outlining the functions of student ePortfolios, it is helpful to first have a general sense of their overall purpose. According to a survey by the American Association for Higher Education (AAHE, n.d., summarized by Myers, n.d.), two key reasons higher education institutions implement student ePortfolios are: (1) to give students a context in which to *reflect* upon their social and academic experiences, and (2) to improve upon the current state of *career and résumé planning.*

In order for ePortfolios to meet these key purposes, they will need to function in a variety of ways.

FUNCTIONS

Student ePortfolios will be summarized according to what have been identified as their five most basic functions: (1) storage, (2) information management, (3) connections, (4) communication, and (5) development. Each of these functions will be clarified with examples of practical applications and grounded in the real needs of undergraduate students at Berkeley.

Storage

Repository for Documents (Artifacts): An ePortfolio is a Web-based repository for documents. Students store artifacts (academic records, résumés, letters of recommendation, mixed-media files, personal and professional development-related content, etc.) within a number of different organizational categories. The following chart illustrates some of the categories used in the University of Minnesota's ePortfolio system (Treuer & Jenson, 2003, p. 5).

Access and Control: Although students will control access to their ePortfolios and the

Table 2. Examples of categories of documents stored in ePortfolios

Categories	Sub-categories	Elements
Professional Practices	Identification Data	Name
	Contact Information	E-mail Address, Phone numbers
	Personality Inventory	Myers-Briggs Results
	Documentation	Biographical Statement
Education	Education History	Current enrollment
	Academic Record	Registration Record, Degree Audit
	Assessment Results	ACT Scores
	Documentation	Research Paper, Course work
Career	Career Plan	Current Career Plan
	Career Inventory	Strong Interest Inventory Results
	Documentation	Resume
Skills	Computer Skills	Self Assessment
	Learning Skills	Language Skills: French
	Documentation	
Professional Practices	Presentations	Conference Presentation
	Performances	Theatre performance
	Service	Volunteer Project
Recognition	Awards	Academic Honors
	Certifications	Tutor, Level II

majority of the content, the university also maintains some of the content, such as transcripts and class schedules. The idea is that ePortfolios will be dynamic systems, updated automatically by campus systems and enriched by students.

Identifying a Need: According to *Getting Smarter about Online Portfolios,* "(S)tudents need an online space where they can collect all the artifacts of their education, including formal course work as well as objects of personal significance. Students should have complete control over the organization of this space and access to it" (Fournier & Satwicz, 2002, p. 1). When surveyed by LDP, Berkeley undergraduate students expressed a similar need for an online space to access and store both academic and personal information. The fact that ePortfolios are Web based and linked into university administrative departments makes this quite different from students simply storing information on their personal computers. It is not surprising that Berkeley students expressed a need for an online space and for access to certain documents in order to prepare quickly for job or internship interviews. The LDP survey also offered insight into what specific documents Berkeley students would choose to store within an ePortfolio and what documents they would choose to share with others. Table 3 lists the top five choices.

Table 3. Berkeley student needs and ePortfolio content

Berkeley students rate, in order of importance, what they would store in an ePortfolio:
1. Transcript
2. Resume
3. Letters of Recommendation
4. Internship Information
5. Course Work
Berkeley students rate, in order of importance, what they would share in an ePortfolio:
1. Resume
2. Transcript
3. Letters of Recommendation
4. Internship Information
5. Certifications

These choices coincide with the primary documents ePortfolios are being designed to store and share. In conjunction with administrative units, such as the Office of Registrar and the Career Center, the storage function of ePortfolios could benefit students and ease bureaucracy by providing them with a central repository with various levels of access and control.

Information Management

"We've left the information age, and we're now entering the information management age," Paul Treuer, head of the University of Minnesota's (Duluth) ePortfolio system and founding member of Open Source Portfolio Initiative (OSPI), commented to the LDP group. The problem we face today is less a lack of information than an overabundance of it, and difficulty accessing quality information. ePortfolios address these concerns and are, overall, a tool designed to manage information.

Qualitative Filtering: Today's students are challenged with filtering what is most useful out of the barrage of information thrust upon them. To meet this challenge, students will need technical and organizational knowledge, as well as an understanding of how people obtain, evaluate, use, and categorize information. That is to say, students will need information management skills.

Collect, Select, Reflect: Information management practices are inherent in the creation and maintenance of an ePortfolio. Dr. Helen Barrett (2001), an expert on electronic portfolio development, has identified several such practices:

- **Collection:** Students gather, save, and store information.
- **Selection:** Students review and evaluate information, identifying that which is useful and important.
- **Reflection:** Students become reflective practitioners by documenting and evaluating their own growth over time. (p. 111)

ePortfolios offer students an opportunity to develop their information management skills as they create and maintain their ePortfolio over the life of their education.

Identifying a Need: Professionals and scholars alike believe it is essential that students practice effectively managing and qualitatively sorting information. Beyond the general need for basic information management skills in today's high-tech world, student surveys at Berkeley also identify examples of specific needs in this area:

- 59% of undergraduate students have not used Open Computing Facilities at Berkeley.
- 92% of undergraduate students list computer skills as important to learn during college. And yet, 35% say they have made "little to no progress" in developing such skills; 36% say they have made only "some progress."
- 80% of undergraduate students do not have a personal Web site. (Berkeley Undergraduate Experience Survey, n.d.)
- Bear Facts is currently the most frequently used electronic system by undergraduate students on campus, but it does not promote or enhance the development of information technology skills. Bear Facts is simply an online portal to student information such as registration, billing financial aid, grades, registration, and class schedules. (Bearlink, n.d.)

The information management function of ePortfolios would address these needs by giving students a tool to qualitatively sort through information, while at the same time teaching valuable basic information management and computer skills.

Table 4. Examples of connection functionality in ePortfolios

Category	Sub Categories	Office	Dept.	Resources
Career Documentation	Planning	Student Affairs	Career Center	Web-based Career Planner
				CalJobs
				Information Lab
	Statement/Grad School	Student Affairs	Career Center	Counselor
	Letters of Rec.	Student Affairs	Career Center	Letter Service
	Resume	Student Affairs	Career Center	Workshops
Skills Matrix	Leadership	Student Affairs	Student Life	Cal Corps
		Undergrad Education	Student Center	Leadership Program
Non-Academic	Volunteer Opportunities	Student Affairs	Student Life	Cal in the Community
				Peer Advising

Connections

Navigate by Categories: ePortfolios provide a way for students to navigate through the vast networks that make up a university or college. By linking administrative and academic resources directly to the ePortfolio categories, students will, in the process of managing and storing information, become connected with resources that are often underutilized.

Awareness of Resources: Giving students a tool to connect with the larger educational community will improve student awareness of what resources are available and why they are valuable. Table 4 highlights examples of how the connections function could point students toward valuable campus resources within the offices of Student Affairs and Undergraduate Education at Berkeley.

By working within the "Career" category of the ePortfolio, students would find themselves connected, or linked, to a number of valuable resources offered by the Career Center, including letter services, counselors, workshops, and internship or job postings. Also, by working in the "Leadership" category, under "Volunteer Opportunities," students would see links to Berkeley programs that offer or promote volunteer opportunities.

Identifying a Need: A Berkeley undergraduate survey found that many students were not connecting with or, worse, even aware of valuable resources that are available to them. The following are some examples:

- 93% of undergraduate students believe "Preparation for a specific career or job" is important during college. And yet, 36% say they have made "little to no progress" and 37% say they have made only "some progress."
- 92% of undergraduate students believe "Preparation for graduate or professional school" is important during college. And yet, 32% say they have made "little to no progress" and 38% say they have made only "some progress."
- 93% of undergraduate students believe "Leadership skills" are important to develop during college. And yet, 35% say they have made "little to no progress" and 36% say they have made only "some progress."
- 57% of the undergraduate student population have not done significant community service work during the academic year.
- 65% of undergraduate students have not used the Career Center.
- 68% of undergraduate students have not used the Student Learning Center.
- 80% of undergraduate students have not used the Student Life Center. (Berkeley Undergraduate Experience Survey, n.d.)

Students need more guidance toward resources that they clearly want but do not seem to be able to connect with, particularly those offered by Student Services and the Office of Undergraduate Education. The connections function of an ePortfolio would meet this need by raising student awareness of what resources are available and how to find them, helping students reach their stated goals.

Communication

ePortfolios involve more than collecting and storing artifacts, managing information, and learning about campus services. Students would also learn purposeful communication through the process of sharing artifacts and receiving feedback.

Presenting Artifacts*:* ePortfolios would have one main interface (a private Web page), from which students would navigate and manage information, as well as "presentation pages" (public Web pages). Satwicz and Fournier (2002) have outlined some of the processes involved in creating an ePortfolio designed to present artifacts:

1. **Developing a Collection:** Students will need "to think broadly and creatively about the kinds of evidence that might best illustrate their skills, progress, interests, etc."
2. **Selecting Artifacts for a Purpose:** Students will need to ensure their presentation pages do not "resemble scrapbooks or filing cabinets [by] using criteria to guide their selection: What is the purpose of the ePortfolio presentation page? Which items from the collection are the best examples for their intended purpose?"
3. **Considering Audience:** "Portfolios [online presentation pages] are tools for conversation, designed with a particular audience in mind. Students will have opportunities to consider how, for instance, a professor, advisor, potential employer or best friend might respond to the artifacts in the [e-]portfolio, the language and content of reflections, and the look and feel (design) of the presentation pages."
4. **Writing About an Artifact:** "Essential to a successful presentation page is the ability to effectively describe an artifact and explain its significance." Students will need to learn to constructively reflect upon and write about artifacts relative to specific audiences. (pp. 2-3)

By creating presentation pages to meet specific objectives, students will learn how to communicate with various audiences, how to present documents for a purpose, and how to constructively reflect on and write about artifacts. Students would control access via passwords to these presentation pages, thereby restricting them to certain audiences, such as classmates, faculty, employers, graduate schools, friends, or family. In the end, students would have several presentation pages, all built from the student's main interface, and each designed for a specific purpose and audience.

Receiving Feedback: ePortfolios are very much a collaborative tool. They allow students to solicit and receive feedback about shared documents in their collection. In fact, some ePortfolios are being linked directly to classroom learning systems. Such linking allows faculty, advisors, and others to communicate with students about the artifacts in their collection, such as papers or résumés. By granting access to certain categories and files, students can allow faculty to offer feedback on coursework or Career Services staff to access and review a resume. ePortfolios could also enable students to track graduation requirements more closely, allowing for more effective communication with advisors.

Table 5 highlights how students could receive feedback using the communication functionality of an ePortfolio.

Identifying a Need: The communication function is closely tied to the connection function. Both raise awareness of campus resources. The communication function not only connects

Table 5. Examples of the communication functionality in ePortfolios

CATEGORIES	ITEM	VIEWED BY	PURPOSE/ FEEDBACK
Education			
	Research Paper	Faculty Member	Reviewed/Graded
	Transcript	Advisor	Progress Report
Career			
	Resume	Career Center	Feedback
	Resume/Cover Letter	Potential Employer	Review
	Letter of Recommendation	Faculty Member	Review
Skills Matrix			
	Self-Assessment	Career Counselor	Guidance

students with faculty and staff, though, it also facilitates dialogue. Some of the highest levels of student dissatisfaction with their educational experience are related to faculty advising and accessibility and staff advising (Berkeley Undergraduate Experience Survey, n.d.). ePortfolios could address this by facilitating communication between students, staff, and faculty. The communication function also builds upon information management skills as students learn to effectively present and articulate their skills and experiences to employers, graduate schools, faculty, and so on. Such experiences will provide students with opportunities to reconsider career or educational goals in light of their own reflections and others' responses, and to revise them proactively. Overall, the ability to present and communicate artifacts publicly and through technological systems is a skill students need in today's high-tech society.

Development

Commitment of Student Affairs: According to Student Services: A Handbook for the Profession, the history of student affairs is one of an enduring and distinctive idea: "the consistent and persistent emphasis on and commitment to the development of the whole person" (Nuss, 1996, p. 23). Much has changed in higher education over the years, but the "profession's adherence to this fundamental principle should not be overlooked or underestimated" (Nuss, 1996, p. 23). Perhaps the most significant and often discussed function of ePortfolios is how development theory can be applied to the categories of ePortfolios, in order to deepen the commitment of student affairs to the enhancement of the whole student.

Developmental Theory: Over the last 50 years, a considerable amount of research on how college affects students has identified a number of quantitative and qualitative skills students may develop over the course of their higher education. Feldman and Newcomb (1969) published the groundbreaking *The Impact of College on Students,* a work which reviewed 1,500 studies conducted over four decades. Continuing and updating this research, Pascarella and Terenzini (1991) synthesized more than 2,600 additional studies in *How College Affects Students,* summarizing much of what is known about how students change and benefit as a consequence of attending college. Pascarella and Terenzini (1991) identified a number of different skills and skill-sets students potentially acquire. Table 6 lists a number of the different skills they identified.

Table 6. Skill-sets potentially developed by higher education

COGNITIVE	QUANTITATIVE
• Reasoning • Critical Thinking • Reflective Judgment • Objective Evaluation of New ideas • Self-Esteem	• Subject Competence • Mathematical Skills • Verbal Skills • Social Self-Concept • Personal Adjustment
SELF-SYSTEM	**RELATIONAL SYSTEM**
• Identity Status • Ego-Development • Academic Self-Concept • Morals & Values	• Autonomy • Authority • Intellectual Orientation • Interpersonal Relations • Maturity

Adapted from Pascarella and Terenzini (1991, pp. 62-269)

An important role of student affairs is to raise student awareness of these skills and, when possible, ensure that students have access to services and resources designed to assist in their development. And yet, according to much of what was reported in the AAHE survey of colleges and universities, little is known specifically about how students acquire and employ the skills they accumulate over the course of their college career. ePortfolios could change this by allowing students to apply developmental expertise more explicitly than has been possible in the past, giving students the ability to oversee more concretely their own skill development.

Skills Matrix: Although there are currently no examples of ePortfolios specifically designed relative to the skills identified by Pascarella and Terenzini, some universities and colleges are now using ePortfolios to implement what they call skills matrices. In a skills matrix, specific developmental skills are cross-referenced with ePortfolio categories, for example, communication skills could be cross-referenced to specific courses and/or professions. A skills matrix gives students the ability to understand how to acquire and track these skills themselves. Table 7 is based upon a skills matrix currently being implemented at Florida State University (FSU, n.d.).

A skills matrix provides students a context in which to understand how to acquire and employ the skills they accumulate over the course of their college career. A skills matrix also allows students to see the big picture in terms of their educational requirements, to visualize a trajectory of their development, and to articulate competencies and experiences to employers and graduate schools in a more concrete manner.

Identifying a Need: During the LDP program, Vice Provost of Undergraduate Education at Berkeley, Christina Maslach, discussed with LDP participants the need for a capstone experience for all students and the need for technology to enhance the undergraduate education. Maslach's comments were made in light of recommendations made by the recent Western Association of Schools and Colleges (WASC) accreditation review. The development function of ePortfolios could potentially meet both of these needs. It could technologically enhance undergraduate education by giving students the ability to create a trajectory of

Table 7. Example of an ePortfolio skills matrix

	Experiences				
Skills	Courses	Jobs/ Internships	Service/ Volunteer Work	Memberships/ Activities	Interests/Life Experiences
Communication	*Link*	*Link*	*Link*	*Link*	*Link*
Creativity	*Link*	*Link*	*Link*	*Link*	*Link*
Critical Thinking	*Link*	*Link*	*Link*	*Link*	*Link*
Leadership	*Link*	*Link*	*Link*	*Link*	*Link*
Life Management	*Link*	*Link*	*Link*	*Link*	*Link*
Research	*Link*	*Link*	*Link*	*Link*	*Link*
Social Responsibility	*Link*	*Link*	*Link*	*Link*	*Link*
Teamwork	*Link*	*Link*	*Link*	*Link*	*Link*
Technical and Scientific	*Link*	*Link*	*Link*	*Link*	*Link*

their educational experience at Berkeley (i.e., a capstone experience). As one respondent to the AAHE survey commented:

(S)tudents will benefit from organizing their diverse experiences into coherent and articulated formats and from using this accumulated information to plan and assess their progress." More, as a Berkeley staff member commented in the LDP survey, "The holistic approach to student services would allow us to develop students in a more meaningful and specific way. This tool would allow me to ask specific and targeted questions based on trends I see. [It would] also be very useful for [the] career center to help students with their post-undergraduate aspirations. It would be extremely helpful for students in their development and their future goals.

Simply stated, in keeping with the commitment of Student Affairs, an ePortfolio could provide knowledge of developmental processes directly to the students.

CONCLUSION

Taken together, the five key functions of student ePortfolios—storage, information management, connections, communication, and development—along with their practical applications, could transform higher education by placing students at the center of their learning, better prepared to draw connections across subject matters and across realms of student life. With a clear-cut and practical overview of each of these functions, grounded in student needs, implementation can proceed more efficiently. There is definitely valuable substance behind the attention ePortfolios are receiving, and there are also many specific needs that ePortfolios can meet, if they are used to their full potential.

ACKNOWLEDGMENT

I want to thank and acknowledge each of the members of the LDP team: Tony Christopher, Ally Finkel, Linda Finch Hicks, Mei-Mei Hong, Ben James, Joan Shao, and Alicia Vanderpol. This chapter developed out of the LDP Student E-Portfolio Report, something that was very much a team effort. In particular, many thanks to Ally for significantly contributing to this chapter.

REFERENCES

AAHE (American Association for Higher Education). (n.d.). Retrieved December 2003, from http://ctl.du.edu/portfolioclearinghouse/index.cfm

Barrett, H. (2001). Electronic portfolios= multimedia development+portfolio development: The electronic portfolio development process. In B. Cambridge (Ed.), *Electronic portfolios: Emerging practices in student, faculty, and institutional learning* (pp. 110-123).

Bearlink. (n.d.). *Student e-portfolios.* Retrieved December 2003, from http://bearlink.berkeley.edu/e-portfolio/

Berkeley Undergraduate Experience Survey. (n.d.). Retrieved December 2003, from http://osr2.berkeley.edu/Public/STAFFWEB/TC/ucues2003/ucues2003_menu.html

Cambridge, B. (2001). Electronic portfolios as knowledge builders. In B. Cambridge (Ed.), *Electronic portfolios: Emerging practices in student, faculty, and institutional learning* (pp. 1-11). Washington, DC: American Association of Higher Education.

Fournier, J., & Satwicz, T. (2002). Getting smarter about online portfolios: Efforts at University of Washington. In *Proceedings of the NLII October 2002 Focus Session on Electronic Portfolios.* Retrieved December 2003, from http://www.educause.edu/ir/library/pdf/NLI0 236c.pdf

FSU (Florida State University). (n.d.). Retrieved December 2003, from http://www.career-recruit.fsu.edu/careerportfolio/enter/login.html

Komives, S., & Woodard, D. Jr. (1996). *Students services: A handbook for the profession* (3rd ed.). San Francisco: Jossey-Bass.

Myers, G. (n.d.). Retrieved December 2003, from http://www.plu.edu/~myersgm/index.htm

Pascarella, E., & Terenzini, P. (1991). *How college affects students: Finding insights from twenty years of research.* San Francisco: Jossey-Bass.

Treuer, P., & Jenson, J. (2003). *Setting standards for electronic portfolios: A broader vision for an educational revolution.* Retrieved December 2003, from http://www.theospi.org/resources/portfolioStandards.pdf

KEY TERMS

Communication Function: By presenting artifacts (objects stored in the ePortfolio) within presentation pages (public Web pages based upon a student's underlying ePortfolio), students are able to create public spaces, share artifacts with others (friends, classmates, professors, potential employers), and receive feedback.

Connections Function: By linking administrative and academic resources directly to the components and categories of ePortfolios, students will be able to navigate though the vast networks that make up a university or college, gaining an awareness of what resources are available and how to find them.

Development Function: By applying developmental theories to the design and categorization of an ePortfolio, students are given a context in which to understand how to acquire and employ the skills accumulated over the course of a college career.

Information Management Function: According to its design, an ePortfolio will assist students in qualitatively sorting and filtering information through its different categories and through the process of ePortfolio development (the collection, selection, and reflection process).

Skills Matrix: An element of the development function which helps students map a trajectory of their skill develop while attending a college or university. Students chronicle skills and experiences attained through coursework, employment, and other activities.

Storage Function: A Web-based repository of documents, linked to university administrative and academic units (e.g., Registrar's Office). This function provides students with an online space where they can collect and save various artifacts, as well as access official university documents (e.g., transcripts).

Student-Centered Learning and Development: Compared to teacher-focused/transmission-of-information instructional formats, students have more choice in what to study, and more understanding of how and why the topic is important and fits within their own overall educational trajectory.

Student ePortfolio: A highly personalized, customizable Web-based information management system, which allows students to demonstrate individual and collaborative growth, achievement, and learning over time. An ePortfolio can be used in support of career planning and résumé building, advising and academic planning, academic evaluation and assessment, and as a tool for reflection.

Student ePortfolio Function: What an ePortfolio is used for and expected to perform. This chapter identifies five of the most basic functions: storage, information management, connections, communication, and development.

Chapter XX
eLearning Tools for ePortfolios

Uri Shafrir
University of Toronto, Canada

Masha Etkind
Ryerson University, Canada

Jutta Treviranus
University of Toronto, Canada

ABSTRACT

This chapter describes eLearning tools that focus the learner's attention on meaning, rather than rote learning of text and rehearsing problem-solving procedures. These tools are the Interactive Concept Discovery Learning Tool and the Meaning Equivalence Reusable Learning Object (MERLO). Results of several evaluative implementations of these novel instructional methodologies, which encourage learners to interact directly with the conceptual content of to-be-learned material, demonstrate their potential to enhance learning outcomes and to provide authentic, credible, evidence-based demonstration of mastery of learning and formative assessments of learning processes and outcomes for inclusion in 'learning ePortfolios'.

INTRODUCTION

It is generally agreed that an important function of a "learning ePortfolio" is to store records that provide authentic, credible demonstration of an individual's mastery of learning. However, at present there are no accepted standards and therefore the format of such records and their content are open to interpretation by individual learners and institutions alike. For example, a large university in Canada has been recently offering workshops to students and faculty on "How to Use our Learning Management System (LMS) to Create Presentations of

Students' Learning" for inclusion in their ePortfolios. Such presentations usually contain graded assignments, including term papers, problem sets, and so forth. While such presentations may be viewed as authentic demonstrations of learning, the precise interpretation of "mastery of learning" remains open. This is a crucial issue; it is clear that future success of learning ePortfolios is critically dependent upon the credibility of the records as an authentic demonstration of mastery of learning. In this chapter we describe two novel eLearning tools that were designed to generate such records including their rationale, details of the instructional methodologies, and results of several evaluative implementations.

WHAT IS "MASTERY OF LEARNING"?

Credible evidence for mastery, or deep comprehension, of learned material is a necessary component of successful completion of a learning experience. However, what particular evidence is required and what lends credibility to such evidence are the subjects of a lively debate among experts in the learning community (Bransford, Brown, & Cocking, 2004). The development of the novel eLearning tools described in this chapter was motivated by a rationale that views deep comprehension as good knowledge of the conceptual content of learned material. Indicators of deep comprehension are various manifestations of an ability to identify and flexibly adapt conceptual content to different situations, and the spontaneous generation of different representations that highlight and clarify various relevant features of the conceptual situation under consideration. Learners who attain deep comprehension of a particular subject area can produce multiple representations (statements) that share equivalence of meaning, recognize that a statement encodes a particular conceptual content, and also recognize other statements that may or may not "look like" that specific statement, encode equivalent meaning.

In the next part of this chapter, we will offer an operational definition of *concept* in the context of semantic analysis; describe concept parsing algorithm (CPA), a generic semantic procedure that identifies the lexical labels and building blocks of concepts in unstructured text (Shafrir & Etkind, 2005); and describe two applications of CPA in eLearning that result in the generation of digital records particularly suitable for inclusion in learning ePortfolios, one for learners who explore the conceptual content of digital text through the Interactive Concept Discovery Learning Tool, and the other for domain experts and instructors who use CPA for detailed and accurate mapping of the conceptual content of course material and for the construction of Meaning Equivalence Reusable Learning Objects (MERLOs) that focus learners' attention on meaning (patents pending).

What is "Concept"?

Unlike words in natural language, "concept" in a discipline must be precisely and clearly defined; for conceptual content of a scientific discipline to be successfully captured by language, the meaning of the words must first be disambiguated. "Concept" is a regularity, an organizational principle behind a large collection of facts, an invariant, a pattern in the data. How are concepts—patterns in the data—encoded and communicated? All content areas use "code words" to communicate meaning; it is easy to verify that such codes exist in all disciplines: science, medicine, social science, humanities, as well as in the professions.

Lexical Labels of Concepts

The use of "code words" as lexical labels of concepts within a context in a discipline differs from the use of these same words in ordinary language in two important ways:

1. Lexical labels of concepts do not encode the literal meanings associated with their constituent words in the daily use of the language; rather, each such label encodes a connoted meaning, a meaning rooted in the regularity being considered, that differs from the literal meaning of the word(s).
2. Lexical labels of concepts do not have synonyms; rather, each label functions like a proper name of the signified concept.

The implications of this formulation will be examined in this chapter; as we shall see, they are considerable. For example, it is easy to verify that textbooks and articles in learned journals, while discussing conceptual content of the particular discipline, "read like" natural language. In other words, while containing a "secret code" that re-defines parts of the lexicon (by using "ordinary words" as lexical labels that denote precisely defined, abstract concepts), text in these books and journals still obeys syntactical, morphological, and grammatical rules of the natural language in which it is written. This seems to hold across disciplines and across languages.

There is no uniform format of lexical labels of concepts. A lexical label may be a single sign or a sequence of signs in a mono-level sign system—namely, words in natural language. For example, the words "strangeness," "color," and "spin" are lexical labels of concepts in particle physics, where they encode meanings that are very different from their literal meanings in English; "scaffolding" is a lexical label of a concept in learning theory, unrelated to the construction industry; genetics contains the lexical label "bi-directionality"; and "flying buttress" is a lexical label of a concept in architecture that is unrelated to flying. A lexical label may also be one or more words borrowed from another primary sign system (i.e., another natural language; for example "bulimia nervosa"), or signs borrowed from a secondary sign system (e.g., CO_2; ♫), or a combination of several such elements in a multilevel sign system (e.g., F# Major). As one can see, lexical labels function like proper names of concepts.

What is the Meaning Attached to a Lexical Label of a Concept?

A paragraph in a textbook that contains a lexical label may provide an approximate definition of the concept associated with it. However, in order to qualify as a *concept statement that specifies the meaning of the concept,* the paragraph must provide a comprehensive encoding of the regularity under consideration. Concept statements may be found in textbooks or may be formulated by domain experts, and must include not only the lexical label of the concept but also describe its building blocks—that is, all the important features of the concept. Here is an example of a paragraph that may be identified as concept statement (Sternberg & Williams, 2002):

As children mature, their cognitive functioning changes. They acquire new mental skills that enable them to better perceive, process, encode and memorize information. Cognitive development is the study of changes in mental skills that occur through biological maturation and experience. Cognitive development does not stop when children mature, but continues throughout the lifespan. (p. 40)

While this paragraph provides a broader background, the core sentence of interest is the definition of the concept here identified by the lexical label *cognitive development* in the context of child development:

Cognitive development is the study of changes in mental skills that occur through biological maturation and experience.

A close examination reveals that the concept with the lexical label *cognitive development* is defined here by co-occurrence of three other subordinate concepts (mental skills, biological maturation, experience), and particular relations between them (changes, occur through). Schematically, this sentence may be parsed into three sets:

Cognitive development = {[mental skills, biological maturation, experience], [changes, occur through], [linguistic descriptors]}

We may denote these sets as:

[Ci] = [mental skills, biological maturation, experience] is a set of co-occurring concepts [C_1, C_2, C_3].
[Rj] = [changes, occur through] is a set of relations [R_1, R_2].
[Lk] = [linguistic descriptors] is a set of additional linguistic elements [L_1, L_2,...] that obey syntactical, morphological, and grammatical rules of the language.

Concept Parsing Algorithms (CPAs)

Systematic examination of concept statements in different disciplines reveals that they may be parsed in a fashion similar to the above example. This may be formulated as the following generic rule:

$$C' = \{[Ci], [Rj], [Lk]\} \quad (1)$$

Where C' is a superordinate concept, and [Ci], [Rj], and [Lk] are the three sets described above. We use equation (1) as an operational definition of a concept, a generic format that may be used as concept parsing algorithms—a formula that provides guidance for discovering the meaning of a lexical label of a concept by identifying its "building blocks." Superordinate concepts whose building blocks contain only subordinate concepts, but no relations (i.e., [Rj] is an empty set) are called *containment concepts* (Laurence & Margolis, 1999). Superordinate concepts whose building blocks contain both subordinate concepts and relations (i.e., [Rj] is not an empty set) are called *inferential concepts* (Shafrir & Etkind, 2005).

INTERACTIVE CONCEPT DISCOVERY LEARNING TOOL

Interactive Concept Discovery Learning Tool is a novel *semantic search* tool based on concept parsing algorithms outlined above. It is an intuitive, interactive procedure that allows a learner to search large digital databases of unstructured text (e.g., World Wide Web, eJournals and eBooks in libraries, organizational eArchives). It allows the learner to discover the building blocks underlying a lexical label of a concept within a particular context (specific content area within a discipline)—namely, co-occurring subordinate concepts and relations—as well as to construct concept maps that clearly identify not only the conceptual content of course material, but also its internal conceptual structure (e.g., hierarchical and lateral relations among concepts and their building blocks).

The learner begins a search in the Interactive Concept Discovery Learning Tool by identifying the lexical label of a particular concept within a context in a discipline, then evaluating the consistency of appearance of co-occurring concepts and their relations across different documents found to contain this lexical label. In each successive iteration, the learner can read/save found documents online, mark/save lexical labels and candidate features of building blocks, evaluate the degree of relevance of a particular found document to the specific conceptual content under consideration, and construct alternative graphical representations of links between concepts and their building blocks.

A stored comprehensive record of a learner's sequence of all iterations allows for a detailed reconstruction of the learning episodes generated by the Interactive Concept Discovery Tool over time; it reveals the learner's consistency of "drilling-down" for discovering deeper building blocks of the particular concept, and the temporal evolution of outcomes of the learning sequence. This digital record is an authentic, evidence-based demonstration of mastery of knowledge that can be used as a springboard for a follow-up class—and chat room discussions—and provide a credible record to the individual's learning ePortfolio.

Discovering the Meaning of "Color"

We will demonstrate some aspects of the Interactive Concept Discovery Learning Tool by exploring the lexical label "color." The *Oxford English Reference Dictionary* lists 15 different senses (11 nouns and 5 verbs) for "color" (presented as "U.S. spelling of 'colour'"). The first example is of a learner in a biology course who is interested in discovering the building blocks of the superordinate concept "color," using the World Wide Web as a database of unstructured text. Following the specification of the lexical label "color" in the discipline of "biology" in the context of "vision" in the Interactive Concept Discovery Learning Tool, the learner finds 111,000 relevant documents. Further guided iterative sequences reveal that the set [Ci] contains co-occurring subordinal concepts 'retina', 'photoreceptor', 'cones', and 'rods', still further 'drilling down' reveal additional, deeper co-occurring subordinal concepts: 'wavelength', 'red', 'green', and 'blue'. At this stage, the Interactive Concept Discovery Learning Tool identified 287 documents that contain all the above mentioned features of the superordinal concept "vision," and ranked them by degree of relevance.

The second example is of a learner in a physics course who is interested in discovering the building blocks of the superordinate concept "color," using the World Wide Web as a database of unstructured text. Following the specification of the lexical label "color" in the discipline of "physics" in the context "chromodynamics" in the Interactive Concept Discovery Learning Tool, the learner finds 4,780 relevant documents. Further guided iterative sequences reveal that the set [Ci] contains co-occurring subordinal concepts 'quark', 'gluon', and 'charge'; still further 'drilling down' reveal additional, deeper co-occurring subordinal concepts: 'red'; green'; and 'blue'. At this stage the Interactive Concept Discovery Learning Tool identified 281 documents that contain all the above mentioned features of the superordinal concept "vision," and ranked them by degree of relevance.

It is interesting to note that "color" is a lexical label of two entirely different superordinate concepts in the disciplines of biology and physics that encode two different meanings in the contexts of "vision" and "chromodynamics," respectively. In both cases, the Interactive Concept Discovery Learning Tool guided the learners to identify, evaluate, and recognize more and more co-occurring candidate subordinate concepts, as features in the building block set [Ci] in equation (1) above.

MEANING EQUIVALENCE REUSABLE LEARNING OBJECT (MERLO)

We now move on to describe a second application of Concept Parsing Algorithms for concept mapping of content areas in the disciplines. At the core of MERLO are comprehensive concept statements that encode the conceptual content of a particular course. In preparation for MERLO construction, domain experts and instructors carry out detailed concept mapping by using the Iterative Concept Discovery Learning Tool. Each important *concept* may be represented by one (or more) *concept statements;* in turn, each concept statement is used to construct several *target statements* (representations), each encoding important features of the concept, as well as features that, in the instructors' experience, present particular difficulties for learners. Each target statement anchors an *item family* (see Figure 1); in addition to the target, an item family also includes additional statements that are thematically relevant to the particular target statement, but that: (1) may (or may not) bear surface similarity to the target; and (2) may (or may not) share equivalence-of-meaning with the target (Shafrir, 1999).

Figure 1. Template for constructing an item-family in MERLO

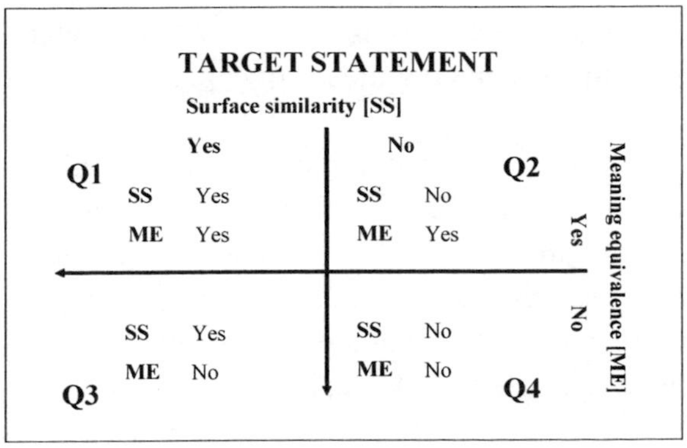

TARGET STATEMENT
Surface similarity [SS]
Yes | No
Meaning equivalence [ME]: Yes / No

Q1	SS Yes ME Yes	
		SS No ME Yes	Q2
Q3	SS Yes ME No	
		SS No ME No	Q4

MERLO is then a multi-dimensional grid of item families centered on individual target statements that encode different features of an important concept; collectively, these item families encode the complete conceptual content of a course (a particular content area within a discipline). Statements in the four quadrants—Q1, Q2, Q3, and Q4—are thematically related to the target statement and are classified by two sorting criteria: surface similarity to the target, and equivalence-of-meaning with the target. Statements in quadrant Q1 (see Figure 1) are similar in appearance to the target and also share equivalence-of-meaning with the target. Statements in quadrant Q2 are not similar in appearance to the target but, nevertheless, share equivalence-of-meaning with it. Statements in quadrant Q3 are similar in appearance to the target, but do not share equivalence-of-meaning with it. Finally, statements in quadrant Q4, although thematically related to the target statement, are not similar in appearance to the target and do not share equivalence-of-meaning with it. In statements that belong to quadrants Q2 and Q3, there is valence mismatch between the two sorting criteria, while in statements in Q1 and Q4 there is no valence mismatch.

MERLO guides the sequential teaching/learning episodes by focusing learners' attention on meaning. Item-families are used to construct individual test items. The novel format for MERLO item construction was designed to assess deep comprehension of conceptual content by eliciting responses that signal learner's ability to recognize and/or construct multiple representations that share equivalence-of-meaning. A typical MERLO item contains a target statement and four additional statements from quadrants Q2, Q3, and Q4. In our experience, inclusion of statements from quadrant Q1 makes items too easy, because the valence match between surface similarity and meaning equivalence is a strong indication of shared meaning with the (unmarked) target statement; hence Q1 statements are excluded from MERLO items. Task instructions in a MERLO test are:

At least two out of these five statements—but possibly more that two—share equivalence-of-meaning. Please mark all statements—but only those—that share equivalence-of-meaning.

In other words, the learner is asked to carry out the task in situations where the particular target statement is not marked, that is, the features of the concept to be compared are not made explicit. In order to perform this task, learners first need to decode the meaning of each stimulus in the set. This process is typically carried out by the learner, by analyzing the underlying conceptual features that define the meaning of each stimulus. Successful analysis of all the stimuli in a given five-stimulus set (item) requires deep understanding of the conceptual content of the specific domain being assessed. MERLO item format requires both rule inference and rule application in a similar way to the solution of analogical reasoning items. MERLO item type is designed not only to be used in the context of formative assessment of deep comprehension, but also to explicitly support instruction and remediation by quantifying partial knowledge of conceptual content, and thus providing detailed diagnostic information in the learner's response set.

MERLO Scoring Algorithms

There are several ways to score MERLO test items. *Quadrant-specific scores* are proportional scores that are first calculated for each item for the target statement and for statements from each quadrant, and then collapsed over all the items in the particular MERLO test. Quadrant-specific scores provide detailed and accurate feedback because they identify and pinpoint 'soft conceptual spots' of individual learners. Quadrant-specific scores also provide helpful cues for classroom and chat room discussions and individual remediation. Specific diagnostic information about comprehension deficits show up as depressed scores on quadrants Q2 and Q3; in these quadrants there is a mismatch between the valence of surface similarity and meaning equivalence dimensions. However, the interpretations of these two scores are very different:

- A depressed proportional score on Q2 indicates that the learner does not include in the 'boundary of meaning' of the group of related concepts certain statements that share equivalence-of-meaning (but not surface similarity) with the target and therefore should be included; such depressed score signals an over-restrictive (too exclusive) understanding of the meaning underlying the group of related concepts.
- A depressed score on Q3 indicates that the learner does not exclude from the 'boundary of meaning' of the group of related concepts certain statements that do not share equivalence-of-meaning (but that do share surface similarity) with the target and that therefore should be excluded; this signals an under-restrictive (too inclusive) understanding of the meaning underlying these concepts.

MERLO test items may also be scored for correctness of the learner's decisions to mark (or not to mark) statements within an item. *Positive partial score* is the proportion of correctly marked statements that share within-item equivalence-of-meaning (these are target and Q2 statements), and therefore should be selected; in a similar way, a *negative partial score* is calculated for the proportion of statements that do not share equivalence-of-meaning (these are Q3 and Q4 statements), and therefore should not have been—and in fact were not—selected by the learner. *Positive* and *negative scores* are calculated for each item separately, then collapsed over all the items in the MERLO assessment of a group of related concepts. Positive and negative scores may be interpreted as two complementary indices of deep comprehension, in that they reveal specific misunderstandings and misconceptions held by the learner about the meaning-equivalence of the ensemble of concepts anchored in the test's target statements.

EVALUATIVE IMPLEMENTATIONS

Evaluative implementations confirmed our expectations of the instructional value of detailed feedback from MERLO assessments and provided individual learners with accurate evaluations not only of what they know but—critically—of what they do not know, namely, their 'soft conceptual spots': quantitative assessments of their partial knowledge of conceptual content. Evaluative implementations of the Iterative Concept Discovery Learning Tool and MERLO-supported pedagogy were carried out during 2001-2005 in several collaborative projects in K-12, post-secondary, and workplace learning environments in Canada and abroad. In each project, detailed concept mapping was followed by construction of MERLO and implementation in the classroom, including assessments, feedback, class discussions, and instructors' reports. Examples are:

1. At Ryerson University in Toronto, seven MERLOs in two courses, History of Western Architecture I and II, have been constructed and implemented; this project has continued since September 2002.
2. In a collaborative project with the Russian Academy of Sciences, MERLOs have been constructed and implemented across the high school curriculum in math, physics, and biology in Lycee Technical-Physical High School of Ioffe Institute in St. Petersburg. This project resulted in more than 60 MERLOs (available in both Russian and English) that cover the complete high school curriculum in math, physics, and biology, as well as introductory university courses in these disciplines. This project has continued since June 2002.
3. At the Ontario Institute for Studies in Education of University of Toronto (OISE/UT), five MERLOs in a pre-service teachers training course, Foundation of Learning and Development, were constructed and piloted during the 2002/2004 academic years.
4. At George Brown College in Toronto, four MERLOs in English Spatial Prepositions were constructed in 2002 and used for assessment of deep comprehension of language in three student populations: native English speakers, ESL students, and students with specific reading disabilities.
5. The Material and Manufacturing Ontario (MMO) Center of Excellence sponsored the construction and evaluative implementation of three MERLOs for an in-depth workshop, "Risk Management in the Supply Chain," during February 2002. Following are two illustrations of typical results obtained in these evaluative implementations.

English Spatial Prepositions

Shalit (2005) conducted detailed concept mapping of English spatial prepositions in four categories—anthropomorphic (e.g., front, back);

inclusion (e.g., in, out); proximity (e.g., near, close to); and verticality (e.g., up, down)—and constructed four MERLOs (each containing eight item-families in a particular category). These MERLOs were then used to compose two Meaning Equivalence (ME) tests, each with 16 items; these tests were administered to three groups of college students: E1 (English speakers), E2 (English as second language—ESL), and RD (reading disabled). Means-proportional scores (standard deviations) and results of analysis of variance (ANOVA), shown in Table 1, reveal that: (1) native English speakers outperformed both the ESL and the RD groups; and (2) in all three groups, Q2 and Q3 proportional scores were depressed compared to T and Q4 proportional scores.

In-Depth Workshop: Risk Management in the Supply Chain

Sixteen supply chain managers from several medium and large Canadian companies participated in this workshop (Shafrir & Krasnor, 2002). In preparation for the workshop, a domain expert conducted detailed concept mapping and constructed three MERLOs with a total of 81 item families. Following each of three weekly sessions, each with a different conceptual content, learners took a 10-item ME test. Following completion of each test, participants were given the scoring code, scored each other's tests, and participated in class discussion. Results show that mean Q2 proportional scores increased from Test #1 (M=0.71; SD=0.13) to Test #2 (M=0.85; SD=.11) to Test #3 (M=0.94; SD=.07); differences are significant at the p<=0.5 level. In other words, learners consistently improved their conceptual thinking and refined the demarcation of the 'boundary of meaning' of the conceptual content of learned material.

Table 1. Mean (SD) proportional scores and results of ANOVA analysis of ME test of English spatial prepositions for the E1, E2, and RD groups

	E1 (n=98)	*E2 (N=54)*	*RD (N=55)*	*F*
T	.85 (.15)	.79 (.14)	.83 (.13)	3.35*
Q2	.76 (.17)	.64 (.17)	.67 (.18)	9.65 ***
Q3	.79 (.15)	.74 (.63)	.66 (.21)	2.61
Q4	.93 (0.9)	.88 (.12)	.85 (.13)	10.71***

Note: ANOVA (p<=0.5; *** p<=0.001)*

CONCLUSION

A total of 1,981 individual digital records of the new eLearning tools for ePortfolios were generated in these evaluative implementations (see Table 2). Results have shown consistently and across different content areas and across disciplines that:

a. The Interactive Concept Discovery Learning Tool enables learners, instructors, and

Table 2. Number of individual digital records generated by the new e-learning tools in various evaluative implementations

LEARNING ENVIRONMENT	*DISCIPLINE*	*NUMBER OF RECORDS*
K-12	Mathematics	504
	Physics	204
	Biology	96
College	English as a Second Language (ESL)	369
University	Architecture	722
	Psychology	38
Workplace	Business	48

researchers to identify building blocks of important concepts, and to create detailed and accurate concept maps in many content areas in several disciplines.

b. These concept maps may be used for the construction of MERLOs that support research and enhance learning outcomes, not only by helping instructors to focus on conceptual content, but also by providing learners with feedback from self-tests that is immediate, accurate, detailed, and that elaborates "soft conceptual spots" in need of reinforcement and remediation.
c. Concept discovery is learner centered and empowers active learning, and it exposes learners to different points of views and varied representations of conceptual content, accommodates different learning styles, and augments English proficiency of new immigrants (ESL) and students with reading difficulties.
d. MERLO pedagogy is effective across different populations of researchers, instructors, and learners, and across disciplines.
e. Initial construction of MERLO by domain experts is consequently improved and refined following feedback from various implementations.
f. MERLOs offer considerable economy by subsequent reuse for the construction of test items that may vary in format, as well as in degree of difficulty.
g. MERLO is technologically scalable and can be implemented in low-tech classrooms as well as online.

These results support the conclusion that these eLearning tools provide clear and authentic evidence for mastery of learning based on measures that are independent of jurisdiction, grading system, or accreditation differences.

ACKNOWLEDGMENTS

We thank our colleagues and friends Vyacheslav V. Ivanov and Victor Erlich for critical comments on earlier versions of this chapter.

REFERENCES

Bransford, J. D., Brown, A. L., & Cocking, R. R. (2004). *How people learn: Brain, mind, experience, and school* (expanded ed.). Washington, DC: National Academy Press.

Laurence, S., & Margolis, E. (1999). Concepts and cognitive science. In S. Laurence & E. Margolis (Eds.), *Concepts: Core readings* (pp. 3-81). Cambridge, MA: MIT Press.

Shafrir, U. (1999). Representational competence. In I.E. Sigel (Ed.), *The development of mental representation: Theory and applications* (pp. 371-389). Mahwah, NJ: Lawrence Erlbaum.

Shafrir, U., & Etkind, M. (2005, January). *Concept Parsing Algorithms: Mapping the conceptual content of disciplines. Version 11.0.* Toronto: PARCEP.

Shafrir, U., & Krasnor, C. (2002). *Increasing competitiveness of Ontario's material and manufacturing companies through enhanced training outcomes in pre-competitive skills.* Meaning Equivalence Design Studio, Resource Centre for Academic Technology, University of Toronto, Canada.

Shalit, R. (2005). *Meaning equivalence tests for deep comprehension of English spatial prepositions in college students.* Doctoral dissertation, Department of Human Development and Applied Psychology, Ontario Institute for Studies in Education, University of Toronto, Canada.

Sternberg, R. J., & Williams, W. M. (2002). *Educational psychology.* Boston: Allyn and Bacon.

KEY TERMS

Concept: A regularity; an organizational principle behind a large collection of facts; an invariant; a pattern in the data.

Concept Map: A textual/graphic representation that clearly identifies conceptual content and the internal conceptual structure (e.g., hierarchical and lateral relations among concepts and their building blocks).

Concept Parsing Algorithm (CPA): A formula that provides guidance for discovering the meaning of a lexical label of a concept by identifying its 'building blocks'.

Concept Statement: A comprehensive description of the meaning of a concept; a comprehensive encoding of the regularity under consideration.

Interactive Concept Discovery Learning Tool: A novel semantic search tool based on concept parsing algorithms; an intuitive, interactive procedure that allows a learner to search large digital databases of unstructured text and to discover the building blocks underlying a lexical label of a concept within a particular context (specific content area within a discipline).

Item Family: Anchored in a target statement, an item family also includes additional statements that are thematically relevant to the particular target statement, but that: (1) may (or may not) bear surface similarity to the target, and (2) may (or may not) share equivalence-of-meaning with the target.

Lexical Labels of Concepts: 'Code words' that serve as proper names of concepts within a context in a discipline.

Mastery of Learning: Deep comprehension of the conceptual content of learned material.

Meaning Equivalence Reusable Learning Object (MERLO): A multi-dimensional grid of item families centered on individual target statements that encode different features of an important concept; collectively, these item families encode the complete conceptual content of a course (a particular content area within a discipline).

Target Statement: A description of a particular conceptual situation that includes some important features of a concept.

Chapter XXI
Toward a Framework/Data Model:
From ePortfolio Thinking to Folio Culture

Franc Feng
University of British Columbia, Canada

ABSTRACT

In this exploratory contribution, the author proposes a framework for re-mapping ePortfolio research around an emergent model of engagement with information. Through an anthropological lens, he casts ePortfolio implementation within communities of practice in complex networks of actors, artifacts, and flows. His work surveys extant approaches in the ePortfolio research, identifying gaps in the literature, towards an inclusive framework around a new model reflecting the changing relationship with information, grounding the theorizing in his practice, designing and teaching online graduate courses in Cultural and New Media Studies in Education.

REVIEW OF THE LITERATURE, LOGIC, AND METHOD

This exploratory contribution sits at the intersection of: (1) research investigating implications over applications of technology; (2) background in cognitive sciences/design; (3) experience with initial implementation of computers into the schools; (4) cybercultural studies, artificial intelligence (AI), artificial life (AL), and cybernetics; and (5) action research with implementing ePortfolios in online learning communities.[1] Concerned with gaps in the literature, that we might be forgetting lessons we learned when we first implemented computers into the schools, with an appreciation of the changing ways we are relating to each other around information, this chapter attempts to theorize a conceptual framework and data model that speaks to these concerns.

When conducting literature reviews on a topic, among work that might at first appear as disparate, it is possible to find commonality. ePortfolio literature is, in this respect, no different. We can group disparate ePortfolio literatures to arrive at broader categories that unfold a measure of homogeneity across approaches. In what follows, I will draw upon this principle to point to an emphasis on applications in the ePortfolio literature, with arguably, consequential gaps for addressing implications. Rather than embark on an exhaustive review to support my claim of gaps in the literature, and my rationale for remapping the field, and theorizing an inclusive framework and model, I adopt a modest approach that samples, in searching for patterns of homogeneity across what appears initially as different approaches to ePortfolio research.

I began with select surveys introducing the basics of portfolios (Easley & Mitchell, 2003; Vancouver School Board, 1993), portfolios as discovery (Deen, 1993), portfolios in terms of self-directed inquiry (Grant & Huebner, 1998), teachers' voices in applying portfolios in the classroom (Smith & Ylvisaker, 1993), mentoring portfolio development (Freidus, 1998), planning portfolios (Crockett, 1998; Martin & Stollenwerk, 1999), portfolios as tools for learning and instruction (Schipper & Rossi, 1997), or portfolios across the curriculum (Cole, Ryan, & Kick, 1995).

Given the relationship of portfolios to testing, I also sampled the literature on large-scale assessments with provincial performance assessment (British Columbia. Educational Programs. Curriculum Development Branch, 1994) and the National Assessment of Educational Progress (NAEP)'s assessments of writing portfolios (Gentile, Martin-Rehrmann, & Kennedy, 1995). On the theme of assessment, I sampled extant literature assessing records portfolios (Sullivan, 1994), the work of children in portfolio practices (Beckley, 1997; Kingore, 1993; Seidel, 1997), portfolios across the curriculum (Cole et al., 1995), development of portfolios for learning and assessment (Klenowski, 2002), rethinking validity for assessment of teaching (Moss, 1998), and balancing between professional development and performance assessment (Synder, Lippincott, & Bower, 1998).

The sampling necessarily recalls the nascent work of Lee Shulman, past president of the American Educational Research Association (AERA), on teacher education and professionalism (Lyons, 1998b; Shulman, 1998). Shulman has a special place in our review, as it was through the imperative of teacher professionalism that Lee shifted evaluation to electronic portfolios (Shulman, 1998, 1992). We include seminal texts that capture historical threads in ePortfolios (Lyons, 1998d) with writings of teachers who viewed portfolios as embedded in narratives (Lyons, 1998a), framed the advent of portfolio in terms of concomitant shifts in culture (Teitel, Ricci, & Coogan, 1998; Wolf, 1998), detected problems with portfolios (Klenowski, 2002; Shulman, 1998), and examined possible consequences of portfolio implementation (Lyons, 1998c).

I also sampled the literature under the notable names of Barrett (2005b, 2005c, 2005d), Batson (2005a, 2005b), and Cambridge (Cambridge, Kahn, Tompkins, & Yancey, 2001), who have influenced, shaped, and directed the evolution of the field. I include here writings on significant questions of interest which lie at the intersection of Course Management Software (CMS) and ePortfolios (Batson, 2005a).[2] Then there is the overlap with the reflection literature on the reflective practitioner (Schon, 1983, 1987), reflection in higher education (Moon, 2005), with forming teams (Davis & Honan, 1998), perspectives (KnowledgeLab), and theory (Feng, 2004). Turning to the recent literature, I sample an exemplary foundational piece of work on emerging practices at multiple levels of ePortfolio implementation (Cambridge et al., 2001) with a body of work across student, faculty, and institutional levels that investigate comparisons between electronic and paper portfolios (Springfield, 2001), reflective Webfolios (Reiss, 2001), composing ePortfolios using common tools (Rice, 2001), and portfolios in practice (Barkley, 2001; Barrett, 2001; Kelly, 2001; Stier, 2001; Tompkins, 2001). I include here contributions on the role of portfolios in institutions, on accreditation (Wexler, 2001), as a tool for departmental learning and improvement (Dorn, 2001), and in institutional research (Borden, 2001) with institutional applications such as the IUPUI institutional portfolio (Hamilton, 2001) and the Portland State University's Electronic Institutional Portfolio (Ketcheson, 2001).

While we could continue sampling the literature, having established the pattern through the sampling review broadly grouped the categories; since the patterning would likely remain similar, we arguably have reached an informed sense of emphasis in the ePortfolio literature. Taken collectively then, with some exceptions (e.g., Barrett, 2005d; Klenowski, 2002; Lyons, 1998c; Shulman, 1998), our sampling detected a measure of homogeneity in emphasis towards applications with positive attitudes towards implementation. The phenomenon can also be empirically verified with a detour online, where one finds that generally, if expressed, concerns, problems, or ethical considerations appear to be around technology or content rather than ePortfolios per se.[3]

Commonality does not stop with emphasis on application of ePortfolios. It is also found at the fundamental level of tacit underlying assumptions. Given most ePortfolios, with the exceptions above, often begin non-problematically within applications, the lack of critique is arguably of a fundamental nature. Conversely, since research that begins with and emphasizes implications over applications subscribes to a different set of underlying assumptions, we have arguably found confirmation of gaps in ePortfolio literature. The finding is especially of interest since the similar trajectory we are retracing appears to suggest that we might have forgotten some of the lessons we learned when we first began introducing computers into our schools. Within the parallels in the computing literature that came to value implications over application in infusing the discourse with historical critique, we seek directions to address the relative lack of critique in ePortfolio literature, towards theorizing a framework and model.

IMPLEMENTATION AS CONTINUITY IN HISTORICAL CONTEXT

Analysis through the historical lens suggests one possibility for contemporary emphasis on applications—contra the lessons of microcomputing in the schools—lies in how the ePortfolio phenomenon might be perceived as a break rather than continuity. There is good reason for this thesis. While the analogy is applicable and a lesson appropriate for comparison, we need to realize the present situation around ePortfolio implementation is qualitatively different. Precisely from having learned from the history of implementation, we have more efficient, reliable, portable, expandable, faster, higher-storage, and multiple-format systems with a variety of application programs.

Still, glimpses offer collective reminders of parallels from our computing history that might help inform our current trajectories with ePortfolios. The historical turn is informative in recalling lessons we have learned. The lens allows us to recall how the bulk of the literature addressed programming, with researchers more concerned with questions of competency than implications, and theories limited in social scope. It also recalls how, as computers entered into classrooms, they became a significant presence, and questions began to percolate around inequity, culture, and representation. Research turned to questions around gender (Bohlin, 1993; Howell, 1993; Shashaani, 1993), class (Muira, 1987; Watson, Penny, Scanzoni, & Penny, 1989), culture (Bowers, 1988), and race (Badagliacco, 1990). We are reminded how we often reversed the process, beginning with computers rather than learning needs.

Importantly, the historical lens reminds us of the consequences of forgetting to be cautious of the implications of technology. In forgetting to ask questions of equity with implementation, we became complicit to creating divides. Forgetting to place value on ethical questions over implementation, we learned while we graduated fully competent students, they often had little or no understanding of responsibility attendant to the skills or power relations created through the exercise of their skills. To address the ethical implications of computing, we learn to widen our attention to historical (Franklin & CBC Enterprises., 1990; Mumford, 1967), anthropological (Ragsdale, 1988; Roszak, 1969), philosophical (Postman, 1986), cultural (Wajcman, 1991), and ecological (Bowers, 1997; Jardine, 1993) contexts, in efforts that situated the critique of computing within the interdisciplinary corpus of humanities, and social sciences critique that, whether or not directed at computing, were nevertheless relevant (e.g., Doll, Feng, & Petrina, 2001; Giddens, 1990; Jagtenberg & McKie, 1997; Merchant, 1980).

Thus, our argument is over the possibility, given these improvements of not seeing or forgetting the continuity, in retracing a similar trajectory, but this time online, in privileging applications over implications, in forgetting to begin with student needs, in not seeing the relevance of the above literature or forgetting to locate critique in the wider historical context. As before, the imbalance of applications over implications suggests we need to expand theorizing along similar interdisciplinary and historical trajectories. With this foregoing laying the groundwork for advocating a shift towards implications within an inclusive framework, I propose a strategy for remapping the field around the changing ways we are learning to interact with information around ePortfolios.

EXPANDING THE FIELD: CULTURAL SHIFTS AND TECHNOLOGICAL CHANGE

What extended literature should we be also reviewing when sketching the broader contours of the literature within which to locate ePortfolio literature? Clues exist within the ePortfolio literature we sampled earlier. We begin with earlier ePortfolio literature theorizing the shift of portfolio from paper to electronic, beyond that of material artifact, equating the advent of ePortfolios with cultural transformation. I am referring to nascent signs in ePortfolio literature, of the shift in attention to the cultural, found within Wolf's (1998) contribution to the Nona Lyon (1998) classic, *With Portfolio in Hand: Validating the New Teacher Professionalism.*[4]

Through this move, we connect the ePortfolio literature in Wolf (1998) that began to view the shift around actors, artifacts, and practice, from paper to electronic portfolio as anthropological, tracing similar shifts as with modes of thought (Havelock, 1963), from orality to literacy (Ong, 1977, 1982), in the interface around orality and writing (Goody, 1987) and advent of print culture and printing as an agent of social change (Eisenstein, 1979, 1983, 1986). When we update these historic shifts through a critical re-

reading of McLuhanian notions of the makings of typographic man [sic] in the Gutenberg Galaxy, the global village and medium as message and extension, (McLuhan, 1962, 1965; McLuhan & Fiore, 1968; McLuhan & Powers, 1989), we situate ePortfolios historically, in technocultural developments generating the electronic signature of the Internet pre-dating the emergence of the ePortfolio phenomenon.

Having surveyed the pivotal literature on technology change and literacy, we also need to review the synoptic literature on cyberculture (Burnett & Marshall, 2003; Lévy, 2001; Murphie & Potts, 2003), followed by focusing on implications of technocultural change in cyberculture. Here we are interested in emergent literature around the changing nature of interactions in cyberspace, bridging literature on changing identities (Jonscher, 1999; Turkle, 1995), the rise of the Net generation reflecting new ways of being (Castells, 2004a, 2004b; Tapscott, 1998), risks and opportunities in an eConnected world (Coleman & Queen's University, 2003), digital divide around globalization (Sernau, 2000), signs of emergent netocracy and attentionalism (Bard & Sèoderqvist, 2002), merging of human and machine into a single planetary consciousness as superorganism (Stock, 1993), simulacra (Baudrillard, 1994a, 1994b), virtual reality (Heim, 1998; Rheingold, 1991), gendered identity (Haraway, 2004; Stone, 1995; Turkle, 1995), virtual communities (Rheingold, 1993), and the cultural body in human/machine-entanglement hypothesis (Dyens, 2001; Haraway, 2004; Pepperell, 1995).

As history is critical by definition, through these moves we build critique into the theoretical framework by locating ePortfolio literature within the historical context from which it emerges. While the relevance of the bulk of the above writing might not be seen as immediately obvious for the ePortfolio literature, one can also understand how being informed in these works would go some way in addressing comparative lack of critique in ePortfolio research. Online issues of gender, identity, and virtuality are, after all, the contemporary correlates of the earlier extension of the computing literature into ethical implications of computing.

Of special relevance to our interests with actors, artifacts, and practices (Latour, 1987), since the open software initiative directly addresses the changing ways in which we relate to data, I pay special attention to the literature on free speech online movements in our theorizing. Thus, the Open Source Portfolio Initiative (OSPI, 2005), with its contribution of non-proprietary, open source electronic portfolio software, is (1) an application and (2) an example of cultural shift that highlights the nature of (3) our changing relationship with information associated with the OSPI initiative. Differently put, the OSPI and Open Source Initiative (2005a), which elicits corporate contributions (OSI, 2005b) inspiring similar initiatives (ELGG, 2005), needs to be theorized in connection with its ambit associated with the general movement towards the freedom of information in cyberspace (Barlow, 2005; Dickinson, 2003; Doherty, 2005), GNU (2005), rise of Linux developed under the GNU General Public License (Linux, 2005), the Wikipedia Commons (2005), and the Creative Commons (Garlick, 2005), through which OSPI obtains its legitimacy around an alternate model of information exchange.

PATTERNING: AN ePORTFOLIO MODEL OF INFORMATION EXCHANGE

I have supported my arguments of gaps in the literature through demonstrating the emphasis of ePortfolio literature on applications. I have briefly surveyed the larger body of literature for addressing the implications gap in which I argue, for situating ePortfolio literature. Having briefly sketched the rough outlines of this framework, I consider next the potential of this corpus of literature for theorizing a model of ePortfolio information exchange associated with flow of data characterizing ePortfolios.

In connecting with the literature on technological change, we established continuity between ePortfolios and other historical forms of technological change. Seen through an anthropological lens around actors, artifacts, and practices, like their antecedents with orality and print, ePortfolios reflect cultural shifts in education and literacy. As such, ePortfolios are also symbolic of our changing relationship with data across (1) sharing behavior inherent to ePortfolios consistent with (2) the movement towards free software (including the OSPI initiative) and (3) the freeing of knowledge from copyright and ownership. To arrive at a model capturing our differential relationship with information, we turn next to emergent systems theory and artificial intelligence (AI) literature.

Casting the question in social terms, when Castells (2001) refers to "individual portfolios [that one] can negotiate with different people," he locates that exchange of personal information within a network of change through which identity connects with global social movements and technological change. It is instructive that Castells (2000) argues this greater system around the rise of the network state, and change from state to identity politics occurs not in "a space of places" but in "a space of flows." The notion of flows lends new fluidity and scope to our anthropological lens of actors, artifacts, and practices. Focusing on the language of flows, Castells' words locating the exchange of portfolios are consistent with the corpus of literature under the rubric of systems theory or complexity theory (Bateson, 1979; Capra, 1996; Cohen & Stewart, 1994; Gleick, 1987; Lovelock, 1995; Murphie & Potts, 2003).

Under this rubric, the theme of flows is consistent with Deleuze and Guattari's (1987) writing on machinic flows, Levy's (1997) theorizing on collective intelligence, Hayles' (1999) shifts around patterns, and De Landa's (1997) work on self-organizing and emergence. Consistent with Bausch's (2001) efforts to apply complexity principles to social theory in synthesizing an emergent consensus in social systems theory, I theorize the ePortfolio phenomenon (characteristic of emerging practices around the rise of social software like wikis and blogs) fits well with notions of complexity as expounded by systems theory. The cybernetic model—with its attention to unpredictability, linkages, possibilities, spaces, complexity, and community, characteristic of the nature of not only data, but all cybernetic organisms that self-regulate around information and representation—is arguably our best candidate for a theoretical model.

Such a system is capable of explaining the phenomenon: under a self-regulating model; the shift to freedom of information might be seen as inevitable, given the near saturation the Earth has reached under the extant commodified models of information flow (Lovelock, 1995; Meadows, Meadows, & Randers, 1992; Meadows & Rome, 1972). The fit of model is reinforced when one remembers that not only are the citations above also drawn from the systems literature, but concepts around flow/patterning (Minsky & Papert, 1988), turbulence (Clark, 1997), actor network theory (Latour, 1987), embodied cognition (Varela, Thompson, & Rosch, 1991), distributed cognition (Hutchins, 1995), learning and adaptation (Winograd & Flores, 1986), and autopoiesis (Maturana & Varela, 1980) are core to systems theory.

The applicability of systems theory extends to events. Under the tenets of systems theory, when systems are far from equilibrium, conditions are created for a shift in which higher order emerges from lower (Prigogine & Stengers, 1984). I posit a similar change in order might have occurred as society began systematically behaving differently around data. Given the connections with the flows literature, and the notion of "pattern" consistent across the literature of flows and AI, I further submit that "patterning" makes an appropriate gerund for the ePortfolio phenomenon in associating the emergence of the phenomenon with the global shift for individuals to make sense of patterns in mutual exchange of information as identities are forged in the mix. Applying the anthological lens, as we were, with writing and printing, we are "patterning." Our artifacts and practices—whether through ePortfolios, blogs, or wikis—bear the unmistakable signature of cultural transformation in which the changing nature of our relationship with data as exemplified in the free software and free online speech movement should be seen as a marker for the change related to the rise of the mass phenomenon of "patterning."

It is, therefore, not an odd coincidence that founders of the movement advancing free flow of information are software coders like Richard Stallman or Linus Torvalds (2005; Williams, 2005). In retrospect, perhaps this changing attitude with information was documented as early as two decades ago by Roszak (1986) when he likened the rise of personal computers to an "electronic populism" (p. 138), coincident with rise of the counterculture. This point is underscored by Castells (2001), albeit differently; when referring to the same phenomenon, he argued that the idea of "a personal computer…was subversive by definition," eventually manifesting in complex relationships between identity, social movements, and technological change. We note the global connection between the actors, artifacts, and practices in Castells' claim. Interpreting Roszak's characterization in hindsight, the populist movement can be seen as a signal of the coming expansion of the public domain, return of the commons, and rise of the open software initiative.

The upshot of this brief review leads to this intriguing possibility and postulate. Contrary to conventional views of ePortfolio as largely commercial, when analyzed through the historical lens, the technocultural shift to "patterning"—in which "pure" exchange is emphasized over commodified exchange as exemplified by the ePortfolio phenomenon—might perhaps be better understood as rumblings of an altering relationship with information seeking to free knowledge as a commodity.

GROUNDING THEORIZING: BRIDGING DESIGN, PRACTICE, AND THEORY

By way of review, I surveyed the extant ePortfolio literature with my unit of analysis at the categorical level, located ePortfolio implementation in continuity with the historical advent of computers into schools, re-located ePortfolio research in literature of technological change, surveyed the relevant literature for inclusion into my framework, proposed a gerund for ePortfolio phenomenon, reviewed literature at the intersection of system theory and AI, and argued for aptness of systems theory for framing an ePortfolio model reflecting our changing relationships with data. It is significant that my theorizing does not appear *ex nihilo,* but rather, grounded within my practices with implementing ePortfolios in an online graduate course I co-author and co-teach on "Cultural and New Media Studies in Education," where my practice with implementing ePortfolios is informed by systems theory. Appropriately, I close with empirical support for my theorizing through a glimpse of learning in the online community that seeds my ePortfolio theorizing[5].

In our ePortfolio implementation, rather than adopting a package, and proceeding with that package, we reverse the process beginning with student needs, bearing in mind those earlier lessons on introducing computer to schools. With deliberately vague notions of ePortfolios, the portfolio work is emergent, as students implement ePortfolios, wikis, and blogs seamlessly without regard for distinctions. With more than 50 students working with WebCT as the CMS, we have exhausted the limitations of WebCT, whether with discussion boards, chats, or e-mails. Teaching and learning in these conditions far from equilibrium, our students are aware of both the autopoietic potential of ePortfolios in unfolding spontaneity in online communities and of collective intelligence. Excited with notions of sharing data, energized with applying Lave and Wenger's (1991) notions to online community in which learning and care are co-implicated, on their own volition our students eagerly choose free software initiatives as topics for assignments. Our students use ePortfolios to document the unfolding nature of their communication, and to generate theory and theorizing on material they share with their class. It is significant that students' concerns revolve around implications, confirming Castells' empirical research and theorizing locating exchange of portfolios at the nexus of identities, concerns for the world, and interest in the potential for social change.

In this small piece of a larger conversation, I proposed a theory, model, and gerund for the ePortfolio phenomenon from which my work has itself become emergent. If the above holds, I call for action research that shifts the models of ePortfolio as cold, static folders and routines to one of a vibrant and active learning community. As conceived, active design calls for embedding both curriculum and facilitator into communities of pattern-forming sharing learners, wherein ePortfolios reflect a different relationship with information. For myself, I am interested in applying my extant work on narrative (Feng, 2002) that draws from MacIntyre's (1981) notion of narrative as unity of life, to connect with Barrett's (2005a, 2005d) notion of digital narratives. If Castells (2000) is to be taken seriously, out of this environment in which information is shared where students help each other with ePortfolios in the digital community, profound changes could result in sharing of digital initiatives. In rearticulating the weaves between being, knowing, and doing, we need to pay attention to the effects of active ePortfolios on student identity and praxis.

REFERENCES

Badagliacco, J. M. (1990). Gender and race differences in computer abilities and experience. *Social Science Computer Review, 8,* 42-63.

Bard, A., & Sèoderqvist, J. (2002). *Netocracy: The new power elite and life after capitalism.* London: Reuters.

Barkley, E. (2001). From Bach to Tupac: Using an electronic course portfolio to analyze a curricular transformation. In K. B. Yancey (Ed.), *Electronic portfolios: Emerging practices in student, faculty, and institutional learning* (pp. 117-123). Washington, DC: American Association for Higher Education.

Barlow, J. P. (2005). The economy of ideas. *Wired.* Retrieved 2006, from http://www.wired.com/wired/archive/2.03/economy.ideas.html

Barrett, H. (2001). Electronic portfolios = multimedia development + portfolio development:

The electronic portfolio development process. In K. B. Yancey (Ed.), *Electronic portfolios: Emerging practices in student, faculty, and institutional learning* (pp. 110-116). Washington, DC: American Association for Higher Education.

Barrett, H. (2005a). *Digital storytelling (in e-portfolios) for reflection and deep learning.* Retrieved from http://72.14.207.104/search?q=cache:BP5kR-an0bgJ:electronicportfolios.com/portfolios/NCCE05W.pdf+concerns+with+e-portfolios&hl=en

Barrett, H. (2005b). *Electronic portfolio handbook.* Retrieved June 15, 2005, from http://electronicportfolios.org/

Barrett, H. (2005c). *Electronic teaching portfolios: Multimedia skills + portfolio development = powerful professional development.* Retrieved June 15, 2005, from http://electronicportfolios.com/portfolios/site2000.html

Barrett, H. (2005d). *E-portfolio as story.* Retrieved June 15, 2005, from http://homepage.mac.com/e-portfolios/iMovieTheater13.html

Bateson, G. (1979). *Mind and nature: A necessary unity* (1st ed.). New York: Dutton.

Batson, T. (2005a). *CMS and e-portfolio: At the crossroads.* Retrieved June 15, 2005, from http://www.campus-technology.com/news_article.asp?id=10041&typeid=155

Batson, T. (2005b). *The electronic portfolio boom: What's it all about?* Retrieved June 15, 2005, from http://www.campus-technology.com/article.asp?id=6984

Baudrillard, J. (1994a). *The illusion of the end.* Stanford, CA: Stanford University Press.

Baudrillard, J. (1994b). *Simulacra and simulation.* Ann Arbor: University of Michigan Press.

Bausch, K. C. (2001). *The emerging consensus in social systems theory.* New York: Kluwer Academic/Plenum.

Beckley, W. L. (1997). *Creating a classroom portfolio system: A guide to assist classroom teachers in kindergarten through eighth grade.* Dubuque, IA: Kendall/Hunt.

Bohlin, R. M. (1993). Computers and gender differences: Achieving equity. *Computers in Schools, 9*(2/3), 155-165.

Borden, V. M. H. (2001). The role of institutional research and data in institutional portfolios. In K. B. Yancey (Ed.), *Electronic portfolios: Emerging practices in student, faculty, and institutional learning* (pp. 192-202). Washington, DC: American Association for Higher Education.

Bowers, C. A. (1988). *The cultural dimensions of educational computing: Understanding the non-neutrality of technology.* New York. Teachers College Press.

Bowers, C. A. (1997). *The culture of denial: Why the environmental movement needs a strategy for reforming universities and public schools.* Albany: State University of New York Press.

British Columbia. Educational Programs. Curriculum Development Branch. (1994). *Performance assessment.* Victoria: Curriculum Development Branch Ministry of Education.

Burnett, R., & Marshall, P. D. (2003). *Web theory: An introduction.* London; New York: Routledge.

Cambridge, B. L., Kahn, S., Tompkins, D. P., & Yancey, K. B. (Eds.). (2001). *Electronic portfolios: Emerging practices in student, faculty, and institutional learning.* Washington, DC: American Association for Higher Education.

Capra, F. (1996). *The Web of life: A new scientific understanding of living systems* (1st ed.). New York: Anchor Books.

Castells, M. (2000). *The rise of the network society* (2nd ed.). Malden, MA: Blackwell.

Castells, M. (2001). *Identity and change in the networked society*. Retrieved from http://globetrotter.berkeley.edu/people/Castells/castells-con0.html

Castells, M. (2004a). *The network society: A cross-cultural perspective*. Cheltenham, UK/Northampton, MA: Edward Elgar.

Castells, M. (2004b). *The power of identity* (2nd ed.). Malden, MA: Blackwell.

Clark, A. (1997). *Being there: Putting brain, body, and world together again*. Cambridge, MA: MIT Press.

Cohen, J., & Stewart, I. (1994). *The collapse of chaos: Discovering simplicity in a complex world*. New York: Viking.

Cole, D. J., Ryan, C. W., & Kick, F. (1995). *Portfolios across the curriculum and beyond*. Thousand Oaks, CA: Corwin Press.

Coleman, S., & Queen's University, S.o.P.S. (2003). *The e-connected world: Risks and opportunities*. Montreal: Published for the School of Policy Studies Queen's University by McGill-Queen's University Press.

Crockett, T. (1998). *The portfolio journey: A creative guide to keeping student-managed portfolios in the classroom*. Englewood, CO: Teacher Ideas Press.

Davis, C. L., & Honan, E. (1998). Reflections on the use of teams to support the portfolio process. In N. Lyons (Ed.), *With portfolio in hand: Validating the new teacher professionalism* (pp. ix, 276). New York: Teachers College Press.

De Landa, M. (1997). *A thousand years of nonlinear history*. New York: Zone Books.

Deen, M. K. (1993). Portfolios as discovery. In M. Ylvisaker (Ed.), *Teachers' voices: Portfolios in the classroom* (pp. 49-59). Berkeley, CA: National Writing Project.

Deleuze, G., & Guattari, F. (1987). *A thousand plateaus: Capitalism and schizophrenia*. Minneapolis: University of Minnesota Press.

Dickinson, T. (2003, February 3). *Cognitive dissident*. Retrieved 2006, from http://www.motherjones.com/news/qa/2003/02/we_268_01.html

Doherty, B. (2005). *John Perry Barlow 2.0. The Thomas Jefferson of cyberspace reinvents his body—and his politics.* Retrieved from http://www.reason.com/0408/fe.bd.john.shtml

Doll, W. E., Feng, F., & Petrina, S. (2001). The object(s) of culture: Bruno Latour and the relationship between science and culture. In M. Morris (Ed.), *(Post) modern science (education): Propositions and alternative paths* (pp. 25-39). New York: Peter Lang.

Dorn, D. S. (2001). Electronic department portfolios: A new tool for departmental learning and improvement. In K. B. Yancey (Ed.), *Electronic portfolios: Emerging practices in student, faculty, and institutional learning* (pp. 203-208). Washington, DC: American Association for Higher Education.

Dyens, O. (2001). *Metal and flesh: The evolution of man: Technology takes over*. Cambridge, MA: MIT Press.

Easley, S.-D., & Mitchell, K. (2003). *Portfolios matter: What, where, when, why and how to use them*. Markham, Ontario: Pembroke.

Eisenstein, E. L. (1979). *The printing press as an agent of change: Communications and cultural transformations in early-modern Europe*. Cambridge; New York: Cambridge University Press.

Eisenstein, E. L. (1983). *The printing revolution in early modern Europe*. Cambridge; New York: Cambridge University Press.

Eisenstein, E. L. (1986). *Print culture and enlightenment thought*. Chapel Hill, NC: Hanes Foundation Rare Book Collection/University Library University of North Carolina at Chapel Hill.

ELGG. (2005). *Personal learning landscape*. Retrieved from http://elgg.net/

Feng, F. (2002). Pedagogical implications of critiquing the ecotechnocultural crisis of modernity through narrative research. In *Proceedings of the AERA 2002 Chaos and Complexity SIG Conference*, New Orleans, LA.

Feng, F. (2004). At the intersections of pedagogy, technology, digital narratives and communities of learning/practice: An exploratory approach augmenting course management software as electronic portfolios. In *Proceedings of 'Reflection Is Not A Mirror, It's A Lens'*, Chan Centre, Vancouver.

Franklin, U. M., & CBC Enterprises. (1990). *The real world of technology*. Toronto: CBC Enterprises.

Freidus, H. (1998). Mentoring portfolio development. In N. Lyons (Ed.), *With portfolio in hand: Validating the new teacher professionalism* (pp. 51-68). New York: Teachers College Press.

Garlick, M. (2005, June). *Open democracy*. Retrieved from http://creativecommons.org/text/opendemocracy

Gentile, C. A., Martin-Rehrmann, J., Kennedy, J. H., Educational Testing Service, National Assessment of Educational Progress (Project), & National Center for Education Statistics. (1995). *Windows into the classroom: NAEP's 1992 writing portfolio study*. Washington, DC: Office of Educational Research and Improvement, U.S. Department of Education.

Giddens, A. (1990). *The consequences of modernity*. Stanford: Stanford University Press.

Gleick, J. (1987). *Chaos: Making a new science*. New York: Viking.

GNU. (2005). *GNU free documentation license*. Retrieved from http://en.wikipedia.org/wiki/GNU_Free_Documentation_License

Goody, J. (1987). *The interface between the written and the oral*. Cambridge; New York: Cambridge University Press.

Grant, G. E, & Huebner, T. A. (1998). The portfolio question: The power of self-directed inquiry. In N. Lyons (Ed.), *With portfolio in hand: Validating the new teacher professionalism* (pp. 156-171). New York: Teachers College Press.

Hamilton, S. J. (2001). Snake pit in cyberspace: The IUPUI institutional portfolio. In K.B. Yancey (Ed.), *Electronic portfolios: Emerging practices in student, faculty, and institutional learning* (pp. 159-177). Washington, DC: American Association for Higher Education.

Haraway, D. J. (2004). *The Haraway reader*. New York: Routledge.

Havelock, E. A. (1963). *Preface to Plato*. Cambridge: Belknap Press/Harvard University Press.

Hayles, N. K. (1999). *How we became posthuman: Virtual bodies in cybernetics, literature, and informatics*. Chicago: University of Chicago Press.

Heim, M. (1998). *Virtual realism.* New York: Oxford University Press.

Howell, K. (1993). The experience of women in undergraduate computer science: What does the research say? *ACM SIGSCE Bulletin, 25*(2), 1-8.

Hutchins, E. (1995). *Cognition in the wild.* Cambridge, MA: MIT Press.

Jagtenberg, T., & McKie, D. (1997). *Eco-impacts and the greening of postmodernity: New maps for communication studies, cultural studies, and sociology.* Thousand Oaks, CA: Sage.

Jardine, D. W. (1993). Ecopedagogical reflections on curricular integration, scientific literacy and the deep ecologies of science education. *Alberta Science Education Journal, 27*(1), 50-56.

Jonscher, C. (1999). *Wired life: Who are we in the digital age?* London: Bantam Press.

Kelly, T. M. (2001). Wired for trouble? Creating a hypermedia course portfolio. In K.B. Yancey (Ed.), *Electronic portfolios: Emerging practices in student, faculty, and institutional learning* (pp. 124-129). Washington, DC: American Association for Higher Education.

Ketcheson, K. A. (2001). Portland State University's electronic institutional portfolio. In K. B. Yancey (Ed.), *Electronic portfolios: Emerging practices in student, faculty, and institutional learning* (pp. 178-191). Washington, DC: American Association for Higher Education.

Kingore, B. W. (1993). *Portfolios: Enriching and assessing all students, identifying the gifted grades K-6* (1st ed.). Des Moines, IA: Leadership Publishers.

Klenowski, V. (Ed.). (2002). *Developing portfolios for learning and assessment: Processes and principles.* London; New York: Routledge Falmer.

KnowledgeLab. (2005). *Insights and reflections on e-portfolios.* Retrieved from http://www.knowledgelab.dk/now/e-portfolio/

Latour, B. (1987). *Science in action: How to follow scientists and engineers through society.* Cambridge, MA: Harvard University Press.

Lave, J., & Wenger, E. (1991). *Situated learning: Legitimate peripheral participation.* Cambridge, UK/New York: Cambridge University Press.

Lévy, P. (1997). *Collective intelligence: Mankind's emerging world in cyberspace.* New York: Plenum Trade.

Lévy, P. (2001). *Cyberculture.* Minneapolis/London: University of Minnesota Press.

Linus Torvalds. (2005). Retrieved from http://en.wikipedia.org/wiki/Linus_Torvalds

Linux. (2005). *Linux online!* Retrieved from http://www.linux.org/

Lovelock, J. E. (1995). *Gaia: A new look at life on earth.* Oxford: Oxford University Press.

Lyons, N. (1998a). Constructing narratives for understanding: Using portfolios interviews to scaffold teacher reflection. In N. Lyons (Ed.), *With portfolio in hand: Validating the new teacher professionalism* (pp. 103-119). New York: Teachers College Press.

Lyons, N. (1998b). Portfolio possibilities: Validating a new teacher professionalism. In N. Lyons (Ed.), *With portfolio in hand: Validating the new teacher professionalism* (pp. 11-22). New York: Teachers College Press.

Lyons, N. (1998c). Portfolios and their consequences: Developing as a reflective practitioner. In N. Lyons (Ed.), *With portfolio in hand: Validating the new teacher professionalism* (pp. 247-264). New York: Teachers College Press.

Lyons, N. (Ed.). (1998d). *With portfolio in hand: Validating the new teacher professionalism.* New York: Teachers College Press.

MacIntyre, A. C. (1981). *After virtue: A study in moral theory*. Notre Dame, IN: University of Notre Dame Press.

Martin, D. B., & Stollenwerk, D. A. (1999). *The portfolio planner: Making professional portfolios work for you.* Upper Saddle River, NJ: Merrill.

Maturana, H. R., & Varela, F. J. (1980). *Autopoiesis and cognition: The realization of the living.* Boston: D. Reidel.

McLuhan, M. (1962). *The Gutenberg galaxy; the making of typographic man.* Toronto: University of Toronto Press.

McLuhan, M. (1965). *Understanding media: The extensions of man.* New York: McGraw-Hill.

McLuhan, M., & Fiore, Q. (1968). *War and peace in the global village: An inventory of some of the current spastic situations that could be eliminated by more feedforward* (1st ed.). New York: McGraw-Hill.

McLuhan, M., & Powers, B. R. (1989). *The global village: Transformations in world life and media in the 21st century.* New York: Oxford University Press.

Meadows, D. H., Meadows, D. L., & Randers, J. (1992). *Beyond the limits: Confronting global collapse, envisioning a sustainable future.* Post Mills: Chelsea Green.

Meadows, D. H., & Rome, C. O. (1972). *The Limits to growth; a report for the Club of Rome's project on the predicament of mankind.* New York: Universe Books.

Merchant, C. (1980). *The death of nature: Women, ecology, and the scientific revolution.* San Francisco: Harper & Row.

Minsky, M. L., & Papert, S. (1988). *Perceptrons: An introduction to computational geometry* (expanded ed.). Cambridge, MA: MIT Press.

Moon, J. (2005). *University of Exeter.* Retrieved from http://www.heacadcmy.ac.uk/resources.asp?process=full_record§ion=generic&id=72

Moss, P. A. (1998). Rethinking validity for the assessment of teaching. In N. Lyons (Ed.), *With portfolio in hand: Validating the new teacher professionalism* (pp. 202-219). New York: Teachers College Press.

Muira, I. T. (1987). Gender and socioeconomic status differences in middle-school computer interest and use. *Journal of Early Adolescence, 7,* 243-254.

Mumford, L. (1967). *The myth of the machine: Technics and human development* (1st ed.). New York: Harcourt Brace Jovanovich.

Murphie, A., & Potts, J. (2003). *Culture and technology.* New York: Palgrave Macmillan.

Ong, W. J. (1977). *Interfaces of the word: Studies in the evolution of consciousness and culture*. Ithaca, NY: Cornell University Press.

Ong, W. J. (1982). *Orality and literacy: The technologizing of the word.* New York: Routledge.

Open Source Initiative (OSI). (2005a). *The open source definition.* Retrieved from http://www.opensource.org/

OSI. (2005b). *Products.* Retrieved from http://www.opensource.org/docs/products.php

OSPI (Open Source Portfolio Initiative). (2005). *Welcome: The Open Source Portfolio Initiative (OSPI).* Retrieved from http://www.theospi.org/

Pepperell, R. (1995). *The post-human condition.* Oxford, UK: Intellect.

Postman, N. (1986). *Amusing ourselves to death: Public discourse in the age of show business.* New York: Penguin Books.

Prigogine, I., & Stengers, I. (1984). *Order out of chaos: Man's new dialogue with nature.* New York: Bantam Books.

Ragsdale, R. G. (1988). *Permissible computing in education: Values, assumptions, and needs.* New York: Praeger.

Reiss, D. (2001). Reflective Webfolios in a humanities course. In K. B. Yancey (Ed.), *Electronic portfolios: Emerging practices in student, faculty, and institutional learning* (pp. 31-36). Washington, DC: American Association for Higher Education.

Rheingold, H. (1991). *Virtual reality.* New York: Summit Books.

Rheingold, H. (1993). *The virtual community: Homesteading on the electronic frontier.* Reading, MA: Addison-Wesley.

Rice, R. (2001). Composing the intranet-based electronic portfolio using "common" tools. In K. B. Yancey (Ed.), *Electronic portfolios: Emerging practices in student, faculty, and institutional learning* (pp. 37-43). Washington, DC: American Association for Higher Education.

Roszak, T. (1969). *The making of a counter culture: Reflections on the technocratic society and its youthful opposition.* Garden City, NY: Doubleday.

Roszak, T. (1986). *The cult of information: The folklore of computers and the true art of thinking.* New York: Pantheon.

Schipper, B., & Rossi, J. (1997). *Portfolios in the classroom: Tools for learning and instruction.* York, ME: Stenhouse.

Schon, D. A. (1983). *The reflective practitioner: How professionals think in action.* New York: Basic Books.

Schon, D. A. (1987). *Educating the reflective practitioner: Toward a new design for teaching and learning in the professions* (1st ed.). San Francisco: Jossey-Bass.

Seidel, S. (1997). *Portfolio practices: Thinking through the assessment of children's work.* Washington, DC: National Education Association.

Sernau, S. (2000). *Bound, living in the globalized world.* West Hartford, CT: Kumarian Press.

Shashaani, L. (1993). Gender-based differences in attitudes towards computers. *Computers and Education, 20*(2), 169-181.

Shulman, L. S. (1992). Portfolios in teacher education: A component of reflective teacher education. *Proceedings of the American Educational Research Association Conference,* San Francisco.

Shulman, L. (1998). Teacher portfolios: A theoretical activity. In N. Lyons (Ed.), *With portfolio in hand: Validating the new teacher professionalism* (pp. 23-37). New York: Teachers College Press.

Smith, M. A., & Ylvisaker, M. (Eds.). (1993). *Teachers' voices: Portfolios in the classroom.* Berkeley, CA: National Writing Project.

Springfield, E. (2001). Comparing electronic and paper portfolios. In K. B. Yancey (Ed.), *Electronic portfolios: Emerging practices in student, faculty, and institutional learning* (pp. 76-82). Washington, DC: American Association for Higher Education.

Stier, M. (2001). Teaching great books on the Web. In K. B. Yancey (Ed.), *Electronic portfolios: Emerging practices in student, faculty, and institutional learning* (pp. 106-116). Washington, DC: American Association for Higher Education.

Stock, G. (1993). *Metaman: The merging of humans and machines into a global superorganism.* New York: Simon & Schuster.

Stone, A. R. (1995). *The war of desire and technology at the close of the mechanical age.* Cambridge, MA: MIT Press.

Sullivan, M. (1994). *Assessment records portfolio.* Richmond Hill, ON: Scholastic Canada.

Synder, J., Lippincott, A., & Bower, D. (1998). Portfolios in teacher education: Technical or tranformational. In N. Lyons (Ed.), *With portfolio in hand: Validating the new teacher professionalism* (pp. 123-142). New York: Teachers College Press.

Tapscott, D. (1998). *Growing up digital: The rise of the net generation.* New York: McGraw-Hill.

Teitel, L., Ricci, M., & Coogan, J. (1998). Experienced teachers construct teaching portfolios: A culture of compliance vs. a culture of professional development. In N. Lyons (Ed.), *With portfolio in hand: Validating the new teacher professionalism* (pp. 143-155). New York: Teachers College Press.

Tompkins, D. P. (2001). Ambassadors with portfolios: Recommendations. In K.B. Yancey (Ed.), *Electronic portfolios: Emerging practices in student, faculty, and institutional learning* (pp. 130-131). Washington, DC: American Association for Higher Education.

Turkle, S. (1995). *Life on the screen: Identity in the age of the Internet.* New York: Simon & Schuster.

Vancouver School Board. (1993). *Portfolios.* Vancouver: Vancouver School Board.

Varela, F. J., Thompson, E., & Rosch, E. (1991). *The embodied mind: Cognitive science and human experience.* Cambridge, MA: MIT Press.

Wajcman, J. (1991). *Feminism confronts technology.* Cambridge, UK: Polity Press.

Watson, J. A., Penny, J.M., Scanzoni, J., & Penny, J. (1989). Networking the home and the university: How families can be integrated into proximate/distant computer systems. *Journal of Research on Computing in Education, 22*(1), 107-117.

Wexler, J. G. (2001). The role of institutional portfolios in the revised WASC accreditation process. In K. B. Yancey (Ed.), *Electronic portfolios: Emerging practices in student, faculty, and institutional learning* (pp. 209-216). Washington, DC: American Association for Higher Education.

Wikimedia Commons. (2005). Retrieved from http://commons.wikimedia.org/wiki/Main_Page

Williams, S. (2005). *Free as in freedom: Richard Stallman's crusade for free software.* Retrieved from http://en.wikipedia.org/wiki/Free_as_in_Freedom

Winograd, T., & Flores, C. F. (1986). *Understanding computers and cognition: A new foundation for design.* Norwood, NJ: Ablex.

Wolf, D. (1998). Creating a portfolio culture. In N. Lyons (Ed.), *With portfolio in hand: Validating the new teacher professionalism* (pp. 41-50). New York: Teachers College Press.

KEY TERMS

Cybernetics: Concerned with discovering what mechanisms control systems, and in particular, how systems regulate themselves. (http://www.webopedia.com/TERM/c/cybernetics.html)

Educational Technology: Using multimedia technologies or audiovisual aids as a tool to enhance the teaching and learning process. (http://www.emsc.nysed.gov/technology/nclb/definition.htm)

Intellectual Property Rights: Temporary grants of monopoly intended to give economic incentives for innovative activity. IPRs exist in the form of patents, copyrights, and trademarks. (http://dret.net/glossary/ipr)

Learning Outcome: Specification of what a student should learn as the result of a period of specified and supported study.

Literature Review: Critical analysis of a segment of a published body of knowledge through summary, classification, and comparison of prior research studies, reviews of literature, and theoretical articles.

Online Community: Set of users who communicate using computer-mediated communication and have common interests, shared goals, and shared resources. (http://www.amazon.ca/exec/obidos/ASIN/0805835075/702-7447084-8105636)

Pedagogy: Art or profession of teaching. (http://www.thefreedictionary.com/pedagogy)

Virtual Community: A community of people sharing common interests, ideas, and feelings over the Internet or other collaborative networks. (http://whatis.techtarget.com/definition/0,,sid9_gci213295,00.html)

Virtual Reality: An artificial environment created with computer hardware and software, and presented to the user in such a way that it appears and feels like a real environment. (http://www.webopedia.com/TERM/v/virtual_reality.html)

Web-Based Training: A generic term for training and/or instruction delivered over the Internet or an intranet using a Web browser. (http://www.webopedia.com/TERM/W/WBT.html)

ENDNOTES

1 This chapter owes its origin to: (1) University of British Columbia (UBC), through the Teaching and Learning Fund from Teresa Dobson's grant, funding my postdoctoral fellowships (PDFs) towards my participation in UBC's ePortfolio Community of Practice on evaluation and implementation of ePortfolios; (2) Centre for Cross Faculty Instruction (CCFI), then known as the Centre for the Study of Curriculum and Instruction[CSCI]) in the Faculty of Education (FoE), UBC, where I completed my doctorate specializing in exegetical, hermeneutic, phenomenological, and narrative approaches for my dissertation in curriculum and instruction at intersections of technology, culture, and nature; (3) Curriculum Studies in the FoE at UBC; and (4) Computer Science Department at UBC for coordinating my interdisciplinary research examining implications of gender learning setting and prior experience on computing competency with my Gates-Tangorra-Feng scale (my gratitude to Rosenberg Boutillier,

Casselman, Coatta, Forsey, Kirkpatrick, Little, Pai, Pippinger, Tsiknis, Velthuys, and Zhu of Computer Science, UBC, for validating my computer competency scale developed through my interview with Bill Gates, Microsoft); (5) National Academy of Engineering (NAE) commissioned review on how people learn technology; and (6) College of Engineering Technology, University of Houston in the United States of America, where I learned microprocessor design. I acknowledge my gratitude to Robert Tierney, Dean of the FoE, UBC; Jon Shapiro, Senior Associate Dean, FoE, UBC; James Gaskell, Associate Dean, External Program and Learning Technology, FoE, UBC; Michelle Lamberson, Director, Office of Learning Technologies (OLT), UBC; Kele Fleming, Coordinator, Community of Practice, (OLT), UBC; Teresa Dobson, FoE, UBC; Stephen Petrina, FoE, UBC; Karen Meyer, FoE, UBC; Carl Leggo, FoE, UBC; members of the UBC/OLT community of practice, especially Bjorn Thomson, Alison Wong, and mentors/colleagues, UBC: Ted Aoki, Walter Boldt, Roger Boshier, John Brine, Bob Bruce, Mary Bryson, Alice Cassidy, Graeme Chalmers, Chan Choon Hian, Jerry Coombs, Pamela Courtney-Hall, Leroi Daniels, Brent Davis, Stuart Donn, Frank Echols, Gaelen Erickson, Lynn Fels, Don Fisher, Hillel Goelman, Ricki Goldman-Segall, Rita Irwin, Nand Kishnor, Don Krug, Cynthia Nichol, Jim Sherrill, Charles Ungerlieder, Munir Vellani, Harold Ratzlaff, David Robitaille, Leslie Roman, Bob Walker, Walt Werner, Marv Westrom, John Willinsky, Doug Wilms; menotrs, students enrolled in ETEC 531, in the UBC and Tec de Monterey Masters of Education MET program that Stephen Petrina and I co-taught, which I elaborate in endnote 5, for seeding empirical foundations of my theorizing/contribution.

[2] Having adapted the WebCT CMS software for ePortfolio application, we will likely be revisiting the informative Batson argument.

[3] Take the cursory raw "test" for your own empirical verification. Searches for these key words—"problems," "concerns," "ethics," or "ethical implications"—with ePortfolios likely yields results directed towards problems or concerns around the technology and content rather than the ePortfolio itself. Helen Barrett stands as a notable exception online with her concerns directed at implications of ePortfolios.

[4] Wolf's work was an important watershed for my theorizing, what Wolf saw as the creating of "portfolio culture" (p. 41) was for myself an emergence in historical continuity with paradigmatic shifts in our relationship with information.

[5] As indicated in endnote 1, I would like to thank all the graduate students who were enrolled in ETEC 531, Cultural and New Media Studies in Education, in the joint University of British Columbia - Tec de Monterey online Masters of Education (MET) program for summer 2005, co-taught by Stephen Petrina and myself, for their interactions in cyberspace that seeded my theorizing in ePortfolios, patterning, complexity, and online/virtual learning communities.

Chapter XXII
Integral ePortfolio Interoperability with the IMS ePortfolio Specification

Darren Cambridge
George Mason University, USA

ABSTRACT

Interoperability that enables the distribution and migration of portfolios as integral wholes between venues requires the ability to describe, encode, and transmit the relationships between assets within the portfolio and its information architecture and visual design in a format that both human and computer audiences can understand. This chapter will discern interoperability challenges fundamental to ePortfolios. It will explain how fundamental issues begin to be addressed by the IMS ePortfolio specification and will consider the challenges that lie ahead as adoption of this specification grows.

INTRODUCTION

Electronic portfolios are integrative in every sense. Rhetorically, they provide an integrated representation of what a person knows, believes, values, and can accomplish. Pedagogically, they integrate diverse learning experiences and sources of evidence. Technically, supporting their development and use requires integrating numerous systems and applications. Because of this integrative nature, an exhaustive account of the interoperability issues that confront the developers of ePortfolio technology would be impossible. This chapter, therefore, will discern interoperability challenges fundamental to ePortfolios.[1] It will explain how these fundamental issues begin to be addressed by the IMS ePortfolio specification and will consider the challenges that lie ahead as adoption of this specification grows.

PORTFOLIO AS DIGITAL COMPOSITION WITHIN A VENUE

Focusing on fundamental interoperability issues for ePortfolio software requires identifying some defining features of an ePortfolio. Most definitions maintain that an "ePortfolio" contains a collection of evidence about the learning and performance of an individual, group, or organization. Some definitions go on to imply that an electronic portfolio is a software application in and through which this collection is developed and used. However, a genuine portfolio is conceptually distinct from, if technically related to, the software through which it is composed and read.

More than a collection of information about learning, an electronic portfolio is a *digital composition* within a rhetorical *venue*.[2] As a composition, a portfolio is a message about what a person or group has learned and can do, composed by an author and delivered to an audience. Not just a repository of learning-related information, it is an argument that explains past learning and performance and predicts future capabilities. As a digital composition, an ePortfolio uses the affordances of the digital, networked medium to make this argument; therefore, the hypertextual arrangement and the visual design of the portfolio are important to its success.

Because a portfolio is a message within a rhetorical situation, a venue must be available through which portfolio authors and audiences can connect. Although this portfolio venue is not the portfolio itself, it is essential as the "place" where the portfolio is read. A primary advantage of electronic media for portfolios is the availability of powerful venues, such as the Web. As part of a venue, ePortfolio software can provide important services to portfolio authors and audiences. Venues can enable the provision of evidence for use in the portfolio, guidance during portfolio composition, feedback on the results, tools for analysis, and connections to new audiences. Within a given venue, a portfolio author is likely to have multiple portfolios, composed using overlapping collections of assets, targeted at multiple and overlapping audiences.

Portfolio learning occurs within this venue *through* the process of composition. The portfolio does not simply record past and inform future learning. The composition of the portfolio itself is a central learning activity. Rather than a collection of reflections on other learning experiences or learning in general, the portfolio is composed through reflection *on* the assets, or artifacts, collected for use within the portfolio. Through this reflective process, the portfolio author articulates the relationships between assets to convey what they mean. In reflectively composing the portfolio, the author makes meaning through relating different assets within the context of a larger narrative about his or her learning. *This making of meaning through synthesizing a network of relationships is at the heart of portfolio practice.*

When portfolio information is moved between venues, it must travel with sufficient structure to represent information within the context of this synthesized whole. It must maintain its integrity as portfolio information, rather than simply reverting to atomized data that happened to have been part of a portfolio. While assets like goals, samples of work, and competencies may be important components of a portfolio, they cease to be portfolio information if they lose their place within the network of relationships that join them into an integrative portfolio argument.

Portfolio venues can powerfully shape both the ways in which portfolios can be arranged and delivered to audiences and the range of options readers have when experiencing portfolios. Much of this capacity is dependent on the software that powers the venue-understanding elements of the underlying semantic structure of the portfolio. For example, a system might enable an author to organize portfolio information within a matrix of competencies that could be analyzed by its audience in comparison with other portfolios utilizing this same structure. When portfolio compositions are moved between venues, they must carry with them sufficient semantic information to allow the new venue to connect the portfolio to a new set of services.

AGGREGATION, SYNDICATION, DISTRIBUTION, AND MIGRATION

The interoperability needs of portfolios can be divided into four categories: aggregation, syndication, distribution, and migration. The first two categories, aggregation and syndication, are important to creating powerful portfolio venues. However, they are not fundamentally linked to portfolios, because they do not engage portfolios as integral digital compositions. *Aggregation* is the process by which information that is needed for the composition of the portfolio is made available within the portfolio venue. For example, a collection of competencies by which an educational institution certifies an individual might be aggregated within a portfolio venue for use in a portfolio. *Syndication* is the process of making information that is part of a portfolio available beyond the portfolio's venue. For example, a course management system might access a set of reflections stored within a portfolio. In both the processes of aggregation and syndication, the information is divorced from its context within the network of relationships and interpretations that make up the portfolio's argument. The aggregated assets have yet to be linked purposefully, and the syndicated assets no longer bear the traces of their place within the synthesized whole. Nonetheless, aggregation and syndication are important aspects of portfolio venues.

Aggregation and syndication require lightweight, flexible standards and specifications. Scott Wilson of the Center for Educational Technology Interoperability Standards has begun exploring the use of specifications often associated with blogs, such as RSS and Atom, for aggregation of portfolio information (Wilson, 2005). RSS, which stands for rich site summary or really simple syndication, is a widely used format for making summaries of frequently updated information resources, such as blogs, available in a machine-readable format over the Web. Atom is an alternate format used for similar purposes. David Tosh and Ben Werdmuller have employed similar specifications in their ELGG, a free system which combines simple portfolio functions with social networking and blogging, for the syndication of information used with portfolios and use the Friend of a Friend (FOAF) format to share profile information (Brickley & Miller, 2005; Tosh & Werdmuller, 2005). Although the power of these specifications is largely untapped by the leading enterprise ePortfolio systems, they hold much promise for improving portfolio venues. Also useful for aggregation and syndication are simpler common eLearning specifications, such as the IMS Reusable Definition of Competency or Educational Objective (RDCEO), which are being used in portfolio-related Web services being developed in the UK and Europe, such as Web Services for Reflective Learning and Skills Profiling Service (see Grant, this volume; Cooper & Ostyn, 2002). However, these standards and specifications are certainly not unique to ePortfolios, and they do not address the need to make interoperable the fundamental, integral nature of portfolios. Aggregation only becomes integration through the portfolio author's articulation of relationships and information architecture as the aggregated assets are synthesized into an argument.

Distribution and migration, in contrast, do address the integral nature of ePortfolios. *Distribution* encompasses the processes by which portfolios are shared between venues as integral wholes. Successful distribution requires that portfolio venues can understand and can represent the full complexity of the digital composition: its relationships, hypertextual organization, visual design, and diverse types of assets. Submitting a portfolio developed with a university's ePortfolio software to a potential employer evaluating the portfolio through a different ePortfolio system is an example of distribution. *Migration,* on the other hand, is the process of moving multiple, overlapping portfolios along with the contents of the repositories of assets from which they draw. Moving an author's complete set of portfolios and her archive of assets from her high school's ePortfolio system to a personal set of tools at graduation is an example of migration. On a larger scale, another example of migration is moving the portfolios and portfolio data for all a firm's employees when the firm switches portfolio software vendors. Distribution and migration require more robust and complicated standards and specifications than aggregation and syndication. ePortfolio-specific specifications, therefore, are needed to enable sharing of portfolios as integral wholes.

IMS ePORTFOLIO SPECIFICATION

The IMS ePortfolio specification is the first open specification developed to support distribution and migration. The IMS Global Learning Consortium is the leading international organization developing technical specifications to support eLearning, with members across North America, Europe, and Australia from a variety of educational and industry sectors. While much work remains to fully support these processes, the release of the specification marks a significant milestone. The body of practice emerging as ePortfolio technology developers adopt the specification will launch subsequent work, further developing standards that support integral portfolio interoperability.

History and Scope

The IMS ePortfolio specification is the result of two years of work by a diverse group of learning technologists. The IMS ePortfolio Group, formed at a meeting in Sestri Levante, Italy, in May of 2003, was formally chartered by IMS that December. After a base document was released in April of 2004, a public draft became available in September 2004. The final specification, approved by the IMS Technical Advisory Board in June 2005, was publicly released on July 5, 2005 (Cambridge, Smythe, & Heath, 2005).

The scope of work defined in the charter was based on use cases contributed by both IMS member organizations and other members of the educational community following a widely publicized open call. Use cases were received from the U.S., Canada, Europe, and Australia; from those in higher education, lifelong learning, and training; and from both technical and content experts. In the U.S., the EPAC virtual community of practice held several meetings in which pedagogy and assessment experts, in addition to technology developers, wrote and contributed use cases (EPAC, 2005).

The development team for the charter, co-led by Andy Heath of Sheffield Hallam University and Darren Cambridge of EDUCAUSE and George Mason University, included members from the U.S. and the UK. Commercial vendors were represented through the participation of Blackboard, IBM, Texas Instruments, Thompson Learning, and FD Learning. Participating higher education institutions included The Pennsylvania State University and the University of California at Berkeley. The team was rounded out by delegates of non-profit organizations and NGOs, EDUCAUSE, the Center for Recording Achievement, and CETIS. Andy Heath served as a link to the EPICC project, which involved additional UK and European higher education institutions and Italian vendor Giunti Labs in gathering European requirements for ePortfolio interoperability. Work was closely coordinated with the British Standards Institute's UKLeaP project, which produced the BSI 8788 standard, a UK standard for recording learner information throughout life.

Most use cases in the development process described scenarios focusing on the distribution or migration of complete portfolios between venues. Success in these scenarios requires three types of alignment between the venue in which the portfolio originates and its destination venue. First, the technology that supports each venue must share a common data format for moving portfolios into and out of it. Second, the two venues must agree on a method of communication for sharing portfolios encoded in that format. Finally, the ways in which authors and audiences classify and interpret portfolios must be sufficiently aligned between the two venues to enable audiences at the destination to make sense of what they receive. This final coordination is not primarily a technical problem, although it does have some implications for how technical specifications are put into practice, as discussed below. Because interpretation is largely a policy and pedagogy challenge, it was clearly beyond the scope of the specification effort. The second alignment, communication protocols, is essential, but it is not specific to ePortfolios. Many other eLearning activities require the exchange of complex, structured collections of information. Because guidelines for defining these protocols, based on emerging Web services standards and practices, were in the process of being formalized by the IMS General Web Services project, the ePortfolio team decided to wait until this work is complete to define ePortfolio-related services. Therefore, the scope of this first iteration of the ePortfolio specification project focused on defining a data format for portfolios for the purposes of distribution and migration.

While the use cases centered around these two processes, and it was clear that a common data format was the first step to supporting them, the requirements gathered also dictated that the specification support diverse portfolio practices, utilizing multiple types and combinations of tools, across educational sectors. The level of detail in the specification needed to be sufficient to capture the semantic structure fundamental to a portfolio's integrity, but it also needed to be flexible and extensible enough to accommodate the significant diversity of local technology and practice. The requirements also revealed a rapid pace of change in both pedagogy and technology that made a definitive and exhaustive analysis of existing practice impossible. The team was shooting at a moving target. Without a body of practice in portfolio distribution and migration on which to draw, it was unlikely that it would get the balance between detail and flexibility exactly right prior to the release of the specification. Therefore, it proceeded expecting that the specification it developed would need significant revision over time as the eLearning community gained experience using the specification to distribute and migrate portfolios.

Both the practices and systems in use to support portfolios had significant overlaps and interrelationships with other eLearning activities and technologies already in widespread use. While the requirements focused primarily on distribution and migration, implicit within them was a need to integrate with other systems within an organization or individual's technical ecology. In addition, we discerned that many components needed for the specification had been developed in other contexts and could be easily adapted to ours. In order to facilitate enterprise integration and to minimize duplication of work, we chose to incorporate and build upon existing standards and specifications whenever possible.

The final decision necessary to fix the scope of the specification was to determine technology to which to bind the information model. Topics maps, resource description format (RDF), and related semantic Web technologies seemed to offer particularly compelling ways to accommodate diverse practice and to represent complex relationships. However, existing IMS specifications, as well as most of the other open standards and specifications members of the team deemed related, used eXtensible Markup Language (XML), the nearly ubiquitous "markup language for documents containing structured information" (Walsh, 1998). IMS staff also expressed a strong preference for XML, based on their perception of the maturity of the two technologies and the state of the eLearning market. With some misgivings, we settled on XML. The packaging mechanism defined in the final specification does facilitate the inclusion of portfolio information encoded using other technologies when XML is insufficient.

Structure

The IMS ePortfolio specification consists of four primary documents: an Information Model, a Binding, a Best Practices Guide, and a Rubric Specification. The Information Model specifies the normative structure of a portfolio, independent of any specific technology. The Binding specifies how the XML is used to implement the information model. It includes both normative guidelines for packaging portfolios and a set of XML schemas, which incorporates elements from several other IMS specifications. The Best Practices and Implementation Guide provides non-normative suggestions for implementation, conceptual background, vocabularies for some elements, and a set of example portfolios encoded using the binding. The Rubric Specification is a separate document because the rubric structure defined therein may find applications not directly related to portfolios.

The information model defines the primary components of a portfolio (see Figure 1). A portfolio consists of four primary components. First, it includes a collection of heterogeneous Parts, the assets used to make the portfolio's argument. Second, these parts are associated with an Owner, the author of the portfolio. Third, the portfolio includes a set of Relationships between the parts. These relationships define how the parts of the portfolio are synthesized into an integral whole in a manner that can be understood by the systems supporting ePortfolio development and use. Fourth, a portfolio may also include Presentations, instruc-

Figure 1.

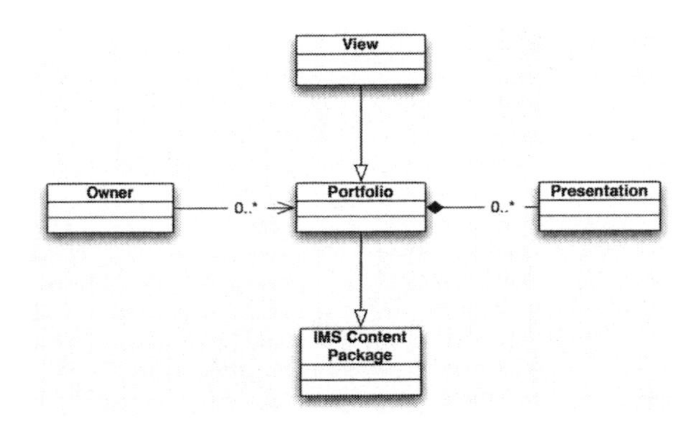

tions on how an audience should experience the portfolio that specifies its hypertextual structure and visual design. Finally, to facilitate migration, a portfolio may also include *views,* which are selections of parts, relationships, and presentations for a particular audience or purpose. All of these components are bundled together to be shared across venues within a portfolio package. More than a simple collection, a portfolio encoded using the IMS ePortfolio specification represents the complete structure of a portfolio as an integral digital composition so that it may be used by other software and audiences in a manner that engages its semantics.

A portfolio contains some number of Portfolio Parts, each of which has a type. The set of types is intended to define the most common types of assets and information the authors may wish to include within their portfolios. The types are listed in Table 1. While a few of these types are unique to ePortfolios, most are taken from existing IMS specifications (Smythe, Tansey, & Robson, 2001) (see Figure 2). From the IMS Learning Information Package (LIP) specification come the Portfolio Part types: Activity, Affiliation, Competency, Goal, Identification, Interest, Product, QCL (Qualification), Security Key, and Transcript. Definitions of competencies are included using RDCEO. Accessibility information may be included through a part defined using the IMS Accessibility for LIP (ACCLIP) specification (Norton & Treviranus, 2003). While a participation element is defined in LIP, the ePortfolio specification uses its own definition for the participation Portfolio Part type based on the IMS Enterprise Services specification to better enable repre-

Table 1. Portfolio part types in the IMS ePortfolio specification

Portfolio Part Type	Purpose
Accessibility	Describes preferences for interacting with systems and content
Activity	Describes relevant activities
Affiliation	Describes organizational affiliations
Assertion/Reflexion	Represents reflections upon, or assertions about, a Portfolio Part, including comments and explanations
Competency	Describes skills acquired
Goal	Describes personal objectives or aspirations
Identification	Indicates the owner
Interest	Describes hobbies, recreational activities, etc.
Other	Accommodates portfolio information of other types
Participation	Group of people (who participated in an activity, created a document, etc.)
Product	Materials produced by the owner
QCL (Qualification)	Describes qualification, certifications, and licenses
Rubric	Represents guidance about how a portfolio has been or is to be assessed
RubricCell	Refers to outcomes at the intersection of dimensions within a rubric
SecurityKey	Represents passwords, security codes, etc.
Transcript	Store summary records of academic performance at an institution

Figure 2.

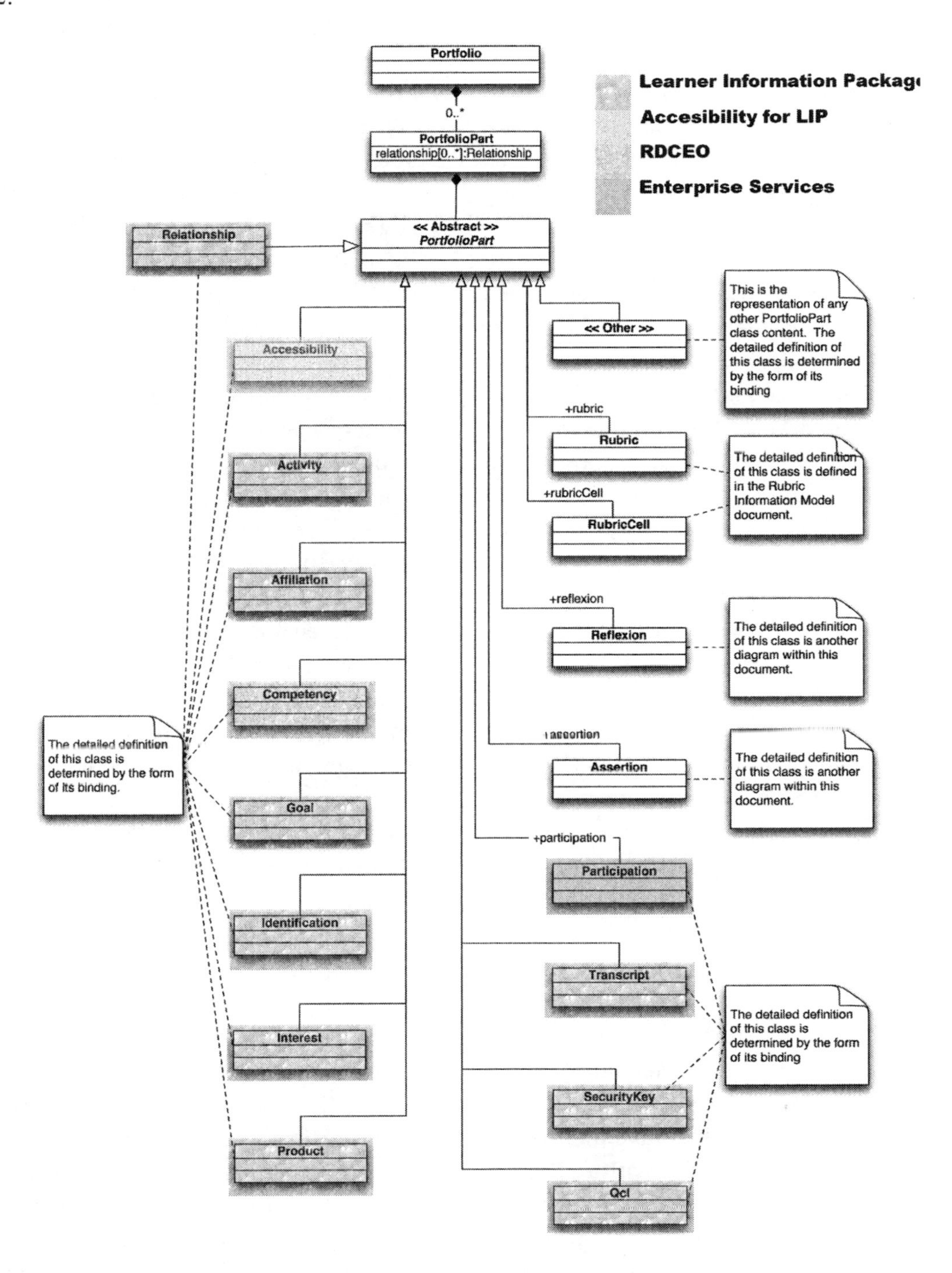

sentation of group participation (Smythe, 2004). In addition, four types of Portfolio Parts are defined that are new. Portfolio Parts of the type Assertion and Reflexion are used to represent reflections and comments about other Portfolio Parts. The structure of the Assertion and Reflexion elements is identical with those proposed for BSI 8788 (UKLeaP). The Rubric type enables inclusion of rubrics, multi-dimensional matrixes of competency definitions and scores, and the RubricCell type allows relationships to be defined between other Portfolio Parts and cells within a Rubric. Portfolio information that cannot be easily included using one of the defined types may be incorporated using the Other type.

Relationships between Portfolio Parts are encoded using the Relationship element, taken from LIP. Each relationship tuple has a type, which defines its purpose within the portfolio's argument. The Best Practices guide includes a vocabulary for relationship types, which is aligned with the vocabulary incorporated into BSI 8788, a vocabulary that merged from an extensive investigation of practice conducted by Simon Grant for the Center for Recording Achievement. Scott Wilson of CETIS has usefully grouped the relationship types into five categories: types for representing basic relationships, such as shows-up, supplements, supports, and precedes; types for representing assessments and evidence, such as attests, evaluates, evidences; types for indicating commentary, such as reflects-on; types for showcasing content, such as presents; and types for representing motivation, such as aims-at.

Presentations define how the set of Portfolio Parts and their relationships are to be presented to the portfolio's audience. They define the information architecture and visual look and feel of the portfolio. While the technical format of a presentation is left open, we anticipate that presentations will most often take the form of an XSL or set of XSLs, coupled with a CSS, that may be used to transform the IMS ePortfolio data into an XHTML or set of XHTML pages. Other possible formats include XML Formatting Objects (XML-FO), which could be used to create a PDF version for printing. Views, similarly, take the form of XSLs that create a new portfolio that is simply a subset of the old one.

All the Portfolio Parts, Relationships, Presentations, Views, and other supporting resources, such as the media files referenced by Products, within a portfolio or set of portfolios are gathered together with a Portfolio Package. The format of a Portfolio Package is complicated, requiring fairly in-depth knowledge of several other specifications, and is likely to be simplified in future versions. In its present form, the packaging format is based on the IMS Content Package specification. Each Portfolio Part, Relationship, Presentation, and View is included as a separate XML file. A Content Package-style manifest describes all of the included components. Within the manifest, the organization and title elements are used to indicate the purpose and type of each resource through a set of naming conventions. Learning object metadata (LOM) records may be included for any component (Learning Technology Standards Committee, 2002). These metadata records may be used to indicate the importance of a component to the portfolio. For example, metadata could be included to indicate that a presentation is essential to understanding a portfolio designed to persuade its audience that its author is a superior graphic designer.

Implementation

As of the fall of 2005, the final version of the specification was just released, so most ePortfolio tool builders are only now working the specification into their plans. A number of major ePortfolio software developers have expressed their intention to adopt and implement the IMS ePortfolio specification, including the vendors Angel Learning, Avenet, Blackboard, Nuventive, and the Open Source Portfolio Initiative (OSPI). Guinti Labs' recently released Learn eXact ePortfolio, which fully supports and is based on the specification. It was demonstrated at the ePortfolio Plugfest in Cambridge, England, in October 2005 (Giorgini, 2005). Also at the Plugfest, UK vendors and developers demonstrated the PebblePAD, ePortfolio Extensions Toolkit (ePET), and LUSID implementations of UKLeaP, which is very similar to the IMS ePortfolio. These implementations were certified using a tool developed by Technology Enhanced Learning Conformance—European Requirements and Testing (TELCERT), which tests conformance to ePortfolios, UKLeaP, and several other standards and specifications. The IMS team has additionally been in contact with university-based developers in Australia, France, and Norway who are conducting pilot development projects based on the specification. Because IT acquisition policies encourage the adoption of open standards and specifications, adoption is likely to be more rapid in Europe, and U.S.-based vendors will be motivated by the needs of the European market in the short term.

Among the open source implementation projects of which the IMS team is aware, OSPI is furthest along. Led by Chris Arnett at the University of Minnesota, OSP developers are building the ability to import and export IMS ePortfolio packages into version 2.1 of the Open Source Portfolio, to be released in the first quarter of 2006 (Open Source Portfolio Initiative, 2005). An export tool will also be developed for use with version 1.x of OSP and will serve as an option for migration between 1.x and 2.x, as well as for migration and distribution to other vendors' tools.

The University of Minnesota system and Minnesota State Colleges and Universities, which includes all other primary public higher education systems in the state, have an immediate need for interoperability because they use different systems. The University of Minnesota system, which uses OSI, has a concrete need to make the 50,000+ portfolios they host interoperable with the 35,000+ portfolios supported by the eFolio Minnesota project, which uses Avenet. Although OSPI is working with Avenet to achieve two-way distribution and migration, Avenet's software is much less data centric than OSP, making the process of mapping to the IMS specification more complicated. In 2005, Avenet is developing new tools to add more structured data to eFolio Minnesota portfolios. These new tools will produce assets that map to core Portfolio Part types, primarily those from LIP.

Because OSP's architecture is particularly well aligned with the structure of the IMS ePortfolio format, OSPI's progress has been more rapid.[3] All data items within OSP are stored natively as XML documents. The import-export tool simply translates between items in OSP XML and the appropriate IMS ePortfolio Portfolio Part or Relationship using two XSL documents. Uploaded material and other pertinent files are included and referenced in the Portfolio Package, along with the transformed XML documents. Mappings between a set of core OSP data elements, developed in November 2005 by representatives from the OSPI community based on existing hierarchies in use at member institutions and IMS ePortfolio Portfolio Part types and relationships, will be included in the 2.1 release. OSP 2.0 already includes a presentation export feature that produces files appropriate for inclusion within an IMS ePortfolio package as Presentations.

However, the OSP core elements include more detail than is supported automatically by the IMS ePortfolio specification. For example, the OSP elements include at least two dozen different types of activities, which are categorized hierarchically. The IMS specification includes only a generic Activity Portfolio Part type with no associated vocabulary. However, each Portfolio Part within an IMS ePortfolio may be assigned a type, which can be defined within a controlled vocabulary. In order to capture such additional detail, OSPI will create a community vocabulary, making use of IMS's Vocabulary Definition Exchange specification (VDEX) (Cooper, 2004).

The set of mappings that define how IMS ePortfolio elements will be used with OSP and the controlled vocabulary together will constitute an application profile of the IMS specification. As OSPI works with its partners, this application profile will be refined and expanded to include the practices that OSPI and other developers agree upon. Because the specification is intended to support a broad range of practice across sectors and regions, application profiles will likely be necessary in many applications in order to capture the needed level of detail. Application profiles have frequently been developed by organizations and national coordinating bodies to ease the implementation of other eLearning specifications. As vendors and institutions begin using the specification for the distribution and migration of portfolios, multiple application profiles will be developed. For example, the EPICC project is developing an application profile of the specification that meets the needs of medical education. Other application profiles might map the details of de facto standards for employment information, such as the academic CV format from Community of Science or the résumé format from Monster.com, to the ePortfolio specification. TELCERT has developed an open source tool that generates profiles that may be of use to communities developing such profiles (Riley, 2005).

As common patterns of use emerge from these multiple profiles, IMS will incorporate the resulting elements and vocabularies back into future versions of the ePortfolio specification. However, a significant range of local and sector-specific needs will probably always exist. As integral, individually controlled representations of the richness and diversity of human learning, portfolios are too complex to define globally, except around the edges. The IMS specification can serve as the organizing framework for capturing and sharing this complexity, but, in itself, is unlikely to represent it exhaustively. Even within the OSPI community, individual institutions create their own unique data elements, which will need to be mapped to both the OSP and IMS types and vocabularies.

As Arnett argues, the success of the IMS ePortfolio specification—indeed, ePortfolio standards and specifications in general—depends on developing and putting into practice effective mechanisms for articulating between vocabularies. The need for articulation is not unique to ePortfolios. Developers at this year's Alt-I-Lab collectively identified the need for a specification for such articulation, and IMS is likely to take on such a project in the near future. Developing such a specification in a form that proves usable may mean moving beyond XML and embracing semantic Web technologies, such as topic maps and the OWL Web Ontology Language, which are designed specifically to deal with multiple, distributed systems of representation (Berners-Lee, Hendler, & Lessila, 2001). Promising work is underway in Scandinavia putting topic-map-based ePortfolio systems, such as BrainBank, into practice (Nordeng, Dicheva, Garchol, Ronningsbakk, & Meloy, 2005).

INTERPRETATION

Ultimately, however, portfolios can only be distributed or migrated successfully if both the originating and destination venues share common interpretive practices. Having effective means for translating between vocabularies is an important technical support for interpretation across the boundaries or venues. However, portfolio authors and audiences must move beyond alignment of technical semantics to shared ways of making meaning out of the portfolios they share. While shared practices of meaning-making can be supported by technical standards, they must also be forged through bi- and multi-lateral articulation agreements, such as the one being developed between the University of Minnesota and MnSCU, through research on how individuals and institutions make sense of and use portfolios in the wild, and through building shared conceptual frameworks through communities of practice. True ePortfolio interoperability requires aligning technical specification development with research initiatives such as the National Coalition for Electronic Portfolio Research and communities such as EPAC (National Coalition for Electronic Portfolio Research, 2005). When technology, research, and communities themselves interoperate, we will then be able to share portfolios in a manner that celebrates the power of their integrity.

REFERENCES

Arnett, C. (2005). *Mapping OSP portfolios to the IMS e-portfolio specification: Implementation overview.* Minneapolis, MN: OSPI.

Berners-Lee, T., Hendler, J., & Lessila, O. (2001, May 16). The semantic web. *Scientific American,* 35-43.

Brickley, D., & Miller, L. (2005, June 3). *FOAF vocabulary specification*. Retrieved July 6, 2005, from http://xmlns.com/foaf/0.1/

Cambridge, D., Smythe, C., & Heath, A. (2005). *IMS e-portfolio specification v1.0.* Retrieved July 6, 2005, from http://www.imsglobal.org/ep/

Cooper, A. (2004). *IMS vocabulary definition exchange v1.0.* Retrieved July 5, 2005, from http://www.imsglobal.org/vdex/

Cooper, A., & Ostyn, C. (2002). *IMS reusable definition of competency or educational objective v1.0.* Retrieved July 6, 2005, from http://www.imsglobal.org/competencies/index.cfm

EPAC International. (2005). *EPAC international.* Retrieved September 30, 2005, from http://epacinternational.org/

ePortConsortium. (2003). *Electronic portfolio white paper.* Retrieved July 6, 2005, from http://with.iupui.edu/WhitePaper/whitepaperV1_0.pdf

Farrell, T.B. (1993). *Norms of rhetorical culture.* New Haven: Yale University Press.

Giorgini, F. (2005). Portability and interoperability between e-portfolio management systems: From the EPICC project to the eXact Portfolio solution. In *Proceedings of the E-Portfolio Conference 2005,* Cambridge, UK.

Learning Technology Standards Committee. (2002). *1484.12.1-2002 learning object metadata.* Retrieved July 6, 2005, from http://ltsc.ieee.org/wg12/files/LOM_1484_12_1_v1_Final_Draft.pdf

National Coalition for Electronic Portfolio Research. (2005). Retrieved September 30, 2005, from http://ncepr.org/ncepr/drupal/

Nordeng, T. W., Dicheva, D., Garchol, L. M., Ronningsbakk, L., & Meloy, J. R. (2005). Topic Maps for integrating e-portfolio with e-curriculum. In *Proceedings of the E-Portfolio Conference 2005,* Cambridge, UK.

Norton, M., & Treviranus, J. (2003). *IMS learner information package accessibility for LIP v1.0.* Retrieved July 5, 2005, from http://www.imsglobal.org/accessibility/index.cfm

Open Source Portfolio Initiative. (2005). Retrieved July 6, 2005, from http://www.theospi.org/

Riley, K. (2005). *TELCERT.* Retrieved November 3, 2005, from http://www.imsglobal.org/telcert.html.

Smythe, C. (2004). *IMS enterprise services v1.0.* Retrieved July 6, 2005, from http://www.imsglobal.org/es/index.cfm

Smythe, C., Tansey, F., & Robson, R. (2001). *IMS learner information package v1.0.* Retrieved July 5, 2005, from http://www.imsglobal.org/profiles/index.cfm

Tosh, D., & Werdmuller, B. (2005). *ELGG personal learning landscape.* Retrieved July 6, 2005, from http://elgg.net/

Walsh, N. (1998). *A technical introduction to XML.* Retrieved September 30, 2005, from http://xml.com/pub/a/98/10/guide0.html?page=2#AEN58

Wilson, S. (2005). Creating e-portfolios using Atom and FOAF. *Scott's Workblog.* Retrieved September 30, 2005, from http://www.cetis.ac.uk/members/scott/blogview?entry=20050603020705

Yancey, K. B. (2004). Postmodernism, palimpest, and portfolios: Theoretical issues in the representation of student work. *CCC, 55*(4), 738-761.

KEY TERMS

Application Profile: An adaptation of one or more open standards or specifications to fit the needs of a particular community of users.

Digital Composition: A digitally represented message within a rhetorical situation linking an author to an audience.

Electronic Portfolio (ePortfolio): A digital composition, which includes authentic evidence, within a rhetorical venue that communicates a story or theory about what a person or group knows, can do, or has learned.

IMS Global Learning Consortium: An international membership organization, composed of a group of software companies, higher education institutions, training providers, government agencies, and publishers, that develops technical specifications to support eLearning.

Interoperability: The ability to conduct an activity across multiple, independently managed systems and/or institutions in a manner as transparent as possible to users.

Open Source Portfolio Initiative (OSPI): "A collaborative, open-source, software development project" with a mission to "create and sustain leading production ePortfolio software, build a software platform to accelerate ePortfolio innovation for teaching and learning, influence and reflect best practices in portfolio thinking, [and] influence the movement of open source in education" (OSPI, 2005).

Venue: The setting through which communication takes place.

ENDNOTES

1. For an overview of the full range of interoperability issues related to ePortfolios, see the ePortfolio Whitepaper (ePortConsortium, 2003).
2. For more on electronic portfolios as digital compositions, see Yancey (2004) who coined the term. For a discussion of the rhetorical conception of venue, see Farrell (1993).
3. For a fuller account of the OSP implementation work as of the summer of 2005, see Arnett (2005).

Section II

ePortfolio Case Studies

Chapters within this section investigate the development of ePortfolio projects, and case studies for such projects are provided along with success rate reports. The section is subdivided progressively into three sections detailing information about ePortfolio systems in various stages of implementation: (1) reports by authors writing of investigative projects or task force findings, (2) accounts of ePortfolio trials using limited implementation, and (3) case studies revealing observations and data after full implementation of an ePortfolio system. The final chapter summarizes a survey of ePortfolio projects.

Chapter XXIII
How "White Papers" in ePortfolios Document Student's Learning Skills

Paul A. Fritz
University of Toledo, USA

ABSTRACT

This chapter describes the "Undergraduate ePortfolio Project" used in the Department of Communication, University of Toledo. The author argues, from a constructivist perspective, that the success of an ePortfolio project lies in its content, not its form. Included are the theoretical underpinnings of this project, the pedagogical design, and the assessment rubrics. The pedagogical section describes how the department revised its writing assignments for the portfolio, offers suggested writing projects, describes the generic assignment sheet used by the department, and offers sample student papers. The assessment section presents specific rubrics for evaluating the practical nature of portfolio writings.

INTRODUCTION

This chapter describes the "Undergraduate ePortfolio Project" used in the Department of Communication (600 undergraduate majors) at the University of Toledo, installed in Academic Year 2000-2001. The description below contains the theoretical underpinnings of this project, the pedagogical design, and the assessment rubrics applied to students' portfolio submissions. We found the success of an ePortfolio project lies in its content, not its form.

THEORETICAL MODEL

At the heart of the ePortfolio is the end user; the faculty envisioned two: students and employers. We wanted students to enjoy *using* their ePortfolios to publish, manage, and display their academic projects. But in a larger sense, we wanted students to begin a *lifelong* habit of displaying portfolio projects to document their professional development as their careers unfolded (Jafari, 2004).

Also, we wanted employers to enjoy *reading* students' documents. A prospective employer would probably prefer to read entries like "Communication and Management Errors: Animal Deaths at the Toledo Zoo" or "A Critique of Trade Publications of the Public Relations Profession" rather than ubiquitous academic topics: "My Merit Scholarship Essay" or "Diversity and Women's Sports at Enormous U." Focusing on these two end users, we asked students to fill their ePortfolios with real-life narratives revealing students' depth of professional interests and their abilities to link class constructs to professional problems(Fritz, 1999, 2003). These narratives began life as class writing assignments.

To avoid charges that such assignments were nothing more than "creeping vocationalism" (Folsom & Reardon, 2001; Goldstein; Reardon, Zunker, & Dyal, 1979), our faculty asked ourselves: Would any educational theory support this "practical" approach? Our project was informed by two educational theory models and focused by one educational action research project.

The first theory family was social *constructivism.* For constructivists, knowledge is not demonstrated by replicating professors' lectures on exams. Instead, knowledge is built when students identify examples of lecture constructs in *their* social contexts, communicate the meaning of those phenomena, imagine the future, and act according to what they think *might* happen (Bandura, 1977; Brown et al., 1979). Students take in (assimilate) new experiences, and using schema (learning styles) they render the unfamiliar familiar and (accommodate) that new information in line with others' expectations (Piaget, 1970; Gagnon & Collay, 2001; Shulman, 1979). We argue that *students* create knowledge by applying lecture "constructs" to actual contexts outside the classroom and constructing plausible explanations and solutions to realistic communication problems.

A second family of theory, often called cognitive experientialism, sharpens the constructivists' focus: *how* do students transform their experiences into knowledge that others can use? Students group and transform information in social contexts by their information processing styles (schemata). Heavily influenced by Manturana and Varela's (1987) concept of "autopoiesis," Kolb, Baker, and Jensen, (2002) argue that students transform their experiences by lifelong dialogues which differentiate contradictions between the "real" world and their own experiences. Students use four types of experiential skills: affective complexity (convergers), perceptual complexity (divergers), symbolic complexity (assimilators), and behavioral complexity (accommodators). They use these preferences to develop profession-specific vocabularies (Vygotski, 1986), to structure explanations (Norman, 1980) and develop "deep learning"—knowledge that links assertions to specific contexts (Weigel, 2002). The faculty designed assignments where students would plunge into professional contexts *outside* the classroom, and analyze these experiences using not only their own dominant learning and communication styles, but also the learning styles of their readers. These writings become a type of *field research* for the portfolio content.

Our project was further guided by a seven-year action research project in Boston. Twenty public school teachers, together with Harvard education professor, Martha Stone Wiske (1998), discussed the topic "What Is Worth Understanding?" Emerging from those discussions, her text, *Teaching for Understanding*, generated standards or "categories of tasks" for presenting "demonstratible" knowledge. For example, Wiske asserts, students demonstrate knowledge when they reason with rich conceptual webs, assess information quality, describe the consequences of knowledge, and so forth. Her full list of categories appears in the "Assessment" section below. These categories became rubrics for evaluating students' writings.

We concluded that students' field research could *stand for* knowledge if they fulfilled three criteria for qualitative data: if they analyze multiple dimensions of a site, if they are heuristic, and if they are "thick" [richly descriptive] (Merriam, 1998; Lincoln & Guba, 1985). In short, can students' written field studies be understood and appreciated by a prospective employer unacquainted with course content? The example below models these aims (see http://www.utoledo.edu/~pfritz/resources/e-christy%20horn.htm).

PEDAGOGICAL DESIGN

At first glance our students' ePortfolios were similar to other universities' portfolios. We asked students for three standard pages: résumé, letters of recommendation, and internship (departmental requirement) summary. The rest of the portfolio was a different story. One of our best student's work is at: www.geocities.com/deanna024/homesite.

How did we achieve this end? We helped students produce the narratives as class assignments. First, we restructured traditional writing assignments. Second, we developed a step-by step method for incorporating these new writing assignments into each professor's courses. Third, we developed broader types of generic exercises which could be adapted to a variety of courses. Last, we assisted students in mounting their assignments on their own Web sites.

Restructuring the Writing Assignment

A majority of faculty members replaced the typical "term paper" writing assignments with "white papers." The typical class assignment would simulate a research project a CEO might assign to a division head. A professional example of a white paper can be found at: http://www.utoledo.edu/~pfritz/resources/cinci%20white%20paper.pdf.

The white papers were based on students' observations of field sites: restaurants, "big box" stores, TV studios, hospitals, and so forth. After observing the sites, students reflected on the scenes relevant to specific assigned course content and wrote analytic white papers. For example, if the class were studying a unit on nonverbal communication, they would collect instances of "distance," "activity," "hedonic tone," and "competence" as observed in a hospital ER waiting room, a customer service desk at K-Mart, or court proceedings during jury selection.

Of course, writing an analysis only of *bad* communication would be supercilious. Instead, these assignments asked students to identify fractured communication norms. Then, in the last portion of the analysis (usually 50% of the grade), students wrote plausible *corrections* to the sites' communication problems. Students played the role of the "Vice President for Human Resources" or "VP of Training," writing a white paper to the CEO of the organization.

We find students often need specific training in writing to master the white paper. Many students do not know how to "think of the reader" as they write; they often cannot "see" the reader. Therefore students' papers often read flatly. To assist students, we found the Kolb Learning Style Inventory (LSI) was a durable tool for training students to imagine their white papers' readers. The LSI analyzes readers' preferred patterns of communication. Convergers prefer "pragmatic applications," divergers desire "rich descriptions," assimilators" favor orderly plans," accommodators enjoy "active engagement." We assessed students' information processing styles using the LSI. We also coached them to write to all four styles their readers might prefer. In the following example, the reader can "see" the patrons' exchanges at the gym (see http://www.utoledo.edu/~pfritz/resources/e-faith%20hill.htm).

Usually assignments were organized in three parts: description of the problem (10%), analysis of the problem (40 %), and correction of the problem (50%). Students analyzed the sites using pre-assigned course constructs. Students were required to define, explain, and apply those terms to the observation site, but use the terms in written language a naïve reader (i.e., potential employer) would understand. A sample of a "white paper" may be found at http://www.utoledo.edu/~pfritz/resources/e-keven%20ankney.htm (search for the word string "the very first mistake"). Here a student adroitly connects definition, explanation, and application. Note the careful amelioration of the "text book" jargon.

Step-By-Step Instructions

To help students unacquainted with field research, a model "generic" assignment sheet was written (see http://www.utoledo.edu/~pfritz/resources/e-portfilio%20-%20analysis.htm). The assignment sheet contained the outline for a white paper and the role the students were to play. For a "Conflict in Communication" class, the student might observe the customer service desk at a K-Mart; or for a public relations class, the student might observe a "media event" at the local zoo, knowing the zoo had just fired the veterinarian for animal neglect. For a communication ethics class, the student might observe a press conference of a local firm announcing its default of payments to its employee retirement accounts. These assignments tended to give students confidence to mingle in the adult professional community.

Instructors also explained assignments sharing the rubrics from the final portfolio assessment sheet (see http://www.utoledo.edu/~pfritz/resources/e-portfolio-grade%20sheet.htm). The instructors designated each assignment consistent with four types of learning tasks (Angelo & Cross, 1993). These learning tasks answer the question: "What is the goal of your paper?" A "declarative" paper focused on defining phenomena and organizing information drawn from the analysis; a "procedural" paper explained how to achieve a correction; a "conditional" paper explained the cause of a problem; a "reflective" assignment weighed the meaning actors in the setting gave to their communication. By using these "goal titles," students were given yet another tool for increasing readership: clear expressions of the purpose of the writing—the first canon of writing: "clarity."

Examine the Assignment Sheet's Right Column

The target course concepts are listed at http://www.utoledo.edu/~pfritz/resources/e-portfilio%20-%20analysis.htm. In this assignment students were to draw five of the constructs into the analysis. The instructors can easily assess a student's mastery of concepts if he/she can (1) define, (2) explain, and (3) apply the construct correctly. These terms can be adjusted for most courses and focused for the unit of study in the course. Many faculty weight these writing assignments (usually four per semester) at 60% of a student's final grade. Of course, grammatical and syntactical purity was stressed. Most professors permit only five errors before the paper is refused as "unacceptable."

Broader, More Generic Types of Assignments

Aside from the specific generic model, we created numerous broader and more elaborate ePortfolio projects. These project suggestions could be shared among several courses, could be disassembled for parts of an independent study, or could be used as cornerstone course projects for our majors.

The first of these broad assignments was an interview with a high profile leader in the student's vocational field. We wanted students to gain a sense of access to persons of high rank. Too often undergraduates denigrate how interesting they really are to professional leaders. One ambitious student planned interviews with officials from the Department of Energy and the National Institutes of Health (the federal consortium controlling research on the Human Genome Project) in Washington, DC. Her career interest in law was intellectual property rights. On the same trip, she interviewed the CEO of Celera Genomics (the privately funded firm controlling research on the human genome). Passing back through New York, she also interviewed one of the science editors of *The Wall Street Journal* whose specialty was genomic research. Writing a small grant to fund her travels, planning appropriate questions and having them okayed by interviewees, and submitting her plans to the Institutional Review Board of the university (since she recorded their responses) all led to her Honors Thesis. Her work was published by our Department Chair in his text on business communication (Jackson, 2002).

Another student traveled to Tampa, Florida, to interview leaders at Media General's WFLA. Media General owns both WFLA and *The Tampa Tribune.* While the FCC prohibits joint ownership of two outlets in the same market, this unique purchase was made prior to the FCC ruling. Capitalizing on this pairing, the owner built a multi-purpose facility in Tampa, housing both the TV station and the newspaper. Writers, producers, and staff members of both media all interact on each floor of the building. There is no "TV floor" or "newspaper floor." TV reporters routinely publish in the newspaper and journalists frequently appear on television news productions. The facility is considered a model for future media development. The student analyzed this complex scene and synthesized a "composite skill description" that young professionals may need when working in innovative organizations such as this one.

"What shall I ask him/her?" was a frequent question. Here faculty members assisted the students by quizzing them on content of former courses, suggesting appropriate background reading and showing them how to install "newsgroups" on their browsers to capture immediate news developments in the official's profession. Eventually a full quiver of open-ended questions was fashioned: "Where do you see your firm in 10 years?" "How has the Internet changed your profession?" "What did you find most useful in your education?" "What advice would you offer a new hire fresh from college in your organization?" In our courses students were trained to listen for generalities in interview replies and to ask for examples to substantiate generalizations. We found that students had to be trained to "hear" the information given to them from professionals.

Students wrote analyses of their interviews, selecting at least five major constructs from our discipline and showing how the interviewees' examples clarified those constructs.

Another general exercise in this series is the "Community Players" paper. Students are asked to interview a practitioner in the student's field and ask for the practitioner's community "connections." This information was obtained with an open question such as: "If your firm wanted to raise funds for a local child in need of a kidney transplant, which three people would you contact?" The student harvests the answers, then interviews the referrals with the same question. Of course the student explored "network" topics with each interviewee: "What are good professional organizations to join in this community?" "Who are the 'leader' practitioners in this community?" The finished white paper can take several forms: "A Network of Professionals in Jackson County" or "How Professionals Mobilize for Community Service." This exercise helps students connect the academic term "communication network" with powerful community leaders. Students' writing shows how they sought and identified resources beyond their own experience. An employer reading these white papers can recognize how the student models problem solving, how he/she gained access to busy power practitioners in the community, and how he/she analyzed effective norms of discourse within the community.

A third type of general exercise is the "Trade Publications Bookshelf." Here students interview professionals to learn what media—print or online—they use "to keep up to date" with the market. After the interviews, students analyze the publications. First they analyze the sources for the quality of the information, considering accuracy, authority, objectivity, currency, and coverage (Ward & Hansen, 1997). Then the students write annotations about each source. Finally, they rearrange the sources on a continuum from "popular" to "technical" publications. As presented in the portfolio document, the bibliography demonstrates the student's ability to rank-order discrete variables and it displays his/her interest in the target profession. The student learns industry leaders, case studies, corporate culture specific to that profession, and scores of nuggeted professional information hidden in trade publications. For example, Bob Garfield has a standard column in *Advertising Age* magazine critiquing the effectiveness of TV commercials. However he is often heard on National Public Radio and appears on numerous TV shows as a guest commentator. He has become a good model for young professionals who must be prepared to present their "story" in a wide range of media.

A highly successful project is called "Staying Out of Trouble." This is a lunchtime focus group of professionals discussing the topic, "How to Avoid Making Unintended Mistakes." Students ask the internship supervisor for a list of five of his/her peers and call a lunchtime meeting. The colleagues are asked to discuss the topic, "A Big Mistake I Made and How I Got Out of it." The student harvests a feast of errors and ingenious solutions to correct the errors. Reflecting on the answers, students content-analyze the responses and draw themes from the replies. The finished paper tells a reader the student has an awareness of valued norms in organizations and how to avoid fracturing them.

Other generic projects include:

- "The Clients in my Field and How I Communicate With Them"
- "A Clipping File of a Current Community Problem" (see http://www.utoledo.edu/~pfritz/resources/zoogate.htm)
- "A Guidebook for the Next Intern"
- "A Survey of Community Action Projects at Giant Computer" (showing how an organization publicizes its core community values)

- "Logistics for the Launch of 'The Race for the Cure'" (analysis of the organization and execution of a major fund-raiser)
- "Correcting First Impressions" (see http://www.utoledo.edu/~pfritz/resources/deanna%20lytle-correct%20first%20impression.htm)

Faculty further helped students by offering special orientation sessions for freshmen communication majors. Here we urged students to save digital copies of *all* their college assignments. These (in re-written form) could become grist for the senior ePortfolio course (COMM 4910, required of majors). In these sessions, faculty encourage students to begin interviewing professionals in their career interest areas to focus their career goals. During orientation, we also distribute copies of our professional organization's publication, *Pathways to Careers in Communication* (Morreale & Westphal, 2003), which contains hundreds of specific job descriptions organized under broad headings, such as Careers in Government, Careers in Law, and so forth. Most disciplines publish a similar booklet on career guidance. The final Senior Portfolio Assessment Sheet for the portfolio was distributed and explained to each student. Faculty explain the rubrics of "clear purpose" (Angelo & Cross, 1993), the rubrics of "demonstratable knowledge" (Mansilla, 1998), and the grade levels for each assignment (Mansilla, 1998). Students are encouraged to begin mounting papers on a Web server of their own choosing. During their senior year they will select five papers on their site and present them to their senior portfolio instructor for grading (see http://www.utoledo.edu/~pfritz/resources/e-portfolio-grade%20sheet.htm and http://www.utoledo.edu/~pfritz/resources/e-portfolio-wiske%20grades.htm).

It appears the success of this project depends on how seriously a student begins to visualize him/herself in a professional role. At our university (urban, largely non-residential, students work to fund education), a majority of our majors enjoy this "constructivist" approach. Problem students are those who expect to play a passive role in their education: they expect to be *offered* a job upon graduation. By contrast, examples of "learning involved" follow: "discourse analysis" (http://www.utoledo.edu/~pfritz/resources/e-pam%20roth.htm), "information storage at a non-profit organization" (http://www.utoledo.edu/~pfritz/resources/e-rebecca%20woodward.htm), and "gender marketing" (http://www.utoledo.edu/~pfritz/resources/e-tiffany%20hill.htm and http://www.utoledo.edu/~pfritz/resources/e-whitney%20walker.htm).

Mounting White Papers on Web Sites

White papers were mounted on Web sites of the students' own choosing. We found that students tended to "own" the content more if they were required to obtain their own server and maintain the content themselves. Once the content issue of a student's Web site was solved, the carrier issue was a minor problem. Fortunately GeoCities.com at http://geocities.yahoo.com/ps/learn2/HowItWorks4_Free.html from Yahoo provides a free "starter kit" for students. We were surprised by savvy students who turned to various and sundry technicians to obtain server space. Even the University Webmaster could be "sweet-talked" into providing space. We encourage students to add their URLs at the top of their résumés and to print inexpensive business cards containing those URLs for distribution during job interviews.

ASSESSMENT RUBRICS

How did the department assess these white papers in the ePortfolio format? Students sign up for a pass/fail course (COMM 4910) their senior year. Each semester, approximately 60 communication majors graduate. Each semester, half the faculty (six professors) divide the 60 graduates into six sections and select one section to assess. Each student selects five manuscripts in his/her portfolio for "grading." Students meet frequently with their assigned "graders." The faculty person surveys the five submissions as "rough drafts," suggests changes, and reviews the grading rubrics. When the student is satisfied with revisions, he/she mounts the five selected papers on his/her Web site and gives the appropriate URLs to the faculty member.

The instructor assesses the papers and completes one grade sheet per submission. First, all five pieces must represent at least one of Angelo and Cross' (1993) criteria (see http://www.utoledo.edu/~pfritz/resources/e-portfolio-grade%20sheet.htm): declarative, procedural, conditional, reflective. If each of the five submissions do not meet at least one of the criteria, grading ceases and the student fails.

Next, the professor evaluates the five samples using the Wiske (Manssilla, 1998) model (What knowledge can you demonstrate?). Does the student demonstrate: (1) a transformation from naïve inquirer to antonymous learner; (2) an ability to reason with rich conceptual webs of meaning in a specific field: from general to specific and from specific to general; (3) an ability to assess the information quality: accuracy, authority, objectivity, currency, coverage; (4) an ability to build at least one tool the professionals might use—annotated bibliography, clipping file, a blog on current professional debates, such as RFID tags, Sarbanes-Oxley compliance, medical digitalization of records, Homeland Security, and so forth; (5) an ability to know how knowledge is validated in different fields: the profit mode, the health model, the dialogue model, the crime-reduction model, the statistical model, the compliance model, and so forth; (6) an ability to demonstrate knowledge of the consequences and applications of knowledge in the student's particular field; (7) an ability to demonstrate personal ownership of the knowledge and commitment in the student's chosen field; (8) an ability to communicate knowledge to a professional in his/her field; (9) an ability to use a variety of symbols to explain professional jargon to a naïve audience; and (10) an ability to understand clients' information needs in his/her field.

Each submission must demonstrate at least three of the Wiske criteria on an "A" or "B" level (see http://www.utoledo.edu/~pfritz/resources/e-portfolio-wiske%20grades.htm). The professor makes additional notes on the summary sheet and then writes a summary of all five pieces. A "Pass" grade is given to the student whose five papers individually meet at least one of the Angelo and Cross rubrics, and whose five papers individually meet at least three of the Wiske rubrics at an "A" or "B" level. A "Fail" is given to students not meeting these two evaluations, who may then retake the course. Students tell us this exercise is good preparation for employment interviews.

The use of white papers has given our faculty an ability to assess students' commitment to their discipline. The assignments seem relevant for the student and revealing for the faculty members—in class and in final assessment mode. Using the ePortfolio, students can demonstrate their bridge-building skills—connecting classroom to the community.

REFERENCES

Angelo, T. A., & Cross, K. P. (1993). *Classroom assessment techniques: A handbook for college teachers* (2nd ed.). San Francisco: Jossey-Bass.

Ankney, K. J. (2004). *Description and analysis of how first impressions affect communication patterns at BD's Mongolian Barbeque.* Unpublished manuscript, University of Toledo, USA. Used with permission.

Bandura, A. (1977). *Social learning theory.* Englewood Cliffs, NJ: Prentice-Hall.

Brown, J. S., Collins, A., & Duguid, P. (1989). Situated cognition and the culture of learning. *Educational Researcher, 18*(1), 32-42.

Folsom, B., & Reardon, R. (2001). *The effects of college career courses on learner outputs and outcomes: Technical report no. 26.* Tallahassee, FL: The Center for the Study of Technology in Counseling and Career Development, Florida State University. Retrieved from http://search.netscape.com/ns/boomframe.jsp?query=creeping+vocationalism&page=1&offset=0&result_url=redir%3Fsrc%3Dwebsearch%26requestId%3Dfbb0e740b86090e3%26clickedItemRank%3D1%26userQuery%3Dcreeping%2Bvocationalism%26clickedItemURN%3Dhttp%253A%252F%252Fwww.career.fsu.edu%252Fdocuments%252Ftechnical%252520reports%252FTechnical%252520Report%25252026%252FTechnical%252520Report%25252026.html%26invocationType%3D-%26fromPage%3DNSCPIndex2%26amp%3BampTest%3D1&remove_url=http%3A%2F%2Fwww.career.fsu.edu%2Fdocuments%2Ftechnical%252520reports%2FTechnical%252520Report%25252026%2FTechnical%252520Report%25252026.html

Fritz, P. (2003, November 20). Assessment guide for the portfolio project. In *Proceedings of the National Communication Association Convention,* Miami Beach, FL.

Fritz, P. (1999). Digital portfolios: Issues and solutions. In J. A. Chambers (Ed.), *Selected papers from the 10th International Conference on College Teaching and Learning* (pp. 41-48). Jacksonville, FL: Florida Community College at Jacksonville.

Gagnon, G. W., & Collay, M. (2001). *Designing for learning: Six elements in constructivist classrooms.* Thousand Oaks, CA: Corwin Press.

Goldstein, M. (1977). *The current state of career education at the post-secondary level* (A paper for the National Advisory Council for Career Education). Washington, DC: U.S. Government Printing Office.

Hill, T. (2005). *Description and analysis of gender marketing at BW3.* Unpublished Manuscript, University of Toledo, USA. Used with permission.

Hill, F. (2005). *Description and analysis of gender marketing at World's Gym.* Unpublished manuscript, University of Toledo, USA. Used with permission.

Horn, C. (2005). *Publishing a brochure entitled "Explaining the Internet to Our Clients."* Unpublished manuscript, University of Toledo, USA. Used with permission.

Jackson, J. E. (2002). Mapping the genome: A case study on the communication of information to the public. In R. J. Knecht & D. E. Tucker (Eds.), *Professional business communication: In an interactive setting* (pp. 271-287). Boston: Pearson Custom Publishing.

Jafari, A. (2004). The "sticky" e-portfolio system: Tackling challenges and identifying attributes. *Educause Review, 39*(4), 38-49.

Kolb, D. A., Baker, A. G., & Jensen, P. J. (2002). Conversation as experiential learning. In A. C. Baker, P. J. Jensen, & D. A. Kolb (Eds.), *Conversational learning: An experiential approach to knowledge creation* (pp. 51-66). Westport, CT: Quorum Books.

Lincoln, Y. S., & Guba, E. G. (1985). *Naturalistic inquiry.* Thousand Oaks, CA: Sage.

Lytle, D. (2005). *Correcting the first impression messages clerks communicate to customers.* Unpublished Manuscript, University of Toledo, USA. Used with permission.

Mansilla, V. B. (1998) What are the qualities of understanding? In M.S. Wiske (Ed.), *Teaching for understanding: Linking research with practice* (pp. 161-198). San Francisco: Jossey-Bass.

Manturana, H., & Varela, F. (1987). *The tree of knowledge: The biological roots of human understanding.* Boston: New Science Library, Shambhala Publications.

Merriam, S. B. (1998). *Qualitative research and case study applications in education.* San Francisco: Jossey-Bass.

Morreale, S., & Westphal, J. A. (Eds.). (2003). *Pathways to careers in communication.* Washington, DC: National Communication Association.

Norman, D. A. (1980). What goes on in the mind of the learner. In W. J. McKeachie (Ed.), *Learning, cognition and college teaching* (pp. 85-93). San Francisco: Jossey-Bass.

Piaget, J. (1970). *Structuralism* (*Le Structuralisme*). C. Maschler, trans. New York: Basic Books.

Reardon, R., Zunker, V., & Dyal, M. (1979). The status of career planning programs and career centers in colleges and universities. *Vocational Guidance Quarterly, 28,* 154-159.

Roth, P. (2005). *How "noise" affects communication and productivity at Bob Evans.* Unpublished manuscript, University of Toledo, USA. Used with permission.

Shulman, L. (1999). Taking learning seriously. *Change, 31*(4), 11-17.

Vygotski, L. S. (1986). *Thought and language.* Cambridge, MA: MIT Press.

Walker, W. (2005). *Description and analysis of gender marketing at Jed's Barbeque and Brew.* Unpublished Manuscript, University of Toledo, USA. Used with permission.

Ward, J., & Hansen, K. A. (1997). *Search strategies in mass communication.* New York: Longman.

Weigel, V. B. (2002). *Deep learning for a digital age: Technology's untapped potential to enrich higher education.* San Francisco: Jossey-Bass.

Woodward, B. (2005). *How I solved the information storage problems at H.O.P.E. Marketing, Inc.* Unpublished manuscript, University of Toledo, USA. Used with permission.

KEY TERMS

Accommodator: One of the four information processing categories introduced by Donald Kolb. This person prefers to process information (learn) by trial and error, by hands-on experience, by not fearing to make mistakes in obtaining a learning goal.

Assimilator: One of the four information processing categories introduced by Donald Kolb. This person prefers to process information (learn) by organizing data into orderly and logical lists or charts. This person enjoys putting apparently disparate items into a unified whole.

Autopoiesis: A state of mind where the participant creates his/her own meaning of a scene by experiencing it. By contrast, some epistemologists argue that meaning is imposed on a person outside his/her own experience.

Converger: One of the four information processing categories introduced by Donald Kolb. This person prefers to process information (learn) by applying theory to practical matters. This person values the "bottom line" in a project and values the "final practical application" of any learning task.

Diverger: One of the four information processing categories introduced by Donald Kolb. This person prefers to process information (learn) by watching others perform a task. This person values observation, quiet contemplation, and trying to read the motives of others.

Rubrics: Rules for operating a specific project or endeavor. The meaning is: if these rubrics have been followed, the endeavor is successful. There are two types of rubrics: permissive (meaning these are optional to the success of the endeavor and may be followed), and directive (meaning these are not optional to the success of the endeavor and must be followed).

White Paper: A term applied in large organizations to mean a research project commissioned by organizational leaders for the benefit of the firm. Often these white papers are offered to other members of the profession as solutions for common professional problems.

Chapter XXIV
Purpose, Audience, and Engagement in Spelman College's eFolio Project

Margaret Price
Spelman College, USA

ABSTRACT

This chapter reports on the pilot phase of a longitudinal study that tracks Spelman College's transition from a paper-based First-Year Writing Portfolio to an electronically based one. It presents data from interviews with students, faculty, and administrators, as well as surveys administered to a pilot section of students composing eFolios. These data indicate that the transition will require a re-evaluation of the First-Year Writing Portfolio's current conception of audience and purpose. Further, they indicate that assigners of eFolios should discuss audience and purpose directly with all stakeholders in the eFolio composition process, including students, administration, and faculty, since these elements may be differently conceptualized by different individuals and/or across different contexts.

Unless we develop a habit of thinking in new ways about technology and technologically-based texts, electronic portfolios are as likely to be used by teachers to support those practices we now see as reprehensible in our educational system (e.g., surveillance, competition, outdated assessment methods, and the continued oppression of women and students from underrepresented groups in our culture) as they are by teachers who employ those practices we see as positive (e.g., collaboration, the valuing of individual expression and creativity, and the productive exploration of difference).

—Hawisher and Selfe (1997, p. 318)

My feelings are more or less honestly "Why do we have to do this again?"

—Dee, Student Participant in Spelman College's eFolio Pilot Project

INTRODUCTION

Electronic portfolios (eFolios) have exploded in popularity across college campuses. In 1996, Kathleen Blake Yancey guest-edited a special issue of *Computers and Composition* on electronic portfolios, but remarked in her introduction that she had begun the task wondering, "Would there be enough people who had worked with electronic portfolios to fill an issue like this?" (p. 129). Only six years later, Batson (2002) notes that eFolio programs are already in place at many schools, with technology vendors including WebCT and BlackBoard scrambling to develop and market eFolio tools. However, critical consumers of these products—and indeed, critical consumers of the notion of eFolios in general—are stepping back to ask questions. Early in the process of eFolio development, Hawisher and Selfe (1997) called for "a more tempered view of what we can and cannot expect from writing portfolios and computers" (p. 308). The existence of this collection speaks to the rise of interest in eFolios as well as the urgent need for critical research on eFolios.[1]

Two concerns highlighted in this chapter are *audience* and *purpose*. We need to consider carefully how imagined and real audiences may impact the development and success of eFolio programs. The faculty and/or administration who sponsor electronic-composing projects often assume that their notion of a "real audience," such as users on the Web, is the same as students' (Price & Warner, 2005). This leads to divergent senses of purpose for the eFolio, with faculty and administration viewing an eFolio as a marvelous tool to facilitate critical reflection, assessment, and "real-world" preparation, while students may view it as simply another bureaucratic hoop through which they must jump, or worse, as an updated version of the ominous "permanent record" that follows one through school.

The purpose of this chapter is to report on the pilot phase of a *longitudinal study* in progress at Spelman College. The study tracks Spelman's transition from a paper-based First-Year Writing Portfolio to an electronically based one. Presenting data from the first pilot group to have completed eFolios, this chapter shows how the issues of audience and purpose have impacted the implementation of Spelman's eFolio program thus far, describes revisions being made to the program on the basis of this research, and offers suggestions aimed at "temper[ing]" (Hawisher & Selfe, 1997) our continued teaching and research in these areas.

DEFINING "eFOLIO"

Definitions of eFolios may be quite general, like the one offered by Chen and Mazow (2002): " ... purposeful collections of artifacts that characterize the learning experiences of the portfolio owner." Or they may be quite specific, like Batson's (2002) distinction between the "Webfolio," which he identifies as static and HTML-driven, and the "electronic portfolio," dynamic and database-driven. Often, as a starting point, researchers cite the portfolio catchphrase "collection, selection, reflection," but it is also recognized that the shift into an electronic medium has brought changes to that familiar triad.

In her earlier work on electronic portfolios, Yancey (1996) defines a portfolio as a "metatext with seven defining features": collection of work; selection of work; reflection upon work; demonstration of development, whether implicitly or explicitly; demonstration of diversity between types of work and between portfolio authors; communication; and evaluation (p. 130). Several years later, continuing her exploration, Yancey (2004) draws a key distinction between eFolios which might be called "print uploaded" (p. 745)—that is, a collection of texts which are available electronically but which in other ways imitate hard-copy texts—and those that are "Web-sensible" (p. 745). Web-sensible eFolios do include print texts, but "include as well images and visuals, internal links from one text to another, external links that provide multiple contexts, and commentary and connections to the world outside the immediate portfolio" (p. 746). Much of the promise of eFolios derives from their potential Web-sensibility; without this important change, an eFolio is simply an attractive storage container.

Drawing upon the sources cited here, faculty participants in Spelman's eFolio Pilot Project collaboratively developed a definition of an eFolio as a purposeful, Web-sensible collection of texts which represents and reflects upon learning across time, contexts, and/or in terms of future achievement. At present the project focuses on the First-Year Writing Portfolio, which asks all first-year Spelman students to present a portfolio at the end of the year. However, the project envisions future possibilities for adapting this portfolio for use within students' majors, as a capstone writing experience, and/or for professional purposes including private-sector jobs and graduate school.

PANACEA, PANOPTICON, AND EVERYTHING IN BETWEEN

Like their paper predecessors, eFolios have been greeted with enthusiasm by faculty and administration (Hawisher & Selfe, 1997; Batson, 2002; National Council of Teachers of English, 2004a). Particular eFolio programs report positive effects such as fostering students' senses of ownership over their writing, encouraging a greater sense of engagement in learning, or increasing student retention rates (Wall & Peltier, 1996; Yancey, Peagler, & Winchell, 2002; Yancey, 2004). The NCTE *Council Chronicle* quoted the director of one eFolio pilot program as saying that her school's eFolio pilot program had been "wildly successful" (National Council of Teachers of English, 2004b).

However, as Yancey and Weiser (1997) point out: "Each opportunity is just that: an opportunity that has quite possibly equal potential to do harm" (p. 7). Thus, each potential benefit carries with it its ominous flip side. For example, easier storage and retrieval of texts are true not only for students who compose eFolios, but also for faculty, administration, and (if the eFolio is a publicly accessible Web site) anyone with a computer and Internet access. This leads to a panopticon effect through which one's "permanent record," which follows one through school and is usually invoked as a threat, now appears in a more portable, updatable form, accessible to more people. Or, to take another example, the potential for deeper and/or larger-scale assessment with eFolios also invites co-option by assessment practices which seek to use assessment for sorting and exclusion rather than revision and learning (Lucas, as cited in Yancey & Weiser, 1997). The effect of this is to encourage assessment practices that perpetuate inequities already rampant in our educational system. Finally, eFolios add a host of new problems, one of which is that students dazzled by the "flash" (either literally or figuratively) of constructing an eFolio will neglect the reflection upon and revision of its content (McIntire-Strasburg, 2001).[2]

Batson (2002) suggests that since writing programs have been working with portfolios for more than 25 years, these programs may be able to offer insight into the challenges of eFolios. And in fact, a common exhortation in the literature on eFolios has been to treat them rhetorically (Carney, 2004; McIntire-Strasburg, 2001; Neal, 2005; Yancey, 2001). Treating eFolios rhetorically means placing issues including author, context, purpose, and audience at the center of program development rather than making these issues secondary to considerations such as tools, technical training, and equipment.

Educators who assign eFolios (including myself) like to think that a student's sense of ownership, and hence investment in his or her work, will increase as a result of various features of the new technology, including its accessibility by a "real" audience. However, the in-progress eFolio Pilot Project at Spelman demonstrates that this process is not automatic. As previous researchers have warned, and as I have found out to my chagrin, the shift to an electronic medium may simply replicate problems which already exist in the design and implementation of a portfolio program. However, one finding of this study to date is that these problems are not merely replicated, but in fact thrown into relief by the shift to eFolios, and therefore represent an opportunity for revision as well as cause for chagrin.

SITUATING THE STUDY

Spelman is an all-women's, historically Black college with about 2,000 students. Most students are aged 17 to 22, and most graduate in four years. Demonstration of writing proficiency is required of all students at two points: at the end of their first year, and again in their majors. The first-year requirement comprises two parts: the English course First-Year Composition, which must be passed with a grade of "C" or higher, and the First-Year Writing Portfolio, collaboratively administered by the Comprehensive Writing Program, the African Diaspora and the World Program, the English Department, and the Office of Undergraduate Studies. The portfolio is designed to aid in the development and assessment of several of the "behaviors" Spelman sets as goals for students, including an interdisciplinary approach to learning; critical and creative thinking skills; communicative and technological skills; and assessment of his or her own "qualities, talents, skills, values, and interests" (Spelman College, 2004b, p. 5). The First-Year Writing Portfolio requires each student to present several essays, including an academic argument, a research essay, and an essay written in response to a provided prompt, along with a "letter" (audience unspecified) that reflects on the portfolio's contents and "your writing skills in general."[3]

Since its inception in 1994, Spelman's portfolio has been paper based: students generate hard copies of their essays and house them in manila folders. Portfolios are assessed by an interdisciplinary committee of faculty and returned to students with comments, along with an assessment of "Pass" or "Resubmit." According to Anne Warner, Director of the Comprehensive Writing Program, the current portfolio system is unsatisfactory for a number of reasons. First, the "Resubmit" rate has been high, ranging between 17% and 37% for the last several years. Second, and more disturbing, students clearly are not invested in the portfolio-building process. They generally regard the requirement with annoyance and, according to Warner, rarely seem to grasp the purpose of the portfolio as envisioned by the college. For these reasons, in 2004 Warner began researching the possibility of shifting the medium of the portfolio from paper to electronic, in hopes that this shift, along with other revisions, could increase the "Pass" rate and improve students' senses of ownership over their portfolios. As a member of the English Department's Writing Committee and (at that time) the department's only specialist in writing research, I was recruited to lead the investigation into this possible shift in medium.

The research team based its thinking on two assumptions: (1) problems in the design and implementation of the First-Year Portfolio Program do not stem only, or even primarily, from its paper-based format; and (2) a shift to eFolios will require that the program undergo consistent re-evaluation, not only in terms of the shift to digital learning, but in terms of its success in helping students meet its stated goals. With this in mind, and knowing that our study would need to begin on a small scale and span a number of years, we established these research questions:

- How do students and faculty view the First-Year Writing Portfolio in its current form? How do they view the possibility of a shift to electronic form?
- What changes need to be made to the portfolio's design and implementation, and how can a shift to an electronic format help achieve these changes?
- What will be the impact on student engagement of a shift to an electronic portfolio?
- How does the First-Year Writing Portfolio assessment committee currently define "success" in writing proficiency? In other words, what differentiates a "Pass" portfolio from a "Resubmit" portfolio?
- What impact will a shift to eFolios have on these standards? What impact will it have on the success of students' portfolios in meeting these standards?
- What support will students and faculty need during and after a transition to electronic portfolios?
- How can the First-Year Writing Portfolio be better integrated into students' continuing work as composers, throughout their work in college and beyond, as a means to achieving the behavioral goals stated in the college's "Statement of Purpose"?

This chapter focuses on one small part of that larger, ongoing study: three interviews conducted with students and faculty in order to learn their views of the paper-based portfolio, and two questionnaires administered to the first wave of students piloting eFolios. For this first wave, I selected one of my own sections of First-Year Composition, comprising 20 students. These students were given an expanded set of guidelines for the First-Year Writing Portfolio, which included the same written requirements but were adapted to the criteria for the electronic environment. For example, one criterion states, "Design of site demonstrates clear organization and is accessible to a wide range of users." These 20 students received support in the form of training seminars on topics including Web design, Web editors, accessibility, editing and uploading images, and intellectual property. In addition, they received support from the Writing Program's coordinator of instructional technology and several student assistants working in the Writing Program.

Before moving on to describe the study's findings, I want to include a brief note about my own situatedness—indeed, embeddedness—in this study. As the primary researcher of the eFolio Pilot Project at Spelman and a member of the project team itself, I am invested in this project's success. However, I am most interested in implementing a program that achieves *critical* success. By "critical" I mean involving both one's own and others' experiences and theories, subject to constant revision, and aware of the sociocultural phenomena that link technology and literacy.[4] I hope these eFolios will help students become more critical users, not simply consumers, of electronic technologies. This last goal is particularly important for Black women, who, as Knadler (2001) argues, are often implicitly left out of discussions of women's presence in electronic spaces. "If women's e-spaces are not going to become just more white spaces," Knadler writes, " ... I think we need to pay greater attention to what it would mean to represent, to have representation online" (p. 254). I hope to construct Spelman's eFolio project as an occasion for paying this sort of attention.

ATTITUDES TOWARD THE CURRENT PAPER-BASED PORTFOLIO

A group interview of seven faculty members and administrators from across the disciplines, with experience in the First-Year Writing Portfolio ranging from extensive (Anne, director of the Writing Program) to very limited (Rochelle, a new faculty member in the English Department), was conducted in order to learn more about faculty views of the paper-based portfolio and their reactions to a potential shift to an electronic form.[5] All interviews were tape-recorded and transcribed. Transcripts were analyzed using rich feature analysis (Barton, 2002), a form of *discourse analysis,* in order to locate themes for further investigation.

Although faculty and administrators spoke at length about the positive effects that the portfolio could have, it was generally agreed that the assignment as written could achieve those effects better. One faculty member, for example, pointed out that when she sat on the committee to evaluate portfolios, students' "argumentative" papers were often "not what we as readers thought was argumentative," and that this problem stemmed in part from the failure of faculty to assign papers that called for argumentation. Other participants expressed confusion about the overall goal of the portfolio, wondering whether it was intended to be aimed at assessment (looking back over the first year), prediction (looking forward into the majors), or both. The main theme characterizing faculty comments was lack of communication: between teachers assigning first-year writing and sponsors of the First-Year Writing Portfolio; between first-year students and the portfolio assessment committee; and between different departments on campus, or even faculty within departments, about what the criteria for "good writing" should be.

Of the faculty members present, only Anne had seen an eFolio before. Two samples of eFolios were shown, and participants were asked how they imagined a shift to an electronic medium might affect the process of Spelman's First-Year Writing Portfolio. Reactions were enthusiastic. Several theorized that the medium would increase engagement: one said, "A student files [the paper portfolio] with something she did her freshman year, and it never comes out again. This [the eFolio] I see as a living document that would have meaning and significance for the person who creates it and anybody who looks at it." Another added, "Students will take it more seriously and spend more time on it." Finally, it was suggested that the electronic medium would be more enjoyable for students: "So they don't realize that it's just, that it's a writing assignment, that they think it's part of this big neat project." Notably, in this comment, the speaker assumes that students do not find writing enjoyable—in fact, at another point this participant also suggests that the electronic format could be a way of "disguising [writing] assignments for students"!

The positive reaction from participants at the interview was echoed at an all-campus faculty meeting several weeks later, where, when the idea of the eFolio was presented, several faculty spoke about ways they believed the eFolio could benefit students' work in their majors, and an anonymous on-paper poll recorded positive responses from over 90% of attendees. The enthusiasm of these reactions corresponds to observations in the literature that eFolios have an "enchanting" (Batson, 2002) quality, at least for faculty and administrators. However, when students were interviewed in a group setting identical to the one used for faculty, their responses—both about the current, paper-based program, and about the possibility of a shift to eFolios—were quite different.

Two groups of students were interviewed, both composed of sophomores who had recently completed paper portfolios, numbering 13 students in all. Their descriptions of their experiences while composing (or a better word might be "assembling") their paper portfolios were, to say the least, trenchant. Participants agreed that few first-year students pay much attention to the requirement. Catherine, for example, reported that "no one really took any notice of it until it came up to the time. And everybody was like, 'Oh, yeah, we have to do this.'" She described her process of building the portfolio by saying, "I slapped 'em [the papers] in a folder and took them over there [the Writing Program], and went right back to studying [for exams]." In the other interview group, all participants except one reported assembling their portfolios, and doing all additional required writing (the prompt essay and the reflective letter), the same day it was due.

Strikingly, students in both groups repeatedly used the same gesture to illustrate their process of portfolio development: a pantomime of placing something in a folder, clapping the folder shut, and pushing it away from her. In their comments, students connected their lack of engagement with the portfolio to its apparent lack of purpose, as in this remark from Carol:

I didn't want to do it because I was tired of writing and I was like, why are we writing this? Like I said earlier, if I don't know why I'm writing it, I tend not to want to do it. Because I'm like, what's the purpose? So, I'm doing this for my health? You know, why?

Students' comments about the reflective letter give further indication of the link they perceive between their lack of engagement and the portfolio's apparent lack of purpose. Several stated that they "made up" the letter in response to what they believed the portfolio assessment committee would want to hear. Tjazha reported, "The letter, to me, was, I don't want to say dumb, but useless. It was hardest for me to write, because it had to be, like, two pages, and I couldn't even fill up one page ... So to fill up that page requirement, I made up some stuff that just sounded good." Chandra, participating in the same interview, responded that she found reflective writing "easy," but added, "At the end, if I didn't have anything to say, I would just make up something."

Students consistently linked their lack of engagement to their perception that the portfolio is purposeless. In some cases, they also linked it to the portfolio's unnamed, but evidently authoritative, audience. Melissa theorized that the audience might be Spelman's faculty, so that they could see "where the staff, or whatever, needs to improve." Tjazha took this idea one step further, suggesting that the portfolio's ultimate audience might be Spelman's accrediting agency: "Somebody said they had to do it to be accredited ... or just keep up with other schools. I really didn't see a purpose besides that." Important to note here is that the portfolio assignment itself does not specify an audience: even the reflective "letter" is not explained in terms of whom the addressee might be.

Eleven students said they had not seen an eFolio before; two (Jasmine and Jamita) said they had. When shown the same sample eFolios that had been presented to the faculty, students' reactions were mixed. Some said they believed they would like to have built eFolios instead of paper portfolios, but several concerns were raised as well. Concerns included the additional time it would take to build an eFolio, disadvantages to students who do not "have a computer background" (Jamita), overfocus on "special effects [and] visual effects" rather than on "the actual work" (Jasmine), having work plagiarized from an online portfolio, and increased competition among students. Perceptively, these students identified some of the most pressing concerns debated in eFolio literature today: equality of access, management of intellectual property, and balancing emphasis on the various literacies (verbal, visual, aural) involved in eFolio building.

New concerns, however, show that students brought to this discussion an assumption that the portfolio offers little, if any, benefit to them. Objections that an eFolio will take "more time," for example, seem to assume that the less time spent on a portfolio, the better.[6] In fact, one of Tjazha's comments about the eFolio seems to take for granted the value of composing a portfolio in a short period of time. Describing what she viewed as a potential drawback, she stated, "[An ePortfolio] will take a lot longer, and obviously people can't wait until the day of or the day before." Overall, students' objections seem to fall into two broad categories: philosophical concerns such as intellectual property, fairness, and competition; and practical concerns about time and new skills required.

Comments from students who saw potential benefit in the eFolio centered almost exclusively on specific purposes and/or audiences. For example, Melissa suggested that the eFolio might be useful in a job interview: "Like, sometimes you might go to an interview or something and ... sometimes they'll say, like, do you have any copies of what you've done or whatever, and then you can show them a Web page of something you've done." Carol said that she might like to show an eFolio to her family: "I know it seems small, but you can go be like, 'Mom, this is what I was able to do at Spelman College. Like, this is one of the actual activities I did.' ... She would be impressed by that, that the school actually took the time to help you prepare that and it's going to be useful." In each case, the speaker names a specific audience for whom she can imagine the eFolio might be relevant, and in each case, the specificity of the audience seems to lend the project a potential purpose for her. In other words, when students named audiences for the project (which the current First-Year Writing Portfolio does not do), their assessments of its purpose became more specific, and their estimations of its potential value to them increased.

Interestingly, students seemed to separate this sense of personal investment from school work in general. For example, Chandra said that she would like to compose an eFolio, but:

> *I wouldn't really want to do it for school. Because, for me, it would take me a long time. I'd have to put music on it, get every picture that I want, I would have to get it perfect for me ... But for school I'd rather do something like what we had to do [the paper portfolio]. Just a little something to do and be over with.*

This comment is telling for two reasons. First, Chandra makes a distinction between her school work and her work "for me." She identifies schoolwork as something she would prefer to keep quick and uncomplicated ("a little something to do and be over with") and work "for me" as something in which she would like to be much more invested, "tak[ing] a long time" and "get[ting] it perfect." Most significant, perhaps, is the reiteration of the two words *for me*. Chandra positions herself as the primary audience for and authority over an eFolio, and it therefore becomes something she would not expect to achieve in school, but only outside it.

eFOLIOS: THE FIRST PILOT SECTION

The rich-feature analysis of interview transcripts, as shown here, indicates that purpose and audience are crucial to understanding students' and faculty's views of the current First-Year Writing Portfolio and its possible shift into electronic form. These themes informed the design of the assignment given to the 20 members of the first wave of eFolio pilot, as well as the questions posed on the entrance and exit questionnaires given to them at the beginning and end of our First-Year Composition class.[7] Although these questionnaires recorded students' responses on a number of topics, including experience with and attitudes toward computer use, for the purposes of this chapter, I focus here on two particular questions. One asked students to rate their sense of satisfaction in the eFolio project:

Entrance questionnaire:
Although we have not yet begun this project, how would you rate your anticipation of the amount of satisfaction you will take in the experience?

Exit questionnaire:
When you worked on your ePortfolio, how would you rate the amount of satisfaction you took in the experience?

Students were offered a range of six responses: "None," "Poor," "Fair," "Good," "Very Good," or "Excellent." The other question asked, upon both entry and exit, was: "Which of the following potential uses for an ePortfolio are important to you? Select all that apply." Possible responses included: "Create an archive of my written work," "Reflect on my written work," "Express myself," "Enable self-assessment of my written work," and "Enable assessment by others (professors, peers, or administrators) of my written work," as well as a space for students to specify an additional response of their own. Amplifying data from these two relatively closed-ended questions are students' responses to various open-ended questions in the questionnaire, including: "Describe what you believe building an ePortfolio will require/has required of you" and "Describe your feelings when you think about building/having built an ePortfolio."

As the teacher of the class that housed the first eFolio pilot group, I can report from observation that students' initial views of the eFolio seemed skeptical. For example, when I explained the assignment and its role in the First-Year Portfolio research project, one student, Dee, asked, "So, we're going to be guinea pigs?" Other students expressed concern about whether their computer expertise would be up to the task; Angel, for instance, wrote on her entry questionnaire, "I am not electronically inclined." However, all students completed eFolios, which were turned over to the First-Year Portfolio Committee for assessment.[8]

Analysis of student responses on these questions indicates two strong themes. The first is that working on eFolios increased students' senses of investment in the project, at least to the extent that the infamous First-Year Writing Portfolio, and/or their fears about learning new technologies, became less intimidating and more manageable over the course of the semester. Some students' comments indicate that the medium itself was part of what motivated them.

Cassandra, for instance, wrote on her exit questionnaire, "I always wanted to know how to create a Web page," while Allison wrote, "I feel very proud and up-to-date because I created my own personal Web site." It should be noted that the electronic medium did not automatically lead to investment; Vanessa, for example, wrote, "I'm glad it's over because building a Web page is not exactly an interest of mine." These responses, then, corroborate previous research on eFolios which argues that electronic technologies in and of themselves do not necessarily increase student engagement. Rather, only when such technologies are used rhetorically (with attention to purpose, audience, and so on) will they reliably have this effect.

The theme I did not anticipate was students' emphasis on having created these eFolios for themselves, not for an anonymous authority such as the First-Year Writing Committee or Spelman's accrediting agency. Allison's comment, quoted earlier, in which she calls her eFolio a "personal Web site," is one example of this. Another indication is students' responses to the entry/exit question asking which potential uses for an eFolio are important to them. Of the 10 students who returned both entry and exit questionnaires, five checked "self-assessment" upon exit without having checked it upon entry. (Two students checked it upon both entry and exit; one student checked it upon entry only.) At the same time, the number of students who checked "Assessment by others" dropped from three to two. Although the sample is too small for significance, this theme warrants further exploration. This issue is especially salient given students' emphasis on the personal satisfaction and pride they felt from having created eFolios: 7 of the 10 used "proud" or other self-directed positive terms, such as "good about learning" or "very big accomplishment," to describe their feelings about having created an eFolio. Overall, the first wave of students completing eFolios seemed to experience an increased sense of engagement. Some of this increase, again, is no doubt due to the additional guidance these students received. The challenge for Spelman's First-Year Portfolio Project, if it continues to go electronic, will be to remedy the problems stemming from the current model's lack of clarity around purpose and audience, while increasing students' opportunities to work as critical users and authors within an electronic medium.

CONCLUSION

eFolios tend to highlight questions of *audience* and *purpose* in the composing we ask our students to do. This highlighting effect occurs for two major reasons. First, eFolios move us out of familiar, relatively static technologies such as pen/paper or word processor/page, and into less-familiar, relatively dynamic settings such as interlinked and/or public Web sites. This creates a defamiliarizing effect which enables us to re-examine for whom eFolios are composed, and what the purpose of an eFolio is or might be. Such re-examination is often led by students, who ask questions such as: "So, I'm [just] doing this for my health?" (Carol) or "Why do we have to do this again?" (Dee). Second, eFolios tend to transcend bounded settings such as classrooms or departments, in which we are accustomed to treating questions of audience and purpose as givens. Therefore, when students begin to compose eFolios, which typically move outside of individual classes and departments (and often outside of academia), the question of audience/purpose suddenly becomes paramount.

As a result of this highlighting effect, the polite fiction that students' purposes for their writing generally coincide with those set forth by faculty and administration becomes more apparent as a fiction. Attempting to force students to adopt faculty and administrative purposes does not have the desired effect, and may—as seems to have occurred at Spelman—result in decreased engagement and hence an even wider schism between the groups' respective purposes. Therefore, I recommend that faculty and administration assigning eFolios consider the following suggestions. These considerations are ones to which we should "pay attention" (Selfe, 1999) in our teaching and research—including that of Spelman's continuing eFolio project.

1. **Discuss Audience and Purpose Directly with Students Engaged in Composing eFolios:** For what purpose(s), and for what audience(s), in their *own* view, are they building the eFolio? What audience(s) and purposes(s) do they wish to have? Even if eFolios will be published on the Web, project designers must avoid the assumption that this "real" audience will be imagined similarly by faculty, administration, and students. The probability that audience/purpose will shift as the project goes on should also be recognized and discussed.
2. **Keep Projects and Discussions Context Sensitive, Noting the Specificity of the Site in which the Project Takes Place and of Individuals Composing eFolios:** For example, Knadler (2001) found that eFolios composed by Black women at Spelman challenged previous research because their tendency was to use the electronic medium to reinforce, not escape from or play with, their sense of physical existence.
3. **Although it May be Uncomfortable, We Must be Willing to Question and Possibly Revise our own Purposes:** The critical use of technology, as I am defining it here, requires constant re-visioning (Lee, 2000) by faculty and administration as well as by students. For example, if an eFolio is required for some reason, what is that reason? Who is invested in that reason? How do these investments translate into the design and assessment of the eFolio? Ideally, eFolio projects should be used to assess not only students' work, but our own goals and methods in assigning that work.

New technologies are like new diets: although the fact that they do not cure anything may be an open secret, we—and by "we" here, I mean all of us engaged in educational enterprises—still desire that magic ingredient, that *one thing* that will rescue us from the slow, difficult, and messy process of teaching/learning. Unfortunately, no new technology, no matter how captivating, will rescue us from this. In their prescient article, Hawisher and Selfe (1997) argue, "It is too easy to see computers and writing portfolios as 'tools.' We need instead to view them as the richly embroidered artifacts of a culture, artifacts which ultimately embody the values and ideological directions of our society" (pp. 317-318). The most important conclusion I draw from this study to date is the eminently practical one suggested by Catherine's question, "So, I'm doing this for my health?" Her question is one we would benefit from keeping in mind: For whose health (whose purpose, whose imagined audiences) do we assign eFolios?

REFERENCES

Barton, E. (2002). Inductive discourse analysis: Discovering rich features. In E. Barton & G. Stygall (Eds.), *Discourse studies in composition*. Cresskill, NH: Hampton Press.

Batson, T. (2002). The electronic portfolio boom: What's it all about? *Campus Technology*.

Retrieved May 20, 2005, from http://www.campus-technology.com/print.asp?ID=6984 (original work published in *Syllabus*, 2002).

Carney, J. (2004). *The role of theoretical knowledge in electronic portfolios.* Retrieved August 1, 2004, from http://dl.aace.org/14234

Chen, H. L., & Mazow, C. (2002). *Electronic learning portfolios and student affairs.* Retrieved July 20, 2004, from http://www.naspa.org/netresults/PrinterFriendly.cfm?ID=825

Hawisher, G. E., & Selfe, C. L. (1997). Wedding the technologies of writing portfolios and computers: The challenges of electronic classrooms. In K. B. Yancey & I. Weiser (Eds.), *Situating portfolios: Four perspectives* (pp. 305-321). Logan: Utah State University Press.

Knadler, S. (2001). E-racing difference in e-space: Black female subjectivity and the Web-based portfolio. *Computers and Composition, 18,* 235-255.

Lee, A. (2000). *Composing critical pedagogies: Teaching writing as revision.* Urbana, IL: National Council of Teachers of English.

McIntire-Strasburg, J. (2001). *The flash or the trash: Web portfolios and writing assessment.* Retrieved June 2, 2005, from http://english.ttu.edu/kairos/6.2/coverweb/assessment/strasburg/index.htm

National Council of Teachers of English. (2004a). Electronic appeal: Writing portfolios go digital. *The Council Chronicle*. Retrieved May 29, 2005, from http://www.ncte.org/portal/30_view.asp?id=115623

National Council of Teachers of English. (2004b). A quick tour of four portfolio programs. *The Council Chronicle.* Retrieved May 29, 2005, from http://www.ncte.org/portal/30_view.asp?id=115624

Neal, M. (2005, June). Using electronic portfolios: Definitions and descriptions. In *Proceedings of the 24th Annual Writing Across the Curriculum Conference,* Atlanta, GA.

Price, M. (in press). *Writing from normal: Critical thinking and disability in the classroom.*

Price, M., & Warner, A. (2005). What you see is (not) what you get: Collaborative composing in visual space. *Across the Disciplines, 2.* Retrieved December 10, 2005, from http://wac.colostate.edu/atd/visual/price_warner.cfm

Selfe, C. L. (1999). *Technology and literacy in the twenty-first century: The importance of paying attention.* Carbondale and Edwardsville: Southern Illinois University Press.

Spelman College. (2004a). *The 2004-05 first-year writing portfolio at Spelman College.* Comprehensive Writing Program, Spelman College, Atlanta, GA.

Spelman College. (2004b). Statement of purpose. *Spelman Bulletin 2004-2005.* Atlanta, GA: Spelman College.

Wall, B. C., & Peltier, R. F. (1996). "Going public" with electronic portfolios: Audience, community, and terms of student ownership. *Computers and Composition, 13,* 207-217.

Yancey, K. B. (1996). Portfolio, electronic, and the links between. *Computers and Composition, 13,* 129-133.

Yancey, K. B. (2001). Introduction: Digitized student portfolios/Conclusion: General patterns and the future. In B. L. Cambridge, S. Kahn, D. P. Tompkins, & K. B. Yancey (Eds.), *Electronic portfolios: Emerging practices in student, faculty, and institutional learning.*

Washington, DC: American Association for Higher Education.

Yancey, K. B. (2004). Postmodernism, palimpsest, and portfolios: Theoretical issues in the representation of student work. *College Composition and Communication, 55,* 738-761.

Yancey, K. B., Peagler, S., & Winchell, D. (2002). *Portfolios on the Clemson campus: What students tell us.* Unpublished manuscript, Roy and Marnie Pearce Center for Communication, Clemson University, USA.

Yancey, K. B., & Weiser, I. (1997). Situating portfolios: An introduction. In K. B. Yancey & I. Weiser (Eds.), *Situating portfolios: Four perspectives* (pp. 1-17). Logan: Utah State University Press.

Yancey, K. B., & Weiser, I. (Eds.). (1997). *Situating portfolios: Four perspectives.* Logan: Utah State University Press.

KEY TERMS

Audience: The imagined, invoked, and/or actual readers/receivers of a text.

ePortfolio (eFolio): A purposeful, Web-sensible collection of texts which represents and reflects upon learning across time, contexts, and/or in terms of future achievement.

Historically Black College or University (HBCU): An institution of higher education established prior to 1964 with a principal mission of educating Black students.

Longitudinal Study: A study progressing over a long period of time, typically years.

Purpose: The rationale underlying the composition of a text. Can be seen as constructed by author(s) and/or audience(s). Sometimes categorized as operational or taxonomic.

Rich Feature Analysis: A form of discourse analysis developed by Ellen Barton.

ENDNOTES

1 Many thanks to the people who contributed to the ideas in this chapter, including all research-project participants, as well as Anne Warner, Danielle Bascelli, Iretta Kearse, Michael Neal, Michael Salvo, and Kathleen Blake Yancey.

2 I am wary of distinctions drawn between "style" and "content" in discussions of print or electronic texts. For example, I believe that a student's critical abilities can and should be applied to the visual design of a site as well as to the argument expressed in a paper displayed on that site. However, when teaching with eFolios, I also have noted that sometimes a student's revision of an eFolio's design will supplant rather than accompany revision of the texts she chooses to include as part of her eFolio.

3 Guidelines for the 2005-2006 portfolio have been revised in response to this research. This article cites guidelines from 2004-2005.

4 This definition, which draws in part upon Selfe (1999) and Lee (2000), is a distillation of a fuller definition developed in *Writing from Normal: Critical Thinking and Disability in the Classroom* (Price, in press).

5 All participants are identified by pseudonyms or by their own names, according to each participant's stated preference.

6 This is not intended as a value judgment against students, who, after all, do have to view their schoolwork from a practical point of view. However, because one of this study's concerns is student engage-

ment, it is important to note that minimizing the amount of time invested in a portfolio appears to underlie some student comments as an assumed benefit. This is especially significant in light of Chandra's "get it perfect" remark.

7 Of the 40 questionnaires distributed, 30 were returned. Ten students returned both entry and exit questionnaires, so for the purposes of the following analysis, only these 10 students' questionnaires are included.

8 The committee slightly adapted its criteria for evaluation of portfolios in order to accommodate the eFolios; for example, when considering organization, they looked at the site's global organization as well as organization within each document. However, since I gave my students the same set of requirements that all other students received, including the "reflective letter," for the most part assessment criteria remained similar. Seventeen percent of the eFolios were assessed "Resubmit," which places this group within the low-normal range of "Resubmit" rates for First-Year Writing Portfolios in general. Comprehensive Writing Program Director Anne Warner reported after assessment was completed that two assessors observed that the writing in the eFolios seemed to demonstrate greater "engagement" than in their paper counterparts. However, because the pilot project has so far included only one class of students, conclusions based upon this observation would be premature.

Chapter XXV
Developing an ePortfolio for Health Professional Educators: A Case Study

Mary Lawson
Monash University, Australia

Debbie Kiegaldie
Monash University, Australia

Brian Jolly
Monash University, Australia

ABSTRACT

This chapter describes the development and implementation of an ePortfolio to support the Graduate Certificate in Health Professional Education (GCHPE) at Monash University, Australia. The GCHPE addresses the skills and knowledge of teachers working in health, and encourages the development of a professional approach to teaching practice. The ePortfolio was developed primarily to enable the preparation and sharing of reflective tasks and assessment items constructed from the workplace of the course participants, and to facilitate written peer and tutor feedback. The first interprofessional cohort completed the course in 2003. In this chapter, the development process, evaluation methods, and results of the first year of implementation will be summarized. Problems experienced in the development and implementation process are identified along with recommendations for further action.

INTRODUCTION

Monash University is the largest university in the Southern Hemisphere, operating out of several campuses in various Australian and international locations. As such, there is a plethora of organizational and quality assurance challenges in delivering high-quality education to large numbers of students in diverse locations both nationally and internationally. To achieve the goal of mass-dispersed higher education of high quality, Monash has developed a strategy and set of associated aims. In this, the university statement of purpose is summarized as follows:

Monash University seeks to improve the human condition by advancing knowledge and fostering creativity. It does so through research and education and a commitment to social justice, human rights and a sustainable environment. (Monash Directions 2025, 2005)

Monash's strategies are directed toward achieving or enhancing excellence in education, management, research and scholarship, innovation and creativity, diversity, international focus, fairness, engagement, integrity, and self-reliance. One means to achieve excellence in teaching is to use information technology creatively; for example, to increase flexibility in teaching and learning, whether on or off campus. Additionally, staff are encouraged to implement the principles of student-centred, flexible learning, emphasizing the discovery, analysis, and integration of information, problem-solving, communication, and a preparation for a lifetime of learning.

With this strategic vision and pursuit of educational excellence as central tenets of institutional activity, academic staff at Monash are required to be at the forefront of contemporary educational practice. This encompasses "eLearning" and is actively promoted within the organization. Monash actively encourages innovative practice in eLearning via a number of schemes. In the Faculty of Medicine, Nursing, and Health Sciences (the faculty in which the authors are located), an IT committee organizes an annual competitive funding scheme. Under this scheme, staff are invited to submit proposals for funding to develop innovative educational projects supported by any aspect of information technology. It was under this scheme that the authors received funding to develop the ePortfolio to support teacher training on the GCHPE within our faculty. It was envisaged that this would be a pilot for similar activities in the larger and more complex undergraduate arena across the various disciplines in the faculty.

This chapter describes the ePortfolio and also appraises how successful its development has been. Major obstacles to its development, implementation, and further application and refinement are identified and a variety of practical recommendations made for others considering similar projects. The authors will describe what the tutors were trying to achieve in terms of meeting principles of student-directed learning and how they went about achieving it. Strengths and weaknesses will be outlined from the participants, tutors, and institutional perspective. In addition, the case study will be critically appraised for educational best practice.

BACKGROUND

Traditionally, academics in higher education have not been trained for their teaching role (Laurillard, 2002). This is true of most health professional groups, with the notable exception of the nursing profession. Typically, it has been widely assumed that in-depth content or discipline-specific knowledge is enough to ensure that lecturers are able to pass on their knowledge to future generations of learners. There would be public concern if this were the case for our children's teachers in school, or even if there were widespread recognition in society that students at university are not routinely taught by staff with a formal teaching qualification. However, this is changing now, and an increasing number of stakeholders in higher education are insisting that academics should develop teaching skills.

In recognition of this, Monash University introduced a policy of compulsory probationary training in teaching and learning in 2000. This policy applies to all new academic staff appointed at half-time fraction or above. A course in higher education is provided for new staff from all disciplines. In recognition of the unique teaching contexts and nature in the health professions, an additional course was developed (the GCHPE) specifically aimed at those who teach in clinical contexts. The aims of both courses are to ensure quality of educational planning, delivery, assessment, and evaluation, and to encourage educational innovation.

There are essential differences between how health professional students engage in learning and teaching activities and how other students undertake their university studies including the importance and, frequently, the presence of the patient. Differences also arise in the very wide variety of settings in which learning takes place. In some other professional courses, clients also maintain a high profile¾teaching, law, and architecture all have their versions of "patient contact." But when the French, Economics, or History student steps outside the lecture theatre, the lab, or the library, this tends to be for only a small proportion of their time. However, in the health professions, clinically based learning can be as much as 100% of a course or unit of study. Also, in other professional courses, many client settings are public (the classroom or the courtroom), many are dangerous (the building site), and some are intimate (the prison cell, the confessional). But only in the health professions do all three come together¾the operating theatre, the Accident and Emergency Department, the sexual health clinic.

The GCHPE is necessarily aimed at a broad cross-section of the health professions, including medicine, nursing, optometry, paramedic studies, pharmacy, dietetics, physiotherapy, radiography, and psychology. Participants to date have reflected this diversity of occupations. The course uses the capacity of participants to bring experience from their own profession and to compare this experience with the perspectives and approaches of other professional groups. This is one of the key underpinning principles that has guided course development.

Overall there are some global aims for providing the GCHPE, and these include:

- Supporting excellence in undergraduate and postgraduate course development and delivery for the health professions
- Improving the learning experience of students in clinical environments
- Increased scholarship in health professional education, including the adoption of evidence-based decision making and involvement in high-quality research pursuits
- The formal development of career pathways for clinicians wanting to focus on education

The course achieves these aims by developing participants' skills as health professional teachers in course development, the theoretical underpinnings of teaching and learning, clinical teaching, student assessment, course evaluation, and educational research and development.

There are four core units offered together to help participants develop their expertise in all the major components of a teaching role in health professional education. The GCHPE is usually completed on a part-time basis over one year. The course is taught and assessed via a series of study days and supported workplace activities. The ePortfolio supports reflection on teaching practice from the workplace and assessments linking theory to practice.

In the past 20 years, courses in education for health professionals have come to be seen as needing different approaches and content from those used to develop other university teachers. This has happened on a worldwide scale. Lecturing and tutorial management are still important, but so are bedside teaching and psychomotor skills development. The health professions are almost unique in their need to blend cognitive skills with the kind of expert artisanship normally associated with portraiture, plumbing, and cabinet making.

In the GCHPE the tutorial team also strives to prepare participants for a world of work that is changing rapidly; where supervision, teamwork, multi- and inter-professional working, and learning are becoming more common; and where governments and patients are demanding an increase in seamless health care and in effective communication among professionals providing that care.

The philosophy of the GCHPE reflects the need to be eclectic and pragmatic in the educational theories and practices that we employ. Health profession courses across the world currently employ radically different techniques, from total lecturing to total self-directed learning. For health professional teachers, educational proficiency involves being comfortable using a range of techniques and being able to engage colleagues and students in a rapidly expanding horizon.

It is virtually inconceivable that a course of this nature could exist without demonstrating at least some component of eLearning as an example of contemporary educational practice. It was with this in mind that the application was made to fund the development of an ePortfolio.

CASE STUDY: AN ePORTFOLIO IN A POSTGRADUATE COURSE IN HEALTH PROFESSIONAL EDUCATION

The initial development focus for the ePortfolio was to support an interprofessional course for any teacher in the health professions. The course has run as a one-year, part-time program since 2003, has four core units, and is approved by Monash University for probationary training. However, some underlying assumptions in the development process ensured that the ePortfolio could be developed beyond this primary focus to support a number of other educational initiatives across the faculty.

The ePortfolio was developed to enable reflection and feedback to occur wherever our course participants teach (i.e., in a geographically dispersed participant cohort). This is common at both undergraduate and postgraduate levels, where learning is based in diverse and dispersed clinical sites. Other goals in developing the ePortfolio included:

- To provide an example of contemporary educational practice for clinical teachers;
- To integrate the assessment of professional teaching behaviour into all units of the course
- To enable the preparation, sharing, and submission of assessment items in the actual workplace of the course participants and to facilitate self-, peer, and tutor feedback

Assessment tasks inserted into the ePortfolio incorporate formative and summative tasks throughout the four course units. Via the ePortfolio, course participants can immediately record written reflections on their clinical teaching practices, retrieve and collate reflections for assessment submission, gain access to peers' work, and receive feedback. The ePortfolio has participant, tutor, and administrator views, and the functionality in each view will be described.

For course participants there are two areas within the ePortfolio. The first is a private space in which a reflective journal of teaching activities can be maintained, and the other is a dedicated space for assessment planning, submission, and feedback. It is acknowledged that individuals may have other mechanisms which they prefer to adopt or maintain reflective journal writing, and so this is not an essential component of course participation. For participants, the ePortfolio activities and features are summarized as follows:

- Password-protected access to a secure Web-based learning environment
- Personal journal space to document teaching experiences in the clinical environment (this area is not accessible to tutors and participants all sign an "Acceptable Use of Information Technology Facilities Policy" to prevent inappropriate use of this secure area)
- Space for submission of assessments to share with tutorial group members, tutors, or the whole cohort prior to submission if desired
- Opportunities to exchange views with other participants
- Access to Web-based feedback (this includes receiving feedback themselves on their assessment items, but also the opportunity to develop their own skills in written feedback with their colleagues; it also includes their assessment grades)

For tutors and administrators, the ePortfolio provides them with their own unique online environment. Tutors are provided with "anytime, anyplace" access to assessment submissions. They also have the opportunity to mark work and provide written feedback in this environment. Prior to submission deadlines for assessment tasks, it is the participants who control whether access is provided to their own personal tutor or not.

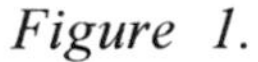
Figure 1.

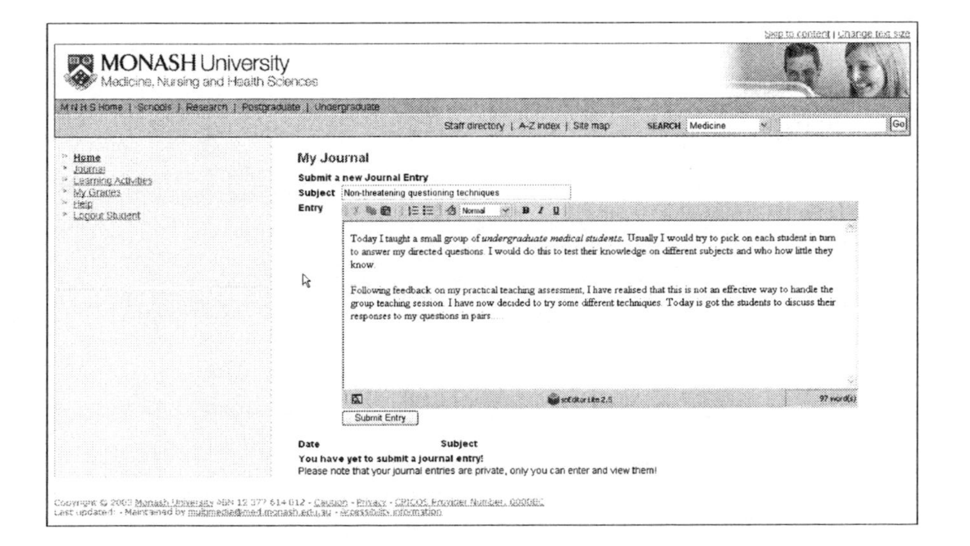

For administrators, it is possible to create simple and flexible assessment tasks in text-based format. They can allocate course participants and tutors to units of study and to tutorial groups, and this information is picked up from the university central records system for tutors and participants. Within the administrative arena, records are maintained of participants' assessment submissions, and tutors' feedback and marking progress. E-mail reminders of impending assessment deadlines are generated via the system.

The development of the ePortfolio represented collaboration between academic staff and the faculty Web team. A form of electronic learning was also considered essential for a course of this nature to demonstrate contemporary educational practice and to role model innovative teaching practice. In summary, the ePortfolio was developed to support learning on a postgraduate course for health professional teachers and to demonstrate best educational practice, act as an initial step in the development of a managed learning environment to support the whole course, and be a pilot for a similar need in the undergraduate medical program.

The faculty innovative teaching grant, which supported the development, paid for Web design and also an external consultancy visit from an expert in the field of multimedia in education to advise on design, process, and implementation issues. The development process adopted an iterative format with regular meetings between academic and Web design staff. Commercially available platforms were considered but did not appear to support the educational objectives required. A small academic team worked collaboratively with a Web design group to produce a specialized electronic system. This system is written in ColdFusion MX and hosted on a Microsoft SQL Server 2000. Administrator training was provided for academic staff, and the ePortfolio was introduced in Semester 1 of 2003. The infrastructure to support the innovation was also provided by the faculty.

Assessment tasks include identification and analysis of critical incidents. These incidents involve teaching in the clinical environment as part of the participants' work experience The tasks also include opportunities to practice written feedback, which the course identifies as an important skill within a teaching role.

Figure 2.

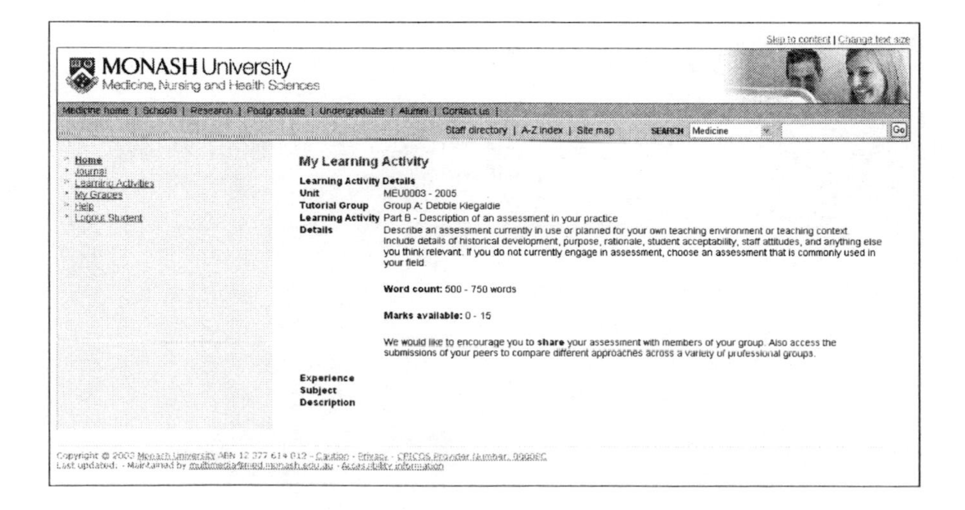

The ePortfolio was designed to embrace person-centred learning principles (Rogers & Freiberg, 1994). As an example, participants are helped to achieve results they appreciate and consider worthwhile by allowing them to select assessment tasks that are closely aligned with their working practice. The fact that a Web-based tool is available also means that there can be a consistent emphasis on the workplace, as tasks can be completed and reflections recorded as and when they occur. The provision of a completely personal journal space was designed to enhance trust between teacher and participant. Participants are able to determine and control the level of access that was given to peers and tutors during preparation of assignments. In this way, "work-in-progress" can be shared between peers and with tutors. This feature, together with the facility to make ongoing entries and revisions prior to the assessment deadline, was designed to aid reflection and promote deeper levels of thinking.

In the first iteration of the ePortfolio, participants were very closely involved with piloting of and feedback on the system. While sometimes frustrating to be involved in an educational pilot (and the inevitable troubleshooting that is associated), participants did find this aspect stimulating and, as teachers themselves, welcomed the opportunity to engage with an example of contemporary educational practice.

Person-centred learning principles were also reflected in the opportunities for self- and peer review and revision prior to submission of items for assessment. The immediate access to participants' work by tutors also provides the potential for immediacy in feedback.

The person-centred learning principles embodied in the ePortfolio were supported in other aspects of the course (e.g., by the provision of formal teaching on ways of giving effective feedback). The nature of the feedback provided from peers and tutors, including the use of "non-final vocabulary" and of "authentic" assessments, are in line with recommendations for assessment in professional courses (Boud, 1995).

In data obtained at the conclusion of the first year of the course, participants reported that the ePortfolio was relatively easy to use, although they expressed mixed levels of confidence in the technology (e.g., lack of trust that work submitted online will be received successfully by teaching staff, issues regarding timing-out of sessions, and loss of text formatting). Their own technical abilities were found to be highly varied, and subsequently skills assessment, remedial training, and peer tutoring have been introduced to address this (Lawson, Bearman, Jolly, Kiegaldie, & Roberts, 2004).

For tutors, one of the major benefits identified in evaluation was the easy electronic access to all student assessments. Conversely, this can also be seen as a disadvantage, as some models of eModeration can be intrusive, interfere with work life balance for tutors, and be difficult to limit (Salmon, 2000). Also, rather perversely, as a group of tutors, we have found that "anytime" access to participants' assignments has prevented us from being as efficient as previously in our marking habits!

Another advantage identified was the reduction in paper and the central repository of course information. Confidentiality was also thought to be easier to maintain in a paper-free environment. Opportunities for cross-marking and quality control mechanisms for marking were facilitated by the introduction of the electronic system. Finally tutors appreciated having a central repository of assessment information, marking criteria, and participant instructions, including milestones (Lawson, Kiegaldie, & Jolly, 2004).

From the Web team's perspective, what worked well was the close collaboration with the academic team and the use of a development site for ongoing piloting and refinement. However, improvements in participants' preparation for engagement in learning activities in a Web-based environment, in the ability to deal effectively with participants online, and in the provision of clearer instructions for users were needed. An online FAQ section has now been added and is now provided in the course handbook.

From tutor and participants' perspective, what worked well was the experience of an educational innovation and remote access at any time. What needed alteration was a technical error leading to multiple reminders of due dates for work and issues with loss of work and formatting. There were two outstanding issues for action, one technical and the other academic. The technical issue related to the inability to extend deadlines on an individual participant-negotiated basis. Currently all participants are "locked out" of assignments on a single due date. The academic issue concerned the minimal use by participants of the personal journal space. Some participants reported that this space acted as a prompt for them to record their reflections in other formats (either notebooks or simple Word documents), but others did not appear to be engaging at all in the reflective component of the course as anticipated.

A number of educational limitations and institutional barriers were also identified in the implementation of the ePortfolio. For example, the assessments in the ePortfolio can only ever assess professional attributes at a self-reported level rather than at performance-based level in the actual workplace (Miller, 1990). It would be advantageous to shift from the assessment of self-reported professional behaviour for participants to actual observation of practice. This could not be achieved with the confines of the ePortfolio.

At an institutional level, we have been unable, as yet, to move to wider-scale implementation in other courses. This is largely due to a funding mechanism with restricted capacity to support the small ongoing development that would be required to extend the use of the ePortfolio into other courses and disciplines. There is also a lack of willingness to share ideas with external partners due to issues of intellectual property.

FURTHER DEVELOPMENTS, CONCLUSIONS, AND RECOMMENDATIONS

One of the major lessons learned from the project was the need for close cooperation and liaison among tutors, Web designers, and users or course participants in the piloting stages. The ePortfolio achieved its goal of demonstrating contemporary educational practice. It was also possible to record teaching activities in the workplace, and to encourage the development of reflective skills and also those of providing written feedback. The ability for students to review draft work by their peers was thought to be instrumental in developing both of these skills.

Further work is needed to clarify instructions to participants and to improve the baseline assessment of participants' skills in use of Web-based resources and IT in general. Training in use of IT needs to be incorporated in the course delivery and individually tailored to need at least at the current time. A statistics server has been linked to the ePortfolio site to enable more objective evaluation of participant use, and in the future the ePortfolio will be embedded in a networked learning environment. It is also being explored currently for the potential to plug in seamlessly to other commercial platforms and for use in an undergraduate group of students where the numbers will be increased by a factor of approximately 10. Other refinements are required to allow the assessment tasks to be more person centred. For example, the setting of individually negotiated deadlines for tasks would be beneficial.

In summary, an ePortfolio in a graduate course in health professional education is one way in which reflection and feedback skills can be fostered. Despite initial apprehensions from the participant group, it can be used effectively as an adjunct to other more traditional forms of assessment. In general, including some components of the activities of the ePortfolio in the summative course assessment was important to provide a clear indication to the participants that the demonstration of appropriate professional behaviours in relation to their teaching role is as important as the acquisition of teaching skills and theoretical knowledge. A final observation from the development of this ePortfolio is that the process for educational innovation supported by IT needs to be driven by people who understand learning and pedagogical principles.

REFERENCES

Boud, D. (1995). Assessment and learning: Contradictory or complementary? In P. Knight (Ed.), *Assessment for learning in higher education.* London: Kogan-Page.

Ende, J. (1983). Feedback in clinical medical education. *Journal of American Medical Association, 250*(6), 777-781.

Laurillard, D. (2002). *Rethinking university teaching.* London: Routledge-Falmer.

Lawson, M., Bearman, M., Jolly, B., Kiegaldie, D., & Roberts, C. (2004, July). Assessing the readiness of students in professional healthcare education for e-learning. In *Proceedings of the Ottawa Conference in Medical Education,* Barcelona.

Lawson, M., Kiegaldie, D.J., & Jolly, B.C. (2004, June). Using an ePortfolio in a postgraduate course in health professional education. In L. Cantoni & C. McLoughlin (Eds.), In *Proceedings of the ED-MEDIA 2004 World Conference,* Switzerland.

Miller, G. E. (1990). The assessment of clinical skills/competence/performance. *Academic Medicine, 65,* S63-S7.

Monash Directions 2025. (2005). Retrieved June 6, 2005, from http://www.monash.edu.au/about/monash-directions/

Rogers, C., & Freiberg, H. J. (1994). *Freedom to learn* (3rd ed.). New York: Macmillan.

Salmon, G. (2000). *E-moderating.* London: Routledge-Falmer.

KEY TERMS

Authentic Assessment: A form of assessment in which students are asked to perform real-world tasks that demonstrate meaningful application of essential knowledge and skills. Student performance on a task is typically scored on a rubric to determine how successfully the student has met specific standards. The concept of 'model, practice, feedback' in which students know what excellent performance is and are guided to practice an entire concept rather then bits and pieces in preparation for eventual understanding. A variety of techniques can be employed in authentic assessment. The goal of authentic assessment is to gather evidence that students can use knowledge effectively and be able to critique their own efforts.

Bedside Teaching: Teaching and learning that takes place with a patient or in the vicinity of a clinical facility. In general this term covers contact with all patients and not just those that are actually bed-ridden, for example those in a general practice surgery, in outpatient or ambulatory settings, or visited at home.

Cognitive Skills: Mental abilities that help us process external stimuli.

eLearning: The delivery of a learning, training, or education program by electronic means. E-learning involves the use of a computer or electronic device to provide training, educational, or learning material (from www.intelera.com/glossary.htm).

ePortfolio: A portfolio based on electronic media. It consists of a personal digital record containing information such as personal profile, and collection of assessments, assignments, or other achievements; personal reflections on those tasks; and other information that relates to the owner of the ePortfolio and the people (peers, other students, teachers) and organisations to whom the owner has granted access.

Information Technology (IT): A term that encompasses all forms of technology used to create, store, exchange, and utilize information in its various forms including business data, conversations, still images, motion pictures, and multimedia presentations.

Non-Final Vocabulary: This term is coined from Rorty's view that there are no absolutes by which individuals can be assessed; for example, nothing is ever 'right' or 'wrong'—it all depends on perspective. Attempting to describe students' work using 'non-final' vocabulary is both a challenge and potentially very beneficial to students because it validates their work, but can contrast it with other perspectives and value systems without pejorative implications.

Psychomotor Skills: Physical actions or activities (body movements) that people perform which involve coordinating perceptions and cognitive processes with that action—for example surgery, particularly laparoscopic surgery.

Reflection: Takes place when the learner observes, interprets, and reflects upon his or her own learning or clinical practice experience. This reflection would include the who, what, where, and why of the learning experience and an attempt to understand how that experience can best be used to foster learning.

Student-Centred Learning: An approach to education focusing on the needs of the students, rather than those of others involved in the educational process, such as teachers and administrators. This approach has many implications for the design of curriculum, course content, and interactivity of courses. For instance, a student-centred course may address the needs of a particular student audience to learn how to solve some job-related problems (from Wikipedia, the free encyclopaedia).

Chapter XXVI
ePortfolios in Graduate Medical Education

Jorge G. Ruiz
University of Miami, VA GRECC, and Stein Gerontological Institute, USA

Maria H. van Zuilen
University of Miami, USA

Alan Katz
University of Miami, USA

Marcos Milanez
University of Miami, USA

Richard G. Tiberius
University of Miami, USA

ABSTRACT

Residency education is the period of clinical education that follows graduation from medical school, and prepares physicians for the independent practice of medicine. The Accreditation Council for Graduate Medical Education (ACGME) is an organization responsible for accrediting residency education programs. The ACGME is increasingly emphasizing educational outcomes in the accreditation process. The authors will discuss the experience of GME programs using ePortfolios for both formative and summative evaluation of residents and the integration of ePortfolios as part of institutions' learning management systems. ePortfolios can be especially useful for evaluating and documenting mastery of educational outcomes such as practice-based improvement, use of scientific evidence in patient care, and professional and ethical behaviors that are difficult to evaluate using traditional assessment instruments. The authors also review the literature describing the use of ePortfolios as a tool that is both powerful and reflective, for the assessment of program outcomes by administrators and faculty.

BACKGROUND

Residency education or graduate medical education (GME) is the period of clinical education that follows graduation from medical school, and prepares physicians for the independent practice of medicine. Depending on the specialty, resident physicians require between three to seven years of full-time experience in a training program to graduate as qualified specialists ready to practice. Resident physicians care for patients under the direct supervision of teaching physicians. The clinical experiences occur in a range of venues from community settings and outpatient practices to institutional environments such as hospitals and long-term care facilities. These clinical experiences are integrated into a comprehensive educational program that includes didactic activities and research.

Keeping track of residents' progress and assuring that all residents acquire the necessary knowledge, skills, and attitudes to become competent physicians in their areas of specialty can be a challenge given this variety of training experiences. Increasingly, accrediting agencies are holding training programs accountable for documenting outcomes. Traditionally, the Accreditation Council for Graduate Medical Education (ACGME) has focused on evaluating the adequacy of the process or structure of the residency programs to educate residents. In 1999, the ACGME introduced a new paradigm, the Outcomes Project, which places greater emphasis on a program's actual accomplishments through an assessment of program outcomes (ACGME, 2004).

In order to accomplish this goal, the ACGME has outlined six competencies: patient care, medical knowledge, professionalism, interpersonal and communication skills, practice-based learning and improvement, and systems-based practice. The rationale for this emphasis on outcomes is the need to ensure that physicians become and remain competent to meet the health care needs of their communities. At the end of their training, physicians must develop competence in lifelong learning strategies, reflective clinical practice, skills, and appropriate attitudes. Achieving these outcomes and documenting the achievement presents challenges for planners of postgraduate teaching, learning, and assessment. Medical educators and trainees must meet these new challenges in the face of dramatic changes in the U.S. health care system. Mounting clinical and academic activities due to changes in health care delivery and advances in medicine have increased demands on academic faculty, resulting in less time for teaching and mentoring (Ozuah, 2002).

To be able to assess this expanded range of competencies, training programs must redefine their current assessment approaches. Graduate medical education programs need to move from an almost exclusive reliance on traditional evaluations such as global subjective ratings of performance and written examinations, towards a competency-based model that requires multidimensional evaluations such as objective structured clinical examinations (OSCEs), standardized patient exams, chart reviews, and peer and patient evaluations. Even these additional assessment methodologies will not enable us to effectively evaluate all of the competencies. The assessment methodologies appear to be more effective in the evaluation of patient care, knowledge, and communication than they are in the evaluation of competencies such as practice-based learning and improvement (Lynch, Swing, Horowitz, Holt, & Messer, 2004), systems-based practice (Ziegelstein & Fiebach, 2004), and professionalism. There is a need for new tools with which to conduct valid and accurate assessments of these competencies. Moreover, these new tools should be compatible with the learner-centered model that emphasizes self-reflection and self-directed learning, critical skills that put learners in control of their own learning.

PORTFOLIOS IN MEDICAL EDUCATION

Portfolios document the evidence that demonstrates a doctor's education and practice achievements (Wilkinson et al., 2002). Medical educators have used portfolios at the undergraduate, graduate, and continuing medical education levels across various medical specialties such as psychiatry (Jarvis, O'Sullivan, McClain, & Clardy, 2004), obstetrics and gynecology (Lonka et al., 2001), internal medicine (Hayden, Dufel, & Shih, 2002), pediatrics (Carraccio & Englander, 2004), and emergency medicine (O'Sullivan & Greene, 2002). Medical education experts advocate the use of portfolios at each level of training to aid these specialties in the evaluation of competencies set forth by accrediting agencies such as the ACGME. Some portfolios focus primarily on assessment and reflect a learner's achievement of competency in specific areas of medicine. These types of portfolios are often used for summative evaluation purposes. Others are more developmental in nature and present evidence of improvements in learning over time. Such portfolios can be used by program directors and by the learners themselves for formative purposes to track progress. Yet other portfolios might showcase a person's best work or achievements in specific areas such as clinical work, research, or education. Most portfolios contain a combination of elements. The table lists some components that have been included in medical portfolios (Carraccio & Englander, 2004; Hays, 2004; Ozuah, 2002).

Portfolios can be tailored to the medical trainee, and the content can be determined by the trainee's learning needs. They can accommodate a diversity of practice and academic evidence. They foster self-directed learning, lifelong learning, critical thinking, and self-reflection (Carraccio & Englander, 2004; Challis, 2001; Hayden et al., 2002; Lynch et al., 2004; Stanton & Grant, 1999).

There are some disadvantages to the use of portfolios. Portfolios are time consuming to complete and assess, and immediate documentation of an experience is not always practical, given competing clinical obligations. Portfolios sometimes lack structure and standardization, making their use in evaluation difficult. Finally, portfolios do not really tell us much about the actual level of performance in many clinical activities (Challis, 2001; Snadden, 1999; Stanton & Grant, 1999).

RATIONALE FOR THE USE OF ELECTRONIC PORTFOLIOS

Electronic portfolios (ePortfolios) can circumvent some of the difficulties with hardcopy portfolios. Portfolios in their traditional written form are difficult to update, store, search, access, and distribute. These problems are compounded by the rotation of residents through different clinical venues. ePortfolios enable program administrators to gather and keep track of all the portfolio components that need to be submitted by residents, supervising faculty, and other contributors, especially when these persons are geographically dispersed. ePortfolios give residents access to their portfolio at all times, so they can document their clinical training in a timely fashion and allow their physician mentors and colleagues to review their progress.

Most ePortfolios are based on Internet technologies that offer multiple useful features such as accessibility, easy updating, learner control, distribution, standardization, tracking, and monitoring. Accessibility refers to the trainee's ability to find in the ePortfolio what is needed, when it is needed. Improved access to ePortfolio content is crucial, as learning is often an unplanned experience. Updating electronic content is easier than updating printed material (Chu & Chan, 1998); ePortfolios allow trainees to revise their content simply and quickly. Learners have control over the content, learning sequence, pace of learning, time, and often media, thereby allowing them to tailor the ePortfolio to meet their own personal learning objectives (Chodorow, 1996). Internet technologies allow the widespread distribution of ePortfolio content to many users simultaneously, anytime and anywhere (Chu & Chan, 1998). An additional strength of ePortfolios is that they may standardize content and delivery. Automated tracking and reporting of a trainee's activity lessens the faculty administrative burden. Moreover, ePortfolios can be designed to include learner assessments to determine whether learning has occurred. Since documentation of outcomes is the new ACGME mandate for residency programs, ePortfolios will likely grow in popularity.

There are some downsides to the use of ePortfolios in medical education, including issues related to computer server space, technical support and maintenance, use of portfolio software, and security and confidentiality. Medical educators considering the use of ePortfolios need to work with their local information technology staff to identify whether the level of expertise is available to develop the electronic platform and have access to dedicated support. There are a variety of commercial products available, but these are generally limited in their ability to meet the specific needs of medical education programs and may not fulfill the needs of learners, faculty, and program administration.

ePORTFOLIOS IN GRADUATE MEDICAL EDUCATION

ePortfolios can be especially helpful in documenting the ACGME competencies for graduate medical education. The ACGME has suggested methods for the evaluation of each competency (ACGME, 2004). Data from these evaluation methods can be effectively captured in the ePortfolio. For example, discipline-specific medical knowledge can be documented in the ePortfolio by including oral, written, or MCQ test results. Most of these tests can easily be administered electronically, which greatly facilitates the inclusion of results in the ePortfolio. The patient care competency can be documented through a variety of information sources, including record reviews, chart-stimulated recall exercises, patient surveys, and results from performance-based competency assessments such as standardized patient exams and OSCEs. The interpersonal and communication skills competency can also be effectively assessed through patient surveys and the performance-based assessments. Some of this data can be gathered electronically. For the other elements it is relatively easy to enter the results in an online template.

ePortfolios offer particular benefits for the remaining competencies, which are more difficult to assess. Aside from the evaluation methods proposed by the ACGME, medical educators can experiment with a wide array of innovative evaluation methods to assess these competencies (Carraccio & Englander, 2004). The practice-based learning and improvement competency requires residents to be able to investigate and evaluate their own patient care practices, appraise and assimilate evidence-based scientific evidence, and consequently improve their patient care. ePortfolios provide an accessible platform where residents can document evidence of their patient care practices, allowing them to reflect upon these experiences, analyze their thought processes, identify strengths and weaknesses, and under the guidance of supervising faculty with access to the same ePortfolio, set up a plan for improvement of overall clinical performance. These reflective activities can also provide evidence for the professionalism competency, as it fosters residents' commitment to ethically perform their professional responsibilities to an increasingly diverse patient population. Finally, the documentation of medical errors, the critical incidents during patient care activities, and the performance of quality improvement projects serve to fulfill the systems-based practice competency where residents must demonstrate an awareness of and responsiveness to the larger health care system, and an ability to provide optimal patient care by effectively mobilizing the health care system resources (Carraccio & Englander, 2004).

There are several examples in the literature of how ePortfolios have been used in graduate medical education to address the above ACGME competencies. Fung et al. (2000) described a learner-driven ePortfolio that was successfully implemented in an obstetrics and gynecology training program. They demonstrated improved self-directed learning and lifelong learning attitudes. Since then, their ePortfolio, called KOALA, has been used successfully with other trainees. Carraccio and Englander (2004) developed a Web-based ePortfolio to evaluate pediatric residents' performance in ACGME competencies. Their ePortfolio consists of self-assessment, a learning plan, tracking features, asynchronous discussion boards, and a system to address critical incidents during pediatrics training. Chisholm and Croskerry (2004) present an ePortfolio entry that can assess the Practice-Based Learning and Improvement competency. An example is of a senior faculty member who describes a medical error that occurred, say "delay in diagnosis." The learner is encouraged to reflect on the system errors and personal errors that might have contributed to the delay in diagnosis. The faculty member can also identify a number of personal learning points. This case study can then be distributed to residents and faculty in an emergency medicine residency. This type of portfolio entry promotes introspection and self-reflection. The authors note that senior-level faculty may need to model the portfolio for novice learners such as students and residents that have little experience with this process.

ePORTFOLIOS IN A GRADUATE GERIATRICS EDUCATION PROGRAM

The Geriatrics Fellowship at the University of Miami Miller School of Medicine is a one- to two-year training program following residency. Currently, nine residents (called fellows at this level) are enrolled in training. The fellowship includes several affiliated institutions with diverse training venues through which the fellows rotate including the nursing home, acute and sub-acute care settings, hospice, geriatric evaluation and management, home care, and outpatient settings. Although the training program is based in Miami, the fellows rotate at locations geographically distant from the home institution.

At the beginning of the 2004-2005 academic year, the fellowship committee decided to incorporate the ACGME recommendations, anticipating the full implementation of the outcome project in 2006. Our technical group, in conjunction with fellowship faculty and fellows, initiated a pilot ePortfolio program to capture the ACGME outcomes. To meet the challenge of reliably measuring all of the six competencies, the committee expanded the assessment of the fellows from global subjective evaluations to a more comprehensive assessment methodology based on multiple assessment tools and multiple raters. One example of a multiple assessment tool is the 360-degree evaluation in which fellows are evaluated by different members of the interdisciplinary teams they work with. A 360-degree evaluation can address aspects of several ACGME competencies, including interpersonal and communications skills, professionalism, patient care, and systems-based practice (ACGME, 2004). These evaluations are integrated with other training materials and self-reflection components as part of an electronic portfolio. Most of these evaluations were previously in written format, which complicated the ongoing evaluation of fellows. The use of an ePortfolio offers the opportunity to enhance documentation and reduce the administrative burden of dealing with nine fellows dispersed across different locations.

The Geriatrics Fellowship relies on a learning management system (LMS) called GeriU: the Online Geriatrics University (http://www.geriu.org). GeriU is based on the Angel LMS platform, a SCORM (Sharable Content Object Reference Model) conformant LMS which is a database-driven eLearning platform. This LMS offers several collaboration features such as e-mail, chat, and discussion groups. It also serves as a repository for digital materials ranging from digitized text documents to highly interactive multimedia eLearning tutorials. The fellowship homepage was built as an ePortfolio to allow fellows to document the clinical, educational, and research activities they engage in during their fellowship.

DESCRIPTION OF THE GERIATRICS FELLOWS' ePORTFOLIO

The ePortfolio our fellows use is organized into four major sections: toolbox, clinical, education, and research, reflecting the major components of the fellowship training program. A description of each section follows:

Toolbox: This section contains guidelines for completion of the ePortfolio, pertinent articles about ePortfolios, the ACGME competencies, an overview of the assessments used to evaluate each competency, and a frequently asked questions section.

Clinical: This section contains information related to the supervised clinical activities of Geriatrics fellows. For each clinical rotation, the portfolio includes an evaluation of the fellow by the attending physician, an evaluation of the attending completed by the fellow, and a learning objective checklist that allows fellows to check whether they have completed a core set of activities for that rotation. After finishing each rotation, fellows complete a reflective exercise in which they describe some of their key learning experiences. The clinical section of the portfolio also contains a patient log, patient surveys, 360-degree evaluations, chart reviews conducted by the fellows, and an analysis of critical incidents.

Education: The education section comprises fellows' educational activities, products, and evaluations. Fellows conduct teaching and assessment sessions for medical students, residents, their peers, and sometimes other audiences. A list of educational activities conducted by fellows is included in the ePortfolio, as well as any teaching materials the fellows developed such as PowerPoint presentations, journal club reviews, and morbidity and mortality case conference summaries. The education section also contains evaluations of some of these teaching sessions from the learners.

Another aspect included in this section is a list of educational activities the fellows have participated in, as well as results from competency assessment activities. This section also contains a reflective component asking fellows to describe what they learned from each of these experiences.

Research: Each Geriatrics fellow completes a research project under the mentorship of Geriatrics faculty. This section includes the description of the research project with its goals, objectives, research plan, result, discussion, and conclusions. Any abstracts, manuscripts, or presentations resulting from this and other research in which the fellows are engaged are included in this section. Fellows' reflections on their experience with the research project are also included.

Assessment Process: The program director and associate program director are in charge of conducting the ePortfolio evaluation. These two faculty members will review each fellow's portfolio independently following an agreed-upon rubric. After completion of their summative evaluations, they will meet to discuss their evaluations and try to reach agreement. If no agreement is reached, the ePortfolio will be reviewed by the fellowship committee, which will then arrive at a final decision.

Preliminary Indications: The Geriatrics fellows who are currently using the ePortfolio have given some preliminary evaluations. They find the ePortfolio to be a very useful component of their training and describe it as easy to use and navigate. They are very satisfied with the opportunity to analyze their performances and see the milestones during their training clearly documented. The fellows gave mixed evaluations about the reflective exercises for the different sections. A clearer explanation of the rationale for self-reflection may be needed. Fellows indicated they would like to continue having access to their ePortfolio at the end of their training.

CONCLUSION

Medical educators have used portfolios for both formative and summative evaluation of trainees. Portfolios promote self-directed learning, lifelong learning, critical thinking, and self-reflection—important characteristics for competent physicians. The introduction of electronic portfolios offers medical educators advantages over hardcopy portfolios by making it easier to access, update, store, search, and distribute portfolio content. This greatly facilitates the documentation of the training experience. The ACGME is increasingly emphasizing educational outcomes in the accreditation process of graduate medical education programs. ePortfolios can be used to evaluate all six ACGME competencies, but they are especially useful in evaluating practice-based improvement, professional and ethical behaviors, and systems-based practice—competencies that are difficult to evaluate using traditional assessment instruments. The authors described their experience implementing an ePortfolio as part of a graduate medical education program in Geriatrics and provided examples of how their portfolio entries address the ACGME requirements. The ePortfolio can easily accommodate a broad variety of materials and reflect the spectrum of academic activities that medical trainees participate in. Setting up an initial ePortfolio structure that is capable of capturing this broad array of information is time consuming and costly. The authors will refine their existing ePortfolio structure based on feedback from the different stakeholders, with the goal to provide a template that can readily be adapted by other graduate medical education programs to document their outcomes.

REFERENCES

ACGME (Accreditation Council for Graduate Medical Education). (2005). *ACGME outcome project: Enhancing resident education through outcomes assessment.* Retrieved May 5, 2005, from http://www.acgme.org/Outcome/

Carraccio, C., & Englander, R. (2004). Evaluating competence using a portfolio: A literature review and Web-based application to the ACGME competencies. *Teaching and Learning in Medicine, 16*(4), 381-387.

Challis, M. (2001). Portfolios and assessment: Meeting the challenge. *Medical Teacher, 23*(5), 437-440.

Chisholm, C. D., & Croskerry, P. (2004). A case study in medical error: The use of the portfolio entry. *Academic Emergency Medicine, 11*(4), 388-392.

Chodorow, S. (1996). Educators must take the electronic revolution seriously. *Academic Medicine, 71*(3), 221-226.

Chu, L. F., & Chan, B. K. (1998). Evolution of Web site design: Implications for medical education on the Internet. *Computers in Biology and Medicine, 28*(5), 459-472.

Fung, M. F., Walker, M., Fung, K. F., Temple, L., Lajoie, F., Bellemare, G., et al. (2000). An Internet-based learning portfolio in resident education: The KOALA Multicenter Program. *Medical Education, 34*(6), 474-479.

Hayden, S. R., Dufel, S., & Shih, R. (2002). Definitions and competencies for practice-based learning and improvement. *Academic Emergency Medicine, 9*(11), 1242-1248.

Hays, R. B. (2004). Reflecting on learning portfolios. *Medical Education, 38*(8), 801-803.

Jarvis, R. M., O'Sullivan, P. S., McClain, T., & Clardy, J. A. (2004). Can one portfolio measure the six ACGME general competencies? *Academic Psychiatry, 28*(3), 190-196.

Lonka, K., Slotte, V., Halttunen, M., Kurki, T., Tiitinen, A., Vaara, L., et al. (2001). Portfolios as a learning tool in obstetrics and gynecology undergraduate training. *Medical Education, 35*(12), 1125-1130.

Lynch, D. C., Swing, S. R., Horowitz, S. D., Holt, K., & Messer, J. V. (2004). Assessing practice-based learning and improvement. *Teaching and Learning in Medicine, 16*(1), 85-92.

O'Sullivan, P., & Greene, C. (2002). Portfolios: Possibilities for addressing emergency medicine resident competencies. *Academic Emergency Medicine, 9*(11), 1305-1309.

Ozuah, P. O. (2002). Undergraduate medical education: Thoughts on future challenges. *BMC Medical Education, 2*(1), 8.

Snadden, D. (1999). Portfolios—attempting to measure the unmeasurable? *Medical Education, 33*(7), 478-479.

Stanton, F., & Grant, J. (1999). Approaches to experiential learning, course delivery and validation in medicine. A background document. *Medical Education, 33*(4), 282-297.

Wilkinson, T. J., Challis, M., Hobma, S. O., Newble, D. I., Parboosingh, J. T., Sibbald, R. G., et al. (2002). The use of portfolios for assessment of the competence and performance of doctors in practice. *Medical Education, 36*(10), 918-924.

Ziegelstein, R. C., & Fiebach, N. H. (2004). "The mirror" and "the village": A new method for teaching practice-based learning and improvement and systems-based practice. *Academic Medicine, 79*(1), 83-88.

KEY TERMS

ACGME: The Accreditation Council for Graduate Medical Education (ACGME) is responsible for the accreditation of post-MD medical training programs within the United States. Accreditation is accomplished through a peer-review process and is based upon established standards and guidelines.

Competencies: Complex set of behaviors built on the components of knowledge, skills, attitudes, and "competence" as personal ability.

Geriatric Fellows: Geriatric fellows are physicians who are first trained in family practice or internal medicine and then complete additional years of fellowship training in geriatrics.

Geriatrics (or Geriatric Medicine): The branch of medicine dealing with the medical management and care of older people.

Graduate Medical Education: Residency education or graduate medical education (GME) is the period of clinical education that follows graduation from medical school, and prepares physicians for the independent practice of medicine.

Resident: A medical resident is a physician who has received a postgraduate medical degree (M.D. or D.O.) and is enrolled in a clinical training program in the United States of America.

Chapter XXVII
A Flexible Component-Based ePortfolio:
Embedding in the Curriculum

S. J. Cotterill
University of Newcastle, UK

J. F. Aiton
St Andrews University, UK

P. M. Bradley
University of Newcastle, UK

G. R. Hammond
University of Newcastle, UK

A. M. McDonald
University of Newcastle, UK

J. Struthers
St Andrews University, UK

S. Whiten
St Andrews University, UK

ABSTRACT

This chapter provides case studies of embedding the ePortfolio in the curricula of two medical schools in the UK, one of which is outcomes based, while the other uses a series of patient scenarios to inform the teaching of clinical skills within a curriculum that emphasises the scientific basis of medicine. These case studies describe the implementation, evaluation, and process of embedding the portfolio within the respective curricula. They also illustrate the flexibility of a component-based ePortfolio to serve different pedagogic requirements. Research and evaluation issues are discussed, including an action-research approach with "fine-tuning" of technical features and pedagogy during the evaluation phase.

OVERVIEW

A component-based ePortfolio has been developed using open source software as part of a collaborative project (http://www.e-portfolios.ac.uk). The ePortfolio has been applied to a range of settings including dentistry, biosciences, postgraduate research students, and contract research staff. This chapter provides case studies of embedding the ePortfolio in the curricula of two medical schools in the UK, one of which is outcomes based, while the other uses a series of patient scenarios to inform the teaching of clinical skills within a curriculum that emphasises the scientific basis of medicine.

The first case is from the University of Newcastle where the ePortfolio was first implemented in the medical program in September 2003. The portfolio, initially developed as a stand-alone application, was integrated into the bespoke VLE used by the medical program. A new tool was developed for the ePortfolio to support Year 4 student-selected components (SSCs); its completion was mandatory. Students in Years 1 and 2 initially had the choice of completing a portfolio on paper or online. Following two years of experience implementing the ePortfolio, an assessed element was included, focusing on evidencing professional attitudes and behaviours.

The second case is from the University of St Andrews where the ePortfolio was implemented in September 2004. This implementation included a number of existing ePortfolio components and a novel patient scenario component designed by curriculum staff of the medical program. Following group work sessions, students used the portfolio to set objectives and tasks related to each patient scenario in the domains of knowledge, skills, and attitudes. Learning diaries have also been completed and shared with mentors.

These case studies describe the implementation, evaluation, and process of embedding the portfolio within the respective curricula. They also illustrate the flexibility of a component-based ePortfolio to serve different pedagogic requirements. Research and evaluation issues are discussed, including an action-research approach with "fine-tuning" of technical features and pedagogy during the evaluation phase.

POLICY REQUIREMENTS

A key policy driver across the UK Higher Education (HE) sector has been the requirement to support PDP (NCIHE, 1997). This is defined as "a structured and supported process undertaken by an individual to reflect upon their own learning, performance and/or achievement and to plan for their personal, educational and career development" (QAA, 2001). Many institutions are implementing portfolios (electronic or paper) as a way of facilitating these PDP requirements. One issue is that many programs already have elements of PDP (such as reflective learning and action planning), though not necessarily referring to under that label. There may therefore be an issue of whether to (1) implement PDP as a distinct "add-on" to the curriculum, or (2) embed the PDP processes within the curriculum. Also, the employability and widening participation agendas also impact on PDP, as do subject-specific requirements and local factors, such as staff resources, access to careers services, and established practices in academic tutoring.

In medicine, in common with most modern professions, there are requirements for independent learners who are able to play an active role in their continuing development and career progression (GMC, 2002). The processes involved in maintaining an ePortfolio may help in the transition towards independent learning by fostering self-analysis, awareness of transferable skills, personal development planning

(PDP), and other lifelong learning skills. The experience of evidencing learning outcomes may also help in preparation for appraisals, assessments, and re-accreditation required in professional medicine.

DESIGN RATIONALE

A component-based ePortfolio (Cotterill, McDonald, Drummond, & Hammond, 2004b) was developed at Newcastle University as part of a FDTL-4 project (http://www.e-portfolios.ac.uk). The ePortfolio was designed to be flexible and easy to customise, in recognition that requirements and assessment strategies will vary considerably—both between institutions and subject areas, and over time within each specific context. The portfolio includes a set of generic tools, many of which can be used to support PDP. However, the component-based architecture of the ePortfolio gives the scope to add context-specific tools which share common features such as the facility to share files, add comments, and include integrated action planning. This flexible design also follows the philosophy that it is beneficial to embed PDP and related processes within the curricula.

Course leaders can select from a bank of generic components, including a learning diary, CV, log of meetings with tutors, learning outcomes/skills log, and tools (see Figure 1). Different sets of components can be selected for specific courses and year groups. The title, icon, and other features of each component can also be modified. Outcomes/skill sets, nomenclature, and "look-and feel" can also be customised for each course. New components can be created by developers using open source software. These can draw on the built-in features to support content sharing, commenting, attaching objects (files, etc.), and integrated action planning. Administrators can also create structured tools, without the need for any programming skills, using simple Web forms.

Figure 1. Selecting portfolio components at the course/program level

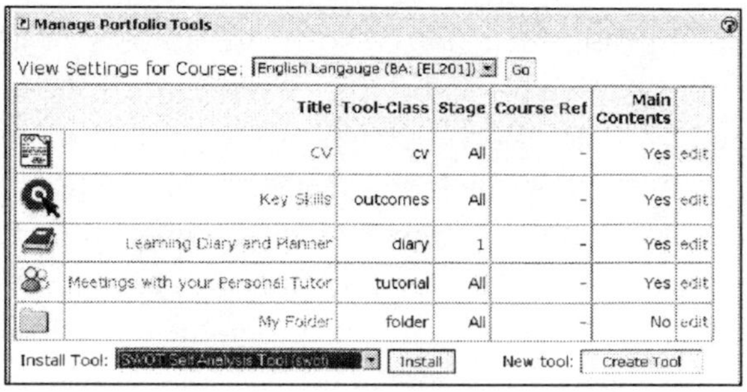

Manage Portfolio Tools

View Settings for Course: English Langauge (BA: [EL201]) Go

	Title	Tool-Class	Stage	Course Ref	Main Contents	
	CV	cv	All	-	Yes	edit
	Key Skills	outcomes	All	-	Yes	edit
	Learning Diary and Planner	diary	1	-	Yes	edit
	Meetings with your Personal Tutor	tutorial	All	-	Yes	edit
	My Folder	folder	All	-	No	edit

Install Tool: SWOT Self Analysis Tool (swot) Install New tool: Create Tool

Access to portfolio content is primarily controlled by the learner. By default only the learner will have access to their content and they choose who can see specific parts of their portfolio. However, course leaders can also prospectively define access policies for each component, for example where the ePortfolio is being used to support assessment.

CASE STUDY 1: UNIVERSITY OF NEWCASTLE

Context

The undergraduate medical program at the University of Newcastle supports over 1,400 students. The program is nominally five years in length with the first two years (Phase I) at Newcastle and the final three years (Phase II) being hospital based. There are three different entry points into the program: a standard five-year program, an accelerated four-year program for students with a prior science degree, and a joint program with Durham University. During Phase II, students are based in hospitals which are dispersed over a wide geographical area. A new curriculum was introduced in 2003, with training and administration for Phase II being formally provided by four regional clinical centres called Base Units. The program is an outcomes-based curriculum, with learning outcomes derived from professional requirements defined by the General Medical Council. Students are familiarised with the learning outcomes from the onset of their studies. Their assessment marks are given for the three "top level" learning outcomes.

The medical program uses a bespoke virtual learning environment (VLE) initially developed in 1997 and utilises Open Source technologies (Skelly & Quentin-Baxter, 1997). It is continually developed and refined in response to changing curriculum and policy requirements (Cotterill, Skelly, & McDonald, 2004a). There was significant development and restructuring of the VLE (now referred to as the Learning Support Environment) in 2004. It includes personalised portal views (to support multiple versions of the curriculum, which has changed over time, and also varies according to the entry route onto the program). The VLE includes study guides, a timetable, communications, self-assessment, learning resources, online evaluation, and numerous other features. It is integrated with the university's management information systems and library systems.

Customising the ePortfolio

The ePortfolio, initially developed as a standalone application, was incorporated into the bespoke VLE for Medicine at Newcastle (see Figure 2). It was tied into the style sheets and authentication system (LDAP) used by the VLE. A selection of generic tools (CV, learning diary, meetings with tutors, learning outcomes log, action planning, and SWOT) were selected, and some context-specific tools were also developed. One of the key context-specific tools to be developed was a portfolio to support the Year 4 student-selected components (SSCs). Also, a different subset of components was selected for the students in the accelerated program.

Figure 2. The Learning Support Environment for Medicine at Newcastle

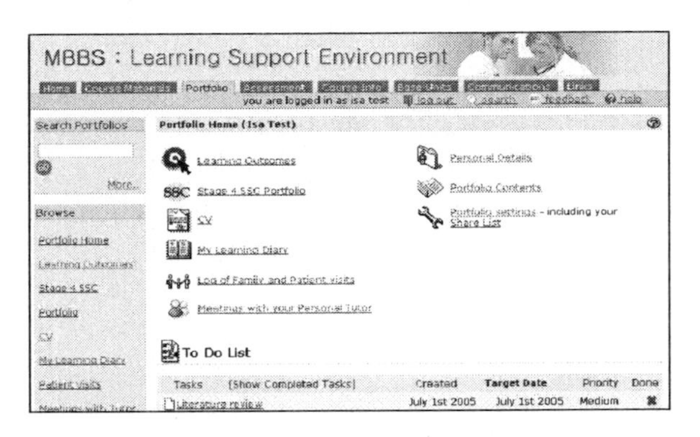

Implementation

The ePortfolio was implemented in the undergraduate medical program at the University of Newcastle beginning in September 2003. Students in Years 1 and 2 (n=450) had access to a learning diary, log of learning outcomes, action plan, CV, record of meetings, SWOT, and a log of patient and family visits within the ePortfolio. Using the ePortfolio was non-compulsory for Years 1 and 2; students were given the option of completing sections of a portfolio either in a paper logbook or in the ePortfolio. An overview of the ePortfolio was included in the induction to the wider Learning Support Environment and was referred to in subsequent teaching sessions.

Students continue to have access to the ePortfolio as they progress. In Year 4 it was mandatory for students to complete an SSC component within the ePortfolio (see Figure 3)

Figure 3. Overview of the SSC portfolio

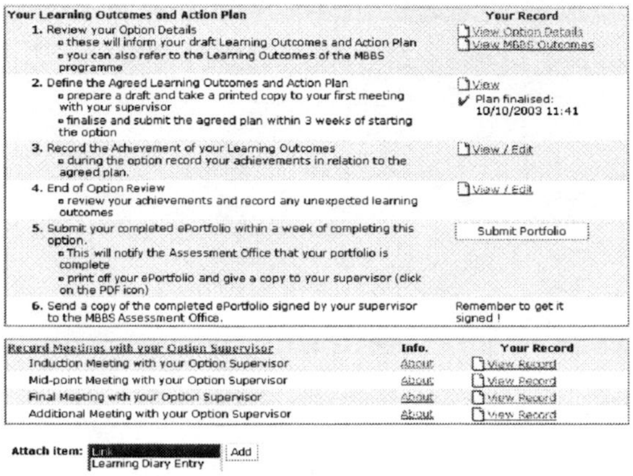

for one of their three SSCs which run between January and June each year. The SSC portfolio was not formally graded; however, its satisfactory completion and sign-off by the SSC supervisor was required in order for the student to progress. A structured "Learning Outcomes and Action Plan" was specifically designed to support the SSCs. Students were required to identify intended learning outcomes (in negotiation with their supervisors). For each outcome, students stated how they would achieve it and how its attainment would be measured/quantified. Once finalised, these learning outcomes could not be edited. During the SSC, students reflected against the outcomes and evidenced their achievements. At the end of the SSC, both intended and unintended learning outcomes were reviewed. Upon completion the SSC portfolio was submitted, at which point the content was "locked." A printed copy was signed by the supervisor and sent to the exams office (electronic sign-off was not considered feasible at the time, as many supervisors were not registered with the university IT facilities).

Evaluation

Two evaluation studies were undertaken, both with external ethical approval. An overview of results is included in Table 1.

The first study was designed to evaluate student perceptions of the paper logbook and ePortfolio used by students in Years 1 and 2 in 2003/2004. Two focus groups, involving 12 Year 1 students were facilitated by a fourth-year student as part of his/her SSC in medical education. Issues raised in the focus groups were used to inform the design of a questionnaire for the wider year group.

The ePortfolio proved to be generally acceptable, navigable, and easy to use. Most students thought that the ePortfolio was "a good idea," but some questioned the motivation to use it when it was not assessed. The focus groups and questionnaire indicated that there was a need for better clarity of purpose (i.e., a training issue). There was positive feedback on the facility to browse the learning outcomes of the curriculum. The structured learning diary was perceived as useful at first, but less so over time.

The second evaluation study related to the Year 4 SSC portfolio. A questionnaire-based evaluation study was granted ethical approval, and students provided written informed consent to participate prior to commencing their SSC. Participants were asked to complete two questionnaires. These were designed to assess potential changes in awareness of learning outcomes, factors influencing use of the ePortfolio, attitudes and perceptions of educational impact, and usability.

A total of 186 students completed the ePortfolio (100% compliance), and 165 students completed the questionnaires. The SSC ePortfolio proved to be feasible and acceptable, and facilitated the evidencing of learning out-

Table 1. Key evaluation findings (quantitative data)

Evaluation Questions (selected)	Disagree			Agree		
	a	b	c	d	e	f
	%	%	%	%	%	%
Year 1 Students 2003/2004 (n=232)						
I had sufficient information and guidance on how to use the ePortfolio.	11	18	18	21	24	8
The ePortfolio was easy to use.	5	10	20	33	26	6
Year 4 Students 2003/2004 (n=165)						
I found it difficult to navigate around the ePortfolio.	12	40	21	14	7	5
The online instructions for completing the ePortfolio were easy to understand.	1	8	13	22	45	11
Using the 'Learning Outcomes and Action Plan' was quite intuitive.	1	6	17	33	38	5
I discussed the intended learning outcomes with my supervisor at or near the beginning of the [SSC].	1	2	6	13	38	40
Having clearly defined intended learning outcomes influenced the way I approached the [SSC].	2	9	14	25	42	8
I feel that I have recorded good evidence that I have achieved specific learning outcomes from the [SSC].	0	4	6	29	42	19
I discussed my completed ePortfolio with my supervisor.	3	12	9	16	35	25
At the end of the [SSC,] I spent time considering what I had learned from it.	1	4	4	24	46	21
My supervisor showed no interest in my ePortfolio.	22	32	21	18	5	2
Building the ePortfolio was a useful learning experience.	4	5	10	34	38	9

Code: a = strongly disagree, f = strongly aggree

comes. Most respondents perceived it as being beneficial (80% thought it was a useful learning experience). Both the quantitative and qualitative data indicated that the process had a positive impact on the planning and organisation of learning:

It encouraged me to really give thought to what I wanted to achieve during the [SSC], which was especially useful as this was my first [SSC]. As a result of the portfolio I think I got much more out of the option than I would have otherwise.

The quantitative and qualitative data suggests that the ePortfolio had a positive impact on the way some students approached learning during their SSCs. The process may have also prompted reflection in some students (72% spent time considering what they had learned from their SSC). Barriers to using the ePortfolio were access to computers (students predominantly used computers on location at their SSC, at home, and/or at the university) and limited time.

Conclusions

The use of the ePortfolio has been very successful in the context of the Year 4 SSCs. With the Year 1 and Year 2 students, it has proven to be both feasible and acceptable. While many students have used the ePortfolio, its widespread uptake is unlikely without an assessment driver. Therefore, from 2005/2006 on, it will be mandatory for Year 1 students to complete a section of the ePortfolio which will focus on evidencing learning outcomes associated with professional attitudes and behaviours.

CASE STUDY 2: UNIVERSITY OF ST ANDREWS

Context

The Bute Medical School at the University of St Andrews introduced a new medical curriculum in September 2004 in response to general recommendations made by the General Medical Council's Education Committee and to specific comments from invited external reviewers. The school has an annual intake of around 130 students, and after three years of pre-clinical studies, the students graduate with an Honours Degree in Medicine. Students then complete a further three years of clinical training at the University of Manchester Medical School. Since St Andrews medical students merge with a cohort of Manchester students who have completed their Phase 1 training (two years of a PBL course), the aims and philosophy of the new St Andrews curriculum were developed to address national standards while retaining the qualities that characterise our own unique course. The new program is designed to deliver the foundations of medical science through an integrated curriculum with a strong clinical context. The delivery of the program is essentially through a taught knowledge stream which includes lectures, small-group teaching, and whole-body dissection supported by self-directed learning elements designed to encourage the application of medical sciences to clinical problems. Ethics, communication skills, and behavioural and health psychology are also included within the pre-clinical course. A major component of the clinical context is provided by a customised series of patient-based tutorials running through the entire course, and there is a substantial program of clinical skills training throughout the course.

Staff were instructed to make the best use of technology to support both the administration and delivery of the new curriculum. The curriculum is available online via the school's own Web-based course management system, with each time-tabled element linked to resources, learning objectives, and formative assessment. In addition, a major innovation for us was the adoption of an integrated curriculum resulting in a move away from the subject-based approach to medicine—that is, managing learning under traditional subject boundaries such as anatomy, physiology, and biochemistry was adapted to an integrated systems-based approach to the teaching of medicine. It was with these aims in mind that St Andrews decided to implement a Web-based portfolio system that was firmly embedded in the new curriculum.

After reviewing a number of commercial and open source solutions, the Bute Medical School joined in partnership with the University of Newcastle Medical School to use its component-based ePortfolio. In addition to using the existing generic tools already available, the flexibility of the underlying open source architecture of the Newcastle ePortfolio allowed St Andrews to participate in the development of new context-specific components for incorporation into the ePortfolio framework. Here we describe the use of the ePortfolio and implementation of a Patient Scenario tool that encourages students to set their own learning plans and agendas, and link learning to reflection.

Initial training in the use of the ePortfolio and reflective practice was provided though a structured program of events, including three lecture theatre events that introduced the students to the ePortfolio and provided a background to the importance of reflection and self assessment as part of their developing clinical careers.

1. **Introduction to ePortfolio:**
   - Write CV
   - Reflective response to DR and patient strand
   - Start using the learning diary
2. **Guidance on Reflective Writing:**
   - Reflect on their objectively structured practical exam (OSPE) performance and share portfolio with a tutor
3. **Recording Learning Objectives:**
   - Record learning objectives from the patient strand

These introductory sessions were supported by a series of self-study modules, each of which had provided detailed step-by-step instructions, e-mail support, and drop-in support.

- **Reflective Tasks:**
  - Personal experience of the dissection room
  - OSPE (objectively structured practical exam) performance
  - Response to family interview
- **Creating Action Lists:**
  - Patient scenarios
- **Logging Claims of Achievement:**
  - Clinical skills (blood pressure)
- **Mapping to Scottish Doctor Outcomes:**
  - Clinical skills
  - Simulated patient

The analysis of patient scenarios is an important focus for integration in the new curriculum. Students work in small groups with a facilitator to define the core knowledge, skills, and attitudes prompted by each patient. Subsequently, mind-mapping software (MindGenius) is used to consolidate a class overview and define key objectives. Students use their ePortfolio tools to determine their own learning objectives and create an action plan that maps out the routes, methods, and resources they will use to consolidate their learning (see Figure 4).

Figure 4. Patient scenarios

Tasks:
From your knowledge of patient assessment, assess and concisely summarise Andrew
Define any terms which you do not understand in the above scenario.

Make 3 lists: Knowledge, skills and attitudes, which you would like to acquire from this scenario. Note these in your portfolio.

Your objectives and actions

	Specific objectives/goals	Task to achieve objective	Target date	Done	
Knowledge	1. Know treatment, symptoms of tetanus	Find out which of the clinical skills practised might help me with the diagnosis of tetanus	23/03/2005	✓	Edit
	2. Recognise normal X-ray of shoulder	Look at different x-rays of shoulder joint	21/02/2005	✖	Edit
	3. To understand what fasciculation is and the physiology underlying it	Look up fasciculation	21/02/2005	✖	Edit
	4. Learn the anatomy of the brachial plexus	Ensure I can identify the brachial plexus in next dissection class	21/02/2005	✖	Edit
	Add a Task				
Skills	5. Know how to clinically inspect upper limbs	Review procedure on inspection of body	23/03/2005	✓	Edit
	6. Assess tone	Learn the 3 points for assessment of tone	23/02/2005	✖	Edit
	7. Assess power in upper limb	Learn the active movements against resistance for each joint	16/03/2005	✖	Edit
	8. Be able to do the 3 upper limb reflexes (Bicep, Tricep and Supinator)	Practise eliciting reflexes on friends using tendon hammer	09/05/2005	✖	Edit
	9. Know how to assess of sensation	Learn the different sensory modalities and test these on friends	11/05/2005	✖	Edit
	Add a Task				
Attitudes	10. Decide on what information needed to communicate with patient	Decide what are the important points about the injury that I need to communicate to the patient and discuss with them	22/02/2005	✓	Edit
	Add a Task				

The figure shows a student's analysis of a patient scenario with the key objectives listed under the categories of knowledge, skills, and attitudes. Students also decide upon the tasks to be completed in order to achieve their learning objectives, as well as setting a date by which the task must be completed. These tasks also are added to a "to do" list which compiles all the tasks a student has identified for completion. After completing each patient scenario, students then use the Learning Diary in their ePortfolios to reflect on each patient, and identify the strengths and weaknesses of their approach (see Figure 5).

Figure 5 shows an entry in the Learning Diary of a student asked to reflect upon the first encounter with a simulated patient as part of a communication skills training session. Entries in the Learning Diary (and other sections of the ePortfolio) are electronically shared with designated tutors who are able to add comment and feedback to the ePortfolio entry.

Figure 5. Example of a Learning Diary entry

Day 07/05/2005	
Key outcomes achieved	**Week 10 Guided Study on working with simulated patients.**
Observation —What has gone well?	I really enjoyed working with the simulated patients as it gave me a chance to put the skills acquired in communication skills sessions to use. I considered myself to have quite good communication skills compared to some people after coming to St. Andrews, but I soon realised that I have still got a lot to learn and work on ...
Analysis —Why has this happened?	I have thought about the communication skill sessions afterwards and 'tried' to implement them into my everyday thinking and speech. ... I would rather practice communication skills with a group of friends and make a fool of myself in the Bute, rather than in front of professional colleagues on a hospital ward.
Observation —What has gone less well?	... I was constantly thinking about the tactful use of language and the how appropriate certain words are in particular situations—especially the word "die." However when it came to my turn to talk to the patient, I managed to get myself into a situation where I had to say the word "die." I was annoyed at myself for not thinking carefully enough about what I was saying ...
Analysis —How would you approach things differently next time?	In future I will make sure that I think about every word, a bit like a politician ...

Skills Checklist

In order to ensure that students practice and maintain their clinical skills throughout their undergraduate curriculum, we are implementing a "Record of Practice" tool within the ePortfolio for 2005/2006.

Students must ensure that each skill is first practiced prior to review by their peer assessor (either a student from within their cohort or a more senior cohort). Students then are formally assessed by a tutor, and it is the responsibility of the student to confirm these details within the checklist. An automatic confirmatory e-mail is generated so that the examining tutor is available for confirmation (see Figure 6).

Evaluation

A comprehensive evaluation of the ePortfolio was carried out at the end of the first year. The purpose of the evaluation was to inform the school of how well the portfolio had been used by the students and to highlight any training needs for both staff and students. The evaluation focused on both the technical as well as user perceptions of the ePortfolio. The evaluation was delivered as an online anonymous survey within a WebCT course and consisted of a five-point series of qualitative questions ranging from strongly agree to strongly disagree.

Results

The results (see Table 2) indicated that over the entire year, 52% of the students spent between 2-5 hours on their portfolio, 17% of them spending 6-10 hours, and 24.5% spending less than one hour. Over 90% of the responses indicated that the students were confident in the technical aspects of using the ePortfolio; however, only 25% felt that they had benefited from using

Figure 6. Skills list for 2005/2006

Patient	Specific Objectives	Comment Box	No. of Times Practiced	Date Last Practiced	
Recovery Position	*To be completed by student*	*To be completed by student*			Assessment
BLS					Assessment
Airways Management					Assessment
Pulses					Assessment

Clinical Skills: Recovery Position

	Date Assessed	Peer Assessor E-Mail Address	Date Assessed	Staff Assessor E-Mail Address	Passed OSPE
MD2000		*E-mail address*		*E-mail address*	*Date*
MD3000		*E-mail address*		Not required	
MD4000		*E-mail address*		Not required	

Note: MD2000, MD3000, and MD4000 refer to the modules taken during the three-year curriculum

the portfolio. Results showed 32% found it a good way of recording work done and learning achieved, and 39% felt that using the learning diary helped them to think about the process of learning;11% of the students said they used their learning diaries on a regular basis.

In relation to the learning diaries, 87% of the students said that they understood what is meant by critical reflection, 48% found critical writing easy to write, while 45% would like more training in critical reflection.

Conclusions

Our first experience with the use of ePortfolios with entrant medical students direct from secondary (high school) education has been informative. The challenge ahead is to address some important questions that have arisen during the past year:

- How do we make it relevant to student learning?

Table 2. A selection of results from evaluation (n = 105)

Evaluation Questions		a	b	c	d	e
		%	%	%	%	%
I found the portfolio easy to use.		15	38	20	26	10
I feel I have benefited from using the portfolio.		6	17	26	25	26
I have used the learning diary on a regular basis.		3	8	19	35	35
I find the portfolio a good way of recording work done and learning achieved.		4	25	28	22	21
I am aware of the importance of maintaining a portfolio for my future career development.		22	43	16	13	7
I feel that using the learning diary has helped me think about the process of learning.		6	23	22	26	23
I understand what is meant by critical reflection.		27	50	10	8	5
I find critical reflection easy to write.		9	39	21	23	8
I would like more training in critical reflection.		15	34	24	31	17

Code: a= strongly agree, c= neutral, e = strongly disagree

- Who will develop suitable reflective learning tasks?
- How do we motivate student use without summative assessment?
- How much time can staff invest?
- Are we going to undertake staff training?
- How do we best embed the portfolio across the curriculum?
- Will the portfolio be assessed?

DISCUSSION

Here we have presented two case studies of implementing ePortfolios in undergraduate medicine. Many of the findings are relevant to other subject areas.

In both cases it is clear that implementation is a learning process, and ongoing evaluation activities are essential (these are akin to an Action Research approach). Successful adoption and integration with curricula requirements take time and experience. In Newcastle, after successful trialling of the ePortfolio in Years 1 and 2 since 2003, an assessed part of the portfolio is being introduced for pedagogic reasons (to help assess professional attitudes and behaviours) and practical reasons (motivation). At St. Andrew's University, a patient scenario component was designed and implemented within the ePortfolio framework. Its use was concentrated during the second semester, and following the success of the process, it is being extended to include a clinical skills list.

ePortfolios can be used for a diverse range of purposes (formative, summative, presentational, etc.), and pedagogic requirements vary with each educational context. It is therefore important that ePortfolios are flexible and easy to customise. For example, the two institutions here have different curricula. The flexibility of the ePortfolio framework has enabled its use and fine-tuning to these different contexts. The patient scenarios tool developed by St. Andrew's University complements its strategy for implementing clinical skills training within a science-orientated medical curriculum. The tool integrates with the "generic" action-planning and content-sharing features of the portfolio. At Newcastle, where there is an outcomes-based curricula, the portfolio has been adapted to serve both "terminal" learning outcomes and those for particular SSCs.

In both cases, the ePortfolio was introduced at a time of curricula change. The introduction of a new ePortfolio raised further challenges for staff during this demanding time. One of the reasons we think that the Year 4 SSC portfolio at Newcastle has been so successful is that the processes mirrored what most supervisors were already doing (i.e., discussing intended outcomes, etc.) and did not necessarily generate significant new demands on their time. It did make demands on student time, but was successful, in part, because the process was directly relevant to and focused on current activities. This may seem obvious, but it is clearly a challenge for those implementing a "one-size-fits-all" portfolio, for example, to support PDP across an entire institution.

Training is also a key issue when implementing ePortfolios. From the student viewpoint, a key barrier that we need to address relates to the perception that the ePortfolio is an add-on to the "real work" of the curriculum. This may be because we have not been fully successful in conveying the importance of continuing professional development in their medical careers (where they face portfolio-based appraisal, assessment, and revalidation). This may require more explicit training, involving qualified health professionals in explaining the importance of the portfolio in modern-day medicine. Staff also have concerns. Some are naive about reflection and reflective practice. They see it as an additional burden and feel ill-equipped to deal with assessment issues. Though clinical staff are familiar with continuing professional development and logging of clinical experience, non-clinical academic staff have yet to be involved in this type of career development. There also may be an additional difficulty because staff are not always comfortable with the use of an online environment and feel that they require a significant amount of support to become proficient with the tools.

In summary, we have presented two case studies of implementing ePortfolios in medicine. The component-based ePortfolio developed as part of a collaborative FDTL-4 project (http://www.e-portfolios.ac.uk) has proven flexible to support the diverse requirements of different curricula. The technology, however, is only part of the equation. There are key questions of how ePortfolios can best serve curricula and other requirements. Ongoing evaluation and refinement are essential. An evaluation focused on one point in time may be useful, but other factors such as changes in culture, perceptions/expectations, training/experience, and so forth are constantly changing, as is the technology. Furthermore, research into the educational benefits and effectiveness of the wider portfolio processes is essential.

NOTE

On behalf of the consortium developing "Managed Environments for Portfolio-Based Reflective Learning: Integrated Support for Evidencing Outcomes," a FDTL-4 funded project (http://www.e-portfolios.ac.uk).

REFERENCES

Cotterill, S. J., McDonald, A. M., Drummond, P., & Hammond, G. R. (2004). *Design, implementation and evaluation of a 'generic' e-portfolio: The Newcastle experience.* Retrieved June 1, 2005, from http://www.e-portfolios.ac.uk

Cotterill, S., Skelly, G., & McDonald, A. (2004). Design and integration issues in developing a managed learning environment which is responsive to changing curriculum and policy requirements. *Network Learning,* 409-416. Retrieved from http://www.shef.ac.uk/nlc2004/Proceedings/Individual_Papers/CotterillSkellyMcD.htm

GMC (General Medical Council, London). (2002). *Tomorrow's doctors.* Retrieved June 1, 2005, from http://www.gmc-uk.org/med_ed/tomdoc.pdf

NCIHE. (1997). *Higher education in the learning society. Report of the National Committee of Inquiry into Higher Education.* London: HMSO.

QAA (Quality Assurance Agency for Higher Education). (2001). *Guidelines for HE progress files.* Retrieved June 1, 2005, from http://www.qaa.ac.uk/crntwork/progfileHE/guidelines/progfile2001.pdf

Skelly, G., & Quentin-Baxter, M. (1997). Implementation and management of online curriculum study guides: The challenges of organisational change. In *Proceedings of the CTICM Computers in Medicine Conference* (pp. 65-73). Bristol, UK.

KEY TERMS

Fund for the Development of Teaching & Learning (FDTL): The FDTL programme was launched in 1995 to support projects that develop teaching and learning initiatives and that encourage dissemination of good practice. IT is funded by the Higher Education Funding Council for England and administered by the UK Higher Education Academy.

Objectively Structured Practical Exam (OSPE): A form of assessment widely used in health care education where students will complete a number of practical 'stations' with observers grading their competences using agreed criteria. For example, an OSPE might involve taking a medical history from someone playing the role of a patient, making a physical examination, doing a procedure on a mannequin, and providing interpretation of related lab results.

Personal Development Planning (PDP): A term widely used in UK Higher Education defined as "a structured and supported process undertaken by an individual to reflect upon their own learning, performance and/or achievement and to plan for their personal, educational and career development" (QAA, 2001).

Problem-Based Learning (PBL): An approach to learning based on a problem, question, or scenario, designed to raise a number of themes or dimensions of learning. It usually involves facilitated group work.

Student-Selected Components (SSC): Part of a programme of study where a student makes a selection of what they will do (a.k.a. student-selected module: SSM).

SWOT Analysis: A framework for analysing strengths, weaknesses, opportunities, and threats. This may be applied to an individual or group for a range of purposes, including the analysis of a skill or a particular approach to achieving an objective.

Virtual Learning Environment (VLE): An IT system to support a range of teaching and learning contexts, including distance learning and online learning.

Chapter XXVIII
Supporting the Portfolio Process with ONNI–The Learning Journal

Tommi Haapaniemi
University of Kuopio, Finland

Pasi Karvonen
University of Kuopio, Finland

ABSTRACT

The purpose of this chapter is to describe the use of an electronic learning journal in the portfolio process and the construction of a digital portfolio. The authors discuss the problems that have arisen during the learning and tutoring process of various traditional (paper) learning journals. The problems of traditional learning journals and their tutoring have been the following: (1) low extent of tutoring and evaluation during the process; (2) when the learning journal is the object of external assessment, it is not used as a tool for profound reflection (private vs. public dimensions of the learning journal); and (3) there has been a lack of a user-friendly tools with which to construct a Web-based learning portfolio. In this chapter the authors discuss the basic elements of ONNI–The Learning Journal, as well as how this electronic tool can help in solving the problems mentioned above. ONNI is presently being experimented on at the University of Kuopio, but it will also be developed to become a tool for every Finnish college student and to better support learning from peers as well as lifelong learning.

INTRODUCTION

The goal of learning journals is to promote the student's reflection during the learning process via writing. The learning journal can also be used to facilitate tutoring and as a tool for the evaluation of learning. The use of learning journals may, however, present some problems. Some of the problems involve the format (on paper), the possibilities for the teacher to tutor the process, and the private nature of reflection in journal writing. In the following, we throw some light on research that has been conducted on the use of learning journals. In addition we present the main features of ONNI–The Learning Journal, and discuss how this Web-based learning journal can support the portfolio process.

DEVELOPING ONNI-THE LEARNING JOURNAL: THEORETICAL CONNECTIONS

Learning Journals

A learning journal is a tutored or instructed writing process which centers around analysis and reflection. A learning journal can be a lecture journal, a learning log, and a part of a learning portfolio. A learning portfolio is a broader concept than a learning journal, for it is a collection of items that the writer collects during a learning process. A learning journal can thus be part of the writing process of a learning portfolio or a tool with which to construct a portfolio (Lindblom-Ylänne, Levander, & Wager, 2003).

Many researchers recognized the educational value of journal writing in the early 1960s, and since the 1970s learning journals have been used in university-level teaching. In addition, learning by writing was emphasized during the 1970s and 1980s in the United States. In Finland, learning journals have been used and their use researched since the middle of the 1980s. Their use as a teaching method has been grounded on research results on the correlation between writing and the development of thinking (Dyment & O'Connell, 2003; Lindblom-Ylänne et al., 2003; Tynjälä, Mason, & Lonka, 2001).

Aims of the Learning Journal

The learning journal has its theoretical foundations in cognitive-constructivist and humanistic approaches to learning. The pedagogical implications of these approaches are that the student is autonomous in directing his/her learning process and responsible for the choices he/she makes. The cognitive-constructivist approaches underline the ever-changing nature of knowledge and the student's active role and goal direction in interpreting experiences, defining meaning, and connecting new knowledge to existing knowledge structures. The construction of knowledge focuses on the student's knowledge and skills of self-regulation and reflective thinking (Tynjälä, 1999; Mezirow, 1996; Novak & Gowin, 1995; Marton, Dahlgren, Svensson, & Säljö, 1980).

Journal writing enhances learning and reflection during three phases of the process: the planning of writing, conversion of the plan into a text, and the editing and evaluation of the written text. These phases do not necessarily follow each other chronologically, but they are cognitive phases that take place during the writing process (Tynjälä et al., 2001). The best tasks and assignments to develop expertise and diverse forms of learning are the ones in which texts are not only produced, but writing is integrated into various learning processes, for instance into reading or group work processes (Tynjälä, 2001; see also Tynjälä, 1998).

Reflection is a key concept in the pedagogic use of learning journals. It means active thinking, which is directed towards oneself and one's actions in different (learning) situations. The aim of reflection is to self-regulate action in the future or following situation. It can focus on one's own thinking, actions, or emotions in a given situation (Boud, Keogh, & Walker, 1985). Reflection is metacognitive action, which is geared towards altering knowledge structures through thinking, and thus influencing action. Through reflection, metacognitive knowledge of one's learning is transformed into action (self-regulation) (Lindblom-Ylänne et al., 2003; Kolb, 1984).

The aims of tutored learning journal writing have been to help the student to classify and clarify information, concepts, and theories; deepen his/her scientific thinking; promote dialogue between the tutor and the student; and develop the student's capabilities for self-evaluation and reflection (Lindblom-Ylänne et al., 2003; see also Ojanen, 2000). To enhance the student's self-evaluation and self-direction, the learning journal can also include time planning and management, which enable the student to see his/her learning goals, and self-assessment and development of learning skills on a more concrete level (Vänskä, 1999). Journals have also been used as a method in researching experts' (such as teachers) work (see Bray & Harsch, 1996).

Tutoring the Learning Journal

The student can keep the learning journal regularly as part of the portfolio process. As the teacher has access to the student's writing, ongoing tutoring and facilitation of learning is possible (Tobin & Tippins, 1993). The learning journal is a tutored writing process; therefore the instructions or guidelines given by the teacher play an important role. The student directs his/her action and writing on the basis of them (Lindblom-Ylänne et al., 2003).

It is challenging for the teacher to foster critical thinking, and thinking that combines various kinds of knowledge. The purpose of tutoring is to clarify the objectives of the journal writing process. Apart from the instructions and guidelines, the students also need support and encouragement during the learning and writing process. The deeper and more analytic the student's writing process is, the more tutoring he/she needs. The writing process can be supported with small group meetings, peer tutoring, or writing reflective summaries of the learning journal entries (Lindblom-Ylänne et al., 2003).

The students benefit from direct instructions mostly in the beginning of the writing process, but later on, the tutor should have possibilities to comment on the writing and encourage the student to think creatively. There may be problems: the students find journal writing beneficial for learning, but they do not write on a regular basis, which is most important for the development of reflection, or they wish to use the learning journal more as a concrete tool for learning instead of developing thinking (Langer, 2002; Wagner, 1999; see Parer, 1988; Tauriainen, 1989). The factors that hinder the development of thinking with the learning journals are, for example, procrastination, shallowness, non-reflective entries, weak interest or enthusiasm towards active writing, or inability to reflect (Paterson, 1995; see also Cole, 1994).

Doyle and Garland (2001) found out that journal writing enhanced low-achievers' learning and that during the writing process they read more and also comprehended the reading much better than before. Especially the students who make few entries to the learning journal and receive low grades need clear and detailed feedback from the tutor (Lindblom-Ylänne et al., 2003).

Based on learning journal research, Dyment and O'Connell (2003) have drawn some guidelines for teachers and tutors who wish to use the learning journal in teaching. The teacher should be able to give the student thorough and detailed feedback, and consider using a variety of methods for assessing the learning journal. The teacher should also offer training, good examples, and use groups to support learning, but also let students set individual goals for keeping the learning journal. It is essential for the teacher/evaluator to create and maintain a confidential relationship with the writer of the journal. In addition to these, the teacher should recognize that male and female students differ in their views of keeping the learning journal. Finally, the teacher should give enough time for writing and avoid using the learning journal too much, for example in several courses simultaneously.

The research results mentioned above have been the starting points in the development work of ONNI. These results have been applied to the structure and technical functions of the learning journal. The following discussion on ONNI–The Learning Journal is primarily based on our own experiences.

CHALLENGES IN THE USE OF LEARNING JOURNALS

Traditional learning journals have been used at the University of Kuopio for years already. They have been used especially as learning logs in practical training, for instance in the clinical training of medical students, for training of university student tutors, in laboratory experimentation, or during field training periods in Finland or abroad. In addition to these, learning journals have been used to facilitate learning in lecture series.

We have found out that traditional (paper) learning journals have three major problems: (1) low extent of tutoring and evaluation during the learning process; (2) when the learning journal is externally assessed, it is often not used as a tool for profound reflection (the private nature of the journal); and (3) students do not have possibilities (tools) for easy construction of a Web-based learning portfolio based on the reflective learning process and its documentation.

Tutoring and Evaluating the Learning Process

Traditional learning journals are normally handed in to the teacher when the course is over. Students often leave the writing until the last minute. The student is then responsible for keeping the journal, and the tutor does not have possibilities to give the student specific instructions and clarifications on journal writing during the course. In ONNI–The Learning Journal, the teacher can instruct and monitor the student's learning process, and comment on the development of the learning journal—therefore tutor and evaluate the student using the same tool. ONNI has been used in student tutor training at the University of Kuopio. The student tutors have noticed that the Web-based learning journal has altered their writing styles and has fostered reflection during the learning process.

Facilitating Profound Reflection

Traditional learning journals are public documents, if the teacher or someone else reads the entries for example when assessing a course. It is then most likely that the student does not write about his/her private thoughts, emotions, personal reactions, experiences, or comments. This is however in contradiction with the aims of the learning journal as a tool to promote reflection, because in the learning journal, the student reflects his/her learning process on a very personal level: he/she writes the journal mostly for him/herself, not for the teacher. With ONNI–The Learning Journal, the student has the choice: whether to use the learning journal for the purposes of attending a course or for private purposes only. Moreover, the student can make the decision, entry by entry, whether the teacher has the right to read and comment or not. The right to comment on entries gives the teacher the possibility to facilitate the student's learning process. The most public form of a learning product processed with this tool is the learning portfolio published on the Internet.

Constructing a Learning Portfolio on the Internet

In ONNI–The Learning Journal, both the student's private entries and those that are also for the teacher to read can be part of the portfolio process, but as such they are usually not ready to be published in the learning portfolio. ONNI features an integrated tool for constructing a digital portfolio with which it is also possible to publish the learning portfolio on the Internet. The students do not need skills in Web page design to publish the portfolio; they can thus concentrate on the structure and contents of the portfolio. The program creates a Web page address for the portfolio automatically. The student can give this address, for instance, to his/her tutor, if the portfolio is a course requirement. The student can also save the completed portfolio when the course or studies are over or publish the portfolio in his/her personal Web pages.

USE OF THE PROGRAM AND ITS FEATURES

ONNI–The Learning Journal is Web based; in other words, it is used with a browser. Moreover it is authenticated with the student's e-mail account (it is also possible to use other kinds of authentication systems), programmed with PHP, and uses MySQL. ONNI–The Learning Journal is a tool for the student to self-direct and evaluate his/her learning. It is a tool for reflection, with which the student can document the learning process and recognize weaknesses and strengths in his/her learning skills. Students can easily and flexibly write entries to the learning journal whenever they have access to the Internet. The teacher can also monitor the student's learning "in real time" and comment on the learning journal entries when necessary. The guiding principles in developing the program were student centeredness and user friendliness. The students at the University of Kuopio can start using ONNI independently, if they wish, simply by logging in with the university e-mail ID.

Figure 1. Front page: Log in

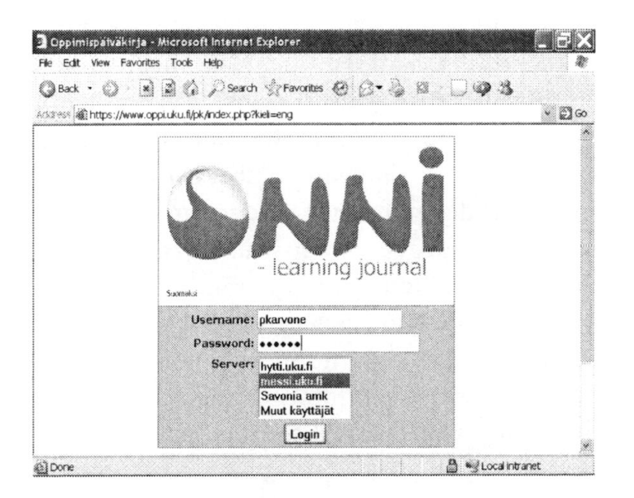

Figure 2. Front page: Five learning journals and the portfolio

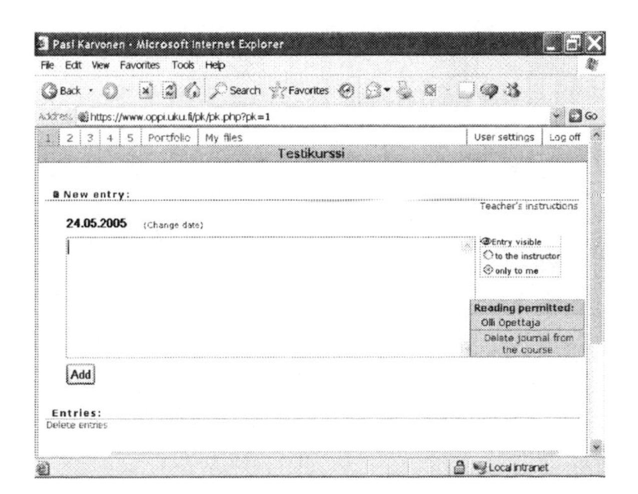

Figure 3. Portfolio: Screen shot of the editing phase

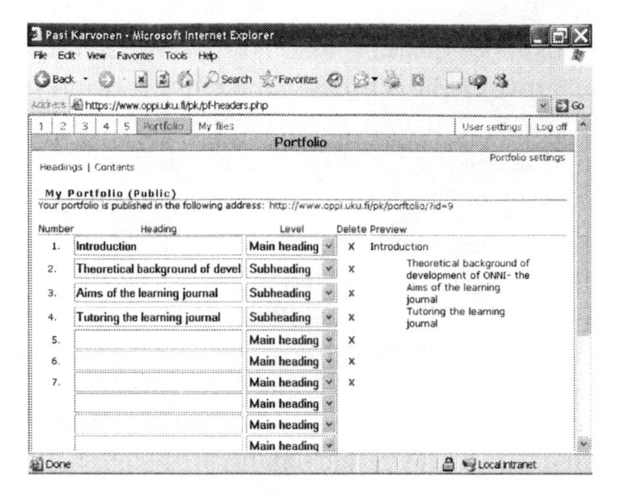

In ONNI–The Learning Journal, the student has simultaneous access to five learning journals and the portfolio. The student can use a learning journal for private purposes or attach the learning journal to a course. If the learning journal is attached to a course, the student can decide whether the teacher can see the entry or not. The teacher can give instructions to journal writing and feedback to the student's entries. It is also possible for the student to attach files to the entries.

With the portfolio tool of ONNI, the user can easily construct a portfolio. The portfolio can be published on the Internet or it can be saved as a Web page. The layout of the portfolio can be chosen from templates. Files can be added and attached to the portfolio.

Figure 4. Screen shot of a published portfolio

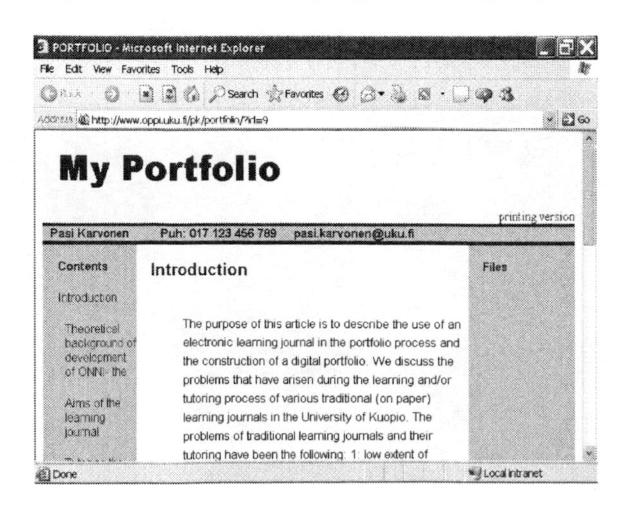

AN UNCOMPLICATED TOOL TO SUPPORT THE PORTFOLIO PROCESS

The importance of process evaluation, which complements the summative assessment of a course, has been under a lot of discussion in the Finnish university circles. Process evaluation can be carried out by using learning journals and/or portfolios. The goal in developing ONNI–The Learning Journal has been to create a tool with which journal writing and the learning process becomes more open, and the student processes it in collaboration with the tutor.

ONNI is a tool that supports the student's reflection during the learning process with which it is possible to tutor and evaluate learning. It is easy for the student to incorporate the learning journal into the portfolio to be published on the Internet. We maintain that ONNI–The Learning Journal solves or at least eases the three major problems of traditional learning journals discussed in this chapter.

ONNI–The Learning Journal is available mainly for the students at the University of Kuopio at the moment. However, in the future, our goal is that every Finnish university student can have access to this program via the Web portal of the Finnish Virtual University. We also aim at developing the program so that it better supports peer tutoring and peer-to-peer evaluation. ONNI–The Learning Journal is each student's personal Web space (see Cohn &

Hibbitts, 2004) during his/her studies, but we feel that students' lifelong learning should be promoted as well. It is our intention to further develop ONNI–The Learning Journal to meet this challenge.

REFERENCES

Boud, D., Keogh, R., & Walker, D. (1985). *Reflection: Turning experience into learning.* New York: Kogan Page.

Bray, E., & Harsch, K. (1996, November 2). Using reflection/review journals in Japanese classrooms. In *Proceedings of the Annual Meeting of the Japan Association of Language Teachers.* Retrieved from http://www.eric.ed.gov/ERICDocs/data/ericdocs2/content_storage_01/00000000b/80/24/bc/e9.pdf

Cohn, E.R., & Hibbitts, B.J. (2004). Beyond the electric portfolio: A lifetime personal Web space. *Educause Quarterly, 27*(4), 7-10.

Cole, P. (1994). A cognitive model of journal writing. In M. R. Simonson (Ed.), *Proceedings of selected research and development presentations at the 1994 National Convention on the Association for Educational Communications and Technology.* Retrieved from http://www.eric.ed.gov/ERICDocs/data/ericdocs2/content_storage_01/0000000b/80/22/2d/d5.pdf

Doyle, M. S., & Garland, J. C. (2001). A course to teach cognitive and affective learning strategies to university students. *Guidance and Counseling, 16*(3), 86-91.

Dyment, J. E., & O'Connell, T. S. (2003). *Journal writing in experiential education: possibilities, problems, and recommendations.* Retrieved from http://www.eric.ed.gov/ERICDocs/data/ericdocs2/content_storage_01/0000000b/80/2a/3a/10.pdf

Kolb, D. A. (1984). *Experiential learning: Experience as the source of learning and development.* Englewood Cliffs, NJ: Prentice-Hall.

Langer, A. M. (2002). Reflecting in practice: Using learning journals in higher and continuing education. *Teaching in Higher Education, 7*(3), 337-351.

Lindblom-Ylänne, S., Levander, L., & Wager, M. (2003). Oppimispäiväkirjat ja portfoliot. In S. Lindblom-Ylänne & A. Nevgi (Eds.), *Yliopisto–ja korkeakouluopettajan käsikirja* (pp. 326-354). Vantaa: Dark Oy.

Marton, F., Dahlgren, L. O., Svensson, L., & Säljö, R. (1980). *Oppimisen ohjaaminen. (Inlärning och omvärldsuppfattning).* Espoo: Weilin & Göös.

Mezirow, J. (1990) *Fostering critical reflection in adulthood: A guide to transformative and emancipatory learning.* San Francisco: Jossey-Bass.

Novak, J. D., & Gowin, B. (1990). *Learning how to learn.* Cambridge: Cambridge University Press.

Ojanen, S. (2000). *Ohjauksesta oivallukseen ohjausteorian kehittelyä.* Saarijärvi: Saarijärven Offset.

Parer, M. (1988). *Students' experience of external studies. Student Diary Project.* Churchill: Centre for Distance Learning, Gippsland Institute.

Paterson, B. L. (1995). Developing and maintaining reflection in clinical journals. *Nurse Education Today, 15,* 211-220.

Tauriainen, P. (1989). Oppimispäiväkirjan hyödyllisyys aikuisopiskelussa. Kokemuksia ideapäiväkirjan käytöstä esimiesten koulutuksessa. *Aikuiskasvatus, 2,* 52-55.

Tobin, K., & Tippins, D. (1993). Constructivism as a referent for teaching and learning. In K. Tobin (Ed.), *The practice of constructivism in science education* (pp. 3-22). Mahwah, NJ: Lawrence Erlbaum.

Tynjälä, P. (1998). Traditional studying for examination versus constructivist learning tasks: Do learning outcomes differ? *Studies in Higher Education, 23*(2), 173-190.

Tynjälä, P. (1999). *Oppiminen tiedon rakentamisena. Konstruktivistisen oppimiskäsityksen perusteita.* Tampere: Kirjayhtymä.

Tynjälä, P. (2001). Writing, learning and the development of expertise. In P. Tynjälä, L. Mason, & K. Lonka (Eds.), *Writing as a learning tool* (pp. 37-56). The Netherlands: Kluwer.

Tynjälä, P., Mason, L., & Lonka, K. (2001). Writing as a learning tool: An introduction. In P. Tynjälä, L. Mason, & K. Lonka (Eds.), *Writing as a learning tool* (pp. 7-22). The Netherlands: Kluwer.

Vänskä, M. (1995). *Antoisaan opiskeluun. Käsikirja opiskelun ja opetuksen kehittämiseen.* Helsinki: Yliopistopaino.

Wagner, Z. M. (1999). Using student journals for course evaluation. *Assessment & Evaluation in Higher Education, 24*(3), 261-272.

KEY TERMS

Learning Journal: A tutored or instructed writing process, which centers on analysis and reflection. It can be a lecture journal, a learning log, and a part or a tool of the writing process of a learning portfolio.

Metacognition: A learner's knowledge of his own cognitive and emotional processes. It allows the learner to consciously regulate learning and thinking, for example, self-evaluation and self-guidance of the learning process.

MySQL: An open source relational database management system for adding, accessing, and processing data in a database.

PHP: A scripting language that is used to create dynamic Web pages.

Reflection: Active thinking that is directed towards oneself and one's actions in different (learning) situations. The aim of reflection is to self-regulate action in the future or following a situation. Reflection is metacognitive action that is geared towards altering knowledge structures through thinking, thus influencing action. Through reflection, metacognitive knowledge of one's learning is transformed into action (self-regulation).

Self-Evaluation: A technique where a student is making decisions of the quality of his work for the purpose of doing better work in the future. Its goal is to have an impact on student performance through enhanced self-efficacy and increased intrinsic motivation.

Tutoring: Supporting the learning process by giving individual instructions, based on the learner's self-guidance skills, and tutors and learners' equality in the guidance process.

Chapter XXIX
The ePortfolio:
A Learning Tool for Pre-Service Teachers

Martine Peters
University of Quebec at Montreal, Canada

Jacques Chevrier
Université du Québec en Outaouais (UQO), Canada

Raymond LeBlanc
University of Ottawa, Canada

Gilles Fortin
Université Saint-Paul, Canada

Judith Malette
Université Saint-Paul, Canada

ABSTRACT

The study reported here explored the use of an ePortfolio in teacher education, focusing on its possibilities for development of competencies in technology. The goal was to assess this competency development over a three-month period and to examine pre-service teachers' perception of the ePortfolio as a learning tool. Results show that pre-service teachers' competencies with technology increase while working on the ePortfolio and that they respond favorably to the ePortfolio as a learning tool. Pre-service teachers feel that the ePortfolio fosters reflection and the development of organizational skills and self-esteem while giving them better chances of finding employment. Solutions and recommendations about improving the use of an ePortfolio as a learning tool in a teacher education program are proposed.

INTRODUCTION

The province of Quebec has invested considerable time and effort to reform the curricula for all its programs. Preschool, primary, secondary, and teacher education programs have all been targeted, and all curricula are based on students developing various competencies. With

Figure 1. Professional competencies for teacher education in Quebec

1	To act as a professional inheritor, critic, and interpreter of knowledge or culture when teaching students.
2	To communicate clearly in the language of instruction, both orally and in writing, using correct grammar, in various contexts related to teaching.
3	To develop teaching/learning situations that are appropriate to the students concerned and the subject content with a view to developing the competencies targeted in the programs of study.
4	To pilot teaching/learning situations that are appropriate to the students concerned and to the subject content with a view to developing the competencies targeted in the programs of study.
5	To evaluate student progress in learning the subject content and mastering the related competencies.
6	To plan, organize, and supervise a class in such a way as to promote students' learning and social development.
7	To adapt his or her teaching to the needs and characteristics of students with learning disabilities, social maladjustments, or handicaps.
8	To integrate information and communications technologies (ICTs) in the preparation and delivery of teaching/learning activities and for instructional management and professional development purposes.
9	To cooperate with school staff, parents, partners in the community, and students in pursuing the educational objectives of the school.
10	To cooperate with members of the teaching team in carrying out tasks involving the development and evaluation of the competencies targeted in the programs of study, taking into account the students concerned.
11	To engage in professional development individually and with others.
12	To demonstrate ethical and responsible professional behavior in the performance of his or her duties.

this reform, all pre-service teachers must now develop 12 new competencies (see Figure 1).

The eighth competency focuses on technology. The pre-service teacher must develop the ability "to integrate information and communications technologies (ICTs) in the preparation and delivery of teaching/learning activities and for instructional management and professional development purposes" (MEQ, 2001, p. 92). Furthermore, pre-service teachers are expected to develop critical judgments about ICTs, to understand the various possibilities offered by these tools, as well as use them in different aspects of their job. In addition, they are expected to be able to transmit the ability to use technology to their students.

Unfortunately, many researchers have found that teacher education programs do not adequately prepare future teachers in terms of technology competencies (Laffey & Musser, 1998; OTA, 1995; Schrum, 1999). In many programs, only one course is geared to teaching with technology, and this is judged insufficient to adequately prepare future teachers to integrated technology in their classrooms (Benson, 2000; Wildner, 1999). To better prepare future teachers, one solution proposed has been to integrate technology throughout the program (Gilligham & Topper, 1999; Peters, 2005).

To foster development of competencies with technology in our pre-service teachers, the faculty at the University of Quebec at Montreal (UQAM) decided in 2003 to integrate a technology component throughout our four-year program to teach language teachers. There is the typical compulsory technology integration course offered in the third year of the program. In addition, our students take a course called *Becoming a Teacher* during their first semester which presents all the basic information needed to function during the teacher training program, including some technology components such as searching the Web for references, making an oral presentation with PowerPoint, preparing a table of contents for a term paper, communicating with a discussion forum, and creating an ePortfolio. This ePortfolio becomes a resource to which pre-service teachers contribute throughout their four years of their training.

To make sure that the ePortfolio is best serving the needs of our students, we are conducting studies at each major milestone in its use. The study reported here explored the first development and use of an ePortfolio in our teacher education program. Specifically, it reports on the introduction of ePortfolio in the Becoming a Teacher course, about students' technology competency in using it and their perceptions of it. Data was collected during the fall semester of 2004. Our goal was to assess this competency development over the three-month period of the term and examine students' perceptions of the ePortfolio as a learning tool during this time. A questionnaire (Desjardins, Lacasse, & Bélair, 2001) was used to measure competencies and students' comments on a discussion forum, for the course provided qualitative data to appraise their perceptions of the ePortfolio as a learning tool.

This report first presents a background review of the literature, next presents the methodology, then presents the results, and closes with conclusions and limitations of this study.

BACKGROUND

In this section, we will define portfolios and ePortfolios as well as explain how the ePortfolio can be used to develop technology competencies.

Portfolios and ePortfolios

Traditionally, a portfolio has been defined as any type of case used for holding materials, such as loose papers, photographs, or drawings. They have been used for many years for a variety of purposes: such as to gather similar resources, like a collection of artwork or a collection of investments, and to present a prospective job candidate, such as the portfolio that a graphic designer typically shows when seeking assignments. Portfolios have also been used by educators to evaluate the progress made by students and to show exceptional student work. Specifically, the Quebec Ministry of Education (2002) suggests three major purposes of portfolios:

1. **Learning Portfolio:** shows progress over a certain period of time by showing all the documents and reflections prepared by a student
2. **Presentation Portfolio:** showcases the best work of a student (rather than all of a student's work, as the learning portfolio does)
3. **Assessment Portfolio:** shows student work that is representative of the variety of particular tasks and that will be assessed by their teacher

In recent years, a new type of portfolio is becoming more widely used: the ePortfolio. According to Barrett (2005, p. 5), the ePortfolio "uses electronic technologies as the container, allowing students/teachers to collect and organize portfolio artifacts in many media types (audio, video, graphics, text); and using hypertext links to organize the material, connecting evidence to appropriate outcomes, goals or standards." In Quebec, many teacher education programs have recently adopted the use of the ePortfolio as a learning tool for pre-service teachers. This tool has grown in popularity because of its numerous possibilities for competency development for those who use it.

In our teacher education program, we chose the ePortfolio for our students. At UQAM, the ePortfolio has a dual purpose for our students: it serves as both a learning portfolio and assessment portfolio. As a learning portfolio, students are asked to use it to collect all documents done in the various courses and to reflect on their learning experiences and future profession. As an assessment portfolio, students use it to demonstrate that they have developed the 12 competencies as demanded by the Quebec Ministry of Education.

All first-year students are required to produce an ePortfolio using FrontPage and to 'upkeep' it for the duration of the program. This software was chosen because its interface is similar to other software the pre-service teachers are familiar with as well as for is compatibility with PC and Mac platforms. Learning this software also provides students with the advantage of learning how to build Web pages, knowledge they can transfer to other teaching and learning situations.

When building their ePortfolios, pre-service teachers can choose to start from scratch or use a template provided to them. This template contains 69 Web pages that are grouped into three categories:

1. Information about the pre-service teacher (such as goals, vision of education, and favorite books and links)
2. Compulsory competencies required by the Ministry of Education (see Figure 1 for a complete list of competencies)
3. Courses taken in the program (see Figure 2)

Students learn how to upload the ePortfolio on the Web, but are not required to do so. Those who do not do so can submit their ePortfolio for assessment on a CD-ROM.

This ePortfolio is evaluated formatively at the end of the second year of the program and summatively at the end of the fourth year, when the student teachers are expected to demonstrate mastery of all 12 competencies.

User assistance with the ePortfolio software is available throughout the program for the pre-service teachers. Assistants who are hired for 15 hours a week are available in the computer laboratories at specified times. All pre-service teachers can seek help.

Figure 2. ePortfolio template of courses taken in the program

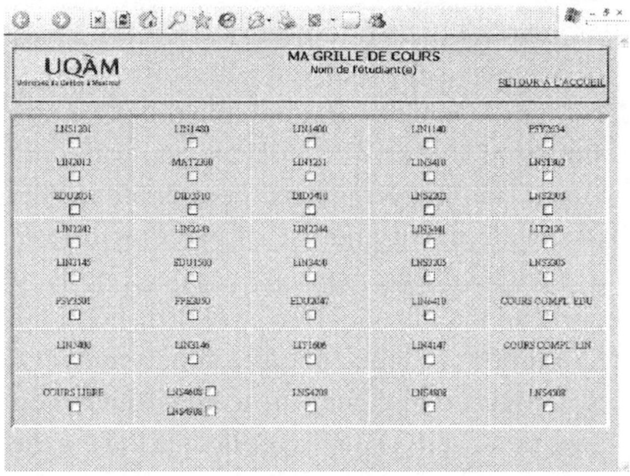

Competencies with Technology

Several researchers have looked at which competencies a teacher needs to properly integrate technology in the classroom (Coughlin & Lemke, 1999; Desjardins et al., 2001; Perrenoud, 1998). Coughlin and Lemke (1999) offer a continuum of competencies that involve curriculum issues, learning and assessment, professional practice, classroom and instructional management and administration. Perrenoud (1999) identified four categories, including the ability to: (1) use word processing programs, (2) adapt computer programs to the learning needs of the students, (3) communicate by means of technology (such as e-mail and instant messenger), and (4) use multimedia tools in the classroom. Haeuw, Duveau-Patureau, Bocquet, Schaff, and Roy-Picardi (2001) propose "families of competencies"—similar to those of Perrenoud—such as communicate and cooperate, organize and manage, document oneself, and create and produce tools and services. The International Society for Technology in Education (ISTE) (2000) has put forward 22 competencies in six different categories which range from technology operations, to conceptual, social, ethical, and legal issues. These standards are used for accreditation in teacher education programs in the U.S.

Another research group has put forward a categorization of competencies and has accompanied it with an instrument that teachers can use to evaluate their own competencies with technology. Desjardins et al. (2001) propose four basic competencies:

1. **Technical Competency:** the capacity to exploit computer hardware and software
2. **Social Competency:** using the computer to communicate with others
3. **Informational Technology:** the ability to exploit technology to find and research content for their classroom, such as using search engines and databases (Dejardins et al., 2001)
4. **Epistemological Competency:** the ability to solve problems and save time using technology (Desjardins et al., 2001)

The questionnaire developed by Desjardins et al. (2001) was used in our research to collect data about these competencies.

METHODOLOGY

This section will present our research questions, our instruments, as well as our participants and their characteristics.

Research Questions

This study had two research questions that focused on the usefulness of the ePortfolio, first as a tool to develop technological competencies and second on the pre-service teachers' perception of the value of this tool in their learning process.

1. Can the students develop technological competencies while creating and using an ePortfolio?
2. What are the pre-service teachers' perceptions of the ePortfolio as a tool in their learning process?

Instruments

Two questionnaires were used for this research project. The first one, the competency questionnaire (Desjardins et al., 2001), was administered to all first-year students at the beginning of the term, September 2004, and again to the same students on the last day of class in December 2004. The competency questionnaire contains 20 questions asking about the students' competency with technology. The survey has five questions about each of the four competencies. Specifically, the survey asks students to grade, on a Likert scale, the extent to which they could perform a particular task with technology. For example, pre-service teachers had to rate on a 1 to 5 scale the extent to which they were able to search for information on the Internet.

The second questionnaire elicited demographic information about the participants and their technology habits. For example, students were asked how often they used computers and for what reason.

In addition, a WebCT electronic discussion forum was used as a data collection instrument. Each week during the semester, a question was submitted to the students for group discussion. Although participation in the forum was compulsory, students were not required to post a response each week. Rather, they were only expected to post a response when the topic was of interest to them. The topic changed each week. ePortfolios were the topic of discussion the week of October 30, 2004. Specifically, we asked students the following question: Do you think creating and using an ePortfolio will help you become a better teacher? Data collected was analyzed qualitatively with the use of ATLAS.ti.

Participants

In total, 54 participants agreed to take part in this study. They were all future language teachers and full-time first-year students in the UQAM language teacher education program. Of the 54 students, 42 were women (78%) and 12 were men (22%). Twenty were between the ages of 18 and 23 (37%), 19 were between 24 and 29 years old (35%), 13 were in the 30-39 age group (24%) and two were over 40 years old (4%).

Of the pre-service teachers, 30 (56%) reported having no training of any kind in technology, while 24 (44%) reported that they had followed one or two courses on the use of certain computer programs (such as MS Word or MS Excel). The pre-service teachers were also asked what type of computer equipment they had at home. A very high percentage (91%) of the pre-service teachers had computers at home, but only 85% of those were linked to the Internet. A little more than a third of the pre-service teachers also had scanners at home. When asked how frequently they used their computer, none of the pre-service teachers replied that they never used it. Seven (13%) answered that they used it only once a week. 23 pre-service teachers (43%) answered that they used computers an average of 4 to 5 times a week, while the rest of the participants (44%) replied that they used the computer every day. Table 1 illustrates the types of computer use that the pre-service teachers reported.

Table 1. Types of computer use by the pre-service teachers

Types of Computer Use	Number of Students	Percentage
Surfing the Web	52	96 %
E-mail	52	96 %
Homework	50	93 %
Bibliographical Web search	29	54 %
Chatting	23	43 %
Scanning images	12	22 %
Using CD-ROMs, games	12	22 %
Creating Web sites	4	7 %
Programming	1	2 %
Others	1	2 %

The two most reported types of computer use by the students are e-mail and surfing the Web. Doing their homework on the computer is also widely performed by the students. Only 54% of the students report using the computer to search the Web for references. Even fewer students (43%) report chatting as a type of computer use. Less than a quarter of the students report scanning images and using CD-ROMs and games. Creating Web sites, programming, and using sound clips were cited as other uses, but by fewer than 10% of the students.

RESULTS AND DISCUSSION

In this section, we first present the results of the survey, then present the results of the analysis of comments posted to the discussion board.

Results of the Survey

At the beginning of the semester, the pre-service teachers' perceptions of their competency with technology were not very high. In addition, they felt that their epistemological and technical competencies were not as developed as their social and informational competencies. By the end of the semester, the pre-service teachers felt that their technological competen-

Table 2. Self-evaluation of technological competencies by the pre-service teachers

Area of Technical Competency	Self-Evaluation in September 2004	Self-Evaluation in December 2004	T-Test Significance
Technical	12.50	14.09	≥0.00
Social	13.60	15.28	≥0.00
Informational	14.82	16.80	≥0.00
Epistemological	11.98	13.70	≥0.00

cies developed, because they self-evaluated their competencies at a higher level. Statistical t-tests for repeated measures indicate that the relationships between the pre- and post-measures are significant.

It is interesting to note that no significant differences were found between the different age groups or between the men and the women. It is possible that no differences were found because of the homogeneity of the group: most participants were women of the same age group.

Analysis of Comments Posted to the Discussion Board

The statistical results are mirrored in the comments the students posted about their competency with technology in the discussion forum. Students commented in general about the ePortfolio and what they thought about the task of producing one. The discussion was very animated, the pre-service teachers building on each other's comments and repeating many key ideas that emerged from the data. Comments were innovative, in that overall they did not reflect what had been said during class time where the conversation concentrated mostly on how to build an ePortfolio, what to include in it, and how it would be evaluated. The discussion forum comments were analyzed qualitatively. In total, over 267 segments of the participants' comments were regrouped in nine categories. Four of the categories were established in advance: these were the competencies established by Desjardins et al. (2001). The five other categories emerged from the data as the analysis progressed. These categories included:

- Usefulness of the ePortfolio as a learning tool in students' personal lives (16 comments)
- Usefulness of the ePortfolio as a learning tool in students' professional lives (21 comments)
- Pertinence of the ePortfolio in the teacher education program (38 comments)
- Use of the ePortfolio for reflection and self-evaluation on their evolution as a teacher (98 comments)
- Use of the ePortfolio process to develop organizational skills (19 comments)

In other words, the pre-service teachers see the ePortfolio in two ways: as a tool for developing competency with technology and as a learning tool in general. The following sections explore the comments in these two general ways.

Perceived Usefulness of the ePortfolio as a Learning Tool for the Development of Competency with Technology

In general, many pre-service teachers commented on the fact that their technological competencies were not very advanced in September and that having a technological prerequisite for the course would be helpful. Also, there were many observations from the participants about how their competency with technology developed during the semester and how this would be useful in their future career. For example, Louise commented:

This course has helped us develop computer skills that will help us all during our program but will also help us when we get to a classroom.[1]

Students were conscious of having developed skills with technology during the semester and attributed a large part of this development to having to create an ePortfolio. Such observations resemble those made by pre-service teachers in Missouri who also felt that technology problems made the production of the ePortfolio more difficult, while clearly showing that they acquired skills with technology while producing the ePortfolio (Placier, Fitzgerald, & Hall, 2001). For example, in our study, Therese commented:

I believe that creating an ePortfolio will give me the chance to master the possibilities offered by a computer which is a learning tool as well as a teaching tool.

Marie added:

I'm not very good with technology and I think this project will help me develop new competencies which should transfer to my teaching eventually.

However, a few students commented that, while they had developed competency with technology during the semester, they were still worried that these competencies were not developed enough and that the task of building an ePortfolio was overwhelming. For example, Marilyn expressed this concern:

I believe the ePortfolio is a wonderful tool but on the other hand I find that it's a huge project for those like me who are very 'basic' with new technologies.

When looking at specific competencies with technology developed through the use of ePortfolios, the pre-service teachers remarked more often on the technical (21 comments) and the epistemological (21 comments) competencies needed to build an ePortfolio than on the informational (3 comments) competencies it developed. There were no comments on the development of social competencies while building an ePortfolio. For example, Beatrice made the following observation on the development of her competency with technology:

If I think about my previous experience, writing a master's thesis is nothing compared to learning a new computer program. I'm sure that creating my ePortfolio will give me a good overview of how it feels to be a beginning language learner who understands nothing and who accumulates mistakes but also how it feels when you finally accomplish something. Eureka! This technological world (of which the ePortfolio is a part of) is for me like a second language. This is where I feel like a learner and I will be able to relate to my future students.

Similarly, Sylvain reported the following perception of the development of his epistemological competency:

The ePortfolio will help us learn how to be good teachers because it will force us to learn how to be well organized and to think about what is important in our Web site.

Most comments about technical competency development focused on the learning of FrontPage to build the ePortfolio. In contrast, comments about the development of epistemological competencies tended to concentrate on the skills of organizing files and folders for the ePortfolio. Comments on the development of informational competencies focused on the use of the Internet either to download or upload information to the ePortfolio.

Perceived Usefulness of the ePortfolio as a Learning Tool

In the discussion forum, students commented on the impact of the ePortfolio on their personal and professional lives, as well as on their teacher education program. The development of the reflective and organizational skills was also the subject of discussion. Following are their comments, and links between the findings here and those of other studies.

ePortfolio and Students' Personal Lives: Many students commented on the usefulness of the ePortfolio on the development of their self-esteem and growth as a person. They were convinced that creating this account of their progress over their four-year program was going to help them learn to know themselves better and, consequently, augment their self-esteem. For example, Nadia commented:

Another thing I understood recently was that the ePortfolio was going to augment our self-esteem because we are going to be working on bringing together all our best work and then work on what is not as good so we will become better persons.

Manon noted that:

I agree with Louise that I'm not quite sure how the ePortfolio will help us on the professional level but I know that on the personal level, it will help me know myself better. It will give me opportunities to examine my strengths and weaknesses.

These comments are consistent with some of the research. McKinney (1998) and Zidon (1996) found that pre-service teachers identified personal growth as an added benefit to building portfolios.

Pertinence of ePortfolio in Students' Professional Lives: If some students were not sure how the ePortfolio would benefit them, the majority of students were positive this tool was going to help them show their best work and that, in turn, will help them find jobs. This is mirrored in the research of Delandshere and Arens (2003, p. 61) who found that their pre-service teachers "believed that the primary purpose of the portfolio is to showcase their teaching performance ... and to prepare in their search for employment." Or, as Stephane observed:

This tool will be an excellent way to promote our program as it was said by Chantal. But it's important to mention that it will promote not only our program but us as education professionals.

Two students did not think the ePortfolio would help them find a job at the end of the program because they believed that school principals and human resource administrators lack knowledge about ePortfolios. Juliane noted:

I don't believe the ePortfolio will give me a lot for my teaching. Let me explain myself. Everyone I have spoken to (teachers, school principals) have [sic] never heard about ePortfolios and are not sure about their usefulness. Nevertheless, I believe that the ePortfolio will be beneficial for myself as a future professional but as for finding a job, now that's another story!"

But most students are optimistic about its value, though one takes a realistic attitude, noting that an ePortfolio is only valuable and useful as a professional tool in the search of a job as long as students invest time and effort in preparing it.

Pertinence of the ePortfolio in the Teacher Education Program: One of the discussions the students had at the beginning of the course was whether or not one is born a teacher or if one develops the skills over time. The students did not reach a consensus, but it did raise many questions, one of which was the role of teacher education programs. Most students tended to agree that whether or not one is born a teacher, the program and the ePortfolio would help them develop the competencies required to become good teachers. Some students commented that the use of an ePortfolio was giving them an edge over students in other education programs. For example, Ronald noted:

I think that our program and the ePortfolio will help us learn how to become a teacher in a modern way and not how to become an old style teacher like they learn in other programs.

Antoine added:

The ePortfolio for me is interesting because it lets us make a link between who we are and what we do in our program, the activities, the discussions like this, etc.

However, it is noteworthy that some pre-service teachers were uncomfortable with the size of the ePortfolio. The notion of linking every course they would take in the four-year program to the development of their competencies seemed overwhelming for some. Others seemed to simply shrug it off and had a "wait-and-see" attitude. When interviewing pre-service teachers, Darling (2001) also found that they thought the task was daunting and the process, intimidating.

ePortfolio and the Development of the Organizational Skills: Many students agreed that the ePortfolio would help them develop organizational skills as well as let them see a sequence of events during their program—a way to tie in all the loose ends, so to speak. For example, Odile noted that:

For me, taking into account my personal history, the ePortfolio will be very important. I was already a teacher in my country and coming here meant taking a step backwards professionally, going back to school to get accredited as a teacher here. I need a link between my past experiences, my present and my future. I think that the ePortfolio will help me build these links.

Victor commented:

Two things will stand out when looking at a student's ePortfolio—on the one hand, the competencies developed and on the other hand the organizational skills used to structure the document.

Peters et al. (in press) also observed how organizational skills can be developed when creating an ePortfolio.

ePortfolio as a Tool for Reflection and Self-Evaluation: Many authors have researched the use of the ePortfolio to promote reflection and self-evaluation (Delandshere & Arens, 2003). Our participants commented profusely on this aspect of ePortfolios. The pre-service teachers recognized the value of the ePortfolio as a tool to facilitate self-evaluation of their learning process and reflection on various aspects of the teaching profession. Consider this reflection from Christine:

The ePortfolio will help us be conscious of our strengths and weaknesses and force us to think of the appropriate means to better ourselves.

Consider, too, this reflection from Gerard:

The ePortfolio can contribute to the process of developing a reflection that will evolve with time about various aspects of education, the goals of teaching, the teacher's role as facilitator in the classroom and the objectives for the students.

Also consider this reflection from Odile:

To conclude I want to say that I think the ePortfolio is a document extremely rich in reflective value and as such is the heart of our teacher education program.

Pre-service teachers seemed to appreciate these reflection and self-evaluation aspects of ePortfolio most. They were quite positive that ePortfolios were excellent tools to help them become better teachers.

SOLUTIONS AND RECOMMENDATIONS

The previous section showed that pre-service teachers are sometimes positive about the benefits of creating an ePortfolio and, at other times, are ambivalent about it. What can teacher trainers do to reassure our students about the value of the ePortfolio as a learning tool? The following sections offer solutions and recommendations for each of the pre-service teachers' concerns.

Technological Competencies

It is unfortunate that many students entering university do not have basic computer skills. When we ask students to start building the ePortfolio in the first session of a teacher training program, those who do not have basic skills, such as cut and paste, and saving and finding files, feel left behind. They scramble throughout the term to keep up with the others.

Three solutions to this problem exist, one which was implemented after the first year of the implementation of the program at UQAM when some pre-service teachers complained about this problem. In January 2003, assistants were hired to work in the computer laboratories to help the pre-service teachers with their ePortfolios. These assistants are graduate students in the field of educational technology. Many pre-service teachers attended skill-building workshops offered by the assistants and showed up for question-and-answer periods that the assistants hosted. These services have been considered helpful by many students and, as a result of the support available, the discrepancy between computer-savvy pre-service teachers and the technological beginners has diminished.

The second solution is easier and less costly to implement. Many of the class activities and homework require teamwork. Teams are formed according to the level of computer knowledge the students have. By pairing a weaker student with one who is more comfortable using technology, the weaker student can learn from the teammate.

The third solution is the most complex because it involves costs, testing, and adding prerequisite courses. Students wishing to be admitted to our program must already submit to language testing. The faculty could require a computer test, too. Students who do not pass the test would be required to take basic computer training during the summer before starting the teacher training program. The problem with this solution is that students usually work during the summer and are not interested in taking a course. If a prerequisite computer course is made compulsory for students who have not passed the test, enrollment in the program might diminish. The other option is to offer this prerequisite course in the first semester and delay the ePortfolio course to the second semester.

ePortfolio as a Learning Tool

The pre-service teachers' major concern about the ePortfolio project was its size; they found it overwhelming. Some were worried that their technical skills would not be sufficient, while others wondered how they would cope with the task itself of linking all they were learning to the development of the competencies.

Our role as teacher trainers is to reassure students about the feasibility of this project and to guide them through the process. The previous section elaborated on ways to make the technical aspects of ePortfolios feel manageable to pre-service teachers. To make the task of linking activities and courses to the development of competencies, our program requires that all teacher trainers specifically outline which competencies are going to be developed in their courses and how students will develop those competencies. With this explicit link stated, pre-service teachers can then see how to relate competencies developed to the competencies covered in their ePortfolios.

Also, during the second year of the program, a formative evaluation of the ePortfolio is scheduled. Pre-service teachers will be required to show how their ePortfolios are advancing, and advice and assistance will be offered to pre-service teachers who need it. This will be implemented for the first time in the winter semester of 2006.

Mentoring for each student that focuses on ePortfolios is another possible solution, but the lack of resources in our department has made this solution impossible.

Finally, the most important solution is to reassure pre-service teachers and show them that the task is not an impossible, one and that the outcomes will definitely be worth the time and effort involved.

CONCLUSION

In this chapter, we have seen that implementing an ePortfolio in a teacher education program can be beneficial for the pre-service teachers in many ways. It helps increase their skills with technology and augments their self-esteem. Also, the pre-service teachers recognize that the use of the tool can help them develop their organizational skills, foster reflection about their future profession, and help them secure jobs in their chosen fields of work. Finally, pre-service teachers note that creating an ePortfolio will help them see links between the activities and courses in their program and the development of their teaching competencies.

However, pre-service teachers are concerned about the size of the task of preparing an ePortfolio and about their lack of skills to undertake this project. Steps are being taken at our university to address these concerns and to make the pre-service teachers aware of the importance of this project. We feel it is important that the pre-service teachers know that we are listening to their concerns and we are offering ways to solve the problems that arise out of the ePortfolio project. In order for this project to succeed, teacher trainers and pre-service teachers have to work together.

Where does that lead us for the future? We are now entering the third year of the project, whose highlight is the first use of the ePortfolio as a means for providing pre-service teachers with a formative evaluation of their education. In 2008, we will pilot the use of ePortfolios for providing pre-service teachers with a summative evaluation of their education as they prepare to graduate. Although we have not yet reached the point where students have completed their ePortfolios, the early results of our work strengthen our belief in our ePortfolio project, and we look forward to the future comments of the pre-service teachers on the value of the ePortfolio after completion.

REFERENCES

Barrett, H. (2005). *White paper researching electronic portfolios and learner engagement*. The REFLECT Initiative Researching Electronic Portfolios: Learning, Engagement and Collaboration Through Technology. Retrieved from http://www.taskstream.com/reflect/whitepaper.pdf

Benson, S. J. (2000). Preparing prospective teachers for technology integration. *Preparing tomorrow's teachers today at NMSU*. Retrieved from http://pt3.nmsu.edu/research.html

Coughlin, E., & Lemke, C. (1999). *Dimension 3: Professional competency continuum*. Santa Monica, CA: Milken Exchange on Education Technology.

Darling, L. F. (2001). Portfolio as practice: The narratives of emerging teachers. *Teaching and Teacher Education, 17,* 107-121.

Delandshere, G., & Arens, S. A. (2003). Examining the quality of the evidence in pre-service teacher portfolios. *Journal of Teacher Education, 54*(1), 57-73.

Desjardins, F., Lacasse, R., & Bélair, L. (2001). Toward a definition of four orders of competency for the use of information and communication technology (ICT) in education. In *Proceedings of the IASTED International Conference, Computers and Advanced Technology in Education*.

Gillingham, M., & Topper. A. (1999). Technology in teacher preparation: Preparing teachers for the future. *Journal of Technology and Teacher Education, 7*(4), 303-321.

Haeuw, F., Duveau-Patureau, V., Bocquet, F., Schaff, J.-L., & Roy-Picardi, D. (2001). Competice: Outil de pilotage par les compétences des projets TICE dans l'enseignement supérieur. *MEN, Direction de la Technologie.*

ISTE (International Society for Technology in Education). (2000) *National educational technology standards.* Retrieved from http://cnets.iste.org

Laffey, J., & Musser, D. (1998). Attitudes of pre-service teachers about using technology in teaching. *Journal of Technology and Teacher Education, 6*(4), 223-241.

McKinney, M. (1998). Pre-service teachers' electronic portfolios: Integrating technology, self-assessment and reflection. *Teacher Education Quarterly, 25*(1), 85-103.

Ministère de l'Éducation du Québec. (2001). *Teacher training: Orientations professional competencies*. Québec: Gouvernement du Québec.

Ministère de l'Éducation du Québec. (2002). *Le portfolio sur support numérique*. Document de travail de la direction des ressources didactiques. Québec: Gouvernement du Québec.

Office of Technology Assessment, U.S. Congress (1995). *Teachers and technology. Mak-*

ing the connection (OTA-EHR-616). Washington, DC: U.S. Government Printing Office.

Perrenoud, P. (1998). Se servir des technologies nouvelles. *L'Educateur,* (3), 20-27.

Peters, M. (2005). Rétrospective de la formation des maîtres en TIC. *La Revue De L'AQEFLS, 25*(2), 130-143.

Peters, M., Chevrier, J., Leblanc, R., Fortin, G., & Malette, J. (in press). Compétence réflexive, carte conceptuelle et Webfolio à la formation des maîtres. *Canadian Journal of Learning and Technology.*

Placier, P., Fitzgerald, K., & Hall, P. M. (2001). "I just did it to get it done"—the transformation of intentions in portfolio assessment in teacher education. In *Proceedings of the AERA Annual Meeting.*

Schrum, L. (1999). Technology professional development for teachers. *Educational Technology Research and Development, 47*(4), 83-90.

Wildner, S. (1999). Technology integration into pre-service foreign language teacher education programs. *Calico Journal, 17*(2), 223-250.

Zidon, M. (1996). Portfolios in pre-service teacher education: What the students say. *Action in Teacher Education, 18*(1), 59-70.

KEY TERMS

Assessment Portfolio: Shows student work that is representative of the variety of particular tasks and that will be assessed by their teacher.

Discussion Forum: Online bulletin board where users can post questions and responses, and where a topic of common interest is discussed by participants.

Epistemological Competency: The ability to solve problems and save time using technology.

ePortfolio: Electronic container used to collect artifacts in many media types.

Informational Technology: The ability to exploit technology to find and research content for their classroom, such as using search engines and databases.

Learning Portfolio: Shows progress over a certain period of time by showing all the documents and reflections prepared by a student.

Presentation Portfolio: Showcases the best work of a student.

Social Competency: Using the computer to communicate with others.

Technical Competency: The capacity to exploit computer hardware and software.

ENDNOTE

[1] All the citations have been translated from French to English and the students' names have been changed in order to protect their anonymity.

Chapter XXX
It was Hard Work but It was Worth It: ePortfolios in Teacher Education

Andrea Bartlett
University of Hawai'i at Manoa, USA

ABSTRACT

Student ePortfolios offer both advantages and challenges for teacher educators. The purpose of this case study is to identify benefits that make the effort worthwhile. Two groups of pre-service teachers—one undergraduate and one graduate—created complex ePortfolios under the direction of a non-technology faculty member. Faculty observations and student evaluations revealed ePortfolios enhance students' educational technology learning, reflection, and collaboration. The author concludes creating ePortfolios was "worth it," and she provides recommendations for making ePortfolios even more valuable for pre-service teachers, their programs, and the schools in which they will someday teach.

INTRODUCTION

Portfolio proponents assert that engaging in portfolio development is linked to self-reflection and the possibility of improved practice; however, few researchers have examined what that involvement has meant for pre-service teachers. (Delandshire & Arens, 2003, p. 58)

In contrast to many other professions, portfolios have been used to assess teaching for only the past 25 years, and electronic portfolios are an even more recent development. Teaching portfolios have been found to provide many benefits, including: (a) a richer, more contextualized view of teaching than standardized tests (Shulman, 1998); (b) enhanced reflection by teachers on their own (McLaughlin

& Vogt, 1996; Valli & Rennert-Ariev, 2002) and students' learning (Fetter, 2003); (c) experience collaborating with peers (Wolf, Whinery, & Hagerty, 1995); and (d) a record of accomplishments for job searches and certification (e.g., Interstate New Teacher Assessment and Support Consortium, National Board of Professional Teaching Standards). Portfolio assessment also contributes to the professionalization of teaching by giving teachers responsibility for their own evaluation (Lyons, 1998a).

The use of multimedia to create ePortfolios provides additional benefits beyond those of traditional paper-based portfolios, such as linking artifacts to teaching standards. This interconnectivity is likely to result in teachers' greater understanding of themselves and the standards, when compared to paper-based portfolios (Norton-Meier, 2003). ePortfolios are also easier to update, store, and share than traditional portfolios. Another important benefit is that pre-service teachers who create ePortfolios learn about technology (Bartlett, 2002). Since ePortfolios may span the teacher education program, they provide an effective vehicle for integrating technology into the teacher education program (Bartlett, 2002) and make it more likely pre-service teachers will implement technology in their classrooms (Goldsby & Fazal, 2000; McKinney, 1998).

While there are substantial advantages, portfolios also present challenges for educators and institutions. Teacher educators who use ePortfolios, in particular, face many hurdles allocating the time, resources, and support necessary to complete a technology-oriented project (e.g., McKinney, 1998; Milman, 1999). Other potential pitfalls include failing to communicate evolving guidelines (Lamson, Thomas, Aldrich, & King, 2001) and focusing on the "bells and whistles" of technology rather than creators' goals (Lieberman & Rueter, 1997).

This chapter is a case study encompassing four years of successful ePortfolio implementation by a teacher educator who began the project with limited technology skills. Two groups of pre-service teachers—undergraduate and masters' students—created complex, standards-based, multimedia portfolios during their two-year programs. Students' perceptions, collected during teacher education and after four months of full-time teaching, are also reported.

Zeichner and Wray (2001) explained the value of such case studies: "It makes little sense to talk about the consequences of using teaching portfolios in general, without an understanding of the particular conditions under which they are constructed and the purposes toward which they are directed" (p. 619). Therefore, the purposes of the chapter are to explain the particular conditions and purposes under which our ePortfolios were created, and to determine whether the implementation was worthwhile through a critical evaluation of successes, problems encountered, and recommended solutions.

BACKGROUND

As a faculty member in Curriculum Studies, rather than technology, I began exploring ePortfolios shortly after receiving tenure. One of my professional roles was coordinator for groups of approximately 25 students as they progressed through their two-year teacher education programs. ePortfolios caught my interest because they appeared to offer the benefits of traditional portfolios, plus the advantages afforded by technology.

After reviewing the literature on portfolios, I decided to go forward, even though I had little idea of what ePortfolios looked like or how I would accomplish my goal. I hoped ePortfolios would benefit my teacher education students, serve as effective performance assessment, and become my new research agenda. Since I had limited technology skills, the technical support offered by a Preparing Tomorrow's Teachers to Use Technology (PT3) Grant in the college gave me the courage to pursue this new interest.

My first experience with ePortfolios was when I created a sample, based on a student's traditional portfolio and videotaped lessons, with the help of a technology assistant. As I edited the videotape into a two-minute teaching clip that would encapsulate this student's strengths as a teacher, I could see the potential for reflection this process offered, and I determined to implement ePortfolios with my next group of pre-service teachers.

Undergraduate Pre-Service Teacher Education Cohort

The ePortfolio sample became the template for a group of 23 undergraduate elementary education majors who developed portfolios over their two-year program, 2000-2002. This portfolio followed Bullock and Hawk's (2001) concept of teaching portfolios:

> *... a teaching portfolio often contains gathered samples of lessons, units of study, and professional documents that reflect the knowledge, skills, and beliefs of the teacher ... The teacher reflects on each piece of work, highlighting strengths, weaknesses, and changes he or she would make in teaching. The teacher's portfolio is used for self-evaluation or external review.* (p. 13)

Furthermore, media were used to put these portfolios into electronic form as defined by Constantino and De Lorenzo (2002):

> *Unlike the paper-based portfolio, the electronic portfolio is a multimedia approach that allows the teacher to present teaching, learning and reflective artifacts in a variety of formats (audio, video, graphics, and text).* (p. 48)

The portfolios consisted of: welcome page, résumé, teaching philosophy, self-evaluation based on state teacher standards, and instructional unit(s). Instructional units included lesson plans with reflections, two to three minutes of teaching video, still photos, and scanned student work samples. The undergraduates used PowerPoint to create their portfolios, which were burned onto CDs and labeled with the college logo.

At the outset of the program, few of the pre-service teachers were familiar with the technology that would be needed to create their portfolios. Since "comprehensive training" has been recommended in the literature (Lamson et al., 2001, p. 13), I arranged for technology assistants, available through the PT3 grant, to provide 17 hours of technology workshops and 18 hours of assistance during class time. Students also had access to a well-equipped and staffed technology center. Despite this high level of support, some students reported they could have used more time, technology instruction, and specific guidelines to complete their portfolios.

A colleague and I used a five-point holistic scoring guide to assess the final portfolios. All but one of the portfolios received a score of 3 or better, meaning they included all required elements in a way that met minimum guidelines. Students received specific comments about the reasons for their scores, focusing mainly on creativity, organization, and use of technology. Levels of reflection were not considered in the assessment, however, and this emphasis would have made feedback even more meaningful (Delandshire & Arens, 2003).

Graduate-Level Pre-Service Cohort

Although pleased with the overall success of our first ePortfolios, I was still far from satisfied. Therefore, I looked forward to a smoother process with my next cohort of 22 students preparing for elementary or secondary certification and a master's degree. In contrast to the traditional teacher education sequence (with student teaching fourth semester), these pre-service teachers student-taught third semester and engaged in a supervised, paid internship fourth semester. This fourth semester internship allowed me to follow students into their first four months as full-time teachers.

Since I had been through the process once, this time I had sample portfolios to show the new cohort. Based on recommendations from former students and the literature (Lamson et al., 2001), I provided a handout with rationale, descriptions of portfolio components, and a timeline for when, over the next three semesters, students would complete each component. We went over the handout at the beginning of each semester, and I referred to it regularly throughout the portfolio process.

The structure of the portfolio was similar to the one the undergraduates had done. Since these students were in a graduate program, I added research activities and career goals to the previous components of welcome page, résumé, teaching philosophy, self-evaluation based on state teacher standards, and instructional unit(s) (see Figure 1 for welcome page template). To create Web-ready portfolios, we changed our software program from PowerPoint to DreamWeaver.

Less technology assistance was available when the graduate-level students created their portfolios than when the undergraduates did theirs. One technology graduate student assisted this second group during the 42 hours of class time and 16 hours of open lab required to complete their portfolios, without benefit of the convenient technology center. Although I originally thought today's students, who grew up with technology, would have little difficulty with DreamWeaver, many struggled. By the middle of third semester, some students had individualistic, creative ePortfolios; however, others had completed little. Knowing something had to be done, cohort faculty asked the technology assistant to develop a template. Once they had the template, struggling students took off and completed their portfolios with much less frustration. Other researchers (e.g., Lamson et al., 2001) have noted the value of templates in creating electronic portfolios, and our experience strongly supports this view.

To improve the holistic assessment process used with the first cohort, I developed a rubric

Figure 1. ePortfolio welcome page template

as recommended in the literature (Goldsby & Fazal, 2001). This rubric more clearly delineated expectations for each portfolio component, including reflection when appropriate. Students critiqued my draft of the rubric, and I incorporated their suggestions into the final form.

WAS CREATING ePORTFOLIOS "WORTH IT"?

In spite of the challenges encountered, there is evidence to support the assertion, "the experience was worth it." This evidence involves both my evaluation of the project and students' perceptions of some of the elements. Students' perceptions were collected through two surveys after submitting their portfolios for evaluation. The first survey was a Likert-scale survey (1 – strongly disagree to 5 – strongly agree), based on Kirkpatrick's Four Levels of Evaluation (1994): (a) attitudes, (b) learning, (c) on-the-job behavior, and (d) organizational impact. The second survey consisted of open-ended questions in which students described what they learned, the benefits, and future uses of their ePortfolios. This evidence will be used to evaluate ePortfolios for their usefulness in enhancing teaching as a career and for assessing student learning and program effectiveness. Findings of the current study will be followed by a comprehensive list of ways to make portfolios even more valuable to students and faculty.

Enhancing Teaching as a Career

Teacher retention is a serious issue for schools today, and I am convinced teachers who renew their teaching expertise by using new teaching methods, engaging in ongoing inquiry about teaching, and assuming leadership positions are more likely to remain in the field. These dynamic, evolving, motivated teachers will create better learning environments for children, and contribute more fully to their schools, than teachers who do not engage in such growth-oriented activities. The following sections discuss evidence collected from students and my own observations concerning the impact of ePortfolios on pre-service teachers' use of (a) technology as an innovative teaching strategy, (b) reflection to improve teaching, and (c) teacher leadership for school improvement.

Technology Expertise and Applications to Teaching

It is widely acknowledged that pre-service teachers (PSTs) need to learn about technology and how to apply it effectively in teaching contexts (Milken Exchange, 1999). PSTs who created portfolios in the present study indicated learning about technology was the main benefit of ePortfolios. These comments are typical: "The ePortfolio forces the student to keep up with the technological curve" and "ePortfolios keep you up with today's technology." These findings support an earlier study by Milman (1999) in which PSTs who completed an electronic portfolio course believed the course provided useful technology skills.

While there was strong agreement among the PSTs that they learned about technology, applications to teaching were less clear. Students who wrote about classroom technology tended to qualify their comments, based on what they knew about local schools: "The technological advantages are great. I can use what I learned to teach my students (if we have the resources) or to help the computer teachers" and "If everyone does it, I see a step towards the future and a new awesome way of teaching." Although students agreed they were more likely to apply technology in their future employment after creating ePortfolios, the PSTs were less likely to anticipate having their own students create ePortfolios. Wilson, Wright, and Stallworth (2003) found this same lack of enthusiasm for implementing electronic portfolios among the secondary PSTs in their study. It is likely students' attitudes would improve if technology were less of an obstacle, and they were given adequate support.

The following semester, these students were full-time interns, responsible for children in local schools. After four months, the new teachers reported using technology in many ways with their students, and two interns actually implemented ePortfolios with their students. The interns did not necessarily credit ePortfolios for this usage, however.

These findings, before and during full-time teaching, indicate a need for ongoing, implicit connections between technology used for ePortfolios and possible classroom applications. To be most effective, these connections would include specific application examples and ways to overcome the roadblocks that often stand in the way of educational technology advancement.

Reflection and Self-Evaluation

Reflection is almost universally considered to be an important goal of teacher education (e.g., Lyons, 1998b). My observations indicate ePortfolios facilitate reflection and self-evaluation, and this was borne out by students' responses to the two surveys. For example, one student wrote the following benefit of her ePortfolio: "Having to organize a portfolio meant I had to organize my thoughts. I found I was more reflective." Another student saw reflection as a future use of her portfolio: "I will use it for reflecting on what I am discovering about myself as I continue to grow as a teacher."

Pre-service teacher reflection on the ability to adapt instruction for diverse learners is an area of particular importance in today's schools. On the quantitative survey, pre-service teachers in the present study did agree their portfolios reflected their understandings of a wide range of learners. Thus, the portfolios addressed, to some extent, the test put forth by Zeichner and Wray (2001):

If the reflection stimulated by teaching portfolios does not help challenge student teacher perspectives that help to maintain the gap between the poor and others in U.S. schooling, then its value is problematic. (p. 627)

While the findings in the area of reflection were encouraging, reflection, like other aspects of teaching, can always be (and should be) improved. Most student reflections were perfunctory analyses of what went well, and I should have led them to consider deeper questions about "... the students, the curriculum, the institutional setting, and the larger social role of schools ... " (Liston & Zeichner, 1990, p. 240).

Assessment rubrics provide further opportunities for enhancing reflection. With the second cohort, I presented a draft rubric to students for their comments, and incorporated their suggestions in the final instrument. Looking back, I see it would have been better to start with students' ideas, instead of my own, and then have students include self-evaluations based on the rubric in their portfolios. Increasing student involvement would have made the process more "student/owner-centric" (E-Portfolio Consortium, 2003, p. 11), and more in keeping with feminist, as opposed to interpretivistic, assessment approaches (Shapiro, 1992, cited in Johnston, 2004).

Collaboration and Teacher Leadership for School Improvement

A teaching career currently requires collaboration with other teachers, administrators, students, and parents. Responses to the quantitative instrument indicated students were slightly positive about whether the process of creating ePortfolios was collaborative, and slightly negative about whether they had sufficient opportunity to view peers' portfolios. Students were even less satisfied with the amount of faculty feedback than with the amount of feedback they received from peers.

These findings indicate students would benefit from appreciably more peer and faculty review. The goal would be to create a "portfolio culture" by "developing a kind of learning environment of intense expectations, care and richness" (Wolf, 1998, p. 41). According to Lyons (1998a), "Validation and understanding emerge through portfolio conversations with peers and mentors, the presentation of portfolio evidence, and the recognition of the new knowledge and practice generated through the process" (p. 5).

In another area related to school improvement, I had hoped my students would come to picture themselves as advocates for electronic portfolios when they became teachers. In actuality, few PSTs planned to advocate for electronic portfolios for either student or teacher assessment at their schools.

This finding led me to consider how ePortfolios could be used as a focus for discussions about teacher leadership. Students should be encouraged to articulate what they believe the benefits and/or disadvantages of portfolios are, and practice presenting their ideas to small groups of peers. More attention should also be paid to school culture and how such cultures can be changed.

Assessments of Student Learning

Delandshire and Arens (2003) found teacher educators and students had different goals for a teaching portfolio. Students considered a portfolio as "an exhibit of their personal development (showing growth and who they are as teachers) and as a useful tool for seeking employment" (p. 61), and instructors were more likely to emphasize performance-based assessment. These goals will be examined in the next sections.

Showcase for Job Searches

Results of the current study indicate students saw multiple purposes for their ePortfolios, with job searches being most prevalent. One student wrote, "After this class is over, I would like to keep adding to this ePortfolio. I would add units from my other education classes and hopefully use the portfolio after our program to assist me in finding a job." A second student stated, "I hope to show it off as I go for my interviews," while a third reported, "It impressed my interviewers with my willingness to use technology."

Pre-service teachers' focus on the usefulness of the portfolio as a job tool is understandable, since most were scheduling job interviews as they finished their portfolios, and other researchers (Meyer & Tusin, 1999; Wilson et al., 2003) have reached similar conclusions. In our case, students emphasized job searches even though handouts listed multiple benefits. Our experience points to a need for ongoing conversations about the uses and purposes of portfolios.

Standards-Based Performance Assessment

Students typically complete a range of assignments as they progress through the foundations courses, methods courses, and field experiences that make up most teacher education programs. However, these assignments are likely to be discarded, along with faculty comments, unless a portfolio is required. A major strength of portfolio assessment, then, is the potential for formative assessment, or the ability to monitor growth over the entire teacher education program.

A critical evaluation of our ePortfolios led me to conclude they function mainly as a summative assessment, and not a formative assessment to the degree I had hoped. The key components—philosophy, teaching unit, and self-evaluation—concentrate on field experiences, and the portfolio could have been expanded to include other parts of the teacher education program. Furthermore, the time spent on the technology of putting the portfolio together meant portfolios remained sketchy until the end of the student teaching semester. While portfolios provided an overall idea of how students were progressing during the program, other assessments were more important in that regard.

The formative assessment value of the portfolio was also affected by the use of performance standards, in our case state teaching standards. The value of standards in teacher education has been a source of some debate. Delandshire and Arens (2003) pointed out teaching standards may lead to fragmented assessments of teaching and serve as substitutes for theory. In our case, students often commented about the overlap among the standards.

For portfolios organized around teaching standards, an overall evaluation that connects to teaching philosophy would make portfolios more meaningful. In this way, standards would function as a "guide to thinking about teaching and learning" (Diez & Blackwell, 1999, p. 359), thereby avoiding some of the pitfalls of standards-based assessment. Ongoing critique of the standards (Darling-Hammond et al., 1998), as they relate to each period in teacher development, would further enhance the portfolio process.

Comprehensive Program Evaluation

ePortfolios have much potential as a means for comprehensive program evaluation. Given the time and technology expertise necessary to complete this type of individualistic ePortfolio, it is unlikely our college would ever receive faculty support for this initiative. An easier, more convenient way to store evidence would need to be found before ePortfolios could be used to assess program effectiveness.

Once these issues are worked out, faculty would be able to use portfolios to determine which aspects of the teacher education program are working and which need to be changed. For example, Snyder, Lippincott, and Bower (1998) found some courses receiving poor student evaluations were mentioned often in portfolios, leading faculty to gain new appreciation for these courses.

In addition to program evaluation, ePortfolios could be used to document teacher education programs' effectiveness when seeking accreditation. In our case, ePortfolios played only a small role in our last National Council for the Accreditation of Teacher Education evaluation, since they were just one of the many types of assessment exhibited.

To be used for accreditation purposes, some teacher education programs are standardizing student portfolios. Allington (2005) pointed out the contradictions: "Our students are pressed to develop standardized ePortfolios (seems oxymoronic to me)" (p. 199). The challenge is to make portfolios that can be used for accreditation purposes, while allowing them to be individualized enough for students to maintain ownership.

Ultimately, student ePortfolios would become part of a teacher education Web portfolio for accreditation purposes (Banta, 2003). Our college is currently moving toward a program-wide evaluation of this type. A university-wide system would further support this program initiative, and some universities currently provide software and servers for student portfolios (e.g., Yost, Brzycki, & Onyett, 2002). This overall structure would help faculty maintain, update, and share information, including portfolio files.

FUTURE TRENDS

Based on our experiences and the literature, I believe ePortfolios of the future should include the following elements:

- **Technology:**
  1. Students take an educational technology course, or show they have the needed skills for making a portfolio, before beginning the portfolio process.
  2. Hardware and software is easy to learn and use. In teacher education, technology with clear applications to classroom teaching is best.
  3. Students have convenient access to computers and software. (In our college, incoming teacher education students will soon be required to have laptops with certain specifications and necessary software.)
  4. Students and faculty have convenient access to technology support. For example, educators in our state are discussing plans to collaborate on a 24/7 technology help line.
- **Reflection:**
  1. Reflections go beyond "How did I do?" to look at larger issues of schools and schooling.
  2. Reflection is emphasized through ongoing conversations and evaluations.
  3. Students use educational literature, such as action research and conceptual articles, to deepen their understandings of classroom experiences (Snyder et al., 1998).
- **Collaboration:**
  1. There are frequent opportunities for peer sharing, faculty review, and input.
  2. Students contribute to the evaluation rubric, and use it to assess their own and peers' portfolios.
  3. There are periodic portfolio presentations to peers, faculty, and others.
  4. Students present their portfolios in a dissertation-style defense to the whole class or a portfolio review committee.
  5. Mentor teachers and other members of the school community participate in the review process.
  6. There is a mechanism for sharing with those in and outside the college (some commercial ePortfolio programs now have this feature).
- **Job Searches:**
  1. Faculty stress multiple purposes of ePortfolios throughout the process.
  2. Students use their portfolios to role play job interviews (Georgi & Crowe, 1998).
- **Standards-Based Performance Assessment:**
  1. Portfolios are organized by state teaching standards, but with connections and continuous critique of standards.
  2. Working files are set up as a learning portfolio, with bins for each standard. Students review their portfolios often and select samples for each semester to show growth.

3. Students write strong philosophy statements, based on theory, which link to all other aspects of the portfolio.

- **Program Evaluation:**
  1. Students provide feedback on the process and how it could be improved.
  2. Student ePortfolios become part of a Web-based institutional portfolio for evaluation and accreditation purposes.

CONCLUSION

ePortfolios have much promise for improving learning and assessment in teacher education and in the schools in which our students will teach. For this promise to be fully realized, new technology will be needed that is simpler and less cumbersome. As Willis (2001) concluded, "Technology should be in the background; it can never be *The Focus*" (p. 4).

This new technology would facilitate reflection and sharing, rather than detract from it, and move us toward a more ideal teaching portfolio that is:

> ... *a structured collection of teacher and student work created across diverse contexts over time, framed by reflection and enriched through collaboration, that has as its ultimate aim the advancement of teacher and student learning.* (Wolf & Dietz, 1998, p. 13)

Putting technology in the background would allow faculty to put the emphasis back on theory, reflection, and collaboration—the way teacher education was meant to be.

Overall, I agree with the student who wrote, "Making an ePortfolio was hard work, but it was worth it." Although not for the faint of heart or risk-adverse faculty member, I encourage other teacher educators to try ePortfolios for the combined advantages that cannot be achieved in the same totality by any other means.

ACKNOWLEDGMENT

The author would like to thank the Lei Aloha Preparing Teachers to Teach with Technology Grant staff for their support with this project. (For a video and student sample from the first cohort's ePortfolio project, please see http://etec.hawaii.edu/oldsite/vr/videos/the_record/feature.htm-teachsource.)

REFERENCES

Allington, R. L. (2005). Ignoring the policy makers to improve teacher preparation. *Journal of Teacher Education, 56*(3), 199-204.

Banta, T. W. (2003). Electronic portfolios for accreditation? *Assessment Update, 15*(4), 3-4.

Bartlett, A. (2002). Preparing pre-service teachers to implement performance assessment and technology through electronic portfolios. *Action in Teacher Education, 24,* 90-97.

Bullock, A. A., & Hawk, P. P. (2001). *Developing a teaching portfolio: A guide for preservice and practicing teachers.* Upper Saddle River, NJ: Merrill Prentice-Hall.

Constantino, P. M., & De Lorenzo, M. N. (2002). *Developing a professional teaching portfolio.* Boston: Allyn and Bacon.

Darling-Hammond, L., Diez, M. E., Moss, P., Pecheone, R. M., Pullin, D., Schafer, W. D., et al. (1998). The role of standards and assessment: A dialogue. In M. E. Diez (Ed.), *Changing the practice of teacher education: Standards and assessment as a lever for change.* (ERIC Document Reproduction Service No. ED417157.)

Delandshire, G., & Arens, S. A. (2003). Examining the quality of the evidence in pre-service teacher portfolios. *Journal of Teacher Education, 54,* 57-73.

Diez, M. E., & Blackwell, P. (1999). Improving master's education for practicing teachers: The impact of the National Board for Professional Teaching Standards. *Teaching and Change, 6*(4), 350-363.

E-Portfolio Consortium. (2003). *Electronic portfolio whitepaper, version 1.0.* Retrieved May 21, 2005, from http://eportconsortium.org

Fetter, W. R. (2003). *A conceptual model for integrating field experiences, professional development schools, and performance assessment in a world of NCATE 2000.* (ERIC Document Reproduction Service No. ED472396)

Georgi, D., & Crowe, J. (1998). Digital portfolios: A confluence of portfolio assessment and technology. *Teacher Education Quarterly, 25*(1), 73-84.

Goldsby, D., & Fazal, M. (2000). Technology's answer to portfolios for teachers. *Kappa Delta Pi Record, 36*(3), 121-123.

Goldsby, D., & Fazal, M. (2001). Now that your students have created Web-based digital portfolios, how do you evaluate them? *Journal of Technology and Teacher Education, 9*(4), 607-616.

Johnston, B. (2004). Summative assessment of portfolios: An examination of different approaches to agreement over outcomes. *Studies in Higher Education, 29*(3), 395-413.

Kirkpatrick, D. (1994). *Evaluating training programs: The four levels.* San Francisco: Berrrett-Koehler.

Lamson, S., Thomas, K. R., Aldrich, J., & King, A. (2001). *Assessing pre-service candidates' Web-based electronic portfolios.* (ERIC Document Reproduction Service No. ED458202)

Lieberman, D. A., & Rueter, J. (1997). The electronically augmented teaching portfolio. In P. Seldin (Ed.), *The teaching portfolio: A practical guide to improved performance and promotion/tenure decisions* (2nd ed., pp. 47-57). Bolton, MA: Anker.

Liston, D. P., & Zeichner, K. M. (1990). Reflective teaching and action research in preservice teacher education. *Journal of Education for Teaching, 16*(3), 235-254.

Lyons, N. (1998a). Portfolio possibilities: Validating a new teacher professionalism. In N. Lyons (Ed.), *With portfolios in hand: Validating the new teacher professionalism* (pp. 11-22). New York: Teachers College Press.

Lyons, N. (1998b). Reflection in teaching: Can it be developmental? A portfolio perspective. *Teacher Education Quarterly, 25,* 115-127.

McKinney, M. (1998). Pre-service teachers' electronic portfolios: Integrating technology, self-assessment, and reflection, *Teacher Education Quarterly, 25,* 85-103.

McLaughlin, M., & Vogt, M. (1996). *Portfolios in teacher education.* Newark, DE: International Reading Association.

Meyer, D. K., & Tusin, L. F. (1999). Preservice teachers' perceptions of portfolios: Process versus product. *Journal of Teacher Education, 50*(2), 131-139.

Milken Exchange on Education Technology. (1999). *Will new teachers be prepared to teach in a digital age? A national survey on information technology in teacher education.* Santa Monica, CA: Author. (ERIC Document Reproduction Service No. ED428072)

Milman, N. B. (1999). Web-based electronic teaching portfolios for pre-service teachers. *Proceedings of the International Meeting of the Society for Information Technology and Teacher Education,* San Antonio, TX. (ERIC Document Reproduction Service ED 432273)

Norton-Meier, L. A. (2003). To e-foliate or not to e-foliate? The rise of the electronic portfolio in teacher education. *Journal of Adolescent & Adult Literacy, 46*(6), 516-518.

Shapiro, J. P. (1992). What is feminist assessment? In C.M. Musil (Ed.), *Students at the centre: Feminist assessment.* Washington, DC: Association of American Colleges.

Shulman, L. (1998). Teacher portfolios: A theoretical activity. In N. Lyons. (Ed.), *With portfolio in hand: Validating the new teacher professionalism* (pp. 23-38). New York: Teachers College Press.

Snyder, J., Lippincott, A., & Bower, D. (1998). The inherent tensions in the multiple uses of portfolios in teacher education. *Teacher Education Quarterly, 25,* 45-60.

Valli, L., & Rennert-Ariev, P. (2002). New standards and assessments? Curriculum transformation in teacher education. *Journal of Curriculum Studies, 2,* 201-225.

Willis, J. (2001). Foundational assumptions for information technology and teacher education. *Contemporary Issues in Technology and Teacher Education, 1*(3).

Wilson, E. K., Wright, V.H., & Stallworth, B. J. (2003). Secondary pre-service teachers' development of electronic portfolios: An examination of perceptions. *Journal of Technology and Teacher Education, 11*(4), 515-528.

Wolf, D. (1998). Creating a portfolio culture. In N. Lyons (Ed.), *With portfolio in hand: Validating the new teacher professionalism* (pp. 41-50). New York: Teachers College Press.

Wolf, K., & Dietz, M. (1998). Teaching portfolios: Purposes and possibilities. *Teacher Education Quarterly, 25,* 9-22.

Wolf, K., Whinery, B., & Hagerty, P. (1995). Teaching portfolios and portfolio conversations for teacher educators and teachers. *Action in Teacher Education, 17,* 30-39.

Yost, N., Brzycki, D., & Onyett, L.C. (2002). Electronic portfolios on a grand scale. *Proceedings of the Annual Meeting of the Society for Information Technology and Teacher Education* (pp. 594-579). Nashville, TN. Retrieved May 28, 2005, from http://dl.aace.org/10835

Zeichner, K., & Wray, S. (2001). The teaching portfolio in U.S. teacher education programs: What we know and what we need to know. *Teaching and Teacher Education, 17*(5), 613-621.

KEY TERMS

The following definitions were retrieved from the Education Resources Information Center, Thesaurus of ERIC Descriptors, http://www.eric.ed.gov/.

Accreditation: Formal or informal assessment of an institution from without, often for accreditation purposes.

Assessment: Data collection and interpretation concerning attainment of educational objectives (nationwide, statewide, or locally) for use in educational planning, development, policy formation, and resource allocation.

Case Study: Detailed analysis, usually focusing on a particular problem of an individual, group, or organization.

Certification: Statement attesting recipient has abilities, aptitudes, achievements, or other personal characteristics that suit an individual to particular positions or tasks.

Educational Technology: Systematic identification, development, organization, or utilization of educational resources and/or the management of these processes—occasionally used in a more limited sense to describe the use of equipment-oriented techniques or audiovisual aids in educational settings. Related term: classroom technology.

Educational Technology Integration: Process of making technological tools and services, such as computer systems and the Internet, a part of the educational environment—includes changes made to the curriculum as well as to educational facilities.

Faculty: Academic staff members engaged in instruction, research, administration, or related educational activities in a school, college, or university.

Rubrics: Evaluation tools, usually grids, that list the criteria for a task or performance, and articulate gradations of quality for each criterion.

Teacher Education: Programs of academic study that prepare students to enter or advance in the education field.

Chapter XXXI
Using ePortfolios to Facilitate Professional Development Among Pre-Service Teachers

Gail Ring
Ball State University, USA

Sebastian Foti
University of Florida, USA

ABSTRACT

The purpose of this study was to examine an electronic portfolio project as it was implemented in a teacher education program in a College of Education to determine how these electronic teaching portfolios affect a student's professional development. Much of the recent portfolio research discusses portfolio implementation in an anecdotal manner, focusing on studies undertaken in a single class, or with a small population of pre-service teachers. This study investigated the implementation of an electronic portfolio project throughout a four-year period, collecting data from students enrolled in the Early Childhood, Elementary, and Secondary Education programs. It explored the impact the development of an ePortfolio had on the professional growth of these students.

INTRODUTION

Mokhtari, Yellin, Bull, and Montgomery (1996) contend that, "In classrooms, portfolios encourage teacher self-direction and reflection and form the basis for professional development" (p. 247). This chapter focuses on the experiences of students during the implementation of an ePortfolio project in a College of Education. The central issue of this chapter pertains to the impact the development of an electronic portfolio has on a student's professional development. Specifically, do students who maintain an electronic portfolio critically understand the standards that govern the profession better, become more reflective practitioners, better collaborators, and more proficient users of technology? Arter and Spandel (1992) stress the significance of these characteristics for students: The perceived benefit for instruction is that the process of assembling a portfolio can help develop student self-reflection, critical thinking, responsibility for learning, and content area skills and knowledge (p. 38). The development of an electronic portfolio, particularly reflection in the process and on the process, can encourage students to take charge of their learning. It is our contention that functioning within the proper framework, portfolio development can aid students in making links between theory and practice—what they learn in their courses to what they do in their teaching internship—thus contributing to their professional development. Kozma (2000) pointed out that if learners are not yet skilled in taking charge of their learning, our tools and environments should help them move in that direction. This chapter justifies the use of digital portfolios as a way to facilitate the professional development of students.

BACKGROUND

Electronic Portfolio Project Goals

Beginning in the 2000-2001 academic year, students enrolled in the PROTEACH (Professional Teacher) program in the College of Education were required to develop and maintain electronic portfolios that demonstrated their competency in the 12 Florida Accomplished Practices (FAPs) (Appendix A). Implemented in the early 1990s by the Florida Education Standards Commission, the FAPs are essentially the best practices of teaching. The Electronic Portfolio Project was designed to provide a forum through which students demonstrate their proficiency in these 12 practices. Campbell, Cignetti, Melenyzer, Nettles, and Wyman (2001) suggest: "As students connect their work to standards, they begin to see the value and relevance of their work" (p. 50). We made the prediction that portfolio development would facilitate students' connection-making, and highlight the value and relevance of their teacher preparation work. In addition to demonstrating their competence in the FAPs, these student portfolios addressed other aspects of the educational experience such as a student's self-assessment and decision-making skills, ability to reflect on teaching and learning, as well as his or her ability to use technology.

Historically the burden of accountability was placed on the professors; however, accountability is becoming a shared responsibility among teacher preparation programs, faculty, and students. Responding to the challenge of shared accountability, faculty in our college decided collectively that each student should be responsible for the selection, storage, and presentation of their illustrations for each of the 12 Florida Accomplished Practices in a Web-based electronic portfolio. The Electronic Portfolio Project was a college-wide innovation that impacted administrators, professors, and students, as well as the curriculum of our teacher education program. As such, it has been a catalyst for change in the teacher education program.

METHODOLOGY

The purpose of this study was to examine an electronic portfolio project as it was implemented in a teacher education program in a College of Education to determine how these electronic teaching portfolios affect a student's professional development. Much of the recent portfolio research discusses portfolio implementation in an anecdotal manner, focusing on studies undertaken in a single class or with a small population of pre-service teachers. This study investigated the implementation of an electronic portfolio project throughout a four-year period, collecting data from students enrolled in the Early Childhood, Elementary, and Secondary Education programs. It explored the impact the development of an ePortfolio had on the professional growth of these students. Of interest is the student's increased understanding of the standards that govern the teaching profession, propensity to collaborate with peers, capacity for reflection, as well as changes in his or her use of technology that may have occurred as a result of participating in this study. It was our goal that students, through the development of their ePortfolios, begin to make connections among practical techniques, the state standards, and the theories of learning development and cognition.

The case study method was used to address the research questions. Case study methods work well for this particular type of study because the focus is on a program or group in a real-life context (Yin, 1994), and it is well suited to a study interested in process (Merriam, 1998). Students were asked to complete voluntary surveys pertaining to the ePortfolio, their knowledge and understanding of the FAPs, and technology proficiency prior to beginning their portfolios (n=345), midway through the PROTEACH program (n=269, and after they graduated, n=126). In addition, the students' electronic portfolios were examined, exit interviews were conducted, and field notes were reviewed as they pertained to the questions under study. The portfolios were examined over the one- to three-year period of development and revision to understand how the portfolios evolved.

Also collected and analyzed were student questions and comments, as well as audiotapes from student exit interviews, which were transcribed and analyzed. Addressing student questions—such as "What do you think of my portfolio?" or "I'm not really sure I understand how to write a rationale statement; would you give me some feedback?"—contributed to greater insight into students' problems and misunderstandings, and ultimately led to additional observations being recorded by the researcher. Moreover, these questions and suggestions contributed to the extensive online support system put in place for students and faculty. Portfolio evaluations were conducted based on the assumption that each student is unique and approaches the project from a unique perspective with varying degrees of proficiency pedagogically, reflectively, and technologically. Descriptive interpretations were constructed explaining features and patterns of each student's and groups of students' level of participation and professional development.

Description of the Site

The PROTEACH program is an NCATE-accredited, three-year bachelor and master's degree program culminating in teacher certification. The PROTEACH faculty undergirds their programs with knowledge drawn from research on effective teaching, teacher reflection, and subject area learning (http://www.coe.ufl.edu). The faculty in the elementary PROTEACH program at the University of Florida has identified the development of critical reflection as the primary goal of their teacher education program (Ross, 1989). Participants in this study were students majoring in early childhood, elementary, and secondary education content areas. Secondary education students develop their ePortfolios over the course of their one-year graduate PROTEACH program, whereas the early childhood and elementary students complete their portfolios during their three-year PROTEACH program. The portfolios of all students were examined, while participation in face-to-face interviews and online surveys was voluntary. All student data were kept confidential and each student assigned a code to protect anonymity.

Participants

The participants in this study were students enrolled in the PROTEACH program. During the four-year period under study, 1,025 students participated in the Electronic Portfolio Project, including 132 early childhood students, 704 elementary students, and 189 secondary education students. Both male and female students participated in this study. Again, all student data were kept confidential and each student assigned a code to protect their anonymity.

SIGNIFICANCE

Although there are many definitions of portfolios found in the literature, the definition that was most closely aligned with the conceptual framework of the University of Florida Electronic Portfolio Project is that of Winsor and Ellefson (1995): "A fusion of processes and product. It is the processes of reflection, selection, rationalization and evaluation, together with the product of those processes" (p. 68). A goal of the ePortfolio project was to move beyond using portfolios solely as an assessment tool to using portfolios as a means through which our students become reflective professionals. The ePortfolio is comprised of various components representing students' instructional and academic experiences (Appendix B). This study is significant because it goes beyond anecdotal information to the evaluation of the use of portfolios throughout a teacher education program. This longitudinal study allowed the researchers to observe the project throughout the first four years of implementation, making it possible to identify emerging problems and implement necessary changes quickly.

DISCUSSION

Students' Increased Understanding of the Standards

Pre-service teachers exhibit professional growth through increased understanding of the standards that guide the profession. One of the goals of the portfolio project was to help students develop a greater understanding of the Florida Accomplished Practices. Students must understand the FAPs enough to engage in reflection upon them and their relationship to coursework and to student teaching in order to develop a comprehensive portfolio. Prior to the implementation of the electronic portfolio project, professors listed the FAPs on their syllabi; some, however, went a step further and connected their assignments to the FAPs. The responsibility of reporting student understanding and application of the FAPs was placed on the individual professor. We argue that simply putting standards on a syllabus is not enough to guarantee that students understand them or their purpose. Although the FAPs were on the syllabus, we could not ensure that our students were reading, understanding, and operationalizing them; and even if they were, we were still faced with the dilemma of proving to college review committees that this was, in fact, happening. Rather then continuing to place this burden on the faculty, the intent of the portfolio project was to include the students in the reporting process. It was to become the responsibility of the students to collect artifacts from their teacher education classes and field experiences, select appropriate artifacts for inclusion into their portfolios, and reflect on these artifacts by informing the reader of why an artifact was selected and how it related to a given practice. Throughout the teacher education program, students produce and gather a variety of illustrations for inclusion into their portfolios such as lesson plans, presentations, tests, written papers, and so forth which demonstrate their increasing abilities as future teachers. For each of these illustrations, students describe how they have demonstrated an understanding of the FAP in the assignment.

Researchers have found that the development of a portfolio aids students in making links between theory and practice (Arter & Spandel, 1995; Campbell et al., 2001; Ring, 2002). The ability to make these links contributes to the professional development of our students. A student's ability to make informed decisions about what best represents him/her as an educator reflects a high level of professional knowledge. According to Barton and Collins (1993):

Teacher education programs that function at the undergraduate and master's levels commonly emphasize practice and expose students to a variety of practical techniques that have been shown to work successfully with learners. Some programs seek to go a step further and link these practices with theories of learning, development, and cognition, although students often fail to make these linkages. (p. 201)

For many students, developing a portfolio made the FAPs more "conscious" and helped them understand and recognize what the state expects of its teachers. In addition, it helped them appreciate the complexity of teaching and examine the appropriateness of their teaching choices.

The FAPs were not explained to me at all, I would sit down and try to figure out what they were talking about, because we really hadn't gone over them. I think the FAPs are valuable, and requiring us to give reasons why an artifact was chosen is also valuable. Some people that I talked to had a problem with that for some reason, but if you can't explain what the assignment has to do with the FAPs then you need to rethink it. (PA1.1)

This student has learned that the development of the rationale statement helps one link theory to practice. For example, if a rationale statement mentions specific elements of the artifact that pertains to the FAP, the viewers of the portfolio will have a greater understanding of the student's perspective on that assignment, what they learned, and the connections the student can make to the FAP.

Students seemed to better understand and apply the FAPs when they became participants in the decision-making process involved in the selection of appropriate FAP illustrations and when they had to articulate how their course work and student teaching related to the particular FAP. This is supported by the following student comments:

I knew that I had done an analysis of my teaching videos, but I never would have thought to call it continuous improvement. But that was what it was, me improving on the way that I was teaching. Before I began to develop my portfolio I just thought about the assignment as something I had to do for a class. Connecting the assignment to a particular practice gave it grounding in my professional education. (PA3.1)

The electronic portfolio helped me to look at assignments through the lens of the accomplished practices, more specifically a "teacher's lens." (PA5.4)

These comments reinforced Dollase's (1996) belief that the portfolio has the potential to be transformative, encouraging student learning through decision making and explanation. Based on student feedback, through the development of an ePortfolio and through the process of collecting, selecting, and reflecting, our students have gained an increased understanding of the FAPs. Learning was taken to a new level throughout the development of the ePortfolio. For example, when the students attempted to articulate why their work was connected to a particular practice, they sometimes came to the conclusion that what they originally thought appropriate was not. It was through their portfolio activity (collect, select, and reflect) and the feedback from their professors and peers that students began to understand the complexity and importance of this task.

Seventy percent of the students (n=345) surveyed at the beginning of the program had no knowledge of what the FAPs were or why they were instituted in the PROTEACH program. Midpoint surveys show that 20% of the students (n=269) surveyed midway through the program could define what the FAPs were, yet few could explain their relevance to the teacher education program, as supported by the following student's statement:

I honestly haven't looked at them, I know they exist, but that's pretty much it. (PA8.1)

Eighty-nine percent of the students (n=129) surveyed after graduation felt that developing an ePortfolio helped them gain a deeper understanding of the FAPs.

It not only defined them for me, but also allowed me to apply my knowledge on each one. (PA9.4)

Because I had to critically think about how to meet them. (PA9.6)

Students' ability to critically examine their work was a key component of the ePortfolio and is essential to a pre-service teacher's professional development.

Enhancing Students' Capacity for Reflection

At a general level, reflection is defined as a way of thinking about educational matters that involves the ability to make rational choices and to assume responsibility for those choices (Goodman, 1984; Ross, 1987a; Zeichner & Liston, 1987). Moreover, Ross (1989) contends:

Preparation of reflective practitioners requires teaching not only the elements of reflection but also increasing the range and depth of knowledge in each student's appreciation system. (p. 29)

Dewey (1933) believed that the development of reflective capabilities also requires the development of several attitudes and abilities, such as introspection, open-mindedness, and willingness to accept responsibility for decisions and actions. Winsor and Ellefson (1995) believe reflection upon practice and beliefs is critical to professional growth and helps teachers learn who they are as teachers and become aware of how they teach.

The study examined changes in the quality of the students' reflection statements over time and the students' final thoughts on the development of an electronic teaching portfolio. According to Johnson and Rose (1997), developing a portfolio is a lifelong skill that is necessary for future success. In addition, the development of an electronic portfolio, particularly reflection in the process and on the process, may aid students in making links between theory and practice and what they learn in their courses to what they do in their teaching internship. It was our hope that developing an electronic portfolio would encourage students to take charge of their learning and develop a habit of reflection.

If portfolios are vehicles for constructing knowledge, then the activity of reflection is central to the development of teaching portfolios. In exploring the use of portfolios, Lyons (1998) contends:

The real power of a portfolio process for teacher interns or master teachers may well be in the acts of constructing, presenting, and reflecting on the contents or the evidence of a portfolio. This reflective, interpretive activity can result in the surety of the realization, 'Yes, I am the teacher. I am ready to take responsibility for a class.' Here the portfolio serves its most significant purpose: as a scaffolding for reflective teacher learning. Instead of presenting a set of courses and credits earned for purposes of credentialing and certification, the teacher apprentice—or expert—stands at the center of his or her own learning, defining and defending the authority of a credential. (p. 5)

The research of Lyons (1998), Schön (1983), and others implies that discussions with pre-service teachers can help them become more reflective about their practice. Moreover, student participation in the selection of information that is placed into the portfolio is one of the key features of an accurate representation of achievement and ability (Defina, 1996; Ring & Foti, 2003). It was when students were engaged in the process of selecting an illustration, connecting it to a Florida Accomplished Practice, explaining the connection (written in the rationale statement), and making appropriate and necessary revisions, that students became more inquiry oriented and more reflective. We believe that providing students the opportunity to engage in critical reflection is essential to their professional development.

In the header (Appendix C) of each illustration, students add a rationale statement. The rationale statements are two to four sentences in length and provide the opportunity for the student to articulate why the illustration was chosen and how it demonstrated proficiency in the practice. These reflective statements contain the evidence that the student has in fact operationalized the assignment, and understands and can articulate, in his or her own words, the purpose of the illustration. Ideally, to understand the level of the students' understanding about a practice, one should be able to simply read the rationale statement. Predictably, early versions of student rationale statements did not demonstrate that our students were moving beyond what Elder and Paul (1996) described as stage one of critical thinking: the unreflective thinker, "thinkers who lack the ability to explicitly assess their thinking and thereby improve it." Nor did these statements provide evidence that students were "reflecting in practice and reflecting on practice" (Schön, 1988) about both the intellectual and ethical dimensions of classroom teaching and learning. Examples of early rationale statements provide evidence of this:

Provide students with opportunities to demonstrate proficiency through a variety of assessments. (PA2.8 Statement 1.1)

The following poem was used in a lesson plan designed to teach students how to use higher order thinking when reading and interpreting poetry. (PA2.1 Statement 4.1)

Coaching and feedback is essential in helping students develop skills of reflection. If we are to enhance a student's reflective capacity, it is important to provide him or her with feedback in the reflection process. Students who began their portfolios in the fall or spring semester were provided extensive feedback from the project director to help them improve the quality and depth of their rationale statements. The following are examples of the above rationale statements revised by students after feedback and coaching:

I chose this lesson plan to demonstrate the variety of assessments I use to evaluate my students. Not all students can demonstrate their proficiency through quizzes alone, so I included a variety of assessments. Students will write journal entries, write a first draft of a science fiction story, take a quiz, and read for comprehension. (PA2.8 Statement 1.1)

Poetry often frustrates readers because to understand a poem, one must solve the riddles of imagery, language, and structure that impart the poem's meaning. I believe that poetry is writing's highest art, requiring a complicated creative and intellectual thought process on the part of the writer and the reader. Teaching students to read, understand, and appreciate poetry means introducing a most Understanding a poem often requires Poetry The following poem was used in a lesson plan designed to teach students how to use higher order thinking when reading and interpreting poetry. (PA2.1 Statement 4.1)

Through the students' further reflection and subsequent revision of their rationale statements, we witness a vast improvement in their reflective dialogue. The improvement of rationale statements provides evidence that, through the opportunity to write reflective statements, and with the necessary coaching on these statements, our students were becoming more reflective. Their reflective ability developed over time, with coaching and with experience.

Predictably, students who began to work on their portfolios early in the program were able to spend more time reflecting on their illustrations and modified their portfolios based on new information. These students moved beyond what Fuller (1969) described as the self or survival stage of teaching, where a student is focused on him or herself, to the task stage where the focus begins to center more around the task of teaching. This is evident in the comments of one student:

The portfolio, in shaping my way of teaching, was an incredibly beneficial experience, for a lot of reasons. One basic reason was that it allowed me to look at the timeline of the teaching I had done, and for that matter the coursework that I had done to look at all of that work and fit it into a timeline or a framework or paradigm to look at myself as a teacher, and also the way I progress as a teacher, and also the way I would create ideas around which to teach. When I was teaching, I was trying to make the connection between what I was teacher and what was printed there. I can't say I did that every time, but I did try to do that. (PA2.1)

Unfortunately, early in the implementation process, students were not encouraged to view the portfolio as a formative experience, and professors were not providing students support in the reflection process. In many cases the only feedback the students received was provided by the project director contributing to their perception that the portfolio was not an integral part of the teacher education program, rather than another assignment tacked on. Lin, Hmelo, Kinzer, and Secules (1999) argued that support is necessary for high-level reflective thinking. The students agree that feedback/coaching is a necessary element of developing an ePortfolio and one that seemed to be missing from their teacher education program.

Increased integration, make it a requirement in completing each PROTEACH course to put up an illustration from that course by the end of the semester. The instructor can then review the illustration and give feedback. This will help the student complete the project continuously throughout the program without waiting until the end. (PA4.5)

More than half the students (64%) surveyed attributed the development of the ePortfolio and engaging in the act of collecting, selecting, and reflecting to helping them become more reflective practitioners.

I feel it helped me become a more reflective practitioner because I really had to put a lot of thought into the portfolio as a whole. You can't just wing a portfolio. It has to be well thought out. (PA9.85)

Not surprisingly, 25% of the students surveyed did not believe that the ePortfolio contributed to their reflective practice; they believed that the lack of integration made the portfolio seem more of an assignment than a tool for reflection.

It didn't [make me more reflective]. It was helpful to look back through my work and see the amount of growth. However, the ePortfolio does not require reflection in order to be completed. It merely asks for perfection of skills. For example, the ePortfolio is considered complete if all of the links work. However, no feedback was given based on the quality of our work, our rationale statement, or our choice of pieces. (PA9.74)

The remaining 11% of the students surveyed believed that the portfolio supplemented a teacher education program already embedded in reflection.

Collaboration

In addition to understanding the standards, reflecting in practice and on practice, Groce, Henson, and Woods (1999) include collaboration with colleagues as evidence of professional growth. Indeed, 98% of the students surveyed stated that they collaborated with their classmates on the development of their ePortfolios. Most of the collaboration was reciprocal; for example, 86% of the students said they helped their peers, and 73% said their peers helped them. Most often students could be seen working in groups in the portfolio lab or one of the college's computer labs. One group of students implemented a *Portfolio Buddy System* where they worked together and kept on task as a group.

Technology Proficiency

Just as innovation diffusion moves along a continuum, appropriate and effective technology use develops over time as a teacher progresses from a novice to a more advanced user. Although 84% of the students surveyed self-assessed themselves as intermediate to highly skilled users of technology, words like fear, frustration, and anxiety were heard repeatedly by students when describing the thought of developing an ePortfolio. This supports the data of Whetstone and Carr-Chellman (2001) who found that, regarding use of a computer, an overconfidence exists in pre-service teachers when compared to actual practice.

Even though many students surveyed (71%) had developed Web pages in their technology class, it became evident that without the opportunity for continued practice—that is, uploading assignments to the ePortfolio throughout the semester—students soon forgot what they learned and remained fearful of the process. Yet throughout the four-year period of the study, student use of technology changed dramatically, as evidenced by Figures 1 and 2. Furthermore, in the final survey, 82% of the students surveyed stated that development of an ePortfolio increased their technology skills.

I was able to use the technology and apply it to something relevant to me. This allowed me to successfully use technology and understand how it works and therefore transfer it to other aspects of my like, i.e. I put this newfound knowledge on my résumé. (PA9.63)

Making students use the technology promotes their understanding of their world. Many students surf the Web or e-mail but rarely understand what is involved. We are in an age where children are more and more inundated with technology and teachers should join them instead of letting them get ahead of us. (PA8.42)

It was awesome to be able to put my Web site link at the top of my résumé and have interviewing principals go there and see what I created. (PA2.9)

TENSIONS

Student tensions revolved around issues of integration, time, and support. Colleges and universities are under pressure to develop a quantitative assessment system, and portfolios simply do not serve that purpose. It is difficult to ensure the validity and reliability of an electronic portfolio, particularly a student-centered one such as ours where student choice and decision making is an essential element. Teachers are also being asked to engage with students in new ways—such as monitoring, small group work, conferencing with students over portfolios, coaching performances in simulations—and to assume more authority for evaluation, but with little assistance or practice in designing and using new instructional and assessment strategies.

Figure 1. Technology-rich artifacts: Year 1

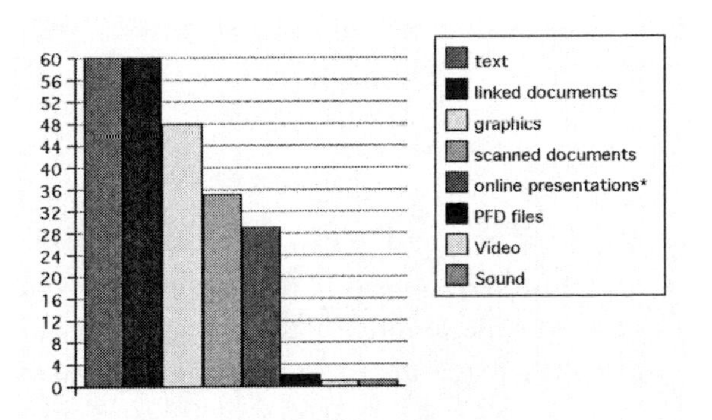

Figure 2. Technology-rich artifacts: Year 4

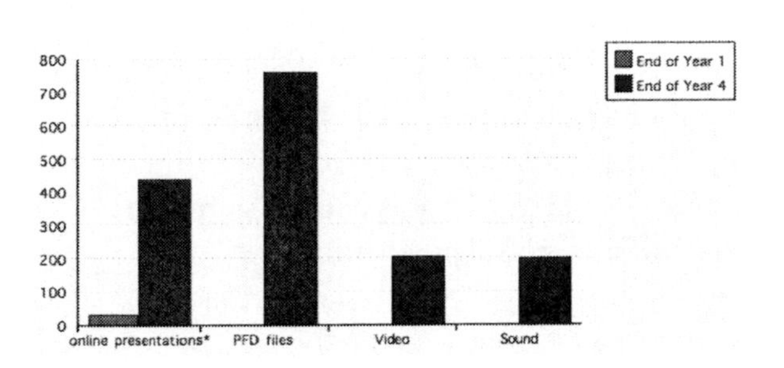

In an environment that has typically rewarded swift, tidy work, many teachers, like their own students, require reassurance that they can take time to ponder and discuss new concepts, participate in a 'grungy' process, as one teacher put it, and make mistakes along the way. Even with such reassurance, however, many teachers are reluctant to lower their tenuous comfort zone by risking the loss of what little control, respect, motivation to learn, and academic success that they are able to command among students in the current school environment. (as quoted by Aschbacher, 1994, p. 28)

Van Sickle and Hoge (1991), however, contend that attention to this complex type of learning and assessment enables students to develop higher-order thinking skills and to develop strategies for learning. When assessment follows constructivist form, then the student will have a more active role in the assessment process. By its very definition, constructivism indicates that assessment should become an ongoing developmental process. According to Nickerson (1989), "If higher-order cognitive functioning is a major goal of education, assessing such functioning is likely to be futile until better methods are developed for measuring success in this regard" (p. 24).

LESSONS LEARNED

The time has come, however, for us to shift our attention away from "how to put a portfolio together" toward a systematic look at the implications of portfolio use in teacher education (Herman & Winters, 1994). While this statement was made prior to the days of widespread electronic portfolios, it is equally germane to the issue of electronic portfolios.

As with any innovation, early proponents predict—indeed, hope—for extreme changes caused directly by the innovation itself. While we agree that statements like "Electronic portfolios have the potential to ... " are necessary to promote their use, in reality, many of the effects credited to new innovations are often related to the context in which they are applied. In our study, for example, the focus of the development process for students was on understanding the relationship between the theory and practice of Florida's Accomplished Practices. This contextual frame cannot be separated from the use of the innovation, that is, the electronic tool. Similarly, the development of a personal pedagogical philosophy, as well as rationale statements, related significantly to the professional development of many of the students. Changes would no doubt also be observed in non-electronic implementations of similar portfolio initiatives. We feel, however, that the building of the electronic portfolio has distinct advantages over its paper counterpart. These advantages, which include the ability to update, maintain, and display indefinitely, and necessitate the monitoring of evolving professional standards, cascade into a variety of professional learning activities that can have a positive impact on a teacher's professional development. Unfortunately, technological aspects of the electronic portfolio process introduce a number of difficulties, some of which may have serious detrimental effects on the success of an electronic portfolio project. A brief discussion of some of these difficulties follows.

Faculty Issues

The mode of instruction in most teacher education institutions is largely teacher directed. Even if teachers promote constructivism in their classrooms, they often do so in non-constructivist learning environments. The application of many technological tools, and electronic portfolios specifically, is best carried out in a more student-centered environment. While there is clearly a way to engage in highly directed teaching while assigning electronic portfolio development outside of regular classroom activity, there must be a level of teacher buy-in that is obvious to the students. The teacher must exhibit an understanding of the portfolio development process. For example, if students are asked to "print out and hand in" their portfolio work, this discourages the use of multimedia by the students. Unfortunately, there is a qualitative gap between understanding how to access portfolio "assignments" and the portfolio development process. In our program, several professors viewed the portfolios as static assignment containers and questioned whether "creating and reviewing portfolios of performance-based work really increase our knowledge of what students know and are able to do." They wonder "if class grades, along with Pathwise documentation of the Florida Educator Accomplished Practices (FEAPs) are not sufficient documentation of the performance of student teachers who ALL pass state certification tests, are ALL judged as eligible for rehire, and who are widely sought by districts in Florida and outside Florida because of their competence" (Bondy & Ross, 2004, p. 286). Fair enough. If we look at portfolio development as a summative assessment tool, we may come to the conclusion that it is unnecessary. However, most proponents of portfolio development view the process as one of building a personal cultural artifact, closely related to long-term professional development, perhaps more related to lifetime learning than to specific curricular goals. They also view portfolio development as being formative, and some reject the use of portfolios as *summative evaluation* tools altogether. This is important as it relates to the development of program goals and faculty consensus building.

The value of electronic portfolios, therefore, cannot be assumed. In any serious electronic portfolio project undertaking, the intended outcomes and perceived values must be established, preferably through consensus. The enterprise involves a large awareness component, and issues of practicality vs. idealistic hopefulness are sure to arise.

A common practical question about portfolio initiatives is whether or not principals are actually willing to look at them. Discussions with principals during and after our study indicate that many principals favor employment candidates that can immediately show and discuss illustrations of professional experience. In addition, demonstrating this knowledge through the use of technology is considered a plus. "A candidate who has developed an electronic portfolio is highly desirable" (Bill Hatcher, Superintendent of the Kern School District, CA, USA). Although principal comments are anecdotal, student surveys (as well as e-mails from former students) included specific comments: "My employer viewed mine and was very impressed." "I gave my Web-address [ePortfolio URL] to potential employers via e-mail for them to look over. I was offered several interviews, and later positions on the first interview." "In an interview where I am teaching now, I actually went to my portfolio online and I think it weighed heavily in my favor, because I got the job." Clearly, some principals are willing to examine student portfolios as part of the hiring process.

While practical considerations related to portfolio implementation projects are important, the idealistic hopefulness mentioned earlier should not be trivialized. There are large issues about the future of education that will no doubt play a significant role in teaching and learning. These issues, related to the transition from 20th and 21st century views of knowledge, have been well documented. The idea of lifelong learning has also matured. Ouane (2001, Preface) put it this way:

What is clear is that the context of lifelong learning has changed and the utopian and generous vision hitherto characterizing lifelong learning has now become a necessary guiding and organizing principle of educational reform.

We know that it will become increasingly important for students to become more self-directed, self-managing, and self-assessing. It is likely that more formative, self-assessment strategies and techniques will become more common, and perhaps even dominant in the 21st century. In an educational context, self-management implies the ability to work associatively—that is, to identify important components of knowledge structures and integrate those components into a coherent whole. Self-management also requires the integration of new knowledge into a more global, or at least a wider, understanding of the world. The learner in a connected world will need to identify specific communities of practice and be able to become situated in those communities in order to make sense, contextually, of the information s/he encounters. This kind of work is enhanced by practices that support reflection in an explicit fashion. Portfolio initiatives support a shift towards more global communications skills and more self-directed work practices. Current assessment procedures often do not. In fact, teachers often use very different language when discussing supporting students' efforts to become more self-actualized than they do when discussing assessment. Ruescas (2005) has found, for example, that teachers view trust as an important element of individual student support, but when queried about assessing students, the same teachers say: "We can't trust them to assess themselves." Electronic tutorials, simulations, referential tools, and even games will steer the landscape of education in more student-centric directions and away from strictly teacher-directed models. We wonder if professors releasing video presentations online as accepted substitutes for class attendance know that many of their students watch the presentations at high speed, making all voice tracks sound "chipmunk-ish." In an odd way, the lessons are becoming more student centric.

Finally, allow us to make one more point about an educational tool that persists, and can be continuously updated, revised, and enhanced. The world of information presented to the students is very post-modern, full of soundbites and soundbytes, fleeting stories, standalone courses, the latest videos, movies, songs, and news stories *du jour*. Debates are often presented as an extreme position being expressed on one side of an issue and another on the other side of the issue. Developing an argument, or even an idea, is often absent in students' human transactions. This may have consequences with respect to identity formation and development. We can think of very few educational tools that allow students to reflect on their growth over time, revise estimations of that growth, and keep versions of their previous beliefs and perceptions as easily as an electronic portfolio. We collected some evidence that this was not lost on our students. For example, in a portfolio video clip, one student stated: " ... in the teaching philosophy and personal statement, where you have to think 'Who am I? Why am I here? Why would I want to give my life to this?'" Another wrote: "Once I broke through the brick wall regarding technology, and when I got to apply my knowledge in my student teaching, I felt like I could handle anything." Still another: "The ePortfolio was conditioning me for the job to come. If I never had been taught reflection, questioning, or higher-order thinking skills, I don't know how successful my second year of teaching would be" [PA9.76].

When we undertake a new project, we often spend disproportionate amounts of time on what we do not know well. In portfolio projects, educators often focus on the technology, forgetting the essential question: What are pre-service teachers learning about themselves personally and professionally? The technology supports the question but does not answer it. The answer is somewhere in the context of the program, somewhere in the attitude of those that promote and apply it, and somewhere in the process of collaboration, reflection, self-assessment, and decision making. When we consider lessons learned, we immediately realize that portfolio development is a human activity, related to human development, and any successful program initiative will begin and end there.

REFERENCES

Arter, J. A., & Spandel, V. (1992). NCME instructional module: Using portfolios of student work in instruction and assessment. *Educational Measurement: Issues and Practice, 11*(1), 36-44.

Aschbacher, P. (1994). Helping educators to develop and use alternative assessments: Barriers and facilitators. *Educational Policy, 8*(2), 202-223.

Barton, J., & Collins, A. (1993). Portfolios in teacher education. *Journal of Teacher Education, 44*(3), 200-210.

Bondy, E., & Ross, D. D. (2005). *Preparing for inclusive teaching: Meeting the challenges of teacher education reform.* Albany: State University of New York Press.

Campbell, D., Cignetti, P., Melenyzer, B., Nettles, D., & Wyman, R. (2001). *How to develop a professional portfolio: A manual for teachers.* Boston: Allyn and Bacon.

Defina, A. (1996). *An effective alternative to faculty evaluation: The use of the teaching portfolio.* (ERIC Document Reproduction Service ED394561)

Dewey, J. (1933). *As we may think.* Chicago: The University of Chicago Press.

Dollase, R. (1996). The Vermont experiment in state mandated portfolio program approval. *Journal of Teacher Education, 47*(2), 85-98.

Elder, L., & Paul, R. (1996a). Critical thinking: A stage theory of critical thinking: Part I. *Journal of Developmental Education, 20*(1), 34-35.

Fuller, F. F. (1969). Concerns of teachers: A developmental conceptualization. *American Education Research Journal, 6*(2), 207-226.

Goodman, J. (1984) Reflection and teacher education: A case study and theoretical analysis. *Interchange, 15*(3), 9-26.

Groce, E. C., Henson, R. K., & Woods, B. (1999). *The examination of pre-service teachers' journals for reflective thought patterns concerning professionalism.* (ERIC Document Reproduction Service ED 436481)

Herman, J. L., & Winters, L (1994). Portfolio research: A slim collection. *Educational Leadership, 52,* 48-55.

Johnson, N., & Rose, L. M. (1997). *Portfolios, clarifying, constructing and enhancing.* Lancaster: Technomic.

Kozma, R. (2000). Reflections on the state of educational technology research and development. *Educational Technology Research and Development, 48*(1), 5-15.

Lin, X., Hmelo, C., Kinzer, C.K., & Secules, T. J. (1999). Designing technology to support reflection. *Educational Technology Research and Development, 47*(3),43-62.

Lyons, N. (1998). Reflection in teaching: Can it be developmental? A portfolio perspective. *Teacher Education Quarterly, 25*(1), 115-128.

Merriam, S. B. (1998). *Qualitative research and case study applications in education.* San Francisco: Jossey-Bass.

Mokhtari, K., Yellin, D., Bull, K., & Montgomery, D. (1996). Portfolio assessment in teacher education: Impact on pre-service teachers' knowledge and attitudes. *Journal of Teacher Education, 47*(4), 245-252.

National Council for Accreditation of Teacher Education (NCATE). (2002). *NCATE 2002 standards.* Retrieved January 20, 2005, from http://www.ncate.org/standards/m-stds.htm

Nickerson, R. (1989). New directions in educational assessment. *Educational Researcher, 18*(9), 3-7.

Ouane, A. (2001). Preface. In V. Tinio (Ed.), *Revisiting lifelong learning for the 21st century.* Hamburg: UNESCO Institute for Education.

PROTEACH. (n.d.). Retrieved from http://www.coe.ufl.edu/school/proteach/

Ring, G. (2002). *Diffusion of an innovation: The Electronic Portfolio Project in the College of Education.* Doctoral dissertation, University of Florida, USA.

Ring, G. L., & Foti, S. L. (2003). Addressing standards at the program level with electronic portfolios. *TechTrends, 47*(2), 28-32.

Ross, D. (1989). First steps in developing a reflective approach. *Journal of Teacher Education, 40*(2), 22-30.

Ruescas, O. (2005, May 26). New teacher and student roles. In *Proceedings of the Seminar on Pedagogic Information,* Mondragon University, Spain.

Schön, D. (1983). *The reflective practitioner: How professionals think in action.* New York: Basic Books.

Schön, D. (1988). Coaching and reflective teaching. In P. P. Grimett & G. L. Erickson (Eds.), *Reflection in teacher education* (pp. 19-29). New York: Columbia University, Teachers College Press.

Van Sickle, R. L., & Hoge, J. D. (1991). Higher cognitive thinking skills in social studies: Concepts and critiques. *Theory and Research in Education, 19*(2), 152-172.

Whetstone, L., & Carr-Chellman, A. (2001). Preparing pre-service teachers to use technology: Survey results. *TechTrends, 45*(4), 11-17, 45.

Winsor, P., & Ellefson, B. (1995). Professional portfolios in teacher education: An exploration of their value and potential. *The Teacher Educator, 31*(1), 68-91.

Yin, R. (1994). *Case study research: Design and methods.* Thousand Oaks, CA: Sage.

Zeichner, K., & Wray, S. (2001). The teaching portfolio in U.S. teacher education programs: What we know and what we need to know. *Teaching and Teacher Education, 17,* 613-621.

Zeichner, K. M., & Liston, D. P. (1987). *Reflective teaching.* Mahwah, NJ: Lawrence Erlbaum.

KEY TERMS

Artifacts: Pieces of evidence developed by students which demonstrate their proficiency in a specific practice.

Case Study: A detailed analysis of a person or group from a social or psychological or medical point of view.

Cognition: Knowledge.

ePortfolio: A Web-based or software-based, organic, evolving, collection of work.

Florida Accomplished Practices (FAPs): Twelve best practices of teaching designed by the Florida Education Standards Commission for which all pre-service teachers enrolled in Florida Colleges of Education must demonstrate multiple examples of proficiency.

Illustrations: Pieces of evidence developed by students which demonstrate their proficiency in a specific practice.

Innovation: A new idea or practice.

NCATE: The professional accrediting organization for schools, colleges, and departments of education in the United States.

PROTEACH (Professional Teacher): The five-year teacher education program at the University of Florida culminating in a master's degree.

Rationale Statement: An explanation of the evidence included in the portfolio and the reason it was chosen for a particular standard.

Simulations: The act of imitating the behavior of some situation or some process, especially for the purpose of study or personnel training.

APPENDIX A

Florida Accomplished Practices

Assessment	Uses assessment strategies (traditional and alternate) to assist the continuous development of the learner.
Communication	Uses effective communication techniques with students and other stakeholders.
Continuous Improvement	Engages in continuous professional quality improvement for self and school.
Critical Thinking	Uses appropriate techniques and strategies, which promote and enhance critical, creative, and evaluative thinking capabilities of students.
Diversity	Uses teaching and learning strategies that reflect each student's culture, learning styles, special needs, and socio-economic background.
Ethics	Adheres to the Code of Ethics and Principles of Professional Conduct of the Education Profession in Florida.
Human Development and Learning	Uses an understanding of learning and human development to provide a positive learning environment, which supports the intellectual, personal, and social development of all students.
Knowledge of Subject Matter	Demonstrates knowledge and understanding of subject matter.
Learning Environments	Creates and maintains positive learning environments in which students are actively engaged in learning, social interaction, cooperative learning, and self-motivation.
Planning	Plans, implements, and evaluates effective instruction in a variety of learning environments.
Role of the Teacher	Works with various education professionals, parents, and other stakeholders in the continuous improvement of the educational experiences of students.
Technology	Uses appropriate technology in teaching and learning processes.

APPENDIX B

ePortfolio Template

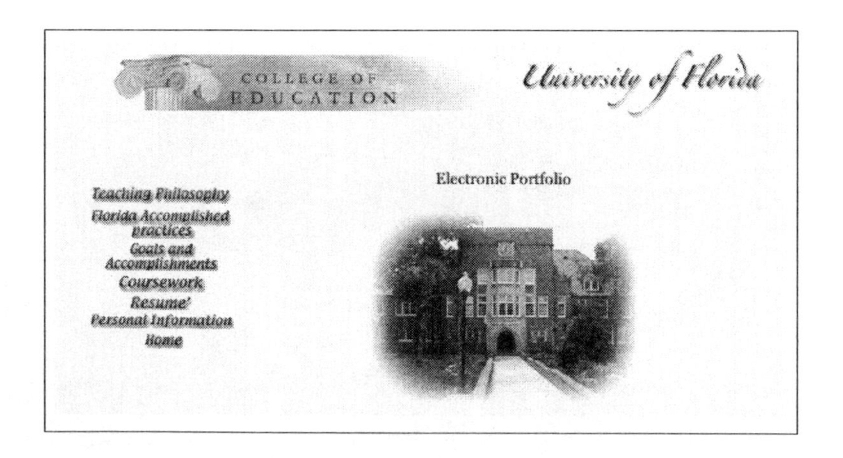

APPENDIX C

Illustration Header

Student Name:
Source of Illustration:
Professor:
Semester Completed in Program:
Acceptable Grade Received on Assignment:
Individual Assignment:

Accomplished Practice:

Description of Assignment:

Chapter XXXII
ePortfolio and Educational Change in Higher Education in The Netherlands

M. W. (Wijnand) Aalderink
Windesheim University for Professional Education, The Netherlands

M. H. C. H. (Marij) Veugelers
Universiteit van Amsterdam, The Netherlands

ABSTRACT

This chapter describes the important role that the concept of ePortfolio plays in new pedagogical paradigms in The Netherlands. ePortfolio can be seen both as a consequence of and a stimulus for the movement towards student-centered, competence-based learning in Dutch higher education. The authors present lessons learned in ePortfolio implementation, derived from experience from the past five years in the Low Countries, both in local institutional projects and in large-scale national projects. They then describe the cases of their own universities, being Windesheim University for Professional Education and the University of Amsterdam. The chapter ends with conclusions and future developments in the field of ePortfolio in The Netherlands.

INTRODUCTION

In Dutch institutions of higher education, the subject of ePortfolio continues to attract increasing interest. This can be explained partly by the focus on competence-oriented education in universities of professional education, in which the emphasis is placed on student development, but also by academic universities' attention to fostering academic maturity. In the process of educational innovation, the ePortfolio is frequently used as an aid for guiding the learning process or as an assessment tool. It also offers the "Net Generation" students

(Aalderink & Veugelers, 2005a) of today the possibility of presenting themselves to various target groups. ePortfolios have the potential to offer clarity and flexibility, for which various stakeholders in education have a particular need, in learning, teaching, and administrative processes.

Much useful experience with the implementation of ePortfolios has been acquired in The Netherlands, through both national projects and initiatives set up by most institutions of higher education. The aim of NL Portfolio[1], established in the spring of 2004, is to combine, share, and expand this experience. NL Portfolio is one of the SURF Foundation's special interest groups. SURF[2] is the Dutch partnership organization for information and communications technology (ICT) in Dutch higher education and research.

LESSONS LEARNED IN ePORTFOLIO IMPLEMENTATION

From the different projects that have been carried out in The Netherlands, different lessons can be learned which are first presented here and will then be illustrated by the cases of Windesheim University of Professional Education and the University of Amsterdam.

Lesson 1: Pedagogy Comes First

In educational change processes using information technology, it is very important to start off from the functional perspective of the learner and the teacher, and to avoid a technology push. In The Netherlands this view is well accepted and is also found to be a key factor in ePortfolio implementation in large-scale, nationwide projects like the E-Folio Project3 and the LMS/DPF (Learning Management System/Digital Portfolio) Project (Kokx, Van de Laar, Veltman-Van Vugt, & Van Veen, 2004). Students in the LMS/DPF Project have reported that the greater amount of self-responsibility in learning with an ePortfolio was a stimulus for them that evoked them into intrinsic learning in which they were motivated to reflect on and improve their learning processes. One of the conclusions of the E-Folio Project was that the extra value of the use of portfolios lays in learning in authentic situations, creating room for individual development, and investing in coaching and alternative assessment. In the model of Van Tartwijk et al. (2003), the pedagogical field is located in the center of the picture, representing an approach that most Dutch institutes share as common ground: it all starts with the learner. The model also shows elements of the lessons that follow (see Figure 4).

Lesson 2: Clear Definition of Goals and Results is Important

ePortfolio tends to be a container term used for a variety of tools in a wide range of approaches. Traditionally, an ePortfolio refers to a file-sharing system used as a showcase for an individual by which he provides an overview of his achievements in a certain field. Another large-scale project in The Netherlands carried out by the Digital University[4] (Veugelers et al., 2004) has shown that different approaches on ePortfolio implementation can be categorized in a scenario model in three major areas according to their primary focus on career counseling and/or assessment and/or personal development planning (see Figure 1).

In The Netherlands, academic universities tend to choose a career counseling portfolio, as the case of the University of Amsterdam will show later on, whereas in universities of Professional Education, like Windesheim, all goals (counseling, assessing, and planning) are at stake in an integrated portfolio approach. From

Figure 1. Scenarios for ePortfolio implementation

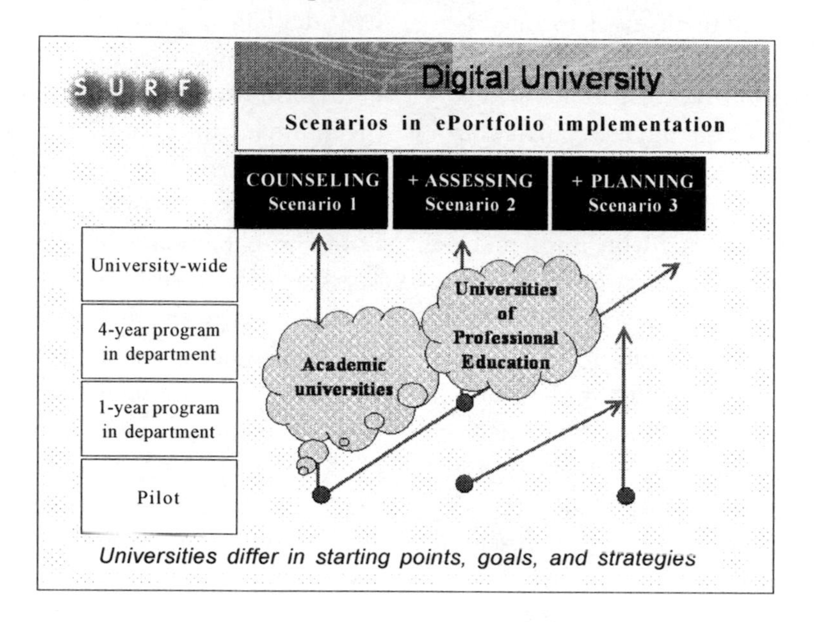

a lot of large- and small-scale projects, it has become clear that implementing a portfolio requires much more than just providing a tool. As concluded in the E-Folio Project: ePortfolios should be tailored to the purposes for which they are used in the learning environment.

Lesson 3: Maintaining Multiple Stakeholders' Perspectives is Vital

At the organizational side, the question in the ePortfolio case is how to keep the different perspectives of involved stakeholders in line with each other. It has become clear that a multidisciplinary approach in development and implementation is essential with the involvement of all of the stakeholders (students, teachers, coaches, assessors, work field, managers, administration employees, and technicians). Depending on the level of implementation from single-class experiments up to institution-wide ePortfolio projects, this multidisciplinary approach becomes more crucial. Project managers and team members have to do a lot of communication and must actively organize sessions for groups of key users that function as a sounding board. The central finding of a lot of experience so far has been that ePortfolio implementation tends to be more successful if the different stakeholders can define the institute's own specific form of folio thinking together. Different processes, whether they are pedagogical, administrative, or technical, should be developed and tested in collaboration.

Lesson 4: Support by Management is Crucial

Support by management is crucial: the lines of development are best chosen as a result of a bottom-up process, but after the decisions are made, management should support, facilitate, and monitor them top-down by defining a clear strategic framework.

Change management is what is needed in ePortfolio projects, bringing about change in effective ways, a process in which existing human resources are a vital link. The art of change management consists of making effective use of existing as well as incoming energy. The Net Generation student, who is much more into technology than most teachers are, is in a position to play a leading part in this process. In different pilots, students have proven to be good change agents in the development and implementation of eLearning. With regard to ePortfolio implementation, the change management approach tallies interestingly with a further shift of accent from tools to processes. When embedded adequately in the processes or workflow of the different stakeholders, their motivation for the application of the ePortfolio system as a tool will be influenced in a positive way.

Lesson 5: Functional and Technical Support is Also Crucial

The different users of an ePortfolio system need tailor-made performance support in an accessible form, since ePortfolio implementation is not another routine project, but in most cases part of a complex educational innovation. Support should be set up both on the functional-pedagogical and on the technical-instrumental side in the local departments in cooperation with institution-wide support units for IT and educational development. A common strategy for implementation in The Netherlands is to start with small-scale pilots in several departments, to explore the ePortfolio case in each specific context, define the workflow, and train the local key players. These "locals" are the ones that play a very important role in the subsequent phases of scaling up. The different local portfolio project managers are then facilitated as a community of practice together with the "central" project managers. In this way support can be co-organized and facilitated in an effective way. The form in which the support is organized may vary from department to department and also within departments. It may be a mix of training sessions, workshops, paper manuals, a good support site with tutorials and best practices, office visits, and so forth.

Lesson 6: Technological Choices Matter Too

Although the "pedagogy comes first" axiom has very strong appeal in The Netherlands, there is of course also the technical challenge of how to create functional workflows in an integrated technical infrastructure. In The Netherlands there is a growing tendency to work with integrated architecture approaches, giving attention to open standards and interoperability[5]. Systems for digital portfolios are in technical terms still in a considerable state of flux; this also applies, for example, to their relationship to digital learning environments and study registration systems. In most cases the ePortfolio is not just a single tool (just one piece of software), it is more often part of a larger technical configuration in which the required functionality may be met by the cooperation of different hardware and software tools.

TWO EXAMPLES OF ePORTFOLIO IMPLEMENTATION IN THE NETHERLANDS

It will be clear from the two cases described below that the implementation of an electronic portfolio in higher education needs a long breath, a lot of flexible attitude, and a strong conviction that this will be the tool for the future in lifelong learning. The implementation struggles and strategies we describe will provide more insight into the learning process that led to the lessons learned of the previous paragraphs.

Case One: Windesheim University of Professional Education – Portfolio in the Heart of the Organization

During the past four years, Windesheim has worked on an integrated and functional strategy for the development and implementation of a campus-wide ePortfolio system (Aalderink, 2004). In the developed pedagogical model, using an ePortfolio is not to be just some extra activity that stands apart for the teachers and the students. Instead it should be a fundamental cornerstone for the pedagogical process on the one hand and the educational institute's administrative processes on the other. When implemented in the heart of both, an ePortfolio can make learning and teaching more efficient and effective. It supports and improves students' acquisition of competencies, and it also brings about a more transparent and flexible workflow for the different stakeholders involved. In this picture, the ePortfolio fulfills vital demands for overview and flexibility.

Windesheim plans to use the ePortfolio as a tool for both students and faculty in all of the courses, starting with the cohort of 2006-2007. The results of two intensive rounds of pilots have shown that it can make learning and teaching more efficient and effective when embedded in the workflow of students and faculty. An important element of ePortfolio development and implementation at Windesheim so far has been that the different stakeholders have been involved from the start of the program in 2001. By working this way, there is common ground regarding the functional specifications, the key processes, and the selected tool.

Windesheim has run pilots in nine of the total number of 10 departments. It is now preparing for an intensive implementation project in terms of educational and administrative processes. Parallel educational standards for the application of ePortfolios in student-centered, competence-based education within the major-minor model are being developed at a strategic level in the so-called Windesheim Educational Standards.

At Windesheim, ePortfolios will eventually cover the following primary functions: career counseling, assessing, and planning in both Windesheim's more classic subject courses and especially in so-called integrated professional tasks that students work on over a longer period of time.

Figure 2 shows the central position of the student from plan to progress in Windesheim's competence-based process model that students go through each half year.

A circular model like this one is common in several student-centered ePortfolio approaches in Dutch higher education; one can see the learning cycle of Kolb (1984) shining through.

In the portfolio system that Windesheim develops in cooperation with Concord[6], assess-

Figure 2. Processes in competency-focused, student-centered education

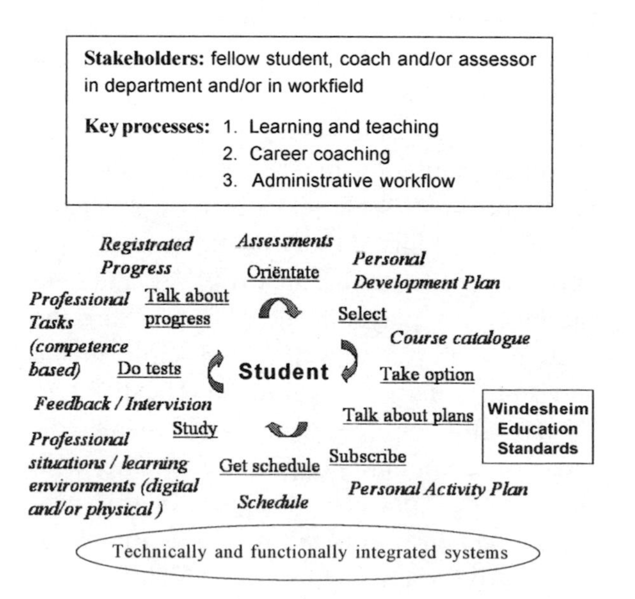

ment matrices provide an actual overview of work in progress and work done by the students. In this manner the system supports the student-centered approach Windesheim chooses, with the focus on competency acquisition in flexible curricula. Students assemble their personal development plan (PDP) within the portfolio system, in a cooperative setting with stakeholders in the institute itself (fellow-students, coaches, assessors) and in the working field (coaches, assessors).

All of the plans, all of the tasks, all of the work in progress, and all of the work done by each student are accessible through the hyperlinks in the matrices in a structured way.

Justification arguments for competency and skills certification in the portfolio system may be circulated for discussion with peers and other selected parties, and be made part of the justification process. Each justification can be held at one of several justification levels (see Figure 3): Proposed, Required, Plan, Draft, Feedback, Closed, Withdrawn, Finished, and Complete. The communication and feedback involved can also be stored in the system. The assessment matrix is where the primary requirements of both reflection and registration are being met. For the students there is always an answer to be found in the matrices on common but vital questions like, "Where do I stand?" and "How did I get here?" and "Where do I move next?"—answers that can be quite relevant to the other stakeholders in a student's learning process as well, especially in a setting where collaborative learning is important. Students are invited to propose learning tasks themselves to give them more responsibility for their own learning.

At Windesheim the ePortfolio project has recently become part of a strategic program, "IT for Student-Centered Education," consisting of the following projects:

1. The upgrade of the student information system
2. The development of an electronic catalog for majors, minors, and courses
3. The ePortfolio project
4. A qualitative approach to the virtual learning environment
5. Information architecture and personalized "my Windesheim" portal

Figure 3. Course matrix following Windesheim Educational Standards

Course matrix following Windesheim Education Standards	
Course-code— Title of course. **Short description from Major Minor-Course Catalogue** **Matrix status: Under construction** **Teacher:** [ ] **Headteacher:** [ ]	
Learning task/product	**Status**
Title learning task / learning product 1	**Required**
Title learning task / learning product 2	**Required**
Title free learning task / learning product	**Proposed (Required)**
Final assessment	**Required**

Pedagogical workflow course
○ **Proposed**
• **Required**
○ **Plan**
○ **Draft**
○ **Feedback**
• **Finished**
○ **Close**
• **Completed**
• **Revise**
• **Withdraw**

6. Reorganization of the processes and tools for scheduling, testing, and progress registration
7. Integrated training and support for the whole set of new systems, developed per stakeholder and implemented per department

The program of projects creates as much synergy as possible in the development (using Internet technology, Web services for system cooperation and integration) and implementation of the different new IT tools involved that will scaffold all of the administrative and pedagogical processes and stakeholders in an integrated way. As a result, the organizational shift at Windesheim University will be supported with information technology in an effective and efficient way, with the ePortfolio as an important key element.

Case Two: University of Amsterdam – A Step-by-Step Three-Pillar Model

The University of Amsterdam is an academic university with "traditional" education: lectures, work groups, and laboratory courses. The departments are reasonably autonomous and formulate their educational concept themselves. Ever since 2001, there have been numerous pilots focused on working with an electronic portfolio (Veugelers, 2004). In the space of three years, the plans have been put into effect at nine of the 24 university departments. Progress was so rapid all over that in January 2003, the decision was made at the central level to draw up a university-wide implementation plan. The situation was described for a two-year rollout in an effort to have 40% of the 22,000 students working with an electronic portfolio by 2005. Due to the great financial investments this would involve, the decision was made to first discuss the matter with all the educational directors to enroll their commitment to the project.

After their commitment was clear, a new strategic plan was written in February 2004 to prepare a Go/No Go decision for December 2004, so the university board could make a decision. This implementation will be based on the University of Amsterdam three-pillar model (Fisser & Dekker 2003) of pedagogy, management strategy, and technology. The following aspects are to be prepared:

- A teacher training program for the new role as coach (instead of the role as an expert), supporting faculty members in their development from sage on the stage to guide on the side
- Best practices with examples of assignment instructions and student portfolios to be shown on the university Web site portfolio
- A pedagogical support framework
- The appointment of a team of professionals to help with the new initiatives
- A format for the technology support at the university
- A proposal for a tool selection
- A financial overview of various hosting models
- A discussion with educational managers about the new challenges in educational innovation at a university
- A checklist of pre-conditions for the management of new initiatives

The model of portfolio and educational innovation attention areas from Van Tartwijk et al. (2003) was used since October 2003 for all the initiatives and appeared to be a useful model (Veugelers & Korterink, 2005). The University of Amsterdam recommends that there should be an extra circle behind the model for the

Figure 4. University of Amsterdam "ePortfolio concept model"

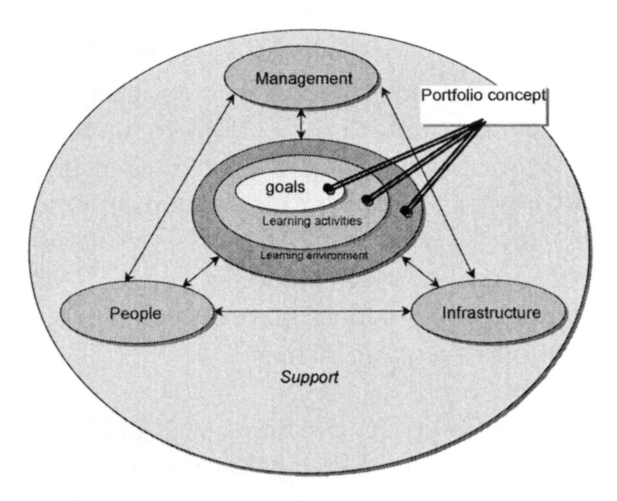

Source: Adapted from Van Tartwijk et al. (2003)

central organized support by the (educational and strategic) implementation in the whole university so that all the knowledge can be shared (see the lessons learned in the first part of this chapter and Figure 4).

Besides, it is maybe better to speak about a "portfolio concept" instead of an ePortfolio system, because the concept is more than the "tool": the concept is the whole idea of taking up self-responsibility as a student for student growth, thinking in reflection, giving stimulating feedback, and so on.

The increasing focus on academic training and skills is the main reason to start with a portfolio at this university without a central concept of competence-based education, like there is at Windesheim in the previously described case. Stimulating the growth of these academic skills and making them visible in an ePortfolio are the bases for all of the pilots. Simultaneously with this movement, there is also renewed interest in arriving at a collective concept of education. And as a result of the collaboration with a local university of professional education, the Amsterdam University of Professional Education, the improvement of the student career counseling is once again on the agenda.

All these movements converge in the University of Amsterdam portfolio implementation route and can be viewed as an example of the Scenario 1 route (see Figure 1). This scenario in which career counseling and personal development predominate is expected to serve as the guideline for the next few years.

In view of the strong autonomous role of the departments at the University of Amsterdam, up to now the change approach—according to the classification by De Caluwé and Vermaak (2002)—has been characterized as a "yellow change" with attention for creating a support base/sharing views/involving the context. The implementation of an electronic portfolio will however require a "blue" approach with a blueprint for a study career-counseling route, with checklists for the managers to steer the pilots and new initiatives. This is an approach that is common practice in the IT world, but not so much at this university. There will also have to be a "red" focus on stimulating and encouraging teachers to grow in their changing role from expert to coach by setting up a route for their professional development.

In 2002 a consortium of 10 universities (the Digital University) introduced a portfolio tool that could be used by various educational universities and commercial firms in The Netherlands. The University of Amsterdam used this tool from the beginning. It is a very "open" tool: students can create their own look and feel; there is not a fixed format for presentations. The system runs on a server outside the organization. During the last two years a lot of the participating universities chose for their own university a system with more possibilities for technical connection to other university tools. For that reason the Digital University has decided that the tool could not become a financial success, and from August 2005 on, the tool will be no longer available.

So in Autumn 2004, the University of Amsterdam decided to select another portfolio system: based on technical requirements (besides the educational functional requirements), the university chose the Open Source Portfolio from OSPI because they believe in the Sakai concept for the future, where OSPI is embedded. During 2005, the university prepared the rollout of version 2.1 (October 2005) and hopes that in April 2006, version 2.5 will be ready for all of the university. As a member of Sakai, the University of Amsterdam shares its knowledge in the OSPI community[7].

CONCLUSION

From the two higher education case studies that were presented above, and from many other projects in other parts of the educational sector in The Netherlands and worldwide, we can learn that developing and implementing an ePortfolio is a challenging job that takes a lot of time and energy. It calls for context-dependent folio thinking that can only succeed when linked closely with educational change in the specific organization at different levels and from different perspectives.

The lessons learned as presented are these: pedagogy comes first; we must work on well-defined goals towards planned results; all stakeholders should be involved in a multidisciplinary approach; management support cannot be missed, as is the case for functional and technical support; and the different IT tools have to interoperate in a technical architecture that is user friendly in a personalized way. We can expect more progress in the field of ePortfolio if we succeed in learning and applying these lessons together.

FUTURE DEVELOPMENTS IN THE NETHERLANDS

Within Dutch higher education, SURF funds special interest groups, a concept that has already been applied successfully for the subjects of streaming audio and video in the "Webstroom"[8] group and for standardization in the "SIX" special interest group[9]. As yet, another of these special interest groups, "NL Portfolio," has defined its activities for the coming two years, including:

- Setting up a coordinating Web site[10] that will be the portal to the subject of ePortfolio for Dutch institutions of higher education
- Participating in existing innovation projects in The Netherlands, grassroots projects, and eLearning research projects
- Initiating its own project tender among Dutch institutions of higher education
- Cooperating internationally in the field of ePortfolio
- Exploring and developing the subject of "lifelong learning" in The Netherlands, thereby cooperating with partners in the educational sector, the government, and the professional field
- Disseminating project-related information by means of national and international conferences and seminars

Cooperation in The Netherlands on ePortfolios has been taken up already, as the following examples make clear (see also Aalderink & Veugelers, 2005b):

- In a trend study on ePortfolio in higher education (Slotman et al., 2005) as part of an eLearning research project by SURF, aiming specifically at the audience of higher education managers, results describe the lessons learned by different institutions regarding ePortfolio, in terms of "actors, factors, and strategies."

- Also, different higher education consortia in the Netherlands, like Apollo[11], E-Merge[12], and the Digital University[13], have done ePortfolio tool studies to explore the future in this field together.
- Across the educational sector, different partners, from primary education up to higher and further education, have worked together on a broad state-of-the-art study on ePortfolio in The Netherlands. The report (Hensen, 2004) describes five possible routes for future development in terms of cooperation: from doing nothing (route 1), up to one system for ePortfolio on a national scale (route 5). The report advises working towards "route 4" by creating "one mutual highway" that will set standards for both functional and technical specifications that can be applied regionally and in different sectors of education.
- Also in other sectors of education, initiatives on portfolios exist. An example is the "Platform Portfolio" in the professional education sector[14].

International cooperation on ePortfolios is also a field in which participation from The Netherlands evolves.

- A recent example of cooperation by Dutch universities was organized by SURF and ALT[15] (UK). Portfolio specialists from both countries have exchanged knowledge and experience in a working seminar and have written a briefing paper together (Cotterill et al., 2004). The paper highlights apparent similarities and differences in approaches between the UK and the Netherlands, as well as opportunities for future collaboration.
- In the 2005 edition of this meeting, ILTA[16] from Ireland also joined the conference and research seminar (Roberts, Aalderink, Cook, et al., 2005).
- The University of Maastricht participates in the European Union-funded EPICC project[17], which describes use cases and scenarios.
- As part of an intensive cooperation program between JISC[18] and SURF, new projects will start soon on ePortfolio. Experts from both countries' joint workforces will exchange information and come up with joint PDP/ePortfolio formats and advices on coordinated future development of assessment models. Also, more collaboration workshops will be planned in the near future.

REFERENCES

Aalderink, W. (2004, June 29-July 2). Digital portfolio: Tool for flexible learning and teaching in competency focused higher education. In *Proceedings of Eunis 2004—IT Innovation in a Changing World,* Ljubljana (pp. 25-29).

Aalderink, W., & Veugelers, M. (2005a, June 20-23). Educating the Net Generation: More focus on the student in the USA. In W. Aalderink & M. Veugelers (Eds.), *Educause 2004: IT from a higher vantage point* (pp. 133-139). SURF Edutripreport 2004, Helsinki, The Netherlands.

Aalderink, W., & Veugelers, M. (2005b). E-portfolio's in The Netherlands: Stimulus for educational change and lifelong learning. In *Proceedings of EDEN 2005-Lifelong E-Learning.*

Cotterill, S., Darby, J., Rees Jones, P, Roberts, G., Van Tartwijk, J., & Veugelers, M. (2004,

April 22-23). *ALT-SURF seminar: E-portfolios and digital repositories.* Edinburgh. Utrecht: Stichting SURF.

De Caluwé, L., & Vermaak, H. (2002). *Learning how to change: Handbook for the change manager.* Deventer: Kluwer.

Fisser, P. H. G., & Dekker, P. J. (2003, July 2-4). Implementing a university-wide electronic learning environment, technology, communication and didactics. In *Proceedings of EUNIS 2003,* Amsterdam (pp. 154-156).

Hensen, T. (2004). *Research e-portfolio: An organizational and infrastructural challenge.* Kennisnet, The Hague.

Kolb, D. A. (1984). *Experiential learning.* Englewood Cliffs, NJ: Prentice-Hall.

Kokx, P., Van de Laar, H., Veltman-Van Vugt, F., & Van Veen, J. (2004). *From wish to reality* (SURF Project LMS-DPF). The Netherlands.

Roberts, G., Aalderink, W., Cook, J. et al. (2005, April 1). Reflective learning, future thinking: Digital repositories, e-portfolios, informal learning and ubiquitous computing. In *Proceedings of the ALT-SURF-ILTA Report on the E-Portfolio Research Seminar,* Dublin.

Slotman, K., Fisser, P., Gulmans, M., Braspenning, C., Van der Veen, J., & Logtenberg, H. (2005). *E-portfolio: Beyond the hype or limited optimism?* The Netherlands: SURF E-learning Research.

Van Tartwijk, J., Driessen, E., Hoeberigs, B., Kösters, J., Ritzen, M., Stokking, K.M., & Van der Vleuten, C. (2003). *Working with an electronic portfolio.* Hoger Onderwijs Praktijk. Groningen: Wolters-Noordhoff. (English version available at http://e-learning.surf.nl/portfolio, see Handbook.)

Veugelers, M. (2004). Electronic portfolio: Be aware of the pedagogical challenges and the technology struggle. In *Proceedings of Eunis 2004—IT Innovation in a Changing World.*

Veugelers, M., Gulmans, M., Van Kayzel, R., Kemps, A., Kinkhorst, G., Meeder, S., & Slotman, K. (2004). *Portfolio-implementatie.* Utrecht: Digitale Universiteit.

Veugelers, M., & Kemps, A. (2004, October 28-29). The manager's challenge: With one toolkit, three scenarios and change management, start the portfolio implementation. In *Proceedings of the 2004 E-Portfolio Conference* (pp. 119-134). La Rochelle, France.

Veugelers, M., & Korterink, A. (2005). Implementation of electronic portfolio, experiences of the University of Amsterdam. *From trend to transformation.* Digital University, The Netherlands.

KEY TERMS

Assessment: The process of documenting, usually in measurable terms, knowledge, skills, attitudes, and beliefs. Assessment is often used in an educational context (to refer, for example, to the work of institutional researchers), but it applies to other fields as well (such as health and finance). Assessments can be classified in many different ways. The most important distinctions are: (1) formative and summative; (2) objective and subjective; and (3) criterion-referenced and norm-referenced.

Career Counseling: Provides one-on-one or group professional assistance in exploration and decision-making tasks related to choosing a major/occupation, transitioning into the world of work, or further professional training. The field is vast and includes career placement, career planning, learning strategies, and student development. Career counseling advisors assess people's interests, personality, values, and skills, and also help them explore career options and research graduate and professional schools.

Competence: In human resources, a standardized requirement for a individual to properly perform a specific job.

ePortfolio: In the context of education and learning, a portfolio based on using electronic media and services. It consists of a personal digital record containing information such as a collection of artifacts or evidence demonstrating what one knows and can do.

Implementation: In engineering and computer science, the practical application of a methodology or algorithm to fulfill a desired purpose.

Pedagogy: The art or science of teaching. Pedagogy is also sometimes referred to as the correct use of teaching strategies (see instructional theory).

Personal Development Planning: A structured process undertaken by the individual to reflect upon their own learning performance and/or achievement, to support personal, educational, and career development. In an ideal world, students' would be enabled to enhance achievement through reflection on current attainment, make strategic decisions based on their strengths and weaknesses, and 'evidence' their learning processes.

ENDNOTES

1. http://e-learning.surf.nl/portfolio
2. http://www.surf.nl
3. http://www.surf.nl/en/projecten/index2.php?oid=62
4. http://www.du.nl/portfolioimplementatie (an English version of this Web site is in preparation)
5. The SURF SiX Special Interest Group is very active in this field of standards. http://e-learning.surf.nl/six
6. http://www.concord-usa.com
7. http://www.theospi.org
8. http://video.surfnet.nl/info/webstroom/home.jsp
9. http://e-learning.surf.nl/six
10. http://e-learning.surf.nl/portfolio
11. http://www.apolloplatform.nl
12. http://www.emerge.nl
13. http://www.du.nl
14. http://www.cinop.nl/projecten/platformportfolio/Default.asp
15. http://www.alt.ac.uk
16. http://www.ilta.net
17. http://www.qwiki.info/projects/Europortfolio/epicc
18. http://www.jisc.ac.uk

Chapter XXXIII
ePortfolio in the UK: Emerging Practice

Colin Dalziel
University of Wolverhampton, UK

Rachel Challen
University of Wolverhampton, UK

Shane Sutherland
University of Wolverhampton, UK

ABSTRACT

This chapter investigates the emergence of ePortfolio systems in the UK and the drivers for their adoption as part of the national agenda for lifelong learning. Beginning with a historical perspective, the chapter highlights UK initiatives that have led higher education institutions toward providing ePortfolio facilities for their students, and highlights why ePortfolios are becoming more popular for supporting learners and learning. The authors aim to provide a context for ePortfolios in the UK, discuss the drivers for change, identify some of the issues faced by institutions, and highlight some of the differences in ePortfolio adoption between the UK and other countries.

INTRODUCTION

EPortfolios are a recent innovation in the UK and, although a number of projects at several UK universities have been funded to investigate the potential of the medium, their use is currently small scale and experimental. This chapter provides a review of activity and looks at the background to ePortfolio including the former use of records of achievement and the process of personal development planning (PDP). Several UK government initiatives are driving higher education (HE) institutions towards the adoption of ePortfolio facilities for students, and the issues surrounding this move are discussed.

Unlike the United States, where ePortfolios are often hosted by commercial companies, with students paying an annual fee, UK systems are likely to be hosted and paid for by universities or government departments as part of the widening participation and skills for life agenda. Some of the implications for individuals, institutions, and the government are addressed in this chapter.

To support this chapter, a survey of personal development planning and ePortfolio use in the UK was conducted. Responses from 26 institutions were recorded, and although a relatively small number, this does reflect the current position of institutions in the UK. As the movement towards ePortfolio use in the UK has been precipitated by PDP initiatives, the survey looked at both PDP and ePortfolio activity.

BACKGROUND

Although increasingly prevalent in the United States, ePortfolios are a recent innovation in the United Kingdom; the process of recording educational achievement has some history in the UK, most notably with the introduction to secondary education of New Records of Achievements (NRAs) in 1991. In this paper-based system, students were provided with a folder in which they could keep a record of assessed academic progress and activities which had not been officially examined: these could then be shared with prospective employers. The information was in a prescribed format, which was designed to give equality in the employment selection process. The current focus on education for the 14-19 age range (Department for Education and Skills, 2003; Tomlinson, 2004; DfES, 2005) has shifted the traditional educational structures in place in the UK (ages 11-16) towards a post-compulsory learning experience, so enforcing the ideology that learning is a continuum. This has in turn made the NRA obsolete, and they ceased to be available after 2004, replaced with progress files. To promote consistency across sectors, higher education progress files were also introduced following work by the National Committee of Inquiry into Higher Education, which became known as the Dearing Report. Progress files were defined by Dearing (1997) as "a transcript recording student achievement and provision for the planning of personal development." The Quality Assurance Agency for Higher Education (QAA) defines personal development planning as:

... a structured and supported process undertaken by an individual to reflect upon their own learning, performance and/or achievement and to plan for their personal, educational and career development.

The QAA goes on to state:

The primary objective for PDP is to improve the capacity of individuals to understand what and how they are learning, and to review, plan and take responsibility for their own learning, helping students:

- *become more effective, independent and confident self-directed learners;*
- *understand how they are learning and relate their learning to a wider context;*
- *improve their general skills for study and career management;*
- *articulate personal goals and evaluate progress towards their achievement; and*
- *encourage a positive attitude to learning throughout life.* (QAA, 2001)

Pressure to deliver the progress files initiative within higher education has come primarily from the government and the QAA. Numerous legislative and consultancy papers, including Burgess (2004) and Tomlinson (2004), have recently heralded the advent of the progress files as a major support for individuals within the UK in achieving lifelong learning. Research by the UK Department of Trade and Industry (DTI) recognized that lifelong learning is a major factor in a country's economic success, and that the resulting 'knowledge economy' is a key component of the competitive edge that is vital if a county is going to achieve economic success (DTI, 1998). The importance of a populous that can not only gain knowledge, but also apply it in diverse situations, creates a population that makes a return on its educational investment. Dearing (1999) acknowledges that higher education is now in a state of progressive change; it has changed necessarily to blend initial learning with lifelong learning to construct the learning society. In contemporary society there is a need to equip the workforce appropriately to operate productively within the global knowledge economy. The challenge in the UK has been to close the gap between a culturally and linguistically diverse population, and to develop key skills to promote lifelong learning. Moser (1999) suggests a 10-point strategy to increase adult basic skills, one of which was a requirement to utilize the benefits of new technology within the emerging adult educational structure. In the past two years, the Department for Education and Skills (DfES) and other agencies have increasingly viewed IT skills as a basic "life skill," and a plethora of IT-related initiatives have helped produce a climate where technical PDP systems and e-portfolios are much more likely to be welcomed and where the end user is much more likely to be able to engage with these tools.

Progress Files and Personal Development Planning

Progress files were introduced after a pilot period and aimed to support a formative lifelong learning process by utilizing the concept of personal development planning. The need for PDP is recognized by Randell (1999, p. 5) who suggests that "concentration upon modular assessment can encourage a learn-it-and-forget-it culture. We should allow more time for reflection upon learning, encourage synoptic analysis and design assessment to look at performance as a whole." Burgess (1999) concurs, asserting that the current honours degree system was outdated for the current educational climate and that each student should provide a detailed transcript of their achievement as they are "crucial translators" of their learning and achievement. A transcript can provide a fuller, richer picture of student achievement; it not only provides the chosen reader with academic and personal success, but allows the student to make contextual sense of their learning. This process can in turn highlight areas of development which otherwise may not be instantly apparent and which can be applied to Action Planning activities for further learning. This process is central to PDP and provides a mechanism for learners to catalogue their learning in a structured manner on a regular basis, with input and dialogue from a tutor. This process guides the learner's development and culminates in a body of evidence that charts their personal and educational development. To underline its commitment to PDP, the QAA (2001, p. 41) has articulated its expectation that "the PDP element of the policy objectives should be operational across the whole HE system and for all HE awards by 2005/06."

From PDP to ePortfolio

Making sure that the progress file is accessible to all users, simple economics and a continuing shift towards technology enrichment are among the reasons for developing an online system for the PDP process. Many institutions are finding computer-based PDP systems have an important economic advantage over paper-based versions. The logistics of providing paper-based PDPs has a financial impact not only in terms of folders, booklets, and paper templates, but also in providing space for storage and in the handling of the portfolio, many of which get misplaced or lost.

Developers of systems that support PDP processes are extending their software to include facilities which go beyond PDP and are increasingly feature rich. Communication, collaborative, and Web publishing tools can add learning value and take the PDP process further into the realms of ePortfolio. These additional facilities create opportunities for using systems for learning and teaching, assessment, professional development, and personal publication. A good ePortfolio system supports both the process of learning and the product, or evidence, of that learning. The assets—the records of experiences, events, ideas, and achievements—that are created within the system can be linked with each other in a manner that allows the user to weave various assessments together and encourages deep reflection on those assessments or activities. An important factor in favour of ePortfolios is that users can access and develop their materials from any computer that has an Internet connection. The records are held on a server, and with proper security and backup procedures, the user's valuable materials can be safely accessed for as long as the user requires or chooses for them to be there. This is particularly valuable for learners moving between institutions or into employment. Computer-based systems also allow the user to publish any chosen element, or collection of elements, from their ePortfolio to a defined audience at any given time. The user can interact with the ePortfolio in a more dynamic and instantaneous way than a paper-based portfolio would allow. Feedback and other forms of dialogue are more immediate in the ePortfolio, further increasing opportunities for learning. Users thus can be much more creative in an ePortfolio environment than in the structured formats and pages of a PDP folder.

The surveys indicate that UK institutions are unsure of how to manage the continued use of ePortfolio systems beyond graduation. Transferability, or ensuring that the record could stay with the user throughout their learning journey, is an aspect to be considered. If the ePortfolio is to be seen in the context of lifelong learning, there has to be a way to transfer the knowledge between educational institutions, and back and forth to the workplace. Typically, students do not have access to institutional computing facilities after leaving the institution, or only for a short period of time. Unless this changes, there will be a need to transfer the contents of an ePortfolio into a central repository directly after the student leaves the institution.

Current interoperability issues and the lack of compatibility between emerging systems means that transferring the contents of one ePortfolio system to another may take some time to resolve. The result of not addressing this issue will be students graduating without access to their institutional ePortfolio system, no way of easily transferring their ePortfolios, and so no incentive to engage with the process in the first place. Hosted ePortfolios managed by external suppliers potentially offer an easy path for continued use after graduation, with the suppliers charging a fee for continued use. With UK institutions preferring to host their own systems, new processes need to be developed to enable them to offer ePortfolio services for graduates. One solution is to include access to computing facilities, including e-mail and an ePortfolio as part of an alumni package. This not only allows users to continually develop their ePortfolio as a lifelong learner record, but also helps the institution maintain a link with its graduates, which could be advantageous in terms of offering continuing professional development courses to alumni—which can then be recorded in their ePortfolio!

While ePortfolio vendors in North America advise institutions that the cost of an ePortfolio system can be passed on to their students, this is not a model that UK institutions support. In our survey, no institution identified students as a source of funding for their ePortfolio; rather, institutions expect costs to be met either by the institution or via funded projects. The initial setup cost of an ePortfolio system is higher in the UK than North America, as locally managed installations rather than remotely hosted systems are the preferred option. In the case of in-house systems, the development and support costs as well as hardware costs contribute to a large initial outlay. However, as full fee paying charges come into effect, institutions will have to become increasingly competitive and offer added value services to attract students. Therefore the initial outlay can be justified not only because it contributes to learning and teaching within the institution, but also because it provides a facility which offers added value to students.

Learners should be able to revisit and re-evaluate knowledge and learning throughout their personal and professional lives. By keeping transferable records of current learning and of past achievements, lifelong learning is encouraged. By using technology to combine lifelong learning and transferable records, a contribution to the knowledge economy is also achieved.

In the context of a knowledge society, where being information literate is critical, the portfolio can provide an opportunity to demonstrate one's ability to collect, organise, interpret and reflect on documents and sources of information. It is also a tool for continuing professional development, encouraging individuals to take responsibility for and demonstrate the results of their own learning. (EIfEL, n.d., p. 1)

EIfEL declared its intention that by 2010 every citizen in the European community should have an ePortfolio, a declaration echoed by their North American partner, LIfIA.

In 1999, the Burgess report (Burgess, 1999, p. 46) categorically stated that ePortfolios in higher education should be made available in a reasonably short timeframe. "(W)e have, perhaps audaciously, set a deadline of the end of December 2005 by which we think clear progress should have been made." Progress has been slower than Burgess suggested, although in 2005 ePortfolios were still seen as a priority area for the DfES, whose E-Learning Strategy (DfES, 2005, p. 22) asserts:

Schools, colleges and universities are working to provide learners with their own personal online learning space and will want to develop eventually an ePortfolio where learners can store their own work, record their achievements, and access personal course timetables, digital resources relevant to their own study, and links to other learners.

The eLearning strategy has been the most significant single document for ePortfolios across all levels of education and into the workplace.

The Joint Information Systems Committee (JISC) funded a number of projects under the MLEs for Lifelong Learning program to develop collaborative activity among higher education, further education (FE), and the schools sector. This led to the development of a number of PDP-related systems and services, and to the open source ePortfolio ePET. Recent JISC-funded programs have reinforced their interest in ePortfolios; for example, the DEL program supports nine ePortfolio projects out of a total of 21 projects. The majority of these ePortfolio projects focus on implementation and research into the plausibility of embedding ePortfolios into the educational system.

Of particular interest are a number of projects that seek to investigate continuity between FE and HE by defining the learner information required from an ePortfolio for admission into HE. The value of a much richer applicational submission to university is recognized by higher education institutions and the admissions body UCAS. They expect that ePortfolio submissions will provide a much more realistic indication of the student's suitability for a particular course than can ever be portrayed by a list of grades alone.

In terms of scale, nearly half of our survey respondents said their institution had an ePortfolio system in place, although only one institution said that more than 10% of their courses supported the use of ePortfolios. Only one institution said that more than 10% of their students used an ePortfolio on a regular basis. So although paper-based PDP is required by the end of 2005, there is still relatively little use of ePortfolio technology, and of those that do have the technology in place, 60% of responding institutions do not currently make the ePortfolio available to all students. Of the institutions that do not currently have an ePortfolio system, only one said it had no plans to implement a system within the next two years, although it has a functioning PDP system in place.

Institutional request was considered the major influencing factor for the adoption of ePortfolios; over half the institutions questioned highlighted this as a key driver. The survey did not investigate the factors that encouraged the institutions to develop ePortfolio practice, although it may be that some institutions are positioning themselves at the forefront of developing practice while others are acting to keep in line with government initiative. Six institutions cited government initiative as being a major driver towards ePortfolio adoption. What was encouraging was that six institutions were investigating or using ePortfolios as a direct result of requests from the student body. As stated, economic factors have influenced some decisions to adopt electronic systems rather than paper based solutions: one respondent to the survey noted that the ePortfolio was "... the only way to make PDP and progress files available to all our students in an economically viable way."

Adopting Solutions

Within the UK, ePortfolio systems generally fall into three categories, though these categories often overlap. Firstly, there are open source ePortfolios that are freely available to institutions within the UK; for example, the ePET system, developed by the University of Newcastle. ePET is a competency-based ePortfolio system designed primarily for medical students, though the competencies can be changed for any required subject. The second type is commercial-based software that is usually hosted within an institution—for example, pebblePAD, developed by Pebble Learning for the University of Wolverhampton, and now commercialized as an off-the-shelf solution. Also in this category are solutions developed as extensions to learner management systems such as Blackboard. These are very attractive to some institutions as they blend well with existing systems and, while often not very flexible, institutions have selected them to capitalize on existing staff capabilities. In the third category are locally created ePortfolios that have been researched and developed by institutions themselves, possibly catering to a certain course or subject area. The emerging nature of ePortfolio technology and folio thinking has caused many institutions to experiment with their own small-scale solutions while they evaluate what is happening in the marketplace. It is likely that the next few years will see the emergence of a smaller number of flexible and interoperable systems able to accommodate many different subjects, courses, and students.

CONCLUSION

The UK education authorities are clearly trying to drive the use of personal development planning and ePortfolio systems. The drive has been supported with project-based funding through JISC as well as by the weight of funding councils with the insistence from QAA that all higher education institutions have as a minimum PDP processes in place in 2005. There is a danger that a heavy-handed, enforced approach will be met with some resistance, which may lead to minimal engagement. This in turn may lead to systems being made available to students, but support and integration within institutional practice may not run parallel. It is therefore important for practice to demonstrate the benefits of PDP and ePortfolio to ensure widespread adoption.

As an emerging field it is natural that there are many areas that need to develop. These include the level of sophistication of the tools available, continuity of use beyond the education sector, interoperability between systems, and the development of methodologies to support the use of ePortfolios in learning and teaching situations, to suggest but a few. In order for these developments to take place, ePortfolios need to be used in practice, pioneers need to develop methods to support learning, and software developers need to respond to user needs. It is encouraging that funding via JISC projects is being targeted at the use of ePortfolios rather than the creation of systems. The development of local champions striving to build up pedagogic expertise in the use of ePortfolios will better support their use than any number of technological developments. The best place to develop the technology lies with the software vendors who can offer long-term support and development that can take ePortfolio applications forward. There is certainly a place for the open source development community although, as with learner management systems, this is likely to be a fringe activity. Whichever route emerges as the preferred development model, software groups must work closely with the user community to ensure that developments meet the needs of both the educational sector and lifelong learning agendas.

Our survey highlighted that a relatively small number of students are currently using ePortfolio systems, which suggests that institutions are moving with some caution towards full-scale implementation. After experiences with expensive learner management systems, many institutions appear to be wary of getting locked into large-scale monolithic software solutions with associated escalating costs. However, set against the costs of paper-based processes, most can see the economic benefits of using computer-based systems and the potential added value ePortfolio systems can offer. It is thus likely that the majority of UK institutions will be implementing some kind of ePortfolio systems before the PDP deadline.

REFERENCES

Burgess. (2004). *Universities UK/SCOP. Measuring and recording student achievement.* London: HMSO.

Dearing, R. (1997). *National Committee of Inquiry into Higher Education. Higher education in the learning society.* Norwich: HMSO.

Dearing, R. (1999, June).The role of higher education in lifelong learning. In *Proceedings of the PADSHE Conference.* Retrieved May 6, 2005, from http://www.nottingham.ac.uk/padshe/conference/dearing.html

DfES. (2003). *The future of higher education.* Norwich: HMSO.

DfES. (2005). *14-19 education and skills.* Norwich: HMSO.

DfES. (2005a) *DfES e-learning strategy 2005.* Retrieved May 8, 2005, from http://www.dfes.gov.uk/publications/e-strategy/

DTI. (1998). *Building the knowledge driven economy.* Retrieved May 22, 2005, from http://www.dti.gov.uk/comp/main.htm

EIfEL. (n.d.). *Europortfolio.* Retrieved May 6, 2005, from http://www.eife-l.org/portfolio

Moser. (1999). *Fresh sum.* Retrieved May 3, 2005, from http://www.lifelonglearning.co.uk/mosergroup/freshsum.pdf

QAA. (2001). *Guidelines for HE progress files.* Retrieved May 5, 2005, from http://www.qaa.ac.uk/academicinfrastructure/progressFiles/guidelines/progfile2001.asp

Randell, J. (1999). The Quality Assurance Agency and national standards: Developing quality outcomes, developing students. In *Proceedings of the PADSHE Conference.* Retrieved May 6, 2005, from http://www.nottingham.ac.uk/padshe/conference/randall.htm

Tomlinson. (2004). *14-19 curriculum and qualifications reform: Final report of the Working Group on 14-19 reform.* London: HMSO.

KEY TERMS

Flash-Based Web Site: Web site developed using Macromedia Flash software. Usually includes higher levels of user interaction than traditional Web pages. End users must install a Flash player on their computer to access materials created in Flash.

Interoperability: The ability of two or more computer-based systems to exchange information and to use the information that has been exchanged. For example a student records systems populating student lists for a group using an ePortfolio management system.

JISC: UK government-funded body supporting the development and adoption of technology in higher education.

Learner Management System (LMS): Web-based software used to support the delivery of course materials. Typically, an LMS will include a range of facilities including discussion forums, content delivery, and chat rooms.

Personal Development Planning: Activity in which individuals develop skills and knowledge to enhance the learning process through reflective activity and planning. Often uses diagnostic tools to evaluate the current position in relation to key learning skills and identify possible resources to support further development.

Plug-In: Software installed into a Web browser to allow the viewing of propriety file types direct from the Internet. For example, QuickTime Video, Flash, and so forth.

Webfolio: A Web site created via an ePortfolio management system which draws upon assets a user has created and stored in his or her personal online space.

Chapter XXXIV
Tracking Capability Using Web-Based ePortfolios in UK Schools

Will Wharfe
TAG Learning Ltd., UK

Karim Derrick
TAG Learning Ltd., UK

ABSTRACT

MAPS, the Managed Assessment Portfolio System (see http://www.maps-ict.com), is a Web-based ePortfolio system that was developed to help both teachers and learners, initially with a focus of helping to raise standards in the teaching and learning of information and communications technology in the UK. MAPS has since developed into a system covering all stages and subjects of school education, and is now being used in further education contexts. This chapter plots the progress of MAPS from an initial sketch idea to its present form: supporting over 57,000 student portfolios. The authors then draw out a number of lessons learned from such extensive use. The chapter finishes with a look at forthcoming ePortfolio issues and consideration of the requirements of lifelong learning ePortfolios.

BACKGROUND: FIRST STEPS

We had just started the process of building online portfolios for teachers as part of the TagTeacherNet portal (http://www.tagteacher.net) when we were contacted in August 2001 by Dave Thomson and Jane Finch from Worcestershire LEA (http://www.worcestershire.gov.uk). They had been researching the use of ePortfolios, and they also had heard good reports of a product previously produced by our company (TAG Learning) called Portfolio Builder. They wanted to know if they could use Portfolio Builder.

After some research, we discovered that Portfolio Builder had been a portfolio system built before we joined TAG Learning. It had been built in Hyperstudio (see http://www.hyperstudio.com) primarily for stand-alone computers, although it was networkable. A cross-curricular system designed for primary schools, Portfolio Builder was very much a learner-centred system. In Portfolio Builder, it was up to the learner to record and describe his/her progress, and the learner was given a framework for describing moments of significant achievement. The framework prompted the learner to review his/her progress at regular intervals during a project and to reflect on that progress after project completion: what worked, what did not, what would they do next time? Portfolio Builder was put together by Tony Wheeler, one of the founding members at TAG Learning, and John Potter of the Newham Local Education Authority. Having reviewed an archived version of Portfolio Builder, we talked to Tony about the thinking and research behind Portfolio Builder.

Tony Wheeler's approach to ePortfolios was influenced by his work for the Assessment of Performance Unit (APU), which was at the time part of the UK government's Education Department, or Department for Education and Science as it was then known. The APU no longer exists, but in the 1980s it was responsible for monitoring school performance by carrying out random sampling; however, before samples could be taken, valid assessment tasks had to be designed. Around 1989-1990, having worked its way through most other subjects, the APU started looking at ways of monitoring standards for teaching and learning in design and technology. Tony Wheeler, together with Professor Richard Kimbell and his team based at Goldsmith's College in Greenwich, had the task of designing a test mechanism that would establish the level of design and technology capability in a sample of 10,000 15-year-olds.

We quizzed Tony about his work for the APU, and later for the Technology Education Research Unit (TERU), which was—and still is—run by Professor Richard Kimbell at Goldsmith's (see http://www.goldsmiths.ac.uk/departments/design/). During this time, one question kept emerging: How do you best assess a pupil's capability? The challenge that Tony and others had faced in previous projects was that it is very hard for a teacher to make a valid assessment of a student's capability by just looking at their work if the work itself did not shed enough light on why and how the student did what he/she did. In many coursework portfolios, all that is placed in the portfolio is the work.

The research by the APU and later TERU (Kimble, 1997) showed that it really was very difficult to make a valid assessment of a student using the work alone. They found that if the student was required to make notes, recording the decisions they made, for example, at the beginning (Planning), middle (Reviewing), and end (Evaluation) of a project, then there was much more evidence for the teacher to use to assess the student's progress compared with just assessing the work. The commentary was in effect a process diary for each project. Then, taking a series of projects together, along with a series of associated commentaries, you have what could perhaps be called a progress diary to chart the student's overall progress, or "distance travelled."

Thus the Portfolio Builder system gave the student the opportunity to write and record comments throughout a project. The system was initially successful and was installed in educational authorities including Newham in East London. However, for reasons that really lay outside of this chapter—the demise of the Acorn computer platform in the UK, for example—the Portfolio Builder project came to an end.

Years later, because of Jane Finch and Dave Thomson's enquiry, we were encouraged to take the time to reinvestigate Portfolio

Builder and to look at the problems involved in trying to make valid assessments of a student's capability using ePortfolios. This process gave us an idea: In addition to the Web-based teacher portfolios we were already designing, why not also have pupil portfolios? In thinking through the teacher's portfolio for TagTeacherNet, we had already confronted a real limitation of the proposal—namely, that while a teacher's network of resources would be useful, it would be much more useful if the teacher assign tasks to pupils linked to the resources. But how could we do that without compromising the teacher's login? Clearly the pupils would need a login too, but that meant completely re-thinking the model. If children needed a login then it meant you would need to be providing the system to the whole school, not just to individual teachers, because the school would need to take responsibility for the security of the children's logins.

By asking us about Portfolio Builder, Jane Finch and Dave Thomson led us to sketching out a design for a full-blown Web-based portfolio system for schools, with the emphasis being on a process that would support valid assessments of pupil capability. When we then met up with Jane and Dave in the early autumn of 2001, we realized that our system could meet most of their requirements, and we decided to work together with them to create a working model.

THE NEED FOR MANAGED ePORTFOLIOS

It is worth taking a moment to look at the context of Jane and Dave's desire for an ePortfolio system for Worcestershire schools. Primarily they wanted to use and ePortfolio system for one subject, known in England and Wales as information and communications technology (ICT). ICT is a core subject in England and Wales from year three to year nine in schools. However, there is currently no test or exam for ICT; instead, there is a mandatory requirement for schools to assess the ICT capability of students at the end of year six, the end of primary school, and at the end of year nine. (A national ICT test for year nine pupils is currently in trial and will be rolled out in 2007.) Schools are expected to build up portfolios of ICT work for all the pupils and to be able to use such a portfolio to justify the levels awarded.

In England and Wales, schools are inspected regularly by a body called Ofsted, or Office for Standards in Education (http://www.ofsted.gov.uk), and schools are acutely aware of the need to provide evidence to back-up assessments. Hence an ICT teacher in England and Wales has a statutory requirement to assess a student's capability based on evidence contained within a portfolio.

Together with Tony Wheeler, we immediately saw the connection between the APU and TERU research and Portfolio Builder. If we could provide an online portfolio where the student could store not only their work and iterative drafts of that work, but also their planning, reviewing, and evaluating comments, then we could potentially provide the teacher with a great tool for assessing capability.

Of note is the fact that, for their work in helping to develop MAPS, Jane, Dave, and teacher Helen Wilkes won the ICT in Practice Award for 2004 from the British Educational Communications and Technology Agency (BECTA). Videos of Jane and Helen explaining their use of MAPS can be found at http://www.becta.org.uk/corporate/display.cfm?section=21&id=3220.

These videos give insight into the problems that they were looking to MAPS to solve. A more detailed presentation given to Nesta Futurelab by Jane Finch, which includes her rationale for using the MAPS system, can be found at http://www.nestafuturelab.org/events/past/be_pres/jf_pc01.htm.

MAPS SYSTEM REQUIREMENTS

Based on our initial work on teacher portfolios for TagTeacherNet, insights from Tony Wheeler and his work with Portfolio Builder, and the needs of the team from Worcestershire, we identified the following requirements of the system:

1. It had to provide portfolios both for teachers and for pupils.
2. The teacher's portfolio would need to have access to resources to support both the teacher (in teaching) and the pupil (in doing the project work).
3. Additionally, the teacher's portfolio had to provide portfolios for the people charged with helping raise standards across an education authority—people like Jane Finch. They needed a place to store and share examples of best practice.
4. The system had to enable the student to provide evidence to the teacher, evidence that would show the student's ICT capability. We felt we needed to support the planning/review/evaluation functionality that we had seen in Portfolio Builder.
5. It needed to be Web-based, because teachers needed to be able to access work to mark it outside of school hours. Additionally, a Web-based solution was the easiest way to give the Worcestershire advisory team the kind of overview they needed of what was going on in schools right across the authority.

There were many other requirements, but they apply to any Web-based system: easy to use, fast, secure, available 24/7, backed up, virus free, plenty of storage space.

At this time we decided to experiment with using open source systems (Linux operating system, Apache Web server, MySQL database, Perl programming language). The main motivation here was to avoid having to pass on to the customer a per-user, third-party licensing fee (which would apply if we used a database application such as Oracle, for example).

The MAPS system was designed, developed, and has continued to evolve through close consultation with the teachers, students, and teacher advisors who use the system. During this process of refinement, although we made many changes, we found increasing and deepening support from the teachers for the fundamental principle of using an ePortfolio as a formative assessment tool to both develop the user's skills and generate evidence of capability.

HOW MAPS WORKS

Within the MAPS system (see http://www.maps-ict.com where there are detailed demonstrations of how the system works), all students, teachers, teacher coordinators, and teacher advisors have their own individual portfolios. Portfolios are the building blocks of the system and can be transferred from one school's MAPS account to another. For the teachers, these portfolios contain their assessment tasks, their classes, and information detailing past attainment, current progress, messages sent from students about their progress, and various other details about their students. For students, their portfolios feature their assessment tasks, the media, comments they have uploaded to evidence their attainment, and the messages that have been sent by their teachers regarding their progress.

Moderation of Teacher Assessments

We begin with a brief explanation of what we mean by "moderation" in this context. In UK education, the word "moderation" is used to describe the process by which teachers compare samples of marked work in order to make sure that they are marking work consistently. Ideally a piece of work that one teacher feels merits an "A" grade should earn an "A" grade from any teacher working to the same assessment criteria. In other contexts the process of eliminating serious divergence in marking may be called standardisation, but in the UK we generally call it moderation.

If you are not marking work as such, but instead forming a view of a student's overall capability based on a portfolio of work, then the possibility of divergence in assessment seems to increase. To help teachers and advisers deal with this issue, we created an online "moderation portfolio." When a teacher marks a piece of work, he/she can opt to put a copy of all the work and messages into the school's moderation portfolio. The teacher can also add some moderation notes to explain and illustrate reasons for the student being awarded a given grade.

Using the MAPS moderation system, any teacher can view exemplars of assessments and can quickly gain an understanding of the reasons why a certain level was awarded. It is easier to make a valid assessment when you can see in one place the drafts as well as the finished work, the student's comments, and the dialogue between student and teacher while the work was being completed.

When opting to put a marked exemplar into the school's MAPS moderation portfolio, a teacher can also opt to put the exemplar into the education authority MAPS moderation portfolio, enabling moderation right across the authority. This was a key requirement from the team from Worcestershire, and they have used it as a way to standardise assessments and to train new teachers.

The MAPS Gallery

When the teacher marks the work, the teacher has the option of putting the work in the school's MAPS gallery. Every student has access to the gallery, but they can only see work for tasks that they completed *and* had assessed. So for example if a student was part way through a task and clicked on the gallery button, he/she could not see any examples of student work for that task. Once their work for the task has been assessed, they can view the gallery. The gallery has been a very successful tool for enabling peer review of work while preventing (at least within the MAPS system) the possibility of students viewing other students' work prior to completing the task themselves.

How MAPS Works Technically

On a technical level, MAPS runs off a server running Redhat Linux. The Web server runs Apache and the database is MySQL. The code was originally written in Perl using *cgi* scripts. However, to enhance the performance of the system, we moved largely to *mod perl,* which effectively means that much of the application runs through Apache. We have been very pleased with the performance and reliability of the system.

HOW HAS MAPS BEEN USED?

MAPS began as a system designed for use by pupils from year six through year nine (ages 11 to 14). It has evolved into a system that covers every stage from year three right through to the top end of secondary education, and we are now piloting use of MAPS in further education contexts, in particular for adults learning to use computers (PC Passport scheme with the Scottish Qualifications Authority, and the CLAiT scheme with Oxford, Cambridge, and RSA awarding body). In June 2005 there were in excess of 57,000 students registered on the MAPS system, with around 281 subscribing schools spread across 36 education authorities in the UK.

In primary schools, pupils are taught all subjects in mixed ability classes. Usually a single teacher teaches these classes. In secondary school students are taught primarily in "setted" classes, where pupils are grouped by ability and varied for each of the main curriculum areas. Assessment of performance is used to determine the "setting." One consequence of this difference is that primary teachers need to be able to see and mark work in all subjects for their pupils, whereas we find secondary teachers just want to look at the work in their subject. We have had to make a number of adjustments so that both primary and secondary teachers can see what they need to.

Use of MAPS in middle and secondary schools has focused on ICT, but the system is now available as an assessment mechanism for all the other subject areas. There are schools using MAPS to support art, business studies, design and technology, music, modern foreign languages, maths, and science. Two main patterns of usage have emerged. In a minority of schools, the assessment is used for all classes all of the time. The system is used for the delivery of materials, as a marking/feedback mechanism as well as for more general assessment according to the statutory requirements of the National Curriculum. A single school may have up to 100 concurrent users of the system. In other schools delivery of teaching materials is varied. MAPS is used primarily as an end-of-unit assessment system. For each student this might mean using the system to complete seven assessment tasks through the school year, in line with the recommended number of assessment tasks modelled in the Qualifications and Curriculum Authority (QCA) Scheme of Work. If the school is using it for end-of-unit assessment, then the pattern of usage tends to be periodic, with pupils uploading work only as they come to the end of a unit. The disadvantages here are that the early drafts of work are not stored, and the capacity of the system to support/record a student's reflections on his/her work is diminished.

In many cases schools report that children enjoy using MAPS and are motivated by it. While we are glad that this is so, we are yet to conduct formal research in to this. We think it is connected with the fact that children can customise their homepage, and also because they can show their work to their parents at home. Perhaps the improved motivation also comes from the fact that they can see their work "on the Web." We have anecdotal evidence of this, but no systematic study has been carried out. Clearly if the system does have aspects that motivate the students, we need to enhance these features.

Transition Between School Phases

In only a small number of schools have all the feeders that feed a secondary school been users of MAPS. Where they are, use of the system has varied between the schools. Some simply have not used the system sufficiently to provide the secondary with adequate data about past attainment and learning, while others have embedded MAPS into the daily routine of setting, handing in, and marking work. In an increasing number of schools, MAPS is being used to develop a new level of relationship between feeder primary and secondary schools. In some instances, secondary schools are using their own budgets to buy MAPS for their primary feeders. One lesson we have learned from our experience of pupil transition through MAPS is that it is the secondary school that drives the transition process. The secondary school needs the information about the pupils coming into the school. An ePortfolio system by itself can help with this, but clearly if the primary school does not actively participate, then the amount and quality of information that is passed to the secondary school will be of limited extent and value. Several schools have developed transition assessment materials for use in transition between primary and secondary education. These are activities that begin in primary school and which then contribute to initial activities in the secondary school, developing a sense of academic continuity. Shared transition activities help to involve both the primary and secondary teaching teams in the process of transition, and the ePortfolio greatly reduces the amount of bureaucracy involved in sharing the transitional work.

Sharing of Assessment Materials

In Worcestershire, LEA materials developed in individual schools have been developed for use across the whole local authority. Teacher advisors have also used the system to promote the use of LEA-developed materials. Warrington LEA has developed an entire scheme of work based on the National Strategy Scheme of work, but with additional multimedia to promote effective delivery.

Qualification Pilots

In England and Wales, students typically take a number of exams at age 16 and many stay on to take further examinations at age 17 and 18 (school years 12 and 13). In order for MAPS to support year 10 onwards properly, we have been working with Oxford, Cambridge, and RSA (OCR), one of the leading awarding bodies in the UK, and we have designed the system so that tasks can be tagged automatically to the assessment criteria for an OCR qualification component. When the teacher marks an OCR task in MAPS, the teacher can press a button to submit the work to the awarding body. We built a system of moderation ePortfolios for OCR so that their staff can then view the submitted work, check the marking, and view the actual files uploaded by the pupil.

In addition to adapting MAPS to support submission of coursework for existing qualifications, we are also working with awarding bodies to support new qualifications where the use of ePortfolios is included in the specification for the qualification. These new qualifications raise new and exciting possibilities, because it should be possible to do a great deal more than just mimic preceding paper-based methods. We are already looking at a range of ways of annotating and layering comments.

Impacts on Attainment

We have not carried out a systematic study of the impacts on attainment levels from using MAPS so we cannot yet shed light on this, but clearly there is a need to carry out such a study. However, on a purely anecdotal level, Worcestershire Local Education Authority, who used MAPS across a large proportion of schools for years six to nine, reported that they saw the assessed levels go down in the first year of use, and that this was because their assessment support team was better able, using MAPS, to view marked examples of work across schools in Worcestershire. Overall the team found that teachers had been marking too generously, and so the net effect of the standardisation of marking as enabled by MAPS was a lowering of assessed grades. By contrast, two schools (King Edward VI Camp Hill School for Boys, Birmingham, and Newlands School, Windsor) pioneering the use of MAPS to collect coursework for ICT GCSE (General Certificate of Secondary Education) have reported significantly higher grades.

Our OCR ICT GCSE short course results for last year are much better than before (92.5% A to B). Much of this can be attributed to improved collection of work through the Internet. We have year nine groups who get one double period (70 minutes in total) every two weeks and the ability to maintain the online portfolio has made a big difference. It reduced the issues students had handing in work to staff and improved and significantly speeded up any feedback to students. MAPS played a big part in this achievement.* (George Rouse, King Edward VI Camp Hill School for Boys, Birmingham)

The introduction of MAPS into the school has really helped in the teaching and assessment of ICT. One of the most noticeable areas of improvement is in the KS4 GCSE course. It has enabled short, achievable deadlines to be set with students having ready access to information that helps them with the completion. In previous years the ICT department has achieved good GCSE results but the advent of MAPS could well see 95% of the students taking the GCSE course achieving A-C grades in their coursework with over 50 % of these being A grades. MAPS has also helped in many other aspects of ICT teaching, such as allowing students to continue with a project easily even if the regular teacher is not available. (Adam King, Newlands School, Windsor and Maidenhead)

The Learner in All of Us

One of the constants over the years of developing MAPS has been the way that we keep on realising that every user is a learner. This is as true for the head teacher and teacher adviser as it is of the pupils. Everyone is learning. Hence the portfolios for the teacher, administrator, and school IT technician will themselves become professional development portfolios, where the teachers/administrators/technicians can evidence their progress and use their portfolio to argue recognition of their professional competence.

Pupils Helping Teachers

We have found that a number of teachers have used the messaging system to ask their pupils for help when stuck using an application at home. It appears that pupils can be teachers too. Many teachers in the UK who are currently fulfilling the role of ICT coordinator are not themselves ICT specialists. We have frequently had teachers comment that they receive valuable support through MAPS from their more able pupils. This might lead us to reflect this support role in the system itself, giving the ability to some pupils to provide guidance or technical support to other pupils and teachers in the system. Clearly this would need to be controlled and supervised by the teachers, but it is interesting to see how actual usage does not follow pre-conceived boundaries of differences between one role and another.

FUTURE DEVELOPMENTS

With more and more systems coming on the market, there is a proliferation of logins. It is becoming increasingly urgent that a system for supporting single sign-ons is developed. Various options are being reviewed at present by the UK government, but as yet no standard has been approved.

In the next version of MAPS, learners will be able to tag their uploaded work against individual assessment criteria, which will then make possible a variety of means of sorting and filtering of work later for a longer term review by the pupil and teacher. We see this as enhancing the view of the pupil's "distance travelled" by enabling both teacher and pupil to review actual samples of work tagged as they were completed, as opposed to tagging all work against the final set of marked outcomes.

We are looking at the possibility of giving students a studio of real online applications, at which point their portfolio in some ways becomes more like a Web-based desktop.

Recent work with Nesta Futurelab (see http://www.nestafuturelab.org) in a project called The Learning Journey (see http://www.nestafuturelab.org/showcase/learning_journey/learning.htm) has opened our eyes to the potential of using ePortfolios to monitor, value, and record teamwork; we may be adding some teamwork features in the next version of MAPS.

Again as part of The Learning Journey project with Nesta Futurelab, we have been looking at using ePortfolios to support new approaches to learning and have been looking at the approach described by Claxton (2002), who identifies the "four Rs" of learning power: resilience, resourcefulness, reflectiveness, and reciprocity. It is still in its early days, but we are thinking of over-arching themes that persist in a learner's lifelong ePortfolio. These might include: how I learn, how I work with others, how I feel about myself, what I feel I have achieved, what others feel I have achieved (enabling the user to collate peer and other assessments of their capabilities), personal milestones, and formal accredited qualifications. Such themes should be viewable filtered by time and by other criteria, probably learner-defined criteria.

We note on page 31 of the UK Government's digital strategy a statement of intent regarding ePortfolios:

> *We will encourage all organisations to support a personal online learning space for their learners that can develop eventually into an electronic portfolio for lifelong learning.*

It will be interesting to see how this translates into practice (http://www.strategy.gov.uk/downloads/work_areas/digital_strategy/report/pdf/digital_strategy.pdf).

PDAs, Smartphones, and ePortfolios

We are working on a project to connect PDAs (and/or smartphones) to Web-based ePortfolios. The idea is for the PDAs to be linked to the Internet via a Wi-Fi (wireless) network. When the pupil saves work on the PDA, it is saved automatically into his/her Web-based ePortfolio. As handheld learning devices offer a computer:pupil ratio of 1:1, they make it possible for pupils to use computers all day. By saving the work automatically to the user's backed-up, virus-protected, Web-based ePortfolio, many of the problems of small, distributed computing devices (they break/get stolen) are mitigated.

The Learner/Teacher ePortfolio

At the moment there seem to be two types of ePortfolio: those that are attached to the institution, and those that are wholly owned and managed by the learner. For a lifelong portfolio, there is a need for an ePortfolio that is managed by the learner, but that can somehow plug into an institution's information management systems. From a fundamental, design concept perspective, perhaps the solution to making such a system work lies first in just seeing people as people rather than as "teacher" and "student." We all have plenty to learn, so we are all potentially students; and if we have managed to learn anything, then we are also potentially teachers too. We are contemplating a dual-function learner/teacher ePortfolio, which may sit in a wider learner/teacher online community. In the learner/teacher ePortfolio, it is up to the user to switch from learner to teacher mode and can do so at any time.

REFERENCES

Claxton, G. (2002). *Building learning power: Helping young people become better learners.* Bristol: TLO.

Kimbell, R. (1997). *Assessing technology: International trends in curriculum and assessment: UK, Germany, USA, Taiwan, Australia.* Maidenhead: Open University Press.

Chapter XXXV
Implementing Electronic Portfolios at Bowling Green State University

Milton D. Hakel
Bowling Green State University, USA

Mark H. Gromko
Bowling Green State University, USA

Jessica L. Blackburn
Bowling Green State University, USA

ABSTRACT

This chapter outlines the implementation of electronic portfolio technology as part of a university initiative to improve learning. The implementation of electronic portfolios, via Epsilen Software, is discussed in terms of key features deemed necessary by Bowling Green State University's assessment committee. One of the key features of the software is the matrix. This matrix is discussed in terms of its use for documenting student learning on the university's learning outcomes. Reactions from current users are also provided. The chapter concludes by providing the current status of electronic portfolio usage at the university and a discussion of future plans for the software.

BECOMING A PREMIER LEARNING COMMUNITY

Bowling Green State University (BGSU) is a large and complex doctoral research-intensive university, with about 21,000 students at associate degree through doctoral levels; nearly 900 full-time faculty; and over 200 baccalaureate degree programs, 65 master's degree programs, two specialist programs, and 16 doctoral programs in seven academic colleges plus the Graduate College.

In 1998 we adopted this goal: Bowling Green State University aspires to be the premier learning community in Ohio and one of the best in the nation. The goal sparked many initiatives, and the implementation of electronic portfolio technology is one of them. Many other initiatives, such as the development of learning communities and enhanced first-year programs, a redesign of our general education program, and a signature student learning experience concerning critical thinking about values, are being carried out as a result of this focus.

In this chapter we tell the story of the electronic portfolio initiative in the pursuit of this goal, discuss its current status, and close with some reflections on what we have learned so far. But before doing so we give a brief sketch of the context in which this work is taking place.

Even before the "premier learning community" goal was adopted, it was clear that assessment of student learning outcomes was an important driver for assuring the quality of student learning. Using a decentralized approach beginning with undergraduate majors, we asked faculty members to define the learning outcomes that students were to demonstrate in each degree program. Analysis of these several hundred outcomes identified seven underlying skills that are now known as the university learning outcomes: inquiry, creative problem solving, valuing in decision making, writing, presenting, participation, and leadership (see http://www.BGSU.edu/offices/provost/Assessment).

The university learning outcomes give us a shared framework and vocabulary for describing student learning and development. With it, we are transforming our general education program from one based on a content distribution requirements model to one that emphasizes the intellectual skills identified in the university learning outcomes. Other programs that connect directly to the university learning outcomes include piloting an initiative on critical thinking about values and a systematic approach to undergraduate research. We created several first-year experience programs and also residential learning communities that have succeeded in improving student retention. Initiatives like these are turning our aspiration and the academic plan devised to implement it into reality (see http://www.BGSU.edu/offices/provost/BGSUAcademicPlan1.PDF).

In this institutional context, electronic portfolio technology is highly attractive because it enables students to document and reflect on their learning, and to prepare showcase portfolios. It also gives faculty a tool to learn much more quickly and directly about what is working well and what needs more attention. We saw great potential for supporting and documenting student learning in early software releases, and we are convinced that electronic portfolio technology is one of the major enabling forces that will make us a premier learning community.

With that potential in mind, the assessment committee enumerated the features it saw as needed in any electronic portfolio system:

- Easy use (especially adding new materials and new users)
- Access anywhere, anytime via a Web connection
- Include audio and video files
- Under joint control, and in institution's possession
- Sophisticated security and access permissions
- Search by title or any indexed attribute
- Trace cumulative patterns of learning
- Compare portfolios of many students
- Scalable

Based on our knowledge of the innovative and dynamic learning practices pioneered and used at Alverno College (see Hakel, 1997; Mentkowski & Associates, 2000; Hakel, 2001), we especially sought software that could support implementation of similar practices at our university. As a small liberal arts college, Alverno has won dozens of awards, including a MacArthur Foundation no-strings-attached "genius grant" for devising and validating its abilities-based curriculum. We sought and continue to seek to learn from their approach and experience.

We searched periodicals and online sources to identify Web applications that might meet our needs. Based on our evaluation of features and technology available at the time, we decided to join the ePortConsortium as a Developing Member in January 2003. We installed the Epsilen software in March of that year and have been using it since then. A year later we were accepted as a member of the founding cohort of the National Coalition on Electronic Portfolio Learning.

TRACING CUMULATIVE PATTERNS OF LEARNING

A principal virtue of the electronic portfolio is its utility as a tool for teaching and learning. It is much more than a repository or showcase for student work. The cumulative record of student performances can be easily bookmarked in an electronic portfolio, with reflections (student self-assessments) and faculty assessments linked to particular passages or elements of the student's work.

Beyond that attribute, however, the ePortfolio software we adopted offers a revolutionary conceptual advantage—a developmental framework for learning. The developmental framework—or matrix—is a vehicle for creating coherence in the student's learning experience. It can encompass learning that takes place in general education courses, courses in the major, research projects not tightly connected to individual classes, service learning experiences, and appropriate extra-curricular activities. While curricula within universities have coherence from the standpoint of the faculty members who design them, from the student standpoint this is less apparent, appearing as lists of required courses for topics that hold little interest and that seem unrelated to one's career goals. For students, the coherence is more likely to be seen in retrospect. The matrix is a two-dimensional array, scalable to different sizes. Figure 1 shows one example of the matrix, based on our university learning outcomes. It is 4x7 in size, but it can be adjusted in either or both dimensions to accommodate the approaches of particular programs or majors, and (of course) different institutions. Alverno College, for instance, has a degree requirement/portfolio program that integrates six levels of achievement in eight abilities (learning outcomes).

The columns of the matrix represent developmental stages. With four levels identified, they might correspond to typical performance of freshmen, sophomores, juniors, and seniors in college. Or they might correspond to goals for development of academic ability that are not tightly connected to year in college. In any event, they are intended to be explicitly developmental in design, rather than an evaluative scale of grades or performance scores. The rows of the matrix represent learning outcomes or different areas of accomplishment. In the example shown, the rows list the university learning outcomes, and represent skills, abilities, and dispositions that underlie effective performance in each of them. There are three groups: thinking (inquiry, creative problem solving, and valuing in decision making), communication (writing and presenting), and social interaction (participation and leader-

Figure 1. Matrix showing the BGSU learning outcomes as rows and four developmental levels as columns

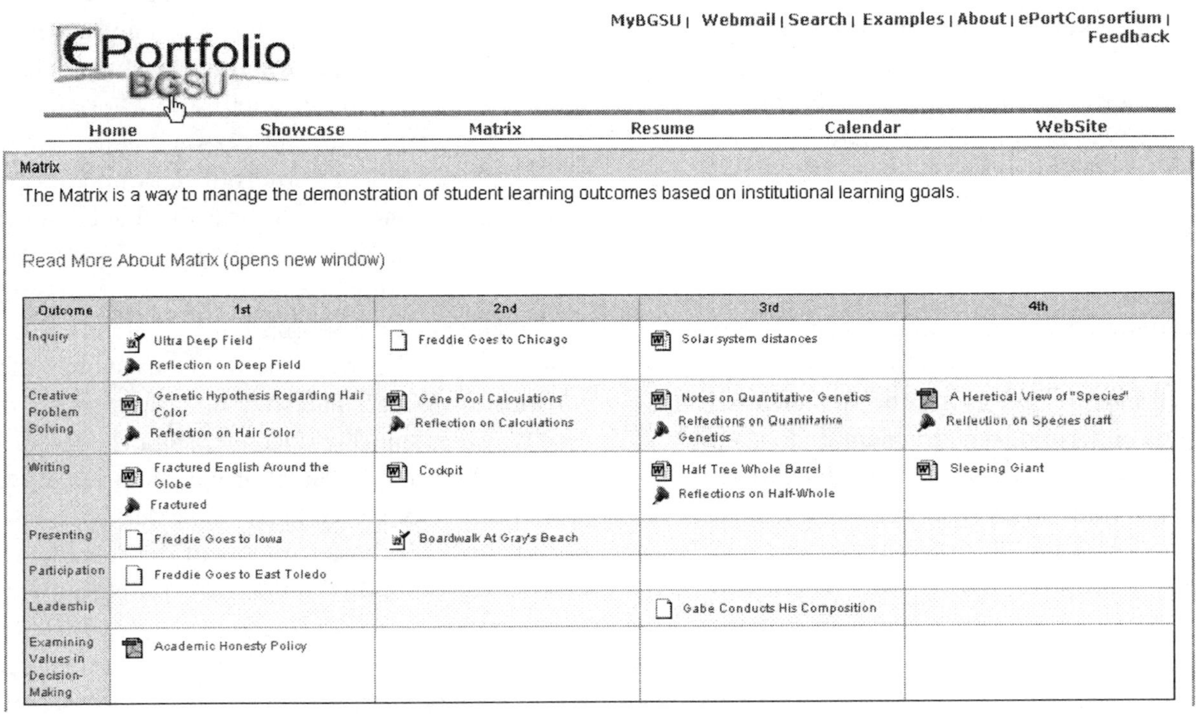

EPortfolio BGSU

MyBGSU | Webmail | Search | Examples | About | ePortConsortium | Feedback

Home Showcase Matrix Resume Calendar WebSite

Matrix

The Matrix is a way to manage the demonstration of student learning outcomes based on institutional learning goals.

Read More About Matrix (opens new window)

Outcome	1st	2nd	3rd	4th
Inquiry	Ultra Deep Field Reflection on Deep Field	Freddie Goes to Chicago	Solar system distances	
Creative Problem Solving	Genetic Hypothesis Regarding Hair Color Reflection on Hair Color	Gene Pool Calculations Reflection on Calculations	Notes on Quantitative Genetics Relfections on Quantitative Genetics	A Heretical View of "Species" Relfection on Species draft
Writing	Fractured English Around the Globe Fractured	Cockpit	Half Tree Whole Barrel Reflections on Half-Whole	Sleeping Giant
Presenting	Freddie Goes to Iowa	Boardwalk At Gray's Beach		
Participation	Freddie Goes to East Toledo			
Leadership			Gabe Conducts His Composition	
Examining Values in Decision-Making	Academic Honesty Policy			

ship). They are not themselves content areas, but skills and abilities important to many different content areas. Moreover, they are keys to success in every career field. They are developed in a wide variety of classes, projects, and extracurricular activities. The rows are, for the student, one of the tangible means to establishing coherence.

To set the stage for the use of the matrix in teaching and learning, it is helpful to contrast it to a different model of education, which we will label the "report card" model. One could represent a report card as a grid, similar in appearance to the matrix of Figure 1. However, instead of developmental levels, a report card has grades. And instead of skills and abilities, a report card lists content areas or courses. The report card would tally the number of grades of A, B, C, and so on, in the many courses completed.

Contrast a static report card ("I got a B in calculus") with the dynamic, developmental model of learning implied by the matrix in Figure 1. "Writing," for instance, is not something one leaves behind in freshman composition ("I got a C in Freshman Comp"). It is a skill that one continues to develop and employ throughout college and throughout life. The particular kind of writing one does will differ in various courses of study and professions (business writing is different from scientific writing, which is different from creative writing), and so the definition of "first-level" and "second-level" writing will differ by content area. But it is an ability that contributes to students' performance effectiveness throughout life. Similarly, thinking (inquiry, creative problem solving, and valuing in decision making) and social interaction (participation and leadership) have different manifestations in the many disciplines and professions. Those differences remain open to exploration and development within the developmental context framed by the matrix. The definitions of the columns, labeled "1st," "2nd," "3rd," and "4th" in Figure 1, are thus of considerable importance. At Alverno College, the faculty undertook an analysis of their curricula as a means to understand and define the developmental stages (Alverno College Faculty, 1994). They "worked from the assumption that there is also a progression of abilities implicit in the movement from introductory survey to advanced seminar." That is, they used established curricula as a means to discover underlying developmental sequences. The result of their analysis was the definition of four developmental levels expected of all students in all eight of the abilities that define their rows (communication, analysis, problem solving, valuing in decision making, social interaction, global perspectives, effective citizenship, and aesthetic responsiveness), plus two additional levels expected of students in their major. Their matrix thus comprises eight abilities defining the rows and six levels defining the columns.

At Bowling Green State University, we have created "rubrics" for each of the developmental stages in each of our seven ability areas. These can be accessed online at_http://www.bgsu.edu/offices/provost/Assessment/Rubrics.htm. They are very much a work in progress. It is the analytical process of identifying the patterns of development of proficiency as a writer, for example, that offers the major curricular impact of electronic portfolio implementation. While an established curricular sequence is an excellent starting point for discerning the presumed path to increasing proficiency, the direct observation of student work products as viewable in electronic portfolios can greatly inform revisions of that curriculum.

A student populates the matrix with work products that demonstrate achievement in a particular learning outcome or ability and at the specified level of proficiency. The work products can be anything that can be represented in a digital format, including text, photographs, graphics, and video and audio files. In deciding what to include in the matrix and where to put it, the student must reflect on his/her work products in light of the definitions of the levels of accomplishment ("rubrics"). To be most effective as a learning device, the student's written reflections or self-assessments should be included in the appropriate cell of the matrix along with the work products to which the reflections refer. The student's understanding of why the items included in the matrix demonstrate their achievement at the specified level should be compared and negotiated with faculty and others' assessments of the same work products. Since this comparison is longitudinal, rather than being confined to a single course or a single semester, long-term improvement (or the lack thereof) in the skills and abilities shaped by coursework and other learning experiences becomes visible.

As the student develops, he or she populates the matrix from left to right, producing a cumulative record of personal development. The matrix—populated by work products, self-assessments, and faculty assessments—provides not only a record of past accomplishment and current ability, it also allows the student to identify what is needed to move to the next stage in development. That is, with reference to the definitions of competencies, or rubrics, the student can set goals for improving their ability in each of the learning outcomes.

For students nearing graduation, the work products in the right-most column can be used as an exhibition or career portfolio. Permissions can be set by the student so that potential employers have access to the work products representing the student's highest level of development and in the learning outcomes most relevant to a particular job.

Finally, electronic portfolios offer programmatic advantages, especially to researchers. A new field of scholarship and application, the science of learning, is emerging. Both laboratory experiments and field studies are starting to reveal new and surprising findings about how people learn (see Bransford, Brown, & Cocking, 1999; Halpern & Hakel, 2003). In this context, electronic portfolios can be construed as observational instruments, not unlike telescopes. Both have the capacity to gather huge quantities of data. Acute focus and skillful interpretation will enable researchers, as well as teachers, not to mention students themselves, to detect and document evidence of learning.

CURRENT STATUS

As of March 2006, 7,736 portfolio accounts had been created by end users. About 75% of the accounts were owned by undergraduates, 16% by graduate students, and 9% by faculty, staff, and administrators. About 20% chose to display at least one file in the Showcase, and the maximum number of files in any single Showcase is 19. About half of the end users created or uploaded information for display in the Résumé section. Fifteen percent uploaded photographs to be displayed on portfolio homepages. Some 700 end users uploaded over 4,000 files, and 65% placed files on display in Matrix. The growth in usage to these levels has happened largely through informal faculty and student networking, and with no formal or central promotional efforts.

We turn now to reviewing the first two years of using Epsilen in the context provided by our original list of desired features. This review is, of necessity, a snapshot of our experience, and it will become obsolete as upgrades are installed. Epsilen Version 2 is now being coded, and we expect to be running it long before this chapter appears in print.

- **Easy Use (especially adding new materials and new users):** Epsilen is relatively easy to use. For end users, uploading files and setting access permissions on them is quick and straightforward, once the end user understands the basic operation of the system. The process for creating new accounts is fully automated.
- **Access Anywhere, Anytime Via a Web Connection:** Browser compatibility has been a frequent challenge in version 1, particularly for Netscape-based browsers and also for Mac users. While Netscape itself is no longer supported on our campus (and accounts for less than 2% of page requests to the university homepage), one of its derivatives, a browser named Safari, is used on many Macs (about 30% of campus machines are Macs). Occasional problems occur for Mac users who are running Internet Explorer. All these issues have become much less severe over the series of upgrades of version 1.
- **Include Audio and Video Files:** Epsilen 1 handles audio and small video files (up to 12 Mb) adequately.
- **Under Joint Control, and in Institution's Possession:** As a Web application offered by the university, and because portfolios are assembled and maintained in part for the satisfaction of curricular requirements, the university acquires certain limited rights to access, monitor, and evaluate student work. The advantage of the Epsilen system is that copies of all work reside on a university server, making institutional access relatively easy. However, in Epsilen 1, the faculty interface for institutional access is quite limited.
- **Sophisticated Security and Access Permissions:** Portfolio items are private by default, and can be made accessible to (1) the public without limitation, (2) any arbi-

trary network ID, or (3) any holder of an access code. Access can be made available through placing the item on a public page or by furnishing a complete URL to a client for direct access via a browser.

- **Search by Title or Any Indexed Attribute:** Epsilen version 1 offers few search facilities, with the Search link being presently limited to searching for dynamic personal portals only by first name, last name, or network ID (these searches accommodate wildcard searching).
- **Trace Cumulative Patterns of Learning:** Epsilen version 1 supports reflections, brief statements about what was learned from the experience represented by the portfolio item(s). There are two types of reflections, the first of which is linked directly to a specific item and is viewable by others only through accessing that specific item, and if a public, network ID or access code viewing right has been granted. The second is independent of specific items. It might contain text pertaining to several or no specific items, and is written and can be viewed only in the context provided by a particular cell of the Matrix (it is public by default). Version 1 end users experienced considerable confusion about why reflections appeared or failed to appear in Matrix.
- **Compare Portfolios of Many Students:** Epsilen version 1 provides an unobtrusive way to collect examples of students' work, and also their reflections on and others' assessments of that work. As such, it provides a solid base for supporting research on student learning and assessment of student learning outcomes.
- **Scaleable:** The .NET framework provides a sound basis for the scalability of Epsilen software, and therefore for institution-wide provision of portfolio accounts, through multi-tier, modular, and object-oriented Web application coding practices. Epsilen version 1 provides installation facilities that configure several parameters to govern local operation. Colleges and universities operate many Web applications, and Epsilen version 1 was designed as a dynamic personal portal that included electronic portfolio services. It is capable of operating as a standalone Web application, authenticating users against LDAP and ADS servers. With significant local adaptation it can interact with other institutional databases.

REFLECTIONS ON IMPLEMENTING THE EPSILEN SOFTWARE

Let us start with a representative sample of comments from students:

I really liked the portfolio system. I had no major problems and I am interested to see what this will bring.

I enjoyed working on this project for the most part and feel that it would serve as a good resource for future employers. However, I did have trouble in the beginning and the trouble shooting links were not as helpful as I would have liked them to be. They were very general and did not have many options. Another problem I had was when I uploaded my résumé it did not stay in the format it was originally in. Overall, I feel that this program can be very successful and has a good start, good luck with the rest of it!

I think that the whole idea of the online portfolio is a good idea. There should be a course or unit to show you how to use it, during freshman year. This would let the freshman get an early start on how they want their portfolios to look and give them an early start on collecting their best pieces of work to put into them. The university might want to think about making this part of UNIV 100, since this is a course that many first-year students take. The only problem that I had with this system is that I thought my password had an 'l' instead of a '1'. Once I figured this out I no longer had to cut and paste it.

The portfolio is very hard to get things to work; it took me until the middle of the semester to get logged in and then it took me forever to upload my info and documents. I am still trying to get pictures uploaded with some of my documents.

I had many problems in the beginning and really did not realize the useful things that this Web site offers until the end. I feel like with proper instruction about this Web site it will be a helpful thing. I also wondered if there was a way to make it more customized. I think that students are more attracted to things that they can make personal, as in color, font, background, etc ...

I am a junior taking EDTL 302. I feel that the Electronic Portfolio was a very interesting and helpful program to use for college students to display their academic goals and knowledge. Thank you and have a great day!

After figuring out my problems, everything works well. I like this idea and think it will be very beneficial.

In general students understand the advantages of this technology and appreciate the availability of persistent storage for their electronic files. The Showcase and Résumé sections are popular and supply immediate benefits to interested students.

Faculty attitudes about electronic portfolios are mixed and fall into three groups. One group comprises the "early adopters," those who are willing to try new technology—their attitudes are the most positive and carry the same general tone as conveyed in the student comments quoted above. At present about 10% are early adopters. A second group, about 70%, comprise the "watchful waiters," those who are aware of the availability of electronic portfolio software for university-wide use, but feel that others should use it first. As the software itself matures and student enthusiasm for using portfolios grows, they will incorporate assignments and activities into their courses that can become portfolio entries. The third group, the remaining 20%, are the "resisters," those who, when presented with a potential change, shoot back with, "OK, if you want me to do *that*, what do you want me to *stop* doing?" They will eventually discover that electronic portfolio technology carries substantial benefits for faculty members as well as for students.

One of the subtleties in the adoption of electronic portfolio software is the shift it can induce from a focus on the teacher and teaching to a focus on the learner and learning. It makes faculty look beyond standalone courses to examine how students learn and develop over the full course of their enrollment. It necessitates consultation about the learning outcomes to be achieved and publication of the standards by which their achievement is to be evaluated. Then it falls to the student to document, with the tangible products collected in the electronic portfolio, what has been learned. Both research and practice demonstrate a key insight: learning goes beyond knowledge to being able to *do* what one knows. Electronic portfolio technology makes it possible to verify the evidence of what one can do with one's knowledge.

PROSPECTS FOR THE NEAR FUTURE

Within the next year we expect to more than double the number of portfolio accounts. Several programs have made commitments to build their courses, assignments, and activities in ways that take advantage of the available technology. The Music Education and College Student Personnel programs are the most advanced in this regard, and strong progress is being made in all teacher education programs, the revised general education program, freshman composition, and a large-scale initiative concerning critical thinking about values.

The bottom line is: Epsilen meets our needs and enables our students to demonstrate that they can *do* what they know.

REFERENCES

Alverno College Faculty. (1994). *Student assessment-as-learning at Alverno College.* Milwaukee: Alverno College Institute.

Bransford, J. D., Brown, A. L., & Cocking, R. R. (Eds.). (1999). *How people learn: Brain, mind, experience, and school.* Washington, DC: National Academy Press.

Hakel, M. D. (1997). What we must learn from Alverno. *About Campus,* 16-21.

Hakel, M. D. (2001). Learning that lasts. Review of Marcia Mentkowski and Associates, Learning that lasts: Integrating learning, development, and performance in college and beyond. *Psychological Science.*

Halpern, D. F., & Hakel, M. D. (Eds.). (2002). Applying the science of learning to university teaching and beyond. *New Directions for Teaching and Learning, 89,* 1-109.

Mentkowski, M., & Associates. (2000). *Learning that lasts: Integrating learning, development, and performance in college and beyond.* San Francisco: Jossey-Bass.

KEY TERMS

Assessment: The practice of specifying measures, collecting data, analyzing it, and using the results to guide changes in performance.

Critical Thinking: Cognitive skills or strategies that increase the probability of a desirable outcome; used to describe thinking that is purposeful, reasoned, and goal directed—the kind of thinking involved in solving problems, formulating inferences, calculating likelihoods, and making decisions when the thinker is using skills that are thoughtful and effective for the particular context and type of thinking task. Critical thinking also involves evaluating the thinking process. *See Reflection and Meta-Cognition.*

Developmental Stages: A sequence or ordered set of descriptors that mark increasing levels of proficiency or effectiveness, such as beginner, intermediate, proficient, and expert.

Epsilen: An open source ePortfolio system licensed by the ePortConsortium, designed by Ali Jafari and his team at the CyberLab in Indianapolis, Indiana.

General Education: A set of courses required of all students at an institution that are intended to develop the ability to think critically and communicate effectively; the ability to understand different cultures and modes of thought; and the ability to investigate forces that shape the social, artistic, scientific, and technological complexities of contemporary culture. *See Learning Outcomes.*

Learning Community: An interdependent group of learners, interacting over some period of time to achieve one or more learning outcomes.

Learning Outcomes: Brief statements that describe what a learner knows and can do at the end of instruction. For example, one learning outcome for Computer Science majors at BGSU is: "Work effectively with a client and members of a software development team to analyze, specify, design, implement, test, and document software that meets the client's needs."

Matrix: A means for displaying organized sets of electronic artifacts. In the BGSU Matrix, the university learning outcomes (or more specific outcomes defined by the academic program) define the rows, and stages of development define the columns.

Reflection: A key strategy for becoming an outstanding performer is to ask yourself, after each and every performance, "What did I learn from doing this?" The practice of thinking about and analyzing your performance is called "reflection." It might also be called "self-assessment," "meta-cognition," "do differents," or "an after-action review."

Rubric: Written criteria or guidelines and definitions that are used for evaluating artifacts or performances.

Chapter XXXVI
Twisting the Kaleidoscope: Making Sense of ePortfolios

Roberta Devlin-Scherer
Seton Hall University, USA

Joseph Martinelli
Seton Hall University, USA

Nancy Sardone
Seton Hall University, USA

ABSTRACT

This exploratory study examines if student perceptions and ePortfolio products match faculty beliefs that ePortfolios are influential learning experiences. Multiple methods of data collection (survey about values and uses of ePortfolios, and content analysis of the quality of ePortfolios) are used to triangulate the results. Student ePortfolios are reviewed for level of difficulty, uniqueness, design, and depth of reflection. Multiple raters help ensure reliability. Bivariate analysis as descriptive statistics is used to determine if any relationship exists between ePortfolio rubric score and academic credits earned in computer technology courses. This research aims to inform the development process of ePortfolios across university campuses, and suggests that the investment of time and resources in this authentic assessment process is yielding some valuable results.

INTRODUCTION AND PROBLEM STATEMENT

Creativity is a lot like looking at the world through a kaleidoscope. You look at a set of elements, the same ones everyone else sees, but then reassemble those floating bits and pieces into an enticing new possibility.

—Rosabeth Moss Kanter

Beginning in 1996, Seton Hall University embarked on a technology initiative that included laptop computers for all undergraduate students and faculty, investing over $25 million to support teaching and learning with technology (Seton Hall University, 2002). In 1999, EDUCAUSE recognized Seton Hall University for superior campus networking. The same year the university was ranked 16th in a survey of Yahoo Internet Life's "America's Most Wired Colleges" among United States' campuses, and first among Catholic universities based on the initiatives in the areas of hardware, academics, and services in technology. Simultaneously, faculty in the Educational Studies department participated in a three-year Preparing Tomorrow's Teachers to Use Technology (PT3) Implementation grant sponsored by the U.S. Department of Education, Office of Postsecondary Education. The project was locally named Project SHURE (Seton Hall University Revitalizing Education). The prime directive of this national initiative was to foster technology-enriched teacher education programs by focusing on practical faculty training. As a result of this grant, use of technology in course offerings has increased. Educational Studies faculty have continued to further investigate ways to use technology to foster students' growth and development both as individuals and future teacher educators, as well as to offer opportunities to develop their reflective thinking skills. The idea for students to develop their own electronic portfolios (ePortfolios) that promoted their professional and technology proficiencies, packaged together with a focus on employment, was the result of this investigation. This preliminary study of ePortfolios has allowed us to learn more about our students through both our observations of their work, and self-perceptions of their electronic portfolio experiences through written survey responses. In the end, we have a renewed sense of the perceived value of this college experience, which has informed our own practice.

The authors view ePortfolios as living documents that allow for students' growth and development over time, and use an adapted version of the living-systems design model for the development of Web-based products (Plass & Salisbury, 2002) in course work. Plass and Salisbury created this instructional design model with the view that the resulting system (or in the case of electronic portfolios, a product) is a living and adapting organism. Their view is that "since growing and sharing knowledge is, by definition, an ongoing and self-modifying process, the goal is to design and build a system that is adaptable to its environment—a living system" (Plass & Salisbury, 2002, p. 39). To further illustrate our view of electronic portfolios as living documents, we found a fitting analogy in Brewster's 1816 invention, the kaleidoscope. Consisting of carefully placed mirrors that reflect off the contents contained within, this instrument produces an endless and ever-changing variety of colors and forms, which can be complex, unique, inspiring, and fascinating. A well-produced electronic portfolio, like the kaleidoscope, can be multi-faceted in design, absorbing to review, and possibly different each time reviewed, offering insight and depth into the teacher candidate's proficiencies.

As proponents for the ePortfolio development process to be part of the teacher preparation curriculum, the authors believe that students who construct ePortfolios benefit from a unique experience that not only develops their reflective thinking and creative skills, but also enhances their learning in other meaningful ways. By exploring the results of an electronic survey with Seton Hall University's College of Education and Human Services alumni (n=9) who volunteered to complete an ePortfolio in their coursework and conducting an analysis of the latent content of individuals' ePortfolios, which can be found at the Web site http://education.shu.edu/portfolios/, the authors sought evidence to determine if survey results and student products corroborated faculty beliefs and observations.

BACKGROUND

Interest in using ePortfolios as tools for students and professionals to store and display artifacts of their work is expanding. Among four-year private colleges, ePortfolio services rose from 12% to 20% during 2003-2004, while public colleges reported an increase of 18% to 32% (Green, 2004). Accrediting agencies have highlighted ePortfolios as one means of assessing candidate performance, and standards boards (e.g., National Board of Professional Teaching Standards, Endodontics, and Nursing) recognize accomplished professionals through stringent portfolio presentations, many of which have evolved into electronic format. In teacher education, portfolios have been used to stimulate reflection about teaching and learning, assess teacher competence, and document K-12 student performance (Barone, 2002; Biddle & Lasley, 1991; Campbell, Cignetti, Melenyzer, Nettles, & Wyman, 2004; Long & Stansbury, 1994; Zubizarretta, 1994).

Electronic portfolios have the potential to provide authentic and valuable learning opportunities for students. Faculty believe ePortfolios facilitate student growth and development (Macedo, Snider, Penny, & Laboone, 2001), and reflective thinking skills (MacDonald, Liu, Lowell, Tsai, & Lohr, 2004). They report that while students find ePortfolios demanding to develop (Irby & Brown, 1998; Milman, 1999), students value learning about instructional design and development (Richards, 1998), honing their technology skills (Hewett, 2004), exchanging ideas with peers (MacKinnon, 1999; Tsai, Lowell, Liu, MacDonald, & Lohr, 2004), and preparing materials for employers (Young, 2002; Hewett, 2004).

As educators in higher education at Seton Hall University who have designed, built, and taught students how to develop ePortfolios, the authors concur that these strengths are inherent in the ePortfolio development process. In the Educational Studies department at Seton Hall, reflective thinking as an outgrowth of self-awareness is viewed as an essential skill to guide future teacher practice. Throughout the current curriculum, teacher candidates are asked to reflect about their experiences, about communities (school and society) that they are working in, and about the effects of their professional work with K-12 students. Therefore, through this study we sought to find out what level of self-awareness and reflective skills are showcased in the ePortfolio product and how important these skills are to students. Traditionally, portfolios in teacher education programs have been created in paper format. However, portfolios in this form do not provide a clear method to determine an individual's proficiency with computer technology or organizational skills to the level that an electronic format can provide. To further refine our study questions, we sought to determine what level of proficiency in computer technology and organizational skills is evidenced in ePortfolios and how important the acquisition of these skills is to students.

METHOD

The authors created an electronic survey using the Seton Hall University Web-based survey tool, ASSET (Academic Survey System & Evaluation Tool), consisting of 29 items and five open-ended questions. Drawn from the literature on ePortfolios which comments on the perceived values of these products, the survey questions relate to the main themes of this study: self, skill, and career development. Respondents were asked to describe the development process of their ePortfolio, their personal growth and computer technology skills development, uses of their ePortfolio, perceived value of the product and its relationship to employment, and continued development. Other data, including demographic information, age, academic credits earned in computer technology courses, current work setting, and professional development experiences, was also collected.

This survey tool generates a Web link to the electronic survey which was distributed via electronic mail to 15 Seton Hall University alumni who volunteered to develop their own Web-based ePortfolios, published in the public domain. All of the alumni constructed their ePortfolios with the support of Seton Hall University faculty within a course. Six graduate and three undergraduate students, age ranges of 21-25 (55.6%), 26-30 (11.1%), and over 35 (33.3%), completed the survey for a 60 % response rate. The undergraduate secondary education students had academic majors in English and history; elementary students majored in the social sciences. Graduate students were from the school library media, teacher education, and instructional design programs. Professional work settings include elementary/middle school teachers (55.6%), high school teachers (33.3%), and instructors in higher education (11.1%).

In addition, the latent content of alumni ePortfolios was evaluated according to a nine-point rubric scale to determine quality of communications, depth of reflections, demonstration of organizational skills, use of instructional design principles, and level of difficulty. The investigator-designed rubric was previously piloted with sample ePortfolios. Multiple evaluators were used to ensure reliability. Data analysis of the ePortfolio contents and demographics used descriptive quantitative methods (Babbie, 2001).

This preliminary study also used bivariate correlations as descriptive statistics to determine if any relationship existed between rubric score and academic credits earned in computer technology courses. No attempt was made to use the resulting correlations as predictors or as an inferential statistical technique. These correlations were used to measure the strength and direction of relationships.

These methods—data collection, alumni surveys about the value and uses of ePortfolios, and content analysis of the quality of alumni ePortfolios using a rubric instrument—were used to triangulate the results. This strategy minimizes the possibility that the research findings reflect the method of inquiry (Babbie, 2001).

RESULTS

The authors meshed the headings of the rubric instrument used to analyze the contents of the ePortfolios with the self-report data provided from the survey. The headings include communication, organization, reflection, presentation, and difficulty. Seton Hall University alumni portfolios and scoring rubrics are available at http://education.shu.edu/portfolios/.

Communication

The investigators reviewed samples of writing throughout each ePortfolio. In analyzing the quality of communication, the evaluators looked for an overall clear, purposeful, focused, and coherent writing style. Most students communicated energy, pride, and passion for their intended profession. In several ePortfolios, reflective entries were missing or yet to be developed. In one undergraduate product, sentences were not well expressed and there tended to be a reliance on reader inference for understanding. However, most products had been carefully edited; only two portfolios had minor spelling errors.

The opportunity to communicate the purpose and value of their college experience through the ePortfolio mechanism was appreciated by the alumni respondents. When asked what they liked best about their finished ePortfolios, themes of personal pride and increased productivity emerged. This user's comment portrayed both pride and planned use of the ePortfolio: "My portfolio really captured who I am and what I would bring to a potential employer." Adaptability of the ePortfolio was highlighted in another response: "I like that I can change the ePortfolio and amend the documents as I grow professionally."

The surveys revealed that the ePortfolio was viewed as a powerful instrument used to seek employment. After developing the ePortfolio product, respondents felt they would promote their ePortfolio during an employment interview or professional introduction. These job-seekers believed that an ePortfolio would make a candidate "stand out a little bit more than others who do not have one" and displayed instructional tools they had developed. As one developer exclaimed: "I am planning to tell potential employers during the interview about the ePortfolio so that they can see my work as an educator and also observe my technological abilities!" Students included their ePortfolio Web address in their employment cover letter or on the résumé (100%), provided a copy of their ePortfolio or the Web link for potential employers (71.4%), or submitted a CD (28.6%). No one converted the electronic format to paper format for potential employers, nor did they plan to do so. When asked about specific feedback they received after sharing their ePortfolios with prospective employers, four respondents indicated that employers expressed satisfaction with being able to use the ePortfolio as a reference before and after the interview. Alumni were also told by potential employers that they were impressed by the ePortfolio product.

Organization

In analyzing the ePortfolio contents for organizational skills demonstrated, the evaluators found evidence that respondents valued and used organizational methodology and strategies. Strong and consistent navigational methodology and appropriate file structures were found throughout the evaluated ePortfolios. The undergraduate ePortfolios had more organizational errors than the graduate-level ePortfolios, such as forgetting to publish links to the Web server, instead pointing the links to their network drives, rendering dead links. In another instance, Web pages were created and linked properly, yet the pages were blank and had no indication of an under-construction status.

When asked to offer words of wisdom to future portfolio preparers, respondents recognized the importance of planning and organizing both materials and ideas. They suggested thinking through ideas first, then organizing materials in folders, and highlighted the value of seeking help. One commented:

Designing an ePortfolio can be somewhat frustrating. It can seem overwhelming at times because you want it to look great. When you are in doubt, ask someone else for advice. Sometimes other people viewing it can be a huge help to perfect your ePortfolio.

Reflection

The investigators reviewed ePortfolio philosophy statements and reflective writing pieces about their included artifacts, in the form of descriptions and explanations. Exhibits demonstrated appropriate professional competencies, although some did not state educational standards explicitly. In analyzing the ePortfolios for level of reflective thinking, the evaluators cited the overall ability of the designers to relate the content to the larger context and purpose of ePortfolio development (employment). It was noted that when developing ePortfolios and including samples of their students' work (if they participated in field experiences), developers need to analyze the actual work and tie it back in to the original teaching objective. Instead, the evaluators found student work samples posted with shallow or missing reflections.

Self-awareness is the gateway to the development of effective reflective skills. All alumni reported that they learned more about themselves by engaging in the ePortfolio development process. One respondent noted that the ePortfolio afforded him/her the opportunity to assess his/her views about education. Statements about "unique background," "identification of special skills," "ability to generate creative thoughts," and developing "creative processes using software" described the abilities the group believed they gained. Others commented on the value of the opportunity to summarize their college experience. As one noted, "I found out I have accomplished a lot over my time at Seton Hall."

Over half of respondents (66.6 %) said that they knew very little or nothing about ePortfolios before they began the development process. Four respondents commented on increased employment marketability and about their previously untapped creative skills which were discovered by working with the technology tools. Employment purposes were cited as their primary reason for developing an ePortfolio (88.9 %), followed by improving software skills (55.6%), earning course credits (33.3%), and developing a better understanding of alternative forms of assessment (22.2%). It was noted that an advantage of ePortfolios is that they "are easier to work with than paper because you can continuously change them to suit your changing needs." All of the respondents felt that the creation of an ePortfolio helped them achieve their desired goals.

Presentation

The origin of *kaleidoscope* comes from the Greek words *kalos* (beautiful), *eidos* (form), and *scopos* (watcher). The authors found this sample of ePortfolios beautiful in composition. In evaluating the ePortfolio contents as to the use of instructional design principles, the evaluators found a kaleidoscope offering of ePortfolios, each differing from one another in design, layout, and use of colors and fonts.

Like any piece of art, beauty lies in the eyes of the beholder, stemming from the individual's intrinsic sense of style. One respondent stated, "I liked the professional look of my ePortfolio and the ability for many people to view my portfolio." Two alums stated: "I think my ePortfolio looks great!" and "I like the design and coloring of my ePortfolio. I also liked the pictures I added that indicate my accomplishments!" Often cited in the responses was an enjoyment of the creative processes involved with using software tools. Respondents stated that professors, peers, and professional mentors influenced their selection of artifacts, but not family members. Despite inherent challenges in the development of an ePortfolio, future preparers can take heart from the promise of ownership and these words of encouragement:

The ePortfolio process is an enjoyable developmental process ... it is helpful for employment, interviews, workshops, and it brings forth creativity. I really enjoyed the various articles, media-music and sounds, actual photos/artifacts, clipart, and unusual fonts with 'cool' transitions that you can incorporate in your very own ePortfolio.

Difficulty

In evaluating the ePortfolio for level of difficulty as indicated by learning curve of software programs and the incorporation of advanced multimedia objects, the evaluators found that almost all of the ePortfolios were published onto a Web server using the Microsoft FrontPage product, and all but two were constructed using this program. Of the two exceptions, one alumnus created her ePortfolio using Microsoft Word, imported the completed pages into FrontPage, and subsequently published her work to the Web server. The other alumni used a Web-based template, TeacherWeb.com, and the site resides on the TeacherWeb.com server. Both of these developers had an easier time in the construction process, as the Word program and the template offering are far easier products to use than the FrontPage software program.

When looking at the ePortfolios to determine the array of software programs used to design and create not only the ePortfolio shell but also the actual artifacts resident in the ePortfolio, our observational findings confirmed the survey results. Additional software programs included Microsoft Word (88.9%), various photo editing software (66.7%) of Adobe Photo Elements, Microsoft Image Composer, and Microsoft Paint, PowerPoint (44.4%), Publisher (22.2%), with the other category reporting uses of Adobe PDF, Macromedia Flash, and Director. (In some instances, total percentages may exceed 100% because multiple responses were permitted). These files were most often created in other classes, uploaded to the Web server, and linked as file attachments as a way to demonstrate learned knowledge. Graphics were used in every ePortfolio created, while 33.3% included sound and/or audio clips.

The importance of providing interactivity in their Web sites was apparent to 66.7% of respondents who included an e-mail link as a way to elicit responses from Web visitors, and 22.2% of respondents went a step further, creating interactive Web-based forms. The use of these software elements demonstrates extended thinking processes and proficiency at a higher level. This is also true of ePortfolios that included advanced software commands such as dynamic effects, embedded files, and use of innovative navigation methods.

The evaluators decided not to rate the inclusion or exclusion of advanced multimedia objects as an indication of difficulty level achieved due to unforeseen obstacles associated with hardware devices (lack of speakers) and software programs (ill-functioning movie players) during classes.

Descriptive statistical tests using SPSS were performed to determine any relationships among courses taken, rubric scores, and level of student. When analyzing technology course credits taken by undergraduates vs. graduates, it was found that the undergraduates had completed less credits (M=10, SD=4.58) than graduates (M=15.0, SD=5.02). In scoring the ePortfolios, the undergraduates' mean scores (M=37.0, SD=7.0) were slightly less than the graduates' (M=39.83, SD=6.55). Using Pearson Product Moment Correlation Coefficients, no significant correlation existed between the total rubric score and number of technology credits for either undergraduate or graduate groups.

Some educators believe that the answer to the question as to whether a student learned the given material is found in what they do *after* the course is over. Most alumni responded that they have shared the ePortfolio strategies they learned with different groups, including peers (66.7%), students (55.6%), co-workers (44.4%), and family (44.4%), and received positive responses. Electronic portfolio development has positively affected their classroom teaching, as respondents commented that their confidence level with technology grew through this process. This newfound competence with technology was what enabled them to use computers for teaching and learning with their own students. This is evidenced by many of the survey responses, such as by the alumnus who commented, "I discovered that I truly can do something even when it seems impossible. I also realized how great technology is as a tool for teachers and educators."

Two respondents maintain Web sites on an active basis as a way to inform parents and students of assigned schoolwork and upcoming events, and one respondent currently has students create ePortfolios of their own to share their work. Others indicated that they maintain their ePortfolios with the addition of new work samples, new instructional tools for collaboration, and new Web links (62.5 %).

DISCUSSION

Respondents believed that the ePortfolio development process was an influential and powerful experience that fostered their learning. The process provided them with a broadened sense of awareness as to the capabilities of technology and an opportunity to develop their technological skills. It also imparted an increased awareness of visual design principles and an enriched sense of style, recognition of their ability to develop new ideas and skills, and increased productivity. Respondents found having an ePortfolio saved time when updating information, was less costly to use than paper-based format, and enabled employers to preview them before the interview process—another timesaver.

An effectively designed portfolio enables the end user to develop a self-portrait over a period of time. It can chart important developmental processes in which goals are continually reached and new goals for improvement are set (Campbell et al., 2004). Information obtained from the students sampled at Seton Hall show that by creating ePortfolios, they have obtained greater insight into their abilities and skills. Study participants believed that as a byproduct of the ePortfolio process, they have grown both professionally and personally. Uneven performance of reflective entries in ePortfolios suggests that faculty need to increase their focus on teaching writing reflections for some undergraduate and graduate students to foster deeper thinking.

Perhaps due to the voluntary nature of these ePortfolio developers combined with the personal nature of the ePortfolio project, students were highly motivated to do well regardless of whether they were at the undergraduate or graduate level. Undergraduate students achieved relatively the same mean rubric score (U: 37.00 vs. G: 39.83) with less college credits in technology courses (U: 10 vs. G: 15) than graduate students. However, graduates students' work was less error prone than that of undergraduates, as evidenced by incorrect structural links.

The purpose of an ePortfolio may change as well as its artifacts, but a well-designed portfolio will be able to show how a student/learner is performing as a professional. It can serve as a de facto digital archive over a student's entire career. The positive comments received in this exploratory study indicate that ePortfolio development indeed results in a tangible, marketable product that is often appreciated by employers. Electronic portfolios provide accessibility and portability features for readers and an opportunity for students to be creative while presenting their best work to a larger community. Survey results indicated that respondents valued the development process of the ePortfolio.

Critics of ePortfolios have thought employers would have not had the time, interest, or knowledge to review them. That was reported in one case in this survey. However, the following statement describes a different kind of reception that will become more common as the use of ePortfolios grows:

When applying for jobs, I included my Web address in my cover letters. It allowed those who were interested to take a look at what I have to offer before I go on the interview. My current employer was very impressed and I was away when I received the phone call to come in for an interview. They called back three times after viewing my ePortfolio. I believe the ePortfolio is what landed me the job!

In addition, the process involved in ePortfolio development is rich in additional learning opportunities and influences. Students become actively engaged in the learning process rather than act as passive recipients. They develop self-confidence in their technology skills, which appears to relate to the use of technology for teaching and learning in their own classrooms. Some continue to update their artifacts, which appears to indicate a belief in the fluid and changing notion of knowledge. Benefits are extended as they share their technology expertise in their own classrooms through the promotion of active learning methods and authentic assessment opportunities.

The scoring rubric used to assess the ePortfolios in this study needs further development to become a more precise scoring tool in the following areas: the presentation section needs to address more instructional design principles, greater consideration needs to be taken in the areas of reflection, and accommodations need to be made for the differences of available multimedia creation tools.

CONCLUSION AND FUTURE TRENDS

Initially at Seton Hall University, faculty involved in the ePortfolio development process have been more concerned that students achieve their personal and professional goals, and that the ePortfolio contain artifacts of quality rather than mandating the use of a specific technology-oriented software product. The problem inherent in a non-prescribed methodology is the lack of data aggregation opportunities that can inform future practice. In addition, the steep learning curve associated with the FrontPage Web-authoring product caused us to seek other options. Currently, customized development is underway at Seton Hall using the developer's toolkit option within the Blackboard Content Management System to build in data aggregation in the form of reports tied to educational standards. Presently, we have the ability to pull aggregate reports on a quantitative basis (number of students by major by standard who have entered a product, complete with a justification as to why they believe it meets the standard). Work continues on to develop an effective tool within the Blackboard management system to evaluate the qualitative data found in product justifications.

Capitalizing on ePortfolios as an authentic assessment method is spreading to a variety of disciplines as shown in an initial sampling of those currently available on the Web in the References section of this chapter. Electronic portfolios require intensive professional support, expensive hardware and software tools, end user skill awareness and development, an extensive time investment, and loads of energy for both student and instructor. This study and the increasing interest outside teacher education suggest that the investment of time and resources are worthwhile.

An ePortfolio offers both the designer and end user a unique look into one's professional and personal experiences. Like a kaleidoscope, depending on the amount of light and number of turns of the mirrors, an ePortfolio may be different with each viewing based on the designer's choices. Our ePortfolio study will continue to evolve and change over time as well, with each new finding providing us the assistance we need as proponents, teachers, and designers of this developmental process.

NOTE

Authors contributed equally to this article.

REFERENCES

Babbie, E. (2001). *The practice of social research*. Belmont, CA: Wadsworth.

Barone, D. (2002). *National board certification handbook: Support and stories from teachers and candidates*. Portland, OR: Stenhouse.

Barrett, H., & Wilkerson, J. (2005, February). *Conflicting paradigms in electronic portfolio approaches: Choosing an electronic portfolio strategy that matches your conceptual framework.* Paper presented at the meetin of the American Association of Colleges of Teacher Education, Washington, DC. Retrieved May 29, 2005, from http://electronicportfolios.com/systems/paradigms.html

Biddle, J., & Lasley, T. (1991). *Portfolios and the process of teacher education.* Paper presented at the meeting of the American Educational Research Association, Chicago.

Campbell, D., Cignetti, P., Melenyzer, B., Nettles, D., & Wyman, R. (2004). *How to develop a professional portfolio: A manual for teachers*. New York: Pearson.

Gibson, D., & Barrett, H. (2003). Directions in electronic portfolio development. *Contemporary, Issues in Technology and Teacher Education, 2*(4). Retrieved May 15, 2005, from http://www.citejournal.org/vol2/iss4/general/article3.cfm

Green, K. (2004, October). *Computing and information technology in U.S. higher education.* Paper presented at the meeting of EDUCAUSE, Denver, CO.

Hewett, S. (2004). Electronic portfolios: Improving instructional practices. *TechTrends, 48*(5), 26-30.

Irby, B. J., & Brown, G. (1998, April). *An exploratory study of perceptions of preservice administrators on traditional versus electronic career advancement portfolios.* Paper pesented at the meeting of the American Educational Research Association, San Diego, CA. (ERIC Document Reproduction Service No. ED 421467)

Kilbane, C., & Milman, N. (2003). *The digital teaching portfolio handbook: A how-to guide for educators.* New York: Pearson.

Long, C., & Stansbury, K. (1994, December). Performance assessments for beginning teachers: Options and lessons. *Phi Delta Kappan, 76*(4), 318-322.

MacDonald, L., Liu, P., Lowell, K., Tsai, H., & Lohr, L. (2004). Part one: Graduate student perspectives on the development of electronic portfolios. *TechTrends*, *48*(3), 52-55.

Macedo, P., Snider, R., Penny, S., & Laboone, E. (2001, November). *The development of a model for using e-portfolios in instructional technology programs.* Paper presented at the meeting of the National Convention of the Association for Educational Communications and Technology, Atlanta, GA. (ERIC Document Reproduction Service No. ED 470133)

MacKinnon, G. R. (1999). *Electronic portfolios in science education*. Research report. (ERIC Document Reproduction Service No. ED437029)

Milman, N. B. (1999, February-March). *Web-based electronic teaching portfolios for preservice teachers.* Paper presented at the meeting of the Society for Information Technology and Teacher Education, San Antonio, TX.

Plass, J., & Salisbury, M. (2002). A living-systems design model for Web-based knowledge management systems. *ETR&D, 50*(1), 35–57.

Richards, R. T. (1998, April). Infusing technology and literacy into the undergraduate teacher education curriculum through the use of electronic portfolios. *T.H.E. Journal*, *25*(9).

Seton Hall University. (2002). *Overview of information technology at Seton Hall University.* Retrieved May 15, 2005, from http://technology.shu.edu/page/Projects+and+Initiatives!OpenDocument

Tsai, H., Lowell, K., Lin, P., MacDonald, L., & Lohr, L. (2004). Part two: Graduate student perspectives on the development of electronic portfolios. *TechTrends*, *48*(3), 56-60.

Tosh, D., & Wermuller, B. (2004). *E-portfolios and Weblogs: One vision for e-portfolio development.* Retrieved February 2, 2005, from http://www.eradc.org/papers/e-portfolio_Weblog.pdf

Young, J.R. (2002, March 8). E-portfolios could give students a new sense of their accomplishments. *The Chronicle of Higher Education*, *48*(21), A31.

Zubizaretta, J. (1994, December). Teaching portfolios and the beginning teacher. *Phi Delta Kappan, 76*(4), 318-323.

KEY TERMS

Alternate Assessment: Other tools and methods to evaluate instruction that diverges from the traditional methods of quizzes and tests, for example. One alternative assessment method is the use of a rubric, or a scoring guide used to assess specified criteria.

Authentic Activities: Instructional activities designed with real-world relevance to provide opportunities to problem-solve and explore, consider different perspectives, and are often collaborative.

Instructional Design: A set of events embedded in a range of purposefully planned and developed activities to engage and facilitate learning.

Kaleidoscope: A tube-like instrument with colored glass and mirrors which the user turns to reflect designs and patterns.

Latent Content: Existing content made evident through analysis.

Living-Systems Design Model: An instructional design model developed by Plass and Salisbury (2002) which views the resulting system or product as a living and adapting organism.

Reflection: The ability and skills to think about learning experiences in new and meaningful ways.

A SAMPLING OF WEB-BASED PORTFOLIOS IN DIFFERENT DISCIPLINES

Web site addresses occasionally change or information is removed. All Web sites listed below were available as of October 1, 2005.

- **Agricultural Education:** http://cast.csufresno.edu/portfolios/scripts/ItemList.asp?user=96
- **Architecture:** http://home.earthlink.net/~hughbaun/
- **College of Business Guidelines for portfolio:** http://www.bus.msu.edu/learcenter/students/portfolio.html
- **Computer Science:** http://www4.cord.edu/mathcs/CS_assessment_files/portfolio.htm
- **Endodontics Portfolio Guidelines:** http://www.aae.org/certboard/examinations/abecasehistory.htm
- **Facilities Management:** http://geocities.com/Eureka/8429
- **Geography Teaching Assistant:** http://www.birgitm.com
- **Guidelines for Portfolios in Science:** http://www.accessexcellence.org/LC/TL/CGSE/contents.html
- **Medical Case History Evaluation Form:** http://www.aae.org/NR/rdonlyres/883A5A58-2141-4AE4-A1F4AE37D1D5D8ED/0/CaseHistoryEvaluationTable.pdf
- **Nursing Portfolio as Professional Development:** http://www.clinical-supervision.com/john_driscoll_files/portfolios_article.pdf
- **Professional Multimedia/Photography Portfolios:**
    - **Doug Finley:** http://www.dfinley.com/index.html
    - **Loren Fisher:** http://www.elfmultimedia.com/
    - **Steve Smith:** http://stevesmithphotography.com/about/steve.asp

Chapter XXXVI
Creating a Strategy for the Implementation of the QUT ePortfolio

David Emmett
Queensland University of Technology, Australia

Wendy Harper
Queensland University of Technology, Australia

Kim Hauville
Queensland University of Technology, Australia

ABSTRACT

This chapter introduces the Queensland University of Technology (QUT) ePortfolio project as an example of a successful collaboration and integration strategy within a higher education context. Following extensive piloting and testing, the portfolio was released to all students and staff late in 2004, and by May 2005 in excess of 10,000 portfolios had been commenced. This chapter will present insights into this project which reveal some key collaboration and integration strategy decisions that were taken by both the university and the portfolio design team. In order to support these insights, preliminary student, academic, and employer feedback is provided based on research carried out from 2003 to 2005. The authors hope that this chapter will provide insights that will enable other institutions to enjoy similar success.

INTRODUCTION

The Queensland University of Technology (QUT) Student Electronic Portfolio (the Portfolio) is a distinctly innovative addition to the experience of being a student at an Australian university. This assertion is made on the basis of its student centeredness, its alignment with teaching and learning policy and with the whole student experience, its flexibility and comprehensiveness, and its university-wide integrated architecture.

The Portfolio's design and development was a direct consequence of the strategic harnessing of a wide spectrum of skills, knowledge, and technology across the university. Its goal is to enhance the student experience, making it more reflective, more personally valuable and continuous, and more enduring than was possible before the development of comprehensive digital facilities at the university.

This chapter will firstly present reflections on the collaboration and integration strategies used for the successful development and implementation of the Portfolio, and secondly provide preliminary student, academic, and employer feedback to the Portfolio based on research carried out during 2003 to 2005.

THE NEED

The impetus for this project was twofold: firstly, the opportunity to create an innovative university framework that helped students to gain a "bird's-eye" perspective on their learning, as well as their goals for the future. If students could achieve this, then it would be possible for them to become more excited about learning and to strategize to reach their own goals. In brief, the project was propelled by a vision to add value to students' learning by empowering them through reflective thinking. As QUT's DVC for Teaching, Information, and Learning Support, Tom Cochrane, said:

There existed genuine potential to help students 'pull it all together' so that they could see how their experiences added up and made sense as a whole.

Secondly, the Portfolio was driven by Col McCowan, the manager of the Careers and Employment section at QUT, who clearly saw the Portfolio as providing a competitive advantage to QUT students over other university graduates in an increasingly competitive labour market.

QUT Portfolio Structure

The Portfolio comprises an online tool that students utilize to record, catalogue, retrieve, and present reflections on experiences and artefacts that support the development of graduate capabilities. The Portfolio extends the student journey beyond the classroom: it allows students to write about their personal, community, and work life, as well as their life as an undergraduate and beyond. From the students' perspective it is holistic, allowing them to build a picture of themselves as a whole person, a picture that cannot be seen in an academic history or curriculum vitae alone.

The Portfolio is available to all of QUT's 40,000 students (12% from overseas) and to all staff (3,500). The Portfolio comprises five main structural areas:

1. **Portfolio Management:** Where students are able to add, edit, and manage experiences and artefacts, and to create, release, and export their Portfolio.
2. **Portfolio Display:** Where authorized users can view released Portfolios.
3. **Portfolio Support:** Where students and staff have access to sample portfolios, electronic and print guides, and tutorials.
4. **Résumé Builder:** Where students can create, release, and manage their résumés.
5. **File Manager:** Where each student can store up to 128mb of artefacts.

Access to the Portfolio is via "QUT Virtual," the university's intranet for students and staff. QUT Virtual provides a simple portal style entry to all of the above areas of the Portfolio for users and visitors.

QUT Portfolio Features

The success of the Portfolio is due, in no small part, to its innovative features; the Portfolio is student driven, it was strongly supported by academics, it supports students during their life at QUT and beyond, it is flexible, and it is comprehensive and fully integrated. As detailed below, these features have been the result of a deliberate policy of collaborating with all stakeholders and integrating with the QUT Information Technology infrastructure.

- **Student Driven:** Students take responsibility for their portfolio. They have control over the input of experiences and artefacts, and assigning who can view their work. The Portfolio offers a dynamic environment for students to seek feedback from peers, academic staff, and Careers officers. Students can also undertake a skills self-assessment and create personal action plans based on the results.
- **Support by Academics:** Vital support was provided for the design and implementation of the Portfolio by the academic community. Academics are now actively integrating the Portfolio into their teaching and research through linkages to the QUT Online Learning and Teaching tool, and through the incorporation of graduate capabilities into the curriculum.
- **Lifelong:** The Portfolio supports the student undergraduate journey and provides graduates with continued access for one year. Returning postgraduate students are able to re-engage with their Portfolio archive for a further nine years.
- **Flexible:** The Portfolio supports teaching and learning activities while remaining student driven. The Portfolio is also able to accommodate course- or industry-specific capabilities, and provides flexibility for students who change courses and capabilities; for example, from Education's Teacher Practitioner Attributes to Law capabilities.
- **Comprehensive:** It supports all three styles of portfolios which enable students and academics flexibility in construction and presentation (Greenberg, 2004):
    - **Structured:** Where students add experiences and artefacts against a matrix of graduate attributes and settings.
    - **Learning:** Where the work evolves dynamically as a result of interest, motivation, and reflection.
    - **Showcase:** Where students reflect on experiences to make new connections, personalize their learning experiences, and gain insights about current and future activities.
- **Integrated Architecture:** The Portfolio is embedded within the university technical infrastructure and accessed via the university intranet, QUT Virtual. This positions the Portfolio at the forefront of a student's online interaction and enables students to link their student details, résumé, photograph, and academic history to their portfolios. Academics can easily link to the Portfolio from the Online Learning and Teaching system, enabling the provision of scaffolding to support reflection and links to assessment.

QUT PORTFOLIO DEVELOPMENT STRATEGY

The keys to the successful development and implementation of the Portfolio included:

- Building on existing knowledge and experience at QUT
- Support and vision from senior management
- Support from Teaching and Learning Committees, faculty deans, and academic staff
- Extensive research and project feedback from all stakeholders
- Collaborative development and implementation strategies
- Provision of extensive support resources
- Enthusiasm and drive from the Project Team

Building on Existing Knowledge and Experience at QUT

QUT had a well-documented history of the use of journals and e-journals (Ballantyne & Packer, 1995; Bruce & Middleton, 1999; Dillon & Nalder, 2002). Building on this research and activity, the first proposal to provide an electronic portfolio tool at QUT was formulated in 2002. This proposal built on existing work with the Student Capability Profile (SCP) tool from the faculty of Built Environment and Engineering.

The SCP was academic driven and focused on formative assessment underpinned by graduate attributes. Evaluations of the SCP tool revealed many guiding principles which later influenced the design of the Portfolio. For example, many students felt that in the absence of defined objectives, completion of SCP activities was not perceived to be as important as completion of assessable items. Motivation was a key, as there appeared to be some resistance to being forced to put down their reflections in the activities from mature-aged and part-time students. However, final-year students perceived the SCP as an opportunity to complete a self-audit before graduation. Students also expressed the desire to have access to the data in the SCP after they graduated. Students felt that it would allow students who were more committed to extend themselves and show their lecturers what efforts they have made: "For the people who put a bit more in, it will be really worthwhile for them." Paradoxically, first-year students saw little value in the tool, while final-year students wished they had had access to the Portfolio in first year.

Support and Vision from Senior Management

Based on the results of the SCP and further research, a new proposal was approved by the deputy vice chancellor, Technology, Information and Learning Support (TILS). This Portfolio development was to be university-wide and closely aligned with key policies of the university; for example, the 2003 QUT Blueprint which provides the overarching strategic direction for QUT has as one of its three key ambitions:

> *... to provide outstanding learning environments and programs that lead to excellent outcomes for graduates enabling them to work in, and guide in a world characterised by increasing change.* (p. ii)

A project steering committee was established under the sponsorship of the DVC (TILS) and consisted of managers from Corporate Information Services, Learning and Teaching Support, and Careers and Employment. Continuing support from senior management at QUT has been an important factor in the successful design, implementation, and funding of the Portfolio project, and lent credibility and visibility to the project across the university.

Project Support from Teaching and Learning Committees, Faculty Deans, and Academic Staff

From the outset of the project, the Portfolio team liaised with a reference group that was established to provide support and feedback. This group consisted of academic staff, library staff, and experts across QUT, employers, alumni, and students. This group also lent credibility and gave visibility to the project across the university and provided avenues for the spread of information. Importantly, it also provided a strong sense of ownership of the Portfolio within each faculty and stakeholder group.

Extensive Research and Project Feedback from all Stakeholders

One of the first tasks undertaken by the project team was to develop a framework of employment-focused graduate capabilities for the Portfolio and then map these against the student academic capabilities identified by QUT. Additional mapping was completed against the standards of specific industry groups—for example, the Employability Skills Framework, as identified by the Business Council of Australia and the Australian Chamber of Commerce and Industry (BCA/ACCI, 2003). As Maria Tarrant, director of Policy of the Business Council of Australia, commented:

The work QUT has done developing the Portfolio and aligning this to the Employability Skills Framework is terrific. Employers will certainly feel more confident that their needs in terms of future employees will be met and it will help graduates achieve employment. Partnerships like this between industry and universities are so important. (Tarrant, 2004)

The final list of capabilities was endorsed by the faculty deans and the QUT Teaching and Learning committees, and were identified as: communication, teamwork, problem solving and critical thinking, life management/lifelong learning, technical/professional/research, managing/organizing, social/ethical responsibility, leadership, creativity/design, and initiative/enterprise.

During the research phase, QUT developed a strong relationship with Florida State University (FSU), and we wish to acknowledge their ongoing support, in particular Dr. Janet Lenz, who is the ePortfolio project leader at FSU. Dr. Lenz visited QUT in April 2005 and commented about our Portfolio project:

I am very impressed with the number of significant developments you have made in the past few months at QUT with your Portfolio. I particularly like the way you have made the skill set both portable and directly applicable to suit a range of audiences and needs. Also, your skill self-assessment capacity is something I would now like to build into our ePortfolio at FSU. Well done. It is great to be able to bounce ideas against a team of developers with similar interests and goals. (Lenz, 2004)

Comments such as this have provided strong motivation for the team and, importantly, validation of our work within the university environment.

Collaborative Development and Implementation

A collaborative strategy was endorsed to develop the Portfolio that involved a multi-disciplinary team from Information Technology Services (ITS) and Teaching and Learning Support Services (TALSS), Careers, and Academic staff. A full set of business requirements were developed which defined the purpose of the Portfolio and functional specifications. This document was approved by all the stakeholders and reflected their shared understanding and satisfaction that the Portfolio met QUT's business needs and was achievable within the scope of project resources and timeframes.

The system design process involved a thorough and exhaustive analysis and design phase, in which many technical and pedagogical issues were resolved. Interface design and development was driven by QUT's inherent systems architecture and took place over an intensive six months. Initial release for extensive pilot testing was carried out with students and academics from a variety of year levels and academic disciplines. Feedback was subsequently evaluated and incorporated into the Portfolio design.

The implementation strategy adopted by the project team in conjunction with the divisional marketing group attempted to reach as many academics and students as possible while remaining conducive to feedback and design comments. This was an extension of the collaborative approach that had been adopted for the design and development phases. The strategy included the development and writing of support resources, marketing materials, and articles and success stories in several university publications. Early in 2004 as part of a six-month preliminary release phase for all staff to access the Portfolio, the team conducted information sessions for academics and helped early adopters with pedagogical assistance. This helped alert staff to the impending release and enabled them to begin the curriculum integration stage prior to student release. A launch of the Portfolio occurred in June 2004, attended by state government politicians, industry leaders, and senior academics from QUT. Success story presentations were made by an academic and a student who had been involved in the pilot group.

The Portfolio was subsequently released to specific course groups late in 2004, comprising 4,000 students for further technical and pedagogical testing. Interestingly, many students from other courses who found out about the Portfolio began requesting access and support, and the number of users grew rapidly. In December 2004 the Portfolio and Résumé Builder were quietly released to all students over the summer break. Surprisingly, 8,000 students began creating résumés, and the number of Portfolios created rapidly grew to over 10,000. Despite little fanfare and direct support, this was a vindication of the Portfolio design, the self-access support material available, and the level of interest and need among the student body. Follow-up workshops have now begun, directly supporting academic initiatives within the unit framework and addressing faculty needs, including assessment of portfolios, reflective practices for workplace learning, and integration into the curriculum.

Provision of Support Resources

Student and academic support resources were developed, including a dedicated Web site, marketing materials, quick reference guides, multimedia presentations, structured workshops, tutor guides, animated tutorials, and workshop sessions. A Portfolio e-mail help desk was established to support students and academics with technical, pedagogical, and career issues. Resources are also currently being developed which relate more closely to student stories than a technical "how-to."

Unsurprisingly, the workshops were the most successful resource tool, as one participant commented:

I probably wouldn't have used the student portfolio had I not done this course and found out the true benefit of it.

Unfortunately, with a small, dedicated team, the provision of wide-scale workshops is not possible and hence sessions are now being directed at academic and library staff that will provide much of the support in the future.

Enthusiasm and Drive from the Project Team

Another key to the successful implementation has been the infectious enthusiasm of the small project team. This enthusiasm has been communicated to users and has provided at least initial enthusiasm for the task of using the Portfolio. Conversely, hearing stories from students about how the Portfolio has changed their lives, about how it has improved their learning, and how enthusiastic they are to show off their Portfolios and talk to other students, has been uplifting for the project team. The project team has also been encouraged to tell others about our work, and to help other universities and organizations where we can. For example, we have begun trialling the Portfolio at a local secondary college with year 11 students, and in 2004 the team consulted with an Australian government initiative, The Le@rning Federation. As Alan Bevan, chief operating officer of The Le@rning Federation, commented:

The manner in which QUT has used the generic employability skills to structure the Portfolio is particularly impressive, as is the way the university has reached agreement on the structure and functionality despite the inevitable diversity of views and needs within an institution the size of a university. The manner in which the Portfolio could be used for teaching purposes rather than solely focusing on the end product was an outstanding feature. (Bevan, 2004)

PORTFOLIO FEEDBACK

The Portfolio team commenced evaluating the implementation process and the Portfolio software in 2003 using a multi-faceted approach involving surveys, interviews, focus groups, and observation. A summary of the feedback we have received is presented below.

The Portfolio team found that students engaged better if provided with the opportunity to participate in hands-on, instructor-led laboratory sessions. Although students did not appear to have a problem with the technology, they did have difficulty with knowing how to reflect and how to connect their life and academic experiences to the graduate capability framework. However, once students had been guided through the process of reflecting in their Portfolio, they appeared to make strong connections about the value of doing this over the long term. The Portfolio also challenged students to reflect on a broader range of experiences and to present themselves as a "whole" person, not just a student. As one Business student commented:

Learning about the Student Portfolio was fantastic. I think it is an amazing tool that will greatly benefit me in preparing job applications in the future. Getting to know my personal strengths and weaknesses, and doing the online portfolio. Now I can work on my weaknesses and plan how to strengthen my strengths.

We also discovered that without the provision of adequate scaffolding, students had difficulties with understanding the graduate capabilities. For example, as a member of the Portfolio team commented:

Each student had a different interpretation of what lifelong learning was, such as: just related to learning environments; related to everything they 'learn' in life and actions that they take to continue to grow and learn; professional memberships.

A third-year education student, when asked what she would put into her portfolio, answered:

What goes into the Portfolio? Definitely practicum experiences. But also voluntary work. I go to the Girls Brigade [where] I take a Grade 6 class. I learn a lot through that because I take them from 6:30 to 8:30 ... they've just had a day at school and are ready to muck up. [Anyway] I have learnt how to talk to them and how to organise them.

The importance of the Portfolio was highlighted by one of the early adopter academics who stated in 2003:

The Portfolio is especially important [because it encourages] learning that draws on student's prior knowledge and understanding to create new meaning in their learning outcomes. Its structure offers students the framework for reflective practice, enabling them to consider their achievements holistically and to recognise that the different dimensions of their lives ... contribute to their professional persona.

Employers as one of our important stakeholder bodies were invited to participate through focus groups and interviews. Employer focus groups felt that the main benefit for them was in the student's ability to organize and reflect on their experiences towards more successfully addressing selection criteria, not necessarily through viewing actual portfolios. They did, however, believe that the use of the Portfolio would provide QUT students with a competitive advantage over other university graduates.

From a recruiter's perspective the Student Portfolio is a great innovation. It allows students to be able to present information from their studies and about themselves in a way that they have total control over." "In the future I can see recruiters using the Student Portfolio as a way of understanding the person behind the resume. Giving us more detail about who the person is. What they are looking for in their professional career.

Student feedback has also indicated changes to the way students write and learn about themselves, as a second-year education student commented:

Reflections required me to commit course content to long-term memory. Reinforcing my learning and making it clearer and more permanent in my mind. I noted down instances when I began to understand something through one piece of assessment, such as the first time I really understood how to use the core learning outcomes.

One of our more interesting comments came from another second-year student:

The good thing about the Portfolio is that it's your own—it makes it so much easier. Because there is no pressure you don't have to be somebody else and that's what I was worried about. So it's almost taken the pressure off a bit realising that it's not an assignment ... I think my writing will be a lot better because there'll be meaning behind it now instead of I have to do it. I actually went home and I went 'MUM, it's not an assignment. The pressure is off.' I think it changes the content and everything. Everything you write is really structured and academic; there is no real meaning and expressing your own way of talking.

Feedback from academics included comments such as:

I teach in the area of Library Science and in one of the units of the course students are asked to complete a portfolio as part of the coursework. We have embedded it into the program. One of the big benefits has been that we can help the students use reflective practice to consider what they're learning has meant to them.

A director of Academic Programs commented:

I think what the Student Portfolio has the potential to do is to encourage students to focus on a wider range of graduate capabilities than they sometimes do, particularly in content-based disciplines. The focus that they have I think then will extend through to an opportunity for academics to promote authentic learning experiences and use field, project, clinical, problem-based approaches which cover a wide range of graduate capabilities in one holistic pattern. And finally, I think in the context of lifelong learning it will be very positive in terms of encouraging students to identify their strengths, but also areas for further development. And as they take responsibility to develop these areas further that's the first step in genuine lifelong learning.

The Portfolio has clearly transformed the student experience at QUT at a basic but critical level. It adds a new, intimate dimension for learning, and it orients students to lifelong learning. That is, it gives students a place to call their own. As one QUT Education student summarizes it:

Everything I write at Uni is for someone else. This [Portfolio] is something I write for me.

The Portfolio, has also transformed the teaching landscape at QUT, allowing students to systematically use reflective practice for deeper learning. As the assistant dean (Teaching & Learning), Faculty of Law, stated:

So many students had never engaged in reflective thinking, or had only done so in part, before the Portfolio was created. By changing this, we are now looking at a whole new opportunity for teaching at the university.

CONCLUSION

The success of the Portfolio at QUT has been for several reasons. The strong vision and sponsorship by the deputy vice chancellor for Teaching, Information, and Learning Support has been crucial. This lent credibility and gave visibility to the project across the university. The formation of a cross-sectional project group made for shared ownership, rather than the project being the proprietary responsibility of one section, as well as a small, highly motivated team, sometimes overloaded but always driven by the positive feedback from students, academic, and industry.

University-wide consultation was critical. The team continually kept stakeholders focused on outcomes and working towards mutually acceptable resolutions of issues. In addition, the university is aware that it has just begun a journey of discovery with the Portfolio:

more features, better integration, and more marketing are clearly on the agenda. Ongoing research is also required to ensure that the outcomes and vision are being met and that the Portfolio meets the needs of all stakeholders.

REFERENCES

Ballantyne, R., & Packer, J. (1995). *Making connection: Using student journals as a teaching/learning aid.* HERDSA. Canberra: ACT.

Bevan, A. (2004). *Interview with QUT Portfolio Team.*

Bruce, C., & Middleton, M. (1999). Implementing assessment by portfolio in a professional practice unit. In *Proceedings of the HERDSA Annual International Conference,* Melbourne.

Dillon, S., & Nalder, G. (2002). *Constructing a new conceptual framework for using digital technologies in achieving better arts assessment.* Retrieved May 23, 2005, from http://dmap.ci.qut.edu.au/Papers/DMAP.html

Greenberg, G. (2004). The digital convergence—extending the portfolio. *Education Review, 39*(4), 38-48.

Lenz. J. (2004). Interview with QUT Portfolio Team.

QUT Manual of Policy and Procedures. (2005). Retrieved May 23, 2005, from http://www.qut.edu.au

Tarrant, M. (2004). Interview with QUT Portfolio Team.

KEY TERMS

Artefacts: Examples of student work gathered for a particular reason and audience.

Electronic Portfolio (ePortfolio): A collection of student work, reflections, and experiences that provides a picture of self, of growth and achievement organised, and referenced to graduate attributes.

Graduate: Capabilities are those elements of professional knowledge and skills, of personal attitudes and skills that are desired of a graduate of higher education by government, industry, and the higher education sector.

Learning: The processing of information gained from engaging and reflecting on experiences, which leads to changes in the brain and an increase in our knowledge and abilities.

Motivation: The reason(s) behind a persons actions or behaviour; motivation can be extrinsic (from outside) or intrinsic (from inside) or elements of both.

Reflection: A form of mental processing, of critically thinking about information gained and experiences encountered.

Self-Assessment: A process in which the learner determines his or her own level of professional knowledge and skills, and of personal attitudes and skills.

Student Centeredness: An approach that focuses on how students learn, what they experience, and how they engage in the learning environment. Students are encouraged to construct their own meaning by talking, listening, writing, reading, and reflecting on content, ideas, and issues.

Chapter XXXVIII
The Art of ePortfolios:
Insights from the Creative Arts Experience

Steve Dillon
Queensland University of Technology, Australia

Andrew Brown
Queensland University of Technology, Australia

ABSTRACT

This chapter examines the creative production context as a vehicle to reveal the issues, problems, and complexities that may be encountered when working with ePortfolios. We utilize metaphors from the creative arts as tools to provide new perspectives and insights that may not otherwise occur in other disciplines to provide a unique critique of the performativity of ePortfolios. Through reference to case studies drawn from drama, dance, music, new media, and the visual arts, the authors' research has problematized ePortfolios from the teacher, student, institutional, and pedagogical perspectives. They identify the issues and propose approaches to resolving them, and illustrate how these ideas derive from creative arts knowledge and outline how they are transferable to other disciplines using ePortfolios based on rich media forms of presentation. In conclusion, we examine the performing arts as temporal art forms attuned to the unfolding of a narrative and examine the notion that the audience experiences the reading of a portfolio as a performance.

INTRODUCTION

The intensive media-rich nature of creative production contexts is particularly challenging for ePortfolio application. This chapter argues that an examination of the use of ePortfolios in creative production contexts reveals the issues, problems, and complexities that may be encountered when working with ePortfolios more generally and can indicate protocols for the use of media rich ePortfolios in any field. Through reference to case studies drawn from drama, dance, music, new media, and the visual arts, we identify issues and propose ways to resolve them. Along the way we illustrate how these ideas can provide transferable outcomes based on the media forms and modes of presentation they employ rather than being limited to a particular discipline context.

WAYS OF EXPRESSING

Think of the paintings in prehistoric caves. Thanks to them, we now know what certain prehistoric mammals looked like! [Cave paintings] preceded the invention of writing by 30,000 years! Those people left us with veritable archives of the fauna of their time. (Eco, Gould, Carriere, & Delumeau, 2000, p. 40)

There is historical and scientific evidence of the role of arts as a technology for expression, storage, and communication of important information about the community. Human societies use sound, gesture, and story expressively as symbolic representation. Print technology has become both a filter and framework for storing, representing, communicating, and expressing valuable cultural ideas. However, there has not been much consideration of "textualized" experiences or products and in what ways words filter meaning. ePortfolios provide an opportunity to redress this imbalance and to manage media-rich expressions and representations of human activity in an integrated fashion. To that end, we need to acknowledge and re-examine what those who have always worked in these ways can tell us about media-rich expression and reflection.

When creative product and experience are textualized, the explanation is privileged over a representation of the knowledge itself in its original symbolic form. Artefacts of artistic practice can be organized into a system that documents creative practice in a way that combines both the experience of the work and explanation of the work to provide a rigorous, accountable, and compelling presentation of the work (Dillon, 2002; Dillon & Nalder, 2003, 2004; Dillon, Nalder, Brown, & Smith, 2003a, 2003b, 2003c; Nalder, Dillon, Brown, & Smith, 2004; Smith, Dillon, Nalder, & Brown, 2004). This form of organization and presentation is able to more readily capture the assessable aspects of the work than traditional methods that reduced observations simply to text and numerical grades. ePortfolios have the potential and the capacity to awaken the silenced voice and embodied knowledge, and to get closer to representing the presence of artistic practice for reflection, analysis, or assessment. As the opening quotation suggests, this is not so much a new methodology, but the re-conception of ancient methods of storing, communicating, and referencing important cultural information—that is, using a variety of non-textual symbolic forms. For example, digitization reconceptualises Australian indigenous concepts of knowledge referencing, management, and communication (Mackinlay, 2004; Mackinlay & Dunbar-Hall, 2003; Martin, 2003; Will, 2000) that provides a model of data management that is as accurate and enduring as oral/artistic knowledge systems, but with the addition of the recall and relative permanence of print.

Arts practitioners are experienced users of physical portfolio systems for education and practice. Particularly in the visual arts, these systems have been used for organizing, reflecting, and evaluating artistic work. Indeed, the Arts Propel research program at Harvard Project Zero (Davidson, 1992; Scripp & Gray, 1992; Seidel, 2001) utilizes highly developed process portfolio systems as central to the learning process, and recognized their role in assessing the products and processes of learning, which involves multiple intelligences (Gardner, 1993). Artistic practice then offers many metaphors and examples for portfolio design, and the different qualities of artistic knowledge provide a means of problematizing the idea of ePortfolios. Digital media and information systems present the opportunity to capture, store, and manage multiple forms of evidence (visual/aural/kinaesthetic) about artistic products and processes that are compatible with the more personal, qualitative meanings with which artistic practice is concerned. Effective ways of utilizing these media are well established in the arts and can be usefully transferred to other disciplines.

An Example of a Creative Arts ePortfolio

See Figure 1. In our new media and music education classes, ePortfolios provided sites for a reflective discourse about the work. Each student was able to upload sound files, computer code, HTML versions of notated arrangements, and compositions alongside text document tasks. The ePortfolio acted as a virtual seminar or networked forum where students and teachers could critically listen to the work exhibited by other students each week. They could discuss the process of interpreting the weekly and longer-termed tasks, and provide annotated exegetical explanations in the presence of an artefact of the work or an example of the process. Performance students were able to see QuickTime movies of their conducting of compositions, and thus isolate critical moments and insights into their learning. Students responding to stimulated recall interviews and reflections about their experiences with these ePortfolios made the following statements:

- The process lent itself to accountability.
- The focus was on understanding rather than outcome alone and upon proving understanding.
- There was a power shift to the student, or at least a responsibility shift—a democratization of the assessment process.
- It provided a demonstration of outcomes.
- Better teaching and better learners. (Dillon et al., 2003c)

In this case study example, the ePortfolio provided both a networked forum for reflective interaction with products and processes and a virtual exhibition space.

Figure 1.

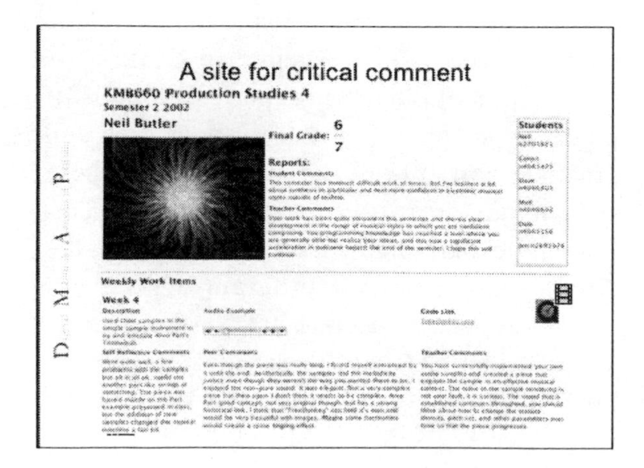

USING DIGITAL MEDIA BEYOND THE ARTS

A solid understanding of non-text digital representations is becoming increasingly important for people in all disciplines, not only those in the creative arts. The digital medium at the heart of ePortfolios has provided a level playing field for different modes of expression, in particular for text, numbers, vision, and sound. This greatly expands the opportunities for expression and communication of ideas beyond those of print media. A widely accepted advantage of ePortfolios is that they allow data to be presented as videos, spoken descriptions, charts and graphs, illustrations and storyboards, as well as text. This trend toward multimedia presentation with computers can be observed in the increasingly media-rich nature of digital "slide" presentations.

Effective expression and communication is essential in all fields, and the continued reliance upon face-to-face meetings underscores the communicative value we place on physical gesture, spoken inflection, and spatial cues. Capturing, or compensating for the loss of these aspects of presence in digital records within ePortfolios, has been the focus of our previous research into digital portfolios, and in this chapter we outline the lessons learned from the creative arts, which we believe are applicable to ePortfolios in any discipline.

The arts are a good vehicle for problematizing ePortfolios because the subject and object of artistic experience are inherently difficult to assess in textual or numeric forms. The arts also represent all fields of expressive human behaviour. Concepts of the body in space and time are expressed in dance; sound in time and space in music; colour, texture, shape, and form in the visual arts; and in dramatic performance a unique blend of text, body, voice, and narrative. In the performing arts, assessment is problematic because the product and experience are ephemeral and time dependent. In the visual arts, the product is often tangible; however, the meaning may not be clear or literal. To assess or evaluate the arts, both product and experience reach into the philosophical realm of aesthetics, and to evaluate these we need to identify the qualities of artistic knowing. This is indeed the first step for any discipline in the creation of educational activities, including ePortfolios. The creative arts are inherently media rich, and this provides us with problems in capturing a suitable artefact of the performance or production so that it can be reviewed and accounted for. Secondly, they present problems in terms of creating an appropriate representational and evaluative framework, which recognizes graduations of technical and expressive ability inherent in the product and process. Furthermore, it should be acknowledged that an ePortfolio is part of a system that includes the technology, teacher, students, and wider community. In all assessment, but especially in the arts, there is a need to recognize that the teacher is a valid instrument of assessment, and their aesthetic judgment informs decisions about quality of work. They interact with the folio and the students and a qualitative experience of the "live" work. The portfolio provides a layer of accountability by allowing the work to be revisited and increases the rigor by providing multiple lenses on the phenomenon.

Metaphors from the creative arts are useful as tools as they provide new perspectives and insights that may not occur in other disciplines. In music, for example, we are concerned with both analytical and intuitive aspects of knowledge (Swanwick, 1994). The analytical aspects of musical knowledge are reasonably easy to measure, as they deal with quantifiable values such as tempo and pitch and rhythmic accuracy, but the intuitive aspects of music making that deal with the expressiveness which activates the technical expertise and communicates the meaning of the sounds in context are only able to be understood by those who have embodied experience of the symbol system. In dance, gesture intertwines with music, and in drama further complexities of language are added. Because these performing arts forms are temporal, multimedia documentation can provide insights into how digital representations of gesture, sound, and still and moving image can be understood as artefacts of moments in time, as samples or frames that may be sequenced to recreate the illusion of movement.

Such a conception starts to reveal the frameworks for understanding the creative arts perspective of digital representations as mostly empty residue of the intuitive or tacit dimensions (Polanyi, 1967) of human experience and production at the core as artistic expression. Providing ways of adequately translating continuous multidimensional knowledge into discrete digital space is at the core of the challenge that creative arts present to ePortfolio designers.

A study of creative production generates complex relationships and issues. This is because the experience of making and perceiving the work is difficult to capture, and once captured may not be a true representation of the work. Digital videotape of musical or dance performances fails to capture the spatial and ambient qualities of a work unless it is recorded using several cameras and then subsequently edited. This raises the question of whether the artefact of the production is sufficiently representative of the quality of the work. Certainly when considered in isolation, this is problematic, but interestingly, when included as part of multiple evidence forms in a portfolio, we found that the users felt more comfortable with a portfolio which contained even poor quality audiovisual artefacts than they had been in the past with a number or description alone. The portfolio became a site for stimulated recall and reflective interaction.

Working in non-alphanumeric media—in particular sound, visuals, and space—has been the traditional domain of the creative arts and design disciplines. As digital media have enabled the interoperability of these on the one platform, their integration has been labelled "multimedia," and the reliance upon skills from these disciplines in the broader society has increased. Drawing on the deep understandings of and research experience with these multiple media in the creative arts, four areas of significance for the use of multimedia in ePortfolios become apparent: representation, offline objects, presentation, and reflection.

Representation

All media—be they textual or statistical descriptions, sound or video recordings, diagrams, or maps—are representations. Most people are well versed in the potential flaws in a textual description of an event because of its referential and interpretative nature; however, the abstractness of other media is less obvious. Inherently, multimedia forms (such as video) are particularly subject to the misunderstanding that they are not abstract and interpretive. The designers of ePortfolios need to consider that a sound recording is a biased representation of the sonic event influenced by the number of microphones, their position, pick-up pattern, orientation, and quality. For example, in an extreme case, comments by one person in a recorded conversation may be completely absent due to poor capturing technique. Similar framing considerations relate to the shooting of video footage. Video and audio recordings of the conventional type are also less dimensional that the original. A stereo recording is a one-dimensional version of a three-dimensional event, and a video recording is a two-dimensional version of a three-dimensional event (leaving out time as a dimension for now). An effective ePortfolio will take into account these framing and flattening effects of the digital representations, either by supplementing them with additional material to compensate and/or by deliberately highlighting the fact that data in these forms is reductive so that the viewer takes that into consideration.

Offline Objects

A related difficulty with the incorporation of media-rich elements in portfolios is enabling appropriate citation or reference to primary sources that are not in digital form. For example, a video documentary of a visual art sculpture would ideally link to the physical object offline. This is usually achieved by adding metadata or annotations to the description which detail the location of the offline object and how to access it if required. Providing this data trail to the source is an important authentication consideration. The variety of media types that are offline may also change depending upon the ability of the asset management system to handle multiple media forms. For example, some years back, audio and video materials would have been considered offline objects, but now their digitization enables them to be online documents. Physical objects, such as buildings and plants, will be offline for the foreseeable future, and ephemeral objects such as theatre performances and sporting events will always be impossible to revisit, even offline, thus their documentation requirements are even more stringent in terms of accurate representation within the portfolio.

Presentation

Fundamental to a creative arts understanding is the performative nature of experience. ePortfolios present work in a structured fashion, and the viewing of the portfolio has a temporal unfolding that can be understood as a performance. The way the ePortfolio is structured and the types of interactions with it that are allowable frame the presentational opportunities and thus the performativity of the ePortfolio.

There is also a notion of the performativity in constructing or adding to the ePortfolio. This is enhanced by effective interaction and user interface design of the ePortfolio itself. This enhancement needs to be based on the understanding that the computer has a special position where it is both the tool for constructing the portfolio and the medium in which the construction takes place. The digital media used for portfolios has properties that enable and limit the scope of the ePortfolio. Sensitivity to these properties can be compared to the artistic skills developed by the sculptor as they work with wood or by a potter as they work with clay. As McCullough (1996, p. 200) notes:

Understanding affordances and constraints is exactly what engineers, designers, artists and craftspeople do well. Each of these expertises involves deep familiarity with possibilities and practicalities of particular media.

ePortfolios could indeed be more effective if the developers paid attention to the experience of the creative arts practitioners whose work is guided by aesthetic theories and experiential intuitions as much as it is by understandings of media properties or functional requirements.

Laurel (1991), in her book *Computers as Theatre,* established the metaphor of the computer as a performative space in the context of computer game development. According to Laurel, computer-based and theatrical representations have a fundamental similarity, that through them "a person participates in a representation that is not the same as real life but which has real-world effects or consequences. Representation and reality stand in particular and necessary relation to one another" (Laurel, 1991, p. 31). The implication for ePortfolio development and use is that there is a theatrical aspect to ePortfolio development and presentation, the user *directs* scenarios within the folio by manipulating the materials at hand to convey or realize a narrative or find a meaning, and they *act* according to the opportunities afforded them by the portfolio features. An ePortfolio is an interpretive presentational activity, at least, and possibly an artistic activity in its own right at its best, and not in a decorative way but through intense engagement with contextualizing or framing activities that have real-life consequences.

Representational biases or distortions are likely to be reinforced during the use of the ePortfolio for reflection or assessment. As outlined in the new media case study, one of the primary purposes of an ePortfolio is to assist with the reflective practices that underpin ongoing improvement (Schön, 1987). These reflections will be based on synthesis of and patterns within data, and therefore will inherit and amplify the representational features of the data. For example, if a set of photos of an event were all taken by one participant, it is likely that the participant will not appear in any of the images; therefore, reflection upon their participation in the activity would be significantly limited compared to the other participants who appeared in the images.

ePORTFOLIO MODELS FROM THE CREATIVE ARTS

The creative production context reveals the complexity and problems that may be encountered when working with ePortfolios. These are things that can potentially arise in many contexts, but may not be immediately evident. Artists and teacher/artists using ePortfolios presented the following issues in our research:

1. **Access and Control:** Who controls the use of the portfolio and how much control is appropriate? In media arts, users may have a great deal of technical skill to manipulate the portfolio.
2. **Ethics and Rights Management:** Confidentiality, intellectual property, copyright: Who sees and owns the work?
3. **Implementation – Technical and Policy Constraints:** What are the technical constraints that prevent quality representations from being uploaded, or who has the skills of access to the technological gateway? What policies prevent or enhance this access?
4. **Representation and Recognition:** How is the work to be represented and what is the quality of the work that is acceptable as an artefact? Can the collection of artefacts capture the qualities of artistic knowledge effectively?

In working with these issues, a number of models of ePortfolios have arisen in the creative arts. The models reframe the ePortfolio either by redefining the role of the portfolio itself, positioning the ePortfolio uses in light of existing arts practices, or establishing an arts-based interpretive spin on the way the ePortfolio is presented. These frames for understanding the ePortfolio are based on traditional expressive dimensions of artistic practice and arts education.

A person creating the portfolio sees that as a creative act. Potentially then an ePortfolio could evolve into a new art form. Already the Word Wide Web is undergoing a change from text-heavy sites to becoming a communication design exhibition, which combines metaphors from the visual arts notions of exhibition, the sonic arts concepts of installation, and the dramatic arts concepts of non-linear narrative. Viewing ePortfolios from the perspective of the creative arts provides a number of interesting metaphors for the use of the ePortfolio, beyond a conception of it as a "shoe box" or "folder" for storing, archiving, and reflecting on materials.

These new usage metaphors open up different horizons of possibility for the application and value of the ePortfolio. For example, the performing arts are temporal art forms attuned to the temporal unfolding of a presentational narrative and thus pay attention to the fact that the audience experiences the reading of a portfolio as a performance. While the visual arts provide us with the metaphor for storing and viewing two-dimensional artefacts in a folio of work, it was the dramatic arts and particularly the more contemporary use of digital video that alerted us to the concept of an electronic portfolio as a documentary of a student's learning experiences. This was also apparent in dance students and involved the act of selecting critical moments from video recordings and putting them together in a form that privileged the performance and allowed the arts-makers to select, reflect, and interact with their own work and provide a stimulated recall and a dialogue with the teacher with the work present in the discussion. The student was also able to edit together a short and powerful representation of critical moments of their work when they achieved personal and institutional goals.

Documentary

Students suggested that the concept of selecting critical moments on a DVD and presenting it in a documentary of artistic performance was a powerful multimedia résumé that they could use to demonstrate their ability to employers or agents. The practice of encapsulating important knowledge into story is ancient in origin. Participants in Arts Propel portfolios (Davidson, 1992; Scripp & Gray, 1992; Seidel, 2001) talk about their work in a presentation to peers, parents, and teachers that is integral to the learning process and in the provision of feedback to the student. Collaborative spaces can be easily constructed using digital systems that allow networked interaction with a narrative flavour; this allows the artists to tell the story of the making process, intentions, and influences. ePortfolios can be considered as documentaries where the act of creating a narrative to frame a series of works or experiences provides an opportunity for a discourse about the work and potentially provides useful feedback to the artists (Megarrity, 2002).

Curated Exhibition

The presentation of materials from an ePortfolio can be understood as an exhibition of works, curated to draw attention to a particular facet of the materials. At one level this perspective can be used to assemble materials that represent a show reel of the best or most diverse work of the portfolio owner. However, a more interesting implication of the curated exhibition metaphor is the assemblage of selected materials that follow a particular theoretical or historical thread. This type of thematic sorting of the portfolio contents is itself an active reflection on the material and may lead to unique insights into the owner's work or skills.

Performance

An ePortfolio could use the arts metaphor of performance where live and digitized recordings are utilized in real time. For instance, an intermedia student whose focus was song writing presented a DVD portfolio of works where the DVD sound and vision became part of her mixed media live performance. She sang and played guitar while a dancer moved in the space, and projected visual images, short films, and enhanced digital audio instrumentation were projected on screen and from loudspeakers. While this represents a complex, media-rich performance with the use of both live and recorded materials, such a presentation is not uncommon in the performing arts. Adequately representing such events in an ePortfolio provides a significant challenge, but considering the presentation in the ePortfolio as another performance helps in making decisions about how best to do so.

The act of taking an ePortfolio to a job interview with a potential employer is in fact a performance where the ePortfolio is used to support the live dramatic performance of the interviewee and a compelling performance for the audience. This is becoming common among teacher education students who not only want to present their résumé in more compelling ways but want to demonstrate their artistic control over information technology.

Installation

In an installation there is no single way of viewing or experiencing the work. The interactive nature of the installation, and the typically media-rich form installations take, shape an interesting model for hyperlinked data in digital archives. The capacity of ePortfolios to present materials in a nonlinear, hyperlinked fashion opens up opportunities to think about portfolio presentations from a formalized (visual arts) or serial (music) perspective. That is a presentation whose structure is determined by following rules that select or link materials. This can give rise to surprising confluences of portfolio contents, the juxtaposition of which may reveal new connections and insights into the portfolio. The ability to have dynamic and programmatic Web sites can provide an ever-changing folio presentation that, like an installation, may never be the same at each visit. Such algorithmic structuring of materials can be manually prepared, as were the original art and music works that used these procedures, or they can be automated with scripts that select materials for presentation based on specified rules. The latter can be stored for reuse or swapped between portfolio owners with interesting effect as the same rules of material presentation are allied to different sets of data.

Choreography

The data stored in the ePortfolio can be understood as occupying information space, and choreography is a creative arts metaphor for navigating space. In a choreographed dance the dancer moves through space in an elegant fashion. Similarly we can conceive of choreographing movements through portfolio space. A presentation can be designed as a dance through the material and the principles of choreographic design—symmetry, balance, flow, and coverage might be used to guide an ePortfolio presentation.

The lesson for ePortfolio designers and users from the creative arts is that media have properties that need to be respected, and it is important to have processes that adequately allow for those properties. It is the fundamental understanding of media properties that the creative arts bring from their long-term engagement with their artistic practice through those media. Observations in the creative arts where there is a heightened sensitivity to the appropriate treatment of media types have led to the development of protocols for using ePortfolios (Dillon et al., 2003c; Nalder et al., 2004; Smith et al., 2004). We believe that these protocols have application beyond the creative arts to those using ePortfolios incorporating multimedia in any discipline because they focus on working with particular media.

ePORTFOLIO LESSONS FROM THE CREATIVE ARTS

We have developed new perspectives by looking at ePortfolios through the lens of arts practice. While this provides some creative fuel for the future design processes and implementations of ePortfolios, we have—through examining the use of ePortfolios in the creative arts—

also been able to identify areas where usage protocols need to be developed. The emergent themes raised earlier in this chapter documented the following outcomes.

Access and Control

The student must maintain control over creativity and expressivity. Students must maintain their creative integrity and input into the selection of the ePortfolio content within institutional protocols and the context of ePortfolio—in formative assessment.

Implementation

The onus is on teachers to equip the students with skills and abilities that will enable them to produce an ePortfolio of quality. With these developed skills, it is understood that the students then have responsibility for populating and maintaining the portfolio. This will vary according to developmental level of the students.

The technological expertise appropriate to attaining suitable ePortfolio quality (standards implication) has consequences for the assessment process. The development of the expertise must be facilitated by the institution and has system-wide implications. The system needs to be developed in an iterative process with users so that it responds to users' practice rather than alters users' practice to fit the technical limitations of the system. We must also expect novel and creative uses of the system and provide an appropriate means of this interaction occurring rather than stifling it with policy or restrictive access protocols.

Ethics and Rights

Given that the intention of the educational institution is to use the created artefacts for subsequent teaching and learning purposes, the ePortfolio contains a representation of the work, not the actual work. This means that "permissions" and "informed consents" are required. The student owns the work and the intellectual property associated with the work, and the laws of copyright extend to the maker. Essentially, as with research ethics, the fundamental right of the user to withdraw the work at any time or restrict access is a primary rule of thumb. The institution as host to the exhibit/artefacts has a teaching and learning contract with the student that does not extend beyond the course of study.

Recognition and Representation of Artistic Learning

All students should be aware of the limitations, functions, and purpose of the ePortfolio process so that the assessment process does not limit the artistic product and making experience. Interestingly, through several research cycles we observed that the quality of the representation was not an issue that concerned artists using ePortfolios. As teachers who had experienced the live moment, we expressed more concern about it than the students. This suggests that the focus here is that it is not the folio alone that represents the work. The portfolio presents an opportunity for a dynamic discourse about the work to be facilitated between students, peers, community, and teachers that provides both useful feedback to all participants and a potentially rigorous, accountable, and transparent assessment system where the qualities of artistic knowledge can be experienced (Dillon et al., 2003a).

These areas of focus provide analytical tools that we can use to ask how they relate to our context/discipline. We can do this by simply translating the arts discipline into their fundamental media forms as sound, gesture, narrative, and still and moving image. The key to what we have discovered in the arts is that it is important to understand how the knowledge is used in the discipline, therefore it is important to determine the way in which knowledge is understood and represented in your field. The four areas described above are the questions we ask about the application and context of portfolios. They can be used as analytical tools to determine appropriate policy.

Toward Usage Policy

By constructing a conceptual framework for using digital technologies in achieving better arts assessment (Dillon & Nalder, 2003), we identified protocols for the use of ePortfolio systems. These protocols can be used as analytical tools in the process of ePortfolio design. Essentially, protocols alert you to ask questions about issues arising from application and context through a process of deliberate problematizing of the space. The problematic issues for ePortfolios in the arts began with the question of what constitutes knowledge in the discipline. In each arts discipline we asked, what are the qualities of artistic knowing? While this seems like a difficult philosophical question, we found that each discipline had a clear understanding of what constituted artistic knowing, and which were common and which were discipline specific. In music, for instance, we identified that musical knowledge exists within a complex and dynamic interaction between the maker, the audience, and the culture in which the practices are embedded. The way individuals within that specific context express themselves and organize sound is interdependent and is as much structured by context as influenced by it; it expresses "to" and "for" the context and either responds "syncretically" (Vella, 2000) to changes in the context or acts as a repository for "traditional" cultural knowledge. Harwood suggests that music is engendered:

1. *according to expectations of performers and audience,*
2. *according to standards of judgement proper to the culture,*
3. *in terms of context proper to particular performance, and*
4. *in terms of analogies with the listener's way of perceiving the world in general.* (Nattiez, 1990, p. 66)

It is these understandings that then inform the construction of appropriate means of capturing and determining the quality of the knowledge.

Secondly, we examined how artefacts of this knowledge can best be represented in media so that they remained close to the symbolic form: sound as sound, gesture as gesture, vision as vision. Once this had been determined, we identified the appropriate media to capture the artistic product. At this point the technical aspects of quality, digital size, and format need to be selected, and generally this involves data compression and selection of standard or readily available formats such as PDF, MP3, WMV, MPEG, or html. Once the artefact is ready to be uploaded, the issues of ethics, intellectual property, and access and control should be determined through institutional policy which privileges the rights of the students to control the portfolio within frameworks of appropriate use (Chan, 2003).

What is essential here is that we begin the process from the viewpoint of knowledge, then capture and storage, followed by the provision of structures for storage and management by the institution that acknowledge the control of the student over IP and recognize the need for ethical and appropriate presentation of the data. Unfortunately most institutions begin this process in reverse by imposing limitations and structures that potentially mask the knowledge.

CONCLUSION

Digital systems can capture data from a wide variety of media types, and ePortfolios are particularly useful because they can incorporate and integrate the wide variety of media types. However, there is a strong tendency both within the history of digital systems and our culture to prioritize text and numerical modes of description. In order to redress this imbalance, we have examined the use of ePortfolios in the creative arts where this media prioritization is reversed. We suggest that all users of ePortfolios can benefit from examining the ways they are used in the creative arts, and by following the protocols we are developing around media representation and use within ePortfolios.

Understanding the ways of knowing within a discipline is critical to the effective use of ePortfolios, and understanding within the creative arts is tightly bound with the mediums of those practices, hence musicians are sensitive to appropriate expression and representation in sound, and visual artists to the treatment of images, and so on. In this chapter we have argued that because of this sensitivity and familiarity with these mediums, the ways in which ePortfolio usage has developed in these disciplines can transfer to their use in other disciplines. We have identified considerations for the effective implementation of ePortfolios, which are likely to lead to the development of policies for effective use. In particular we presented guidelines for media treatment within portfolios in the form of protocols that were designed to ensure that activities and understandings were represented accurately within the portfolio, that the personal expressions captured in the media were handled ethically and sensitively, and that decisions made based on the represented data took account of the distorting effects of the media representations.

In conclusion, we have examined the performing arts as attuned to the unfolding of an expressive narrative in media-rich contexts. We utilized metaphors from the performing arts as tools to provide new perspectives and insights that may not occur in other disciplines to provide a unique critique of the art of ePortfolio development and use.

REFERENCES

Chan, S. (2003). *Legal considerations in the creation and use of digital media portfolios in tertiary assessment* (No. 1). Brisbane: Queensland University of Technology; Faculty of Creative Industries DMAP unpublished research report. Retrieved from http://dmap.ci.qut.edu.au/Papers/DMAP.html

Davidson, L. (1992). *Arts Propel: A handbook for music (with video of evaluation methods and approaches)*. Cambridge, MA: Harvard Project Zero.

Dillon, S. (2002, November 14-15). *Digital multi media portfolios (D-MAP) in music learning.* Closing the Loop: 2002 Evaluations and Assessment Conference, Brisbane, Queensland, Australia [CD ROM].

Dillon, S., & Nalder, G. (2003). Constructing a new conceptual framework for using digital technologies in achieving better arts assessment. *Queensland Journal of Music Education, 10*(1), 59-72.

Dillon, S., & Nalder, G. (2004). *A preliminary research paper examining the need to construct a new conceptual framework for using digital technologies in achieving better arts assessment.* Retrieved from http://dmap.ci.qut.edu.au/Papers/DMAP.html

Dillon, S., Nalder, G., Brown, A., & Smith, J. (2003a). *Digital media assessment portfolios.* Paper presented at the Critical Review Colloquium, Brisbane, Queensland, Australia.

Dillon, S., Nalder, G., Brown, A., & Smith, J. (2003b, August 30-31). *Digital multi media portolios (D-MAP) in music learning.* Paper presented at Loud & Clear: Making Meaningful Music in the Middle Years, Melbourne, Australia.

Dillon, S., Nalder, G., Brown, A., & Smith, J. (2003c, September 27-30). Digital multi media portfolios (D-MAP) in music learning. In *Proceedings of the Artistic Practice as Research: 25th Annual Conference of the Australian Association for Research in Music Education,* Brisbane, Queensland, Australia.

Eco, U., Gould, S. J., Carriere, J., & Delumeau, J. (2000). *Conversations about the end of time.* London: Penguin Books.

Gardner, H. (1993). *Frames of mind: The theory of multiple intelligences.* London: Fontana Press.

Laurel, B. (1991). *Computers as theatre.* Reading, MA: Addison Wesley.

Mackinlay, E. (2004). *Without a song you are nothing.* Lecture notes presented at Music and Spirituality lecure series, Queensland University of Technology, Brisbane, Queensland, Australia.

Mackinlay, E., & Dunbar-Hall, P. (2003). Historical and dialectical perspectives on the teaching of Aboriginal and Torres Strait Islander music in the Australian education system. *The Australian Journal of Indigenous Education, 32,* 29-40.

Martin, K. M. (2001). Ways of knowing, ways of being and ways of doing: Developing a theoretical framework and methods of indigenous re-search and indigenist research. *Journal of Australian Studies,* (76).

Megarrity, D. (2002, November 14-15). *Devising new mean: A discussion paper.* Paper presented at Closing the Loop: 2002 Evaluations and Assessment Conference, Brisbane, Queensland, Australia [CD ROM].

Nalder, G., Dillon, S., Brown, A., & Smith, J. (2004, December 20-23). *Arts education for a "telematic" future.* Paper presented at Imagine Future Possibilities: National Summit of the Australian Institute of Art Educators [CD ROM].

Nattiez, J.-J. (1990). *Music and discourse: Towards semiology of music.* Princeton, NJ: Princeton University Press.

Polanyi, M. (1967). *The tacit dimensions.* London: Routledge and Kegan Paul.

Scripp, L., & Gray, J. (1992). *The Arts Propel video handbook.* Cambridge, MA: Harvard Project Zero.

Seidel, S. (2001). *The evidence project: A collaborative approach to understanding and improving teaching and learning.* Cambridge, MA: Harvard Project Zero.

Smith, J., Dillon, S., Nalder, G., & Brown, A. (2004). *Digital multimedia portfolios supporting authentic learning in the arts.* Paper presented at ePortfolio 2004—Transforming individual and organisational learning, La Rochelle, France [CD ROM].

Swanwick, K. (1994). *Musical knowledge: Intuition, analysis and music education.* London: Routledge.

Vella, R. (2000). *Musical environments: A manual for listening, improvising and composing*. NSW, Australia: Currency Press.

Will, U. (2000). *Oral memory in Australian Aboriginal song performance and the Parry-Kirk debate: A cognitive ethnomusicological perspective* (pp. 1-29). Ohio State University.

KEY TERMS

Artefacts: Representations of artistic products or experiences. For example, a DVD of a dance performance, a recording of music in wave, MP3 format, a MIDI files. It is argued that digital audio and sound artefacts remain truer to the symbolic form of the artistic work or experiences than a textualized explanation, which makes artefacts more authentic.

Artistic Knowledge: Describes the embodied understanding of arts practice often described as involving analytical and intuitive knowledge. It is knowledge that can be stored, transmitted, or used as a cognitive amplifier in a non-alphanumeric form. Many indigenous knowledge systems utilize song, dance, visual art, and story as a means of storing and communicating important cultural knowledge.

Creative Arts Metaphors: This term refers to how we design and use ePortfolios. It is argued that the creative arts provide metaphors, which model artefacts using a range of media forms and practices. For example, use of ePortfolios as curated exhibition, as a performance: dancing through information space.

Media-Rich: Refers to environments where a diverse range of audiovisual and computer code in a variety of formats is present. ePortfolios are capable of being media-rich environments, but many are merely textual explanations or reflections without links to more compelling representations available through rich media.

Non-Alphanumeric Media: Refers to media that are not text or numbers. The term refers to audiovisual or media comprising a range of media.

Performativity: Modes of presentation and activity within an ePortfolio, seen as a performance suggesting that the viewer of an ePortfolio is audient to the experience rather than a 'reader'. The term is a metaphor for the more media-rich presentation of ePortfolios, suggesting they need to be considered as a performance and that a 'reading' metaphor will limit the experience of the ePortfolio.

Physical Portfolio: Like an artist's folio of works, this term refers to portfolios containing sketches, designs, tape recordings, and music scores—non-digitised artefacts. This term refers particularly to the portfolios used in the style of the Harvard Arts Propel Project Zero for assessment of creative arts.

Representation: The capture and presentation of an artefact in another media. Associated in the manuscript with symbolic form—that is, music is a symbolic form and it can be represented as sound waves or in common practice notation.

Textualized: The capture of experience or artefact by description or explanation using text or print technology. The term usually refers to the filtering of meaning through text description or explanation. Textualized artefacts are generally less compelling as evidence than media-rich ones.

Chapter XXXIX
A Principle-Based ePort Goes Public (and Almost Loses its Principles!)

Sharon J. Hamilton
Indiana University-Purdue University Indianapolis, USA

ABSTRACT

When an institution-wide electronic student portfolio "goes public" beyond the campus, the processes of its conceptualization, development, implementation, and evaluation appear seamlessly successful. Similar to a published manuscript, all is in place, and the tortuous paths of creation are invisible. Yet we can learn from both the steps and missteps of any innovation. This chapter describes the evolution of the Indiana University (IU) student electronic portfolio from its initial conception as a first-year "electronic report card" of student learning of core skills to a fully integrated enterprise system that enhances, documents, certifies, and evaluates learning. The discussion moves from a 1995 prototype developed at Indiana University—Purdue University Indianapolis (IUPUI) to the 2005 public release with OSPI and Sakai, with the goal that the processes described this case study will be informative and helpful to those wanting to create, adapt, or adopt an ePortfolio structure on their respective campuses.

CONTEXT AND IMPETUS FOR THE ELECTRONIC STUDENT PORTFOLIO

IUPUI is an urban research campus of almost 30,000 students located in the heart of Indianapolis. Combining the Purdue School of Engineering and Technology and the Purdue School of Science with 20 Indiana University academic and professional schools, IUPUI provides the widest array of academic and professional offerings of any single campus in the nation. While such diversity of academic programs has its obvious benefits for students, it also creates an institutional challenge of identity, particularly in relation to a common undergraduate intellectual learning experience. Our 1992 accreditation report described our then current distribution approach to general education as too vague and fragmented, and stipulated that IUPUI needed to define, in more coherent and unified terms, both its approach to general education in particular and its approach to undergraduate learning in general. After considered deliberation of many approaches to general education, involving more than 300 of our roughly 1,500 faculty members at that time, we decided upon a principle-based approach to general education that would occur not just during the first one or two years of the undergraduate curriculum, but that would actually permeate the undergraduate curriculum from first through senior year, and provide transitions to graduate and professional programs. In 1998, the Faculty Council approved six Principles of Undergraduate Learning (PULs) that would be at the core of every academic program, and that would be fully integrated with the discipline-specific learning outcomes of every major. These six principles included: Core Communication and Quantitative Skills; Critical Thinking; Integration and Application of Knowledge; Intellectual Depth, Breadth, and Adaptiveness; Understanding Society and Culture; and Values and Ethics. While assessment would still focus on discipline-specific learning, it was "understood" that these skills and ways of knowing would be developed throughout the curriculum. No process or mechanism for determining where and how these PULs would be taught, learned, demonstrated, or assessed was stipulated, however, and, for the most part, faculty designed their syllabi and taught their classes just as they had done prior to the approval of the PULs.

Also in 1998, IUPUI, together with five other urban universities, was awarded a generous three-year grant by the Pew Charitable Trust to develop a model for institutional portfolios. This Urban Universities Portfolio Project (UUPP), responding to the way in which urban institutions were marginalized by standards of higher education favoring the Ivy Leagues and large research universities, focused on the missions, visions, stakeholders, and constituencies of urban institutions in the conceptualization and development of the first generation of institutional portfolios. In all participating institutions, the notion of how to demonstrate improvement and achievement of student learning became a challenge. While we could all provide aggregated statistics related to incoming SAT scores, outgoing GPAs, self-reports on exit surveys, and graduate school or employment success rates, we realized that these data were secondary sources of information about what our graduates know and can do. We had no way to document, demonstrate, or evaluate growth and achievement, particularly in relation to our PULs.

As a direct consequence of our work on the institutional electronic portfolio (iPort), we began to reconsider the notion of a student electronic portfolio (ePort). Previously, in 1995, the Honors program had developed a prototype of an electronic student portfolio for all Honors students. While the prototype generated much interest and excitement, particularly its focus on students developing their goals and plans for learning, it never evolved into a working infrastructure, for reasons related primarily to funding and assessment issues. However, with the impetus provided by iPort, and the need to provide authentic evidence of improvement and achievement in student learning at both the disciplinary level and with the PULs, interest in ePort was renewed, and at the conclusion of the three-year project funding for the UUPP, in 2001 the founding director of iPort was assigned the leadership responsibilities for ePort.

INITIAL CONCEPTIONS OF ePORT (WITH A FEW FALSE STARTS)

As mentioned earlier, our first investigation into the feasibility of an electronic student portfolio came about in 1995 as the result of two campus-level initiatives: the reorganization of the Honors program and, at long last, legislative support for increased campus housing on our primarily commuter campus. We thought that an electronic Honors portfolio might capture both the curricular and residential learning experiences of the students. The prototype was developed primarily around a student profile, wherein first-year students thought through their academic goals and outlined their plans for achieving those goals. In this design, students could upload artifacts of their choice to demonstrate their progress along their academic path. Both faculty and students were intrigued by the possibilities, but began to raise questions about its restriction to just Honors students, the potential for it to develop into yet another form of assessment, and the human and financial resources required for development. As a result, the prototype was not developed into a working infrastructure.

The second foray into developing a student electronic portfolio came three years later, in 1998, during the development of our electronic institutional portfolio (iPort). The iPort focused on our mission of providing excellence in research and creativity, teaching and learning, and community engagement, by creating a culture of evidence to demonstrate how effectively we were achieving specific goals related to our mission. While our office of Information Management and Institutional Research (IMIR) provided extensive secondary data about learning, we had no primary, authentic evidence of what our students know and can do beyond the level of individual students. We decided that an electronic student portfolio would be an ideal way to provide authentic evidence of student learning that ranged from the level of the individual student to the programmatic, department, and institutional levels.

The Honors prototype was briefly resurrected, but did not seem to garner even the support it had initially engendered. Our provost then established a committee to explore alternative conceptions of electronic portfolios, but more questions were raised than answered, and that initiative also faltered. Finally, our provost decided, near the conclusion of the three-year funding for iPort, to appoint the founding director of the IUPUI iPort project to become the founding director of the IUPUI ePort, building on her in-depth experiences with electronic portfolios. The initial charge was to develop a first-year electronic portfolio that enabled students to demonstrate what they knew and could do in relation to the Principles of Undergraduate Learning upon completion of their first year, or after 26 credit hours. An oversight committee of faculty and academic staff from across the campus was set up to conceptualize the design of the portfolio, while several multidisciplinary campus committees were established to develop a set of rubrics or expectations for each of the PULs at the first-year level. The faculty member who had designed our university-level course management system, Oncourse, was asked to oversee the design of the technological infrastructure, and by the year 2001, we had our first proof-of-concept pilot with one class.

To say the concept did not prove itself immediately feasible would be to put it mildly. The whimsicality of the technological structure guaranteed frustration for both students and faculty, and the notion of yet another initiative on the horizon that would generate additional work for students and faculty created considerable resistance. Even so, both faculty and students could envision the potential. They saw promise beyond the immediate problems. Possibly the best (and most surprising) result of this proof-of-concept trial of the first-year electronic student portfolio was the agreement of the oversight committee that, if we were going to put all this effort and all these resources into an electronic student portfolio, it should represent learning throughout the entire undergraduate curriculum, and not just the first year.

THE LEARNING CORE OF ePORT: MATRIX + LEARNER PROFILE

One of our first challenges was to understand collectively what we mean by "student learning." What constitutes student learning? Who decides if students have learned? What does learning look like? While on the face of it, these questions seem obvious, the answers are definitely less so. Even once we agreed that class assignments provide the best available tangible evidence of student learning, we still had to determine how to show that learning. We determined that a portfolio is much more than a collection of student work; it is a collection of work thoughtfully selected and organized to demonstrate both improvement and achievement in learning. The resultant design challenge was how to represent that learning in more than 20 different academic and professional schools within a common institutional framework. Our Principles of Undergraduate Learning, common to all undergraduate programs, provided the solution.

The next decision point involved collection points of evidence. Should evidence just accumulate amorphously throughout the undergraduate years? Should there be definite stages? Should the portfolio become a capstone requirement, with completion required just at the end of a student's undergraduate experience? Should each class or each major simply do its own portfolio, without the need for a common framework? Adherents of each of these perspectives had reasonable arguments, and examples of each of these approaches can be seen in the student portfolios developed at different institutions across the country. After considerable discussion, our faculty decided that if the PULs were going to be at the center of our portfolio, then it made sense to have staging points at the end of the first year (so that students would have a baseline for what they know and can do right at the start of their undergraduate work), at the end of the sophomore year (because students qualify for Associate Degrees, and the portfolio would provide evidence of learning for that set of graduates), and at the end of the senior year (to provide evidence of both improvement and achievement of the PULs in relation to the major). Additionally, both faculty and students wanted to be able to demonstrate learning that occurred beyond the classroom in co-curricular, extra-curricular, and work-based experiences. Ultimately, we came up with four levels of learning: Introductory (what all students should know and be able to do in relation to the PULs after 26 credit hours); Intermediate (what all students should know and be able to do in relation to the PULs after 56 credit hours); Advanced (junior and senior level); and Experiential (co-curricular, extra-curricular, and work-based learning in relation to the PULs).

While agreeing that the selection and organization of artifacts of learning in the curriculum, co-curriculum, and extra-curriculum would provide evidence of learning, and might possibly enhance learning during the selection and organization process, the planning group did not consider that potential sufficient to warrant the portfolio effort. Consequently, building on the use of reflection in the Alverno Digital Portfolio, and portfolio work being done at Kalamazoo and Clemson, we included reflection on the group of artifacts for each Principle of Undergraduate Learning as a key component of the learning matrix.

During one memorable three-hour meeting at an AAHE Conference, the project director for ePort and the director of the CyberLab collaborated to envision all of the above ideas graphically, and created on a conference napkin the matrix that became the basis for both the Epsilen and the OSPI infrastructures. This initial matrix looked something like the following (see Figure 1).

Learning Matrix of the IUPUI Student Electronic Portfolio: 2000

The IUPUI CyberLab conceptualized and developed a stand-alone technological infrastructure based on the above matrix, using the ANGEL system to build the prototype, and we conducted our proof-of-concept pilot in 2001-2002. The results of that pilot held significant consequences for future development.

First, the technological infrastructure was not always reliable, resulting in an affirmation of faculty concerns about yet another time-consuming technological innovation eating into their class time, and frustrating their relationship with their students.

Second, we realized that a learning matrix decontextualized from students' academic plans and goals provided an insufficient intellectual platform to track and enhance student learning, and began to develop a learner profile based on the 1995 prototype to provide a more informative academic context for the matrix.

Third, we had sufficient support from the faculty and students in the pilot that we felt encouraged to move forward with our plans,

Figure 1. PUL Pre-Survey

Principle of Undergraduate Learning	Introductory	Intermediate	Advanced	Experiential
1a Core Skills: Written Communication	Add/Edit Help Reflection	Add/Edit Help Reflection	Add/Edit Help Reflection	Add/Edit Help Reflection
1b Core Skills: Analyzing Texts	Add/Edit Help Reflection	Add/Edit Help Reflection	Add/Edit Help Reflection	Add/Edit Help Reflection
1c Core Skills: Oral Communication	Add/Edit Help Reflection	Add/Edit Help Reflection	Add/Edit Help Reflection	Add/Edit Help Reflection
1d Core Skills: Quantitative Problem Solving	Add/Edit Help Reflection	Add/Edit Help Reflection	Add/Edit Help Reflection	Add/Edit Help Reflection
1e Core Skills: Information Literacy	Add/Edit Help Reflection	Add/Edit Help Reflection	Add/Edit Help Reflection	Add/Edit Help Reflection
2. Critical Thinking	Add/Edit Help Reflection	Add/Edit Help Reflection	Add/Edit Help Reflection	Add/Edit Help Reflection
3. Integration and Application of Knowledge	Add/Edit Help Reflection	Add/Edit Help Reflection	Add/Edit Help Reflection	Add/Edit Help Reflection
4. Intellectual Depth, Breadth, and Adaptiveness	Add/Edit Help Reflection	Add/Edit Help Reflection	Add/Edit Help Reflection	Add/Edit Help Reflection
5. Understanding Society and Culture	Add/Edit Help Reflection	Add/Edit Help Reflection	Add/Edit Help Reflection	Add/Edit Help Reflection
6. Values and Ethics	Add/Edit Help Reflection	Add/Edit Help Reflection	Add/Edit Help Reflection	Add/Edit Help Reflection
		Intermediate PUL Survey		**Senior PUL Survey**

and therefore developed for the campus an information brochure outlining a proposed timeline for implementation.

Fourth, we agreed that a stand-alone model would not work as effectively as a fully integrated model with just one portal. That meant that we needed to develop an enterprise system that integrated our course management system (Oncourse), our digital library system, and our student information system (which was about to be transferred to PeopleSoft).

Fifth, the director of the CyberLab at IUPUI became so excited by the potential of electronic portfolios to influence the higher education learning and assessment landscape that he formed a national consortium, using the learning matrix as the basis for his entrepreneurial consortial development. This began the process of "going public" with the learning matrix.

We presented these five consequences of our pilot to the upper-level administrators of our University Information Technology Services (UITS), the most authoritative of whom responded with the following statement: "You are hurtling at 800 miles an hour toward a brick wall and that brick wall is me!" The politics of campus-level innovation, involving the integration of the ePortfolio with other technological services, met the politics of university-level innovation, involving the setting of technological priorities for the entire university system, and the future of the ePortfolio reached its most vulnerable moment. The aforementioned brick wall, built of internecine politics involving previous interactions between our technology person and UITS, meant that if we wanted our portfolio to be integrated with our homegrown course development system, Oncourse, we needed to rebuild our portfolio infrastructure, using JavaScript and following newly evolving national standards for interoperability and transportability. We also had to leave the E-Portfolio Consortium formed by our first technological developer, and start again with a new technological developer from UITS, thereby losing two years of conceptual and technological work.

This was indeed a tricky moment in the development of the IUPUI portfolio. The faculty serving as principle investigator (PI) of the project at the CyberLab and the ePortfolio project director had worked closely together to conceptualize the principle-based learning matrix, and both recognized its importance. Concurrently, the leadership of UITS recognized the potential of the principle-based learning matrix for documentation and assessment of student learning at the level of the individual student, the academic program, and the entire university system. The director of the CyberLab was already using the matrix for his ePortfolio consortium, but had stripped it of its ties to the Principles of Undergraduate Learning in order to make it useful for other institutions. In short, the original principle-based matrix went public and lost its principles. However, the university-level technological developers determined that since the ePortfolio project director and the director of the CyberLab had mutually envisioned the principle-based matrix at an Indiana University campus, we could continue to rebuild the infrastructure around it (see Figure 2).

Figure 2.

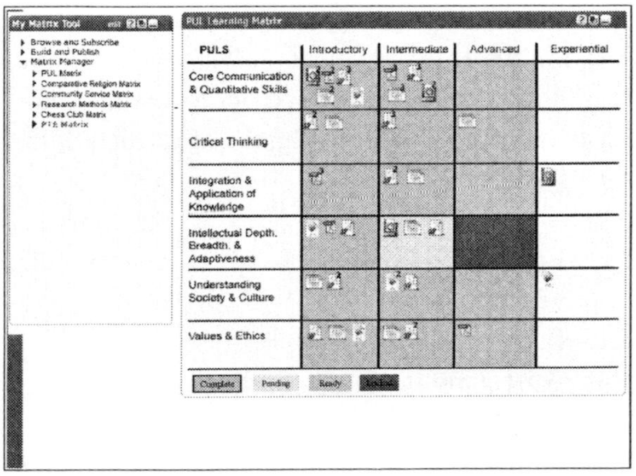

We also developed a learner profile that, in this particular iteration, asked for students to identify their academic goals and their plans for achieving those goals. The intention was to provide links to learner profiles, such as the Myers-Briggs Inventory, the Keirsey Profile, and readiness-for-online-learning profiles, so that students could build and present a developmental and dynamic contour of themselves as individual learners, while also documenting their learning on an institutional basis, organized around the Principles of Undergraduate Learning, in the learning matrix.

Concurrently, however, we began to develop this new iteration of our ePortfolio within the standards of the Open Knowledge Initiative (OKI) and the Open Source Portfolio Initiative (OSPI). Our IUPUI principle-based learning matrix was chosen as the model for the OSPI 2.0 release, which was intended to present an assessment portfolio that could be customizable to meet the needs of a wide range of individuals, courses, departments, academic programs, and institutions. All research and design priorities focused on the learner matrix, and our learner profile was put on hold until the OSPI 2.0 release in the spring of 2005.

IMPLEMENTATION

Concurrent with the technological development of the electronic portfolio was the conceptual development, involving faculty, students, and academic staff. There have been several challenges with these early phases of implementation:

a. Faculty resistance, involvement, and development
b. Pilots and reviewing reflections
c. Assessment, grants, and initial findings

Faculty Resistance, Involvement, and Development

Faculty have been both intrigued and resistant throughout all stages of the development of the IUPUI ePortfolio. Considering the burgeoning demands on faculty time and the increasingly busy schedules of students in higher education, faculty were understandably skeptical of any innovation that would require additional faculty or student time, and particularly dubious about one that united a new technological tool with assessment and that might be mandated as an academic requirement for graduation. We have used four main strategies to reach out to faculty. The first has been to engage as many faculty as possible in the design and decision-making processes. The second has been to identify potential "early adopters" of the ePortfolio and ask them to participate in the pilots. The third has been to provide interesting faculty development opportunities, such as the "ePort Airport" (building on the "pilot" faculty), a full-day workshop offered several times throughout the year to provide interested faculty a comprehensive introduction to the "why" and the "how" of the ePortfolio. And fourth, to be willing to move slowly, encouraging faculty and students to discover how the ePortfolio *can* meet their needs, rather than didactically telling them how it *may* meet their needs. At this stage, after three successive pilots during which the technological infrastructure has been on a local developer server rather than the main server and consequently has been frustratingly unreliable at times, most participating faculty are still willing to remain involved in the upcoming pilot phase and have even persuaded some of their colleagues to join them. On the other hand, at the level of faculty governance, we are encountering the most resistance, since these elected faculty representatives are concerned at the level of policy, and want to protect faculty time and faculty autonomy over their teaching. We are currently working with the executive committee of our faculty senate to keep them informed of developments and findings. Keeping faculty informed has proven to be the best way, not necessarily to overcome faculty resistance, but definitely to create dialogue and an opportunity to respond to their concerns, both verbally and in the development of the portfolio.

Pilots and Reviewing Reflections

One of the most powerful intellectual components of electronic portfolios on many campuses both nationally and internationally is the focus on reflection. Having students not only demonstrate the work they have done in several courses, but also reflect on that work in larger intellectual contexts, is proving to play a significant role in enhancing student learning. The National Coalition for Electronic Portfolio Research, of which IUPUI is a charter member, has spent the last year and a half exploring the impact of reflection on student learning. In the IUPUI portfolio, students are encouraged to upload into the PUL matrix selected examples of their regular coursework that have already been completed and graded as discipline-specific assignments. In that scenario—for example, in order to demonstrate critical thinking—students might include a history essay, a mathematics exam, a speech, and a lab report from science. The purpose of the reflection is to consider all those artifacts in terms of how they demonstrate critical thinking. For support, students are provided, in the portfolios, with a faculty-approved definition of critical thinking, as well as with four faculty-determined learning expectations for critical thinking at the introductory level. Students are guided through a process whereby they identify the evidence they have provided, write a statement wherein they explicitly connect the evidence to the expectation for learning, and then, after they have done that for all four expectations, write an intellectual growth statement that articulates how their understanding of critical thinking has improved as a result of their having done this work. Our working definition of reflection in this portfolio is as follows:

Reflection involves connecting evidence of learning to expectations for learning in order to discover and describe intellectual growth.

The function of the reflections, particularly in the first year, is to engage students in metacognitive thinking about their learning, and to help them begin to see connections among the learning done in different subjects. The function of the review of these reflections is primarily formative, to help students maximize this opportunity through helpful and supportive feedback.

Since these reflections could easily reference work done in a variety of courses, our initial conception, inspired once again by Alverno, was to have them reviewed by external reviewers, including alumni, and members of our Senior Academy—retired faculty members wanting to remain involved with campus initiatives. After our initial pilot, during which reflections were reviewed by several members of our Senior Academy, we learned the following:

1. Off-campus faculty whose preferred e-mail address was not an IUPUI e-mail address could be provided with only very limited and very slow access;
2. Reviewers wanted to know more of the classroom context for some of the assignments provided as evidence;
3. Reviewers wanted to be able to "dialogue" with the students in order to heighten the formative aspect of the reviews;

4. Reviewers wanted to ensure that students had similar in-class preparation for writing the reviews; and
5. Reviewers wanted students to have an opportunity to rewrite weak reflections.

While the first concern was primarily technological and could eventually be rectified, the other concerns were pedagogical in nature. They forced us to reconsider who should be reviewing student reflections. Concurrently, research coming out of the United Kingdom, based primarily on experiences with electronic portfolios to support the nationally mandated Personal Development Plan, was indicating that, for any student portfolio to be effective, it had to be embedded in the curriculum and evaluated as part of the work of the curriculum. Consequently, while we had originally shrunk away from involving faculty in reviewing portfolio reflections, out of consideration for their time, we have now determined that faculty who teach the students are the best ones to both require and review the reflections as part of their regular coursework.

Of course, that presents further challenges, not only those of time, but also those of course autonomy. The pilot faculty have developed a range of models of how to include portfolio reflections based on the Principles of Undergraduate Learning into regular coursework to make the inclusion more integrative than additive. Their sample assignments are used in our faculty development sessions in order to provide guidance for other faculty piloting the ePortfolio. However, we are anticipating a very high learning curve in this area, and are working to develop ways to alleviate that through our faculty development program, and through the growing numbers of faculty involved in the pilot.

Assessment, Grants, and Initial Findings

Designing and implementing an electronic student portfolio is expensive in terms of both human and financial resources. We want to ensure that the ePortfolio achieves our goals for it, and that the processes we are using to implement it are being effective. We have therefore included assessments throughout the development, pilot, and implementation phases. Our initial assessments, conducted as a combination of survey and focus groups of pilot faculty and students, focused on proof of concept and on usability. Using similar methods, our next step of assessments expanded to include curricular, pedagogical, and technological support. In 2004, we received a grant from the National Postsecondary Education Cooperative and Association of Institutional Researchers to assess the impact of the portfolio on learning and retention. We soon discovered that assessing a technological innovation for its impact on learning and retention while it is still in its pilot phase is like assessing the effectiveness of a marriage before the wedding gown has been sewn. When students and faculty are working with a frustratingly unreliable infrastructure and are using new terminology and new constructs for thinking about their learning, the addition of another layer of responsibility over the course of one semester—particularly their first semester with the technology—was simply premature. Even so, our early findings, using questions from the National Survey of Student Engagement, show that students in the classes that piloted the ePort were more engaged, on the whole, than students in classes not in the pilot. Whether that relationship is correlative or causative has yet to be determined. Before we can establish the nature of that relationship, we need first to find out whether faculty who volunteer for a pilot tend to engage their students more actively in their learning than faculty who do not volunteer for new pedagogical initiatives.

Matrix Thinking

One of the most promising intellectual developments to emerge from our early work with the ePortfolio has been the notion of "matrix thinking" in relation both to organizing artifacts already completed and to writing reflections on those artifacts. Each cell of the main principle-based learning matrix contains two dimensions: a principle of learning, and the discipline-specific work done during a given year or semester. In order for students to select an artifact for that cell, they need to reconsider work they have done for a specific course-related concept or set of concepts in terms of one (or more) of the Principles of Undergraduate Learning. That, in itself, constitutes an additional intellectual pass over their work, helping students to envision it in a larger context. But even more, when they write their reflections, they must discover and articulate connections among several pieces of work, done in different courses, in relation to the selected principle of learning. Benefiting from the heuristic capacity of writing to extend or deepen learning through newly articulated connections, students re-engage with their work in a very different intellectual way, resulting in a greater understanding of what they have learned and are in the process of learning.

Our ePortfolio has the capacity to be customized so that it can also be used to track or demonstrate learning in a specific course. Below you will see the customized matrix for a senior seminar in English. Since these students had their first access to the ePortfolio only during their final semester, the default principle-based portfolio, which covers the entire undergraduate experience, would not have worked for them. We therefore asked each student to identify the principle of undergraduate learning that had played the most important role in their undergraduate education, the English Department goal that had been most important to their work in their major, and their main reason for having decided to become an English major. These variables were different for each student in the class. They were then to find completed work from their entire undergraduate career that exemplified their individual learning goals in relation to their goals for lifelong learning, their goals for their career, and their conceptualization of who they are, right now, this semester, as citizens of the world (see Figure 3).

Once they had located, organized, and uploaded their artifacts, we assigned them the task of writing a reflection for each cell of the matrix. We introduced them to the concept of matrix thinking, advising them to consider their artifacts not just in terms of each one of the two

Figure 3.

INDIVIDUAL LEARNING GOALS	LIFELONG LEARNING	CAREER	WHO I AM IN THIS WORLD
My most important Principle of Undergraduate Learning			
My most important English Department goal			
My most important reason for becoming an English major			

dimensions, but rather to look at the intersection of the two ideas. In other words, if their most important principle is critical thinking, and one of their goals is to get a PhD in English, how do these notions interact with each other, and how do their artifacts exemplify this interaction between the two concepts?

While students found this difficult for the first couple of reflections, they soon caught on, and the difference in their thinking, and their articulation of that thinking, changed significantly. Early reflections were primarily additive, for example:

My poem, "Along the Way" uses critical thinking to resolve the problem of how to use an extended metaphor throughout the poem without overdoing it. It also relates to my goal to get an MFA, in that it exemplifies my early attempts at poetry.

This student's revised reflection, done later in the semester, shows the impact of matrix thinking:

Critical thinking plays just as important a role in a Fine Arts degree as creative thinking does. Whether writing a poem or creating a visual image, there are always problems and challenges to resolve, no matter how creative or innovative the idea. These problems and challenges might be resolved through creative thought, but most often they rely on a combination of analyzing the problem, reviewing how others have resolved the problem, and using both critical thinking and creative thinking to solve the problem. My poem, "Along the Way", shows that, in how I developed the extended metaphor of a cyclist without a helmet to exemplify a stage in my life's journey.

While we are in the earliest stages of investigating the power of matrix thinking, we think that it shows promise for enhancing student learning. And that resonates with one of the most consistent messages we have received from faculty: the ePortfolio must not only be able to document and evaluate student learning, but it must also enhance student learning. Matrix thinking may provide one significant way to achieve that goal.

Students Have the Last Word

There is so much more to say and so much left unsaid about the development and evolution of the IUPUI student electronic portfolio, now becoming affectionately (or otherwise) known as "ePort." This chapter has traced the major areas of its history and the significance of the Principles of Undergraduate Learning in its development. It now remains for those most directly involved in using the portfolio, our students, to have the final say:

I no longer see what I have to offer as an English job hunter in mere terms of degree possessed and years of experience... I look at what I have to offer in a larger context. Beyond the essential in my résumé that I share with all other graduates, I now see capacities in critical thinking, communications, and multi-project analyses. All these capacities can be supported with the creative and scholarly material in my matrix.

If students and professors use this archive throughout, then I believe it will naturally become a comfortable companion that in its own use and growth will reach a commonplace acceptance beyond the academic career of the student.

And, finally, to show both the warts and the wonders:

It's a good thing we were asked to write this near the end of the semester. Were we made to write this at the beginning, my response would have been something like, 'good idea?' You honestly think this is a good idea? Hell no, this isn't a good idea ... we all had to learn how to navigate the darned thing, how to put in artifacts, and place them in the correct cells. I suppose that would have been easy ... if the technology was working and the Web site was up. Nope, no dice—at the beginning of the semester I had a very far from high opinion of the ePortfolio system. Then something happened. The techie gods smiled on us, and the ePort Web site was up. NOW, we could start putting stuff up. And, I have to admit, after awhile I was able to see how and why the matrix is a valuable learning tool ... The idea that the ePort is a valuable tool for faculty and students is evident. Any advisor who wants to track the progress of his or her students would be able to open an ePortfolio and view the student's documents. Students could use ePort with professors or collaborate with other students to discuss strengths and weaknesses. Finally, a graduating student would be able to have his or her entire college career in one easily accessible area. Sounds like a fabulous idea to me ... I have to confess something. I was totally wrong about the ePort program. My reluctance to accept the new system was strong until recently, and I resented having my senior capstone serve as a guinea pig for the university's new pet project. Where was Chaucer? Where was Joyce? Why couldn't we read a big, heavy, boring novel? I have to admit that this was much more valuable to me. The ideas and concepts to which I've been exposed through ePort will help me with my career ... So, despite my reluctance to say otherwise, I was wrong. I admit it. The ePort is a wonderful tool.

By spring of 2005, over 300 students had participated in the proof-of-concept and beta pilots of ePort. In fall of 2005, almost 400 first-year students were to be introduced to ePort. Additionally, four departments received Integrative Learning Grants to explore how best to use ePort to help them evaluate student learning in relation not only to the PULs, but also to their own discipline-specific learning goals. Now that ePort has found a stable environment in our revised course management system and is being adopted at the department level, the number of users is expected to grow exponentially over the next three years.

REFERENCES

2004 AIR/NPEC Grant Final Report. (2005, November). Retrieved from http://www.imir.iupui.edu/oie

Academic Affairs Committee of the IUPUI Faculty Council. (1998, May 7). *IUPUI Principles of Undergraduate Learning*. Retrieved from http://www.iupui.edu/~fcouncil/documents/principlesofundergraduatelearning980507.htm

CyberLab at IUPUI. (2003). Retrieved from http://www.cyberlab.iupui.edu

ePort at IUPUI. (2002). *Information site*. Retrieved from http://www.eport.iu.edu

Information Management and Institutional Research. (1993). Retrieved from http://www.imir.iupui.edu

IUPUI Institutional Portfolio (iPort). (2000). Retrieved from http://www.iport.iupui.edu

Oncourse Course Management System. (1995). Retrieved from http://oncourse.iu.edu

Open Source Portfolio. (2005). Retrieved from http://www.osportfolio.org

KEY TERMS

Assessment: The process of documenting, usually in measurable terms, knowledge, skills, attitudes, and beliefs. Assessment using electing portfolios embraces a wide range of student activity ranging from the use of a word processor to on-screen testing. Due to its obvious similarity to eLearning, the term eAssessment is becoming widely used as a generic term to describe the use of computers within the assessment process.

General Education: The North American term for the underlying intellectual foundations of undergraduate learning that provide the basis for disciplinary learning and lifelong learning.

Higher Education: Refers to tertiary education, generally college-level learning.

Innovation: The implementation of a new or significantly improved idea, good, service, process, or practice which is intended to be useful.

Integration: Involves the merging of originally discrete traditions in order to assert an underlying unity.

Learning Outcomes: The expectations for learning specified in particular assignments, courses, or academic programs.

Matrix Thinking: A matrix is something that provides support or structure, especially in the sense of surrounding and/or shaping. Matrix thinking refers to the nature of metacognitive thinking that is shaped by the concepts of a matrix, as in a portfolio matrix.

Pedagogical: Related to the art or science of teaching.

Principle-Based: A principle is a norm or a set of norms that regulates the behavior or expectations of a group of people. An educational program that is principle based is a program based on an agreed-upon set of norms or expectations.

Chapter XL
Community Through Constructive Learning

Patricia McGee
The University of Texas at San Antonio, USA

Misty Sailors
The University of Texas at San Antonio, USA

Lucretia Fraga
The University of Texas at San Antonio, USA

ABSTRACT

This case study illustrates a community-based constructive learning approach to ePortfolio development, and the subsequent phenomena and outcomes that came from the initial implementation. The authors discuss why and how an ePortfolio system was chosen, as well as faculty engagement, student engagement, and recommendations to others based on the University of Texas at San Antonio experience.

INTRODUCTION

Electronic portfolios are typically designed for specific purposes: individual assessment, program or course assessment, metacognitive exercise for the learner, institutional assessment, and employment (Barrett, 2003). The many potential uses of ePortfolios are one reason why community development is so attractive. When building a system with the input and investment of the learning community, institutions can customize their system to fit their needs and context, and resolve problems of functionality as well as interoperability (McGee & Robinson, 2004), while building "what works" and what is valued within the institution (Demarest, 1997) rather than making "what works" fit into a preordained structure. This chapter describes the processes and emerging outcomes that came from an ePortfolio development project on an urban university in South Texas.

ISSUES, CONTROVERSIES, PROBLEMS: PROJECT BACKGROUND

The University of Texas at San Antonio (UTSA) offers 55 bachelor's, 38 master's, and 12 doctoral programs in a broad array of subjects. The university has three campuses with courses and programs offered on two campuses within city limits. Faculty members and students travel between campuses, and therefore reliance of information and communications technologies (ICTs) has become critical. There are currently 522 tenured and tenure-track faculty, 98% of which hold doctorates or equivalent terminal degrees, and 4,537 full-time and part-time staff. The predominance of adjunct faculty has challenged campus administration to provide resources and strategies to ensure a coherent and connected program. In the fall of 2004, enrollment at UTSA was 26,175, of which 59.4% were minority.

As do many portfolio projects, this one began with a teacher preparation program. However, interest across campus was sparked not just by the functionality but also the potential of community development. Faculty initially embraced the concept of an ePortfolio initiative as a way to align course activities to professional standards and document student achievement of the same. For reasons explained later in this chapter, an open source system was chosen as a strategy to engage faculty in the development of the system; however, as faculty and administrators came to understand the concept of an ePortfolio system, their vision exceeded the capability of the adopted platform. Nonetheless, the project served to engage and trigger changes in both programs and individuals.

Faculty and Program Issues

Ely (1999) notes eight conditions that facilitate adoption of technology innovations: dissatisfaction with the status quo, knowledge and skills of the users, adequate resources, adequate time, rewards or incentives, participation, and leadership. From the outset the ePortfolio team recognized that the community as a whole was lacking in some of the conditions specified by Ely, but with grant funding and support, there was a belief that with the support of a very active dean, the project would succeed and indeed be adopted.

A variety of challenges arose throughout the development process and initial implementation. Working with an open source developer alleviated many of the limited campus technical support. However, each institutional culture provides unique as well as universal values and norms (Thomas, 1994) through which the goals of the project intersect with institutional conditions, requiring negotiation, accommodation, and flexibility. The challenges articulated in this chapter may represent the unique conditions and resources that shaped the processes and experiences of the project, but reflect much of the barriers and challenges documented in other portfolio literature (see Cambridge, 2001).

Institutional Support and Acceptance of Open Source

There was little institutional use of open source tools at the time of the project inception, and this required a knowledge-building approach to get support and resources for such a project. Although stakeholders were supportive and even enthusiastic, their lack of knowledge made decision making about design and development all that much more challenging. At the beginning of the project, information sessions were held, and institutional and college-level administrators "toured" the system with enthusiastic response. A new server was purchased, and the ePortfolio team installed and configured the software with the assistance of r•smart, with whom we had contracted. Part of the appeal of open source was the potential of interoperability with other institutional systems (e.g., registrar, course management system). It was not until transitions of staff and administration did institutional support wane, indicating the truly social and political nature of software in 21st century higher education.

Articulation of Required Functions

During the development of the system hierarchy, faculty, staff, and students contributed ideas and reviewed various incarnations of processes and content of the system. However, there was little to show in the form of examples since existing examples were so customized that they did not resemble what we envisioned. It was difficult for users to understand the nuances of building such a system without their participation in the development process; few had time to devote to such participation, and for those who did, the lack of examples, much less exemplars, proved challenging.

Development of a Coherent Hierarchy

Because the software was essentially database driven, a hierarchy of fields had to be created. What appeared to be a clear and self-evident process turned out to be much more complicated than we anticipated. There were several factors that made this process challenging: the configuration and limitations of the system, the newness of OSP V. 1.5[1] which was in beta testing at the time of installation, and the review process that necessitated changes from trials by a number of users. Additionally, those developing the hierarchy were charged with generating a hierarchy that was robust, could withstand the test of time, and would represent the interests of current and future needs. This was not a realistic (or we feel necessary) set of expectations when working with a system that is modifiable. Most critically, although our community had used paper portfolios, the conceptual transfer to a digital system was not easy. It is difficult, if not impossible, to envision how something should work when you have never used it.

Security

UTSA is unique in that security is an academic focus. UTSA offers an undergraduate degree in Infrastructure Assurance and Security and also offers a concentration at the master's level with plans to offer a PhD in the near future. It is also home for the Center for Infrastructure Assurance and Security (CIAS, see http://www.utsa.edu/cias/). This creates a culture in which security is of heightened importance and required (to our eventual benefit) close and constant attention to security-related issues: user accounts and authentication, user agreements, and location on a secure server.

Student Issues

We decided to pilot the ePortfolio initiative with one group of pre-service teachers who were enrolled in a community-based, learning community known as the Literacy and Technology Learning Cohort (LTLC). This group of 21 pre-service teachers was focused on learning to teach in a school that served low-income Hispanic families. They were charged with the challenge of incorporating technology into their teaching in ways that support constructive learning (see Lonka, 1997; Lyons, 1998). While other instructors introduced their classes to the ePortfolio system, students enrolled in the LTLC were the first group to complete their ePortfolios by the time they graduated from UTSA.

There were several issues that this cohort faced throughout the three-semester-long ePortfolio process that involved technology, infrastructure, and support. First, because the LTLC was a field-based cohort, we were at the mercy of the school district's server. There were many instances in which the server was down and students were not able to upload documents to their ePortfolios. Other times, the firewall had been reconfigured and the pre-service teachers did not have access to preplanned Web sites. Although they learned to be flexible in their teaching, these were sources of frustration for the pre-service teachers.

Additionally, the pre-service teachers faced frustrations with working in an online environment they had not encountered before. For example, pre-service teachers were not accustomed to saving information at the end of each page in which they were working as they uploaded their portfolio information. Perhaps this was because they had not worked in an environment like this, or perhaps it was because they had been "spoiled" by the automated save function employed by their publishing program (i.e., Microsoft Word™). Whichever, pre-service teachers lost valuable information from not saving at the bottom of each page. This was a huge source of frustration for many of them until they "trained" themselves to remember to save at the end of each page.

For others, each time they uploaded text into their ePortfolio, they were directed to sign back into the system as the system kicked them out, and this also was a source of lost data. Other pre-service teachers found that they were not able to upload some types of files into their portfolio while their colleagues were able to do so with no problem. While some of the students recognized that their experiences with the ePortfolios were intended to be an exercise in monitoring their development as beginning teachers, many others felt like the portfolios were an exercise in "filling in the blanks of an electronic worksheet." Thus was the problematic nature of the structure set forth by the ePortfolio committee. We provided structure so that we could best capture the learning outcomes of our program. But in retrospect, we believe that the environment may have been too structured. As a result, the final presentation of the ePortfolios were primarily text based and were void of individuality of the students who created them. Further, the majority of the pre-service teachers did not describe the ePortfolios as helpful in their learning to teach; contrarily, they described the ePortfolios as time consuming and burdensome.

FOCUS ON FACULTY

College of Education faculty involved in the implementation of the ePortfolio initiative have benefited greatly over the past three years' progress toward technology adoption. However, most still fit into Early or Developing Tech (CEO Forum, 2000) or levels of Awareness and Exploration (Moersch, 1995). This section will describe and illustrate faculty engagement and shifts in pedagogy and course design, and utilization of technology to support teaching and learning.

Faculty Engagement

Resisting the impulse to purchase a system and provide faculty with a model, the planning team followed a modified version of Yancey's (2001) heuristic and began with a series of faculty meetings, starting with a discussion of why we should take on such a project, what we wanted to come from such a project, what the barriers or concerns were, and what we envisioned the system to be and how it should work. From this came an action plan and a committee that developed a conceptual framework. After a review of several commercially offered products through the use of an EPAC[2]-generated evaluation tool, it became clear that if we were to have a system that would serve all of our needs, we should consider an open source system. During the development of the underlying hierarchy that would organize the system database, faculty members from each program area in the teacher preparation area worked with the ePortfolio coordinator to develop a course map that aligned college, state, department, program, and course elements (see *Focus on Program*). Indeed, faculty came to see the idea of ePortfolios as "the wave of the future" and representations of the "breadth and depth of knowledge a student possesses about their chosen profession."

Shifts in Pedagogy and Course Design

In working with faculty by program areas to align our ePortfolio design to program requirements, an analysis of syllabi and course activities indicates that technology is used for lower levels of thinking rather that to support social, engaged, contextually relevant, and active learning (Carmean, 2003). By their own admission, faculty members expected to see changes in their practice as this project was implemented. We have found the analysis of course artifacts (as limited in access as they have been) very useful in gaining insight into levels of adoption, regardless of the model (LoTi, CBAM, StarChart, etc.). Some faculty began to create course portfolios to share with the high percentage of adjunct faculty, and in these cases shifts in their methods of communication and disseminating information became evident.

Although the system is still in its initial adoption and has not been widely used in program areas, or as a requirement for degree completion, there is evidence that, by going through the process of considering issues, faculty came to focus on teaching and learning more than the nuances and policies associated with the system. For example, the project triggered an interest in translating traditional projects and activities into ones that could be delivered or situated in digital tools or formats. Over the course of the first year of the project, the College of Education became the largest user of the campus course management system. Additionally, technology use became a part of the annual review process, indicating the community value placed on its use.

Shifts in Technology to Support Teaching and Learning

Prior to the development and implementation of the system, teacher preparation faculty members were predominately assessed at the Awareness level[3] and a few at the Exploration level[4] of the LoTi (Moersch, 1995). Faculty members were surveyed three times over a four-year period to document shifts in both their practices and their beliefs. Additionally, requests for support and equipment reveal the increased use of technology, as well as the increased sophistication of those requests. Once meetings and activities for the implementation of the ePortfolio project increased, so did the requests for support as faculty members struggled with technical issues similar to those of students. The basic skills that the technology support office had tried to encourage for several years (e.g., uploading documents, using CMS functions for communication and information dissemination, Webquests, etc.) became priorities for some faculty who managed to move beyond Awareness to Exploration, and for a few, Infusion[5] and Integration.

Although faculty members were the ones who most strongly encouraged the ePortfolio project, there exists a gap between their enthusiasm and technology skills. The relatively intuitive and straightforward functionality appeals to faculty who require sporadic support and ongoing training. This issue, we suspect, will lessen over the course of time and universal adoption.

FOCUS ON STUDENTS

We know that portfolios are an effective strategy to evoke metacognition in learners and specifically with educators (see Collins, 1990; Lyons, 1998; Shulman, 1998). We also know that creating public and professional personas supports the acquisition of professional skills and attitudes. Currently the ePortfolio project is being implemented in a cohort model over the course of several semesters, and we have examined the development of professional identity of students over time, not only through development of their own portfolios, but also as first members of an innovation within our campus learning community. We have also examined how mentoring and scaffolding unfolds or can be strategically utilized for future cohorts. In this way, we believe professional collegiality is mentored and nurtured.

This section describes and illustrates learner shifts in knowledge and skill acquisition, as well as confidence in their professional practice.

Student Knowledge Acquisition

The electronic documents contained in the ePortfolio documented the shifts that occurred in student thinking about the content of their educational methods and reading courses. For some students, learning was mediated by the presence of the ePortfolio. For example, students were more careful with the documents they created that were going to be placed in their ePortfolio. Whether it was ensuring that their lesson plans were free of conventional errors or representing their creativity in a PowerPoint™ presentation used with children, the students were careful to make sure that documents that would be placed in their portfolios were representative of their best work.

In other cases, the ePortfolios were the mechanism by which students assessed their learning. For example, the students were asked to select three lessons written and taught during their student teaching semester. Many students elected to pick their "best" while others selected three that represented their growth as learners themselves (i.e., lessons represented their growing confidence and ability to teach math) and their growth as teachers. Regardless, the empowerment to select those documents that represent "who you are as a teacher" was a powerful choice for students as they were able to assess their own learning.

Student Skill Acquisition

In addition to their content learning, the members of the cohort reported that they learned "tons" of things about technology through their participation in the cohort. We were not surprised that they did not specifically point to the importance of the ePortfolio in their skill acquisition, as it was the placeholder for those electronic files they created for themselves and the children they taught. We considered it to be the end product of process-oriented learning rather than the reason for the creation of the files and documents. Regardless, the ePortfolios of these students included many different types of files and documents that demonstrated the many new applications they learned; in some cases students reported that they were amazed at what they did not know before this cohort experience. Their ePortfolios included evidence of publishing software to create books for their young children using RealeWriter™ (2005) software and Microsoft Office™ products to create traditional documents as well as Web pages. In addition, there was evidence of student use of mapping software (Inspiration™) to create graphic organizers, and presentation software (PowerPoint™) to create games for their children. Finally, there was evidence of student use of production software (iMovie™) to create multimedia movies to document their growth as teachers.

Although there was much evidence of the growth in specific skills in these pre-service teachers, the learning was not trouble-free. For many of the students, there were technical problems that they faced as they uploaded their files to their ePortfolios. Probably just as important as learning the technology itself (and how to use it to support their teaching), the students learned how to be creative in working around the technical difficulties. Some of them simply changed computers (they worked from their home desktop computers rather than their laptops), while others uploaded documents for each other. Although these encounters were frustrating for the students, the encounters did contribute to the sense of "collegiality," the cohort members reported in their exit interviews.

Student Confidence in Professional Practice

Just as we have documented a shifting in student knowledge and technology skills acquisition, we believe that the ePortfolios helped these beginning teachers understand and describe the changes in their professional practices. The students in this cohort fully attributed their growth as teachers to the reflections that accompanied the electronic artifacts of their ePortfolios. They believed that if they had not been asked to reflect on their practices inside this environment, they would not have grown as teachers. Further, they believed that the documents they included in their portfolios were instrumental in helping the in-service teachers with whom they worked (both their cooperating teachers and others on their grade levels) become better teachers because the pre-service teachers were sharing their electronic files with their neighboring teachers.

Further, there was evidence that this cohort was extremely supportive of each other throughout their experiences with the ePortfolio. For example, we often saw students helping each other before, during, after, and outside of class. There were many impromptu lessons between cohort members on how to get online, how to find a signal, and how to move between electronic documents when working on their ePortfolios. We also heard stories about ePortfolio "parties" that were held at the houses of cohort members with high-speed and wireless Internet access. During these gatherings, students worked together on their ePortfolios, supporting each other not only technologically but also as writers (within the system). Autonomy was not the goal of this group. On the other hand, this group seemed to be driven by their undying and often explicated support for each other; these students were living a life of socio-constructivist learning because of their use of the ePortfolio system. We can only hope that the environment they co-created with us carries into their own classrooms during their induction years of teaching.

Now that the second cohort has entered into the development of their ePortfolios, we continue to see patterns of behavior and changes in students, as well as programmatic shifts that have accompanied the initiative.

FOCUS ON PROGRAMS

The ePortfolio system has come to trigger programmatic reflection and articulation that heretofore had not occurred for a variety of reasons: our faculty are separated by two campuses, we have a high percentage of adjunct faculty who are not always engaged in decision making, and our teacher preparation program is primarily field based. Throughout the initial implementation, it became clear that there was a need for a visual tool that would support students and faculty to better understand the relationship between the program of study and the system. McGee (2004) developed a framework for a program map (see Table 1) that aligns teacher preparation program guiding questions, State Board of Educator Certification (SBEC) Technology Standards for All Beginning Teachers[6], program courses, artifacts that are indicators of SBEC standard mastery, and ePortfolio component. The program map was reviewed and discussed with faculty at the beginning of the semester during a faculty meeting. Explanations of the map and specific instructions on how to complete the map were given. Each faculty member was then given a template of the program map to complete for his or her course. Although assistance was provided for those who needed it, two-thirds of faculty struggled to make sense of the concept of alignment. Even though only one part of the map ("ePortfolio Category") was related to the system and was not completed by faculty, faculty members had never participated in an alignment activity to such an extent. Remarkably the program map has been used as a programmatic focus, exclusive of the ePortfolio initiative.

The ePortfolio system has supported interactions that are new or different than those that had occurred prior to the introduction of the system. The current design of the system represents an attempt to satisfy Wilcox and Tomei's (1999) portfolio model that includes reading (collecting evidence of new knowledge), writing (through thoughtful narratives), thinking (making new connections and perspectives), interacting ("sharing, critiquing, publishing, and demonstrating" (p. 12) through group discourse), and demonstrating (application of learning for critique and dissemination). Our current system allows for all of these functions except for group discourse. Such limitation can be worked around by linking external tools (e.g., course management systems, wikis, blogs, etc.) to the user tips that are embedded. For example, if a component of an entry needs to be discussed by all members of a specific course, a link to a course discussion area can be included in the tip so that after reviewing the artifact, the users can proceed to a discussion area. Another strategy that works within the context of a course is to link to the ePortfolio within the CMS so that users access the system within the context of course activities. Strategies such as these take the learning experience beyond the course and help the learner (and instructor) reinforce the larger programmatic learning experience.

Table 1. Excerpt from teacher preparation program map

Guiding Principle	Questions	SBEC Standards	Course Number	Indicator of Standards	ePortfolio Category
Personal Knowledge: Belief Systems and Emotional Aspects of Teaching & Learning	Who am I?				
	What is my philosophical stance about teaching and learning?	PPR 1.24k•1.31K PPR 1.24s•1.29s	ECE 4203		Aspects of Teaching and Learning
		S – 2.2k, 2.4k, 2.5k, 2.6k2.1s, 2.2s, 2.6s, 2.8s, 2.9s, 2.10s	C&I 4403		
		PPR 1.5s	RDG 3823	What do you belief about reading activity	Philosophical stance section

Faculty and Staff Understanding of Potential and Operation

Because faculty members were engaged in the development of the hierarchy, the system operation was the biggest challenge for them. However, the system provided a straightforward, text-based interface. Most faculty members began by creating a course portfolio that required that they consider how best to represent their work so that when it was shared with others, the organization and content could be understood.

Although paper portfolios were required of students in some courses and in their student teaching semester, and most faculty members had experience with paper versions, there lingered a persistent belief in some faculty that there was no need to adopt a system. Faculty opinions were divided into three groups: those who wanted to use a system, those who wanted students to create their own portable digital portfolio, and those who felt paper portfolios were adequate. Eventually the majority of faculty members agree that the system benefits the learner and potentially the program. Administrators, however, have not recognized the potential of the system to provide programmatic data or as a support for accreditation activities.

At the writing of this chapter, approximately 300 students and faculty had been using the system for the past year. Each semester, at least 50 new students are added to the system.

RECOMMENDATIONS

Although this case represents a limited view of an ePortfolio initiative that may not be transferable to every context in higher education, we do believe that there are policy, programmatic, and pedagogical considerations that we have gleaned and can inform other projects.

Policy issues relate to the acceptance and adoption of the systems by faculty members, staff, and students. Four categories of policy that relate to the needs of the users and existing institutional policies emerged over the course of the system development and required prolonged discussion with faculty and administration.

- **Membership, Ownership, and Access:** Early on it was decided that users own their own portfolio and control access. However, the portfolio user agreement specified that if stated in a course syllabus, access to specific areas must be given to the course instructor, and that advisors should be given access upon request and the institution can generate reports about usage.
- **Content:** Content is organized in such a manner that institutional policies, vision, and designated conceptual frameworks are reflected and embedded in the organization of the system.
- **Review or Progress:** A periodic review for user progress or achievement or benchmarks ensures accountability and authenticity of portfolio. Collection of data as relates to courses, programs, or degrees can inform administrators about a variety of topics: achievement of instructional goals, faculty implementation of technology, alignment of activities to program goals and standards, and so forth.
- **Support:** The institution must plan to provide sustained support to users and maintain a secure and functional system through the duration of the project and the life of the system even though systems may be transparent to the user.

From our experience, programmatic and learner recommendations relate to the constructive learning environment in which both faculty members and students worked. We acknowledge that success for us was relative to the entry-level skills of our community. Progress, however, is measured by change. The engagement of faculty in developing the system allowed them to consider issues they would not have done if we had purchased a system off the shelf. By engaging faculty in the work, they became critical participants in the process, perhaps often more critical than the ePortfolio team would have desired. Students were intentionally engaged in constructing knowledge through their immersion into technology-rich contexts that provided them the opportunity to generate artifacts for their portfolio. Engagement of both populations provides ownership and contribution, investing efforts towards a sustained and systematic part of the university experience.

FUTURE

Although the ePortfolio team felt adoption and implementation was slow and at times difficult, both faculty members and administrators raised their expectations for the functional requirements of the system and user interface within one year of use. The primarily text-based and limited configurability of the open source system has proven to be a barrier and constraint for programmatic adoption. Even though faculty members were engaged in the review of systems for adoption initially, their level of understanding and knowledge about what they wanted was missing, and now they can clearly articulate what they want. As a new system is adopted, faculty approvals will be paramount. The authors continue their use and study of the initiative as members of the National Electronic Portfolio Coalition, as they compare student and faculty beliefs about the curricular use of portfolios and learner professional identify as reflected in the ePortfolio.

CONCLUSION

For the authors, the ePortfolio initiative has represented the struggle between the known brick-and-mortar norms and systems and the digital environment that increasingly influences communication and interaction in K-20 education. Paper has been used to create a trail of reasoning; however, seldom are practitioners required to read through historical trails or original artifacts. Digitized information, surrounded by information systems, triggers the overt accessibility to knowledge that is easier to overlook in printed form. Most importantly, the human reflections and metacognition that is triggered, through both the process of constructing a portfolio and the maintenance and sharing, exceed what is accomplished through pen-and-paper processes. For those of us who embrace, and indeed expect, such accessibility, the transfer from print to digital is self-evident. However, we cannot assume that everyone sees the transformation as reasonable, rational, or necessary. We believe that the adoption and implementation of systems such as ePortfolios represent rethinking praxis and in turn creates dissonance. The truth of our project is manifested in the interest and belief of the learner who sees the usefulness (if not awkwardness) for their own purposes beyond the institution. As theory informs us (see Carmean & Haefner 2002; Dabbagh 2003; Wiegel 2002) and the marketplace demonstrates to us, higher education must use digital technologies to be learner centered, and by doing such we can truly sustain and transform teaching and learning (Buckley, 2002; Jamieson, Fisher, Gilding, Taylor, & Trevitt, 2000; Moore, 2002) to meet the needs and expectations of a digitally connected world.

REFERENCES

ATIS (Alliance for Telecommunications Industry Solutions). (n.d.). *Interoperability. ATIS Committee T1A1.* Retrieved November 28, 2005, from http://www.atis.org/tg2k/_interoperability.html

Barrett, H. (2001). Electronic portfolios. In A. Kovalchick & K. Dawson (Eds.), *Educational technology: An encyclopedia.* Santa Barbara, CA: ABC-CLIO.

Buckley, D. (2002). In pursuit of the learning paradigm. *EDUCAUSE Review,* (January/February).

Cambridge, B. L. (Ed.) (2001). *Electronic portfolios: Engaging practices in student, faculty, and institutional learning.* Washington, DC: American Association for Higher Education.

Carmean, C. (2003). *Learner-centered principles.* Retrieved on February 28, 2005, from http://www.educause.edu/DeeperLearningandLearningTheories/2623

Carmean, C., & Haefner, J. (2002). Mind over matter: Transforming course management systems in effective learning environments. *EDUCAUSE Review, 38*(1).

CEO Forum. (2000). *Teacher preparation StarChart: A self-assessment tool for colleges of education.* Retrieved February 28, 2005, from http://www.ceoforum.org/reports.html

Collins, A. (1990). Cognitive apprenticeship and instructional technology. In B.F. Jones & L. Idol (Eds.), *Dimensions of thinking and cognitive instruction* (pp. 121-138). Hillsdale, NJ: Lawrence Erlbaum.

Dabbagh, N. (2005). Pushing the envelope: Designing authentic learning activities using course management systems. In P. McGee, C. Carmean, & A. Jafari (Eds.), *Course management systems for learning: Beyond accidental pedagogy* (pp. 171-189). Hershey, PA: Information Science Publishing.

Demarest, M. (1997). Understanding knowledge management. *Long Range Planning, 30*(3), 374-384.

Ely, D. P. (1999). Conditions that facilitate the implementation of educational technology innovations. *Educational Technology, 39*, 23-27.

EPAC. (n.d.). Retrieved from https://worktools.si.umich.edu/workspaces/dcamrid/002.nsf

Glaser, R., & Bassok, M. (1989). Learning theory and the study of instruction. *Annual Review of Psychology, 40,* 631-666.

Hord, S. M., Rutherford, W. L., Huling-Austin, L., & Hall, G. E. (1987). *Taking charge of change.* Alexandria, VA: Association for Supervision and Curriculum Development.

Jamieson, P., Fisher, K., Gilding, T., Taylor, P., & Trevitt, A. (2000). Place and space in the design of new learning environments. *Higher Education Research and Development, 19*(2), 221-237. Retrieved from http://www.oecd.org/els/pdfs/EDSPEBDOCA 027.pdf

Lonka, K. (1997) *Explorations of constructive processes in student learning.* Doctoral dissertation. Finland: Department of Psychology, University of Helsinki.

Lyons, N. (1998). Portfolios possibilities: Validating a new teacher professionalism. In N. Lyons (Ed.), *With portfolio in hand: Validating the new teacher professionalism* (pp. 11-22). New York: Teachers College Press.

McGee, P. (2004, December 1-4). Breaking "one size fits all" thinking: The faculty perspective. Presentation at the *Open Source Summit,* Phoenix, AZ.

McGee, P., & Robinson, J. (2004, July 21-25). The digital divide: Making a case for open source. Paper presented at the *International Conference on Education and Information Systems: Technologies and Applications,* Orlando, FL.

Moersch, C. (1995). Levels of Technology Implementation (LoTi): A framework for measuring classroom technology use. *Learning and Leading with Technology, 23*(3), 40-42. Retrieved May 30, 2005, from http://www.learning-quest.com/software/LoTiFrameworkNov95.pdf

Moore, M. G. (2002). A personal view: Distance education, development and the problem of culture in the information age. In V. Reddy & S. Manjulika (Eds.), *Towards virtualization: Open and distance learning* (pp. 633-640). New Delhi. Kogan Page, India.

OSI (Open Source Initiative). (n.d.). *The Open Source Definition version 1.9.* Retrieved April 14, 2004, from http://www.opensource.org/docs/definition.php

RealeWriter (2.1). [software program]. (2005). Arvada, CO: RealeStudios.

Shulman, L. (Ed.). (1998). *Teacher portfolios: A theoretical activity.* New York: Teachers College Press.

Thomas, R. (1994). *What machines can't do: Politics and technology in the industrial enterprise.* University of California Press.

Weigal, V. (2005). From course management to curricular capabilities: A capabilities approach for the next-generation CMS. In P. McGee, C. Carmean, & A. Jafari (Eds.), *Course management systems for learning: Beyond accidental pedagogy* (pp. 190-205). Hershey, PA: Information Science Publishing.

Wilcox, B. L., & Tomei, L. A. (1999). *Professional portfolios for teachers: A guide for learners, experts, and scholars.* Norwood, MA: Christopher-Gordon.

Yancey, K. B. (2001). General patterns and the future. In B. L. Cambridge (Ed.), *Electronic portfolios: Engaging practices in student, faculty, and institutional learning* (pp. 83-90). Washington, DC: American Association for Higher Education.

KEY TERMS

CEO Forum StarChart: This diagnostic tool helps educational institutions determine their readiness for technology implementation (see http://www.ceoforum.org/reports.html).

Concerns-Based Adoption Model (CBAM): This model is used to predict and articulate reactions to change (Hord, Rutherford, Huling-Austin, & Hall, 1987). The threefold diagnostic includes stages of concern, levels of use, and innovative configurations.

Course Management System (CMS): A server-based, password-protected system designed to manage course interactions, data, information, and access, typically at the enterprise level.

Deeper Learning: The learning that occurs when the learner participates in activities that support social, engaged, contextually relevant, and active learning (Carmean, 2003).

Interoperability: "The ability of systems, units or forces to provide services to and accept services from other systems, units, or forces and to use the services so exchanged to enable them to operate effectively together" (ATIS, n.d.).

Levels of Technology Implementation (LoTi): The LoTi scale identifies levels of technology implementation in the classroom (Moersch, 1995). The levels reflect the complexity of thinking that develops as the use of technology becomes so sophisticated (see http://www.loticonnection.com/lotilevels.html).

Metacognition: An individual's reflection about their own thinking and thereby developing strategies that support thinking.

Open Source Software: Open source software must meet the following conditions (OSI, n.d.): has no-cost distribution, includes source code, allows modifications and derived works, keeps the integrity of the author's source code, any license does not discriminate against anyone or group, license does not restrict how the code is used, rights associated with the program apply to all who receive it, license cannot be dependent on proprietary software, license cannot restrict what other software can be distributed with it, license must be technology neutral.

ENDNOTES

1. See http://www.theospi.org/modules/cjaycontent/index.php?id=6
2. EPAC: The Electronic Portfolios Virtual Community of Practice jointly sponsored by EDUCAUSE's National Learning Infrastructure Initiative (NLII) and AAHE, engages in the creation, use, publication, and evaluation of electronic portfolio projects and tools in higher education and beyond for teaching, learning, and assessment.
3. Use is primarily an add-on to regular instruction and takes place in computer labs with centralized instruction about technology functions typically taught by someone other than the course instructor.
4. Use is treated as enrichment or extension of course activities.
5. Use of pre-existing or template-formatted activities that are formulated.
6. See http://www.sbec.state.tx.us/SBECOnline/standtest/standards/techapps_allbegtch.pdf

Chapter XLI
Transition to ePortfolios:
A Case Study of Student Attitudes

Corey Hickerson
James Madison University, USA

Marlene Preston
Virginia Polytechnic Institute and State University, USA

ABSTRACT

This project focused on student development in the freshman year as displayed in students' ePortfolios. The experimental design allowed analysis of student attitudes about ePortfolios with results that may be useful to faculty and students at other institutions. Researchers found that careful alignment of an ePortfolio with the learning goals of a course can help students to adapt easily to the new technology and recognize it as a useful academic tool.

INTRODUCTION

The interest in ePortfolios has evolved almost intuitively as faculty and administrators across the country recognized the neat fit of ePortfolios with various academic programs. Along with other institutions across the country, Virginia Tech decided to implement an electronic Web-based portfolio system that held great potential for increasing student reflection and expanding assessment far beyond the classroom. In the Department of Communication, faculty embraced the use of this new technology for a particular course and developed an experimental design to evaluate students' perceptions about the use of standard portfolios and electronic portfolios. This case study explores this department's incorporation of ePortfolios at the beginning of students' academic careers. The success of this project led to a complete transition from paper portfolios to ePortfolios in the freshman course and the implementation of ePortfolios across students' academic careers in the department. Along with the research findings, this report includes a discussion of future considerations for this department, with implications and recommendations for others who may be using ePortfolios for the assessment of student growth, course design, and/or departmental objectives.

BACKGROUND

Institutional Initiative

Virginia Tech's Office of Educational Technologies agreed to participate in the ePortfolio program sponsored by the Open Source Portfolio Initiative. Faculty in the Department of Communication participated with the initial planning of the ePortfolio project and then the pilot stage. Some faculty in this department were very experienced with traditional portfolios and excited by the possibility of a Web-based system. For years, faculty had been using portfolios successfully in their freshman classes. Additionally, upper-class students regularly created professional portfolios for potential employers since portfolios are a standard practice in many communication careers, such as public relations, journalism, and film.

Course Selection for ePortfolio Integration

The freshman sequence of Communication Skills (CommSkills) seemed the likely place to experiment with ePortfolios. The two courses were a fit for the following reasons:

- The courses already included a paper portfolio assignment to allow students to collect and reflect on their work.
- Sections of the course are standardized so that students in all sections complete the same assignments, regardless of instructor, making data collection and comparison feasible.
- The ePortfolio research team was composed of faculty who taught these two courses.
- The capacity to capture student work early in students' academic careers was important to the department as part of ongoing assessment initiatives.

The course design for CommSkills blends a traditional hybrid communication course with a traditional freshman composition course. The result is a two-semester sequence in which students study written and oral communication in order to build personal skills and to meet a general education requirement. Students from various majors enroll in the first course in the sequence and then stay together with the same instructor and fellow students for the second semester. The sequence has been in place for seven years, so the department already had data about the success of the course, including a previous research project that had produced student feedback regarding the usefulness and importance of the paper portfolio—a component of the course that students seemed to value.

Meeting Needs with ePortfolio

The ePortfolio project had the potential to meet various instructional needs: students' developmental needs, students' major and professional needs, and students' needs as related to their university experience. Of course, these student needs are echoed by departmental and institutional needs.

Student Needs Related to Personal Development: The CommSkills sequence is aimed at first-year students who need support as they transition into a new discourse community. As learners they need tools to help them reflect on their growth, set their own goals, and connect various aspects of their educational experience. Once they are able to integrate the various experiences, they can begin to build strengths and identify new goals. Before students can construct personal meaning from new coursework, they have to be able to see themselves as learners and consider their own strengths and expectations.

Along with samples of student speeches, the CommSkills ePortfolios would include letters of introduction, goals memos, progress reports, conflict analysis assignments, research papers, and reflection essays. These artifacts from their first year at Virginia Tech would provide a valuable baseline for students to reflect on and compare to as they move through their college careers. Students would have concrete markers by which to monitor their changing perspectives, their growing content knowledge, and their evolving professional expectations.

Student Needs Related to Their Major: So that students can intellectually connect their work in the major, they need to track their progress across four years. Communication majors have multiple opportunities for performance—speeches, case studies, film analysis, article writing—and they need a vehicle to organize these products for themselves and for future employers. Students *and* the department could assess student growth, enabling an individual student to fine-tune his or her course selections and the department to fine-tune its course offerings and curricula. This monitoring of students' growth over time would also allow for assessment of student skills and of the first-year program.

Student Needs Related to the Institution: Integrating the work of the major with the work of the general education program and/or the work of a minor is an ongoing challenge for students themselves and for institutions in general. The ePortfolio system would allow that integration across the entire undergraduate career. From an institutional standpoint, Virginia Tech had identified the potential importance of ePortfolios as they relate to student learning; results from this department's project would contribute to the understanding of the process and the obstacles that may be involved in expanding this project. Also, assessment demands from the State Council of Higher Education in Virginia and other external bodies require consideration of student writing and speaking; collecting samples via ePortfolios could facilitate this assessment.

IMPLEMENTATION

As the ePortfolio project unfolded, the research team attended to two aspects of implementation: (1) logistical and curricular details to enable the use of ePortfolios in the course, and (2) the incorporation of the research plan to capture data about student attitudes.

Implementation of ePortfolios in the Classroom

As the project began, the research team had a goal of videotaping speeches at two points during the spring semester: group speeches at mid-semester and individual speeches during the last two weeks of the spring semester. The team was admittedly naïve about the complexity of the project—not only the capturing of speeches, but also the encoding, sharing, and storage of the materials. As a result of detailed planning, the team formulated a list of tasks that were required in order to implement the ePortfolios. First, the training and curriculum modification included the training of faculty members and students to use the ePortfolio system, and the revision of course assignments and class calendar to capitalize on the ePortfolio

Figure 1. Transition to ePortfolio: Checklist

I. Program Planning
____Consider goals, audience, uses
____Determine fit—value to the department; connections across the major
____Determine fit—faculty and courses
____Create/choose template—design of the ePortfolio site

II. Expense Planning
____Provide system, server, storage (institutional costs)
____Provide equipment for recording speeches—cameras, lights (departmental costs)
____Provide equipment for translating/preserving speeches—CDs, laptops (departmental costs)
____Provide funds for student wages—technical support
____Consider external and/or internal funding possibilities

III. Assessment Planning
____Determine value to students as course component
____Determine value to students as professional tool
____Determine value to department as assessment tool
____Plan multiple assessment methods

IV. Implementation with Faculty
____Procure equipment and provide faculty training sessions
____Provide support for instructional redesign
____Set up ongoing support as faculty use new systems

V. Implementation with Students
____Introduce ePortfolio—short-term, long-term benefits; models
____Provide opportunities for training and practice
____Provide ongoing support
____Integrate opportunities for reflection

VI. Assessment and Refinement
____Conduct assessment, including student and faculty feedback
____Refine approaches for subsequent use
____Advertise changes to students and faculty
____Arrange re-training sessions as necessary

system. Second, materials and services were secured with a grant from Virginia Tech's Center for Excellence in Undergraduate Teaching. These included the researching of strategies, equipment, and sources for the videotaping setup; the purchase of digital movie cameras, lights for a portable studio setup, software, and tapes; the hiring of student workers for the encoding of speeches; and the purchase of CDs for student and departmental copies of speeches. Third, plans were made to capture and store speeches, including the videotaping of group presentations and individual presentations, the encoding of presentation videos for Web site delivery, and the creation of CDs to deliver encoded materials to students and provide departmental backup.

As the research team attended to the logistics and the curricular plan, they also kept track of other tasks and then developed an implementation checklist for the use of colleagues in other departments or institutions (see Figure 1).

Implementation of Survey Methodology

Furthermore, the research team developed the survey approach that would reveal student attitudes about ePortfolios and allow for evaluation of the process. To determine students' attitudes about the use of ePortfolios, an experimental design was implemented during both years of the team's research. Because of the standardization of assignments across section and the two-semester sequence of the CommSkills classes, the researchers had a unique opportunity to seek student reaction to the creation and use of paper portfolios and ePortfolios. (The paper portfolios were standard three-ring notebooks that included a table of contents, organizers, all work from the semester, and a reflection essay.) The creation of a portfolio each semester was part of the final examination.

Across both years of the project, survey questions were created to address the following topics: ease of use, fit with course, helpfulness with reflection, future use, and sharing with others. Surveys were administered at the end of each semester via the university's Web-based survey tool. Instructors did not see the students' individual responses but did check that students took the survey and awarded participation points as part of the grade for the course if students completed the survey.

Year One (2003-04)

The first year of the study involved two instructors and two groups: (1) an ePortfolio-only group that created ePortfolios in both spring and fall, and (2) a mixed-user group that created paper portfolios in the fall and then switched to ePortfolios in spring. Each group consisted of a total of 48 students who were enrolled in two sections. The instructors used the same materials and tutorials to introduce students to ePortfolios; they also used the same ePortfolio assignments in spring. As described previously, students completed surveys each semester. However, the two experimental groups took slightly different surveys in the fall to allow for customized questions about the ease of use for the specific type of portfolio.

Year Two (2004-05)

The previous year's surveys were examined, and the researchers selected the most useful questions to be included in the course-wide survey administered every semester. This reduced the number of questions, but allowed all 22 sections of the course to take the survey as part of the normal course administration. The topics remained the same, and the questions matched the wording of the previous year's survey. Along with an increase in the total number of participants, the number of ePortfolio users was expanded to six sections of 24 students each. The increased numbers in both paper portfolio and ePortfolio users allowed for a more complete assessment of student attitudes about each format. With the expansion in the numbers of ePortfolio users and overall students surveyed, the second year of the case study included approximately 284 paper portfolio users and 144 ePortfolio users.

Another change was made in the types of groups. During the second year, students created the same kind of portfolio both semesters, either a paper portfolio or an ePortfolio. The mixed-use group was discontinued due to the negative responses of the previous year's students.

The process for administering the survey and awarding participation points remained unchanged from the first year.

RESULTS

The research team retrieved and compiled the data from the Web survey. However, each year's data were kept separate because of the change in group types and the number of students involved. Therefore, the following section is divided according to year of implementation. Overall, the findings from year one about the differences between paper portfolio and ePortfolio users were confirmed with the second-year survey. Since both years' findings were similar, only year-two results about the differences between paper portfolio and ePortfolio users are described in detail.

Year One (2003-04)

The 85 surveys from the first semester included the mixed-use group with 42 respondents, and the ePortfolio-only group with 43 respondents.

Table 1. Summary of findings for Fall 2003 and Spring 2004

Research Group	Mixed-Use Group		ePortfolio-Only Group	
Semester	Fall 2003	Spring 2004	Fall 2003	Spring 2004
Type of Portfolio	Paper	ePortfolio	ePortfolio	ePortfolio
Helpful in reflecting on class progress	54.8%	30.5%*	Overall: 35.6% [a]	
Fit with learning goals *Significant differences between research groups in Spring 2004 ($p < 0.05$)*	59.5%	30.5%**	Overall: 56.3%	
Continue to use ePortfolio next year in the course	Not asked	37.0%	48.8%	72.7%*
Paper portfolio easy to assemble	64.3%	Not asked	Not asked	Not asked
ePortfolio interface easy to navigate	Not asked	26.1%	Overall: 57.5%	
ePortfolio sharing easy	Not asked	28.2%	53.5%	47.6%*
Uploading of files to ePortfolio easy	Not asked	41.3%	72.1%	61.9%*
Use in the future beyond this class	Overall: 26.1%		Overall: 21.0%	
Add information in the future beyond this class	Overall: 19.5%		Overall: 22.8%	
Have shared with anyone *Significant differences between research groups in Fall ($p < 0.001$) and Spring ($p < 0.001$)*	Overall: 51.1%		Overall: 95.5%	
Plan to share with anyone in the future	23.8%	45.7%*	32.6%	63.6%**
Shared with faculty member *Significant differences between research groups in Fall ($p < 0.001$) and Spring ($p < 0.001$)*	2.4%	34.8% ***	Overall: 87.4%	
Plan to share with faculty member in the future *Significant differences between research groups in Fall ($p < 0.001$)*	9.5%	23.9%*	55.8%	27.2%*
Shared with academic advisor *Significant differences between research groups in Fall ($p < 0.001$) and Spring ($p < 0.001$)*	Overall: 17.0%		Overall: 89.7% [b]	
Plan to share with academic advisor in the future *Significant differences between research groups in Fall ($p < 0.05$) and Spring ($p < 0.05$)*	19.1%	23.9%**	48.9%	27.2%**
Shared with friend *Significant differences between research groups in Fall ($p < 0.05$) and Spring ($p < 0.001$)*	Overall: 15.9%		Overall: 54.0%	
Plan to share with friend in the future *Significant differences between research groups in Fall ($p < 0.001$)*	57.1%	8.7%***	Overall: 3.5%	
Shared with family member *Significant differences between research groups in Spring 2004 ($p < 0.05$)*	Overall: 8.0%		Overall: 19.5%	
Plan to share with family member in the future	21.4%	10.9%**	9.5%	0.0%*
Shared with potential employer *Significant differences between research groups in Fall ($p < 0.001$)*	9.4%	6.5%***	Overall: 2.3%	
Plan to share with potential employer in the future *Significant differences between research groups in Fall ($p < 0.001$)*	8.1 %	15.2%***	Overall: 28.7%	

Note: [a] Overall findings for the research group are reported when the differences across semesters are not significant ($p > 0.05$); [b] Sharing with advisor was required for these sections

** The differences within the research group are significant across semesters ($p < 0.05$)*

*** The differences within the research group are significant across semesters ($p < 0.01$)*

**** The differences within the research group are significant across semesters ($p < 0.001$)*

In spring, 90 responses were collected: 46 from the mixed-use group, and 44 from the ePortfolio-only group. Complete year-one results are available in Table 1.

One aspect that was unique to the first year was the switching of students from paper portfolios to ePortfolios. Overall, the students in the mixed-use group preferred the paper portfolio to the ePortfolio. Additionally, the mixed-use group's rating of ePortfolios was lower than that of the ePortfolio-only group. In most questions, responses from the mixed-use group were less positive in spring when using ePortfolios, but the responses for the ePortfolio-only group were stable across both semesters.

The mixed-use group's preference for paper portfolios is evident in the responses about the portfolio as an aid to reflection and a fit with the learning goals. Students in the mixed-use group when using paper portfolio were the most positive about the portfolio's place in the reflection process. During fall, 54.8% of the mixed-use group stated that paper portfolios were helpful for reflection. The next semester, when those students were using ePortfolios, the affirmative responses fell by a statistically significant 24.3%. The ePortfolio-only users' responses did not statistically vary across semesters. Overall, 35.6% of this group found the portfolio helpful in students' reflection on course progress.

While many students identified the portfolio as fitting with the learning goals of the course, a statistically significant difference across semesters was found for the mixed-use group but not for the ePortfolio-only group. Using a paper portfolio in fall, 59.5% of the mixed-use students responded that the portfolio fit with learning goals. This percentage dropped to 30.5% in spring when these students switched to ePortfolios. The ePortfolio-only group's responses were 56.3% positive over both semesters. The only questions that showed a positive increase for the mixed-use group when switched to ePortfolios were about sharing the portfolio with others. In the questions about sharing with anyone, faculty members, academic advisors, family, and friends, the switch to ePortfolio increased the students' affirmative responses.

Year Two (2004-05)

In the second year of the case study, the original survey was reduced in number of questions and added to the annual course survey. While the number of questions was reduced, all students were included in the survey. The fall survey had 241 valid survey responses from paper portfolio users and 99 valid responses from ePortfolio users. In spring, 231 valid responses were collected from paper portfolio users and 97 from ePortfolio users. Surveys were invalidated when students did not indicate what type of portfolio they used.

The description of results in this section includes all topics and focuses on the more significant findings. Complete year-two results are available in Table 2.

Reflection and learning goals. As with the year-one data, these data showed that students thought the portfolio was helpful with reflection and fit with the learning goals of the course. A majority of both paper and ePortfolio users answered affirmatively to these two items, yet the affirmative percentage was lower by a statistically significant amount for ePortfolio users. In fall, 83.8% of paper users and 74.7% of ePortfolio users answered that the portfolio was helpful in reflecting on class progress. The difference was larger for spring when 77.9% of paper users and 55.6% of ePortfolio users answered that the portfolio was helpful for reflection. The 19.1% drop in affirmative responses from ePortfolio users between semesters was statistically significant. Even more students thought that the portfolio fit with the course learning goals. In fall, 92.5% of paper users and 84.9% of ePortfolio users answered that the portfolio fit with the learning goals. In spring, 86.6% of paper users and 71.1% of ePortfolio users answered that the portfolio fit with learning goals. The 7.6% drop across semesters by paper users who answered that the portfolio fit learning goals was statistically significant; the difference across semesters for ePortfolio was not.

Ease of use. A large percentage of students answered that both types of portfolio were easy to assemble. The lowest affirmative response was for spring when 79.4% of ePortfolio users answered that assembly was easy. The percentages were high for both paper and ePortfolio users, but statistically significant differences did exist. In both semesters, fewer ePortfolio users than paper users found the assembly easy. The ePortfolio users' responses were not statistically different across semesters, but the paper users' responses were.

Future use. Students answered two questions about future use of portfolios. First, stu-

Table 2. Summary of findings for Fall 2004 and Spring 2005

	Fall 2004		Spring 2005	
Type of portfolio	Paper	ePortfolio	Paper	ePortfolio
Helpful in reflecting on class progress *Significant differences for ePortfolio users across semesters* *($p < 0.05$)*	83.8%	74.7%**	77.9%	55.6%***
Fit with learning goals *Significant differences for paper users across semesters* *($p < 0.05$)*	92.5%	84.9%***	86.6%	71.1%***
Easy to assemble *Significant differences for paper users across semesters* *($p < 0.05$)*	95.0%	81.8%***	93.5%	79.4%***
Definitely or maybe use in the future beyond this class	Overall: 67.7% [a]		69.2%	57.8%**
Definitely or maybe add information in the future beyond this class	Overall: 55.6%		Overall: 47.6%	
Shared or plan to share with anyone	56.0%	67.7%*	64.1%	77.3%*
Shared or plan to share with family member	Overall: 32.9%		44.2%	23.7%**
Shared or plan to share with friend	Overall: 35.6%		38.5%	22.7%**
Shared or plan to share with academic advisor	Overall: 14.7%		Overall: 11.9%	
Shared or plan to share with faculty member	17.4%	50.5%***	13.9%	62.9%***
Shared or plan to share with potential employer	Overall: 13.2%		Overall: 13.7%	

Note: [a] *Overall findings for the semester are reported when the differences between research groups are not significant ($p > 0.05$)*
* *The differences between the research groups are significant during that semester ($p < 0.05$)*
** *The differences between the research groups are significant during that semester ($p < 0.01$)*
*** *The differences between the research groups are significant during that semester ($p < 0.001$)*

dents answered if they would use this portfolio in the future beyond this class. The second question was about adding information to the portfolio in the future. In fall, no statistically significant differences existed between the two groups for either question. The students responded that 67.7% would use the portfolio in the future and 55.6% would add items to the portfolio. In spring, a statistically significant difference did exist for future use, but not for adding items in the future. As to future usage, 69.2% of paper users and 57.8% of ePortfolio users answered positively. Overall, the spring respondents answered that 47.6% would add items to the portfolio in the future.

Sharing. Some of the largest percentage differences existed in the questions about sharing portfolios with others. Students were asked how they had shared or planned to share their portfolios with a family member, friend, academic advisor, faculty member, or potential employer. A statistically significant difference existed between the groups each semester when looking at sharing with someone in general instead of a specific type of person. In fall, 56.0% of paper users and 67.7% of ePortfolio users had shared or planned to share with someone. The same pattern was found for spring, when 64.1% of paper users and 77.3% of ePortfolio users had shared or planned to share. In general, ePortfolio users were more likely to share their portfolios than paper users.

Sharing with Faculty Members: The largest difference between paper and ePortfolio users was found in the question about sharing with faculty members. In both semesters, a much larger percentage of ePortfolio users shared with faculty members. For example,

17.4% of paper users shared with a faculty member in fall as compared to 50.5% of ePortfolio users. The percentage difference was larger in spring when 13.9% of paper users shared with faculty members, but 62.9% of ePortfolio users did the same. Additionally, sharing by ePortfolio users with faculty members was the largest percentage in the sharing section.

Sharing with Family and Friends: Students shared with family and friends at approximately the same levels. During fall, no significant difference between type of users existed, but this changed for spring when paper users indicated that they were more likely to share with family and friends. During that semester, 44.2% of paper users and 23.7% of ePortfolio users shared or planned to share with family. Similar numbers were found in the question about friends: 38.5% of paper users and 22.7% of ePortfolio users shared or planned to share with friends.

Sharing with Academic Advisors and Potential Employers: When asked about sharing with academic advisors and potential employers, both types of users answered statistically the same. In general, the fewest students shared with advisors and potential employers. Respondents—14.7% in fall and 11.9% in spring—answered that they shared or planned to share with an academic advisor. Similar numbers were found for sharing with a potential employer. Respondents—13.2% in fall and 13.7% in spring—answered that they shared or planned to share with a potential employer.

DISCUSSION

After data collection and analysis, the results offered useful information for instructors and the department. The student attitudes confirmed the usefulness of the ePortfolios while they also shed light on some gaps in the process.

Consistency and Ease of Use

Students who shifted from one type of portfolio to the other (paper to ePortfolio) were less positive about the use of portfolios. Of course, they had only one semester to learn the electronic system, so they did not establish much of a comfort level. Also, the fall semester's paper portfolio seemed familiar and appropriate to them, so learning the new technology may have seemed unnecessary.

On the other hand, the data showed that student responses in the ePortfolio-only group remained stable across both semesters. Students who used ePortfolios both semesters overwhelmingly indicated that ePortfolios were easy to assemble. Students who were switched to ePortfolios may have been reacting poorly to the switch as opposed to the ePortfolio format itself.

Fit with Learning Goals

Students found that portfolios, regardless of type, were a good fit with the learning goals of the course and helped them not only to enhance their skills but also to reflect on their progress. In both years, paper portfolio and ePortfolio users responded that either type was successful in encouraging reflection and fitting with course learning goals. According to one student, "The portfolio was a valuable tool for reflecting our progress because we would get honest feedback from you and it helped us improve on the skills we needed to become more effective writers."

Another student commented, "I personally have a strong liking towards the portfolio and I think it is something that should be carried along with the course."

Another said, "I thought ePortfolio was useful. I enjoyed having an easy way to reflect on my schoolwork. Sometimes during a writing assignment I would look back at previous papers to see how much my writing has improved compared to the ones in the beginning of the semester."

Nine out of 10 pilot students thought ePortfolios should be used again in the CommSkills classes. One student said, "The ePortfolio is a great tool, and I think it will only get better the longer it is being utilized and the more people that are involved with it. Hopefully next semester all the CommSkills classes will use it." The same overwhelmingly positive attitude was seen among students during year two. The researchers believe that this in part is related to the effective incorporation of traditional paper portfolios into the course. The well-integrated paper portfolio made the transition to ePortfolio logical and successful.

Future Uses

The CommSkills courses proved to be a good introduction to ePortfolios, but students did not have high expectations for adding materials to the portfolios once the course ended.

By spring semester, the paper portfolio users reported a higher likelihood of using the ePortfolios in the future. One student described his use of the portfolio after the class:

I do believe that my portfolio will be valuable because I have already found myself going back to it to look at, for example, how a memo or progress report should be compiled. I have an engineering job this summer ... and I have found my portfolio to be a world of help, and I know that if it is already helpful a month after class, it will be even more of an asset as the years go by.

Students may see the paper portfolio as a "book" that they can access in the future, something they can flip through as a reference.

However, the students had no frame of reference for the ePortfolio uses beyond the class, and the department had no infrastructure to support that use. Despite in-class discussions about the potential for future uses of ePortfolios, students seemed to rely on the prior experience, leading them to believe that class tools became relics once a class ended.

Of course, some students did recognize the potential of ePortfolios. One student said, "I think it's important to have a portfolio that really reflects progress and is up to date with technology. I think that viewers will appreciate the fact that my portfolio is online."

Sharing

While both groups indicated some likelihood of sharing their portfolios, the paper portfolio users expected to share their portfolios with their families or their friends. They apparently saw the portfolios as a kind of artifact or memento of their work—almost in the way they might save a concert t-shirt or a copy of a research paper. One student described this kind of sharing:

I sat down with both of my parents and we went through each piece of the portfolio together. I have always had an incredibly supportive background and they were very curious as to what I had done all year. Although I had sent home some papers to hang on the fridge throughout the year, they were definitely excited to look at the mysteriously immense binder that I brought through the door. I was also happy to share it with them because I was proud of all the work that I had accomplished and the grades that I had earned.

Another said:

I shared my portfolio with my mother, and it really showed my progression as a student throughout the year. She loved reading some of the inserts, and it made me proud to show her the thick binder with all my work (especially with the picture on the front).

The ePortfolio users, however, were more likely to share their products—most likely with faculty. This may indicate that students see the ePortfolio as a more academic or professional product. Some of their comments follow:

- *I have shared it with my advisor and my family. They just wanted to get a better idea of what I had done in school so I thought this would be the best and easiest way. They especially liked the videos that I had posted.*
- *I think my portfolio will be useful because it includes a wide variety of my work. The assignments in my portfolio show my writing style as well as my personality. Since ePortfolio is so easy to access, I will be more willing to share it with them.*
- *It gives people a chance to get to know you as well as see your writing and speaking skills. It could be valuable to me professionally because I want to work in the television industry so if I apply for a job I could send them my portfolio and they would be able to see how I work on camera.*

Although students did not have any personal experience with this long-term use of the ePortfolios, their intuition about the benefits of ePortfolio seemed to parallel the initial sense of the research team.

IMPLICATIONS

Based upon the findings from students across two years, the researchers identified implications for the future growth and success of the ePortfolio program.

Matching ePortfolio to the Learning Goals of a Course

Faculty and departments need to articulate the goals of an ePortfolio before adding the technology just because it is a new and exciting technology. Students clearly recognize and appreciate the value of a technology that is a good fit with a course, just as they recognized the portfolio's usefulness in meeting course goals and enhancing reflection.

At Virginia Tech, students found the ePortfolio system to be appropriate for the course and easy, so the CommSkills team was comfortable mandating the move to ePortfolios for all sections of the class. While the initial study affected 100 students the first year and 144 students the second year, eventually all sections of CommSkills will incorporate use of ePortfolios. This will be a first step in students' compilation of materials across the years in the major. As a start, all 2004-2005 freshman communication majors will have an ePortfolio with required elements including documents from the required state assessment of oral communication skills.

Infrastructure to Support ePortfolio

Optimally, ePortfolios should be part of larger institutional and departmental frameworks. A structure should be in place that will require the use of the ePortfolio over the years so that students can see the long-term value of the system and can gain expertise in their use of the system's features. Faculty should explain the use of the ePortfolio over the course of their academic careers and should promote students' sharing of their work with faculty, advisors, and employers.

Faculty and administrators must also consider the logistics required to train faculty and to preserve these artifacts from student essays and speeches. Not only must the department provide instruction for faculty; it must also provide necessary equipment for the immediate use of faculty and students and for the long term. While a department may be able to provide the equipment, institutional support may be necessary to provide the technology resources to update software and maintain servers.

Figure 2. Public relations template for ePortfolio items by course and year

	ePortfolio Items			
	Required Assignment	Required Items	File Type	Approximate Size
First-Year Foundation				
Required				
1014	No Required Assignment			
1015	Introduction Project	Visual Project	.mov, .ppt or .jpg	0.5 MB to 40 MB
		Introduction Letter	.doc	60 KB
	Reflection Essay	Reflection Essay	.doc	60 KB
	Technology Assessment	Word Assessment	.doc	60 KB
1016 (or 2004)	Group Project	Group Assessment Paper	.doc	60 KB
	Persuasive Project	Persuasive Paper	.doc	150 KB
		Persuasive Speech	.mov	15 MB (10-minute presentation)
		Visual Aids	.ppt	3 MB
		Speech Outline	.doc	60 KB
		Linked Research	urls and .pdf	5 MB
	Reflection Essay	Reflection Essay	.doc	60 KB
Second-Year Foundation				
General Foundation				
Required				
1024 Intro to Comm Rsch	Field Research	Field Research Report/Finding	.doc	60 KB
	Literature Review	Annotated Bibliography	.doc	100 KB
2024 Media Writing (WI)	Feature Writing	Feature Story	.doc	60 KB
	News Story from Supplied Information	News Story	.doc	60 KB
	News Story from Collected Information	News Story	.doc	60 KB
Students Take One From:				
2034 Visual Media	Final Project	Varies	pdf	1 MB
2094 Comm, Internet	Final Project	Essay	.doc	60 KB
3814 TV Prod	Final Project	Video Clip	.mov	30 MB
Area Foundation				
Required				
2044 Principles of PR	No Required Assignments			

continued on following page

Figure 2. continued

Junior /Senior Years—Advanced Study (18 hours)				
Required:				
3144 Adv Media Writing (WI)	Client Portfolio	Brochure	pdf	200 KB
		News Release	.doc or pdf	60 KB
		Brochure	pdf	200 KB
4054 (Revised as Cases)	Case Analysis	Case Analysis Paper	.doc	120 KB
Take Three From:				
3244 Political Comm	Submit One Project from One of the Three Classes	Most Will Be Papers	.doc	120 KB
4064 Persuasion				
4074 Org Comm				
4044 International Comm				
4024 Comm Law				
4374 New Comm Tech				
Senior Capstone Experience				
Take One From:				
4xxx Topics in Campaigns	Capstone Project	Situational Analysis and Campaign Plan	.doc	240 KB
		Three Sample Items from Implementation Materials	.pdf	6 MB
		Presentation to Client	.mov	60 MB (30-minute presentation)
		Visual Aids	.ppt	15 MB (large file with many graphics)
4364 Issue Mgmt	Capstone Project	Issue Frames Paper	.doc	240 KB
		Final Culminating Analysis	.doc	350 KB
		Presentation	.mov	20 MB (10-minute presentation)
		Visual Aids	.ppt	10 MB (large file with many graphics)

At Virginia Tech, within the next few years, all 750 Communication majors are expected to have ePortfolios. This change will help students to envision the ePortfolio as a living system that does not end with the completion of one course. The department is continuing the expansion of the ePortfolio project within the major to enhance learning, to facilitate students' progress into the professional world, and to facilitate departmental assessment. As students move through the undergraduate curriculum, they will be prompted at various points to update the ePortfolio. The next step in implementation is the creation of curriculum templates for each of the department's program areas. The template for public relations is created already, and the remaining three templates are under construction with possible completion this summer (see Figure 2). The department has a goal of using ePortfolios for assessment at the student, course, program, and department levels. To facilitate assessment and student usage, a one-credit class in portfolio development is being considered.

At the university level, more server space is being dedicated so that students will be able to use ePortfolios beyond the requirements of a class and to support them in their career development even after graduation.

CONCLUSION

This case study examined one department's transition from paper portfolios to ePortfolios in the first-year course sequence. Students found the ePortfolio a strong fit with course goals, helpful in the reflection progress, easy to use, and potentially helpful in the future, especially as an academic tool. One ePortfolio user summarized the success of the project by stating, "It is a very professional and valuable resource to be able to hand a potential employer, professor, or even peer—a link to a gateway of accomplishments, insight, or other personal information." Based on the results of the pilot, the department is expanding the use of ePortfolios to all sections of the first-year course sequence and to other courses within the major. With careful integration with course learning goals and institutional support, other departments also could find success with ePortfolio.

KEY TERMS

Communication Field: The Association for Communication Administration states: "The field of communication focuses on how people use messages to generate meanings within and across various contexts, cultures, channels and media. The field promotes the effective and ethical practice of human communication." Academic programs in the communication field include communication studies, media studies, organizational communication, journalism, public relations, film studies, health communication, political communication, and radio and television.

Curriculum Assessment: A systematic process of analyzing a curriculum and its student outcomes for strengths, weaknesses, and omissions leading back to curriculum refinement and revision.

ePortfolio: A Web-based collection of student work and data organized to demonstrate mastery of specific objectives for a particular audience or person.

Open Source Portfolio Initiative: A group of individuals and institutions working together to create open source software for electronic portfolio systems. More information is available at http://www.osportfolio.org.

Video Encoding: The process of taking recorded video presentations and converting it to a computer format.

Chapter XLII
How ePortfolios Support Development in Early Teacher Education

Victor McNair
University of Ulster, Northern Ireland

Kevin Marshall
Trinity College Dublin, Ireland

ABSTRACT

This chapter reports on a pilot study which examined how student teachers of a one-year Post Graduate Certificate in Education course in Northern Ireland developed reflective ePortfolios and then used them to embed ICT in their first (Induction) year as qualified teachers. Two central themes emerged. First, the process of constructing the ePortfolio developed confidence among the beginning teachers which supported them when faced with the challenges of starting teaching. Second, the ePortfolio was used to ease the transition from Initial Teacher Education to Induction, but where there is a lack of critical reflection, barriers to professional development can emerge. These issues are discussed within the context of technology policy, teacher training, and emerging technology in Northern Ireland.

INTRODUCTION

Our society is undergoing profound changes, with a resulting increase in the demands placed upon our education system. At the same time, technology is opening up new possibilities regarding when and how learning can take place. Educating teachers in the effective use of information and communications technology (ICT) in the classroom is a key requirement to ensure that the learning potential of new technologies is fully exploited. But ICT can also extend beyond how it can be used to improve children's learning (Wishart & Blease, 1999) to create more effective teaching resources (Barron, 1998) and to generate new learning models (Somekh, 2000). Increasing the ICT literacy of teachers, particularly at the early stages of their teacher education, can enhance how and when they themselves learn about teaching.

This chapter reports on a pilot study which examined how 36 of the 125 student teachers of a one-year Post Graduate Certificate in Education (PGCE) course at the University of Ulster in Northern Ireland developed reflective electronic or ePortfolios, and then used them to embed ICT in their first (Induction) year as qualified teachers. Their practices and concerns are highlighted through an analysis of how they used the ePortfolio as a tool for critical reflective practice, and as a catalyst for initiating professional dialogue with their school-based colleagues in order to improve their teaching. Teacher tutors in schools were also interviewed to determine the use they made of the information and structure of the ePortfolio.

Central to the chapter is how they articulated their professional competence, how they identified appropriate professional development trajectories, and how, when qualified, they continued to develop those trajectories. The support roles of their Induction tutors are also examined to determine how they identified specific needs and how they provided accurate and appropriate support pathways. The study discusses the implications for Northern Ireland's eLearning policy framework, and also comments on how ePortfolios have the potential to enhance the professional development of beginning teachers by providing access to a range of data that can support more targeted progression pathways.

BACKGROUND TO THE STUDY

In Northern Ireland, the Education Technology (ET) Strategy (DENI, 1998), derived from the United Kingdom "National Grid for Learning" (DfEE, 1997), laid the policy foundation that gave rise to a development program called Classroom 2000 (C2K). The program provided a comprehensive computing infrastructure for Northern Ireland's 1,245 schools, and mandatory ICT training for its 20,700 full-time teachers. It also procured high-speed connectivity with 40,000 networked computers. A managed learning environment (MLE) now supports this infrastructure with administration and professional development services (Department of Education, 2004), with ICT strongly integrated into teaching through the provision of a wide range of curriculum-based and specialist software. More recently, the ET strategy has been replaced by "*em*Powering Schools" (Department of Education, 2004) which further centralizes eLearning, online collaboration, and the widespread use of digital technologies to support lifelong learning for all teachers and children (Anderson & Stewart, 2004). Where the ET strategy was characterized by varying rates of development and different ICT practices in schools (Clarke, 2000; Anderson & Stewart, 2004), "*em*Powering Schools" has set targets for individualized learning, greater coherence across schools in the use of ICT, and better access by teachers and children to rich multimedia resources.

For higher education institutions (HEIs) responsible for initial teacher education (ITE), *em*Powering schools offers the possibility of more focused professional support for student teachers through greater online collaboration, and more reliable and faster connectivity. Primarily, however, the continuously converging and improving ICT practices of schools mean that professional support dialogue with student teachers can focus more on effective teaching and learning and on reflections about that teaching. These can be better recorded, accessed, and commented on by peers and others. The now ubiquitous use of ICT means that an emerging data-rich personal history can be summarized in ways that allow both the user and support personnel to identify salient professional development issues, to articulate the potential impact of those issues on teacher progression, and to plot pathways for future development and growth.

Moving Toward Reflective ePortfolios

Traditionally, the portfolio was a simple way of archiving a student's finest work in folders (Herbert, 1998). In essence, it was viewed as a container of work. Of late, however, the portfolio has become a central component in the debate regarding alternative methods of assessment. Proponents of authentic assessment argue that portfolios offer students the opportunity to display creatively who they are and what they can do (Darling-Hammond & Falk, 1997; Gensishi, 1997; Wolf, 1999). Thus, the opportunities to demonstrate growth as opposed to static assessment methods (i.e., tests) are afforded to students.

The debate about the use of portfolios has intensified in the domain of teacher professional development (Campbell, Cignetti, Melenyzer, Nettles, & Wyman, 2000). Ellsworth (2002) argued that the development of a portfolio has led to a deeper understanding of teachers' professional practices. Similarly, Wolf (1995) argued that portfolios document teacher effectiveness and provide opportunities for reflection, collegiality, and professional dialogue. Moreover, the time and effort spent by students reflecting on teaching episodes create a deeper awareness of the characteristics of effective teaching (Dutt-Doner & Gilman, 1998). In short, the process of developing a portfolio encourages students to think about the type of teachers they want to be. Additionally, development throughout any teacher education course can be used to document learning and may ease the transition from ITE to Induction by allowing those in schools responsible for beginning teachers to review their history and experiences. McLaughlin and Vogt (1996) argued that portfolios present what candidates have learned; they also validate the credibility of the teacher training program and increase the candidates' self-confidence. Similarly, they can have the added advantage of being used as a marketing tool when the prospective teacher is seeking employment.

In recent years, technology has enabled the move from portfolios to ePortfolios that facilitate focused interrogation of their contents through hyperlinking and searching tools in ways that allow different support personnel to target quickly those issues that they can help address. In the same way, portability offered by either Web-based or hard-disk-based storage methods means that distribution to, and access by, a range of interested support personnel are not bounded by time or distance. Moreover, the mechanisms for commenting on, collaborating with, and discussion of issues raised in the ePortfolio are more easily accommodated through tools such as comment features, online discussion groups, and synchronous forums. The benefits of ePortfolios include the integration of ICT-based teaching into the means of displaying its teaching potentials and gains through reflection, critical thinking, and evaluative comment. More easily can teachers present a wide range of materials, along with different forms of media to offer an expanded picture of achievement (Goldsb & Fazal, 2000). In a growing climate of ICT use, therefore, ePortfolios serve as an integral part of a process for monitoring ongoing professional growth.

To realize the full potential in their teaching, student teachers must come to view them as tools for reflection on practice and for assessing professional growth over time. Reflective thinking is the "active, persistent and careful consideration of any belief or supposed form of knowledge in light of the grounds that support it

Figure 1.

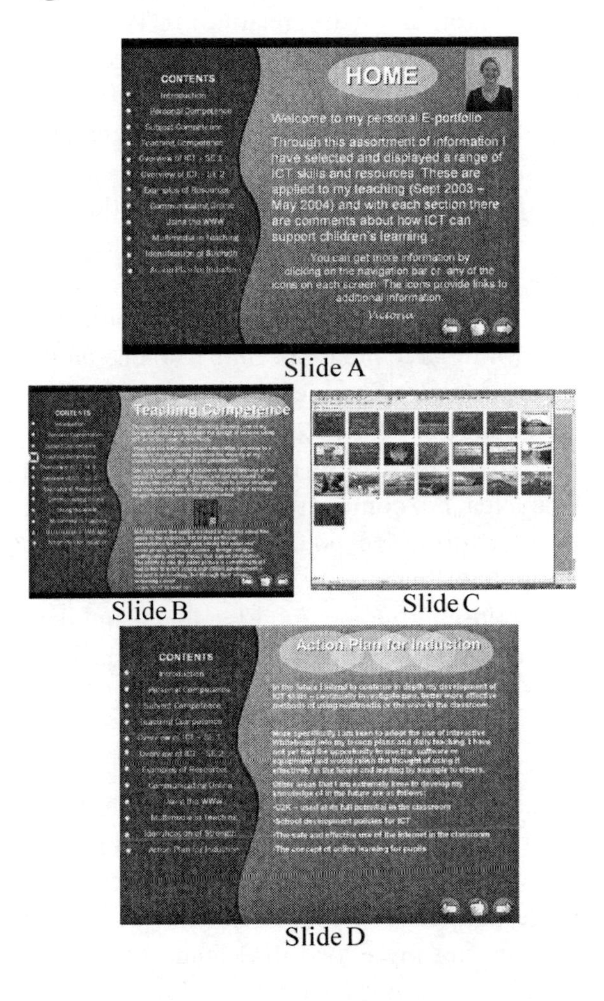

and the further conclusions to which it tends" (Dewey, 1933, p. 9). Consequently, to be useful, ePortfolios must be clear, organized, and goal driven, and must provide evidence that documents the attainment of the knowledge, skills, and dispositions required to be a successful teacher. In addition to discussing ePortfolios as an effective tool in teacher professional development, the concepts of "reflection" and "critical reflection" have entered the vernacular regarding teacher education and particularly that of ITE. There is a body of research arguing that reflection supports the development of teaching competence by providing a framework in which student teachers can think critically about their teaching (Convery, 1998; Hatton & Smith, 1995; Harrington, 1992). However, it is insufficient to provide such a structure without the opportunity for student teachers to reflect on their own thinking and experience. This study aimed to provide such a framework, and consequently, we have defined a professional ePortfolio as:

A digital profile of teaching experiences and reflections through which a community of practitioners can engage in online professional dialogue and support.

To demonstrate this, as part of their assessment of teaching, students were required to build a reflective ePortfolio during their PGCE year. The focus for the assessment was the application of ICT in their teaching, an example of which is shown in Figure 1. Slide A shows the front of the "Home" page with its linked sections (the navigation column on the left). Each section has an introductory slide similar that that of Slide B, with further links (shown as an icon) that, when clicked, open up more detailed evidence and comment about the use of ICT in that section (Slide C). Finally, a summary comment allows the student to highlight areas for development in his or her Induction year (Slide D).

METHODOLOGY

For this pilot study, 10 Art and Design, 15 Geography, and 11 Technology and Design students developed ePortfolios, while all other PGCE students compiled traditional paper-based accounts of ICT in their teaching. Semi-structured interviews were conducted with 19 of the 36 former students after six months of teaching (some had not secured teaching posts, some were teaching in other countries, and some could not be contacted). The interviews sought to probe whether the ePortfolio had been used in their teaching, if it had, in fact, been the expected catalyst for dialogue in their employing school, and if the trajectories they had established had been maintained. Conversely, if the ePortfolio had not been used, it was important to identify the barriers to dialogue and to determine what professional development strategies were needed to reverse this in future.

To support triangulation, semi-structured interviews were conducted with six of their teacher tutors in schools to determine how they viewed the former students' use of ICT to support learning and teaching activities, and whether the ePortfolio had been a source of professional dialogue and support. All teacher tutors had been involved with the beginning teachers we interviewed.

RESULTS

From the data, two main themes emerged and are summarized as follows:

1. How the process of construction and the ePortfolio itself developed confidence among the student teachers, but also how that confidence was set against the challenges of starting teaching.
2. How the beginning teachers used the ePortfolio to ease the transition from ITE to Induction, and how—when there is a lack of reflection—barriers to professional development can emerge.

The ePortfolio as a Basis for Developing Confidence

Confidence was the strongest theme and was mainly derived from teachers' reflections on the increased range of teaching strategies ICT gave them, and their claims for children's increased motivation as a result of ICT in teaching. In relation to varying teaching strategies, teachers linked the process of compiling the ePortfolio to the development of child-centered learning: "[The process of analyzing my actions] changed my teaching in that I allow the pupils to work by themselves more." They also linked the ePortfolio to children's deeper levels of understanding of the subject: "[Compiling the ePortfolio] gave me more time to focus on the initial principle of a topic." In relation to how the use of multimedia in their teaching was reported to increase pupil motivation, one art and design teacher commented: "Well, [compiling the ePortfolio] opened up my eyes to the ways in which ICT can be used in an art classroom ... The children give me good feedback and they seemed to be very pleased with themselves, thinking they had achieved something that looked good ... "

Confidence also related to beginning teachers' ability to make deeply reflective comments about their teaching, going beyond pragmatic surface analysis (Kyriacou, 1985) and examining deeper pedagogical beliefs (Davies, 2003): "[Compiling the ePortfolio] made me totally rethink my attitudes to teaching. I realized that every pupil is an individual and they have their own needs, they all have to be reached on different levels." These deep levels of analysis were also recognized by teacher tutors in schools. One tutor reported " ... very well thought-out applications of ICT ... ," and another teacher tutor indicated that "the beginning teacher knew enough to go beyond simple use of ICT but to integrate it into pupil learning."

The above comments show how the focus on ICT in teaching was enhanced by beginning teachers' reflections, to the extent that teacher tutors recognized their teaching as effective. What is interesting about these comments is that the beginning teachers linked the *process* of compiling the ePortfolio to positive influences, pupil learning, and motivation. Other confidence indicators were more utilitarian in nature and were linked to the ePortfolio as a *product* from which to draw the accumulated resources. Teacher confidence arose from the view that they had seemingly rich material to support their planning, offering choices for teaching strategies that were easily accessible and adaptable: "... it is good to have it all on disk and bring the information if and when you need it, it's like having your own teaching file." This teacher valued the accessibility of the ePortfolio as a resource, while others valued its availability as a source from which to review their own skills: " ... you know that when it comes to teaching a topic you have the resources you need to recap on how it is done." Other comments linked the ePortfolio to their range of skills and experiences: "I think [the purpose of the ePortfolio] was so that I had a log of all of the work I had completed to date ... " "Well [the ePortfolio] enables me to look back over everything I know in relation to ICT ... "

Skill range was an important issue when it came to validating their competence to their more experienced colleagues: "Putting all of your skills, not just from the PGCE, into one file to prove you are ICT competent, and to make you feel more confident in yourself." Or when seeking employment: "[Citing examples from the ePortfolio] sounds impressive when you are in an interview and when you are writing a CV." Indeed, teacher tutors in schools promoted the use of the ePortfolio as a confidence builder: "(T)he ePortfolio has an intrinsic value to the induction teacher ... it summarizes what they can do."

Some caution, however, needs to be used when attributing a positive attitude to the development of the ePortfolio. We acknowledge that to have this resource as a "good start" when seeking employment is a high priority for beginning teachers. Teacher comments above show the contrast between those reflections that view the ePortfolio as an accumulation of resources, and those that foster a deeper understanding of the nature of teaching. The former are, of course, essential, but we view them as the starting point for competence. The latter represent more developed understanding of the function of the ePortfolio and, indeed, reflective practice in teaching. The contrast between these issues will be further discussed in the conclusion.

Transitional Issues Related to ICT in Teaching

The beginning teachers reported both positive and negative Induction experiences which, respectively, were seen as supports for and barriers to the transition from ITE to Induction. Predominantly, beginning teachers' own perceptions shaped their dialogue with schools, and two main issues emerged. The first was that the ePortfolio was used as a means of personal development, and the second was that the beginning teachers were seen as having expertise that the school could use, not an uncommon finding (McNair & Galanouli, 2002, p. 193). Regarding personal development, comments related to how beginning teachers had identified their own strengths and weaknesses through constructing the ePortfolio. One teacher, on commencing employment, continued the process, making judgments about how her needs matched those of the school: "I have been developing my ePortfolio as part of my induction ... The actual practice of putting together the ePortfolio made me push myself further than I would have ... " This aspect of the benefit of the portfolio was also highlighted by her teacher tutor who noted that the beginning teacher "was very good at augmenting ICT into her teaching."

On the basis of the previous section, most beginning teachers had a strong reflective view of their teaching, and it was important, therefore, to determine if they were able to translate these positive views into actions and to establish dialogue about their use of ICT with other teachers. Where this was the case, dialogue tended to focus on the beginning teachers as "experts." For example, when the ePortfolio was presented to their employing schools, the roles were reversed and experienced teachers were supported by the beginning teacher. In one situation the ePortfolio was " ... being used in the geography department ... ," indicating a possible emphasis on content rather than on any process of professional development. (By content we mean resources, such as worksheets and other teaching media, rather than emphasis on the teaching skills and understanding that gave rise to them.) However, it shows how the teacher's work, even as a resource, can be a potential initiator of dialogue. Other participants reported that dialogue was more focused on their own development:

I explained that I had completed an ePortfolio and the interview panel seemed very interested, it was from here that the Head asked to see the work when I got the job and asked me to become involved in the whole school's eLearning program.

Other initiators of dialogue were seen either in a whole-school context or with close subject specialists:

I have shown it to my fellow teachers and my teacher tutor, they think it is a good idea to have a record of all that you know and can do in relation to ICT.

This comment again shows how the perceptions of the ePortfolio can focus on content rather than the process of building effective teaching practices. Nevertheless, there was evidence of reflective practice itself being used as an initiator of dialogue: "[The process of compiling the ePortfolio] did make me ask for more help in ICT." Other data, though, showed that the beginning teacher's dialogue was strongly influenced by the school's reactions. For one, dialogue stopped as a result of the school's apparent lack of knowledge about the ICT-focused ePortfolio: "I have mentioned it to [the staff in school], but I felt like they quickly skimmed over it because they didn't know what it was." Some beginning teachers, in spite of their confidence in the use of ICT, were reluctant to broach any discussion about this, possibly because they saw a contrast between their expertise and the use they had observed in the school: "As I was a new teacher I did not think colleagues would have an idea what it is for and how it should be used." Others were more reluctant to initiate dialogue in schools for reasons based on their own perceptions of the need for it: "[I assumed that the ICT portfolio] was only for myself, for resources and for reflection" or "I was unsure of its relevance to the school." Others seemed to prefer to leave any initiative to the school: "No one asked to see [the ICT portfolio]."

These comments may indicate a school-dominated agenda that inadvertently suppresses dialogue, at least in this area of teaching. The reasons behind these comments are not certain. One teacher tutor deliberately focused, for the first term, on immediate issues such as "survival ... getting established ... and coping with the workload." Indeed, when asked about ICT-related dialogue, it was said that she and the beginning teacher "had other things to talk about." Beginning teachers in such situations may prefer to adhere to the school's agenda and continue to teach in their established ways—happy, it seems, that other teachers left them to it: "I don't think anyone else has asked about it because they just assume I know about ICT." This comment was borne out by one teacher tutor who stated that, " [The] beginning teacher's competence in ICT was such that they could integrate it into their lesson with ease."

With the exception of the last two comments, these findings contrast with the established culture of the PGCE course from which the beginning teachers have emerged, where they are required to routinely engage with subject-department teachers and student-tutor staff on a range of issues (PGCE, 2005). For example, one beginning teacher showed how the dialogue with her former placement school supported her work, "I had no problems asking for help. I found my placement school [during the PGCE course] very accommodating ... which really helped." While former students may regard the university requirements for dialogue as no longer necessary, it is also possible that as beginning teachers they defer such dialogue in favor of more pressing issues suggested by the teacher tutors. In these cases, some eight months between taking up post and being interviewed for this study, the lack of discussion may inhibit the Northern Ireland-wide implementation of ICT and may indicate the need for senior school management and education support personnel to provide a more explicit structure for initial professional development in ICT-related issues. These beginning teachers' apparent reluctance to initiate discussion may point to the need for ITE tutors to develop a more proactive approach to engaging in professional dialogue with schools so that interaction patterns and skills are more established. Similarly, Subject Heads and Senior Teachers responsible for beginning teachers may need to promote more structured and sustained dialogue. This was illustrated by one beginning teacher who decided to defer any dialogue: "I will discuss [the ICT portfolio] when I get established." This stance was supported by that of another who blamed the lack of dialogue regarding the ePortfolio on the belief that it was new to the school: "I felt that the whole experience was new for everyone including the staff."

Beginning teachers demonstrated awareness of the need for schools to be more proactive in initiating dialogue based on the ePortfolio. The comments below indicate their beliefs about how schools could make very good use of the information they receive: "I feel that if the schools [examined] it more they would realize that it is an untapped resource, that would be useful for the whole school, teachers and pupils." Another beginning teacher could see the contrast between previous experiences and the school's stance on the ePortfolio: "[ePortfolios] will become more relevant when the schools learn how to use them properly."

DISCUSSION

There are two major issues that emerge as a result of this study, namely, how the use of ePortfolios can move from pragmatic to strategic application, and how HEIs and schools can best identify development pathways that synergize their acceptance by all support personnel.

From Pragmatic to Strategic Application

The study has highlighted confidence as a major positive influence on beginning teachers, one that resulted from being able to demonstrate ICT competence and from having the ePortfolio as a resource bank that allowed them a "pragmatic" start in teaching. This, in turn, supported them in initiating and sustaining dialogue with peers. While this "pragmatic" role of the ePortfolio is, perhaps, secondary to the aims of HEI and school tutors, it is clear that the workload of beginning teachers is alleviated through drawing on such resources. However, such dialogue was initiated only in a minority of cases investigated, beginning teachers preferring to leave the initiative and the agenda for professional development to schools. Faced with the opportunities that the ICT ePortfolio offered, this trend suggests that there are significant differences between what HEI tutors saw as student needs and what teachers saw as beginning teacher needs. This "needs gap" leaves students with the expectation that the practices they develop in ITE will further be fostered in Induction. The study has shown that this expectation can be realized, and when it is, there is positive professional development that highlights the consistency of approach between schools and HEIs. Other less consistent experiences highlight the need for schools to liaise with HEIs to develop the common approaches to support.

Effective professional development ensues, we believe, when beginning teachers' individual needs are augmented with more strategic use of the information provided within the ePortfolio. Under these conditions, students have the confidence to identify their own needs and articulate them to others in the school in ways that support both sets of needs. The strength of the ePortfolio lies in the variety of access it provides to a range of support personnel. We found limited use of the ePortfolio in this way, in spite of strong guidance provided in ITE about how best to use it. This is, of course, partly to do with teacher tutors allowing students to get started in the school and also allowing main themes to emerge through observation, not least, the issue of classroom management. However, we take the view that there is a range of data that would be of interest to different support personnel and that the culture of identifying, discussing, and acting on a range of data needs to be developed. The link between the pragmatic and strategic approaches is illustrated in Figure 2, which shows that effective professional development is fostered by integrating both.

Figure 2. The link between the pragmatic and strategic approaches

ePortfolios: Development Pathways

In the context of Northern Ireland's developing eLearning infrastructure, opportunities are emerging that allow the data-capturing, synchronous and asynchronous access properties of ePortfolios to provide different forms of support than are currently the case. At present, support is largely concentrated in the schools where close colleagues and the teacher tutor provide the bulk of support. ePortfolios allow a broader constituency to form partnerships with the schools by allowing access to, and comment on, emerging issues that the strictly sequential transition from Initial to Induction prevents. ePortfolios allow HEIs and schools to *overlap* their support, thus providing, for the beginning teacher, greater continuity. In Northern Ireland, school autonomy and HEI funding need to be reviewed for such collaboration to take place.

We suggest three development pathways. First, while the data in this study was essentially text-based with graphic media, the emerging ICT infrastructure in Northern Ireland will soon support a wider range of media. HEIs and schools should investigate the technical and professional development implications of the wider use of multimedia to formatively evaluate teaching. Second, protocols for access to ePortfolios need to transcend the Initial Induction sequence in which HEIs, in practice, have limited involvement in Induction. Rather, an integrated and mutually inclusive support mechanism based on multimedia and online formats would allow overlapping support and would provide consistency and consensus in how to use data and what actions to take following their analysis. Third, such partnerships have to evolve within a policy framework agreed upon and supported by all teachers and HEIs. This will require a major shift in thinking towards a culture where support is asynchronous, collaborative, and inclusive of comment beyond the school. The major question facing all support personnel is how to agree on such an ePortfolio structure so that students, teachers, and HEI tutors have a common approach to its development and use.

Finally, we add a word of caution. Harrington (1992) argued that reflection is a habit of mind central to the development of effective teachers. Consequently, the recording of reflective practice should, therefore, lie at the heart of this process. The temptation may be to develop the technology to its full potential while ignoring our guiding principle of developing confident, competent, and effective teachers. In effect, technology enables the practice of reflection and profession dialogue, but is not the driver in this process.

CONCLUSION

Over the next 10 years, technology will enable more collaboration and partnership among a range of institutions, with greater remote access to a wider range of information that can be managed better and provide a more accurate picture of beginning teacher needs. The challenge facing the education community is that, with the variety of mobile and wireless technologies set to increase, the accumulation, management, and dissemination of professional development support should be based on a consensus of what constitutes valid information, how it informs good teaching, and how development pathways can improve pupil learning.

ACKNOWLEDGMENTS

This project was funded by the Northern Ireland E-Learning Partnership (http://elearningfutures.co.uk) and the Microsoft Ireland Innovative Teachers Programme (INTP) (http://microsoft.com/ireland/education). The Innovative Teachers Programme (INTP is part of the Partners in Learning (PiL) programme aimed at providing a framework for teachers to integrate technology in their respective subjects.

REFERENCES

Anderson, J., & Stewart, J. (2005). Relevant, reliable and risk-free. In M. Sellinger (Ed.), *Connected schools*. London: Cisco Systems.

Barron, A. (1998). Designing Web-based training. *British Journal of Educational Technology, 29*(4), 355-370.

Barton, J., & Collins, A. (1993). Portfolios in teacher education. *Journal of Technology for Teacher Education, 44*(2), 200-211.

Campbell, D., Cignetti, P., Melenyzer, B., Nettles, D., & Wyman, R. (2000). *Portfolio and performance assessment in teacher education.* Boston: Allyn and Bacon.

Clarke, L.M. (2002). Putting the 'C' in ICT: Using computer conferencing to foster a community of practice among student teachers. *Technology, Pedagogy and Education, 11*(2), 163-180.

Convery, A. (1998). A teacher's response to 'reflection-in-action'. *Cambridge Journal of Education, 28*(2), 197-205.

Darling-Hammond, L., & Falk, B. (1997). Supporting teaching and learning for all students: Policies for authentic assessment systems. In A.L. Goodwin (Ed.), *Assessment for equity and inclusion: Embracing all our children.* New York: Routledge.

Davies, D. (2003). Pragmatism, pedagogy and philosophy: A model of thought and action in primary technology and science teacher education. *International Journal of Technology and Design Education, 13*(3), 207-221.

Department of Education. (2004). *Empowering schools in Northern Ireland.* Bangor, NI: Department of Education.

Department of Education for Northern Ireland. (1988). *A strategy for education technology in Northern Ireland.* Bangor, NI: Department of Education for Northern Ireland.

Dewey, J. (1933). *How we think.* Lexington, MA: D.C. Heath.

DfEE (Department for Education and Employment). (1997). *Connecting the learning society.* London: DfEE.

Dutt-Doner, K., & Gilman, D. (1998). Students react to portfolio assessment. *Contemporary Education, 69*(3), 159-165.

Ellsworth, J. Z. (2002). Using student portfolios to increase reflective practice among elementary teachers. *Journal of Technology for Teacher Education, 53*(4), 342-355.

Genishi, C. (1997). Assessing against the grain: A conceptual framework for alternative assessments. In A. L. Goodwin (Ed.), *Assessment for equity and inclusion: Embracing all our children.* New York: Routledge.

Goldsby, D., & Fazal, M. (2000). Technology's answer to portfolios for teachers. *Kappa Delta Pi Record, 36*(3), 121-123.

Harrington, H. (1992). Fostering critical reflection through technology: Preparing prospective teachers for a changing society. *Journal of Information Technology for Teacher Education, 1*(1), 67-82.

Hatton, N., & Smith, D. (1995). Reflection in teacher education: Towards definition an implementation. *Teacher and Teacher Education, 11*(1), 33-49.

Herbert, E. A. (1998). Lessons learned about student portfolios. *Phi Delta Kappan, 79*(8), 583-586.

Kyriacou, C. (1985). Conceptualizing research on effective teaching. *British Journal of Education Psychology, 55*(1), 148-155.

Littlejohn, A. (2002). Improving continuing professional development in the use of ICT. *Journal of Computer Assisted Learning, 18*(2), 166-174.

McLaughlin, M., & Vogt, M. (1996). *Portfolios in teacher education.* Washington, DC: International Reading Association.

McNair, V., & Galanouli, D. (2002). Information and communications technology in teacher education: Can a reflective portfolio enhance reflective practice? *Journal of Technology for Teacher Education, 11*(2), 181-196.

Rees, R. (2002). Second year teacher education candidates reflect on information technology in Ontario secondary schools: How it is being used and the challenges it presents. *Technology, Pedagogy and Education, 11*(2), 143-162.

Somekh, B. (2000). New technology and learning: Policy and practice in the UK, 1980-2010. *Education and Information Technologies, 5*(1), 19-37.

Wishart, J., & Blease, D. (1999). Theories underlying perceived changes in teaching and learning after installing a computer network in a secondary school. *British Journal of Educational Technology, 30*(1), 25-41.

Wolf, K. (1999). Teaching portfolios and portfolio conversations for teacher educators and teachers. *Action in Teacher Education, 17*(1), 30-39.

KEY TERMS

Electronic Learning (eLearning): Developing new understandings using any form of technology as a medium.

Initial Teacher Education (ITE): The preparation of teachers before they gain employment.

Lifelong Learning: Learning that is continuous throughout life, irrespective of employment, lifestyle, or age contexts.

Managed Learning Environment (MLE): A virtual workspace in which curriculum, resources, and online activities are supported, monitored, and facilitated.

Professional Competence: Levels of knowledge and understanding that are applied to professional activities in ways that produce meaningful outcomes.

Reflective Practice: The act of evaluating previous activity with a view to future action.

Teacher Induction: The work-based learning that teachers engage in once they have gained employment in an education context.

Chapter XLIII
Facilitating Reflection Through ePortfolio at Tecnológico de Monterrey

Marco Antonio Mendoza Calderón
Tecnológico de Monterrey, Mexico

Joaquín Ramírez Buentello
Tecnológico de Monterrey, Mexico

ABSTRACT

The chapter describes the Tecnológico de Monterrey implementation of an original ePortfolio model at the Mexico City campus. This model is grounded on student reflection in three broad areas of students' lives designed by Jesus Meza, PhD. The implementation was launched in August 2002, with 60 students studying two different majors. By January 2005, the number of student portfolios had grown to 5,000, covering 18 different majors. According to the mission of the Tecnológico de Monterrey for the year 2015, the authors consider that the ePortfolio model will evolve into a comprehensive communication tool reflecting the personal, academic, and professional achievements of the community at the Tecnológico de Monterrey.

INTRODUCTION

According to the report to UNESCO of the International Commission on Education for the 21st century (1998), the main objective of academic education is to develop the potential of each student so they can be mentally independent and socially compromised, and so they are equipped with the knowledge, capabilities, values, and attitudes that will help them to have a full life and perform a positive role in their communities.

In order to achieve this, our educative institutions face a challenge in the form of changes in our educative models, and also the integration of the holistic concept of education with its benefits, comprehending the development of the person and the integration of basic elements in the social culture, inside the frame of institutional culture. Other authors, such as Porres (2004), mentions the unquestionable use of new educative models that attend the conformation of new social models that help to solve the 21st-century problems.

According to this, in 1997 the Tecnológico de Monterrey undertook an important change in its educative model (MET) that gave insight to the Proyecto Portafolio Electrónico (Electronic Portfolio Project) released in 2002. This project arises as an initiative of Jesus Meza, PhD, academic member of the Research and Innovation in Education Center (CIIE), who was in charge of the project until the midterm of second stage (January 2004). Meza received other assignments, so the Office for Academic Development (DDA) decided to expand the project and bring together the authors of this chapter. The first assignment was constructing a conceptual frame and assures the continuity of ePortfolios at the Tecnológico de Monterrey.

CONCEPTUAL FRAME OF THE ePORTFOLIO PROJECT AT THE TECNOLÓGICO DE MONTERREY

To establish the purpose for the ePortfolio, we adopted the constructivist approach to teaching-learning processes, the postulates of significant learning, and those of knowledge management. These postulates, as we understand them, follow.

The Constructivist Frame

There is certain consensus about the role of education to promote the integral development of people and the learning of some cultural contents so that they may become members of the sociocultural reference frame. Yet, some discrepancies occur when one tries to explain what is understood as development and learning, and what the relationships between those processes are. The development can be understood as a process whereby people acquire the social group culture in which they are submerged, through the structures available at each moment. Even though people development has internal dynamics, according to Piaget, this is possible due to the social interactions between the individual and the many agents acting as mediators of culture, parents, and teachers, according to Vigotsky's postulates.

In this development conception, learning is understood as an individual building process to make a personal and unique interpretation of such culture. From this perspective the learning processes are not a mere association between stimuli and responses, or a knowledge accumulation, but qualitative changes in the existing structures and schemas of increasing complexity. Learning is not just a copy or internal reproduction of reality or external information. This makes the learning process unique and unrepeatable each time. Individual construction is not opposed to social interaction; on the contrary, they complement each other. The same as development, learning is an internal process: nobody can learn for us, but we learn due to the social interaction process with other people acting as mediators of culture's contents. In the educative environment, students learn culture's contents established in the real curriculum, thanks to the processes of interaction and communication with their professors and classmates.

The Postulates of Significant Learning

The constructivist conception, having as an explicative frame the teaching and learning process, is nurtured by many theories, Ausubel's "Significant Learning" being the most useful, since it was formulated inside the classroom and for the classroom. Ausubel, Novak, and Hanesian (1990) think there are many kinds of learning, but it must tend to promote significant learning, comprehensive and related by definition. From this point of view, the act of learning entails a change in previous conceptions and the understanding that such learning is useful to keep on learning. Conditions that make it possible are related to the person and the material. In this case the student assumes an active role in knowledge building and rebuilding.

The integral development of the student must take into account the four learning pillars proposed in the report to UNESCO of the International Commission on Education for the XXI Century, presided over by Jacques Delors (1998). These pillars are the following:

- "learn to know"
- "learn to do"
- "learn to be"
- "learn to live together"

Knowledge processes are inseparable from teaching processes; moreover, they are interdependent. Our teaching plan approach is decisive, because it can help us (or not) to accomplish that the students build significant learning. From the constructivist conception, teaching does not mean to transmit finished knowledge to the students; it must also provide the required aid to the students so that they can build the basic knowledge mandated by the formal curriculum.

Knowledge Management

The knowledge management movement was born in the mid-1990s. Its main mission is to create an environment in which knowledge and information available in an enterprise are easily accessible to stimulate innovation and improve decision making. In a more personal aspect, a new concept named personal knowledge management (PKM) was formed, combining knowledge management and personal information management.

Davenport and Prusak (1998) conceive personal knowledge management as a set of processes to organize and integrate the information that individuals consider important, and then one can make it part of one's personal knowledge database. They also mention that it is mandatory that workers in the age of knowledge have tools to transform random pieces of information into something systematically applicable and capable to increase their personal knowledge.

The new knowledge-based economy and the changes emanating from there have demonstrated to us the fact that, to be a competitive individual or community, one cannot apply a set of identical recipes to every situation; on the contrary, we need activities and dynamic solutions with many factors included, and that prevents us from forecasting what will happen in the future. This situation compels professionals and their communities to review and constantly reflect upon their practices to identify the factors and strategies they will use to promote competitiveness in their regions. In other words, they will build knowledge through the significance of their professional acts.

The understanding of global processes by the students and future graduates requires a deep knowledge about thought, language, intelligence, and the activities and mental processes of attention, perception, memory, representation, reasoning, decision making, problem solving, and so on. Besides these aspects, it is very relevant to know the affective and emotional aspects, given their great influence in the processes of student learning and people well-being. These skills are essential in a world gradually more changing and uncertain, where the individual uses some information-demanding capabilities, related to the improving of their processing capabilities and the use of thinking strategies that maximize the learning ability to build knowledge.

THE ePORTFOLIO PROJECT

The portfolio model in education was born in the beginning of the '90s, as evidenced by the publications of Paulson, Paulson, and Meyer (1991). These writings emphasized the documental compilation for its later evaluation. The portfolios were defined as a documental compilation made by the student, according to an evaluation purpose that enables the identification of students' learning of concepts, procedures, and efforts. These paper or traditional portfolios acquired new validity with the writings of Helen Barrett, PhD, a researcher at the University of Anchorage, Alaska. In 2000, Barrett proposed a new portfolio model with an electronic (online) foundation, whose axis is the reflection and not an accumulative work gathering.

Besides Barrett's works, Levin and Camp's (2002) writings influenced the creation of a unique electronic portfolio's model for the Tecnológico de Monterrey. Levin and Camp (2002) established that professionals who do not reflect upon their work are inefficient to link theory with practice. With this vision in mind, in August 2002, Jesus Meza, PhD, presented his preliminary idea for the Tecnológico de Monterrey's electronic portfolios model.

Meza's (2002) ePortfolio model is grounded on students' reflections in three broad areas of students' lives, the first being personal reflection—including students' values, feelings, and attitudes. The second is the academic area, where students reflect about their life plan and goals in relationship to their major. The last area deals with reflection about the way students construct their competencies for their future careers. Taking as a starting point the mission statement of the Tecnológico de Monterrey's toward 2005, the ePortfolio project is an endeavor to give the students the ability to be educated while they reflect upon the contents that they regard as significant and important in their professional studies. The main purpose is that the students focus themselves on learning, not on their grades. By these means are conformed student records and profiles about their time at the university, as well as the academic and extracurricular activities that contribute to the students' personal and professional formation in a holistic manner.

STAGES OF THE PROJECT

First Stage (August 2002-August 2003)

In its beginnings, the project was proposed as a tool to close the deal in a recruitment process, in the same way as some European and U.S. universities did. The portfolios were pages created in a crafty way: the students received a basic HTML programming course, and each page was the result of the skills and knowledge of each student. The result was a great variety in design along with the frustration of people lacking technical skills.

To begin this stage, we performed a test with two groups of 30 people. The students were supposed to integrate all their portfolios, starting with the first semester, paying special attention to the personal part. Nevertheless, experience showed us that in order for the students to achieve this objective, the project must be explained in different subjects to develop simultaneously the academic growth of the student, and also to seek subjects adequate for the contents they were asked to create. Sixty portfolios were made in this stage with only two assigned professors in two majors.

Second Stage (August 2003-November 2004)

To help students with technical difficulties, we designed HTML templates with the main sections and links. This reduced the design difficulties, but there were still some problems in uploading the Web page to the server and then publishing it. Some sort of standard was achieved, but some students still had problems. The sites were stalled and there was no information backup. Each student was responsible for his/her site; that caused lost information lost and the lack of updates for future semesters. A total of 2,500 portfolios were made in this stage with the incorporation of eight professors in eight majors.

Third Stage (December 2004-November 2005)

In this stage the system was developed to create and manage ePortfolios, which generates the portfolio with PHP programming and the information was saved in a database. The procedure to generate an ePortfolio is similar to the process to obtain a blog.

These circumstances allowed tracing the Web pages, saving them in a database, and offering personal services to the students through their ePortfolios as direct communication, diagnostic applications, and so on.

The necessity to have teachers leading the class is reduced, since this system gives students the necessary options to solve the process by just having a basic knowledge of the Internet. As a result there are just two teachers attending to all the groups.

There is no individualization in the page design, as they all use the same standard design. There are about 1,500 students and therefore the same number of portfolios each semester. In this stage 5,000 portfolios were made in 18 majors with only two professors.

Fourth Stage (August 2005-Present)

We now can observe a revamping of the MET (Tecnológico de Monterrey's educative model) as one of the strategies to comply with the new mission of the Tecnológico de Monterrey towards the year 2015. In this new mission one can identify a deeper attention to the formation of the student within a humanistic and integral educative model.

Tecnológico de Monterrey's mission is to educate upright and ethical persons with a humanistic vision, competitive in the international environment of their professional field, and also citizens committed with the economical, political, social and cultural development of their community, in addition to the sustained use of natural resources.

Because of this change at the MET, the future we foresee for the electronic portfolio system includes the convergence in a system provider of different communication services between students and the academic and extracurricular areas of the institute. In this way we will achieve an integration of student information in different areas; also this will expedite the students' management and development by their career director and other areas related with the student development. That enables the creation of a virtual community, a non-academic space that eases the communication among users—students and professors—outside the strictly academic environment. The community allows keeping its members informed about recent studies, job offers, articles, interesting pages, resources, and/or services on the Web, in a prompt and convenient way. The system's name is Sistema Electrónico de Apoyo al Desarrollo Integral (SEADI—Electronic System to Support Integral Development).

FUTURE TRENDS

SEADI

How can we use information technologies for the benefit of educative managers? How do we trace our students' development through an electronic solution? Until now the learning management system solutions have brought educative managers closer to the classes, with the purpose to trace students. However, these tools do not bestow the option to trace what students learn or their integral education (that is to say, their academic and extracurricular education). Not only are records important, but also students' learning and development as integral persons are important.

In light of these new proposals and the emphasis posed on integral education, the electronic portfolio project is now repurposed as a content management system (CMS), named SEADI. In this new proposal, SEADI will be more than proof of the students' efforts in an institution: now it will be an authentic space for the individual virtual reflection and for collaborative tracing, and will serve as a tool to create a virtual learning community with inherent benefits supporting the Tecnológico de Monterrey's new mission.

Emergent technologies opened the possibilities for the learning of communities increasingly diverse and not necessarily concurrent in time and space, what is experimented with in the Tecnológico de Monterrey's educative model (2002). These technologies are support tools for new methods in teaching, learning, research, creation, and assessment. Their integration makes it necessary to conceive the design of learning environments including various activities, in addition to virtual education experiences linked to the rest of the world.

According to Levin and Camp (2002), this linkage will be achieved through the reflective and critical awareness that allows understanding and transforming the educative experience into responsible actions of personal, professional, and social nature.

The ePortfolio (now SEADI) proved to be an effective tool to promote a systematic reflection of the significant learning and the transforming action in the students, but also to record these reflections in a virtual public space able to develop the students' responsibility and awareness.

In the SEADI our students will have a tool to reflect upon their learning and self-assessment, and they will also have virtual spaces of expression and non-academic linkage with the Tecnológico de Monterrey community. These reflection spaces will let students recognize their significant learning, go deeper into their beliefs and practices and value them, with the intention to validate them and confirm them, or to repurpose, enrich, and transform them. To achieve these goals, the SEADI works as a tool that eases the reflection in action and the transformation of our students. Also, the SEADI allows us to identify and relate to the student in a space outside the formal curriculum, with the different academic and non-academic areas congruent with the Tecnológico de Monterrey's educative model.

Each student in these reflection spaces builds new knowledge and is receptive to the transcendence of this way of thinking, creating a linkage between technology and practice in their formation. The SEADI gives our students the opportunity to interpret their formative experiences, be they personal, academic, or professional. By these means the students are trained to get involved in the knowledge society, since they assess their own knowledge building.

The SEADI is part of an intensive effort to innovate and change our institution. Hence, it has the potential to transcend the curriculum, the technological integration level, and the learning process through reflection, as well as the administrative decision making related with the program assessment.

Purposes and Reach

An electronic portfolio shows a thorough compilation of exemplar evidence that lets the student demonstrate his/her knowledge, capabilities, and dispositions through his/her work and the evolution of the latter. Use of technology makes this process easier to be systematic, perdurable, and practical. Some benefits obtained by using SEADI are:

- **Stimulates Expression:** It allows the students to explore multiple individual forms of their expressive ability.
- **Promotes Technological Competence:** It offers the students opportunities to develop technological competencies in the use of information and new technologies.

Figure 1.

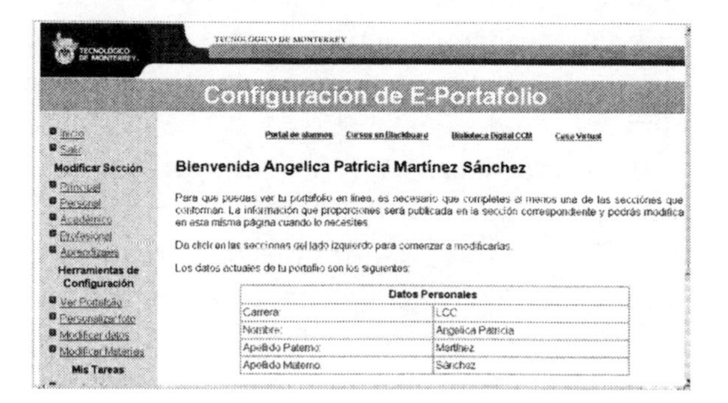

- **Motivates Cooperation:** Students shall invite professors and their mates to appraise their portfolios in the SEADI and ask them for opinions. This action encourages collaboration in the virtual learning community.
- **Eases Communication:** It provides a space for collaboration and electronic feedback hardly ever achieved by paper portfolios, due to the promptness in communication. As a consequence, the communication is faster between professor-student, student-student, and student-academic administrator.

How SEADI Works

SEADI is based on the system designed to create and manage ePortfolios implemented in stage three. This system generates the portfolio as a dynamic Web page with PHP programming (a free and open source technology), using and storing the information in a MySQL database (free and open source technology).

The procedure to generate an ePortfolio is similar to the process to acquire a Web-based e-mail address or Weblog, and therefore the

Figure 2.

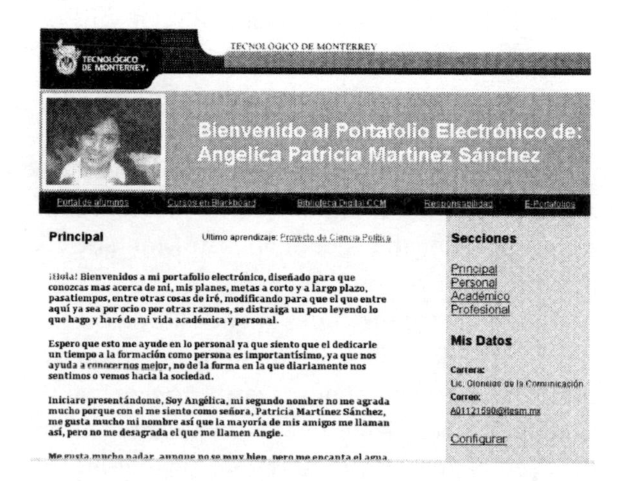

students do not need to have advanced skills in computing, HTML programming, or Web page edition. This ease of use has increased the acceptance by students, especially in careers traditionally resistant to technology, such as law or psychology. SEADI works in modules, and nowadays it has an information edition area named work portfolio that serves as an interface for students, and an open area named public portfolio (see Figures 1 and 2).

The Work Portfolio

The work portfolio is the place where students find access to electronic resources offered by the Tecnológico de Monterrey, Mexico City Campus. This is the case of courses in the Blackboard platform, the Campus' Digital Library, the Virtual Center of Attention and Service to Students, and the Student Portal (see Figure 3). In the left navigation bar are the sections to edit their public portfolio or to modify their account data.

The most important information in the portfolios are the compilation of evidence from the most transcendental and representative knowledge of their careers. This evidence demonstrates the efforts, progress, and achievements of our future graduates—what is useful in the moment and retrospectively—because they turn into a reminder of the goals previously set up; that allows repurposing the personal and professional course of the student and the professional guiding them (see Figure 4).

Figure 3.

CONCLUSION

Our experience with the students let us observe that the process to develop an ePortfolio helps the students to set themselves challenging, but realistic goals, and to achieve them gradually and in an organized way. The students get accustomed to having a register of their ad-

Figure 4.

vancements and have the ability to recognize their deficiencies in the future. In this way the project has contributed to the registration of the professional profile of the student, given the expertise and the results of the former students in job interviews.

The use of technology of dynamic pages with databases lets us have a better management of human resources for training, and also saves time devoted to update the students' profiles. As a result, the students better accept the instrumentation of the electronic portfolio.

We are convinced that the electronic portfolio is more effective when it is supported and integrated in a system of electronic communication and registration, one that facilitates the tracing of the academic performance. This system will ease the tracing of portfolios and go further, for it uses databases to create dynamic Web pages, which creates an opportunity to add interaction and offer personal services as direct communication, diagnostic applications, or group management. That generates something bigger than a space for virtual reflection and gives birth to a virtual and non-academic community.

This virtual community is a non-academic space that enables easy communication among users, students, and teachers outside the strictly academic environment. This will keep the members of the university community informed about recent studies, job offers, articles, interesting pages, resources, and/or services in the net, in a prompt and convenient way.

REFERENCES

Ausubel, D., Novak, J., & Hanesian, H. (1990). *Psicología educativa: Un punto de vista cognositivo.* Mexico City: Editorial Trillas.

Barrett, H. C. (2000, April). Create your own electronic portfolio (using off-the-shelf software). *Learning and Leading with Technology.*

Davenport, T. H., & Prusak, L. (1998). *Working knowledge: How organizations manage what they know.* Cambridge, MA: Harvard Business School Press.

Delors, J. (1998). *La educación encierra un tesoro.* Paris: UNESCO.

Levin, B., & Camp, J. (2002, March). Reflection as the foundation for e-portfolios. In *Proceedings of the Society for Information Technology and Teacher Education International Conference.*

Martín, M. (2002). *El modelo educativo del Tecnológico de Monterrey.* Monterrey, México: Instituto Tecnológico y de Estudios Superiores de Monterrey.

Meza, J. (2002). *Marco conceptual del proyecto portafolio electrónico en el Tecnológico de Monterrey (e-portafolio).* Retrieved January 10, 2003, from http://www.ccm.itesm.mx/dda/eportafolio

Paulson, L. F., Paulson, P. R., & Meyer, C. (1991). What makes a portfolio a portfolio? *Educational Leadership Magazine, 48*(5), 60-63.

Porres, M. (2004). La construcción de un modelo educativo. In C. Sola (Ed.), *Aprendizaje basado en problemas de la teoría a la práctica* (pp. 24-36). Mexico City: Editorial Trillas.

Ramírez, J., & Mendoza, M. A. (2004). *Nuevo marco conceptual del proyecto portafolio electrónico con enfoque en la misión al 2015 del Tecnológico de Monterrey (SEADI).* Retrieved September 22, 2004, from http://www.ccm.itesm.mx/dda/eportafolio

KEY TERMS

Blogfolio: The union and combination of a Weblog and electronic portfolio. It uses the customization power of the Weblog and the evidence showroom of an ePortfolio.

Educative Model: A set of intentions and directives that orient and guide the action in the academic functions for the formation of the people. Through this set, one looks to respond to the necessities of formation of the society, but from a vision of the society itself—the culture, the values and principles—from a conception of the man and his insertion in the different dimensions of life. The model constitutes the reference framework for the curriculum.

Learning Community: A group of students who are not necessary enrolled in the same classes for a semester or a year, who are engaged in intellectual interaction for the purpose of learning. McLellan (1998) describes a VLC as a place to encourage student participation and collaboration without individual competition.

MySQL: A general public license database management system; it is often combined with PHP.

Online Learning Community: Also known as a virtual learning community; same as a learning community which is technology supported.

Personal Information Management: The action of collecting and preserving useful personal information such as e-mails, address books, calendars, and so forth, by a person for his own purposes.

PHP: An open source programming language used to create server-side applications and dynamic Web pages.

Chapter XLIV
Whose Portfolio Is It, Anyway? Implementing Digital Portfolios in K-12 Schools

David Niguidula
Ideas Consulting, USA

ABSTRACT

For every creator of a portfolio, there needs to be a reader. In this chapter, we look at several samples of how the issue of audience has affected a digital portfolio system. Our samples come from high school and elementary schools, and from the original research on digital portfolios in the 1990s to schools using them today. As students and teachers become clearer about the purpose and audience of their school's digital portfolio, they can better understand how to build and read the portfolio's contents.

INTRODUCTION

Back in the 1990s, elementary and secondary schools were just beginning to have the capacity to build digital portfolios. Multimedia and hypertext technologies were moving from research labs to their first commercial incarnations. Even so, when a team from the Coalition of Essential Schools began looking at what it would take to implement digital portfolios in schools, we found that technological innovation was just part of the picture. Far more important then, and still important today, is the notion that portfolios can be a catalyst for school change. To make that change, schools need to consider not just *how* the portfolios will be developed, but be able to describe *why* they are creating the portfolios in the first place.

From the Coalition's initial research on digital portfolios (Niguidula, 1997a), we know that purpose and audience matter a great deal. Students and teachers need to be clear about why they are collecting the work into the portfolio, and what audience will be viewing—and reviewing—the contents. Without answers to those "essential questions," schools have trouble justifying the time required for students to make the portfolio and for teachers to examine them.

A tension arises, however, when multiple purposes come into play. Students want to show their "best work"—which they often equate with their highest grade or with the projects that require the most effort. Teachers must pay attention to the standards of their institution, and may be looking for a breadth of knowledge or skills. As students determine what entries go into the portfolio, and teachers determine how they will assess the work, seemingly small details—such as deciding how many entries will be placed in the portfolio—take on added significance.

This chapter discusses how schools have dealt with this tension. From our work in the last 12 years in approximately 50 different K-12 schools, we have seen that the schools that successfully navigated this tension were those that found purposes that work for both teachers and students.

BACKGROUND

The "essential questions" of digital portfolios emerged from a research project of the Coalition of Essential Schools in the mid-1990s. The Coalition is not an organization primarily concerned with technology; its mission is to create a community of schools interested in reform using a set of "common principles" (Sizer, 1984). These principles include the idea that the primary form of assessment in school should be one of "exhibition," where students demonstrate what they know and are able to do.

The Exhibitions project, funded largely by a grant from IBM, was an exploration of how assessments can help to drive reform and, not incidentally, how technology could be of some help. The project yielded a number of critical concepts, including descriptions of the conditions for successful use of alternative assessments, and protocols for looking at student work (McDonald, 1996; Allen, 1998).

The approach of the Coalition's digital portfolio work was not to focus on technology, but on assessment and school change. In the initial research project, six participating schools in a variety of settings—an urban high school in the Bronx, a rural school in New Hampshire, a suburban high school in Kentucky, and a small school district in Westchester County, New York—experimented with digital portfolios. The resulting portfolios were quite different, but observations from the schools led to the original set of essential questions (Niguidula 1997b): guiding questions that each school needs to answer to make a digital portfolio more than an interesting gimmick.

- **Vision:** What should a student know and be able to do?
- **Purpose:** Why are we collecting the student work?
- **Audience:** Who will be reading the portfolios?
- **Assessment:** What tasks should students perform? How will we know what is good?
- **Technology:** What systems will we need? How is it supported?
- **Logistics:** When does this happen? Who will select and reflect on the work?
- **Culture:** Is the school used to discussing student work? How can the school build the portfolio into its daily life?

In the decade since this initial work, technology has improved greatly; the first round of portfolios were done with the first generation of video cards and in the days before the Web gave a common language to multimedia. However, the essential questions have held up well. Schools still need to look seriously at these issues to make the digital portfolio a part of its culture.

THE ISSUE OF AUDIENCE

The questions of purpose and audience seem to be straightforward. Determine the persons who are most likely to be the reviewers of the portfolio and their reasons for examining the student work, and then it becomes much easier to select the appropriate work to put into the portfolio. Artists, of course, have been doing this for generations. The works that they select to bring to a showing will vary depending on the audience; an in-depth examination of landscapes will suggest a different set of work than a show designed to show a range of media. Yet, the idea of conveying work to an audience is trickier than it first sounds.

In the original Coalition research, one high school asked students to use the portfolio to show their "best work." Late in the spring of the first year, we went to visit the school. As one group of students was showing us their portfolios, we noticed that there were very few entries from their science class. Asked about this, one boy said, "We don't do anything in science." The students acknowledged that they had received grades and had to study for tests. But, when asked to produce evidence of their accomplishments, all they could point to were handouts and lab reports from "experiments" where they already knew what was going to happen. For better or worse, these students did not think the work they produced in this class represented their "best." These students felt a personal stake in their portfolios; best work, as one put it, was work they "could be proud of." Worksheets—even if they generate a good grade—did not feel like a good representation of what they considered "science."

These students had completed the assignments as asked; they had no problem submitting their work to their science teacher. But when asked to submit the work to a portfolio, they balked. Why? The students had a sense that the portfolio, in a digital form, would be something that would be shown to an audience. The specifics of that audience were, at this early stage, very vague; students talked about potentially using the digital portfolios for college interviews or for employers, but for most of these students that was a couple of years away. Still, the act of selecting "best work" meant that students had to make decisions about which work would show their best efforts. These students also had a sense of the production values inherent in technology demonstrations. At the time, the state of the art in multimedia was represented by videodiscs and early CD-ROMs such as the first editions of Microsoft Encarta. When students envisioned handing a portfolio to a reader, they imagined something like giving them a pre-packaged CD-ROM. The digital component of the portfolio was an opportunity to show their work in an environment that went beyond the paper and pencil of worksheets; when students saw themselves reflected in the work appearing on the computer screen, they wanted to be represented by something more substantial.

BUILDING TOGETHER

At the high school described above, students could select any set of work as their "best." This is certainly a valid form of selecting work, and it can serve a number of purposes.

In a number of places, portfolios are seen as a potential supplement, or even replacement, for high-stakes testing. If the portfolio is going to be used for critical decision making (such as determining if a student is ready for graduation) or for accountability reasons, the portfolio has to serve additional purposes—and thus the choices of what goes into the portfolio go beyond the student selecting the best work.

In Rhode Island, for example, students (starting with the graduating class of 2008) will need to "graduate by proficiency" (Rhode Island Department of Education, 2004). Schools can choose various ways for students to demonstrate proficiency, including portfolios, senior or capstone projects, and Certificates of Initial Mastery. (Sample portfolios can be seen at http://www.richerpicture.com.) These modes of assessment are accompanied by other components (e.g., students need to complete a certain number of credits, and will still take standardized tests in English language arts and mathematics); the overall idea is that students can demonstrate proficiency in multiple ways.

To meet this requirement, the state has given some broad outlines; a portfolio, for example, must contain demonstration of skills in English Language arts, mathematics, science, social studies, the arts, and technology. The Department of Education has defined standards (known as "Grade Span Expectations") in some areas, but not all. A group of practitioners, working with personnel from the state department, has provided recommendations on elements of the assessment process (such as the notion that a graduation portfolio must be assessed by more than one person). However, the schools still have a great deal of discretion in defining their portfolios.

When Ponaganset High School (the one high school for the Foster-Glocester school district) began to use digital portfolios, the faculty needed to provide guidelines to the students. As a staff, the faculty had already decided on a set of school-wide graduation expectations and accompanying rubrics. The goal was to have each student demonstrate each of the expectations. But how to make it happen?

Ponaganset moved to a three-step approach of "collect, select, reflect." First, students are asked to collect entries for their portfolio. In each class, teachers have identified two to four entries that they expect students to put into their portfolio. Sometimes, the assignments from the teachers are very specific (all students will enter the third-quarter research paper); sometimes, the students have a great deal more choice (select your best lab report for the year; add three pieces of writing, each from a different genre). The key, though, is that each student has multiple opportunities within each class to demonstrate the graduation expectations.

By the end of the year, each Ponaganset student had about 20 entries in the portfolio. The faculty then asked the students to select entries from their portfolio. For first-year students, the selection was based on a simple question: Where have you done your best work? For tenth graders, however, the selection was more sophisticated. Students needed to discuss which expectations had been met, and how the entries represented those expectations. Students also had to select the entries from the two years that showed growth over time, and (potentially) another set to support the student's academic plan.

It was not enough to just select the appropriate pieces. The students needed to reflect on their entries in two ways. First, they had to write essays defending the selections that they made. Students needed to make the connections between the entries in the portfolio and the school's graduation expectations; they also needed to provide a rationale as to why these specific selections are a good demonstration of the student's growth as a learner or of where he or she wanted to improve. Second, the students

Figure 1.

sat for 15-minute interviews with pairs of teachers. That is, each student met with two teachers who had already read the essays; the student's responsibility was to lead the teachers through the portfolio, and again make the connections between the school's goals and the work compiled in the portfolio.

Figure 1 shows a photo from one of these interviews; here, a ninth-grade student discusses her portfolio with two teachers.

As of this writing, more than 800 students at Ponaganset (the entire ninth-, tenth-, and eleventh-grade classes) have worked on their portfolios; among them, over 21,000 entries have been added. As these students move towards graduation, the portfolio will expand further—and undergo more detailed scrutiny. At the moment, though, Ponaganset's goal for its end-of-year reviews is to create a more immediate feedback loop. At least once a year, students have the chance to reflect not just on individual entries, but on the work as a whole. This is a rare occurrence in high schools, since most academic activities focus on a single class.

Students do have choice in this portfolio; it is not solely the province of the teacher to decide what will ultimately be used as graduation material. However, the selection is not completely open-ended either; each teacher allows each student a certain amount of flexibility in his or her selections. Since the overall purpose is to demonstrate that students are meeting the graduation expectations, the strategy of using the teacher's assignments as a first step will help both students and teachers better understand the specific elements of a graduation portfolio.

TAKING CONTROL

Ownership of a portfolio goes beyond the student's ability to select material. Consider two elementary schools. In both schools, fourth graders were asked to assemble entries for the portfolio. At one school, the issue of teacher vs. student control arose over the quality of the entries. Initially, in this school, fourth through sixth graders were taught how to take digital video of each other's reading and writing. The students, in their first round, created video that was of uneven quality; the sound was not always clear and the interaction between the student being filmed and the student behind the camera sometimes distracted from getting a good view of the work. Upon reviewing the videos, many of the students who had been behind the camera figured out some of the ways that they could improve their technical skills, and proceeded to create better video.

In an effort to make the process more efficient, however, the school attempted to resolve this dilemma by handing the video responsibilities to the adults. One member of the faculty, who had observed the earlier filming, decided that she would be behind the camera for the next round. The video that she generated was definitely of a higher quality; however, this faculty member proceeded to complain about how much time was involved in videotaping the students and entering them into the digital portfolio. The students who had been willing to learn no longer had the opportunity to be helpful; the faculty member who took over the taping no longer saw the portfolio as valuable, but as an additional demand on her time. In addition, the students felt further removed from the portfolio; it was no longer their responsibility to videotape, and therefore the portfolio became just one more thing to be done.

Elementary schools in a different district took another approach. In Barrington, Rhode Island, students were asked to demonstrate problem solving. At one school, 50 fourth graders were asked to take pictures of a problem they had solved earlier in the year, and to record, on video, how the problem had been solved. In this case, however, the students had some help in using the camera: parent volunteers helped the students learn how to take a good picture—and how to play it back to see if the end result worked well. Again the quality varied, but students learned how to judge if a picture was good enough and how to take another picture if necessary.

Similarly, a teacher in another class designated a select group of four or five students to learn how to take video. Since the group was responsible for taking the video of the rest of the class, they became an informal support group, advising each other on how to take the video the "right way." Rather than taking the camera out of the students' hands altogether, these classrooms figured out ways to provide support to the students as they learned, even if the teacher was not very comfortable with the equipment.

Digital portfolios hold great promise for both students and teachers. Students can show their best work and express their individuality about who they are as learners. Teachers can examine the progress students are making towards standards and determine how to help the student move forward. Other stakeholders may have their own interests. In the end, however, schools need to negotiate how these purposes can be resolved—and in doing so, find a balance that allows each participant to gain something from the portfolio.

REFERENCES

Allen, D. (Ed.). (1998). *Assessing student learning: From grading to understanding.* New York: Teachers College Press.

McDonald, J. P. (1996). *Redesigning school.* San Francisco: Jossey-Bass.

Niguidula, D. (1997a). *The digital portfolio: A richer picture of student performance.* (Studies on Exhibitions, No. 13a). Retrieved June 28, 2005, from http://www.essential schools.org/pub/ces_docs/resources/dp/getstart.html

Niguidula, D. (1997b). Picturing performance with digital portfolios. *Educational Leadership, 55*(3), 26-29.

Rhode Island Department of Education. (2004). *Initial guidance for the graduation by proficiency component (final version – 2.11).* Retrieved June 28, 2005, from http://www.ridoe.net/careerdev/HighSchool Reform.htm

Sizer, T. R. (1984). *Horace's compromise: The dilemma of the American high school.* Boston: Houghton Mifflin.

KEY TERMS

"Collect, Select, Reflect": A phrase used to summarize the process of creating portfolios. Students *collect* a body of work, *select* specific entries for a particular purpose and audience, and *reflect* on how the work is connected to that specific purpose.

Digital Portfolios: A synonym for electronic portfolios. In early usage, "digital portfolios" referred to portfolios that relied solely on computer media; an electronic portfolio could use analog video or audiotape. In current usage, the terms are interchangeable.

End-of-Year Review: *See Portfolio Conference.*

Essential Questions: Guiding questions that bring focus to a project or lesson plan. In the case of digital portfolios, the essential questions devised by David Niguidula define the critical issues a school needs to address for the portfolios to be successful.

Expectations: A formal set of statements of what a student should know and be able to do. These may be issued by schools, districts, or states.

Graduation by Proficiency: A policy where students meet graduation requirements by demonstrating a set of skills and knowledge through a portfolio or other mode of assessment. Typically, this requirement is in addition to passing a particular set of courses.

High-Stakes Testing: Using an assessment as a requirement for a certificate or for eligibility. For example, requiring high school students to pass an examination in order to receive a diploma makes the test "high stakes." High-stakes testing is not limited to standardized tests, and most assessment experts believe that a single opportunity to take a single test should not be used for high-stakes decisions, such as graduation.

Portfolio Conference: An event where a student shows his or her portfolio to one or more instructors. Typically, the student highlights key areas of the portfolio, and reflects on the portfolio as a whole; the instructor(s) provide feedback on the student's work, and suggestions of how to move forward.

Chapter XLV
Sustaining ePortfolio:
Progress, Challenges, and Dynamics in Teacher Education

Yi-Ping Huang
University of Maryland, USA

ABSTRACT

The teacher education programs at the University of Maryland Baltimore County (UMBC) and its professional community have undergone substantial changes, as developing and sustaining interventions for systemic impact involve changes in culture, policy, and practice. This chapter discusses the progress, challenges, and changing dynamics associated with sustaining an ePortfolio. An ePortfolio is an integral part of a Web-based Education Accountability System (EAS) developed and implemented by the author and the Department of Education to facilitate community-based teaching and learning, to help address national and state accreditation mandates, and to ensure continual improvements.

INTRODUCTION

The teacher education programs at the University of Maryland Baltimore County (UMBC) and its professional community have undergone substantial changes, as developing and sustaining interventions for systemic impact involve changes in culture, policy, and practice. This chapter discusses the progress, challenges, and changing dynamics associated with sustaining an ePortfolio. An ePortfolio is an integral part of a Web-based Education Accountability System (EAS, http://education.umbc.edu) developed and implemented by the author and the Department of Education to facilitate community-based teaching and learning, to help address national and state accreditation mandates, and to ensure continual improvements.[1]

The discussion of ePortfolio endeavors will be provided in the rich context of EAS and the

UMBC educational community. The first section discourses conceptual issues relating to the design of the ePortfolio and the EAS. The structure of EAS with technical specifications is then described, followed by a discussion of the progress, challenges, and changing dynamics in organizational culture and infrastructure; in program, curriculum, and assessment; and in resources, support, and system renewal. Finally, critical factors in sustaining an ePortfolio as a viable profession-based teaching, learning, and assessment medium for preparing teachers within the education community are summarized.

Figure 1.

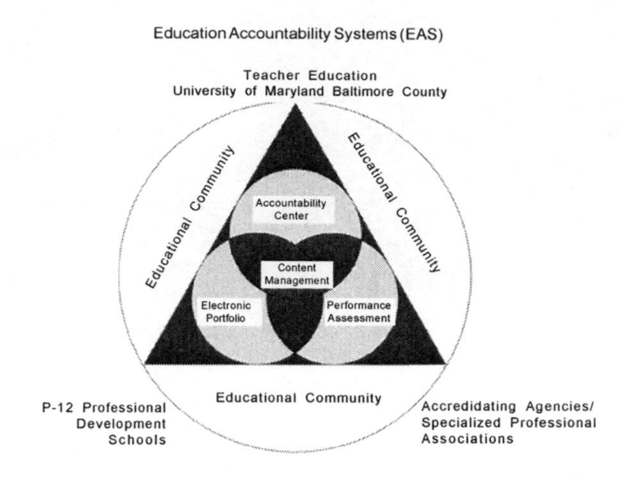

CONCEPTUAL DESIGN

The framework of EAS is built upon capacity and linkage building. Capacity is viewed as existing within discrete yet interconnected policy domains, and is embodied by individuals within these domains. Capacity building for sustainable reform within institutions and communities requires engaging interventions for individual capacity, collective capacity, and material capacity (Spillane & Thompson, 1997; Fullan & Stielgelbauer, 1991; Fullan, 2000). Linkage facilitates connection, communication, and transfer of capacity. Linkage building critically increases the probabilities for successful and sustainable reform. The EAS implementation thus devotes much energy to building structural, relational, ideological, and temporal linkages among the capacities.

Grounded in such a conceptual framework, the EAS model (see Figure 1) takes a holistic approach by actively engaging and encouraging collaborative interactions among stakeholders of the UMBC teacher education programs, its P-12 professional development schools (PDSs), and national and state accreditation agencies. Core to the EAS are three integrated production components: Accountability Center, Performance Assessment, and Electronic Portfolio. These three sub-systems are orchestrated through a centralized content management component. The community-based model enables opportunities for continual observation and influence of interactions among constituents in the community. The fully integrated model further provides viable solutions to the competing and often conflicting paradigms in the assessment management system and electronic portfolio (Barrett, 2004; Barrett & Wilkerson, 2004), as degrees of differences exist in needs, goals, and functionalities.

Education Accountability System (EAS)

The EAS is based on national and state standards. The goals are reflective of UMBC's mission of developing teachers with strong academic background through an authentic professional development continuum. Summaries of major objectives are as follows: First, the learning and assessments are continual and systematic to promote collaboration, encourage reflection, maximize learning opportunities, facilitate growth, and increase effectiveness. Second, the learning and assessments are inclusive of qualitative and quantitative performance opportunities and measures, including coursework, evaluative observations via assessment instruments administrated by the teacher education unit and the institution, process and results of ePortfolio development and review, and results of standardized tests such as Praxis I and II. Third, learning and assessments are conducted and analyzed based on multiple sources and multiple assessments, with multiple indicators in both formative and summative forms to assure reliability and validity. Fourth, learning and assessments are aligned with professional standards, unit-expected competencies, and outcomes within program-specific operations, and are developmentally appropriate at benchmarks. Lastly, results of triangulated assessments (by candidates, supervisors, and mentors) are made available to the various constituents dynamically via the EAS to ensure timeliness of feedback and effective use of data for continual development and improvement. Details of the EAS (see Figure 2) are discussed.

Accountability Center

The Accountability Center is designed to facilitate tracking of candidate performance, monitoring of program quality, and maximizing departmental productivity. It is a centralized database that documents and displays over 550 different fields of personal, academic, and performance data captured by each of the three production components of the EAS. Central to the Accountability Center are functions that allow faculty and administrators to document

Figure 2.

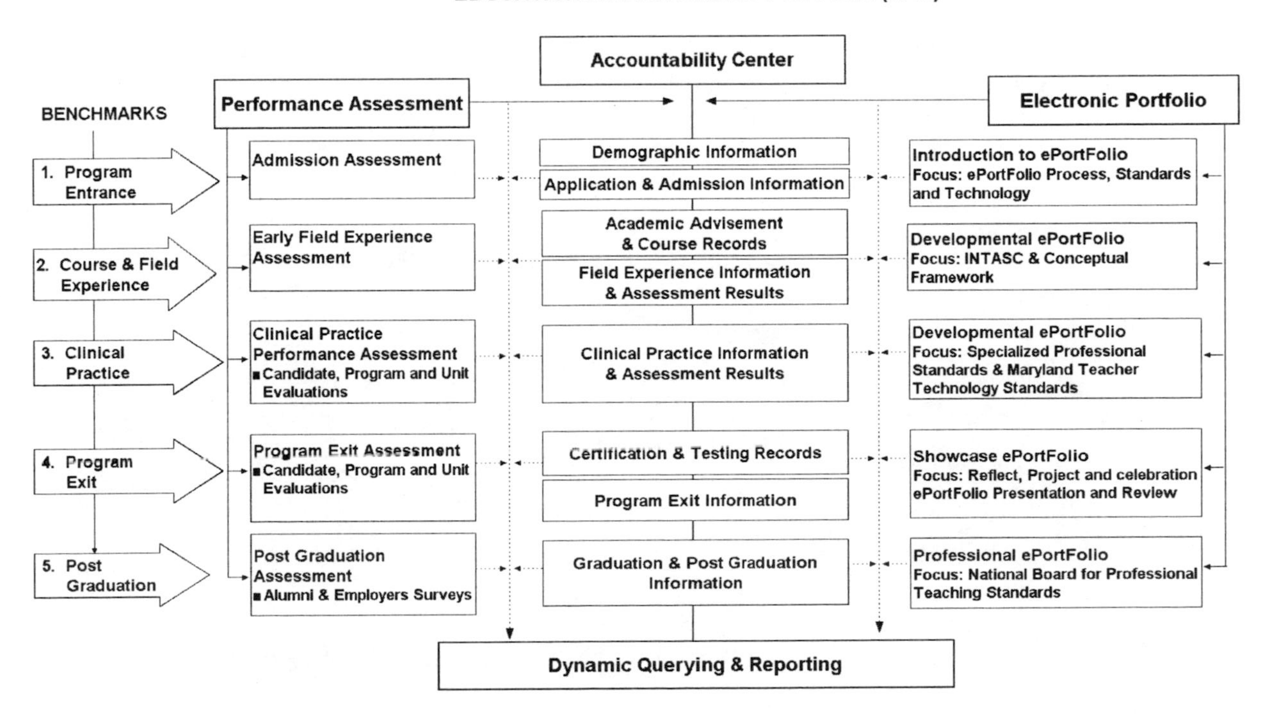

an individual candidate's program outlook, provide academic advisement and services, conduct assessments, review performance, determine remedial needs, and make progress decisions at benchmarks. A live querying and reporting center further facilitates the analysis and reporting of data at individual, program, and unit levels.

Performance Assessment

The Performance Assessment component consists of two integrated tracks: candidate assessment, and program and unit assessment. Candidate assessment emphasizes measurements of candidates' knowledge, skills, and dispositions, and examines the impact of candidates' work on student learning in P-12 settings. Program and unit assessment emphasizes efficacy in aligning instruction and curriculum with professional, state, and local standards; efficacy of courses, field/clinical experiences, and program qualities; and, efficacy of candidates' content, pedagogical, and professional proficiencies that lead to student learning.

A total of 15 assessment instruments, each with a five-point scale, are provided for candidate, program, and unit assessments. A triangulated candidate evaluation was designed to evaluate the candidates' field experience and clinical practice through assessments conducted by clinical instructors, university supervisors, and candidates. A triangulated program and unit evaluation was also designed to assess the efficacy of faculty, curriculum, instruction, and candidate performance by clinical instructors, university supervisors, and teacher candidates. Such triangulated administrations help maximize teaching and learning opportunities, and help ensure validity and reliability. Results of the assessments are made available through the secure, Web-based EAS in real time to provide candidates with ongoing feedback. Aggregated and disaggregated performance data on candidates, programs, and the unit are generated dynamically through querying and reporting functions to facilitate the making of informed decisions for improvement.

Electronic Portfolio

There are three milestones implemented to ease transitions and bridge academic and professional learning and practice: Developmen-

Figure 3. Developmental ePortfolio

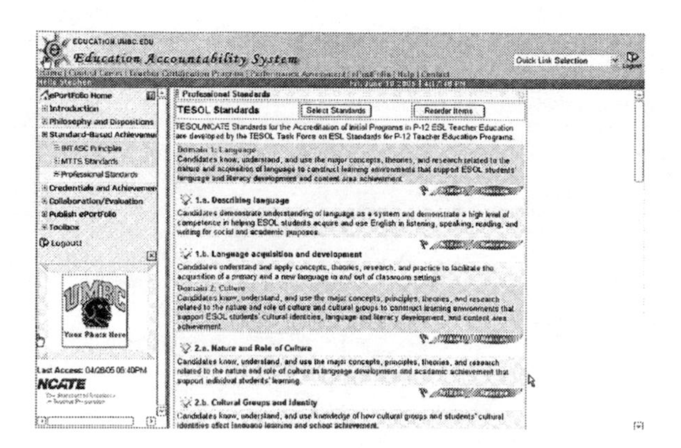

Figure 4. Showcase ePortfolio

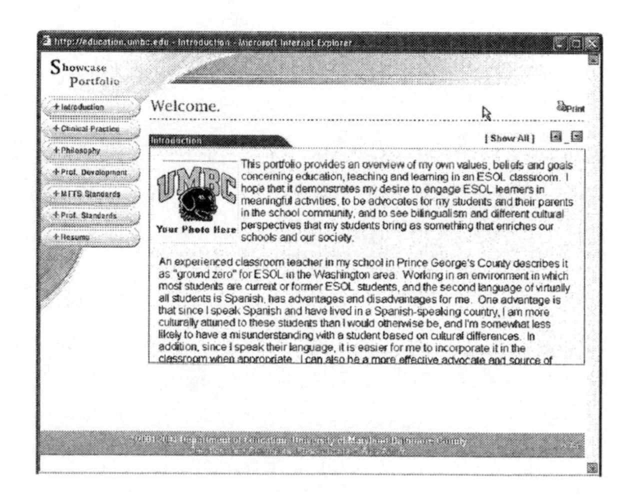

Table 1. Content and organization of ePortfolio

Content Categories	Sub-Categories
Introduction	Introduction Personal and Professional Information Context Studies of Field Experience and Clinical Practice
Philosophy and Dispositions	Philosophy and Dispositions Professional Development Plan Reflective Journals
Standards-Based Achievements	INTASC Principles Maryland Teacher Technology Standards (MTTS) Standards Developed by Specialized Professional Associations (SPAs): ACEI, NAEYC, NCSS, NCTE, NCTM, NSTA, and TESOL Minimum requirements for meeting standards include an interpretive statement, two artifacts, and rationales for each of the standards.
Credentials and Achievements	Résumé Professional Credentials and Achievements
Additional Content Categories	As defined and created by the user

tal, Showcase, and Professional ePortfolios. The Developmental ePortfolio (see Figure 3) provides candidates with opportunities to generate, record, reflect, and assess their growth and performance across the teacher preparation cycle. The Showcase ePortfolio (see Figure 4) is a self-selected, "best evidence" collection of documents and artifacts demonstrating competencies on the standards and on professional growth. The Professional ePortfolio enables UMBC graduates and mentor teachers from the PDSs to continue generating, documenting, and celebrating their performance, growth, and achievement. To this end, the unit is now collaborating with local school systems in customizing professional ePortfolios that are aligned with county review guidelines and national board certification requirements for in-service teachers.

ePortfolio content requirements for teacher candidates are summarized in Table 1. Greater options and control of content and presentation are granted to other types of ePortfolio authors, such as alumni, faculty, and mentors.

TECHNICAL SPECIFICATIONS OF THE EAS

The EAS combines advanced Web application technology with a service-oriented architecture (SOA). SOA enables EAS to interact and potentially integrate with the existing university information systems, such as the student information system (SIS), on data collection and reporting. A three-tiered architecture was utilized to maximize the application's lifecycle by enhancing system reusability, flexibility, manageability, maintainability, and scalability.

Figure 5. Three-tiered architecture of EAS

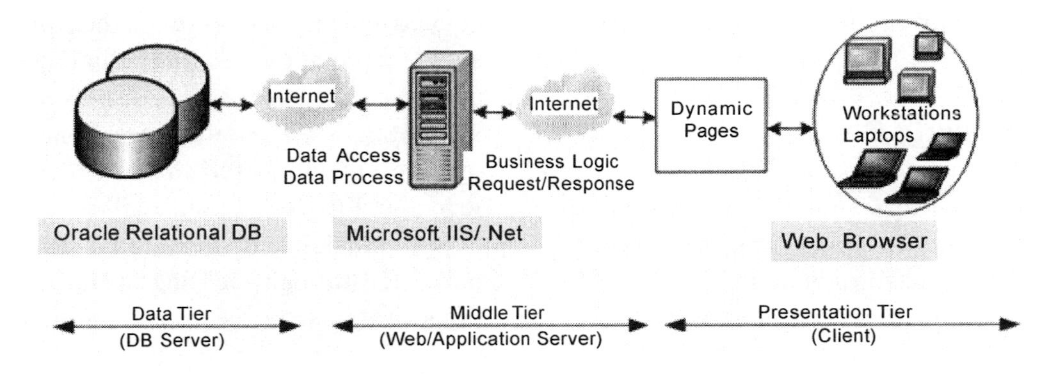

The three-tiered architecture of EAS (see Figure 5) includes the presentation tier, middle tier, and data tier.

The EAS is built on the robust computing platform of Microsoft .NET™ architecture, with a relational database management system at the back end and JavaScript-enabled Web browsers at the front end. A Microsoft Internet information server is utilized in the middle tier to address user requests.

Content Management

Content management provides an integrated online authorizing environment, ranging from text editing to multimedia management, and allows multiple user access with differentiated privileges and responsibilities. This component empowers authorized users at both course and program levels to customize content and assessment needs in an open, flexible, and user-friendly environment. These may include authoring and management of assessment questionnaires, rubrics, reporting criteria, and formats.

A template-driven structure is achieved by the use of back-end Oracle database tables and XML (eXtensible Markup Language) files. Microsoft ASP.NET technology is also used to enable dynamic creation and presentation of content. Interoperability and transportability are enhanced by enabling reusable and exportable content in XML format for exchange with other systems. Stored content can also be published in various formats, such as HTML and PDF.

Accountability Center

The Accountability Center is a centralized data bank that documents and displays personal, academic, and performance data captured by each of the three production components of the EAS. Confidential information, such as Social Security numbers, is encrypted with a Triple-DES algorithm for security. Tasks, structures, access privileges, and responsibilities are as specified in the content management component. Intelligent agents are employed in facilitating secretarial and administrative operations.

Central to the Accountability Center are functions provided by the dynamic query builder which allow the users to document, organize, analyze, and generate qualitative and quantitative reports at individual, program, and unit levels. Metadata are also enabled to document and analyze the levels of congruence among curriculum, assessment, professional standards, and the unit's conceptual framework. The dynamic analysis and reporting functions increase the accessibility and expand the usability of assessment data in monitoring progress, in identifying needs, in defining strategies for improvements, and in compiling documentation for accreditation purposes.

Performance Assessment

Performance Assessment utilizes role-based access control, enabling users to access, conduct, and review predefined assessments tasks and results that are appropriate to the specified user type. The role-based model is particularly important, as a triangulated assessment model is utilized to evaluate the candidate, program, and the unit.

Content of the assessment instruments are created and managed through the content management component. Individual assessment progress and results are displayed through DynaMatrix, a dynamic and personalized content presentation based on the user's role privilege (see Figure 6). Data analysis and reports at individual, program, and unit levels can be generated through querying and reporting functions provided in the Accountability Center.

Figure 6. DynaMatrix

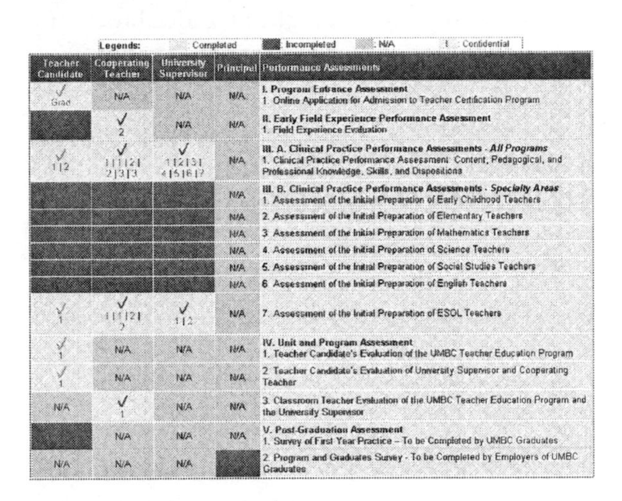

Legends: Completed | Incompleted | N/A | Confidential

Teacher Candidate	Cooperating Teacher	University Supervisor	Principal	Performance Assessments
√ Grad	N/A	N/A	N/A	**I. Program Entrance Assessment** 1. Online Application for Admission to Teacher Certification Program
	√ 2	N/A	N/A	**II. Early Field Experience Performance Assessment** 1. Field Experience Evaluation
√ 1|2	√ 1|1|2| 2|3|3	√ 1|2|3| 4|5|6|7	N/A	**III. A. Clinical Practice Performance Assessments - *All Programs*** 1. Clinical Practice Performance Assessment: Content, Pedagogical, and Professional Knowledge, Skills, and Dispositions
			N/A	**III. B. Clinical Practice Performance Assessments - *Specialty Areas*** 1. Assessment of the Initial Preparation of Early Childhood Teachers
			N/A	2. Assessment of the Initial Preparation of Elementary Teachers
			N/A	3. Assessment of the Initial Preparation of Mathematics Teachers
			N/A	4. Assessment of the Initial Preparation of Science Teachers
			N/A	5. Assessment of the Initial Preparation of Social Studies Teachers
			N/A	6. Assessment of the Initial Preparation of English Teachers
√ 1	√ 1|1|2| 2	√ 1|2	N/A	7. Assessment of the Initial Preparation of ESOL Teachers
√ 1	N/A	N/A	N/A	**IV. Unit and Program Assessment** 1. Teacher Candidate's Evaluation of the UMBC Teacher Education Program
√ 1	N/A	N/A	N/A	2. Teacher Candidate's Evaluation of University Supervisor and Cooperating Teacher
N/A	√ 1	N/A	N/A	3. Classroom Teacher Evaluation of the UMBC Teacher Education Program and the University Supervisor
	N/A	N/A	N/A	**V. Post-Graduation Assessment** 1. Survey of First Year Practice – To be Completed by UMBC Graduates
N/A	N/A	N/A		2. Program and Graduates Survey - To be Completed by Employers of UMBC Graduates

Figure 7.

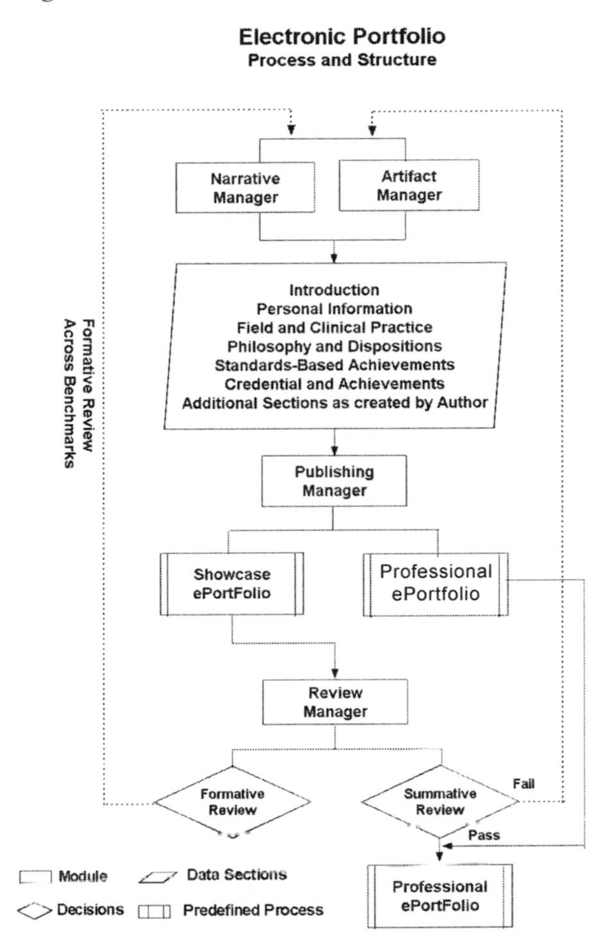

Surveys that are designated anonymous, such as pre- and post-clinical program evaluations, are de-identified. These various functions are enabled by using server-side (ASP.NET) and client-side (Java Script) programming to interface with users and data.

Electronic Portfolio (ePortfolio)

The ePortfolio consists of four core modules: Artifact Manager, Narrative Manager, Review Manager, and Publishing Manager (see Figure 7).

The Artifact Manager module allows users to upload, organize, and control access, display, and share artifacts.

- Artifact types range from basic text files to advanced multimedia files and are organized into categories and elements. Categories may contain file folders and subfolders. Elements are granular units of information which cannot be further divided for sharing purposes.
- Uploading is conducted via the Web with a single file size limitation of 8 MB to prevent potentially dangerous Web site attacks. Space quota is allotted for each user, and adjusted on demand basis.
- Access, display, and sharing of artifacts are provided through a user control interface. The author of the ePortfolio is empowered to finely define and control who, when, and what can be accessed, shared, and/or published.
- Digital rights management is in place to assure the author's intellectual rights. Users are required to clarify ownership of the artifacts and/or acquire release permissions. Once published, images are watermarked with the customized

watermarking function. Authentication and assurance of artifacts and content are being developed.

- Management functions are provided for both individuals and administrators, including creating/deleting/renaming folders and deleting/moving/renaming files. An artifact search function is also provided. Individuals can search artifacts by filename, label, uploading date, or belonging sections associated with her/his ePortfolio. Administrators can search artifacts across all ePortfolios.

The Narrative Manager module enables the author to incorporate narratives in each of the core content sections of Introduction, Philosophy and Disposition, Field and Clinical Practice, Standards-Based Achievement, and Credential and Achievements. An embedded Word-like editor provides users full-fledged editing and formatting capabilities for Web publishing, such as color, font, paragraph, bullets, numbering, hyperlink, and spell-check. A special HTML tidy-up function of the online editor is set in place to ensure that pasted or formatted text conforms to the W3C XHTML 1.0 standard for storing and presentation compatibility. The ePortfolio Narrative Manager module further supports multiple entries to facilitate documentation of learning in and across time, and to encourage reflection and deep learning.

The Review Manager module consists of assessment tasks, rubrics, scoring, reporting, and a commentary section. Content of the showcase ePortfolio, evaluation rubrics, and scoring scheme are displayed in a split window. Multiple reviewers and scores are supported. Inter-rater reliability analysis is enabled as results of multiple reviewers can be compiled and displayed at individual, program, and unit levels. Query and reports can be dynamically generated through weighted calculation of scores at individual, program, and unit levels. Lastly, the commentary section enables further communication and collaboration between the author and reviewer(s). This Review Manager is being tested for implementation in the 2005-2006 academic year.

The Publishing Manager module enables Web-based, computer-based and paper-based presentation and publication.

- The developmental ePortfolio (see Figure 3) interface consists of three frames: top, navigation, and workplace. The top frame contains author identification and links to other components in the EAS. The navigation fold/unfold frame allows the Web browser to populate items on the navigating section that are dynamically retrieved from the backend server. The workplace frame displays details of the selected section.
- The showcase ePortfolio (see Figure 4) interface allows a juxtaposing display of artifacts, interpretive statements, and rationales for the artifacts. The professional ePortfolio is similar to the construct of the showcase ePortfolio, with additional functions allowing greater control over content, structure, and presentation.
- A user control interface empowers the author to finely define and control who, when, where, and what can be accessed, shared, and/or published. A collection of presentation templates are made available for personalizing the feel and look of the ePortfolio. These functions encourage ownership and promote collaboration and sharing, while respecting individual privacy and rights.

- The Publishing Manager is based on a dynamic retrieval and packaging process, allowing storage and presentation on the secured EAS environment, on the open Web, via CD-ROM, and/or in print. For privacy and security reasons, teacher candidates are requested to publish their ePortfolios in the secured EAS environment. Invitations may be issued to viewers without MyEDUC accounts to access the EAS. Teacher candidates may also submit requests to publish on the open Web. Other types of users such as graduates, mentors, and faculty have greater control of accessibility.

PROGESS, CHALLENGES AND CHANGING DYNAMICS

Organizational Culture and Infrastructure

With the vision of community-supported teaching, learning, and assessment, and the high stakes accreditation mandates, the Department of Education began a series of changes in its organizational infrastructure with the implementation of EAS in late 2001. The resulting structure at present is depicted in Figure 8. Structures that existed prior to 2003 are represented by oval-shaped boxes, while structures

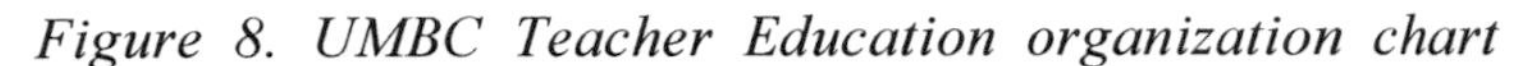

Figure 8. UMBC Teacher Education organization chart

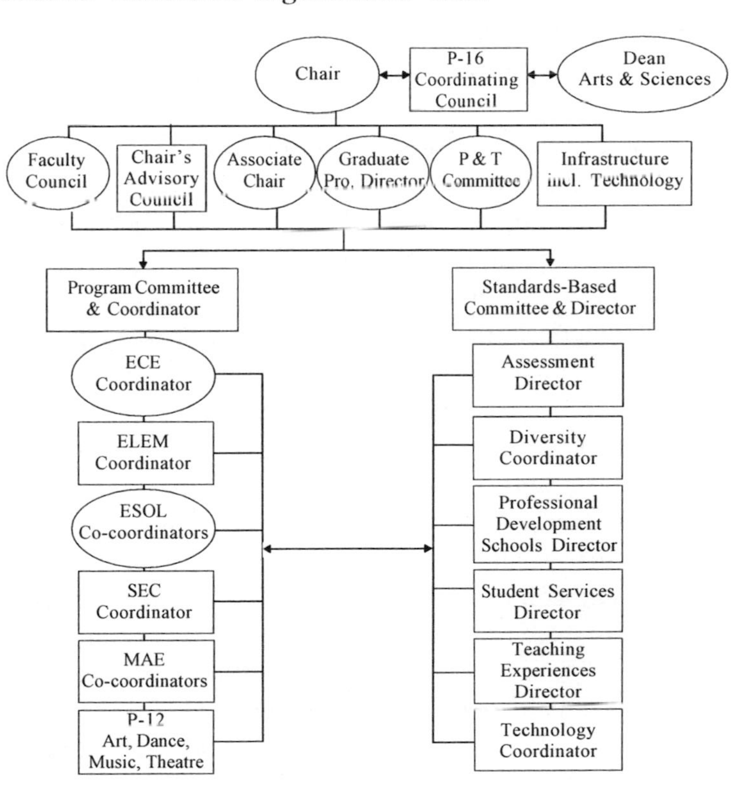

Key: ⬭ *Structure existed prior to 2003,* ▭ *Structure established since 2003*

ECE= Early Childhood Education, ELEM= Elementary Education, SEC= Secondary Education, MAE= Master of Arts in Education program for in-service teachers

that were established after 2003 are represented by rectangle-shaped boxes. In particular, the newly instituted structures are program-based committees addressing programmatic and curriculum issues, and standards-based committees addressing policies and practices relating to NCATE, state, and SPA standards and accountability.

The establishment of specialized committees heightens awareness of capacity and need for change, and encourages the building of individual, organizational, and material capacities. The involvement of a critical mass of faculty in committee activities with often overlapping membership further provides opportunities to create structural, relational, ideological, and temporal linkages necessary for effective and sustained intervention. By actively engaging and challenging members of the department, the organizational infrastructure facilitates shared leadership in creating and adapting to a new culture and environment.

The evolving culture and environment are reflective of the changing dynamic in policymaking and teaching practice, and are critical for institutionalization. Since 2003, the ePortfolio has become a clinical practice exit requirement for all initial teacher certification programs. The initiation, enhancement, and sustenance of processes and procedures leading to institutionalization result both from and in constant interactions among programs, assessment, and standards committees. Examples of these enabling processes and procedures include systemic coordination and collaboration on curriculum planning and execution, on ePortfolio development and evaluation, on professional development and technical support, and on resource allocation and distribution.

The process of organizational change and faculty change is complex (Abbey, 1997; Candiotti, 1998; Waddoups, Wentworth, & Earle; 2004), and is most likely to be successful in an enabling context with a robust support structure and appropriate rewards (Dusick, 1998). In the context of UMBC, the areas that thrive with progress also are areas with persisting challenges. These include leadership, commitment, collaboration, and support. Changing preconceptions and cultivating new understanding and practice call for shared vision and leadership. Sustaining complex infrastructure, nevertheless, requires centralized leadership with champions of change. Systemic interventions demand collaborations in capacity and linkage building. Evolving visions, goals, and needs, however, require careful and long-term management for validity and reliability. The realization of the ePortfolio as a learning and assessment medium relies on long-term commitment. Successful implementation of electronic portfolio is not merely student readiness, but full faculty participation (Gathercoal, Bryde, Mahler, Love, & McKean, 2002). Commitment and participation are energy, time, and resource consuming. Sustained implementation thus requires careful planning on change management, with realistic budgeting of resources, support, and expectations.

Program, Curriculum, and Assessment

Progress, challenges, and changing dynamics persist in program, curriculum, and assessment policy and practice. Renewed views of ePortfolio emerge from changing the preconception of the ePortfolio as mere digitization of paper variation to evolving understandings of the ePortfolio as a means of encouraging and celebrating "deep learning"—learning that is reflective, developmental, integrative, self-directive, and lifelong (Cambridge, 2004). The institutionalization of the ePortfolio, hence, reflects a grounded premise that the construction of the ePortfolio substantiates a persistent, learner-centered, standards-based, and outcome-oriented approach in generating and as-

Table 2. Sample curriculum and assessment master plan: ESOL/BL Program

Benchmark		Course	Title	Cr	Field Exp.	Outcomes/Comments	Portfolio Artifacts from Course, Field Experience, Clinical Practice	Criterion for Progressing to the Next Teacher Education Benchmark
1. Admission								• Pass Praxis I and GRE • Minimum overall GPA of 3.0 • Candidate advisement interview • Online application via EAS • Criminal history disclosure and TB test
2. Early Field Experience	Bridging	EDUC 612	Linguistics for ESOL/Bilingual educators	3	No	• Exhibit knowledge of the fundamentals of linguistics and of the structure of the English language. • Exhibit knowledge of the fundamentals of cross cultural communication. • Observe and analyze students and teaching. • Plan, implement and assess instruction. • Explore and respond to the context of schooling (description of students, school, classroom, etc.) • Demonstrate professional dispositions. • Value linguistic and cultural diversity in schools. • Exhibit appropriate communication skills.	• Reflection logs, tutoring logs, case studies, scholarly papers, linguistic problem sets, and exams. • Lesson and unit plans. • Description of students, schools, classrooms. • Microteaching vignettes. • Statement of teaching philosophy.	• Minimum overall GPA of 3.0. • Continuing advisement • Coursework evaluation Initial professional Development plan • Education foundation courses • Developmental ePortfolio • Early field experience assessments
	Bridging	EDUC 688	Methods and techniques in TESOL	3	Yes			
	Bridging	Ling 494	American English structure for ESL/EFL teachers	3	No			
	Bridging	MLL 625	Intercultural/Cross cultural communication	3	Yes			
	Bridging	EDUC 602	Instructional systems development I	3	No			
	Middle	EDUC 625	Teaching reading and writing to ESOL/Bilingual students, Part I	3	Yes	• Exhibit knowledge of the theories and techniques in teaching reading and writing to ESOL students at all levels. • Demonstrate an understanding of the fundamentals of testing and assessment. • Plan, implement, and assess instruction. • Demonstrate knowledge of the processes of second language acquisition and learning. • Demonstrate knowledge of the theories of learning and apply them in lesson plan and implementation. • Demonstrate professional dispositions. • Exhibit appropriate communication skills.	• Unit plans which incorporate INTASC, TESOL, and Maryland Teacher Technology Standards • Textbook review. • Reflection logs, tutoring logs, case studies, scholarly papers, and exams. • Lesson and unit plans. • Observation and Interview logs of teachers and students. • Samples of student writing and reflections on literact development.	• Minimum overall GPA of 3.0 • Continuing advisement • Coursework evaluation • Education method courses • Developmental ePortfolio including documentation of field experiences • Field experience assessments
	Middle	EDUC 655	Teaching reading and writing to ESOL/Bilingual students, Part II	3	Yes			
	Middle	EDUC 636	ESOL testing and evaluation	3	No			
	Middle	MLL 670	Second language acquisition and learning	3	No			
	Middle	EDUC 601	Human learning and cognition	3	No			

sessing learning and achievement in and over time.

A significant shift in the process toward institutionalization at UMBC is the extension from product ePortfolio in its initial implementation to focusing on process ePortfolio across the teacher education cycle. Process ePortfolio provides a rich candidate development and advisement environment, and facilitates development of transcendental skills that are critical in the twenty-first global society, such as critical thinking, information literacy, and cultural competencies. Product ePortfolio provides opportunities for the reviewer to assess declarative, procedural, and metacognitive knowledge (Huba & Freed, 2000), and empowers authors to construct and celebrate learning and achievements.

The blended approach to process and product portfolios encourages more balanced development across the professional development continuum. This shift, however, demands re-thinking of curriculum, instruction, outcome, and assessment in a systematic manner. Inconsistencies in these areas tend to be magnified in a program-wide ePortfolio where curriculum content and outcomes make up significant portions of the ePortfolio. Commitment to systematic curriculum planning and execution are thus critical to ensure logical and supportive development, leading to candidate mastery of program standards and desired outcomes. The commonly held notion of course ownership needs to be expanded and transformed to program ownership. The faculty needs to reconsider content, instruction, assignment, outcome, and assessment in the context of individual courses, and in relation to other content and professional courses in the program. Processes and mechanisms need to be defined to facilitate community-wide collaborations that take into consideration feedback, and formative and summative reviews provided by the faculty, supervisors, and mentor teachers across the developmental cycle.

UMBC's endeavor toward systemic integration is reflected in the development of the Curriculum and Assessment Master Plan for each of the certification programs. Table 2 is an example from the ESOL/BL program, showing two of the five benchmarks. The top row indicates the benchmarks across the teacher education cycle, course title, credits, field experience component, outcomes, desired portfolio artifacts, and criteria for progressing to the next teacher education benchmark. As with any program improvement effort, the master plans have gone through many revisions based on evolving visions, needs, and goals of the faculty, the programs, and the standards instituted by state and national accrediting agencies.

Concurrent with the mapping of curriculum, standards, outcomes, and assessments is the implementation of a syllabus template to facilitate the coordination and the restructuring of courses to ensure logical and supportive development. The internship seminar, for example, has been subdivided to two separated but related courses, allowing more focused discussion, development, and review of the showcase ePortfolio, a designated clinical practice exit requirement.

Experiences with the new learning and assessment paradigm afforded by the ePortfolio led to renewed interest in interactions and collaborations, and resulted in the creation of a profession-based learning community (see Figure 1). ePortfolio development demands candidates to be self-directed in creating content and constructing meaning. It demands faculty to assume multiple roles as facilitator, conveyor, mentor, and evaluator to actively coordinate and support learning. It demands mentors in the PDSs to provide contextual responses and guidance of real-world experiences. To strengthen collaborative and profession-based learning, the department expanded its ePortfolio services to include all faculty, teacher candidates, alumni, and PDS mentors and coordinators. Specifically, mentors and school administrators are asked to participate in the process of ePortfolio development, review, and system renewal. They are also provided with hardware, software, and publishing services for the creation of their own Professional ePortfolio. The broadened spectrum of participants potentially extends the traditional institution-based evaluation to profession-based learning, assessment, and celebration of achievements.

Another enabling factor in creating and sustaining an ePortfolio culture is a built-in review and renewal process that facilitates organizational and individual learning. In the context of UMBC's teacher education programs, outcome data, process feedback, and experience gained through implementation are analyzed and interpreted by the program, assessment, and the standards committees. The results are translated into change actions for improvement. Examples include curriculum mapping, alignment of outcomes and assessments, and revision of assessment rubric, process, and procedures to address barriers and enhance effectiveness of implementation.

Like benefits, barriers exist on multiple levels and may include:

- **Content Barrier:** Utility, validity, and reliability need to be considered for variations of scope and breadth of content within and among programs. Changing requirements and expectations over time need to be carefully planned, communicated, and monitored.
- **Technology Barrier:** Differences in technological abilities, equity of access to technology, and support need to be taken into consideration for spectrum-wide enterprise services.
- **Process Barrier:** Developmentally appropriate guidance, support, expectation, and feedback need to be provided by faculty, mentors, and supervisors. Time for development and revision should be allotted and honored, as fluency of the ePortfolio process, standards, and technology require time and commitment.
- **Review Barrier:** Review rubric, processes, and procedures need to be clearly articulated and communicated. Formative evaluation at benchmarks requires careful programmatic coordination to avoid conflict and redundancy. Summative evaluation ideally should include multiple reviewers, such as faculty, supervisors, mentors, and other professionals in the education community. Reviewer training and professional development need to be conducted cyclically to ensure coherence and consistency. Lastly, content and construct of assessments and rubric should take into consideration exemplary assessment characteristics—such as those identified by Huba and Freed (2000)—as being valid, coherent, authentic, rigorous, engaging, challenging, respectful, and responsive.

Resources, Support, and System Renewal

Sustaining a comprehensive system requires long-term commitment with resources and support infrastructures, as the institution is accountable to its constituents once implemented. In the context of UMBC, the design, development, implementation, and management of the EAS as a whole are led by the author and a multitasking team, with close collaboration among the various programs and standards committees. The frequent formal and informal interactions facilitate a cyclical review and renewal process, which is particularly important as it epitomizes and encapsulates capacity and linkage building for sustained implementation.

The review and renewal process is based on outcome data, feedback, and experiences gained through implementation. It enables faculty and the management team to refine conceptual designs by further customizing functional and technical requirements and services. It facilitates the revision of software designs that strengthen architectures and interfaces for enhanced interactions. Lastly, the process helps adjust implementation plans that are responsive to the changing culture and environment with evolving visions, goals, and needs.

A multitasking team providing spectrum-wide support and services is another important component, particularly in the context of restricted resources. On the system side, the team is responsible for managing business and operational processes, and software and hardware upgrades. On the user support side, the team is responsible for providing a wide variety of services to candidates, faculty, supervisors, mentors, alumni, and other reviewers from the education community. Candidate support includes development and delivery of instructional modules on the ePortfolio process, standards, and technology in online, blended, and in-person classrooms. The team also develops and distributes Web-based and printed supporting materials, such as the *E-Portfolio Handbook,* which consists of policies, processes, content authoring, evaluation, media release, and process feedback documents. A computer lab, the Portfolio Place, was established and staffed to increase accessibility to technology and services. Support for other stakeholders includes professional development and technical training for members of the department and faculty at P-12 PDSs, and reviewer training conducted at the institution and on site at its PDSs. Publishing services (via CD-ROM and the Internet) are provided to all users.

As with other educational interventions, the necessary resources and support for the ePortfolio and EAS are often greater than what they appear to be or what are available. Advocacy in the institution, strong leaders in the department, and persistent communication among stakeholders help manage expectations and operations for sustained implementation.

SUMMARY

This chapter narrates an institution's experience in designing, implementing, and sustaining an ePortfolio and the EAS in its education community. Factors and conditions that facilitate implementation and correlate to sustainability and effectiveness are summarized below.

- **Capacity and Linkage:**
  - Sustaining effective interventions requires attention at multiple levels that build capacity and linkage, and requires community-wide commitment and engagement.
- **Organizational Capacity and Linkage:**
  - Organizational infrastructure is critical to enabling connections, communications, and transfer of capacities.
  - Institutionalization demands sustained leadership, commitment, collaboration, support, and resources, and requires enabling conditions provided by the organizational infrastructure.
  - Strong leadership with champions of change facilitates change management and encourages creation and adoption of a new culture.
- **Technological Capacity and Linkage:**
  - A robust system needs to be grounded in a coherent conceptual framework,

  and should be capable of realizing evolving visions, goals, and needs of the community.
  - A core team responsible for system design, management, upgrades, and user support is necessary, as the institution is accountable to its stakeholders.
- **Curriculum and ePortfolio Culture:**
  - Commitment to systematic curriculum planning and execution is critical to assure logical and supportive development, leading to candidate mastery of program standards and desired outcomes.
  - Cultivating an ePortfolio culture requires well-articulated policies, processes, and strategies addressing potential barriers in areas of content, technology, process, and review to ensure utility, validity, and reliability.
  - A profession-based learning community inclusive of candidates, faculty, mentors, and other colleagues in the profession potentially extends the traditional institution-based evaluation to profession-based learning, assessment, and celebration of achievements.
- **Support and Resource:**
  - Sustaining the implementation of a comprehensive system requires careful planning on change management with realistic budgeting of resources, support, and expectations.
- **System Renewal:**
  - A built-in review and renewal process facilitates organizational and individual learning, and increases probabilities for successful and sustained reform. Whether in the areas of conceptual, software, or implementation designs, outcomes data, process feedback, and experience gained through implementation need to be analyzed, interpreted, and translated into change actions for improvements.

As progress continues to be made, new challenges continue to emerge. The institution and its community will need to continue to adjust policies and practices in the effort to create a dynamic learning community that takes advantage of the new teaching, learning, and assessment paradigm afforded by systems such as the ePortfolio and the EAS.

REFERENCES

Abbey, G. (1997). Developing a technology-friendly faculty in higher education. In D. Willis, B. Robin, J. Willis, L. Price, & S. McNeil (Eds.), *Technology and teacher education annual 1997* (pp. 351-353). Charlottesville, VA: Association for the Advancement of Computing in Education.

Barrett, H. (2004). Differentiating electronic portfolios and online assessment management systems. In *Proceedings of the 2004 Conference of the Society for Information Technology and Teacher Education.* Retrieved June 2004 from http://electronicportfolios.org/portfolios/SITE2004paper.pdf

Barrett, H., & Wilkerson, J. (2004). *Conflicting paradigms in electronic portfolio approaches.* Retrieved June 2004 from http://electronicportfolios.com/sytems/paradigms.html

Cambridge, B. (2004, February 11). Electronic portfolios: Why now? In *Proceedings of the EDUCAUSE Live Teleconference.*

Candiotti, A., & Clarke, N. (1998). Combining universal access with faculty development and academic facilities. *Communications of the ACM, 41*(1), 36-41.

Danielson, C., & Abrutyn, L. (1997). *An introduction to using portfolios in the classroom.* Alexandria, VA: Association for Supervision and Curriculum Development.

Dusick, D. M. (1998). What social cognitive factors influence faculty members' use of computer for teaching? *A Literature Review. Journal of Research on Computing in Education, 31*(2), 21-36.

Fullan, M. (2000). The return of large-scale reform. *Journal of Educational Change,* (1), 1-23.

Fullan, M.G., & Stielgelbauer, S. (1991). *The new meaning of educational change* (2nd ed.). New York: Teachers School Press.

Gathercoal, P., Bryde, B., Mahler, J., Love, D., & McKean, G. (2002). Preservice teacher standards and the magnetic connections electronic portfolio. In *Proceedings of the Annual Meeting of American Educational Research Association (AERA),* New Orleans, LA.

Hill, D. (2002). Electronic portfolios: Teacher candidate development and assessment. In *Proceedings of the 54th Annual Meeting of the American Association of Colleges for Teacher Education,* New York.

Huang, Y. (2003). UMBC performance assessment system. In *Assessing education candidate performance: A look at changing practices.* Washington, DC: National Council for Accreditation of Teacher Education.

Huba, M. E., & Freed, J. E. (2000). *Learner-centered assessment on college campuses: Shifting the focus from teaching to learning.* Boston: Allyn and Bacon.

Jafari, A. (2004). The sticky e-portfolio system: Tackling challenges and identifying attributes. *EDUCAUSE Review, 39*(4), 38-48.

Spillane, J. P., & Thompson, C. L. (1997). reconstructing conceptions of local capacity: The local education agency's capacity for ambitious instructional reform. *Education Evaluation and Policy Analysis, 19*(2), 185-203.

Waddoups, G., Wentworth, N., & Earle, R. (2004). Teaming with technology: A case study of a faculty design team developing an electronic portfolio. *Journal of Computing in Teacher Education, 20*(3), 113-120.

KEY TERMS

Accreditation: A process of assessing and enhancing academic, educational, and or organizational quality through peer review conducted by national and/or state agencies.

Assessment System: A comprehensive and integrated set of evaluation measures that provides information in monitoring, managing, and improving candidate performance, program quality, and organizational operations associated with teacher education. Definition adopted from National Council for Accreditation of Teacher Education (NCATE).

Benchmark: A description of individual or organizational performance and/or outcome that serves as a standard of comparison for evaluation or judging quality.

Developmental ePortfolio: A process that facilitates the generation, recording, reflection, and assessment of one's own growth and performance throughout the teacher preparation cycle.

Education Accountability System (EAS): A comprehensive and dynamic learning management system developed and implemented by the University of Maryland Baltimore County. It consists of three integrated production components: Accountability Center, Performance Assessment, and Electronic Portfolio.

Professional ePortfolio: A process that encourages practicing educators in the education community to continue generating, documenting, and celebrating one's own performance, growth, and achievement.

Showcase ePortfolio: A self-selected, "best evidence" collection of documents and artifacts that demonstrate competencies on the standards and professional growth.

ENDNOTE

1 The EAS is copyrighted with a technology invention disclosure granted to the author and the lead programmer, Alan Ma. The Performance Assessment component was selected as a part of the National Assessment Examples Project (Huang, 2003) by the National Council for Accreditation of Teacher Education (NCATE). The ePortfolio component was awarded a Preparing Tomorrow's Teacher for Technology (PT3) sub-grant by the Maryland State Department of Education, with the author serving as principle investigator. The technical specification section of the chapter is written with assistance provided by the lead programmer.

Chapter XLVI
Psychology ePortfolios Enhance Learning, Assessment, and Career Development

Benjamin R. Stephens
Clemson University, USA

DeWayne Moore
Clemson University, USA

ABSTRACT

The authors evaluated psychology program assessment measurements derived from self-report and electronic portfolios in the psychology undergraduate major. Their new introductory and senior laboratory courses have been specifically created to provide student-centered learning experiences that lead to ePortfolio construction. This chapter describes the initial stage of an evaluation of our assessment strategy, which centers on the new laboratories. In the lab courses, each student's abilities were evaluated using several measures of achievement derived from national learning outcomes. ePortfolio and non-portfolio-based measures demonstrate promising reliability and validity. ePortfolio laboratories seem to enhance student learning and career planning. These early observations encourage collection of assessment data yearly, from undergraduate majors in each class, to provide longitudinal evaluation of their ePortfolio learning and career planning assessment strategy.

INTRODUCTION

Student portfolios have strong potential as a basis for effective class and program assessment goals (APA, 2003; Panitz, 1998). Assessment strategies should provide a rich source of information concerning student learning and development (Graham, 1998; Allen, Noel, Deegan, Halpern, & Crawford, 2000; Halonen et al., 2002; Shavelson & Huang, 2003). In addition, when integrated into the curriculum, assessment should provide learning experiences that benefit the student as well as improve subsequent teaching methods (Halpern, 1988;

Halonen et al., 2002). Electronic reflective portfolios show promise in meeting these criteria for assessment (Yancey, 2001).

Portfolio-based assessment originated in the arts, architecture, and writing. Their use increased as educators began to emphasize that all students should be able to engage in creative and critical thinking. Open-ended assessment is effective for these skills, and also tends to promote changes in curriculum towards strategies and pedagogy that promote those higher-order skills in students (Gardner, 1992; Herman & Golan, 1993; Resnick & Resnick, 1992).

The potential advantages of portfolio assessment may be best understood by consideration of the construction of the portfolio, particularly a reflective portfolio. Yancy (2001) conceptualizes the formation of the reflective portfolio in terms of three processes: collection, selection, and reflection. These processes are consistent with prevailing cognitive theory and principles, such as an apprenticeship model of cognitive development and assessment (Gardner, 1992), as well as socially mediated cognition that is domain specific (Brown, Campione, Webber, & McGilley 1992; Vygotsky, 1978). These cognitive viewpoints suggest that a reflective portfolio is fertile ground for development of deeper critical thinking skills.

The scope of the reflective portfolio can vary. Class portfolios ask students to indicate their understanding of course material over the course of the term. A program portfolio, located within a discipline, requires students to reflect on and provide evidence of their competence across the discipline. It often includes a résumé, and so provides an integrating theme between the college curriculum, personal development, and career development (Garcia & Clausen, 2000; Kwiatkowski, 2003; Yancey, 1997).

In addition to these functions, we believe that electronic portfolios may share pedagogical elements common to proven techniques for effective undergraduate science education (Stephens & Weaver, 2005). This attribute enhances the value of the assessment program for the science major, engages their attention, and should produce a more valid set of assessment data. One key element of the scientific curriculum is undergraduate research experiences. Assessment data from our NSF-funded Research Experiences for Undergraduates program is consistent with the notion that ePortfolios can enhance undergraduate research training. Students constructed summer program research ePortfolios, documenting and reflecting on their research training. Consistent student and faculty ratings of student learning may have been enhanced by student ePortfolio construction and faculty review of those portfolios (Klein & Stephens, 2005; Stephens & Weaver, 2005).

The reflective ePortfolio may also be effective for integrative learning. One may conceptualize integrative learning as student-constructed connections within and across domain-specific knowledge systems (Huber & Hutchings, 2004; Shavelson & Huang, 2003). We suspect that ePortfolio construction can promote student construction of such connections over the semester. The students make connections for themselves to support a range of ePortfolio goals. In the Intro lab, a common goal is developmental, where students' lab ePortfolios communicate a deepening appreciation of fundamental concepts within psychology. A common goal in the senior lab is a "showcase" program ePortfolio, communicating both psychology and non-psychology themes to graduate schools or employers.

The scale and context of a portfolio assessment strategy may be related to its usefulness. Early evaluations of large-scale portfolio assessment reliability were mixed (Koretz, Stecher, Klein, & McCaffery, 1994; LeMahieu, Gitomer, & Eresh, 1995; Gredler, 1995). However, recent efforts to employ portfolio-based assessment demonstrate acceptable reliability in more limited contexts (Johnson, McDaniel, & Willekel, 2000; Johnson, Fisher, Willeke, & McDaniel, 2003; Ingulsrud, Kimiko, Kadowski, Kurobane, & Shiobara, 2002; Newell, Dahm, & Newell, 2002).

The American Psychological Association (APA, 2003) has expressed a favorable view of the potential of portfolio-based assessment in the undergraduate major. APA also reinforces warnings indicating that portfolio construction and measurement may be challenging problems. We designed our portfolio construction and assessment strategy along APA recommendations so that it would retain favorable characteristics but also prevent pitfalls. Our assessment was situated in the context of laboratory courses. The lab courses introduced students to the learning goals and outcomes for the major as well as the portfolio process. Both the introductory and senior laboratories employ a Web-based laboratory manual to aid consistency and reduce workload (Stephens, 2005).

Effective evaluation and conversion to data is a key element to a successful portfolio program assessment. For each portfolio, our assessment process generated multiple ratings across multiple dimensions of achievement. Different raters (peer and the student author) evaluated the portfolio. In addition, non-portfolio self-report measures of achievement were included as a concurrent measure to our portfolio-based measures. The ease of implementation in terms of cost and time argues for both types of measures. If valid and reliable, measures of students' views of their own and others' competence could provide an important index of student awareness of learning, capability, as well as the impact on career development. Together, we expect that these assessment data should provide an accurate and useful description of student views of their abilities.

National Standards and Assessment

One enhancement for assessment is the use of national standards. The conceptual basis for the construction and evaluation of our measures was the APA-recommended goals and outcomes for student learning (APA, 2003). Table 1 lists the 10 APA goals, which are organized hierarchically, and a sample item tapping each goal. Five goals represent do-

Table 1. Conceptual descriptions and sample items for APA goals and learning outcomes

- **P1–Knowledge Base:** Concepts, theoretical perspectives, empirical findings, and historical trends (e.g., "I can demonstrate knowledge and understanding of theory and research in learning and cognition.")
- **P2–Research Methods:** Understand and apply basic research methods (e.g., "I can formulate testable psychological research hypotheses, based on operational definitions of variables.")
- **P3–Critical Thinking Skills:** Critical and creative thinking, skeptical inquiry, and the scientific approach (e.g., "I can recognize and defend against fallacies in psychological thinking.")
- **P4–Application:** Apply psychological principles to personal, social, and organizational issues (e.g., "I can describe the main elements of clinical psychology.")
- **P5–Values in Psychology:** Balance empirical evidence, ambiguity, ethics, and scientific values (e.g., "I can describe the necessity for ethical behavior in all aspects of the science and practice of psychology.")
- **pG1–Information and Technological Literacy:** Demonstrate information, computer, and technology skills (e.g., "I can formulate a researchable topic that can be supported by database search strategies.")
- **pG2–Communication Skills:** Communicate effectively (e.g., "I can demonstrate effective writing skills in various formats, e.g., essays, correspondence, technical papers, note taking.")
- **pG3–Sociocultural and International Awareness:** Understand sociocultural and international diversity (e.g., "I can explain how beliefs, values, and interactions with others influence individual differences.")
- **pG4–Personal Development:** Understand self-management and self-improvement (e.g., "I can apply psychological principles to promote personal development.")
- **pG5–Career Planning and Development:** Psychological knowledge, in occupational pursuits (e.g., "I can apply knowledge of psychology to formulating career choices.")

mains specific to the science and application of psychology (P1-P5), and five represent general education domains furthered by the psychology major (pG1-pG5). APA identifies four to six elements for each of the 10 goals. Each element has between one and six specific learning outcomes. We based self-report and portfolio assessment on these multiple dimensions.

Alternative conceptualizations of program learning constructs exist, and depending on departmental context, may prove to be more or less efficient. For example, some science educators view learning outcomes as organized in terms of three domains: content, process, and application (National Research Council, 2003). In psychology, Halpern (1993) suggests a somewhat different set of three domains: knowledge base, intellectual skills, and personal characteristics. Other frameworks may be specific to an institution, such as a model employed at Alverno, a liberal arts college, where analysis, problem solving, and social interaction are identified as core developmental constructs in the psychology major, selected from a set of college-wide goals and outcomes (Graham, 1998).

We selected the APA framework for assessment to promote portability and to enhance content validity. Content validity is enhanced by employing as many dimensions and elements of a discipline as are both practicable and reasonable. Such an inclusive approach allows one to identify novel constructs. From a portability perspective, the external validity of our assessment strategy relies on its ability to function across context and time. Broad content better enables such generalization.

Portability is also influenced by the demands of the evaluation procedures. If these embedded in-class measures show acceptable psychometric properties, they could prove to be of immense practical value. Such an outcome would ease the workload of program assessment.

RESEARCH METHODS

The central question for our research was twofold. First, are the measures reliable? Psychometric properties of multiple measures obtained from student and peer raters over time were assessed. Specifically, psychometrically sound measures were assessed across methods (portfolio-based vs. non-portfolio-based), across raters, and across time.

Second, are the measures valid? Specifically, are the patterns of ratings organized in meaningful ways across dimensions and across methods? Are these organized patterns changed over time as a result of the laboratory experience?

Participants

In this project's first academic year, we collected portfolio-based and non-portfolio-based measures from psychology senior majors enrolled in the senior laboratory (n=10), psychology majors in the Introductory laboratory (n=130), and non-laboratory volunteers (n=395). The introductory and senior laboratory participants provided assessment data as part of their normal laboratory activities. Non-laboratory participants volunteered for assessment and received extra credit in their psychology courses. Courses offering such extra credit include Introductory Psychology, Research Methods, as well as several mid-level and senior-level courses for majors and non-majors.

Assessment Measures

Self-report and portfolio rating instruments were similar. Each survey was entitled "Psychology Assessment Survey" (PAS). Each item represented a learning goal or outcome based on the APA task force-recommended goals and outcomes outlined in Table 1. APA has defined each of the 10 goals in terms of three to four sub-goals, and the content of each sub-goal is defined further in terms of one or more specific abilities. To develop the PAS, we translated the sub-goals and learning outcomes into statements indicating the presence of the achieved goal or outcome. In the portfolio version of the survey, each statement began with a prefix, "The portfolio shows that the student can ... ," followed by the targeted ability. In the self-report version, the prefix, "I can ... ," preceded the targeted ability. Sample items are provided in Table 1.

For each statement, the respondents indicated their agreement/disagreement on a six-point Likert scale, ranging from 1 – Strongly Disagree to 6 – Strongly Agree. A response bias scale was added to measure bias (resulting from a "capability" response set, a position preference, agreement bias, etc.) by creating a phantom ability as the target of each statement. The final instrument consisted of 169 items, with item position randomly ordered.

In a preliminary study employing only the self-report ("I can ... ") version of the PAS, each (non-laboratory) participant completed the survey using our department's secure online survey system. Data was obtained from 1,143 students enrolled in introductory and upper-level courses in the psychology department. The student sample included mainly non-majors (11% were psychology majors) and freshmen—61.4% freshmen, 23.4% sophomores, 9.4% juniors, and 5.8% seniors. The initial confirmatory factor analysis of the 10-factor PAS did not indicate a good fit to the data. A second model was tested controlling for "illusion of knowledge" (a measure created by summing the four items designed to measure bias). There was a substantial improvement in the fit. After controlling for illusion of knowledge, absolute fit indices indicated excellent fit (values less than .05), but the incremental fit indices indicated poor fit (values about .75). Modification indices identified several problematic items (one to three per scale). Estimating error co-variances for a few of these improved the fit, but the incremental fit indices still remained below .90. This is likely due to some of the problematic items having near zero co-variances with other items in the PAS when controlling for illusion of knowledge.

The self-report PAS pilot data were encouraging. Importantly, they do not reveal any serious psychometric problems in the PAS, and so do not rule out the potential value of the PAS as an assessment measure. Therefore, we used the PAS for the non-portfolio-based measures of self-reported achievement.

The PAS also was used to assess student achievement as represented in the portfolio. For these portfolio-based measures, each item in the PAS was phrased to reflect demonstration of the targeted ability in the portfolio (e.g., "The portfolio demonstrates that the student can ... "). The instructions also were modified to direct the rater's attention to the need to base each judgment solely on the contents of the ePortfolio. Each portfolio was rated independently by the student and a peer. The task of each rater was to read the portfolio, then to use that reading as the basis for assessment of the student's achievement on each targeted item, using all elements (components) of the portfolio. These elements include the information provided in collection, organization, selection, and reflection phases. No additional training or special scoring instructions were provided beyond the instructions provided in the PAS, along with familiarity with portfolio goals and structure provided in the course of the semester.

Procedure

In constructing ePortfolios, students were told that they were required to represent and document their areas of understandings, as well as areas in need of improvement. The initial self-report PAS was administered in the first two to three weeks of the semester. Data collection procedures used the departmental automated online systems for administration of the PAS (and subsequent end-of-semester, ePortfolio-based PAS). The online system also was used to collect data from non-laboratory students in the beginning weeks of each semester as part of their normal extra-credit participation in assessment.

Construction of the reflective digital portfolio in labs occurred throughout the subsequent weekly meetings of the regular semester. After construction, peer and self-ratings of the portfolios were collected using the PAS. Each student rated his/her own portfolio, and then each was randomly assigned to read and rate a peer's portfolio. Finally, they rated their own capabilities using the non-portfolio version of the PAS.

After the initial PAS assessment measures, a Web-based manual was employed to guide students through the modules of the laboratories (Stephens, 2005; Stephens & Weaver, 2005). To illustrate, in the career modules, students engaged in activities designed to develop an employer perspective and career identity formation. Résumé fine-tuning and graduate school discussions demonstrated the critical elements of the résumé and graduate school applications. In the Job Searching/Networking activities, the value of the Clemson Michelin Career Center network was illustrated, as well as the value of using a portfolio in a job search.

Demonstrations and activities produced electronic products for actual portfolio use, as well as the reflective process of portfolio construction. For example, in the résumé construction module, we used collection, selection, and reflection to guide the student through the creation of a professional résumé. This résumé linked to work samples and artifacts associated with psychology coursework, as well as non-psychology coursework and extracurricular activities. The product of this module was a résumé suitable for Web page and/or CD presentation.

We described and discussed APA learning goals. Students reviewed APA goals and learning outcomes (Halonen et al., 2002) and constructed a matrix of goals and examples of activities that fit single and multiple goals from major courses, non-major courses, as well as extracurricular learning experiences (Levy, Burton, Mickler, & Virgorito, 1999).

Construction of the portfolio began with collection/representation of all artifacts as a process of identifying and preparing lab and coursework summaries, employment narratives, class notes, tests, drafts, finals papers, graded papers, courses and grades, and so on for electronic presentation and potential inclusion in the portfolio. In addition, students collected or created reflective narratives describing these events and what was learned from them.

Organization of artifacts in terms of APA goals initiated the selection phase. Such organization served as a prompt and framework for the selection of artifacts that represented learning, development, and student-valued understandings within a psychology framework. The process and criteria used to identify the elements from the archive that were central to understanding, capability, and personal development necessarily were student defined and required a communicated justification for each selection (Yancey, 1998, 2001).

The reflection on and communication of learning (themes, connections, strengths, interests, all linked to supporting evidence) constituted the final phase. The student organized and identified synthesizing constructs to characterize educational experiences. The communication of these major themes was supported with the selected evidence and communicated in a professional, yet creative student-centered fashion as an online ePortfolio.

Learning and Assessment Results

Figure 1 presents the mean PAS scale scores for students for each of the five psychology (P1-P5) and general (pG1-pG5) dimensions for each of the following conditions: (1) non-laboratory courses at the beginning of the semester using the non-portfolio based PAS (Non-Lab); (2) Intro and Senior Lab at the beginning of the semester using the non-ePortfolio based PAS (Self-Begin); (3) Intro and Senior Lab at the end of the semester using the ePortfolio-based PAS (Self-Port); and (4) Intro and Senior Lab at the end of the semester using the non-ePortfolio based PAS (Self-End). The standard error of the mean averages roughly 0.06 for these mean scores.

In general, there was a consistent trend for mean Non-Lab scores to be lower than Self-Begin scores, which in turn are lower than Self-Port scores, which in turn are lower than Self-End scores. This pattern is somewhat stronger on average for the psychology dimensions (P1-P5) compared to the general dimensions (pG1-pG5). These patterns suggest that across all psychology dimensions (P1-P5), lab students view themselves as more capable than non-lab students at the beginning of the semester. By the end of the semester, lab students view themselves as having greater capability, with a sizable portion of that achievement represented in their ePortfolio.

Similar observations are noted across the psychology-supported general domains of achievement (pG1-pG5). Lab students also view themselves as more capable than non-lab students at the beginning of the semester. By the end of the semester, lab students view themselves as having greater capability, with a portion of that achievement represented in their ePortfolios. Exceptions include the observations that (1) lab students do not indicate gains in Sociocultural/International awareness in their ePortfolios, and (2) increases in ratings across Begin/Port/End measurements are generally less dramatic in the pG1-pG4 dimensions compared to the psychology (P1-P5) dimensions, although notably the pG5 Career Planning and Development dimension is comparable to the increases observed in the P1-P5 ratings.

Figure 1. Mean scale score is plotted as a function of PAS dimensions. Each condition is represented by different bar styles indicated on the side legend.

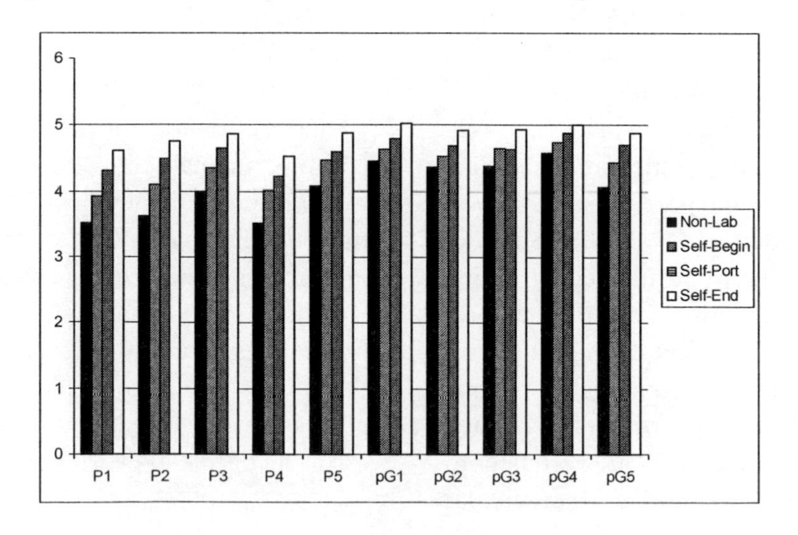

Figure 2. Mean scale score is plotted as a function of PAS dimensions. The two bar styles represent self-assessed ePortfolios (Self-Port) and peer-assessed ePortfolios (Peer-Port).

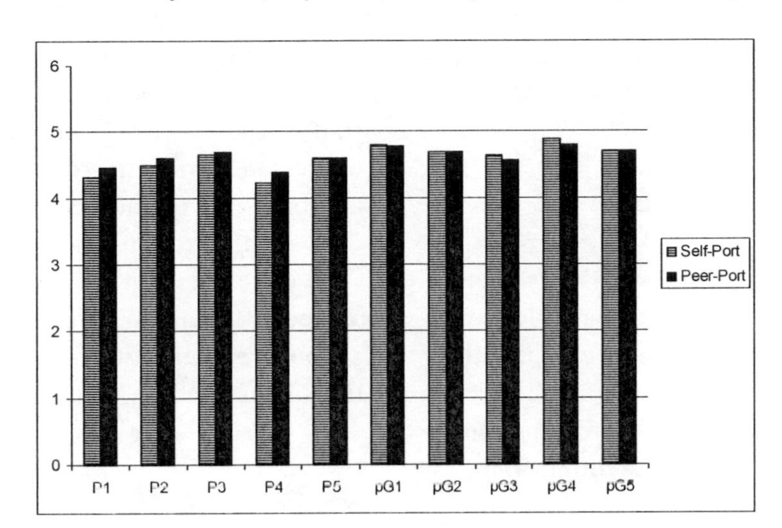

Figure 2 re-plots the Self-Port average scale scores with the Peer-Port scale scores. The Peer-Port scores are a peer's rating of a lab student's ePortfolio using the PAS at the end of the semester. Note the remarkable similarity in the average scores. This convergence in ratings is consistent with the notion that averaged ePortfolio-based PAS measures are reliable.

The validity and value of the ePortfolio and non-ePortfolio scores rest on the reasonableness of the results and the stability of the relative scores across dimensions. Reasonableness is evidenced by the stronger gains in psychology scores relative to general scores, to be expected since the lab students were psychology majors in psychology courses. The stability of the relative scores, regardless of source, also seems reasonable for valid measures, to be expected if these measures are indexes of student views of capability.

Career Planning Observations

The Career Planning and Development average scores (pG5) in Figure 1 are notable, particularly when viewed in conjunction with anecdotal evidence of the effectiveness of the ePortfolio activity for student achievement of broad career planning goals. Examination of the constituent items in the PAS pG5 scale implies that the ePortfolio lab helped students (1) formulate career choices, (2) facilitate entry into the workforce, (3) facilitate entry into post-baccalaureate education, (4) describe preferred career paths, (5) identify and develop skills and experiences relevant to achieving selected career goals, and (6) sustain personal and professional development as the nature of work evolves.

Anecdotal evidence of student involvement and ownership in the résumé portion of the ePortfolio construction, and in the discovery of career-relevant capabilities, confirms these inferences from the pG5 scores. Many students initiated searches for internships and research experiences after constructing résumé portions of the ePortfolio. Many used the résumé and ePortfolio as elements of actual job or graduate school applications. These anecdotal observations suggest that the communication of capabilities, particularly reflected and integrated themes, was a powerful defining exercise for undergraduates. Many students commented that these reflections were invaluable as they considered the next step in their career path.

FUTURE DIRECTIONS

We view these initial observations as showing strong promise for an ePortfolio-based learning and assessment system. The multi-trait, multimethod technique has thus far yielded well-ordered observations that are not only reasonably priced, but also high in potential value.

To be sure, much work is needed to confirm and extend these initial observations. Our data are consistent with the hypothesis that ePortfolio construction mediated and reflected achievement of learning goals and outcomes, but given the non-experimental nature of the design, extensive follow-up work is needed to convince a cautious mind. We need to connect ePortfolios to long-term outcomes that students and theory value. We need to establish the formative functions of ePortfolio learning and assessment in order to communicate their potential and actual import to both internal and external stakeholders.

We suspect that these positives will be realized in the years to come. Part of this expectation rests on the initial data and the various anecdotal sources of success. As an apparent result of the ePortfolio process, students entered graduate school, obtained a passion for a career path, or discovered a central capability, compelling us to pursue the pedagogy. Conversion of these hints into solid empirical foundations will ultimately advance both the science and the practice of this profession.

ACKNOWLEDGMENTS

This chapter was based in part upon work supported by the National Science Foundation under Grant No. SES-0353698. Any opinions, findings, and conclusions or recommendations expressed in this material are those of the authors, and do not necessarily reflect the views of the National Science Foundation.

We are indebted to Jan Murdoch, Kathleen Yancey, Barbara Weaver, and Flora Riley for supportive suggestions that improved innovations in our undergraduate programs.

REFERENCES

Allen, M. J., Noel, R. N., Deegan, J., Halpern, D., & Crawford, C. (2000). *Goals and objectives for the undergraduate psychology major: Recommendations from a meeting of California State University psychology faculty.* Retrieved November 1, 2004, from http://www.Lemoyne.edu/OTRP/teachingresources.html

APA (American Psychological Association). (2003). *The assessment cyberguide for learning goals and outcomes.* Washington, DC: APA. Retrieved November 1, 2004, from http://www.apa.org/ed/guidehomepage.html

Brown, A., Campione, J., Webber, L., & McGilley, K. (1992). Interactive learning environments: A new look at assessment and instruction. In B. Gifford & M. O'Conner (Eds.), *Changing assessments: Alternative views of aptitude, achievement, and instruction* (pp. 121-211). Boston: Kluwer.

Gardner, H. (1992). Assessment in context: The alternative to standardized testing. In B. Gifford & M. O'Conner (Eds.), *Changing assessments: Alternative views of aptitude, achievement, and instruction* (pp. 77-119). Boston: Kluwer.

Graham, S. E. (1998). Developing student outcomes for the psychology major: An assessment-as-learning framework. *Current Directions in Psychological Science, 7,* 165-170.

Gredler, M. E. (1995). Implications of portfolio assessment for program evaluation. *Studies in Educational Evaluation, 21,* 431-437.

Halpern, D. F. (1988). Assessing student outcomes for psychology majors. *Teaching of Psychology, 4,* 181-186.

Halpern, D. F. (1993). Targeting outcomes: Covering your assessment needs. In T. V. McGovern (Ed.), *Handbook for enhancing undergraduate education in psychology* (pp. 23-46). Washington, DC: American Psychological Association.

Halonen, J. S., Appleby, D., Brewer, C. L., Buskist, W., Gillem, A. R., Halpern, D., et al. (2002). *Undergraduate psychology major learning goals and outcomes: A report.* Retrieved November 1, 2004, from http://www.apa.org/ed/pcue/taskforcereport.pdf

Herman, J., & Golan, S. (1993). The effects of standardized testing on teaching and schools. *Educational measurement: Issues and practice, 12*(4), 20-25, 41-42.

Huber, M. T., & Hutchings, P. (2004). *Integrative learning: Mapping the terrain.* Retrieved December 1, 2004, from http://www.cargegie foundation.org/LiberalEducation/Mapping Terrain.pdf

Ingulsrud, J. E, Kimiko, K., Kadowaki, S., Kurobane, S., & Shiobara, M. (2002). The assessment of cross-cultural experience: Measuring awareness through critical text analysis. *International Journal of Intercultural Relations, 26,* 473-491.

Johnson, R. L., Fisher S., Willeke, M. J., & McDaniel, F. (2003). Portfolio assessment in a collaborative program evaluation: The reliability and validity of a family literacy portfolio. *Evaluation and Program Planning, 26*(4), 367-377.

Johnson, R. L., McDaniel, F., & Willeke, M. J. (2000). Using portfolios in program evaluation: An investigation of inter-rater reliability. *American Journal of Evaluation, 21*(1), 65-80.

Klein, N. D., & Stephens, B. R. (2005, April). *Assessment of a summer program for undergraduate research experiences.* Nashville: Southeastern Psychological Association.

Koretz, D., Stecher, B., Klein, S., & McCaffery, D. (1994). The Vermont Portfolio assessment program: Findings and implications. *Educational Measurement: Issues and Practice, 13*(3), 5-16.

LeMahieu, P. G., Gitomer, D. H., & Eresh, J. T. (1995). Portfolios in large-scale assessment: Difficult but not impossible. *Educational Measurement: Issues and Practice, 14*(3), 11-16, 25-28.

Levy, J., Burton, G., Mickler, S., & Vigorito, M. (1999). A curriculum matrix for psychology program review. *Teaching of Psychology, 26,* 291-294.

National Research Council. (2003). *Improving undergraduate instruction in science, technology, engineering, and mathematics: Report of a workshop.* Washington DC: National Academy Press.

Newell, J. A., Dahm, K. D., & Newell, H. L. (2002). Rubric development and inter-rater reliability issues in assessing learning outcomes.

In *Proceedings of the 2002 American Society for Engineering Education Annual Conference and Exposition, Session 2613.*

Panitz, B. (1998). Student portfolios. In F. L. Huband (Ed.), *How do you measure success? Designing effective processes for assessing engineering education* (pp. 49-64). Washington, DC: American Society for Engineering Education.

Resnick, L., & Resnick, D. (1992). Assessing the thinking curriculum: New tools for educational reform. In B. Gifford & M. O'Conner (Eds.), *Changing assessments: Alternative views of aptitude, achievement, and instruction* (pp. 37-75). Boston: Kluwer.

Shavelson, R. J., & Huang, L. (2003, January/ February). Responding responsibly to the frenzy to assess learning in higher education. *Change*, 11-19.

Stephens, B. R. (2005). Laptops in psychology improve organization, e-portfolios, research laboratories, and writing laboratories. In L. Neilson & B. Weaver (Eds.), *New directions for teaching and learning. Special issue: Enhancing learning using laptops in the classroom.* San Francisco: Jossey-Bass.

Stephens, B. R., & Weaver, B. E. (2005). Integrating learning, reflective e-portfolios, undergraduate research, and assessment. In J. A. Chambers (Ed.), *Selected Papers from the 16th International Conference on College Teaching and Learning* (pp. 185-202). Jacksonville: Florida Community College.

Vygotsky, L. (1978). *Mind in society.* Cambridge, MA: Harvard University Press.

Yancey. K (1998). *Reflection in the writing classroom.* Logan, UT: Utah State University Press.

Yancey, K. (2001). Student digital portfolios. In B. Cambridge (Ed.), *Electronic portfolios: Emerging practices in student, faculty and institutional learning.* Washington, DC: American Association of Higher Education.

Yancey, K., & Weiser, I. (1997). Situation portfolios: An introduction. In K. Yancey & I. Weiser (Eds.), *Situation portfolios: Four perspectives* (pp. 1-20). Logan: Utah State University Press.

KEY TERMS

Agreement Bias: A participant's tendency to distort responses toward agreement regardless of the query.

Confirmatory Factor Analysis: A statistical procedure to identify and evaluate the reliability and validity of *a priori* defined constructs in a set of observations.

External Validity: The extent to which measurements, observations, and conclusions generalize beyond the specific sample studied.

Integrative Learning: Understandings represented by connections among learning experiences delivered within a single example or context.

Position Preference: A participant's tendency to distort responses toward a favored location on a scale regardless of the query.

Program ePortfolio: A collection of artifacts representing student learning within a discipline.

Psychometric: Measurements derived from behavior designed to tap psychological variables.

Reliability: The degree to which a measurement or observation may be repeated yielding the same result.

Response Set: A participant's tendency to distort responses in an particular manner regardless of the query.

Validity: The extent to which a measurement or observation accurately reflects the actual conceptual meaning under investigation.

Chapter XLVII
Career ePortfolios in the IT Associates Program at DePauw University

Nathaniel T. Romance
DePauw University, USA

Michael V. Whitesell
DePauw University, USA

Carol L. Smith
DePauw University, USA

Alicia M. (Clapp) Louden
DePauw University, USA

ABSTRACT

DePauw University is a selective, undergraduate liberal arts college of 2,200 students, with an academic year of two 13-week semesters and a three-week January Winter Term. DePauw implemented a career ePortfolio requirement for its Information Technology Associates Program (ITAP) in January 2004. The ITAP ePortfolio serves as both a job-seeking tool and a reflective instrument for students. This case study describes the rationale for introducing ePortfolios into ITAP, the processes used to support students in creating and maintaining career ePortfolios, and the outcomes of the project to this point.

INTRODUCTION

DePauw University is a selective, undergraduate liberal arts college of 2,200 students, with an academic year of two 13-week semesters and a three-week January Winter Term. DePauw implemented a career ePortfolio requirement in its Information Technology Associates Program (ITAP) in January 2004. The ITAP ePortfolio serves as both a job-seeking tool and a reflective instrument for students. While the full outcomes of the program will be realized only after the first complete class of ITAP students required to develop portfolios graduates in 2008, so far 82 students have successfully published ePortfolios. This case study describes the rationale for integrating ePortfolios into ITAP, the processes we use to support students in creating and maintaining their ePortfolios, and the outcomes of the project to this point.

RATIONALE FOR ITAP ePORTFOLIOS

ITAP is a program of distinction that provides opportunities for 160 DePauw students to develop advanced skills in a wide range of information technologies, as well as soft skills. ITAP students have rich opportunities for learning and mastery in areas such as digital video production, Web design, information analysis with spreadsheets and databases, and desktop and network hardware. Students selected for the program spend an average of eight hours per week in internship and training activities. Freshman ITAP students are assigned to four- or five-member cohorts and participate in four six-week training rotations during the first year with leading campus information technology (IT) groups, such as Information Services and the Web Team. As sophomores, juniors, and seniors, ITAP interns participate in semester- or year-long on-campus internships, working closely with faculty members and IT professionals. During their junior year, they have the option to serve a semester-long, IT-related, off-campus internship. Advanced ITAP students mentor, lead, and train other interns while working on DePauw's most important technology-related projects.

Our early research showed that many employers are beginning to pay closer attention to an ePortfolio presented as part of an applicant's materials. In a 2002 national study of employers conducted by the University of Iowa, "seventy-nine percent of the respondents stated that a job seeker's ePortfolio can be a significant selection tool along with references, credentials, transcripts, résumé and cover letter, and interviews" (Achrazoglou, Anthony, Jun, Marshall, & Roe, 2002, p. 20). This same survey produced even more convincing data among the surveyed central office administrators and human resource professionals. Among this group, "81 percent indicated that ePortfolios are an important selection tool" (Achrazoglou et al., 2002, p. 20). Discussions with DePauw's Career Services staff also provided justification for the program, as they emphasized the need for DePauw graduates to provide potential employers with evidence of their skills to help differentiate themselves in the job market. With this increased importance placed on ePortfolios, one goal of the ITAP ePortfolio, then, is to serve as a job-seeking tool that students use to demonstrate their skills and experiences to potential employers.

Further, the principal feature of ITAP is that students engage in authentic, hands-on work activities through which they learn professional skills, both technical and social, that prepare graduates for success. To scaffold their learning, faculty and professional staff members from all parts of the university serve as ITAP hosts—supervisors and coaches who provide a close mentoring environment in which the students work. The ePortfolio process models this strategy. Concurrently with workshops that teach the students technical skills for building ePortfolios, mentors offer constructive advice and feedback related to ePortfolio content and organization. The mentors additionally share professional expertise and advice, helping interns to shape ePortfolios that speak effectively to a targeted audience and that reflect accurately career goals.

Finally, all ITAP students keep personal learning journals, and their hosts periodically offer constructive feedback. Similarly, while part of the ITAP ePortfolio is the compilation and display of one's artifacts and experiences, interns must also write reflectively about those experiences, describing their work in the context of personal professional growth. These ePortfolio strategies provide a rich experience through which the ITAP students engage with diverse role models and professionals who help them exercise and adopt beneficial habits evident among expert reflective practitioners.

ePORTFOLIO CONTENT REQUIREMENTS

While the ITAP interns are given a great deal of flexibility in designing their ePortfolios, they are required to meet minimum content requirements: ePortfolios must contain the students' career objectives, contact information, résumé, and one reflective sample of their work. Mentors evaluate the ePortfolios using a rubric outlining the expectations in terms of general content, artifacts and reflection, organization, design and presentation, and technical accuracy.

ITAP ePORTFOLIO TOOL

Because one of the goals of ITAP is to foster advanced technology skills, ITAP ePortfolios are Web based and created using Macromedia Dreamweaver. Using this tool accomplishes the goals for the program and leverages existing resources, which include DePauw's site license for Macromedia Studio and the Web publishing space available to all students, thus making it a cost-effective means for creating and maintaining ePortfolios.

ITAP ePortfolios were not intended, however, to be simply an exercise in Web design. Rather, to focus attention on developing the content of the ePortfolio, we provide the students with Dreamweaver templates to use as the basis for the overall look and feel. Students are encouraged to personalize their ePortfolios through the organization and presentation of the content. We discourage changing the templates dramatically unless the students have significant Web development experience.

The ITAP templates include five main areas: a graphical banner identifying the ePortfolio as a DePauw ITAP ePortfolio; a header with the student's name; a navigation bar; a main content area; and a footer that includes the student's URL, e-mail address, the date the page was last updated, and again the navigation links. The only area identified in the template file as editable is the main content area, since this is the only section which should vary from page to page. This approach promotes consistency across pages contained within each student's ePortfolio. Other areas students change that should remain consistent across all pages, such as the name in the header, are included as Dreamweaver library items, thus enabling students to personalize the ePortfolio content without the need to actually make any changes to the template itself. See Figure 1 for an example of the ePortfolio templates.

SUPPORT FOR ITAP ePORTFOLIOS

ITAP interns generate their ePortfolios as freshmen and continue to update them throughout their college careers. Entering ITAP students are introduced to the concept of ePortfolios shortly after arrival on campus during the ITAP Institute, an intensive week-long workshop conducted for first-year ITAP students the week before classes begin. The Institute provides an environment in which ITAP students receive instruction on technical skills as well as soft skills, such as customer service and project management. During this week, the students first begin to contemplate their ePortfolios, learning what an ePortfolio is, why it is beneficial, along with details about program requirements. They receive technical training in Macromedia Dreamweaver and Fireworks for creating and maintaining their ePortfolios, they are taught best practices for collecting artifacts as they progress through their first year in the program, and they are encouraged to begin writing reflectively about their experiences. The introductory workshop prepares beginning students to collect artifacts and content during the semester prior to the guided development phase.

The bulk of the interns' work on their initial ePortfolios occurs during the winter term of their freshman year. During this month, they participate in a four-part workshop series to guide them through the processes of organizing, designing, and creating their ePortfolios. All freshman ITAP students are required to attend these workshops, and they are awarded academic credit for doing so. As further incentive and in keeping with ITAP policy, interns are paid for time spent on their ePortfolios outside the workshops.

The first workshop in this series encourages students to plan what they will include in their ePortfolios. During this meeting, they meet their mentor and participate in small group discussions about the importance and potential uses of their ePortfolios during their college years. During the second workshop, the students learn the fundamentals of good Web design. They are provided with the ePortfolio templates and are given an introductory-level Dreamweaver workshop covering the use of templates so they can begin to create their own sites. The third workshop covers more advanced Web authoring techniques and the Web site publishing process. Finally, the fourth workshop consists of team presentations, during which each ePortfolio team showcases examples of their ePortfolios and discusses the challenges and successes they faced during development.

After the initial workshops, the students are expected to continue maintaining their ePortfolios. During the spring, individual ITAP hosts assist the freshman interns with collecting and including artifacts in their ePortfolios. In addition, advanced workshops are available for sophomores, juniors, and seniors to review technical skills for maintenance and learn how ePortfolios should evolve as one's skills mature.

EXAMPLES OF ITAP ePORTFOLIOS

The following figures exhibit features of ITAP ePortfolios. Figure 1 is one of the two templates that the students can use to begin production of their ePortfolio. This template includes the key elements discussed in the "ITAP ePortfolio Tool" section.

Figure 1.

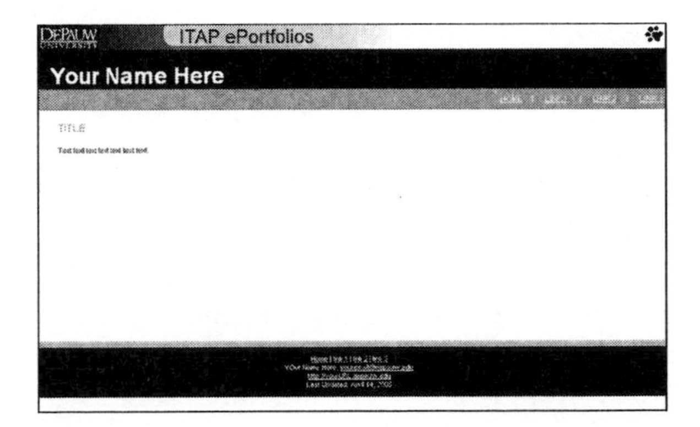

Figure 2.

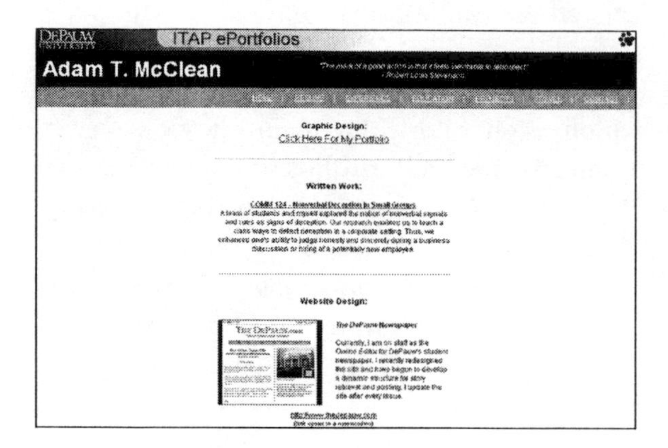

Figure 3.

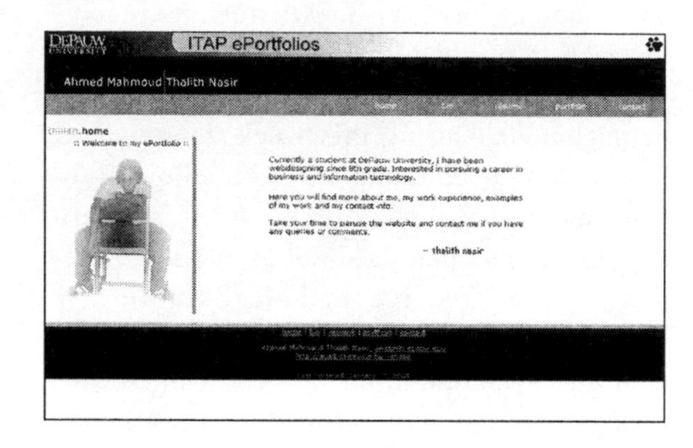

Figure 2 illustrates a common layout scheme chosen by ITAP students. In this case, the student lists examples of his or her work, with links to pages within his or her ePortfolio that provide more details on each project.

Figure 3 is an example of a customized ePortfolio. In this case, the student included a personal photograph along with an introduction to his or her ePortfolio.

Figures 2 and 3 demonstrate how ITAP students can make their own design decisions while maintaining the branding and professional qualities of the supplied ePortfolio templates. We designed the templates using gray and black tones so the standardized elements of the ePortfolios would be less intrusive to the students' colors and artifacts presented in the content areas. They were also kept simple to focus viewers' attention on content.

APPLICATION OF ITAP ePORTFOLIOS

Although there are currently no formal ITAP ePortfolio maintenance requirements, we monitor them periodically to determine how many are actively updated. During the Spring 2005 hiring process, we surveyed interns and on-campus ITAP employers to learn how ePortfolios have changed the way students apply and interview for jobs, and to measure the use of ePortfolios in that process. Eleven of the 40 internship hosts representing a broad range of areas on campus, and almost half (67 of 146) of all ITAP students, responded.

The results of the surveys show that both the students and internship hosts have found the ePortfolios to be a valuable resource. Of the 11 responding hosts, eight reported that at least one of the applicants provided a link to his or her ePortfolio, and nine hosts reported that applicants provided a résumé when applying for the internship. Of the eight hosts who reported that their students submitted a link to their ePortfolios, seven revealed visits to the ePortfolio link, indicating that it may prove to be a useful tool for hiring decisions.

Responses from the students survey yielded similar results on the usage of résumés and ePortfolios. Seventy-five percent (75%) of the student respondents provided a copy of their résumés when applying for on-campus internships. Of the students who maintained an ePortfolio, 47% provided a link to it during their internship search. Further data from the participating students in the ePortfolio co-curricular series is promising for the sustainability of the program. Sixty-six percent (66%) of students indicated that their ePortfolio helped them prepare for the internship search. Additionally, 59% of students agree that they will continue to update their ePortfolio regardless of program requirements. We anticipate that this will benefit students as they apply for off-campus internships and post-graduate employment.

EVOLUTION OF ITAP ePORTFOLIO PROGRAM

In addition to evaluations focused on the manner in which interns maintain and use their ePortfolios, we assess the students' experiences in the creation process and the functionality of the ePortfolios by examining their reactions to the project, evidence of their learning, changes in their behavior, and the overall results of the project. Results of these evaluations drive the planning of future ePortfolio support processes. Some significant changes we made between the first and second years of the curriculum include a new evaluation process, adjustments to the format of the required winter term workshops, and increased technical support.

After the first year, mentors indicated that the evaluation process for rating the quality of the students' work was cumbersome and time consuming. Each ePortfolio was rated by two mentors using four categories: content, organization, design and presentation, and technical accuracy. Because each category contained several associated statements that were rated using a Likert scale, mentors found they needed approximately one hour to evaluate each ePortfolio. This was problematic, since each mentor was volunteering his or her time and each had at least seven ePortfolios to review. Further, inter-rater reliability using this tool was poor, as different mentors had differing opinions on what was average, the basis for the scale used.

To resolve both the time issue and the reliability issue, during the second year we employed a new evaluation tool that uses a rubric with clear guidelines for unacceptable, acceptable, and exceptional ePortfolios in five categories: general content, artifacts and reflection, organization, design and presentation, and technical accuracy. This new tool enables mentors to rate overall quality in key areas rather than a comprehensive series of quality indicators.

After the first year, students indicated a low satisfaction level due to the lack of a conclusion to the project. In the second year, to increase the relevance of the project, we modified the last structured session during the winter term to include time for students to present their final ePortfolios to the rest of the group and discuss their learning experiences.

Finally, although an optional open lab time was offered during the first year, students did not attend sessions that were not mandatory even when they needed more technical support. For example, many students from the first year did not publish their ePortfolios to the Web, and we determined this was likely due to the fact that, while we distributed printed instructions, we did not directly address the topic in a session. In the second year we included open lab time as part of the required sessions, encouraging students to work on the ePortfolios with just-in-time help available to answer technical and conceptual questions. This time also enabled us to help students publish their ePortfolios to the Web. Having a "live" ePortfolio increased the perceived usefulness of the tool for the second group.

CONCLUSION

Because the ITAP ePortfolio program is in its early stages, a complete "bottom line" evaluation of the process is not yet practical. To that end, we are designing methods to track interns' use of ePortfolios through graduation and into the early years of their careers. The results of these evaluations will provide an accurate measurement of the success of the program.

REFERENCE

Achrazoglou, J., Anthony, R., Jun, M., Marshall, J., & Roe, G. (2002). *Performance assessment in teacher education: The Iowa ePortfolio model.* Unpublished white paper, University of Iowa, USA.

KEY TERMS

Career: A chosen pursuit; a profession or occupation. Or, the general course or progression of one's working life or one's professional achievements: *an officer with a distinguished career; a teacher in the midst of a long career.*

ePortfolio: A portfolio based on electronic media and services. It consists of a personal digital record containing information such as a personal profile and a collection of achievements.

Information Technology: The development, installation, and implementation of computer systems and applications.

Internship: A student or a recent graduate undergoing supervised practical training.

Reflection: Mental concentration; careful consideration.

Template: A document or file having a preset format, used as a starting point for a particular application so that the format does not have to be recreated each time it is used.

Web Design: The design or designing of a Web page, Web site, or Web application. The term generally refers to the graphical side of Web development using images, CSS, and XHTML.

Chapter XLVIII
Implementing an Outcome-Based Assessment ePortfolio

Matthew Wagner
Buena Vista University, USA

Elizabeth Lamoureux
Buena Vista University, USA

ABSTRACT

This case study examines the introduction of an ePortfolio requirement as a means of assessing student learning and program effectiveness. The Communication and Performance Studies major at Buena Vista University in Storm Lake, Iowa, began piloting the use of an assessment ePortfolio in the spring of 2003 and has since fully implemented it as a program requirement. Although the potential of ePortfolios is still being realized, research suggests the benefit of involving students in program assessment. Case studies are helpful to further define and articulate the emerging literature on assessment ePortfolios. Using qualitative research methods, strengths and weaknesses of this ePortfolio implementation are identified, and areas of improvement are discussed.

INTRODUCTION

The use of portfolios in education is not a new concept. Portfolios have been popular as a showcase tool in programs such as art, graphic design, business, and communication, and as a certification tool in education. An emerging trend is the adoption of electronic portfolios by individuals, academic programs, and institutions. Advances in technology and evolving network capabilities, as well as a maturing understanding of the uses and capabilities of electronic portfolios (ePortfolios), are allowing educators to reevaluate how student learning can be assessed (ePortConsortium, 2003).

Assessment of the Communication and Performance Studies (CPER) program was the catalyst for the in-house development of an electronic portfolio tool named FOCUS. To implement a more systematic approach to assessment, CPER faculty at Buena Vista University (BVU) began piloting an ePortfolio at the program level in the spring of 2003. Since then, the ePortfolio has been fully implemented as a requirement for CPER majors. In the 2003/2004 school year, six students from the graduating class used the ePortfolio with a total of 42 artifacts uploaded. Since full implementation in 2004/2005, 18 of the 56 majors started or completed their ePortfolios with a total of 170 artifacts.

In addition to assisting with assessment efforts, ePortfolios may be implemented for a variety of reasons, such as personal or professional portfolios. BVU's ePortfolio tool, FOCUS, was developed as a means of actively involving students in the learning process. FOCUS was designed to allow students to associate their artifacts with the core outcomes of the major. As a result, FOCUS may be considered a "structured ePortfolio" since it clearly defines learning outcomes for the students and facilitates more efficient evaluation (Greenberg, 2004). The benefits of this approach are the systematic collection of authentic artifacts coupled with students' thoughtful written reflections.

This approach allows the CPER faculty to examine the program collectively to gain a greater understanding of the overall quality of student work. Electronic portfolios give CPER faculty insight into the program, whereby they can make changes or improvements to existing practices. Since the implementation of an ePortfolio requirement is fairly new, this is an opportune time to investigate the perceptions of the involved faculty. Additionally, since the successes of ePortfolios are tied directly to the efforts of those creating portfolios, perceptions of students must also be considered. A case study approach has been selected to examine the implementation of a structured assessment ePortfolio from both a program and student perspective. By identifying issues from a technological and implementation standpoint, this exploratory study seeks to facilitate improvement of the ePortfolio process, as well as address its subsequent impact on program assessment.

LITERATURE REVIEW

ePortfolios are causing much excitement among administrators, faculty members, and instructional technologists because of their enabling potential for students to connect their assignments, presentations, activities, and other educational endeavors to generate a "big picture" of their experience (Young, 2002). King (1999) likens the college experience for students to putting together a jigsaw puzzle without being able to see the picture on the box. King (1999) also suggests that "students get more out of college when the collegiate purposes are clear and consistently communicated" and "show them a picture of the kind of person we hope to help them become" (p. 2). A structured assessment portfolio that asks students to identify with program or institutional outcomes communicates those intended outcomes in a consistent manner, and provides students and faculty with the framework needed to begin completing the puzzle.

ePortfolio Research

Currently ePortfolios are at a similar stage as the course management system (CMS) of the late 1990s (ePortConsortium, 2003). Similar to the CMS, a great deal of buzz surrounds the implementation of ePortfolios—the true potential and benefits have yet to be discovered. The ePortConsortium (2003) also suggests that until ePortfolios can "demonstrate their effectiveness, ease-of-use, and transparent integration, they will not reach the level of acceptance that the CMS has received in the past few years" (p. 9). For this reason, ongoing evaluation and discussion are important to facilitate the growth and development of ePortfolio software. Equally important is the consideration of how the software is implemented. Ehrmann (2005) suggests that ePortfolio software alone will not lead to any "magical" improvements in education; instead, the measure of success will be if faculty and students can use ePortfolios to improve teaching and learning (para. 3).

Although hard-copy portfolios have been used for many of the same functions as ePortfolios, the digital nature of ePortfolios allows some advantages and flexibility over their paper-based counterparts. Electronic portfolios facilitate reflection, support rubric-based outcomes assessment, organize artifacts, and increase student involvement in assessment (Batson, n.d.). Electronic portfolios also allow for a more comprehensive view into a student's academic career. According to the ePortConsortium White Paper (2003), ePortfolios "more effectively provide both an authentic assessment of learning as well as significantly more information about the learning experience. The aim of the ePortfolio is to present and document the work and the process that the student and the faculty member have used to get to a certain point" (p. 22). From an assessment standpoint, ePortfolios can be instrumental for academic and program reform (Ehrmann, 2004). Similar to the early iterations of course management systems, several challenges are associated with ePortfolios; those challenges must be addressed to promote sustained adoption or to become "sticky" (Jafari, 2004). One of the challenges surrounding the use of ePortfolios is their lack of a clear definition, which is evidenced by their many potential uses (ePortConsortium, 2003). For example, administration, deans, and faculty see the potential as an efficient tool for student assessment, while students may be more interested in showcasing their best work to potential employers (Jafari, 2004). Consequently, students may be confused by the ill-defined nature surrounding the ePortfolio, which could impact adoption (Jafari, 2004). Because of the student-centric nature of ePortfolios, it is important to carefully articulate the specific expectations to encourage student adoption or buy-in.

Assessment ePortfolios provide the CPER faculty a means of student assessment based specifically on program outcomes. The development of the CPER student ePortfolio is somewhat structured, as the categories and outcomes are pre-defined by the academic program. While the challenges of implementing an ePortfolio system may seem daunting, the NLII recommends that instead of waiting to develop the best possible ePortfolio tool, schools should jump in and be reactive in the development and improvement of the process (NLII, 2003). For this approach to be successful, ongoing evaluation of the ePortfolio implementation is paramount.

One method for CPER to systematically evaluate the ePortfolio process is through formative evaluation, which seems particularly appropriate for this case study since the research is limited in context and designed to improve a specific program by focusing on the strengths and weaknesses therein (Patton, 1990). Moreover, formative evaluation does not seek to generalize beyond the specific case being studied; rather, it is assumed that "people can and will use information to improve what they're doing" (Patton, 1990, p. 161).

While a considerable body of literature details the merits and implementation of ePortfolios, research designed to elicit feedback from the primary constituents, students, and faculty is limited. With this in mind, this case study focuses directly on the perspectives of the primary participants. Maintaining the philosophy of formative assessment, participants' perceptions of strengths and weaknesses, as well as the implementation process, are considered.

- **R1:** What are the strengths and weaknesses of the assessment ePortfolio?
- **R2:** How can the implementation of the ePortfolio be improved?

IMPLEMENTATION OVERVIEW

For the purposes of this case study, CPER's ePortfolio software, FOCUS, is defined as a student-controlled Web application that is database driven and contains administrative tools for managing and organizing the presentation of digital artifacts (Batson, n.d.). Similarly, an artifact is any digital file or application (Word documents, PowerPoint presentations, multimedia files) created by the student which can be uploaded into the ePortfolio system. To clarify, these collections of artifacts, coupled with descriptions, reflections, and associated outcomes, create the overall "product" or ePortfolio. Whereas FOCUS is the software used to facilitate creation of the product, an ePortfolio is the product itself.

Project Origins

With nationwide attention focused on greater adherence to accreditation standards, BVU, like many other educational institutions, took a closer look at how it measured student progress and program effectiveness. Because the trend in higher education assessment is moving towards student-centered, Web-based evaluation, the CPER faculty decided to explore technological options for assessment. As a result, they collaborated with in-house technology support to discuss assessment possibilities, and they ultimately designed the FOCUS program. To ensure student commitment with this new, systematic ePortfolio assessment process, faculty discussed how best to introduce the program and monitor student compliance. They then determined the students would be introduced to the program at an annual meeting for all majors, and the actual ePortfolio requirement would be "housed" in the senior capstone course.

In an effort to make the assessment process more intentional and encourage greater ownership of student learning, the ePortfolio became an efficient way of introducing students to the CPER program outcomes. The seven CPER program outcomes are listed below for review:

1. Craft and use effective messages to achieve goals relevant to specific communication contexts and audiences.
2. Critically analyze public and personal communication.
3. Display sensitivity to gender, ethnic, and other cultural factors within all aspects of the process of communication.
4. Work productively with groups of people in a variety of settings.
5. Apply communication theories to current issues and situations.
6. Collect, evaluate, and employ communication research.
7. Demonstrate an understanding of the complexity of the human communication process.

Introducing the ePortfolio

As stated above, all CPER majors were invited and encouraged to attend a 30-minute meeting where the ePortfolio process was unveiled. Students were asked to bring their laptops in order to access the software as it was being discussed. The dean, the director of the Teaching and Learning Center (TLTC), and a representative faculty member led the meeting, where the purpose behind the program was explained and the importance of student commitment to the process was articulated. Students were introduced to the importance of program assessment, including reference to the CPER program outcomes. The message was framed so that students might see the potential advantage to their own learning. Students were given the opportunity to ask questions and to try uploading artifacts on the spot.

The ePortfolio Program (FOCUS)

Because an ePortfolio is designed to bring a student's academic career to greater clarity, BVU's ePortfolio software was named FOCUS. Although the need of the CPER major was the catalyst for development of this ePortfolio tool, FOCUS was designed to integrate with BVU's existing infrastructure, so ePortfolios could easily be adopted by all academic programs. Additionally, an ePortfolio configuration interface was designed so the technological requirements to implement an ePortfolio only take minutes (see Figure 1). In the configuration stage, faculty can create a customizable welcome message and mission statement detailing the purpose of the ePortfolio. At this time, faculty create the specific categories and descriptions to organize student artifacts, as well as input the learning outcomes. Since FOCUS is tied directly to the student management database, for those who have access, to create ePortfolios is automatic.

Figure 1. Focus configuration screen

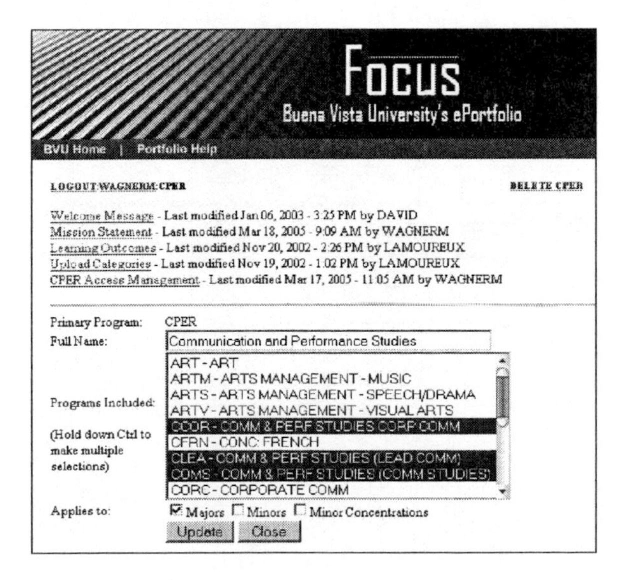

The first time students access the ePortfolio Web site, they are presented with a consistent and concise message about the importance of programmatic assessment, their role in the process, and how to proceed to upload representative artifacts and prepare meaningful reflections. In addition to the welcome message, the program mission statement and learning outcomes are presented. These introductory documents are designed to help positively frame the ePortfolio and encourage its use. After reviewing the preliminary information, students may begin uploading artifacts using a simple Web-based interface (described in further detail).

Students and faculty have two views to choose from when looking at the ePortfolios, by outcome or by category (see Figures 2 and 3). As mentioned earlier, each program at BVU has identified a core group of learning outcomes that are central to the curriculum. When students upload files to FOCUS, they choose which outcomes the assignment achieved. The power of this approach is that students are actively involved in the assessment process. To allow faculty to specify to some degree the types of assignments uploaded into the portfolio, categories were created (i.e., Creative Works, Internships, etc.). For example, setting

Figure 2. "View By Category" screen

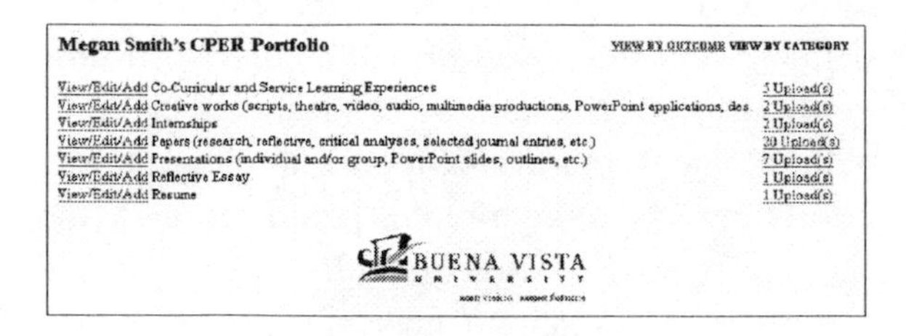

up a category for presentations will guide students as to the types of artifacts expected.

The view of student ePortfolios for students and faculty is almost identical, except on the "View By Category" screen: students have the option to view, edit, or add, while faculty have only the option to view. Students and faculty can choose to view the details of an artifact, including assignment descriptions or the original assignment file, the targeted outcomes, and additional comments or reflections by the student. The details can be accessed by clicking on the "Details" link (see Figure 3) for a specific artifact, which opens the details page (see Figure 4). Similarly, students and faculty may also choose to view the actual artifact or digital file by clicking on the link to that file (also shown in Figure 3). Students have the added capability to archive their ePortfolios to save either locally or reuse for other purposes. To keep record of previous student work, faculty

Figure 4. "Details" screen

Artifact #1 - View Edit Delete

Assignment Details - View
Our whole PR Campaigns class involves a semester long project of handling the PR aspects of a campaign for an acutal client. Our client was the Witter Gallery and we had to handle the public relations aspect of their Da Vinci Caper show for their big fundraiser. It was a success! I have attached the plans book below and the artifact is the initial Power Point we presented to our client and the class.

Student's Comments
This assignment was a good experience for me because I can refer back to it many times during my internship this summer. My campaign group did a lot of initial research on the Witter Gallery, events like the fundraiser we were planning on, and the target audience before we started planning the event. We came up with a survey which we sent to opinion leaders and people with this type of experience. We needed to make sure the invitations and announcements reached our target audience and that we were effective in our messages. This was our plan at midterm and I will post our final evaluation when we are done!

Outcomes Targeted

- Apply communication theories to current issues and situations
- Craft and use effective messages to achieve goals relevant to specific communication contexts and audiences.
- Critically analyze public and personal communication
- Recognize, evaluate and conduct communication research
- Work productively with groups of people in a variety of settings

Figure 3. "View By Outcome" screen

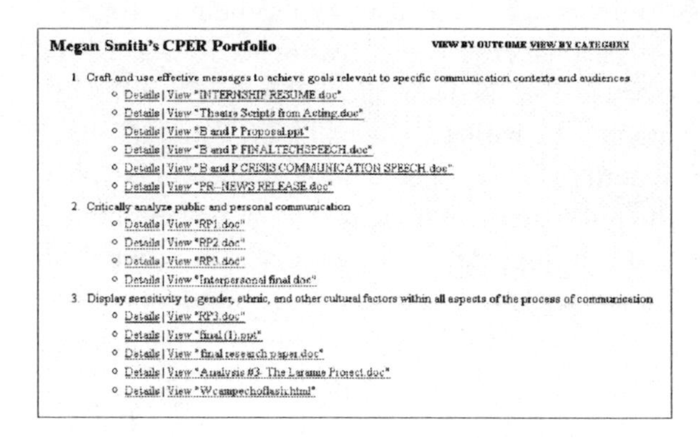

also have the ability to archive multiple student ePortfolios.

To upload an artifact, students choose the most appropriate category and click the "View/Edit/Add" link (see Figure 2). Next they use a simple Web-based interface to upload files into FOCUS and add assignment details or upload the original assignment file (see Figure 5). This process is very similar to creating a Web-based e-mail. At this time, students also select the relevant learning outcomes and add comments or reflections explaining why the item was added and justifying the outcomes chosen. Essentially, students can upload any file in digital

Figure 5. Upload interface

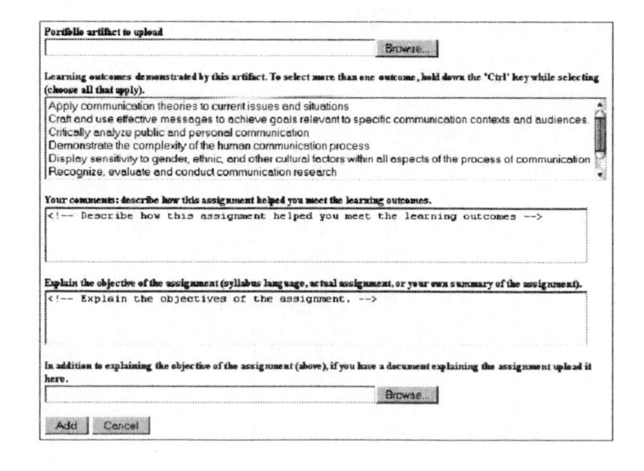

Figure 6. Student list

May 2005

F, Katherine - 8 upload(s) MRKT CCOR
G, Kyle - 7 upload(s) CLEA PHIL EXSC
H, Danielle - 12 upload(s) CCOR WMST
H, Jaclyn - 10 upload(s) SPAN CLEA
K, Courtney MSCM CCOR
K, Sarah - 6 upload(s) CLEA MSCM
L, Tracy - 9 upload(s) MRKT CCOR
M, Laurence CPET MSCM
N, Jenny - 9 upload(s) CCOR ART
S, Sarah - 10 upload(s) CLEA PSYC MUSC
Z, Rebecca - 4 upload(s) CLEA GERN BUSN
Z, Aaron - 9 upload(s) CCOR MGMT

December 2005

D, Jennifer - 13 upload(s) MRKT CCOR
N, Craig - 6 upload(s) CLEA PSCN
S, Jennifer - 12 upload(s) MGMT COMS

format. Additionally the students can either upload the original assignment from the instructor (if available) or describe the assignment to help put the artifact in context for faculty assessment.

The benefit of this process is, it allows students to create an assessment ePortfolio regardless of their technological skills. Students can create and modify their ePortfolios beginning their first year, and faculty members can easily monitor student progress. Faculty can track the types and number of artifacts posted by accessing the "view only" version of student ePortfolios. When faculty access FOCUS, they are presented with a list of all students in their program organized by expected date of graduation. At a glance, they can also see how many artifacts a student has uploaded without having to access that student's ePortfolio (see Figure 6). FOCUS is a closed system, which means only an individual student and the program faculty have access.

CPER's Assessment Process

The final step of the assessment process involves the CPER faculty gathering to systematically assess student work. As is common practice, two to four outcomes are chosen for annual review. A detailed rubric, developed by the CPER faculty, is used to evaluate student artifacts on a four-point scale (Exemplary, Proficient, Marginal, Unsatisfactory). To ensure consistency in assessment, inter-rater reliability is tested. Using a random sample, faculty individually review the artifacts, assessing each based on the selected outcomes. As is sometimes the case, some artifacts are discarded and replaced if they are not appropriate to the outcomes being assessed. After all ratings are recorded, the faculty discuss the results and look for consistent themes that emerge throughout the evaluation process. Based on the evaluation of student work, faculty members draw conclusions about the effectiveness of, or problems with, course design, inclusion, and sequencing. Student skill level, both foundational and those unique to the major, are carefully reviewed. Faculty also ascertain the level of student awareness, recognition, and achievement of program outcomes. This assessment data provides the evidence needed to enhance the quality of the program.

Over time, this dynamic assessment process has also yielded useful feedback related to the implementation of the ePortfolio. More specifically, after the first assessment, the faculty determined the rubric used to assess the artifacts needed to be refined. They also discovered the difficulty in assessing student work without having access to the representative assignment. It has also become apparent that some assignments lend themselves to the assessment process better than others and that some students do not fully understand the learning outcomes and may, in fact, claim to have achieved outcomes that, based on the posted artifact, are not recognizable. Moreover, while students are currently encouraged to begin uploading to their ePortfolio early, the fact that many seem to "wait until the end" has also been addressed. Based on these findings and more, a number of constructive recommendations have been made to enhance the quality of the overall assessment process.

METHODS

To answer the research questions and because this case study was designed to be formative, two methods were utilized—focus groups and a follow-up survey. Patton (1990) explains: "Formative evaluations rely heavily on process studies, implementation evaluations, case studies, and evaluability assessments. Formative evaluations often rely heavily, even primarily, on qualitative methods" (p. 156). Moreover, data generated from focus groups tend to be richer, deeper, and qualitatively different than those supplied by more traditional methods. Focus groups provide the opportunity to observe a significant amount of interaction on a topic in a limited period of time (Morgan, 1988). Despite the primary advantages of focus groups, they are not without limitations. For example, Morgan (1988) explains that the topic may fail to interest some while others may be uninformed. Recruitment of participants is another potential concern. While it may be ideal to have a heterogeneous group, for instance, depending on the constraints of the time, place, or situation, the pool of potential participants may be limited.

Participants

Two focus groups were conducted, one targeting students and one targeting faculty. Six CPER students and five CPER faculty participated in the focus groups led by a trained facilitator. Focus group participants initially completed a brief questionnaire related to their perceptions of the ePortfolio process and implementation. Both a tape recorder and written notes taken by the moderator and assistant moderator were utilized to preserve the accuracy of the group conversations. Based on focus group findings, and because of the small sample size, an electronic follow-up survey was deployed to all CPER majors to gain a better understanding of preconceived notions regardless of students' prior experience with ePortfolios.

RESULTS AND DISCUSSION

Because the ePortfolio requirement is fairly new for CPER, this study uses qualitative means to identify strengths and weaknesses as well as areas for improvement. Because of the malleable definition of ePortfolios, it is important to understand the preconceived notions of both students and faculty before completing a formative assessment. The primary method of gathering this data was an electronic survey. Of the 55 students surveyed, 28 students (51%) responded. When asked about the purpose of the ePortfolio, a common theme emerged. Students seemed to recognize the ePortfolio as a process to help faculty monitor student progress toward meeting outcomes or to assess the quality of the program itself. For example, one student responded, "It is an assessment for the school of communication to evaluate if they are reaching the objectives outlined for the major." Another student responded that the purpose was to assess the program and "learn about improvements they need to make or things they need to change." This was not unexpected considering the manner in which the ePortfolio requirement was introduced to the students.

Despite the students' recognition that the ePortfolio is designed for program assessment, 68% of the respondents viewed this requirement as beneficial to both the faculty and students, while 18% saw the ePortfolio as something that would be beneficial only to faculty and 14% were uncertain. Even though students may see the inherent benefit to themselves, only 25% claim to "look forward to" creating their ePortfolios. Thirty-two percent are not looking forward to the process, while the remaining 43% are neutral. Since the success of this implementation is directly tied to the intentionality and thoughtfulness of the students, it is important to consider ways to increase student motivation and commitment. Based on the data, faculty and students seem to have different ideas of what is important. For example, students appear to be primarily interested in how ePortfolios can help with career aspirations, while faculty seem more interested in how they can improve the assessment process. For an implementation to truly be successful, all participants must see its potential value.

Focus Group Results

One goal of this case study was to identify strengths and weaknesses of the newly implemented assessment ePortfolio. The other goal of this formative review was to recognize areas for improvement in the implementation process. In order to investigate these research questions, respondents were first asked to articulate their understanding of the purpose behind the ePortfolio.

Purpose of the ePortfolio Process: When asked about the purpose, the faculty were fairly consistent in their comprehension of both the purpose and procedures involved. "I think it makes us more intentional in our assessment because we now have clearly defined outcomes and a carefully crafted rubric on which to base our evaluation," commented one participant. "We are certainly more systematic than we've ever been before," another confirmed. The students seemed to echo this understanding of the purpose. For example, one responded, "Going to the meetings, I saw it for the CPER program. It was very much promoted as 'this is going to help our school'. That's okay, but we always like to know what's in it for us."

Benefit to the Students: The faculty participants again were consistent in their perceptions of benefits. "I think the lights are starting to go on in the students' minds," said one, "I think they're starting to recognize the potential power of this tool as a culmination of their undergraduate experience." Another faculty member concurred that especially seniors get "...a sense of wow, look at all I've accomplished!" One student mirrored this sentiment, "It's been beneficial to me because I've found myself saying, 'Wow! I really did learn.' It's also a way for faculty to check and say, 'this works, or oh, this doesn't work.' I like the perspective of this as a work in progress. Students working with faculty on making the program better."

Perhaps more importantly, the process of creating an ePortfolio introduces and reinforces the criterion on which students are evaluated. One faculty member commented, "The students are also catching on that we really have outcomes, although I don't think they fully understand the concept yet, but at least I think they're starting to see that if we all reference this ePortfolio in our classes, they are starting to think, oh, this [assessment] must be something important." Students seemed to agree that it was during the demonstration of the ePortfolio that they were first introduced to CPER's learning outcomes. One student also noted that it should be specifically helpful to faculty since they can be reminded of what is most important for student achievement.

Benefit to the Program: As a result of assessing ePortfolios, actual courses have been added, revised, or reordered based on the systematic review process. One student commented, "I see program changes as a reward. I'm only a sophomore and will reap the benefit from the revisions in the program." Another student added, "This is sure much better than taking a standardized test." The faculty were most enthusiastic with their responses. For example, they unanimously viewed the ePortfolio as a valuable tool since it provides a more sophisticated understanding of students' academic growth and achievement across the curriculum. One faculty member stated, "Not only do I get a better sense of the breadth of student work, but it is fascinating to me to read other assignments in other courses." Another faculty member shared, "I know that I have valued from this assessment process because it has forced me to revisit the learning outcomes in my own individual classes." Yet another responded, "One of the greatest benefits I see, is the dialogue that we share, the coming together as faculty to talk about our program and how to make it better. Let's face it, as busy as we are, we just don't make time for it otherwise. I think this synergistic process is a wonderful way to help build collegiality." "Right," another confirmed, "We don't do enough of this."

Limitations of the CPER ePortfolio: While the merits of the ePortfolio process can be justified, there are also concerns that must be considered. For example, while most students understood the intended purpose, some were under the impression the ePortfolio served a professional purpose. The CPER faculty are aware of this confusion; one commented, "I think some of them see the ePortfolio as a tool for the job search." "Yeah, some do," another agreed. This confusion may affect adoption.

The issue of motivation—for example, how to encourage student use and commitment—was also addressed. One faculty member stated, "It's almost as if they're saying, 'What's in this for me?' Are we doing a good enough job of explaining the purpose so that they don't need anything more?" "Yeah, what's the carrot?" another asked and continued, "How do we get them to take responsibility for their own learning?" "You hate to say this, but students like to see rewards," said one student. "We know it will help the program, but what's in it for us?" The focus group students, as well as many survey respondents, shared interest in increasing the functionality of the ePortfolio to serve an additional purpose as a professional portfolio. This would involve adding the capability to select certain artifacts that could also be showcased publicly to potential employers. As a direct result of this student feedback, developing this functionality is under consideration. This approach has the potential to enhance student motivation immeasurably as well as make the program more "sticky" (Jafari, 2004).

Students also expressed concern over the time involved. "Many see it as something extra that takes time they don't have," said one. Much of this concern centers on the time investment from students to create thoughtful reflections of their artifacts. Some students, for example, perceived the reflections as "busy work" causing some resistance and lack of follow-through. One faculty member counters this idea: "I think as long as the students are aware that their feedback is super-important to the process, this should motivate some to carefully consider the potential power they have for improving the program." This suggests the value of a proper introduction and appropriate framing during the early stages of implementation.

CONCLUSION

The use of an assessment ePortfolio for the CPER program at Buena Vista University has been a dynamic process that has unfolded over time and has been a product of collaborative efforts of faculty, students, and technology support. Although the technology is still evolving, the benefits are already being realized at the program level. As King (1999) suggests, authentic assessment defined by outcomes provides the necessary framework for students to piece together their academic "puzzle." The ePortfolio, in turn, has allowed the CPER faculty to effectively and efficiently utilize the assessment data for program reform. One faculty member said it best: "Assessment is only useful if you're using it!"

REFERENCES

Batson, T. (n.d.). *E-portfolios—bridging the gap left by CMS.* Retrieved February 17, 2005, from http://www.campus-technology.com/print.asp?ID=8669

Ehrmann, S. C. (2004, June 30). *List of activities that electronic portfolios are intended to support (in no particular order).* Retrieved April 8, 2005, from http://www.tltgroup.org/FL-subscribers/FL_Handbook/ePort_Attach.htm

Ehrmann, S.C. (2005, March 23). *Electronic portfolio initiatives: Notes on planning and formative evaluation.* Retrieved April 8, 2005, from http://www.tltgroup.org/FL-subscribers/FL_Handbook/ePort_Strat.htm

ePortConsortium. (2003, November 3). *Electronic portfolio white paper: Version 1.0.* Retrieved April 8, 2005, from http://eportconsortium.org/Content/Root/whitePaper.aspx

Greenberg, G. (2004, July-August). The digital convergence: Extending the portfolio model. *Educause Review,* 28-36.

Jafari, A. (2004, July-August). The "sticky" e-portfolio system: Tackling challenges and identifying attributes. *Educause Review,* 38-48.

King, P. M. (1999, March-April). Putting together the puzzle of student learning. *About Campus,* 2-4.

Morgan, D. L. (1988). *Focus groups as qualitative research.* Newbury Park, CA: Sage.

NLII Annual Review: The New Academy. (2003). *The digital me: Standards, interoperability and a common vocabulary spell progress for e-portfolios.* Retrieved April 8, 2005, from http://www.educause.edu/ir/library/html/nlii_ar_2003/digitalme.asp

Patton, M. Q. (1990). *Qualitative evaluation and research methods.* Newbury Park, CA: Sage.

Young, J. R. (2002). Creating online portfolios can help students see 'big picture,' colleges say. *The Chronicle of Higher Education,* (February 21). Retrieved May 12, 2005, from http://chronicle.com/free/2002/02/2002022101t.htm

KEY TERMS

Artifact: Any digital file or application (Word document, PowerPoint presentation, multimedia file) created by the student which can be uploaded into an ePortfolio system

Assessment ePortfolio: A structured, Web-based portfolio designed to facilitate student and academic program evaluation by matching artifacts to appropriate and clearly defined learning outcomes.

Authentic Assessment: Evaluation of student progress based on multiple performance factors. Portfolios are a means of authentic assessment as an organization of student work demonstrating skills and progress over time.

FOCUS: An electronic portfolio (ePortfolio) system developed at Buena Vista University which gives students Web-based control to manage their artifacts and match them to specific learning outcomes.

Formative Evaluation: A continual process for determining the effectiveness of a project with the goal of ongoing improvement and enhancement.

Learning Outcomes: Statements of what students should achieve as part of a program of study.

Chapter XLIX
Future-Focused ePortfolios at Montana State University-Northern

Jonathon J. Richter
Montana State University-Northern, USA

ABSTRACT

This chapter introduces the idea of using electronic portfolios for enhancing the future thinking of an organization's learners. At Montana State University–Northern, faculty are using ePortfolios to elicit deep learning by encouraging students to reflect on their work in terms of what is possible, what is probable, and what is preferable in their professional lives as educators. By detailing the context that MSU-Northern's ePortfolio system entails, this chapter may assist practitioners to glean some of the advantages of and the factors for getting students to think systematically about the future using electronic portfolios, and researchers to address relevant issues surrounding the application of future-focused ePortfolios.

INTRODUCTION

... Wherein while creating a portfolio system within Teacher Candidate and Graduate Education programs at Montana State University, faculty members employ the sight of three guides: the mouse, the eagle, and the spider.

Developing an electronic portfolio system that is right for your institution as well as for the professional and personal needs of your students is both a challenging and rewarding process. Making clear to all stakeholders the purpose and audience of the portfolio is essential to highlight, as there are multiple possibilities for the "what's," "why's," and "who's" of your efforts. For example, portfolios designed for the purposes of demonstrating professional competencies are likely quite different than those with deep, integrative learning, itself, as the goal. Balancing or creating a transition from one purpose to the other at key points within the student's progress through the program is a laudable, though difficult solution—a design task probably better suited to a beta run, rather than the initial foray into a complicated arena with multiple objectives demanding of many areas of expertise. Even with just a singular purpose, standards-based ePortfolio implementation across a program is undoubtedly one of the more tricky and resource-taxing endeavors in the modern learning enterprise.

Education faculty and administrators at Montana State University–Northern have engaged in persistent, active, and purposeful dialogue on electronic portfolio development on and off for the last five years. Only within the last year have we determined what is believed to be a central tenet, and perhaps a pervasively held lesson in the use of these assessment instruments: juxtaposing the accreditation purposes over the deep learning capacities of the portfolio has a strong, potentially overall chilling effect upon the latter. At MSU–Northern, it has come to the question: which is more important, the learning portfolio or the accreditation portfolio?

At issue here has been the conflation of purposes due to the short period into which faculty have to work with a given student to produce a highly qualified teacher and the weighing of priorities placed upon such a timeframe. In Montana, like many other states without the fortune to have large coffers and progressive legislatures, we have a four-year teacher credentialing program: content and method stuffed into a bachelor's degree designed to meet national- and state-developed teaching standards. Only 128 credit hours to complete the degree ...

Students thus enter into the Department of Education after their first two years of undergraduate study, having taken their general education and prerequisites for the Teacher Candidate program and deciding that this is the career choice for them. Education faculty at MSU–Northern then have two years to impress upon them the methods, practices, and arts of becoming a teacher, just two years within which to construct and implement their electronic portfolios.

The questions then become, do we use this time and effort to create a portfolio for demonstrating our worth in maintaining our hard-won NCATE accreditation? Or should we unlock the power of the learning portfolio and work with our students in a way that does not leave them all too ready to set down the portfolio for the last time on the day they cross the stage, holding the diploma in their hands, and their portfolio "completed and turned in" to a faculty member? How do we empower our new teachers with the vision of learning portfolios, eager to use them as springboards for their own personal and professional lives for years to come? Though these purposes may not be mutually exclusive, the unique combination that would bring students to create, sort, and narratively reflect upon their work in ways that satisfy accreditation needs—while at the same time drawing out the deep, integrative learning potential that ePortfolios possess—is elusive, at best.

One part of the answer to these complex questions may be to focus on the future.

Future Time Perspective

The degree and way in which people integrate their thoughts of the chronological future into their present behavior, a construct known as future time perspective, has been a subject of study for nearly a century. First coined and described by Kurt Lewin, the founder of modern social psychology (1926), statistically significant relationships that correlate to a relatively increased future time perspective have been found with positive health behaviors (Mahon & Yarcheski, 1994; Mahon, Yarcheski,

& Yarcheski, 1997), drug addiction recovery (Henik & Domino, 1975), academic achievement and study habits (Devolder & Lens, 1982), school performance (Murrell & Mingrone, 1994; Nuttin, 1985), life satisfaction among adolescents (Lessing, 1972), non-delinquent behavior (Stein, Sarbin, & Kulik, 1968), and delay in the onset of sexual activity (Rothspan & Read, 1996). It has been argued that having a relatively high future time perspective is tantamount to having a high achievement orientation (Seijts, 1998). Could it be that emphasizing the future, focusing upon it more concertedly in our curricula and institutions, and getting people to actively engage their thoughts more adaptively to the future may improve their individual and our own collective lot? By using the standards as a framework of goals to professionally frame student future-focused behavior, faculty at MSU–Northern believe it is indeed possible to use the ePortfolio system to both deeply engage students in learning and also achieve institutional accreditation. We wish to use educational standards as scaffolding to create compelling visions of the future for our emergent professional educators.

Portfolios as a framework for systematically organizing the performance of an individual over time are, in the estimation of some faculty at MSU–Northern, an ideal vehicle for engaging the student in increasingly future-focused learning and behaving. Especially when constructed for the purposes of encompassing an entire program or even beyond, the portfolio may act as a kind of "historical consciousness" for the learner, effectively engaging him or her in a thread that allows for extension beyond the grade, the term, or the school year, and to see ways in which the work in the past and the present may be harbingers of possible, probable, and preferable futures. Perhaps the most efficacious method for engaging future time perspective through electronic portfolio collaboration is by reflecting on ways in which work achieved may have impact in or on the future. Future-oriented reflection has been referred to as the "highest level of reflection" (Hung, 2004) and is, perhaps, one of the mechanisms by which portfolios may engage the most meaningful sorts of learning.

Reflecting on the Future

Getting students to think about the future is not always easy, however. Perhaps it is due to the preference of many students to focus on the present more than the future. Maybe thinking of the future makes people uneasy or even frightened, or maybe they feel as though casting their minds forward chronologically is not a practical or useful exercise. Perhaps there is something endemic to the schooling experience that suppresses future thinking, or perhaps we have not been using the right methods with our students. In reality, there are probably a lot of individual as well as socio-cultural reasons for the phenomenon in which many of today's people are averse to pondering either the future *or* the past too much, even while a great number of educated and globally aware individuals are alarmed at the prospect of a society that would prefer to stare at the bugs on the windshield than down the road before them. We could, perhaps, intentionally shift this focus in schools, where our learning is intentional and designed.

Wouldn't it be great if we could get students (and teachers) to focus on the relative importance of their learning (and teaching) of any particular subject that goes beyond the test, the grade, and the end of the semester? Wouldn't it be nice if we could reconnect the artificially isolated components of our assembly line curricula to better reflect what occurs in the "real world"? While using purposeful reflection about the personal and technical implications of a learning experience is not a panacea for these systemic problems in education, it may be a start—or as Malcolm Gladwell calls it, a "tipping point" (2000).

At Montana State University–Northern, we first work with our students to "unpack" the standards—deconstructing them into personal key indicators in their own words. This allows them to think about how they can, or could, meet them during their learning, teaching, working, and personal experiences. We then practice identifying the standards that faculty determine the students are meeting in the lessons they are learning: Interstate New Teacher Assessment and Support Consortium (INTASC) Standards for our undergraduate teacher candidates, Montana Office of Public Instruction and program standards for our graduate students, and International Standards for Technology in Education (ISTE NET) Standards for both populations. We work with them by introducing the standards before the lessons, highlight them during the lessons, and encourage them to discuss and write about their experiences after the lessons. We try to practice modeling our own active reflections such that students can better see reflection themselves. As they venture into methods courses and developing their own lessons, we gradually confer more responsibility onto the students to incorporate and interpret these standards themselves. Our intentions are to be continuously working on improving the infusion of appropriate learning experiences surrounding the concept of refection into our teacher candidate curricula. The practices are sometimes agonizingly slow, as students continue to ask for some forms of directed guidance that are not yet in place, faculty members beg for a chance to catch their breath, and the Educational Technology Leadership Team struggles to "build the airplane as we fly it." Remaining steady in our flight, despite apparent design, engineering, or even piloting errors (to stay true to the metaphor), requires that we stay focused on our destination while also paying attention to the navigation controls and indicator panels around us.

It is in the way the reflections within this system are guided and then expected that we elicit "reflections on the future." Our "destination" is not simply to meet accreditation standards with our portfolios, but to use them for teaching and learning about our own futures. Following a model of reflection introduced to us by University of Alaska–Anchorage's Dr. Helen Barrett, Montana State University–Northern uses the "What? So what? Now what?" model. While we have been tinkering with the ways in which we engage in the process of this reflection model, the format has been in use for over five years.

At the beginning of the program, as our students are learning to use program-specific technology and they are being introduced to our program, we focus on the utilitarian, "What?", assisting our students to deconstruct their learning experiences in terms of professional standards and using the stated learning objectives as their guide. For example:

- What have you learned?
- What standards were met during this (particular) learning experience?
- What skills were used or practiced?
- What challenges did you encounter?

Practicing interpretation of their learning experiences assists students to become familiar and personal with the standards, as well as to begin to get purposeful about what they have accomplished as it relates to these desired objectives. Using our airplane metaphor, students learn to read each of the instruments and control panels to navigate with, one at a time. Through such focusing activities, they develop, as Native Americans teach, "mouse vision." Mouse vision allows one to see the details of practice up close, to concentrate on what lies before one's self and not become distracted with anything else. Seeing as the mouse allows one to perform well at the task at hand. Mouse vision helps us guide our airplane by paying attention to what is around us *right now.*

Some faculty have found that the use of short, leading sentences and "recipes" (sentences that students must complete) are useful ways to provide scaffolds for students to begin the task of effective reflection. Once they understand the nature of the standards and can readily interpret them into everyday program activities and learning experiences, faculty then begin to focus on how that relates to their growing understanding of professional practice, or the "So What?" component. For example:

- Why is it important that you, as a teacher of your students, can demonstrate understanding of this standard or lesson?
- This learning experience was important/interesting because ...
- How does this learning experience affect your teaching career and your abilities as a provider of learning experiences?
- What challenges and learning barriers have you encountered that might influence the way that you prefer to teach?
- Who might be a prime stakeholder affected by your mastery or lack of understanding of this standard? Why?

By connecting their understanding to this deeper "So What?", students begin to create a richer, more contextualized perception of the teaching profession such that standards, experiences, and the artifacts from learning become representative of their larger contribution to the field. In our metaphorical airplane, students keep their eye on their destination, gaining perspective of the landscapes and the weather around them. They begin to use, as Native Americans have called it, their "eagle vision." Using eagle vision, students are able to see the bigger picture—seeing larger patterns, themes, and the longer flight path, students can see more clearly where they are going and why. Eagle vision helps us guide our airplane by paying attention to where our actions are taking us and where we want to go.

By the time students are finishing their first semester of their junior year, they are practiced enough in summarizing the nature of the learning experience (what) and how it relates to the profession (so what), and they can begin to focus on the future. The future portends many things related to learning: professional development needs, anticipated challenges and opportunities, and anything related to changes in the environment or the learner from today to tomorrow. The developmental arc of these teacher candidates' experience is, at this point, ready to be increasingly focused on those future horizons.

As the spider in Native American lore represents the animal that connects the past to the future, I like to say that students begin to develop their "spider vision." Allowing for the inevitable comparisons to comic book lore, of course, I tell them it is not enough to simply use the vision of the mouse and of the eagle. To see the task in front of you and to see where you are going from up on high—those are two amazing and useful ways of seeing—are two skills that require practice, and are worthy of attention and of our resources and energy. But if we do not see how the past and the present connect to our futures, then we may end up somewhere other than where we were trying to go in the first place, or we may find that our destination was not, given the context, such a great place after all—as it has transmogrified en route. Perhaps, and of even greater danger to both the program and the individual, without a clear sense of how the past is connected to the future, one's motivation may be significantly less than if one feels that present actions are instrumental to achieving an envisioned, desired future. Spider vision allows us to find the wherewithal to transform along with change to arrive at the best location considering altered environments and circumstances. The spider vision is the navigation instrument that allows us to best alter our course and our destination.

Effectively forecasting into one's future requires both critical and creative thinking.

Students are, at a minimum, asked to think about what is probable for them in their future as a teacher, in addition to what is possible and what is preferable. While creating the environments within which teacher candidates are prepared and feel safe to actively engage in such thinking is an area for much discussion and research, it is felt by many faculty at MSU–Northern that the ePortfolio is an excellent platform from which to engage such learning and development.

MSU–Northern's ePortfolio initiative is constantly undergoing change itself. We have approximately 350 undergraduate and 40 graduate students concurrently developing their own ePortfolios using the faculty-created templates and guidelines. Having started off as a HyperStudio-based system, the process has matured as an Adobe Acrobat Writer process—though the "heavy lifting" involved in having students create nearly all of their portfolio structures from scratch has a number of faculty investigating alternative platforms, including TaskStream and Avenet, Inc. In any case, we are interested in increasing the student-developed interest and maintaining control over the process. This balance between accreditation purposes and deep learning purposes continues to be both the directive and the challenge for our institution.

Faculty at Montana State University–Northern are currently investigating ways to create a spiraling curriculum that will effectively engage their students' senses of their future professional goals. One faculty member, enrolled in her PhD program, plans to continue to investigate the development and practice of the future-focused ePortfolio as an action research project for her dissertation requirement. By beginning with sets of common experiences that students have with the standards, linking them to their ideas of what it means to be a practicing teacher, and then finally creating a sense of movement and direction through engaging them in a process of future-focused activities, the electronic portfolio system in the Department of Education hopes to create a broadly meaningful experience for every learner in the program. As time advances and students gather a deeper sense of their historical progress with the steady collection of artifacts, we hope to further improve their sense of effectively thinking about the future. With the help of two pairs of eyes and one set of eight, perhaps, we believe they will eventually be able to invent an airplane that is really worth flying over those next horizons.

REFERENCES

Devolder, M. L., & Lens, W. (1982). Academic achievement and future time perspective as a cognitive-motivational concept. *Journal of Personality and Social Psychology, 42*(3), 566-571.

Gladwell, M. (2000). *The tipping point: How little things can make a big difference.* Boston: Little Brown.

Henik, W., & Domino, G. (1975). Alterations in future time perspective in heroin addicts. *Journal of Clinical Psychology, 31*(3), 557-564.

Hung, J. (2004). Portfolio reflections. In J. Zubizarreta (Ed.), *The learning portfolio: Reflective practice for improving student learning* (pp. 235-236). Bolton, MA: Anker.

Lessing, E. E. (1972). Extension of personal future time perspective, age and life satisfaction of children and adolescents. *Developmental Psychology, 6,* 457-468.

Lewin, K. (1926). Intention, will, and need. In D. Rapaport (Ed.), *Organization and pathology of thought.* New York: Columbia University Press.

Mahon, N. E., & Yarcheski, T. J. (1994). future time perspective and positive health practices in young adults. *Perceptual and Motor Skills, 79,* 395-398.

Mahon, N. E., Yarcheski, T. J., & Yarcheski, A. (1997). Future time perspective and positive health practices in young adults: An extension. *Perceptual and Motor Skills, 84,* 1299-1304.

Murrell, A. J., & Mingrone, M. (1994). Correlates of temporal perspective. *Perceptual and Motor Skills, 78,* 1331-1334.

Rothspan, S., & Read, S. J. (1996). Present versus future time perspective and HIV risk among heterosexual college students. *Health Psychology, 15,* 131-134.

Seijts, G. H. (1998). The importance of future time perspective in theories of work motivation. *Journal of Abnormal Psychology, 132*(2), 154-168.

Stein, K. B., Sarbin, T. R., & Kulik, J. A. (1968). Future time perspective: Its relation to the socialization process and the delinquent role. *Journal of Consulting and Clinical Psychology, 32,* 257-264.

KEY TERMS

Achievement Orientation: The degree to which and the way in which a person is motivated to achieve or maintain a desired state.

Action Research: Research, usually informal, designed for direct application to behavior or to a situation, as research by teachers in their classrooms.

Electronic Portfolio System: The technological, social, and organizational/policy-level framework created through the intersecting decisions necessary to deploy an electronic portfolio within a school or university.

Future Time Perspective: The degree and way in which people integrate their thoughts of the chronological future into their present behavior.

Professional Competencies: The summation of skills, habits, traits, and dispositions required and/or sought in a professional of a particular given field.

Scaffolding: A teaching strategy in which instruction begins at a level encouraging students' success and provides the right amount of support to move students to a higher level of understanding (http://www.crede.org/tools/glossary.html).

Software Platforms: In computing, a platform describes some sort of framework, either in hardware or software, which allows software to run. Typical platforms include a computer's architecture, operating system, or programming languages and their runtime libraries (http://en.wikipedia.org/wiki/Software_Platform).

Splashpage: An attractive simple graphic homepage usually having no navigation options until you click the main graphic or the word "Enter" leading to the main navigation page or to frames (http://www.247webpages.com/01/pages/pg-glossary.html).

Web Portal: A Web site that provides a starting point, a gateway, or portal to other resources on the Internet or on an intranet.

Chapter L
Can We Talk? Electronic Portfolios as Collaborative Learning Spaces

Gary Greenberg
Northwestern University, USA

ABSTRACT

This chapter describes the Northwestern University Collaboratory Project's ePortfolio. As a resource in the Collaboratory, a Web-based collaborative learning environment, it provides collaborative learning spaces where K-12 students can share and discuss their work. Web document templates are used by students to create media-rich documents that can be viewed with only a Web browser. Of particular significance is how the ePortfolio's document-based communication model is being used to support mentoring, peer review, feedback, and reflection, and to facilitate a community of learning that motivates and encourages students.

INTRODUCTION

The Collaboratory Project

Many portfolio projects today are focused on collecting and organizing student work to *showcase* achievement. However, the Northwestern University Collaboratory Project's ePortfolio was designed to be a *learning portfolio* (Greenberg, 2004). It provides collaborative learning spaces to support the evolution of work; encourages interaction and collaboration among students, teachers, and mentors; and serves as a resource for teacher professional development. The ePortfolio is one of a number of resources and services available to K-12 teachers and their students in the Collaboratory, a Web-based *collaborative learning* environment.

The Collaboratory Project (http://collaboratory.nunet.net) was established in 1996 with a $1.8 million grant from the Ameritech Foundation as a technology outreach initiative for Northwestern University. In creating a network-based collaborative learning environment for K-12 students, the goal was to bring together a large, diverse community of students and their teachers to share information and experience, collaborate on projects, and learn from each other. By removing technical barriers to accomplishing objectives and delivering services, the Collaboratory is making it possible for educators to carry out significant educational activities that would otherwise be technically impossible or prohibitively expensive. The project currently receives support from federal, state, and foundation grants.

The project provides consulting, training, and support to Illinois educators who wish to use the Collaboratory to engage students in *project-based learning* activities that can be aligned with learning standards. Teachers create and manage projects as well as student accounts, give students access to projects and resources, and approve student work through password-protected accounts. Students submit text, graphics, sound, and video files that are saved in a database and are used to dynamically create Web pages.

The Collaboratory is available thorough a standard Web browser from servers at Northwestern University seven days a week, 24 hours a day. Today, more than 6,700 Illinois teachers, over 630 Illinois technology coordinators and media specialists, and almost 38,000 students representing over 1,500 Illinois schools have accounts in the Collaboratory.

Creating a Collaborative Learning Environment

Projects in the Collaboratory are composed of activities that use the ePortfolio and other Collaboratory resources as well as resources available on the Internet. These activities and classroom events appear on each project's calendar. The Project Page provides a framework for teachers to develop *engaged learning* activities for their students. These are made available to students through their Collaboratory accounts, created by teachers or by the Collaboratory Project for the school or district.

Collaboratory Communication Services include messaging, conferencing, discussion forums, invitations, and announcements—all used to support collaboration among teachers and students. Automatic alerts and notifications keep participants up to date about activities, new projects, and events. Search capabilities enable participants to easily find other people and projects.

The ePortfolio is one of the Collaboratory Resources teachers use to develop innovative project-based curricular activities that can be aligned to learning standards. In addition to the ePortfolio, there is a Cybrary that teachers use to create customized, curriculum-specific virtual libraries of Internet resources. MediaSpace is where "electronic multimedia postcards" containing text, graphics, sound, and/or video are used to share projects and information. In the Internet Book Club, teachers create reading lists, and students share book reviews and essays. The Survey Studio is used to create online surveys, questionnaires, and data collection forms for project activities. Teachers can also create Nexus Communities to bring together people with common interests in interactive *online learning communities*. Nexus Communities take the same approach to creating, sharing, and discussing student work as the ePortfolio, but are organized in communities, work areas, and galleries,

The Collaboratory in the Classroom

K-12 teachers in Illinois have been using the Collaboratory for a variety of classroom projects. Elementary students have learned about Illinois prairies, shared book reviews on district-wide reading lists, and written poems under the guidance of an in-class/online visiting poet. Middle school students have studied and reported on 15th and 16th century explorers, conducted school-wide national elections that model the electoral process, and compared life in their communities. High school students have participated in online discussions about literature, designed experiments for the Space Shuttle, collected and analyzed data for environmental science projects, and participated in online writing workshops.

Using Collaboratory resources, the Collaboratory Project created LexiTown, an online foreign language learning environment. It is developing a national astronomy research collaboratory for high school students with the Sloan Digital Sky Survey at Johns Hopkins University and Hands-On Universe at the University of California at Berkeley under a three-year grant from the National Science Foundation. The Collaboratory is piloting an Illinois Virtual School project with the Chicago Public Schools and the Illinois Virtual High School.

THE COLLABORATORY ePORTFOLIO

The Collaboratory ePortfolio

Some ePortfolio projects restrict participation, often out of concern for resources, especially storage, or are limited to supporting a program's specific needs, such as professional certification. However, in the Collaboratory, everyone with an account has an ePortfolio (MyPortfolio). The Collaboratory ePortfolio is a general-purpose *learning portfolio* intended to be used by students and teachers at any grade level and in any subject area.

Figure 1.

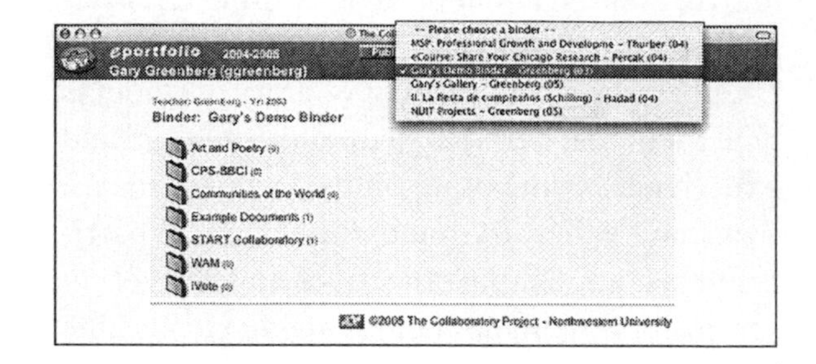

A familiar Binder-Folder-Document metaphor makes it easy for teachers and students to use their ePortfolio (Figure 1). Teachers create, manage, and give students access to the binders and folders used to organize and share work. Teachers also select the Web document templates that students use to create work. Learning objectives for student work can be identified through the Collaboratory's database of Illinois Learning Standards.

In designing the ePortfolio, we needed to address three critical technical issues:

1. Controlling who can view student work
2. Enabling students to create media-rich documents that can be viewed with only a Web browser
3. Supporting communication and collaboration around the work students create

Access Control

In developing the ePortfolio, we had to strike a balance between giving students ownership and control of their work, while ensuring that teachers could provide appropriate guidance for a project and that information about students would be protected. Even though teachers create and manage binders and folders, it is the students/authors who own and control access to their work in the ePortfolio. Access to any document and information about an author is based on one's role in the ePortfolio binder (manager, reviewer, and participant) and the Collaboratory (teacher, student, etc.).

Our work a few years ago with teachers piloting a Repository application to organize and share student work taught us that teachers want to be able to interact privately with students before they share their work with classmates. In the ePortfolio, all new documents are *private*, by default, and can be viewed only by the author and binder manager or reviewer(s). In order to support and encourage collaboration and interaction, when an author is ready for a document to be viewed by other binder participants, s/he can make a document *shared.*

However, to make a document *public,* viewable by anyone on the Internet, students must obtain the approval of the binder manager (teacher). This is to ensure that the work accurately represents the student's accomplishments for a project, does not contain inappropriate materials, and meets the district's Internet Use Policy on sharing student work and information about students. For people who are not binder participants, finding public documents from the ePortfolio search page can be difficult. To address this issue, students can create a Cover Page to organize, archive, and share their public documents as a *showcase portfolio*. Even though teachers do not own student work, they can create a Gallery of public documents their students have created to share what was accomplished in projects as a *professional portfolio*.

The Collaboratory Document Architecture

A critical requirement in designing the ePortfolio was that documents would be viewable to Collaboratory participants, regardless of where or when they choose to work. Of course, the Web can provide ready access to documents. However, to support broad collaboration, the ePortfolio, like other Collaboratory resources, must not require a specific application program in order to view student work that participating schools or students may not have access to. In addition, the Collaboratory Project expects students will work not only with text and images, but with sound and video as well. Therefore, students must be able to see and hear video and audio used in documents, regardless of their school's resources or media production capabilities.

The ePortfolio, like all Collaboratory resources, could not require that students know HTML in order to create documents. The ePortfolio would create Web pages dynamically using the text, graphics, sound, and/or video students submitted. In addition, we wanted students to be able to create more complex documents than is possible with the Collaboratory's MediaSpace.

To address these needs, we developed a document architecture that provides Web document templates composed of placeholders for text, graphics, sound, and/or video (Figure 2). The templates are used by students to create well-designed, media-rich Web pages. Using

Figure 2.

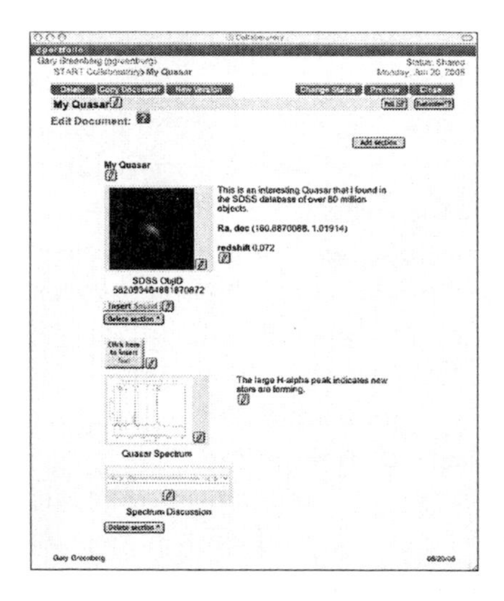

Figure 3.

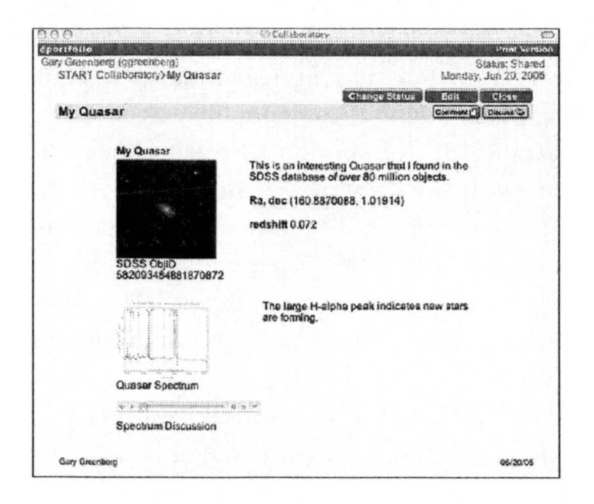

Figure 4.

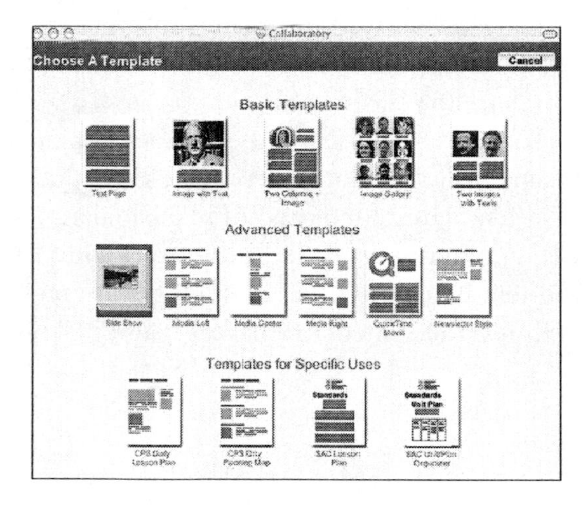

the media students have submitted for each placeholder, the Collaboratory builds the page dynamically when the document is viewed. Empty placeholders disappear (Figure 3).

The Collaboratory Project has created a number of Web document templates (Figure 4) that students use to create simple documents with only a picture and text, as well as complex documents incorporating multiple images, sound and/or video files, and multimedia slide shows. We have also created custom-designed templates with wizards that are used to select learning standards for teacher professional development projects. Application files are also supported, but this limits the document-based collaboration that is at the heart of the ePortfolio. The document architecture is currently being extended to take advantage of Web services to dynamically populate a document with data, information, and media from Internet archives and applications.

To avoid having multiple copies of the same file on the Collaboratory servers, especially if the file is very large, all media used in documents is saved in the author's Media Repository for reuse in other documents. In addition, teachers can create collections of image, sound, and/or video files for their students in shared Media Repositories.

Document-Based Communication

The Collaboratory's document architecture makes it possible to share media-rich documents with only a standard Web browser. This is essential. What makes the ePortfolio truly innovative is how the document architecture enables document-based communication. Much of the ePortfolio collaboration requirements were clarified through EPAC discussions organized by John Ittelson as an NLII Fellow[1]. These discussions brought people together from across the country who were developing electronic portfolio applications and supporting pilot projects that explored the potential of different portfolio models. From these discussions, we determined that the Collaboratory ePortfolio should focus on four learning activities:

- **Mentoring** between a teacher or expert and the student to provide personal attention.
- **Peer review** where students can view and discuss each other's work.

- **Feedback** on specific questions a student may have about work in progress or completed.
- **Reflection** on the learning process that would help students better understand themselves as learners.

Our approach to implementing these interactions was influenced by our experience creating collaborative communities that encourage communication among participants. Of particular importance was our work with Maud Hickey in the Northwestern University School of Music to create *MICNet* (Music Internet Connections). *MICNet* demonstrated how much more compelling it is to attach discussions to work, in this case MIDI and sound files of original music compositions, than it is to take the typical approach of attaching documents to a discussion. On the basis of this experience, we adopted a document-based communications model for implementing mentoring, peer review, feedback, and reflection.

Specifically, the document architecture plays a key role in enabling document-based mentoring and coaching in the ePortfolio (Figure 3: "Comment" button). Each placeholder in an ePortfolio document has a button that authors can use to exchange private comments about any element in a document with the binder manager/teacher. Comments are listed in reverse chronological order next to a copy of whatever is in the placeholder. Helping teachers and students keep track of when comments are requested and if there has been a reply has proven to be particularly challenging.

Regarding peer review and informal student discussions, these are supported by threaded discussions that are an integral part of any document and are open to all binder participants when the document is shared (Figure 3: "Discuss" button). Binder participants can post new topics or reply to existing threads, just as they would in a typical discussion forum. Teachers can choose to participate, or not.

In addition, a student can create a short poll to request specific feedback about a document (Figure 2: "Poll" button). Polls can include simple Yes/No, True/False questions or request a scaled response (e.g., Strongly Agree-Strongly Disagree on a scale from 1-5). A poll can also pose one question that requires a text response.

ePortfolio documents also support reflections (Figure 2: "Reflection" button) with which authors can maintain ongoing journals about their learning process. Reflections are simple text documents that are always available for the author to add to or edit and can be either private or shared.

The ePortfolio in the Classroom

Although a very good use of the ePortfolio is to share and discuss student writing, it is also proving to be a means of stimulating student interest and creative thinking in other types of projects across the curriculum. For example:

- Third-grade students have been sharing and discussing solutions to math word problems as well as to open-ended problems requiring conflict resolution.
- Sixth graders have used video clips to explain Newton's Laws of Force and Motion, and using "The Legend of Lady Ilena" as a vehicle, have shared research about feudalism and gender roles.
- Middle school students in the Chicago region have been sharing and reviewing proposals for renovating the Lincoln Park Zoo's South Pond.
- As part of Project Citizen, students in a Chicago school used the ePortfolio to identify the need for long overdue physical improvements, which led to mounting a campaign for a new school.

The learning community fostered by the Collaboratory's ePortfolio is also benefiting teachers. A pilot project is starting up that will use the ePortfolio to mentor teachers working toward their National Board Certification.

Motivating Students

Beyond specific projects, there are larger issues of student motivation that the ePortfolio seems to be addressing. At the Collaboratory Project's Eighth Annual Symposium, teachers reported the following observations:

- **There are Benefits to Students Sharing Work:** Students seem to pay more attention to their work when they know other students will be reviewing it. Moreover, good ideas can propagate through a folder; even if students are at different skill levels, if they see examples of good work, they are motivated to revise.
- **Private Comments have an Impact:** Students appreciate being able to return to and spend time considering private comments on their work, especially from outside reviewers and experts.
- **Document Discussions can be Productive:** As discussions become more focused in the ePortfolio, students move beyond the casual chat of the Internet and simply contributing a "me too" response, and begin to feel responsible for making substantive contributions to discussion threads.

Teachers and students alike are still discovering the learning potential of the ePortfolio. We are beginning to see teachers and students exploring how to incorporate polling in projects. Teachers who are familiar with using reflection in projects are starting to explore the impact of having reflection immediately available with a document.

Becoming an Effective Facilitator

In exploring the opportunities offered by the ePortfolio, one of the greatest challenges for teachers is how to manage and facilitate effective communication. A first step is for teachers to anticipate an appropriate organization for binders, folders, and the documents so that work posted and comments can be easily found. Teachers can encourage students to use a project's activities and calendar to manage their time so that they meet deadlines for posting documents, comments, polls, or reflections, and so that they know when they should look for replies.

A key to facilitating effective communication is for teachers to move away from specifically directing students. Developing provocative prompts can help initiate student discussions, and providing students with model scripts can make their discussions become more stimulating and productive (e.g., start with a compliment, end with a suggestion or question).

When teachers are facilitators, they can be more selective in how they interact with students. This speaks directly to a concern that many teachers have about the time required to review student work online in the ePortfolio. Just as a teacher might look over students' shoulders at work in progress or write short comments on draft reports, teachers can quickly browse ePortfolio documents, paying as much or as little attention to each student as needed. Because they cannot mark up a document with a red pencil, teachers must use their comments to address higher-level content and organizational issues of student work.

In the role of facilitator, teachers are more likely to find the time to use the ePortfolio regularly and consistently. Regular and consistent use is essential if the goal is to build the kind of rapport that fosters a culture of learning.

Impact on Teaching and Learning

Within the culture of learning promoted by the ePortfolio, we envision significant opportunities for both teachers and students. For teachers, there are opportunities that may elude professional development efforts, including:

- **Customizing the Teaching and Learning Experience for Each Student:** Working in the ePortfolio exposes the learning process and the evolution of ideas. Thus, working in the ePortfolio can help a teacher better understand a student's learning style and how to best support and encourage each student.
- **Identifying, Developing, and Sharing Best Practices:** The ePortfolio maintains a record of all coaching and mentoring, student discussions and peer review, polls and feedback, and student reflections on their learning. Educators can use this record to review the consequences of teacher-student as well as student-student interactions and identify best practices that can be further cultivated and shared with others.

For students, there are the significant personal opportunities, including:

- **Becoming More Self-Directed Learners:** The ability to be creators of media-rich documents, the challenges and inspiration that comes with seeing other students' work, and the pride that comes with peer recognition of accomplishments can motivate students to take more responsibility for their learning.
- **Being Recognized:** The forum provided by the ePortfolio can reveal students' skills and abilities that may not surface in traditional classroom activities. As these skills and abilities are recognized by teachers as well as other students, student self-confidence should increase.

CONCLUSION

The Collaboratory ePortfolio is distinctive in its technical design and practical approach to providing a general-purpose, Web-based learning portfolio. The binder-folder model provides easy-to-use collaborative learning spaces for organizing student work. The Collaboratory document architecture enables students to publish and share well-designed, media-rich documents. Document-based communication makes it possible for ePortfolio participants to exchange private comments with teachers and mentors, participate in threaded discussions with one another, create and respond to polls, and maintain reflective journals with only a Web browser.

Teachers are just beginning to tap the potential of the Collaboratory ePortfolio to create a culture of learning. By motivating students and facilitating effective communication, the ePortfolio provides rich opportunities for customizing the teaching and learning experience, and identifying, developing, and sharing best practices. Students have the opportunity to become more self-directed learners and to be recognized for skills and abilities that may not surface in traditional classroom activities. The result should be a more engaging and rewarding classroom experience for everyone involved.

ACKNOWLEDGMENTS

The ePortfolio was developed under the direction of Bob Davis. Rich Barone is the principal architect of the ePortfolio. Paul Hertz and Jonathan Rochkind contributed, with Rich, to the document architecture, document-based communication, and the underlying Collaboratory architecture, resources, and services. Karen Percak, Bonnie Thurber, and Roxana Hadad work with and support teachers and students with projects using the ePortfolio.

REFERENCES

Chen, H. L., & Mazow, C. (2002). Electronic learning portfolios and student affairs. NASPA NetResults, (October 28). Retrieved from http://www.naspa.org/netresults/PrinterFriendly.cfm?ID=825

Greenberg, G. (2004). The digital convergence: Extending the portfolio model. *Educause Review, 39*(4), 28-37.

Jafari, A., & Greenberg, G. (Eds.). (2003, November). *Electronic portfolios white paper, version 1.0.* Retrieved from http://www.eportconsortium.org/Uploads/whitepaperV1_0.pdf

KEY TERMS

Collaboratory: A network-based collaborative environment that enables participants to communicate and share information regardless of time or place.

Cybrary: A virtual library of Internet resources.

Document-Based Communication: Communications about a document are part of the document. This contrasts electronic mail, threaded discussions, and instant messenging where documents are attached to the communication.

Engaged Learning: Student-driven, self-directed learning in the context of authentic tasks.

Learning Portfolio: A portfolio used to support and track explorations and the learning process, usually with interactions from mentors and coaches.

Project-Based Learning: Learning occurs through a series of activities in the context of a meaningful project.

Showcase Portfolio: A portfolio used to organize and present evidence of accomplishments.

Web-Document Templates: Text, graphics, sound, and/or video files are uploaded to placeholders that determine a Web document's layout and design.

ENDNOTE

[1] The Educause Learning Initiative (formerly NLII) ePortfolios page can be found at http://www.educause.edu/E% 2DPortfolios/5524.

Chapter LI
ePortfolio Thinking:
The Challenge of the Public Research University

Jo B. Paoletti
University of Maryland, USA

ABSTRACT

This chapter examines the trajectory of electronic portfolio development and adoption at large public research institutions. The author frames her research with her own attempt to implement a program-level portfolio for undergraduate majors in her own department. Her investigation of 59 institutions suggests that our largest campuses face unique challenges that may limit the extent to which they adopt electronic portfolios. While some of these challenges are practical and logistical, the more significant barriers seem to be related to campus culture, particularly faculty engagement in undergraduate education.

INTRODUCTION

Research is formalized curiosity. It is poking and prying with a purpose.
—Zora Neale Hurston

Researching this chapter has been an exercise in academic excavation. The top layer, whose odd contours first piqued my curiosity, consisted of my own experiences with student ePortfolios. The second layer was the public record of ePortfolio initiatives at institutions like mine: large public research universities. The deepest layer, obscured by the other two and yet somehow still revealed in them, were the untold stories of trial and error, of disappointment, and perhaps even failure. In this chapter, I propose to examine all three layers in order to illuminate the special challenges posed in introducing student ePortfolios at a large public research university. I have drawn on published reports, conference presentations, and interviews with faculty and administrators at a number of institutions, but my interest in these questions began with my own foray into electronic portfolios for majors in my home department, American Studies.

Because this inquiry grew out of and is still shaped by my own experience, this chapter takes the form of a personal narrative, punctuated by the deeper research findings discovered during the process.

FIRST ENCOUNTERS WITH PORTFOLIOS

It helps to remember that portfolios existed for generations before the digital revolution. Painters, photographers, architects, and writers gathered and displayed their work in portable exhibits that comprised a reflection-informed narrative. The experiential trail that has brought me to ePortfolios reaches back to my undergraduate years, struggling on my own to create a major in theater costuming where it didn't really exist, by combining coursework in design and textiles with a work-study position in the university's costume shop. As I discovered when I graduated, the one thing missing in my preparation was proof that those pieces had actually connected: I had no portfolio, and it was too late to compile one. As a graduate assistant teaching apparel design, I made sure that every student knew what a portfolio was and developed one in my class. In making the transition to teaching history of costume and later, American Studies, portfolios gave way to term papers and essay exams.

This personal history is mirrored in the stories behind many ePortfolio projects. Some practitioners come from programs where student writing or design had traditionally been collected, defended, and assessed using physical compilations of their work. Some come from disciplines which had tended to favor other forms of assessment. Some, like me, have experience in both traditions. Whichever the case, portfolios represent a form of assessment outside mainstream academic practice at large institutions, either an accepted mode within an "exceptional" discipline or an experimental mode in more traditional ones. This essentially marginal existence is the backdrop for the introduction of portfolios at large public research institutions: first, they must be explained for those for whom they are foreign.

PORTFOLIO THINKING: COURSE-LEVEL INNOVATION

The emergence of the World Wide Web in the mid-1990s coincided with a pedagogical experiment and a paradigm shift in my own view of student learning. The experiment was the return of the portfolio, this time in a discussion-intensive course, Diversity in American Culture. In this course, students kept journals and wrote a series of short essays about various aspects of diversity; their final assignment was to incorporate these written materials into a Web-based portfolio and add a reflective essay about their own learning. Soon, I was incorporating electronic portfolios into all my classes.

Although I developed this approach independently, it is clear from the number of course portfolio Web sites that my efforts were echoed on campuses, large and small, around the globe. Love, McKean, and Gathercoal, in their 2004 article on levels of maturity in ePortfolio development, posit a trajectory from "scrapbook" to "authentic evidence," but omit the course portfolio as a common entry point for many institutions (Love et al., 2004). While a few ePortfolio initiatives at large research institutions—notably the Indiana University project begun in 1988 (Cambridge, 2001)—begin as visions of longitudinal collections of student work, an extension of the senior projects found at many small colleges, it is worth noting that most of the ePortfolio initiatives at such institutions can be traced to individual faculty members who implemented portfolios at the course level. This, too, affects the nature and trajectory of ePortfolio initiatives at large universities.

PORTFOLIO THINKING: PROGRAM-LEVEL INNOVATION

In 1999, a committee of two faculty and a graduate student proposed the development of an electronic portfolio for American Studies majors. Such a portfolio was perceived as a way to engage students more directly in planning and rationalizing their own programs, in a major which leaves many choices up to the individual. Our committee combined many of the interests found in many ePortfolio initiatives: I brought the traditional "design portfolio" viewpoint, the other faculty member was an alumna of Kalamazoo College and saw their 1996 portfolio project as a model for ours, and the graduate student, a computer scientist pursuing a doctorate in American Studies, brought a scholarly fascination with the impact of technology on learning. With a grant from the university's Center for Teaching Excellence, we developed a one-credit portfolio course, intended to be the first of three such courses which would eventually be required for all majors.

There is nothing unique to large public research universities in this part of the narrative. In some ways, we represented an archetypal cross-section of the usual actors in ePortfolio initiatives. Like so many of them, we successfully competed for a grant to support the project. We had ambitious plans for the ePortfolio courses and assumed we had the support of our departmental colleagues, who seemed willing to entertain the notion, politely if not enthusiastically. The initial development stage of the course went smoothly, and we soon were anticipating an equally successful pilot project. A search of the literature confirmed that we had plenty of company, with hundreds of institutions reporting pilot projects with student portfolios in 2001-2003.

PORTFOLIO THINKING: THE THORN IN THE ROSE

Progress on the AMST portfolio project proceeded steadily, but increasingly slowly, from 1999 to 2004. The other faculty member was busy in her role as graduate director, so I became the teacher of record for the one-credit course, taking on most of the responsibility for the project. I experimented with different formats for the one-credit portfolio orientation course and tried different tools for creating the portfolios. We had to discard the idea of the other two courses—one at the midpoint of the program and one taken concurrently with our senior capstone—because they proved impossible to assign to any other faculty member but myself, and I was wary of developing a suite of required courses for which there was only one potential teacher. Finally, in Fall 2004, I brought to our faculty a proposal that the one-credit course—and, by implication, the ePortfolio—be incorporated into the undergraduate requirements. After considerable discussion, the decision was tabled indefinitely. The course will not be offered in the 2005-2006 academic year, and it is unlikely that it will ever be required. Ironically, just as the American Studies ePortfolio project stalled, I was invited to participate in a campus-wide pilot of various ePortfolio software programs initiated by the Office of Information Technology. This project is now in limbo, as the administrator who spearheaded has left campus.

Having attended dozens of conference sessions on ePortfolios, I was under the impression that no one else was having these problems. In one PowerPoint presentation after another, faculty from other institutions described their ePortfolio initiatives, similar to ours in all but one respect: they had succeeded, where we had failed. Few even mentioned challenges or barriers to ePortfolio adoption, leaving me to wonder if the problem lay within my department, or perhaps more widely within my college or my university. So I turned my curiosity into research and began to dig a little deeper.

Researchers at Penn State University had asked similar questions, when they surveyed activity in the field in 2001 and 2003. They found that "*implementation* of ePortfolios within the Big-10 has increased since this study was conducted in 2001. However, there remains a noticeable lack of consistency in terms of how these various adoptions have been put into place as evidenced by the scattered range of purposes and support structures in place" (Staub & Johnson, 2003). They noted that the most advanced projects were located in teacher education programs—not surprising, given the nearly $400 million allocated by the U.S. Department of Education's Preparing Tomorrow's Teachers for Technology (PT3) project between 1999 and 2003, when the program ended (U.S. Department of Education, 2005).

LOOKING FOR THE TRUTH BEHIND THE POWERPOINT

So who is successfully implementing ePortfolios? Certainly there is considerable interest in electronic portfolios, with the three major consortia (Open Source Portfolio Initiative, the National Coalition for Electronic Portfolio Research, and the Electronic Portfolio Consortium) drawing members from every imaginable type of institution. The ePortConsortium Web site in spring 2005 listed over 500 institutions in 44 countries, ranging from small colleges such as Alverno and St. Olaf to entire statewide systems, such as the University of Minnesota, and including community colleges and online, for-profit institutions such as the University of Phoenix, in addition to traditional four-year colleges (ePortConsortium.org, 2005). A search of the Web sites of a sample the U.S.-based institutions listed as members of the Electronic Portfolio Consortium suggested large public research institutions were lagging behind small colleges, large private universities, community colleges, and for-profit institutions in implementing electronic student portfolios. Because the large public research institutions were often on the cutting edge of technological innovation, it was surprising to find them playing a different role in the adoption of electronic portfolios in higher education.

Clemson professor and ePortfolio pioneer Kathleen Blake Yancey once asked, "Where student electronic portfolios have worked, why have they worked?" (Yancey, 2001). I attempted to answer a different question: "Where student electronic portfolios have stalled, why have they stalled?" I chose to frame the question in these terms, rather than call them a failed experiment at this point, because it is too early to tell whether ePortfolios will be abandoned by any of these institutions. I also elected to focus only on institutions similar to my own, because my ulterior motive is quite parochial: I would like to see ePortfolios eventually succeed at the University of Maryland.

In defining the scope of this analysis, I have limited myself to those institutions listed as members of the Open Source Portfolio Initiative, the National Coalition for Electronic Portfolio Research, or the Electronic Portfolio Con-

Table 1. Public doctoral-extensive universities having more than 15,000 undergraduate students

Institution	Undergraduates	Freshmen	Graduate Students	Total Enrollment
Arizona State University	38,117	7,147	9,220	54,484
Auburn University	18,899	3,594	3,148	25,641
Bowling Green State University	15,628	3,879	3,080	22,587
Cal Poly State U Pomona	16,484	1,950	2,047	20,481
Cal Poly State U San Luis Obispo	16,565	2,933	943	20,441
California State University Fresno	16,650	2,302	3,131	22,083
Central Michigan University	19,616	3,755	7,767	31,138
Eastern Michigan University	18,485	2,354	4,725	25,564
Florida State University	29,820	6,240	7,146	43,206
George Mason University	16,888	2,262	10,688	29,838
Georgia State University	19,239	2,270	6,709	28,218
Illinois State University	17,806	2,834	2,879	23,519
Indiana U Purdue U Indianapolis	20,844	2,720	6,310	29,874
Indiana University	29,062	6,352	7,335	42,749
Iowa State University	20,993	3,729	4,618	29,340
Kennesaw State University	15,917	1,862	1,882	19,661
Louisiana State University	25,849	5,700	4,804	36,353
Miami University	15,011	3,426	2,092	20,529
Michigan State University	37,107	7,607	8,040	52,754
NC State University	20,302	3,957	6,904	31,163
Northern Illinois University	18,025	2,951	6,463	27,439
Penn State University	33,958	5,907	6,465	46,330
Portland State University	15,159	1,363	6,089	22,611
Rutgers University	26,366	4,847	7,513	38,726
San Jose State University	21,663	2,393	7,381	31,437
SUNY Buffalo	17,509	3,183	7,457	28,149
Temple University	22,780	3,815	7,000	33,595
Texas A&M	35,605	7,068	8,192	50,865
Texas Tech University	23,329	3,951	4,311	31,591
The Ohio State University	36,097	6,057	10,210	52,364
UC Berkeley	22,880	3,672	8,803	35,355
UC Davis	23,018	4,268	5,521	32,807
UC Riverside	15,089	3,456	1,964	20,509
UCLA	24,946	3,724	10,771	39,441
UNC Charlotte	15,472	2,629	3,971	22,072
University of Central Florida	34,940	5,965	7,409	48,314
University of Connecticut	15,260	3,247	6,053	24,560
University of Delaware	16,023	3,385	3,395	22,803
University of Georgia	24,615	4,513	6,792	35,920
University of Houston	26,366	3,367	5,915	35,648
University of Illinois at Chicago	15,397	2,716	7,193	25,306
University of Illinois Champaign Urbana	28,931	7,237	9,985	46,153
University of Maryland	24,590	4,198	9,678	38,466
University of Michigan	24,677	6,037	12,184	42,898
University of Minnesota	28,740	5,588	14,595	48,923
University of Nebraska at Lincoln	17,137	3,266	4,246	24,649
University of Nevada Las Vegas	20,607	3,271	4,857	28,735
University of North Texas	24,274	3,480	6,881	34,635
University of Oregon	16,024	3,183	3,415	22,622
University of Pittsburgh	16,677	3,019	7,756	27,452
University of Tennessee	19,308	4,422	6,010	29,740
University of Texas Austin	36,478	6,795	11,282	54,555
University of Texas El Paso	15,448	2,321	3,326	21,095
University of Texas San Antonio	22,259	3,125	3,638	29,022
University of Washington	26,042	4,871	9,660	40,573
University of Wisconsin Madison	28,217	5,642	8,943	42,802
VPISU	21,247	4,943	5,932	32,122
Washington State University	18,825	3,108	3,228	25,161
Western Michigan University	22,336	3,761	5,327	31,424

sortium which are publicly funded, doctoral granting, extensive (50 or more doctoral degrees per year across at least 15 disciplines), and those which have undergraduate enrollments of 15,000 or more. This resulted in a pool of 59 institutions ranging in size from 15,011 (Miami University) to 38,117 (Arizona State University). A complete list can be found in Table 1. I have also focused my analysis on the use of student-owned portfolios, not institutional portfolios which are used to demonstrate achievement of learning goals in the aggregate but usually do not permit students to create their own portfolios and reflect on them. Those which appeared from an initial survey of their Web sites to have an ePortfolio initiative at or beyond the pilot stage are in bold italics. (It is important to note that not all of these ePortfolio programs were easy to find from the institution's homepage. Multiple searches were required to compile this list, and it is possible that some eluded my efforts.)

In Table 2, I have also indicated the number of institutions found to be at various stages of ePortfolio implementation, defined as follows:

- **Negligible:** Implementation appeared to be at the course level, often by a few isolated faculty members, with no evidence of strategic planning at the department, college, or campus level.
- **Planning:** Evidence of planning activity at the department, college, or campus level. Might include creation of a study committee or publication of a report advocating next steps.
- **Pilot:** A limited trial of ePortfolios at the department, college, or campus level, either to test software or to assess the desirability of ePortfolios, or both.
- **Implemented:** A student-owned ePortfolio is in use, with its own portal complete with instructions and indications of ongoing development, training, and support beyond the pilot level.

Table 2. Implementation stage

Implementation Stage	# of Institutions (N=59)
Negligible	24
Planning	10
Pilot	5
Implemented	20

Another measure of implementation is the range of student use, especially whether the ePortfolio was required or optional. The following categories of use were noted:

- **Negligible:** Student use was either limited to a few courses or there were no student ePortfolios, only institutional ePortfolios.
- **Optional:** ePortfolios were available, but not required for any students.
- **Limited Requirement:** ePortfolios were required for some programs (first-year interest groups, some majors, etc.) but otherwise optional.
- **Requirement:** ePortfolios were required for all students.

Several of these findings are worth noting. First, of the 59 large public institutions listed as members of one or more of the three ePortfolio consortia, 41% appeared to have little or no development activity going on. None of them had instituted ePortfolios as a campus require-

Table 3. Student use of ePortfolios

Student Use	# of Institutions (N=59)
Negligible	34
Optional	10
Limited Requirement	15
Campus Requirement	0

ment, as had several of the small liberal arts colleges, and none seemed to be planning to do so. There are nuances behind the figures as well. The institutions at the "pilot" stage were not necessarily close to adopting some form of student ePortfolio¾the University of Maryland is one such campus, and there are no immediate plans to act on the findings of the pilot study. The more I looked for evidence of ePortfolio initiatives, the harder it seemed to find much going on beyond a few clearly established leaders: the University of Washington, Florida State University, the University of Iowa, and the University of Minnesota were cited repeatedly as having mature ePortfolio programs.

So I began to interview people at institutions where the actual progress of their initiatives was unclear, based on available information. Obviously, this was a touchy subject. A few declined to be interviewed; some preferred to offer anonymous comments. In some cases, the original campus leader had gone to another institution, and the project had in effect been left behind. Some ePortfolio advocates have offered fairly candid comments in print elsewhere, and some were also willing to speak with me on the record. Here are some of their insights about the challenges of implementing ePortfolios at large public research universities. These challenges stem not only from the size and diversity of their undergraduate populations, but from their administrative structure and *campus culture.*

Large public research universities often concentrate considerable power at the college/professional school level, resulting in administrative "silos" which can impede campus-wide initiatives, especially those which originate at the grassroots level. Several informants pointed to Florida State University and the University of Minnesota as institutions whose successful ePortfolio initiatives originated at the campus level.

Large public research universities define faculty roles and responsibilities quite differently from smaller, more undergraduate-oriented institutions. Undergraduate teaching is often delegated to adjunct, part-time, or graduate student instructors, while curriculum changes and reviews are in the hands of permanent, full-time faculty. This may foster a "disconnect" between curriculum development and innovations in teaching and learning. This characteristic could effectively stall ePortfolio development at the point at which it requires coordination with the curriculum.

Many of the most successful ePortfolio programs are found in teacher education programs, driven by two very powerful forces: new accreditation standards that favor incorporating new technologies into existing portfolio programs and the PT3 funding from 1999 through 2003. It remains to be seen if their momentum can be sustained by accreditation forces alone, in the absence of significant funding (Dangel, 2005).

The trend toward ePortfolios coincided with a sharp decline in state and federal funding for higher education, which hit large public institutions especially hard. Though still increasing, the rate of growth of IT budgets has declined, and administrators are looking for ways to reduce costs ("IT Funding ... ", 2005). Large public research institutions tend to develop customized software solutions rather than using generic tools, a choice which can be initially much more expensive, another reason for stalled ePortfolio initiatives (Gibson & Barrett, 2002).

The amount of writing required for student ePortfolios—and the concomitant amount of reading required for their assessment—is far greater than what is usually seen at schools with high student-faculty ratios (Arvan, 2005). This objection was expressed in the discussion with the American Studies faculty about our ePortfolio; most were concerned about the increased workload involved in reading and commenting on them.

If a significant portion of the student body actually participate in ePortfolios, the burden on a large institution's infrastructure would be overwhelming. At Penn State University, which is cautiously moving towards electronic portfolios, beginning with encouraging students to simply publish evidence of their academic work, "the existing infrastructure is sufficient to support participation by about half, but certainly not all…undergraduates" (Johnson & DiBiase, 2004).

ePortfolios that are truly owned by students may represent a level of student accountability and autonomy that faculty at large public research institutions may not be willing to grant. It is a paradox of such universities that students are often left to fend for themselves and expected to navigate our complex structures with minimal guidance, yet in an atmosphere of distrust in the students' ability to actually do so (Dangel, 2005).

THE FUTURE: WHAT ROLE FOR LARGE PUBLIC RESEARCH UNIVERSITIES

Having tabled the ePortfolio initiative, we have instead undertaken a massive overhaul of our undergraduate curriculum, incorporating co-curricular elements more intentionally. While I had hoped that the ePortfolio could be used to make visible the integrative learning our students experience, I am acceding to my colleagues' wishes to see what happens at the campus level before adding it to the requirements for the major. I believe that beneath this request lie concerns about workload, anxiety about new technology, and ambivalence about whether or not this represents real paradigm change or just another "flavor-of-the-month pedagogical trend" (in the words of a skeptical colleague). In others words, what began as an experiment in new technology has led me to a cultural impasse.

Like most other aspects of instruction, electronic portfolios will differ widely from one type of institution to another. Large public research universities will probably never require electronic portfolios for all their students, though accreditation standards in some fields will require them for some. Until the funding picture improves, support for ePortfolios will likely be conservative and limited to those units which require them for accreditation, or paid in part by user fees. The public research universities can still play a leadership role in the development of ePortfolio technology, especially in achieving cost-effective solutions that are scalable for large numbers of users, or which are integrated with course and content management systems. The first hurdle for those institutions that are "stalled" may well be to reclaim and redefine their undergraduate education mission, since the logistical barriers seem more surmountable than the cultural ones.

REFERENCES

Arvan, L. (2005). Telephone interview.

Cambridge, B. L. (Ed.). (2001). *Electronic portfolios: Emerging practices in student, faculty, and institutional learning*. Washington, DC: American Association of Higher Education.

Dangel, H. (2005). Telephone interview.

ePortConsortium.org. (2005). Retrieved June 26, 2005, from http://www.eportconsortium.org/

Gibson, D., & Barrett, H. (2002). Directions in electronic portfolio development. *ITFORUM.*

IT funding continues to be major issue for higher education. (2005). *Administrator, 24*(2), 1-3.

Johnson, G., & DiBiase, D. (2004). Keeping the horse before the cart: Penn State's e-portfolio initiative. *Educause Quarterly, 27*(4), 18-26.

Love, D., McKean, G., & Gathercoal, P. (2004). Portfolios to Webfolios and beyond: Levels of maturation. *Educause Quarterly,* (2), 24-37.

Staub, J., & Johnson, G. (2003). *Assessment of on-line student portfolio initiatives at Big-10 and other institutions.*

U.S. Department of Education. (2005). *Preparing tomorrow's teachers to use technology program (PT3): Funding status.* Retrieved June 2, 2005, from http://www.ed.gov/programs/teachtech/funding.html

Yancey, K. B. (2001). General patterns and the future. In B. Cambridge (Ed.), *Electronic portfolios* (pp. 83-87). Washington, DC: American Association of Higher Education.

About the Authors

Ali Jafari is a professor at the Purdue School of Engineering and Technology, Indiana University-Purdue University Indianapolis (IUPUI), USA. In addition to his teaching duties, Dr. Jafari is the founder and director of the CyberLab at IUPUI, where his research focuses on smart learning environments and intelligent agents; founder and director of ePortConsortium.org; and co-founder of ANGELlearning.com. Dr. Jafari has initiated, directed, and co-developed several high-profile, successful technology solutions for education, including the Oncourse Course Management System currently used by the Indiana University campuses; as well as the ANGEL Learning Management System, now a commercial product; and the new Epsilen Environment.

Catherine Kaufman serves as coordinator of ePortConsortium, an association of individuals within higher education and IT commercial institutions who are interested in the development of academic ePortfolio software systems and the establishment of standards for such systems. She is responsible for maintaining communication among ePortConsortium members regarding news, resources, and events associated with electronic portfolio systems. She previously interned with Ali Jafari within the CyberLab at Indiana University-Purdue University Indianapolis (IUPUI), where she wrote user instructions for the initial version of the Epsilen ePortfolio software system. Her experience includes more than 10 years of editing legal documents, and she is currently on hiatus from enrollment in the MBA program of the Kelley School of Business, Indiana University.

* * *

M. W. (Wijnand) Aalderink, having a background as a linguist, has worked since 1998 in the field of IT and education. As program manager of eLearning at the Windesheim University of Professional Education in The Netherlands, he is currently responsible for different projects aiming at the development of an appropriate learning infrastructure for student-centered competence-based education. Mr. Wijnand has been the head of DigiDidact, Centre of Expertise for IT in Education at Windesheim for five years. He has published and presented several papers both in the national and international arena on topics like streaming audio and video, strategic development of corporate eLearning, and ePortfolio. He is chair of the steering group of NL Portfolio, one of the special interest groups of the SURF-Foundation in The Netherlands (http://e-learning.surf.nl/portfolio).

Teresa Acosta is an instructional designer in the office of Educational Technology and University Outreach at the University of Houston (USA) where she conducts faculty development workshops and studies new educational technologies. Her research interests include emerging technology trends, curriculum development, and effective teaching methods. She can be contacted at tyacosta@central.uh.edu.

J. F. Aiton has taught molecular physiology in the Bute Medical School at St Andrews University (UK) for several years and has been involved with trying to develop and implement eLearning solutions for over 10 years. In the last year, they have established a fruitful collaboration with colleagues in Newcastle who have helped them introduce the Web-based ePortfolio to entrant medical students. His research interests are in the molecular biology of Alzheimer's disease—and on a lighter side, he wishes he was a better golfer!

Susan Amirian received her EdD from Nova Southeastern University in Ft. Lauderdale, Florida. She is currently an assistant professor in the Department of Media Communication & Technology in the School of Professional Studies at East Stroudsburg University in Pennsylvania (USA). Her professional experience includes creative, media, and technology management positions at Condé Nast Publishing, Montclair State University, and the New Jersey Devils NHL hockey club. She has consulted for Prudential Insurance and the Yogi Berra Museum. Her most recent certifications include Adobe Certified Expert in PhotoshopCS and Palm Education Training. Her teaching and research interests include the application of technologies in learning, distance education, and electronic media.

Kathryn Chang Barker is a consulting education futurist with a PhD in Education Administration and Policy Studies from the University of Alberta (1994). She is the founding and current president of FuturEd Consulting Education Futurists Inc., QualitE-Learning Assurance Inc. (in Canada and in the UK), and the Learning Innovations Forum d'Innovation d'Apprentissage. She also serves on the boards of the Canadian Education Association, the *Innovate* online journal, the European Institute for eLearning, and eTQM, Dubai's eLearning college. She has extensive experience in eLearning; workforce development and lifelong learning; education reform in the context of global change; accountability, Return on Investment, and quality assurance in learning systems; international education and national standards development; adult and workplace literacy; learning technologies and distance education; prior learning assessment; human capital assets management; and various other fields related to learning innovations. Her current passion is the ePortfolio, and she is working to animate "an ePortfolio for each and every Canadian—and one ePortfolio for life."

Andrea Bartlett is an associate professor in the Department of Curriculum Studies at the University of Hawaii at Manoa, USA. Over the past 10 years, she has gradually integrated technology into her teaching, culminating in creation of electronic portfolios by two cohorts of pre-service teachers. Her research on pre-service teachers' perceptions of electronic portfolios appears in journals such as *Action in Teacher Education* and *Contemporary Issues in Technology and Teacher Education.* She has also published her research in proceedings of conferences such as the

IFIP World Computer Congress 2000 (Beijing) and the IFIP World Conference on Computers in Education 2005 (Cape Town, South Africa).

Jessica L. Blackburn is a doctoral student in Bowling Green State University's Industrial-Organizational Psychology program (USA). She received her Bachelor of Science degree from Portland State University and her Masters of Arts from Bowling Green State University. Her research focuses on the application of psychology to both workplace and educational settings. She is particularly interested in self-regulatory theories and their application to academic and work-related motivation.

P. M. Bradley is academic sub-dean for teaching, learning, and assessment for the undergraduate medical program at Newcastle University (UK). He has played a leading role in integrating portfolios into the curriculum at Newcastle.

Andrew Brown is a senior lecturer in music and sound in the Faculty of Creative Industries, Queensland University of Technology, Australia. Specializing in computer music and creativity with technology, he is also the Digital Media program manager at the Australasian CRC for Interaction Design. Professor Brown has experience and interest in curriculum development for creativity and design, and in the application of contemporary technology to education. He is an active composer of computer music and a builder of software instruments, and he is the co-author of the jMusic composition library for the Java computer language; jMusic is used around the world for music software development and computer music education.

Joaquín Ramírez Buentello is an educational technology specialist from the Tecnológico de Monterrey in Mexico City Campus. His works have focused on multimedia in education since 1995. He is certificated in eBusiness by the Harvard Business School, and is a specialist in Multimedia and Design from the INBA (National Fine Arts Institute) in Mexico. Mr. Ramírez Buentello has a master's degree in eBusiness from the University of Barcelona in Spain. His academic interests lie in the area of innovation in education and the consulting of electronic process.

Marco Antonio Mendoza Calderón is a member of the Research and Innovation in Education Center (CIIE) at the Tecnológico de Monterrey, Mexico City Campus. Since 1996 he has had experience in consulting, designing, and implementing CBT, WBT, and administrative reengineering programs in organizations in Guatemala, Colombia, Panama, and Mexico. He is associate professor of eCommerce at the Tecnológico de Monterrey in Mexico, and eTutor of Internet economy and online business at the Universidad de Málaga in Spain. His interests focus on virtual collaborative work and learning, and m-business. He has a master's degree in eBusiness from the Universitat de Barcelona.

Darren Cambridge joined New Century College of George Mason University (USA) as assistant professor of Internet studies and information literacy, after several years working with AAHE and EDUCAUSE. As director of Web Projects at AAHE, he worked with academics and technologists to envision, build, and use online collaboration tools to support such programs as the Carnegie Academy Campus Program and Engaged Campus in a Diverse Democracy. As a National

Learning Infrastructure Initiative Fellow, he co-led EDUCAUSE's virtual community of practice initiative and researched ePortfolios and lifelong learning. While at the University of Texas at Austin, he led the design of the award-winning Learning Record Online electronic portfolio system. Currently, he facilitates EPAC: The Electronic Portfolios Community of Practice, and chairs a development group on ePortfolios for the IMS Global Learning Consortium that is developing an interoperability specification for electronic portfolios.

Colleen Carmean is a director of information technology at Arizona State University (USA). She teaches applied computing, online and F2F, and is responsible for faculty development and support using technology at her campus. She recently served as a National Learning Infrastructure Initiative (NLII) Fellow, Frye Fellow, and was a founding co-editor of the MERLOT Teaching and Technology board. Her research is in instructional design for deeper learning, learner-centered technology, and next-generation learning models.

Rachel Challen, following a successful management career in hospitality, has enjoyed working as a lecturer in many colleges within the West Midlands and beyond. Since 2003 she has been working for Pebble Learning, mentoring staff in colleges in developing their understanding of teaching in an online world. This work has included working at a range of levels from school children through to postgraduate students. She also continues to teach teacher education programs at the University of Wolverhampton (UK).

Helen L. Chen is a research scientist at the Stanford Center for Innovations in Learning (SCIL) (USA), co-facilitator of the Electronic Portfolio Community of Practice (EPAC), and represents Stanford's involvement in the National Coalition on Electronic Portfolio Research. Dr. Chen earned her PhD in Communication with a minor in Psychology from Stanford University in 1998. Her current research interests focus on the application of Folio Thinking pedagogy and practices in engineering education, and the design and evaluation of social software and innovative learning spaces to support portfolio-related activities and student learning in higher education.

Jacques Chevrier is a full professor in the Department of Sciences of Education, Université du Québec en Outaouais, Canada. He has a PhD in psychology from the University of Montreal. His research interests are learning styles, learning strategies, experiential learning, transformative learning, and the professional identity of teachers.

Alice Christie, recently named Arizona State University President's Professor, received her PhD in educational technology and language and literacy from Arizona State University (USA) in 1995. She currently serves as associate professor of Technology and Education in the College of Teacher Education and Leadership at Arizona State University. Prior to this, she taught for 25 years in K-12 schools. She speaks nationally and internationally on how technology can enhance student learning and how ePortfolios can be used for authentic assessment. Her well-known educational Web site, found at http://www.west.asu.edu/achristie, averages 45,000 visitors per month. *The Chronicle of Higher Education* cited it as one of the best educational portals on the Web. Contact her via e-mail at alice.christie@asu.edu.

Roger Clark was formerly deputy head of the Psychology Department and then head of the Learning & Teaching Development Center team at Liverpool Hope University College, UK. He designed and implemented numerous innovative eLearning resources including a VLE for Liverpool Hope and discussion software now incorporated into the JISC/LTSN Learning and Teaching Portal. He is currently project manager of the Cheshire and Merseyside regional distributed eLearning network.

S. J. Cotterill is a senior research associate based at the School of Medical Education Development at Newcastle University, UK. He has played a leading role in developing ePortfolios as part of an FDTL-4 project (http://www.e-portfolios.ac.uk), which has gone on to be used in a range other educational and CPD contexts.

Colin Dalziel in 1996 moved from a professional background in media research and design to working in higher education, where he developed systems and processes that support networked learning. In 2003, together with Shane Sutherland, Mr. Dalziel founded Pebble Learning and has worked across the educational sector developing staff use of online systems to support learning. The key success of Pebble Learning has been the development of the PebblePAD ePortfolio system which is now widely used across the UK.

Karim Derrick has been senior developer and project manager for five years at TAG Learning Ltd. (UK), pioneering the MAPS Managed Assessment Portfolio System and a number of online project profiling solutions for a range of organizations. He also edits the TagTeacherNet newsletter, which has over 49,000 subscribers.

Roberta Devlin-Scherer teaches advanced teaching strategies and contemporary assessment to graduate and undergraduate students. Students regularly consult her Portfolio Handbook guide at http://pirate.shu.edu/~devlinrb/indexport.html as they create their own ePortfolios. A review of this handbook is available in Educational Technology and Society at http://ifets.ieee.org/periodical/6_3/15.html. She has presented on ePortfolio uses and development at national conferences. Articles on portfolios include: "The Principal Internship Portfolio" in the *Journal of Research for Educational Leaders* and "Preservice Professional Employment Portfolios for Middle Schools" in *Essays in Education*. Her recently published book *Teaching for Real Learning* features a section on portfolios.

Steve Dillon is a senior lecturer in music and sound in the Faculty of Creative Industries, Queensland University of Technology, Australia, specializing in songwriting and music education. His research focuses on the qualities of meaning and engagement in artistic production, and documenting the transformative qualities of music making. He has experience and interest in curriculum development in the application of contemporary technology to education, and he collaborated on the development of *jam2jam* generative online music software for children which was designed around developing theories of engagement and meaning. He has co-authored six music education resource books and numerous academic articles.

Bob Doig is a senior lecturer in the Faculty of Education and Social Work at the University of Dundee, UK. A former history teacher, he has had an interest in information and communications technology as a tool for learning since the early 1980s. He teaches in the BEd (Hons) Program where he is program leader, the Post Graduate Diploma of Primary Education, and the Post Graduate Diploma of Secondary Education.

Stephen C. Ehrmann directs the award-winning Flashlight Program on the evaluation of educational uses of technology at The Teaching, Learning, and Technology Group (USA). He has also become well-known around the world for his work over the last 20 years in helping educators make more productive use of computers, video, and telecommunications. As an author he is well-known for his articles (e.g., "Implementing the Seven Principles: Technology as Lever," "Asking the Right Question: What Research Tells us About Technology and Higher Learning"), his books, and his blog. Before joining the TLT Group, he served for 11 years as a program officer with the Annenberg/CPB Project and for seven years as a program officer with the Fund for the Improvement of Postsecondary Education (FIPSE). He has a PhD in management and higher education from MIT.

David Emmett is a learning designer of teaching and learning support services at QUT (Australia). David has over 10 years of experience as an instructional designer in a variety of settings and is currently completing a Doctor of Education degree examining the use of the ePortfolio at QUT.

Masha Etkind is a professor in the Department of Architectural Science at Ryerson University, Canada. She teaches design, theory, and history of western architecture; her recent research focuses on language and roots of living architecture. Professor Etkind received a professional degree in architecture from St. Petersburg University of Architecture and Engineering, and an MArch from the University of Toronto.

Franc Feng specializes in ePortfolios, learning technologies, online instruction/learning and curriculum design, background in computer engineering technology and computing studies, programming, microprocessor/Web design, workplace training, business systems, consulting, multimedia, evaluation, administration, systems support, and digital curating. His research interests include science-technology-studies (STS), meta-cognition, assessment, cybernetics, chaos/complexity/systems theory, ethics, cultural studies, ecology, philosophy, hermeneutics, phenomenology, globalization and sociology of knowledge. Dr. Feng recently co-authored a large-scale research on how people learn through technology commissioned by the National Academy of Engineering (NAE), and authored chapters in *(Post) Modern Science (Education): Propositions and Alternative Paths* (Peter Lang, 2001) and *Unfolding Bodymind: Exploring Possibility Through Education* (Foundation for Educational Renewal, 2001). He further published in *Educational Insights.*

Eleanor J. Flanigan received her EdD from Temple University, USA. She is currently a professor in the Department of Management and Information Systems in the School of Business at Montclair State University, USA. Her corporate experiences include being employed as a systems analyst at General Electric Company and as the international marketing manager at Ashton-Tate. She was awarded Educator or the Year by two organizations: Eastern Business Education

Association (1978) and Montclair State University Alumni Association (2004). She was awarded Educator or the Year by two organizations: Eastern Business Education Association (1978) and Montclair State University Alumni Association (2004). Her current teaching and research interests include guiding development of digital portfolios, examining diverse learning styles, and designing case-based problems using advanced software application programs.

Gilles Fortin holds a license in theology from Saint Paul University (Canada), an MA in Psychology from the University of Ottawa, and an EdD from UQAM. He is an associate professor in pastoral counseling at Saint Paul University. He is interested in professional ethics, values as they pertain to counseling, experiential learning, and learning styles.

Sebastian Foti is a Fulbright Scholar who has taught physics, mathematics, and instructional computing courses from Grade 7 through graduate school both in the United States and abroad. He has served as a computer consultant in Europe, Africa, Central and Southeast Asia, and South America, as well as in the United States. Along with colleagues at The Athena-Group, Dr. Foti is currently developing a middle school science learning environment that features a series of photorealistic simulations in virtual settings. He is employed by the University of Florida Alliance, (USA) which is an organization that promotes collaboration between Florida's educational institutions, teachers, and students.

Lucretia Fraga currently is the ePortfolio coordinator at The University of Texas at San Antonio (USA). As ePortfolio coordinator she has trained faculty and students in the use of the Open Source ePortfolio System. She is also a member of the National Electronic Portfolio Research Coalition, and is studying student practice with ePortfolios. She holds a master's degree in Instructional Technology from Our Lady of the Lake University.

Paul A. Fritz has served as an associate professor of communication at the University of Toledo (USA) since 1980. He specializes in courses on communication theory and information technology. His research area is in the scholarship of teaching and learning. His research specialty is learning styles.

David Gibson, Director of Research and Development at the Vermont Institutes and the National Institute for Community Innovations, concentrates on partnership development and new programs, systems analysis, evaluation, strategic planning, professional networks, national partners, and telecommunications in learning. His research and publications include work on complex systems analysis and modeling of education, Semantic Web applications and the future of learning, and the use of technology to personalize education for the success of all students. Dr. Gibson is also the founder and president of CURVESHIFT (USA), an educational technology company that assists in the acquisition, implementation, and continuing design of games and simulations, ePortfolio systems, data-driven decision-making tools, and emerging Semantic Web technologies.

Simon Grant has a PhD in cognitive science. He lectured in HCI and systems analysis and design at City University, London. After post-doctoral applied research at the JRC in Italy, he was employed by the University of Liverpool from 1996-1999, giving Internet skills training; during this time he led the conceptual technical design of LUSID (collaborating with Strivens and Marshall), a Web-based PDP system with some ePortfolio characteristics. Since then he has worked freelance, latterly involved in several ePortfolio-related projects, particularly involving interoperability specifications.

Gary Greenberg is director of the Collaboratory Project, a Northwestern University (USA) initiative, funded by the State of Illinois, and federal and foundation grants, that is helping educators use the Collaboratory, a Web-based collaborative learning environment, to improve student learning and achievement. He is also executive director for Teaching and Research Initiatives for Information Technology at Northwestern University. He works on special projects to develop opportunities for using Information Technology to enhance learning, research, and administration at the university. Dr. Greenberg earned his BA from Stanford University and his PhD from Harvard University. He has taught at Yale University, Rutgers University, and Northwestern University, where he also managed the Advanced Technology Group.

Mark H. Gromko is vice provost for academic programs and professor of biological sciences at Bowling Green State University (USA). He received his PhD in biology from Indiana University in 1978. He is chair of the Program Review Committee, which conducts program reviews of all academic departments at the university; he also chairs the Undergraduate Council, which reviews changes and additions to undergraduate courses, curriculum, and academic policies. He serves on the Student Achievement Assessment Committee, the Learning Community Advisory Committee, the Bowling Green Experience Advisory Committee, and other university committees as called upon. The directors of the Honors Program, the BG Perspective (general education) program, and the Center for Teaching, Learning, and Technology report to the vice provost for academic programs. A focus of Dr. Gromko's work is promoting collaboration and coordination among the university's academic initiatives.

Tommi Haapaniemi is a coordinator in the University of Kuopio, Finland. He trains tutors and university teachers in pedagogy. His fields of specialization include student-centered teaching and guidance methods. He holds a master's degree.

Milton D. Hakel is the Ohio Board of Regents' eminent scholar in industrial and organizational psychology at Bowling Green State University, USA. He received his PhD in psychology in 1966 from the University of Minnesota. At Bowling Green, Dr. Hakel chairs the Student Achievement Assessment Committee and the Electronic Portfolio Steering Committee, committees that have identified learning outcomes in majors and for the university as a whole, and also begun building the means for students to document their own learning and development. He created Springboard, a first-year experience course that involves students and their coaches in meaningful assessment and self-development though a series of activities, some of which are recorded on video for later feedback and reflection. He chaired the team that created BGSU's Academic Plan, and presently chairs a task force that is investigating the creation of a PhD program in learning and teaching with an emphasis on math and science.

Sharon J. Hamilton is associate dean of the faculties, chancellor's professor, professor of English, and director of the Center on Integrating Learning at IUPUI (USA). She also is director of the Indiana University Faculty Colloquium on Excellence in Teaching. She conceptualized and directed the development of both the IUPUI Institutional Electronic Portfolio (iPort) and the IUPUI Electronic Student Portfolio (ePort), which became the prototype for the OSPI 2.0 and 2.1 release. She has written several articles on both institutional and student electronic portfolios, and currently is part of the National Coalition for Electronic Portfolio Research.

G. R. Hammond is the head of the School of Medical Education Development, director of the Center for Excellence in Healthcare Professional Education: CETL4HealthNE (http://www.cetl4healthne.ac.uk), and director for a collaborative FDTL4 ePortfolios project.

Wendy Harper is the intranet services manager at QUT (Australia), where she has worked for 18 years in both ITS and the library. She currently heads the systems development group and is project director of QUT Virtual and the Student Portfolio. She has a special interest in the use of technology to support student transition into the university and the world of work.

Elizabeth Hartnell-Young is a researcher and consultant, author of *Digital Professional Portfolios for Change* (with Maureen Morriss), and founder of Women@the Cutting Edge, an Australian portfolio project in the 1990s. She organized the first ePortfolio Australia Conference in 2004, and encourages people in schools and universities to be actively involved in learning and reflection through portfolio development. She has recently undertaken a research project using mobile camera phones to collect material for ePortfolios supported by Nokia in Finland.

Kim Hauville is a senior corporate systems developer in intranet services within Information Technology Services at QUT (Australia). She has degrees in Information Technology and Behavioral Science, and five years experience in the IT industry. Ms. Hauville has been involved in the development of student portfolios since their inception, and currently leads the system analysis and design team.

Jeff Haywood is director of the University of Edinburgh's Media & Learning Technology Service (MALTS – http://www.malts.ed.ac.uk), which provides eLearning and digital classroom services to the university, and professor of Education & Technology leading the Scottish Center for Research into On-Line Learning & Assessment (SCROLLA – http://www.scrolla.ac.uk). His research interests lie in policy and strategies for the use of technology in education, in the educational effectiveness of different technologies, and in the views of learners about educational innovations. Some of his current projects and publications can be found at http://homepages.ed.ac.uk/jhaywood.

Ronald J. Henry has been provost and vice president for academic affairs at Georgia State University (USA) since July 1994. One of his responsibilities is leadership to promote and recommend changes in public education systems that will improve the success of Georgia students at all levels, pre-school through postsecondary and into the world of work. Current work includes improvement of introductory college courses in science and mathematics through inclusion of activity-based learning. He is also involved in ensuring that assessable learning outcomes are developed for each program, that course learning outcomes are mapped to program learning outcomes, and that use of electronic portfolios to document progress towards mastery of learning outcomes.

Corey Hickerson is assistant professor in the School of Communication Studies at James Madison University, USA. His research focuses on the use of technology in two areas: the classroom and public relations. He holds degrees from the University of Memphis, the University of Alabama, and the University of Virginia. Currently, Professor Hickerson is completing a research project on student use of instant messaging with faculty members.

Yi-Ping Huang currently serves as faculty and director of assessment and information at the University of Maryland Baltimore County (USA). She leads and participates as a researcher, consultant, policy advisor, and system designer on a wide range of educational change projects with teacher education programs and local school systems. Her latest endeavors include technology-integrated education accountability system (EAS), and arts-infused teacher education and renewal. As an ethnomusicologist and prominent musician, Dr. Huang has performed and hosted concerts in Asia, Europe, and the United States, and has presented works for Pope John II, royalty in England and Holland, and at diplomatic and public events around the world.

Barbara Illsley is a senior lecturer in the School of Town and Regional Planning with interests in the fields of environmental justice, community governance, and professional land use planning practice. An active member of the Royal Town Planning Institute for more than 20 years, she served on the QAA Benchmarking Group for Town and Country Planning, is a member of the Higher Education Academy, and is currently Associate Dean, Learning and Teaching, in the Faculty of Arts and Social Sciences.

Brian Jolly has more than 30 years experience in medical education. Prior to moving to Australia, he held positions as head of the Academic Unit of Medical and Dental Education at St. Bartholomew's Hospital Medical College, director of the Medical Education Unit at the University of Leeds Medical School, and professor of Medical Education at the University of Sheffield in the UK. His PhD from Maastricht University involved work on clinical teaching. He has had a significant involvement in the UK's GMC Performance Review project, and on the GMC's Revalidation Technical Group. He was the foundation chair of the Education Committee of the General Osteopathic Council (UK) from 1995-2001. He has interests in assessment, clinical teaching, clinical skills development, and educational research design and statistics. His current responsibilities include the development of research initiatives in health professional education, assisting in the development of undergraduate assessment protocols and fitness to practice initiatives.

Pasi Karvonen holds an MSc and is a coordinator in the University of Kuopio Learning Centre (Finland). He is responsible for planning and coordinating support services for the faculties. His fields of specialization include eLearning and educational technology.

Alan Katz is a second-year geriatric medicine fellow at the University of Miami Miller School of Medicine (USA). His area of research interest is in the application of eLearning in medical education. Dr. Katz is involved in the design, development, and implementation of eLearning materials in the area of geriatric assessment tools, which are used in the training of medical students, residents, and physicians in practice. Most recently, Dr. Katz helped develop the structure of an electronic portfolio for geriatric medicine fellows at the University of Miami Miller School of Medicine.

Debbie Kiegaldie has a background in intensive care nursing, and taught and coordinated postgraduate acute care courses for Monash University (Australia) for over nine years. She took up her current position in 2003 to pursue her interests in health professional education. She has a special interest in the development, implementation, and evaluation of educational technologies and has produced a number of interactive computer simulations such as the CD-ROM titled "The Virtual Patient," "The Virtual Ward," and she is currently working on "Virtual Haemodynamics" with the University of Melbourne. Her research interests include computer-assisted learning, clinical skills assessment, and interprofessional education.

Paul Kim is the chief technology officer at the Stanford University School of Education (USA). He currently teaches eLearning, enterprising higher ed in the digital age, and directed research courses while evaluating and developing education support systems. He also manages the information technology department and serves as the chair for the Academic Technology Advisory Committee. He earned his PhD in educational technology in 1998 from USC. In his career, he has held various positions including chief technology officer for the University of Phoenix Southern California Campus, vice president for Vatterott College, Missouri, and chairman of the Board for Intercultural Institute of California. His recent publications and presentations have focused on "Information Visualization and Performance Evaluation."

Elizabeth Lamoureux is an associate professor of speech communication at BVU (USA) where she has taught for the past eight years. Prior to this, she served on the faculty at Illinois State University, Hope College, and the University of Northern Iowa. Recently named BVU's George Wythe Laureate for teaching excellence, she received her BA from Buena Vista University, her MA from Pittsburgh State University, and her PhD from the University of Kansas.

Mary Lawson joined Monash University (Australia) in 2002 from the UK. She has worked in medical education since 1991. Her previous roles have involved the development of alternative venues for clinical teaching (particularly day surgery, outpatients, and community-based education) and coordination of a national project to define core clinical competencies for undergraduate medicine. She has expertise in problem-based learning (PBL) and has been responsible for staff development to support its introduction, has managed a multi-professional teaching project using this method, and also developed some large-group and electronic models for PBL. Her research interests include teacher training to support curriculum innovation and development, electronic course evaluation, and interprofessional education.

Raymond LeBlanc is a full professor in the Faculty of Education, University of Ottawa, Canada. Since 1981 he has been teaching special education and cognitive education in both the teacher education and the educational studies programs of the Faculty of Education. His areas of expertise and research interests are quality-of-life issues, mental processes from a sociocultural perspective, qualitative methodologies, case study and participatory action research methodologies, mental retardation, learning disabilities, autism, and conduct disorders. He is the director of a collection of books in the field of special education and neuropsychology for a European publisher, DeBoeck University.

Tracy Penny Light is acting associate director of the University of Waterloo's (Canada) Teaching Resources (TRACE) office and adjunct assistant professor in the Department of History. She is founding co-editor of the *MERLOT Journal of Online Learning and Teaching (JOLT)* and a member of the MERLOT History Editorial Board. She has designed, developed, and implemented a number of educational technology programs for both high school and higher education. Her current research focuses on the use of electronic portfolios to promote deep learning, helping students to make connections between their learning experiences. She holds a PhD.

Youmei Liu works as a senior instructional designer in the Office of Educational Technology and University Outreach at the University of Houston (USA). She is also an adjunct faculty member teaching an advanced Web technology course at UH. She provides faculty training and support related to online course design and instructional delivery. Her research interests include faculty development, integration of multimedia components and learning objects in course design, and online assessment. She can be reached at yliu5@uh.edu.

Alicia M. (Clapp) Louden is the coordinator of Student Technology Assessment, Resources and Training (START) at DePauw University (USA). She received a BA in computer science from DePauw in 2003 and an MS in instructional systems technology from Indiana University in 2005. As coordinator of START, she addresses the learning needs of all DePauw students by providing opportunities to enhance their liberal arts education with information technology knowledge and skills through workshops, Web-based training, courses, and one-on-one training. She also works closely with faculty members to provide specific course-related technology training through in-class workshops.

Judith Malette is a clinical psychologist and has been assistant professor in pastoral counseling at Saint Paul University (Canada) since 2001. She received a PhD in psychology from the University of Ottawa and did post-doctoral studies in clinical psychology at that same university. Her research interests are as follows: life review, images of God, attachment, and learning styles.

Isabelle Marcoul-Burlinson is the coordinator for undergraduate and postgraduate courses in the Center for Language Studies at City University in London. She holds BA and MA degrees in English and American literature and civilization from the University of Montpellier III in France. Before she moved to England, she studied linguistics and psychology in Munich, Germany. She is a PhD student in education at the University of Lancaster, UK, and her research interests are eLearning technologies and education organizational development.

Adam Marshall is the senior Java developer for Oxford University's Virtual Learning Environment (the Open Source Bodington System) (UK) and has both managed and developed code for the WS4RL and SPWS JISC projects. He is currently working on implementing a Shibboleth Identity Provider and Service Provider as part of the UK's Guanxi initiative, and has worked with electronic Personal Development Planning systems (especially LUSID) for a number of years. He is an active participant in CETIS LIPSIG, CETIS Enterprise, and JASIG UK. In the past he has been a member of the ANSI X3J3 committee and the HPF Forum.

Kevin Marshall is the academic program manger for Microsoft Ireland responsible for implementation of the Microsoft Partners in Learning (PiL) education program. He is also visiting research fellow at the Center for Research in Information Technology located at Trinity College Dublin. Prior to working in Ireland, he worked in Boston Public Schools where was responsible for the School-to-Work transition. He has a BA in psychology from University College Dublin, an MSc in industrial psychology from the University of Hull, and a PhD from Boston College.

Joseph Martinelli has more than 20 years of experience in higher education, 15 as an administrator at William Paterson University and five years as a full-time faculty member at Seton Hall University (USA) in the Instructional Design and Technology program. He holds degrees in communication, sports science, and education, and is a certified K-12 English teacher. He is currently working toward an EdD in secondary education from Seton Hall University.

A. M. McDonald is assistant director in the Faculty of Medical Sciences Computing within the School of Medical Education Development at Newcastle University, UK. He is involved in a wide range of educational technology initiatives, including having the role of project manager for the FDTL-4 ePortfolio project (http://www.e-portfolios.ac.uk).

Patricia McGee is assistant professor of instructional technology at The University of Texas at San Antonio (USA). As director of PT3 and Microsoft/AACTE Innovative Teaching grants, she has contributed to a number of campus-wide technology initiatives. She serves on state and national committees working on a variety of initiatives involving learning objects, virtual communities of practice, next-generation course management systems, and adoption of technology by educators. Her work as an ASEE/Navy Research Faculty with the Joint ADL Co-Lab and DEOMI, combined with her work as a 2003 National Learning Infrastructure fellow, has resulted in tools and resources involving pedagogical frameworks associated with learning objects and course management systems. Currently she a member of the National Electronic Portfolio Research Coalition; she is studying faculty practice with ePortfolios.

Joseph McLuckie is a senior lecturer and ICT teaching & learning coordinator in the Faculty of Education and Social Work at the University of Dundee, UK. His main interests are in the use of online course delivery systems in a variety of curricular areas. This has led to his involvement in a large number of European Projects involving work in France, Spain, Cyprus, Switzerland, Germany, Norway, Finland, Sweden, Italy, and Iceland. Currently his main research areas are online peer-assisted learning and the integration of blended learning opportunities in higher education course delivery.

Victor McNair is a lecturer at the University of Ulster in Northern Ireland. Following a long career as a school teacher, he has been teaching Post Graduate Certificate in education students at the Jordanstown campus (near Belfast) since 1994. His research interests include the use of ICT in teacher education, effective classroom teaching, and student teacher ePortfolios. He also has a strategic role in supporting the application of ICTs in teaching and professional development through his involvement in a range of strategy and special-interest groups.

Marcos Milanez is a geriatrician and family physician with a Certificate of Added Qualifications in Geriatrics Medicine. Dr. Milanez graduated in medicine in Brazil and completed residency training and fellowship in Miami. He is currently an assistant professor of medicine at the Miller School of Medicine, University of Miami (USA). As associate director of the Geriatric Medicine Fellowship Program, he leads the work on ePortfolios for fellows. Dr. Milanez is also part of the DW Reynolds program at the University of Miami, where medical students in all four years receive training in geriatric medicine.

DeWayne Moore holds a BA in psychology from the University of North Texas and a PhD in developmental psychology from Michigan State University. He is professor of psychology and has been a member of the Clemson Psychology Department since 1980. His numerous publications and expertise in adolescent and adult reading and cognitive development are part of the basis for his active collaborations across a wide range of domains in psychology.

David Niguidula is founder of Ideas Consulting (USA), an educational consulting firm based in Providence, Rhode Island. Dr. Niguidula conducted the first research project on K-12 digital portfolios (1992-1997) while managing the technology group at the Coalition of Essential Schools and Annenberg Institute for School Reform at Brown University. Since then, Dr. Niguidula's firm has worked with schools and districts around the world on the technological and assessment tools needed for successful digital portfolios. He has served on national advisory boards for organizations including the U.S. Department of Education, the Education Commission of the States, and the Australian National Schools Network.

Kathleen O'Brien is the senior vice president for academic affairs at Alverno College (USA). She became academic dean in 1991, serving in that position until 1999 when she was named vice president for academic affairs. She served as the interim president of the college in the 2003-2004 academic year. Dr. O'Brien is a graduate of Alverno College, holds an MBA (with Honors) from Vanderbilt University and a PhD in management from the Graduate School of Business, University of Wisconsin-Madison.

Jo B. Paoletti is associate professor of American studies and a faculty associate with the Center for Teaching Excellence at the University of Maryland (USA). Her original research training is in the history of clothing and fashion, and she has published many articles on children's clothing in America. Her current research focuses on the impact of new technology on humanities teaching and learning, particularly in courses concerning diversity and identity.

Richard Parsons is currently the director of eLearning at the University of Dundee (UK), where he manages the central group of staff and systems that support the campus-wide use of learning technologies. For 10 years before this, he worked as a lecturer in plant sciences, teaching undergraduate and postgraduate students and working with a research team to investigate the physiology of nitrogen-fixing plant symbioses. Mr. Parsons has authored a number of software tools to assist eLearning, including an online self- and peer assessment system.

Martine Peters is a professor in the Linguistic and Second Language Teaching Department at the Université du Québec at Montréal, Canada. She has a PhD in psychopedagogy from the University of Ottawa. Her research interests are the development of technopedagogical competencies in second language pre-service teachers, technology integration in the second language classroom, and learning strategies.

William M. Plater is dean of the faculties and executive vice chancellor of Indiana University-Purdue University Indianapolis (IUPUI) (USA). As the chief academic officer, he has led campus efforts to improve undergraduate retention, enhance the effective use of technology, develop IUPUI as a model for civic engagement, and increase research productivity as a part of the campus vision to become a leading urban research university. Dr. Plater is responsible for faculty appointments and advancements, academic programs, and academic support services. He holds baccalaureate (1967), master's, and PhD (1973) degrees in English from the University of Illinois at Urbana-Champaign. He is a professor of English at IUPUI and teaches in the area of contemporary American literature. His research interests focus on contemporary fiction and the interplay of fiction with other genres.

Marlene Preston is assistant department head of the Department of Communication at Virginia Tech (USA). With research interests in communication education, she serves as course director for Communication Skills I and II, a freshman sequence that she designed to foster student writing and speaking skills. She also directs a campus speaking center for students, CommLab, and is an officer with the National Association of Communication Centers. Former coordinator of the University Writing Program, Professor Preston provides faculty development opportunities and consulting through Virginia Tech's Center for Excellence in Undergraduate Teaching.

Margaret Price is an assistant professor at Spelman College (USA), where she teaches composition, rhetoric, and creative nonfiction, and serves as director of the ePortfolio Pilot Project. Her writing has appeared in publications including *College Composition and Communication; Teaching, Writing, Disabilities: A Professional Resource Book; Across the Disciplines; Creative Nonfiction;* and *Bitch: Feminist Response to Pop Culture.* She is currently at work on a book, *Writing from Normal: Critical Thinking and Disability in the Classroom.*

Serge Ravet is chief executive of the European Institute for eLearning (EIfEL), a cross-sectoral professional body created in 2001, whose mission is to support the development of a knowledge economy and learning society, in particular by recognizing the organic link between individual, organizational, and community learning, and the role played by knowledge, information, and learning technologies (KILT) to achieve this goal. Combining both technological and pedagogical expertise (over 20 years experience in training and human resources development) with working experience in Europe and the U.S., he is retained as an expert in the assessment of research projects and has contributed to numerous European learning initiatives. Publications include *Technology-Based Training* (Kogan Page, 1997); *Valider les Compétences avec les NVQs* (DEMOS, 1999); *A Guide to E-Learning Solutions* (2001), and numerous articles on learning technologies, competencies, and ePortfolios.

Jonathon J. Richter was an assistant professor in the Department of Education at Montana State University–Northern (USA) from 2002-2005, where he was also the founder of the North American Rural Futures Institute. He is now an associate researcher for the Center for Advanced Technology in Education at the University of Oregon.

Bonnie Riedinger is a founding partner of FacultyMentor (USA), an online faculty development and consulting company. She was former associate director of distance learning and director of online assessment at a small private university, and worked in educational technology at Trinity College in Hartford, Connecticut and at the Ohio State University. She has taught English on ground and online, has directed an on-ground university writing center, and developed and conducted training materials and workshops on electronic portfolios, online writing tutoring, and reflection for the Connecticut Distance Learning Consortium. She also was the editor of *Matrix: The Magazine for Leaders in Higher Education.* She received her bachelor's degree from the University of Connecticut and her master's degree from Ohio State University.

Gail Ring is the director of the Center for Technology in Education where she works to promote innovation through teaching, research, and outreach to P-12 in north central Indiana. She also teaches Instructional Technology courses. Her research interests involve the study of innovation diffusion in an academic setting and the use of electronic portfolios in education. She is currently working with middle school science teachers in the implementation of virtual experiments in the science classroom. Dr. Ring received her PhD in instructional technology from the School of Teaching and Learning at the University of Florida, where she implemented the Electronic Portfolio Project in the College of Education.

Nathaniel T. Romance is assistant director of the Information Technology Associates Program (ITAP) at DePauw University (USA), where he earned a BA in economics and management. In his current role, he is responsible for the administration and oversight of ITAP and the coordination of technology internships. In addition, he serves as supervisor for 361° Consulting, a student-run IT Consulting firm in Greencastle, Indiana.

Jorge G. Ruiz is a geriatrician, assistant professor of clinical medicine, and director of the Geriatric Medicine Fellowship at the University of Miami Miller School of Medicine (USA). He is a senior investigator at the Stein Gerontological Institute and director of GeriU (http://www.geriu.org) the Online Geriatrics University, a learning management system for geriatrics education. Dr. Ruiz is also the associate director for education and evaluation and an investigator at the Miami VA Geriatric Research Education and Clinical Center. His research interests include Web-based geriatric education, the use of reusable learning objects, and the blended learning approach in medical education.

Misty Sailors is an assistant professor at the University of Texas at San Antonio (USA). She directs the Literacy and Technology Learning Cohort and teaches graduate literacy education courses. She was recently awarded a Teacher Quality Professional Development grant from the Institute of Education Sciences. Her research interests include pre-service and in-service teacher education and the role of technology-rich environments in teacher education. She is also interested in the ways in which children comprehend in an online environment. She is the chair of the Ad Hoc ePortfolio Committee for her department.

Nancy Sardone has 12 years of experience in sales and marketing in the telecommunications industry. She joined the Seton Hall University (USA) faculty full time in the Instructional Design and Technology program in September 2000. She is currently completing her PhD in business education in higher education at New York University, where her research interest is in the area of active learning to support and enrich learning.

Uri Shafrir is associate professor in the Department of Human Development and Applied Psychology and director of the Adult Study Skills Clinic at the Ontario Institute for Studies in Education of the University of Toronto, Canada; his recent research focuses on text analysis for mapping of conceptual content in the disciplines, and on instructional methodologies for deep comprehension. Dr. Shafrir received a doctorate in mathematical sciences from UCLA in 1962 and a doctorate in developmental psychology from York University, Toronto, in 1987. Before moving to the University of Toronto, he was founder and director of the Institute of Planetary and Space Science at Tel-Aviv University, and adjunct professor at the University of Wisconsin and Columbia University.

Greg Sherman is a faculty member and research analyst for Radford University's College of Education and Human Resources (USA). He was a junior high school science teacher for 10 years before earning a doctorate in the field of instructional technology. He has worked in colleges of education for universities in Arizona, Kansas, and Virginia. In addition to teaching courses in instructional design and evaluation, Professor Sherman also consults with a variety of companies as an evaluation specialist. He also facilitates professional development workshops for K-12 teachers in the areas of electronic portfolio development and the use of educational media in the classroom.

Carol L. Smith, associate CIO for instructional and learning services at DePauw University (USA), holds an MS in instructional systems technology from Indiana University, and is a 2004 Frye Leadership Institute fellow. She has been variously involved with information services at DePauw since 1996, playing a key role in developing the university's Faculty Instructional Technology Support (FITS) program. She currently oversees programs that provide instructional technology training for faculty, students, and staff, including the curriculum of the Information Technology Associates Program (ITAP). Ms. Smith is an active member of several professional organizations, including EDUCAUSE and the National Institute for Technology and Liberal Education.

Benjamin R. Stephens holds a BS in psychology from the University of Georgia, and a PhD in developmental psychology from the University of Texas at Austin. He was visiting assistant professor at Williams College before joining Clemson University's Psychology Department (USA) as undergraduate coordinator and professor. His vision and undergraduate education were funded by NIH, NSF, and AFOSR. In 2005, he received the Award for Innovative Excellence in Teaching, Learning, and Technology at the 16th International Conference on College Teaching and Learning.

Heidi J. Stevenson is an assistant professor of education in the Benerd School of Education at the University of the Pacific (USA). Her current research interests lie in K-12 teacher informal collaboration, emotional regulation, computer-mediated anonymous peer assessment of ePortfolios, and constructivist use of technology. She is particularly interested in pre-service teachers' participation in online communities of practice in order to share resources and provide support.

Janet Strivens has taught in various universities in the UK for more than 30 years and is a registered practitioner of the Higher Education Academy. She leads the educational development team at the University of Liverpool, one of the UK's leading research universities, and is also the senior associate director of the Center for Recording Achievement, the UK's national network for the promotion of personal development planning processes across all sectors of education. She was a member of the team which developed the Liverpool University Student Interactive Database (LUSID), one of the first electronic tools to support personal development planning.

J. Struthers is currently working in the Bute Medical School as a learning technology consultant to support the use of technology in the implementation of the school's new curriculum. Her previous experience includes supporting the use of WebCT at the University of St Andrews (UK) and working as an eLearning officer at the University of Abertay, Dundee, where she collaborated with academic staff, educational developers, and IS staff to deliver a program of prioritized eLearning projects. She recently completed a master's degree in advanced learning technology from the University of Lancaster.

Shane Sutherland is the ePortfolio project director at the University of Wolverhampton (www.wlv.ac.uk) and director of the spin-off company responsible for the development of the PebblePAD ePortfolio system (http://www.pebblepad.co.uk). His background is in teacher education, and he is particularly enthusiastic about harnessing technology to support learning. Professor Sutherland still finds time to teach in areas as diverse as sailing, PGCert HE, and first-year undergraduate studies. Throughout the year, he also leads eLearning retreats for fellow teachers exploring the innovative use of ePortfolios, virtual learning environments, WebQuests, and other Web-based systems.

Richard G. Tiberius is director of the Educational Development Office in the Department of Medical Education and professor in the Department of Medicine at the University of Miami School of Medicine (USA), where he collaborates with medical faculty in designing and conducting educational research and faculty development activities. His scholarly work and consulting practice focuses on the improvement of the teaching and learning process, especially the role of the teacher-student relationship in learning. He has authored numerous journal articles, book chapters, and books in the U.S., Canada, and the UK, and he has conducted workshops and lectured throughout North America and Europe.

David Tosh hails from an inter-disciplinary background, obtaining his first degree in geography, before going on to earn a master's degree in software development. He is currently writing a PhD at the University of Edinburgh (UK), researching educational technologies; he is supervised by Professor Jeff Haywood. For the past four years, Mr. Tosh worked as a Web developer focusing on solutions for higher education. He is currently a U21 visiting scholar at UBC. Other areas of research include working on a learning landscape model and exploring ways to homogenize everyday Web technologies to enhance online learning environments.

Jutta Treviranus established and directs the Adaptive Technology Resource Center at the University of Toronto, an internationally recognized center of expertise on barrier-free access to information technology. She is active in and chairs a number of international interoperability specification groups, including groups in the World Wide Web Consortium and the IMS Global Learning Consortium. She is a project editor within the ISO/IEC JTC1 Subcommittee on eLearning (SC36) and has led many multi-partner research and development projects, including The Inclusive Learning Exchange (TILE), the Canadian Network for Inclusive Cultural Exchange, the Network for Inclusive Distance Education, and the barrier-free project. She holds status faculty appointments in the Faculty of Information Studies, the Faculty of Medicine, and the Knowledge Media Design Institute at the University of Toronto, Canada.

Maria H. van Zuilen is assistant professor of medicine in the Division of Gerontology and Geriatric Medicine at the University of Miami Miller School of Medicine (USA). She received a diploma in geriatric nursing in The Netherlands and a PhD in clinical psychology from the University of Miami (UM). As co-director of UM's four-year longitudinal curriculum in geriatrics, palliative care, and pain management for undergraduate medical students and coordinator of the D.W. Reynolds educational grant for physician competency in geriatrics, Dr. van Zuilen has broad responsibility for medical school curriculum development, implementation, and evaluation.

M. H. C. H. (Marij) Veugelers has served as project manager of portfolio implementation for IT in the Education Department at the University of Amsterdam since 2000. In this position, she is responsible for educational implementation at the nine schools that have been using an ePortfolio since 2001. She was also project manager of the Digital University (consortium of 10 universities) Portfolio Implementation Instruments Project. The results are a toolkit for managers on the Web with several new instruments (see http://www.du.nl/portfolioimplementatie). She had organized the first expert exchange meeting, Portfolio UK-NL, in April 2004. Since September 2004 she has been facilitator (community manager) of the Dutch SIG NL Portfolio of the SURF-Foundation (see http://e-learning.surf.nl/portfolio). Over the last two years she has published and presented several times in The Netherlands and abroad (ALT 2004, EUNIS 2004, ePortfolio 2004, AAHE-CRA London 2005) about portfolio implementation aspects. Her background is as an educational consultant, career/student counselor, and biologist.

Matthew Wagner is the director of the Teaching and Learning with Technology Center (TLTC) at Buena Vista University in Storm Lake, Iowa (USA). In this capacity, he is actively involved in promoting the use of instructional technology as a means to support teaching and improve student learning. He is a 1998 graduate of Buena Vista University, receiving his BA in journalism and mass communication. He received his MS from Iowa State University in 2002 for journalism and mass communication.

Phil Walz is the director of admissions and student affairs for the School of Information, University of California, Berkeley (USA).

Ben Werdmuller has been involved in Web technologies for 10 years, most recently for the Media and Learning Technology Service at Edinburgh University and currently at the Saïd Business School, University of Oxford. He is currently the technical director of Elgg, a learning landscape system.

Will Wharfe has been working with innovative educational IT projects since 1994. As development director at TAG Learning Ltd. (UK), he has worked with Karim Derrick to develop a system of ePortfolios both for teachers and pupils called the Managed Assessment Portfolio System (MAPS; see http://www.maps-ict.com).

S. Whiten is a senior lecturer at the Bute Medical School and jointly organized the foundation year of a newly designed medical curriculum. The curriculum is delivered through a Web-based course management system. Reflection is now considered to be one of the essential skills in professional training, and both the development and early implementation of an electronic portfolio for this purpose is an intriguing challenge.

Michael V. Whitesell serves as coordinator of Faculty Instructional Technology Support (FITS) at DePauw University (USA). He holds a BA in computer science from DePauw University and an MS in instructional systems technology from Indiana University. Mr. Whitesell provides consulting and technical support for faculty members who wish to explore and develop uses of technology in their teaching. He has extensive experience managing and mentoring students in IT internships, and supporting students' technology needs at DePauw University. He is also active outside the university as a member of CIASTD and a participant in events and workshops through the Midwest Instructional Technology Center.

Index of Key Terms

B

C

D

E

F

G

H

I

M

N

O

P

Q

R

S

T

U

V

W

X

Z